Company Law Handbook

THIRD EDITION

D1344932

Other titles available from Law Society Publishing:

Commercial Law Handbook
Edited by David Berry

Data Protection Handbook (2nd edn)
General Editor: Peter Carey

Drafting Commercial Agreements
Stuart Cakebread

Employment Law Handbook (5th edn)
Henry Scrope, Daniel Barnett and Keira Gore

Financial Services for Solicitors
Edited by Ian Muirhead (SIFA)

Insolvency Law Handbook (3rd edn)
Vernon Dennis

Intellectual Property Law Handbook (2nd edn)
Edited by Lorna Brazell (Bird & Bird)

Privacy Law Handbook
Edited by Keith Mathieson

Titles from Law Society Publishing can be ordered from all good bookshops or direct (telephone 0870 850 1422, email **lawsociety@prolog.uk.com** or visit our online shop at **bookshop.lawsociety.org.uk**).

COMPANY LAW HANDBOOK

THIRD EDITION

Stephen Griffin

with contributions by David Southern and Peter Walton

The Law Society

Crown copyright material is reproduced with the permission of the Controller of Her Majesty's Stationery Office

ISBN-13: 978-1-907698-53-8

First edition published in 2007
Second edition published in 2010
This third edition published in 2013 by the Law Society
113 Chancery Lane, London WC2A 1PL

Typeset by Columns Design XML Ltd, Reading
Printed by CPI Group (UK) Ltd, Croydon, CR0 4YY

The paper used for the text pages of this book is FSC® certified. FSC (the Forest Stewardship Council®) is an international network to promote responsible management of the world's forests.

Contents

Preface

As with previous editions of this work, this third edition has been designed to present the essential constituents of company law in a detailed but clear and accessible manner. However, the content of the third edition of this book has been expanded considerably. The purpose behind this expansion is twofold. First, the chapters have been enlarged to project a greater depth and understanding of the subject matter. Second, a number of new subject areas have been dealt with in the book, especially in the context of the regulation of public companies. Here, the object of the expansion is to provide a more thorough and complete coverage of company law.

The book is targeted specifically at those who require an insight into the legal regulation of companies and as such the work should appeal to legal practitioners who deal in company law matters. The book should also be of interest to any student of company law. Hopefully, the book will, as a tool of guidance and reference, enhance the reader's understanding of what is, at times, a most complex subject area.

The Companies Act 2006 and related statutory instruments are the primary legislative source for this work and the legislation and its effect on corporate law principles is subject to extensive analysis. The book, in the context of each subject chapter, explains all the relevant provisions of the 2006 Act and the emerging case law and details if, and how, established corporate law principles have been altered or affected.

Although company law is primarily a creature of statute, the subject area is influenced significantly by the common law and principles of equity. The interpretation of the companies legislation, together with the construction of common law and equitable principles, generate an abundance of case law. The principles derived from the decided cases are explained fully in the text. Working examples and extracts from court judgments are also included as an aid to best explaining complex principles. I sincerely hope that this book will be viewed by the reader as instructive, interesting and as a useful tool to those who require its assistance.

I would like to thank David Southern for contributing his expertise to updating **Chapter 12** (Accounts and reporting structures) and **Chapter 13** (Taxation of companies). Special thanks are also due to my colleague Dr Peter Walton for writing the final chapter of this work (**Chapter 22**). The chapter provides the reader with a comprehensive introduction to insolvency law procedures. As ever, many thanks to my publishers and their staff. I would wish especially to commend the encouragement and assistance of Simon Blackett (commissioning editor) together with Heather Benson (production editor) and Juliet Doyle (copy editor). Finally, my sincere thanks to my wife Donna and my daughters, Vicky and Emily, for their patience, support, tolerance and understanding.

I have endeavoured to state the law as of 30 March 2013. However, at proof stage I was able to expand part of the coverage of the book beyond that date. For example, I have included commentary in **Chapter 11** on the Companies Act 2006 (Amendment of Part 25) Regulations 2013, SI 2013/600 and how these regulations affect the rules relating to the registration of charges (**Chapter 11**). I have also incorporated additions to **Chapters 8** and **10** of the book as a consequence of the implementation of the Companies Act 2006 (Amendment of Part 18) Regulations 2013, SI 2013/999. The said additions are concerned with the legal regulation of employee share schemes and rules relating to a private company's ability to purchase its own shares.

This book is dedicated to the memory of my brother, Mark (1963–2010).

Stephen Griffin
Professor of Law
University of Wolverhampton

Table of cases

Table of statutes

Table of statutory instruments

Table of international legislation

Abbreviations

AA 1996	Arbitration Act 1996
AGM	annual general meeting
AIA	annual investment allowance
AIM	Alternative Investment Market
APB	Auditing Practice Board
ARC	Accounting Regulatory Committee
ASB	Accounting Standards Board
BA 2010	Bribery Act 2010
BCCI	Bank of Credit and Commerce International
BERR	Department for Business, Enterprise and Regulatory Reform
BIS	Department for Business, Innovation and Skills
CA 1985	Companies Act 1985
CA 1989	Companies Act 1989
CA 2006	Companies Act 2006
CAA 2001	Capital Allowances Act 2001
CDDA 1986	Company Directors Disqualification Act 1986
CEO	chief executive officer
CFO	chief financial officer
CGAA	Co-ordinating Group on Audit and Accounting Issues
CIC	community interest company
CJA	Criminal Justice Act 1993
CLR	company law review
CMCHA 2007	Corporate Manslaughter and Corporate Homicide Act 2007
CTA 2009	Corporation Tax Act 2009
CTA 2010	Corporation Tax Act 2010
CTSA	corporation tax self-assessment
CVA	company voluntary arrangement
DTI	Department of Trade and Industry
EA 2002	Enterprise Act 2002
EAT	Employment Appeal Tribunal
ECA 1972	European Communities Act 1972
ECHR	European Convention on Human Rights

EEA	European Economic Area
EEIG	European Economic Interest Grouping
EFRAG	European Financial Reporting Advisory Group
EGM	extraordinary general meeting
EPA 1978	Employment Protection (Consolidation) Act 1978
ERA 1996	Employment Rights Act 1996
FAPL	Football Association Premier League
FCA	Financial Conduct Authority
FL	Football League
FRC	Financial Reporting Council
FRS	Financial Reporting Standards
FRSSE	Financial Reporting Standard for Smaller Entities
FSA	Financial Services Authority
FSMA 2000	Financial Services and Markets Act 2000
FTC	foreign tax credit
GAAP	Generally Accepted Accounting Practice
HMRC	Her Majesty's Revenue and Customs
HP	hire purchase
HRMA	higher relevant maximum amount
HSWA 1974	Health and Safety at Work Act etc. 1974
IA 1986	Insolvency Act 1986
IA 2000	Insolvency Act 2000
IAS	International Accounting Standards
IASB	International Accounting Standards Board
IFRS	International Financial Reporting Standards
IFRSIC	International Financial Reporting Standard Interpreting Committee
IR 1986	Insolvency Rules 1986
ITTOIA 2005	Income Tax (Trading and Other Income) Act 2005
IVA	individual voluntary arrangement
LLP	limited liability partnership
LLPA	Limited Liability Partnerships Act 2000
LPA	Law of Property Act
LRMA	lower relevant maximum amount
LSE	London Stock Exchange
PA 1890	Partnership Act 1890
RBS	Royal Bank of Scotland
SE	Sócietas Europaea
SEC	Securities and Exchange Commission
SME	small and medium enterprises
SOA 2002	Sarbanes-Oxley Act 2002
SOCIE	Statement of Changes in Equity
SOPE	Societas Privata Europaea
SORP	Statements of Recommended Practice

SPE	special purpose entity
SSAP	Statements of Standard Accounting Practice
STRGL	Statement of Total Reported Gains and Losses
TCGA 1992	Taxation of Chargeable Gains Act 1992
TDA 1968	Trade Descriptions Act 1968
TIOPA 2010	Taxation (International and Other Provisions) Act 2010
TMA 1970	Taxes Management Act 1970
UITF	Urgent Issues Task Force
UKLA	UK Listing Authority
USM	Unlisted Securities Market
VAT	value added tax

CHAPTER 1

The registered company

1.1 INTRODUCTION

A company registered in accordance with the provisions of the companies legislation (currently the Companies Act (CA) 2006) is, from the date of its incorporation, a body corporate (CA 2006, s.16). As a body corporate the registered company is a separate legal entity possessing rights and subject to duties in much the same way as a natural person. For example, a company may sue and be sued in its own name, be made liable under the criminal law and will be liable to pay its own form of tax, namely, corporation tax. In addition to its separate legal identity, the vast majority of registered companies are incorporated with limited liability. A company may be limited by shares or by guarantee. The former method of incorporation is by far the most common and, unless otherwise stated, this book will be concerned with a company limited by shares.

A company is a limited company if the liability of its members is limited by its constitution (CA 2006, s.3). In respect of a company limited by shares, limited liability means that a member of a company will cease to incur any liability (unless the member personally guarantees corporate debts) to contribute to the debts of the company once the shares held by that member have been fully paid for, that is, the nominal value (par value) of the share has been paid to the company (price of share when first issued). Accordingly, a registered limited liability company will be responsible for its own actions and will be predominately liable for its own debts. Companies limited by guarantee are commonly used as vehicles for charities or other 'not-for-profit' entities in circumstances where the raising of capital has little relevance. Unlimited companies are used only in specialist corporate structures. (Types of companies are discussed further in **Chapter 3**.)

The immediate result of a company's incorporation is the creation of two independent bodies: first, the distinct corporate entity and second, its membership. The members of a limited liability company take shares in the company and the shares held represent a member's interest in the company. The nature and extent of this interest will determine the member's right to participate in dividend payments and the member's right to participate in the decision-making of the company (discussed further in **Chapter 7**). The purchase price for the newly issued shares is paid to the company ('subscribed') and the new shares are issued to the subscriber

1

('allotted'). The subscription price of a share can be its nominal value or any higher amount (the excess is referred to as a share 'premium'). Shares cannot be allotted at a 'discount,' that is, shares cannot be allotted at less than their nominal value (see CA 2006, s.580). Shares can be issued 'partly paid' (where only part of the subscription price is paid) or 'fully paid' (where the whole of the subscription price is paid). Where shares are not 'fully paid' the company can generally demand ('call') payment of the unpaid subscription monies at such times and in such a manner provided by the terms of its constitution.

1.1.1   Relationship between members *inter se*

The relationship between members, *inter se* and the relationship between members and the company will be determined by the company's constitution (together with any membership agreement – discussed in **Chapter 6**). Other than where a company's constitution provides otherwise, a member of the company may freely sell or dispose of his shareholding interest. In respect of the company's existence, it is quite irrelevant that the identity of its members may change over time. A company's legal existence is not dependent upon the survival of individual shareholders; a company has perpetual succession.

Although an individual may have exclusively owned the property and assets of a business prior to its incorporation as a registered company, following the incorporation of the business, the property vests exclusively in the company (the consideration for the transfer of business property may take the form of shares in the newly incorporated company). A shareholder is afforded no right of ownership in respect of the company's property or assets. For example, in *Macaura* v. *Northern Assurance Co* [1925] AC 619, a timber merchant converted his business into a registered company; the timber merchant held the majority shareholding. The property of the newly incorporated company was destroyed by fire and the merchant sought to recoup his loss by claiming against his insurance company. Although the property was insured, the insurance policy was held in the merchant's name. As the merchant no longer owned the property subject to the claim, the property having been legally transferred to the company, the insurance company was not held to be responsible for satisfying the claim. On the incorporation of the business, the insurance policy should have been transferred into the name of the new owner of the property, namely the company (see also, *Re Lewis Wills Trust* [1985] 1 WLR 102).

Although one person may in effect control and execute the affairs of a company by occupying several positions in the corporate structure – for example, an individual may be the majority shareholder, the company's managing director and at the same time the company's sole employee – such a person is not 'the company'. A company is not a slave in the sense that it cannot be owned by any individual (see, e.g. *Lee* v. *Lee's Air Farming* [1961] AC 12). Indeed, an individual who, as the sole shareholder and director of a company, controls the affairs and destiny of the company will ordinarily, in holding a valid service contract, still be regarded as an employee of the company (discussed further in **Chapter 4**). While a company holds its property and assets for the ultimate benefit of the associated rights of its membership, a member of the company may still be convicted of theft from the company, notwithstanding that the member in question holds all or substantially all the shares in the company (see, e.g. *Attorney General's Reference (No.2 of 1982)* [1984] 2 WLR 447, *DPP* v. *Gomez* [1993] AC 442).

The principal disadvantage of incorporation is the loss of privacy for the business; registered companies are subject to many disclosure requirements. Disclosure is a regulatory requirement imposed on companies for the general benefit and safeguard of the public interest. Information relating to the functioning and financial state of a company offers a degree of transparency, giving to investors and creditors the opportunity to obtain knowledge relating to a company's business functions. Public disclosure requirements are imposed by the companies legislation and are made to Companies House (where registration documents, registers, etc. are kept). Disclosure requirements include the basic registration procedures, compiling and maintaining registers, for example, the members and directors register, details of changes to the constitutional structure of the company, copies of all the special resolutions passed by the general meeting of a company, and information of a financial nature.

1.2 A BRIEF HISTORY OF THE REGISTERED COMPANY

The registered company was born in the mid-nineteenth century and, as such, company law is a comparatively modern legal phenomenon. Nevertheless, prior to the mid-nineteenth century, business associations existed in a form that may be properly described as ancestors of, and necessary catalysts to, the present system of company law.

1.2.1 The chartered joint stock company

Chartered joint stock companies were developed in the seventeenth century, largely as a result of an expansion in global trade. Examples of chartered joint stock companies included the East India Company (formed in 1612), the Massachusetts Bay Company (formed in 1629) and the Hudson's Bay Company (formed in 1670). A joint stock company was a sophisticated form of partnership concern and was created with the consent of the Crown, by means of a Royal Charter. A joint stock company had an association of members and each member contributed capital towards specific trade ventures. Individual charters often provided the association with monopolistic rights in specific trades. The joint stock company had a separate legal identity and, if specifically provided for in the company's charter, could be created with a limited liability status. A member of a joint stock company would take shares in the company in proportion to his initial contribution towards the company's stock.

3

A growth in joint stock companies mirrored an expansion in the number of share dealings and by the early part of the eighteenth century speculation in share values had become another means by which the gentry could indulge their gambling instincts. One such company in which the speculative fervour thrived was the South Sea Company. This company was founded in 1711 with the objective of obtaining a monopoly of trade with colonies in South America. The company prospered and, in an ambitious attempt to expand its wealth, entered into a venture whereby it sought to purchase the national debt. The company proposed to buy out government creditors or to persuade them to take shares in the South Sea Company in exchange for the creditors' claims on the national debt. The rationale behind the venture was that the national debt was a profitable high interest-bearing loan. Confidence in the South Sea Company's proposals escalated. In 1719, the year in which the company had first offered to purchase the national debt, a £100 share in the company was quoted at £136, whereas by mid-1720, the share price had reached £1,000. The surge in confidence in the South Sea shares resulted in a general increase in share dealings and a speculative boom in the general value of share prices of other companies. Unfortunately, companies with dubious corporate objectives, many of which had been formed by purchasing charters of long extinct companies, thrived as a result of the general acceptance by naive investors that a company share could do nothing but escalate in value.

The subsequent collapse of the South Sea Company led to general panic and a decline in confidence in respect of the national share market. The resulting wide-spread collapse in markets was inevitable; fraudulently conceived companies were prosecuted; members of the government who had been involved in the share dealings fell from grace; and Parliament, in an attempt to curb the improper use of the corporate form, passed the so-called Bubble Act of 1720. The purpose of this Act was greatly to restrict share transactions and to impose a stricter regime on the ability of businesses to trade as companies.

1.2.2 Unincorporated associations

The decline in the corporate form as a business medium continued until the start of the nineteenth century. The nineteenth century witnessed an increase in the number of companies created by individual Acts of Parliament; such companies were ordinarily large trading concerns, as the expense of incorporating by this method was extremely prohibitive of smaller business ventures. However, despite the growth in statutory companies (e.g. banks, canal companies, railway companies, etc.), by far the most popular form of business organisation of the time was the unincorporated association. The unincorporated association was formed under a trust deed (the deed of settlement) and in a similar way to joint stock companies, members of the association would invest capital in an association and in return take shares in the association. Yet, unlike joint stock companies, the property and assets of the association were not held by the business as a separate legal entity. Trustees who could sue and be sued on behalf of the association held the property and assets.

The principal disadvantage of the unincorporated association was that the members of these businesses did not have the advantage of a limited liability status. In addition, until the Bubble Act was repealed in 1825, the right of members to freely transfer shares in the associations remained undoubtedly questionable.

1.2.3 The Joint Stock Companies Act 1844

The Joint Stock Companies Act 1844 gave birth to the first form of registered company. As a result of the 1844 Act, a company could be incorporated by a registration procedure providing the company had 25 members or more. The 1844 Act also created the registrar of companies with whom particulars of registered companies had to be lodged. Despite the creation of the registered company, the 1844 Act did not confer a limited liability status on these companies. At that time, limited liability was viewed as a means by which under-capitalised concerns could exploit the corporate form to the detriment of creditors and the investing public.

1.3 LIMITED LIABILITY

The Limited Liability Act of 1855 allowed companies with at least 25 members, each holding shares to the minimum value of £10, of which at least one-fifth of the shares was fully paid up, to incorporate a company with a limited liability status. In accordance with the 1855 Act, a company was required to have not less than three-quarters of its nominal capital subscribed and the word 'limited' added to its name. Prior to the Act, the ability to grant a limited liability status to a small business enterprise had been the subject of much discussion; the discussion centred around the fear that general limited liability would result in under-capitalised concerns and as such be detrimental to corporate creditors and the general public interest (see, e.g. the report of the Royal Commission on Mercantile Law and the Law of Partnership in 1854).

In accordance with the 1855 Act, the liability of a member was (as it still is today) limited to the nominal value of the share. The 1855 Act was incorporated into the Joint Stock Companies Act 1856, which required an obligation on the part of a company to have and register constitutional documents, namely the memorandum and articles of association (these in effect replaced the deed of settlement). In addition, and to encourage smaller business enterprises to register as companies, the 1856 Act removed the restriction relating to the minimum amount of capital that had to be contributed by members. Further, it reduced the minimum number of members required for the purposes of incorporation from 25 to seven members. The companies legislation was consolidated into the Companies Act of 1862. The desire to encourage incorporation was fuelled by acceleration in business activity which had been initially inspired and generated by the industrial revolution and a general increase in global trade.

1.3.1 The *Salomon* principle

In the context of the judicial interpretation of the Victorian legislation and the incorporation of large established business concerns, the recognition of the registered company as a separate legal entity, one vested with a limited liability status, was generally accepted without much dissent. Providing a large business concern was registered in accordance with the companies legislation, it was taken that it could benefit from the advantages of incorporation (see, e.g. the House of Lords' decision in *The Princess of Reuss* (1871) 5 LR 176, a case in which the existence of an enterprise incorporated properly as a limited liability company (under the Companies Act 1862) was unsuccessfully challenged on the basis that its membership was composed of 'foreigners'!)

However, the judicial acceptance of smaller registered companies, often incorporated with only one substantial shareholder, was a matter of some uncertainty. While the 1862 Act, in providing that a company should be incorporated by at least seven members, raised perhaps an expectation that those seven members would all contribute significantly towards the company's capital, in the case of many small private companies the expectation was not realised. At the beginning of the 1860s, the incorporation of small 'one-man type' businesses had been rare, but as the nineteenth century progressed, the incorporation of small businesses increased dramatically. By the start of the twentieth century, the small incorporated concern represented an overwhelming majority of all registered companies.

The case heralded as establishing the registered company as an acceptable and valid form of business medium for small businesses was *Salomon v. A Salomon Ltd* [1897] AC 22 (however, it should be noted that earlier examples of the judicial acceptance of an ability to incorporate small businesses do exist; see, e.g. *Re George Newman & Co* [1895] 1 Ch 674 and *Farrar v. Farrar* (1889) 40 Ch D 395). In the *Salomon* case, the proprietor of a small but successful leather business, a Mr Salomon, incorporated the business as a limited company in accordance with the registration provisions contained within the Companies Act 1862. Section 6 of the 1862 Act provided that seven or more persons together could incorporate a business, provided that it was associated for a lawful purpose. The seven subscribers to A Salomon Ltd were Mr Salomon, his wife and their five children. The company, A Salomon Ltd, purchased Mr Salomon's business in a solvent state for a consideration to a value of approximately £39,000. In respect of this consideration, Mr Salomon received 20,000 fully paid-up £1 shares, an issue of debentures to the value of £10,000 (a debenture acknowledges a loan or other credit agreement between the company and its creditor and is normally secured against the assets of the company; in Salomon's case the debenture was secured by means of a floating charge). (Floating charges are discussed in **Chapter 11**.) Mr Salomon took the remainder of the sale price in cash. The remaining members of the family were each allotted a £1 share in the company.

Unfortunately, A Salomon Ltd did not prosper. Prior to its eventual demise, Mr Salomon's debentures had been transferred to a Mr Broderip in return for £5,000;

this amount was pumped back into the company by Mr Salomon. Yet, despite further efforts on the part of Mr Salomon to keep the company afloat, less than a year after its incorporation, the company fell into an insolvent state. The failure of the business was attributed to disruption associated with trade union activity and the loss of substantial contracts. The company could not meet Broderip's debenture interest payments and, fearful that his investment would be lost, Broderip sought to realise his security (the floating charge) by appointing a receiver. (The role of a receiver is discussed in **Chapter 22**.) The company, which had other creditors, was subsequently put into liquidation. (Liquidation is discussed in **Chapter 22**.) The liquidation of the company's assets realised sufficient funds to meet the company's debt to Broderip but not the debts owed to the company's other creditors; unlike Broderip, the other creditors had no secured interest (debentures). In the High Court (heard as *Broderip* v. *Salomon* [1895] 2 Ch 323), the liquidator admitted the validity of Broderip's prior claim to be repaid from the company's assets. Nevertheless, the liquidator counter-claimed that the company (in effect the company's unsecured creditors) was entitled to be reimbursed by Mr Salomon personally. The trial judge, Vaughan Williams J, agreed with this contention. While admitting that upon its registration a company was a legal entity, distinct from its corporators, the learned judge opined that in the case before him, A Salomon Ltd (the company) was no more than an agent of its principal, i.e. Mr Salomon. As such, the principal was responsible for the debts of its agent. The basis for the agency argument was that the company was a mere alias of its founder and had not been formed in accordance with the true spirit of the Companies Act 1862. Vaughan Williams J considered that the 1862 Act, in its requirement for 'seven persons associated for a lawful purpose' should be interpreted to mean seven persons with a *bona fide* intention of participating in a trading venture, and not, as in the *Salomon* case, a company that was akin to a one-man business.

On appeal, the decision of Vaughan Williams J was upheld, although in the Court of Appeal's opinion the correct analogy between the company and Mr Salomon was that of a trust relationship; the company held its property on trust for its beneficiary, Mr Salomon. As such, the creditors of A Salomon Ltd were entitled to a claim against Mr Salomon through the company. As at first instance, the Court of Appeal recognised that the incorporation of A Salomon Ltd had complied technically with the registration provisions of the 1862 Act. However, in unison with the reasoning of the High Court, the Court of Appeal considered that the correct and legitimate interpretation of the Companies Act 1862 was that the seven required members of the company should have had more than a nominal and superficial interest in the company. Accordingly, the court refused to accept that the liability of A Salomon Ltd should be divorced from that of its founder, Mr Salomon. Although the business had been profitable prior to its incorporation, Lindley LJ was of the opinion that the manner in which the company had been formed indicated that it had been created for an illegitimate purpose, that it was 'a device to defraud creditors' (at p.339). Indeed, in the Court of Appeal's opinion, the company's illegitimacy stemmed from the fact that it was in reality a one-man company.

However, in reversing the decision of the Court of Appeal, the House of Lords rigorously denied any assertion by the lower courts that a company could not be formed by one dominant character together with six other persons divorced of a substantial interest in the business venture. According to the House, the statutory language of the Companies Act 1862 (s.6) was clear. A company could be incorporated providing it had at least seven members, irrespective of whether all seven members had made a substantial financial contribution to the company. In this respect, the House of Lords' interpretation of the separate legal identity of a company was absolute. Lord Macnaghten opined:

> The company is at law a different person altogether from the subscribers to the memorandum; and though it may be that after incorporation the business is precisely the same as it was before, and the same persons are managers, and the same hands receive the profits, the company is not in law the agent of the subscribers or trustee for them. Nor are the subscribers as members liable, in any shape or form, except to the extent and in the manner provided by the Act. (at p.51)

In considering the agency and trust arguments of the lower courts, the House of Lords concluded that both arguments were contradictory to the view that the company was a separate legal entity. Further, the finding of an agency or trust relationship would have rendered as illusory the limited liability of the company's majority shareholder, Mr Salomon. Nevertheless, implicit from the judgments of both Lord Macnaghten and Lord Halsbury was the fact that if the company had been incorporated for a fraudulent/sham purpose, such a finding would have disturbed the otherwise legitimate incorporation of the company. For example, commenting on the judgment of the Court of Appeal, Lord Halsbury LC opined:

> If there was no fraud and no agency, and if the company was a real one and not a fiction or a myth, every one of the grounds upon which it is sought to support the judgment is disposed of. (at p.33)

While it is unfortunate that only two of the five members of the House commented on issues related to the effect of a fraudulent incorporation, the lacuna is understandable, given that the incorporation of A Salomon Ltd provided no evidence of any significant fraudulent/sham conduct (other than perhaps the over-optimistic valuation of the company). However, it is submitted that an ability to disturb an otherwise 'legitimate' incorporation on the basis of a fraud/sham (equitable fraud) should be regarded rightly as a secondary element of the main *Salomon* principle. However, in reality, mention of the 'secondary element' is often disregarded in the context of court judgments related to the justification for the disturbance of a company's distinct legal personality (discussed further in **Chapter 4**). Although a fraud/sham incorporation may be capable of disturbing a company's distinct legal personality, the concept of a fraud/sham is restrictively construed by the courts and does not really marry with the true concept of an equitable fraud, a concept that was envisaged (perhaps) in, for example, the judgment of Lord Halsbury, in the *Salomon* case (discussed further in **Chapter 4**).

1.4   THE REGISTERED COMPANY INTO THE TWENTY-FIRST CENTURY

1.4.1   Advantages and disadvantages of the limited liability company

The principal advantage of incorporating a business is undoubtedly the limited liability status of the enterprise, coupled with the favourable and respectable standing that the public (often mistakenly) afford to the limited liability status of the enterprise. In addition to possible tax advantages (discussed in **Chapter 13**), the creation of a limited liability company is a means by which entrepreneurs may limit the risk of investing funds into a business enterprise. Any member of a company limited by shares will, on the basis of a shareholding interest, only ever be liable to contribute to the debts of the company to the extent that his or her shares have not been fully paid. Therefore, if X holds 100 £1 shares and has partly paid £60 in consideration for the same, X's potential liability to contribute to the company's debts will be £40. Once shares held by X are fully paid, X (and any successor) will cease to be liable to contribute towards the company's debts. A company limited by shares may be either a public company (plc), or a private company. A company which is not registered as a public company is construed to be a private company. A company which proposes to operate as a public company must, as from 1980, have been specifically registered as a public limited company. In accordance with CA 2006, both public and private companies must have at least one shareholder and a public company must have at least two directors; a private company need only have one director. Prior to trading a public company must be registered with a minimum share capital (currently £50,000). Unlike a private company, a public company may offer its securities to the general public. (The types and classification of companies are discussed further in **Chapter 3**.)

The principal disadvantage of incorporation is a loss of privacy for the business. Disclosure is a regulatory requirement that is imposed on companies for the general benefit and safeguard of the public interest. Information relating to the functioning and financial state of a company offers a degree of transparency, providing investors and creditors with an opportunity to obtain an insight into a company's business affairs (see further, the Companies (Company Records) Regulations 2008, SI 2008/3006). Public disclosure requirements are imposed by law and disclosure must be made to the registrar of companies at Companies House (where registration documents and certain public information are filed). The disclosure requirements include the basic registration procedures, filing details in the directors' register, details of changes to the constitutional structure of the company, copies of all the special resolutions passed by the general meeting of a company, details of security created by companies over their assets, and their annual accounts. In addition, every registered company must complete an annual return (a report of the company's affairs and details of its shareholders); this must be filed with the registrar of companies, at Companies House (CA 2006, s.854). Further to the annual return, all companies must submit a directors' report for each financial year to include matters such as the development and business activities of the company and the amount (if any) which the directors recommend be paid as a dividend (CA 2006, s.415 and the Small Companies and Groups (Accounts and Directors' Report) Regulations 2008, SI 2008/409, Sched.5). However, it is to be observed that CA 2006, s.415A provides exemptions to the content required of a directors' report in circumstances where the company in question is entitled to prepare accounts in accordance with the small companies regime. Extended matters must be included in the directors' report in respect of a medium- or large-sized company (see the Large and Medium-sized Companies and Groups (Accounts and Reports) Regulations 2008, SI 2008/410, Sched.7). A company must provide an annual report of its accounts that must give a 'true and fair' view of the company's financial affairs (CA 2006, s.393). (Accounting and reporting matters are dealt with further in **Chapter 12**.)

While many statutory changes have occurred in the field of company law since the creation of the registered company, for example, now both private and public limited companies may be incorporated with just one member, the skeleton of the Victorian legislation remains a definite characteristic of modern company law. Incorporation by the process of registration, the recognition of a company as a separate legal identity and the ability to incorporate a business with a limited liability status are characteristics at the very heart of modern company law. The birth of the registered limited liability company was, and remains, a means by which businessmen are allowed legitimately to limit the risk of investing funds into a business enterprise. Encouraging the growth and expansion of companies is of the utmost importance to the national economy because successful companies generate wealth and employment opportunities. Indeed, limited liability stimulates economic expansion. From the time of its introduction, the concept of limited liability has encouraged capital to be aggregated for investment purposes. Nevertheless, while in the nineteenth century loan funds for small- to medium-sized entrepreneurs were not readily available and therefore the aggregation of capital through the medium of the company was a means to enhance the value and potential of a small business, in more modern times this position has not been so apposite (although in very recent times this is perhaps debateable). As part of the twentieth century's credit boom, the availability of business loans has, in small private companies, deflated a need for the aggregation of capital. Therefore, in the context of a private company, a limited liability status may no longer be viewed as a clear advantage in the funding of the enterprise. In addition, in private companies composed of very few members and where a majority of the membership are also directors of the company (the position in the vast majority of private companies), the advantage of trading an enterprise with a limited liability status may be somewhat illusory. Here, major creditors of the enterprise (usually its bankers and landlords) will often demand personal guarantees from the member(s) of the company to secure the company's potential indebtedness. In such a case, should the company's fortunes decline, the member(s) of the company may gain little from the limited liability status of the company as they will remain personally liable, under the terms of the guarantees, to repay the secured debts.

In relation to public companies, limited liability offers greater advantages and protection to the company's shareholders and directors. Unlike private companies, the expectation of personal guarantees is less obvious in the wake of security represented in the form of substantive corporate assets and significant levels of paid-up capital. Further, unlike the private company, a public company is permitted to offer its shares to the general public, providing an advantageous method of raising substantial amounts of investment capital (usually by having its shares 'listed' on a public stock exchange, which provides a marketplace in which the shares can be bought and sold – discussed further in **Chapter 9**).

1.4.2 The registered company and the legislative framework

Prior to the introduction of CA 2006, the regulation of the registered company was subject to an extensive consultation exercise with proposals for reform advanced by both the Law Commission and the company law review (CLR) undertaken by a Steering Group of the Department of Trade and Industry (DTI) (it is to be noted that the DTI became the Department for Business, Enterprise and Regulatory Reform (BERR), which itself is now renamed as the Department for Business, Innovation and Skills (BIS)). The CLR culminated in the Final Report of 2001, 'Modern Company Law for a Competitive Economy'. In 2002, the government responded to the findings of the CLR and produced a White Paper, 'Modernising Company Law' (Cm 5553). In May 2004, the DTI published a further consultation document, 'Company Law: Flexibility and Accessibility'. On 17 March 2005, the government published a second White Paper, 'Company Law Reform' (Cm 6456). In November 2005, the Company Law Reform Bill was issued but was subsequently renamed the Companies Bill 2006. On 8 November 2006, the Companies Act 2006 received Royal Assent. Unlike its predecessor, CA 1985, the 2006 Act also applies directly to Northern Ireland. The overwhelming majority of the 2006 Act's provisions came into force by October 2009. CA 2006 is supplemented by a substantial body of secondary legislation. CA 2006 is significantly longer than CA 1985 and its effect on some areas of company law may justify it being regarded as a reforming piece of legislation. However, in many areas of company law, CA 2006 does not seek to confer substantial changes to the spirit and intent of the previous companies legislation. As such, a number of changes may be described as cosmetic. Other Acts of Parliament which regulate the registered company include the Insolvency Act (IA) 1986, the Enterprise Act (EA) 2002 and the Companies (Audit, Investigations and Community Enterprise) Act 2004.

CHAPTER 2

The formation and registration of a corporate entity

2.1 THE PROMOTION AND FORMATION OF A COMPANY

For a company to obtain the benefits of a limited liability status, it must comply first with the registration provisions contained in the companies legislation. However, prior to obtaining a certificate of registration, the formation of a company will be undertaken by a promoter. Although the companies legislation has never sought to define a promoter, the promoter is nevertheless essential to the creation of a new corporate entity. To establish a person as a promoter, case law illustrates that it is necessary to show the contribution of some essential element towards the incorporation of the company (see, e.g. *Whaley Bridge Calico Printing Co* v. *Green* (1879) 5 QBD 109). The level of contribution may be substantial: for example, negotiating the purchase of business premises; or, on the other hand, it may be less extensive: for example, a person may be deemed to be a promoter by organising the appointment of a company director. The promotion of a public or large private company is likely to be undertaken by a professional agency, but where a small business is to be incorporated, the promotion will normally, although not exclusively, be carried out by the owner of the pre-incorporated business.

A promoter cannot be considered an agent or a trustee of the company which he or she undertakes to promote, because prior to its incorporation the company will have no legal existence. Nevertheless, a promoter occupies a position which is liable to abuse, to the extent that the position is made subject to fiduciary duties in a manner similar to those owed by company directors (discussed in **Chapter 15**). A promoter is also subject to a common law duty to exercise reasonable care and skill in the performance of his or her duties. As a consequence of their assumed fiduciary position, a promoter will be required to make a full disclosure of any personal interest in the promotion process. Accordingly, the promoter must disclose whether he or she obtained a profit as a result of the promotion of the company. A failure to disclose may render the promoter liable to account to the company for the amount of the undisclosed profit. For example, in *Gluckstein* v. *Barnes* [1900] AC 240, a syndicate of businessmen purchased the Olympia Exhibition Hall in West London from a company in liquidation, for a sum of £140,000. The syndicate then promoted a company which subsequently purchased the hall for £180,000. On the public issue of the company's shares the prospectus disclosed the purchase profit of £40,000. However, the prospectus failed to disclose that, in addition to purchasing the Olympia Exhibition Hall, the syndicate had also purchased certain secured debts, secured against the insolvent company's assets. The syndicate purchased the secured debts for £20,000 and, on the realisation of the insolvent company's assets, made a £20,000 profit on that purchase. The House of Lords held that the promoter of the company, namely the syndicate, was liable to account to the company for the amount of the undisclosed profit, that is, a sum of £20,000.

Disclosure of a promoter's personal interest in the promotion of a company must be made to those persons who have invested in or are about to invest in the company, i.e. the company's shareholders or potential shareholders (see, e.g. *Lagunas Nitrate Co* v. *Lagunas Syndicate* [1899] 2 Ch 392). Where a promoter fails to disclose any benefit obtained as a result of entering into a contract related to a company's promotion, the contract will be voidable. The company, if it is to successfully rescind the contract, must not delay in avoiding it. The restitution of the subject matter of the contract must be possible, although where this is not the case, the court may order financial adjustments to be made between the parties.

It is to be noted that a great part of the relevant case law in relation to the extent and enforcement of a promoter's duties is rooted in the mid to late nineteenth century, a period of time when it was common practice for newly incorporated companies to offer shares to the general public. The duties imposed on promoters were a means by which investors could be protected from any fraudulent attempt on the part of a promoter to obtain undeclared and unwarranted profits from the promotion of what was often an unknown and untested business enterprise. In today's world the vast majority of public issues take place as a result of established private companies electing to become public companies and consequently there is less likelihood of fraud. (Public issues are discussed in **Chapter 9**.)

2.1.1 Pre-incorporation contracts

Prior to the incorporation of the business, the promoter(s) of a company will be required to enter into contractual agreements relating to the pre-incorporated company. However, until a company is incorporated it has no existence as a separate legal entity and therefore cannot be bound by contracts made in its name or on its behalf (see, e.g. *Natal Land & Colonisation Co* v. *Pauline Colliery Syndicate* [1904] AC 120). Even after its incorporation, a company cannot expressly, or by conduct, retrospectively ratify or adopt a contract made in its name or on its behalf (see, e.g. *Re Northumberland Avenue Hotel Co* (1886) 33 Ch D 16). Neither may a company adopt a pre-incorporation contract by including the terms of the contract within its constitution (see, e.g. *Browne* v. *La Trinidad* (1887) 37 Ch D 1). To take the benefit of a pre-incorporation contract the newly incorporated company must enter into a new contract with the party with whom the promoter dealt (a novation). Evidence of the existence of a novation may be found where the renegotiation of the terms of the original pre-incorporation contract result in the express or implied creation of a new set of obligations between the company and the contracting third party (see, e.g. *Howard Patent Ivory Manufacturing Co* (1888) 38 Ch D 156). However, following the Court of Appeal's decision in *Rover International Ltd* v. *Cannon Film Sales Ltd* [1988] BCLC 710, monies paid by a newly incorporated company to a third party in the mistaken belief that a pre-incorporation contract was valid may be recovered as against the third party. In addition, the court may grant a *quantum meruit* award to the company for services which it provided, i.e. for the period in which the company was under the mistaken belief that the pre-incorporation contract was valid. The aforementioned remedies may also be awarded against a company in circumstances where a third party mistakenly believed that the business entity with which it had contracted was, at the time of the contract, an incorporated company.

2.1.2 The liability of a promoter

Prior to the UK's accession to the EC in 1972, common law rules exclusively determined whether a promoter could be regarded as a principal to a pre-incorporation contract. The common law rules operated on the basis of a technical and artificial distinction, related to the manner in which the promoter had signed the contract. Where a promoter entered into a contract signing the contract as the company's agent, or signing it on behalf of a company, the promoter could be held personally liable on the contract (see, e.g. *Kelner* v. *Baxter* (1866) LR 2 CP 174). On the other hand, where a promoter entered into a contract by signing the contract using the company's name and merely added his own name to authenticate that of the company's, then, following *Newborne* v. *Sensolid (Great Britain) Ltd* [1954] 1 QB 45, the promoter would not be regarded as a principal to the contract and would escape any personal liability for a purported breach of the terms of the contract. The contract would be classed as having been made with a non-existent entity and as such would be declared a nullity. However, it should be noted that where a contract was declared a nullity a promoter could still incur liability for breach of warranty in a situation where the promoter, in authenticating the contract, did so as a purported director of the company. By authenticating the contract with his own signature, expressed to represent the signature of a director of the unincorporated company, the promoter would misrepresent his authority because at the time of signing the contract the company had no legal existence and therefore could have had no validly appointed directors (see, e.g. *Collen* v. *Wright* (1857) 8 E & B 647).

As a consequence of the UK's entry to the EC, the UK was obliged to implement art.7 of the First Company Law Directive. As a result of the UK's implementation of art.7, the artificial distinction in the rules of common law as applicable to pre-incorporation contracts, was eradicated. The position is now governed by CA 2006, s.51, which provides:

> A contract that purports to be made by or on behalf of a company at a time when the company has not been formed has effect, subject to any agreement to the contrary, as one made with the person purporting to act for the company or as agent for it, and he is personally liable on the contract accordingly.

The wording of CA 2006, s.51 follows on from its statutory predecessors (CA 1985, ss.36C(1) and 36(4)) the statutory language of all the provisions being derived from the European Communities Act (ECA) 1972, s.9(2). The effect of CA 2006, s.51 is to render a promoter personally liable in respect of a pre-incorporation contract, irrespective of whether the promoter signed the contract in the company's name or on behalf of the company. However, a major difference between art.7, and what is now CA 2006, s.51 is that while art.7 expressly states that a company, once formed, may 'assume the obligations' contained within a pre-incorporation contract, s.51 does not. While the party with whom the pre-incorporation contract was made may agree to enter into a new contract with the company (a novation), the new contractual obligation cannot be deemed an assumption of the obligation contained in the pre-incorporation contract; the present position subsists despite the fact that in 1962 the report of the Jenkins Committee (Cmnd 1749) recommended that companies should be given the statutory power to adopt pre-incorporation contracts.

Where CA 2006, s.51 is applicable, its effect is to remove the technical distinctions found in the common law prior to the UK's implementation of the EC First Company Law Directive. Indeed, in *Phonogram* v. *Lane* [1982] QB 938, Lord Denning stated that the distinction between cases such as *Kelner* v. *Baxter* and *Newbourne* v. *Sensolid*, had been 'obliterated'. In *Phonogram* v. *Lane,* a future company, to be named Fragile Management Ltd, was to be formed for the purpose of managing a musical band known as 'Cheap, Mean and Nasty'. The plaintiff, Phonogram Ltd, agreed to finance the group to the sum of £12,000, a sum payable in two instalments. The first payment was sent to the defendant, the group's manager, in anticipation of a recording contract being entered into within a specified time period; the money was to be returned if the contract had not been completed within the time period. For administrative reasons, the cheque was made payable to Jelly Music Ltd – the defendant (the group's manager) was a director of Jelly Music Ltd. The defendant, at the request of the plaintiff, signed the financial agreement 'for and on behalf of Fragile Management Ltd'.

The proposed management company (Fragile Management Ltd) was never incorporated. The plaintiff sued the defendant for the return of the first instalment (i.e. £6,000). The defendant contended that the then relevant legislation, ECA 1972, s.9(2), only applied (in accordance with the French translation of art.9) to a company already in the course of formation (Fragile Management had never been in the course of formation). The defendant also argued that, in accordance with s.9(2), personal liability could only be imposed where a person had contracted as the company's agent; on this point the defendant argued that as Fragile Management had never been formed there could be no principal for which an agent could act. Notwithstanding the defendant's protestations, the Court of Appeal held that the wording of ECA 1972, s.9(2), and not the French translation of art.9 was to be applied and following the interpretation of s.9(2) the defendant was deemed personally liable to account to the plaintiff for the sum in question.

In order for a promoter to avoid the threat of being made personally liable on a pre-incorporation contract, an express statement excluding the promoter's liability must be included within the contract. Despite the theoretical possibility of the appearance of such a clause, its practical effect would be to prevent the party with whom the promoter dealt from seeking specific performance or damages for non-performance or non-compliance with the terms of the pre-incorporation contract, i.e. neither the company (when incorporated) nor its promoter would be deemed liable. Somewhat surprisingly, s.51 makes no specific reference to the promoter's right to enforce the terms of a pre-incorporation contract. However, in the light of basic contract law principles, both parties will be able to enforce the contract (see, e.g. *Braymist Ltd* v. *Wise Finance Co Ltd* [2002] BCC 514).

2.1.3 A Wider interpretation of CA 2006, s.51?

Given a wide, but nonetheless plausible, interpretation of CA 2006, s.51, its possible application would appear to be not exclusively confined to the standard type of mischief against which it is aimed, i.e. a promoter's ability to escape personal liability in respect of pre-incorporation contracts. Indeed, it is possible to interpret the section as applicable to any situation whereby a person contracts on behalf of a company which was not formed as of the date on which the contract was made. For example, if one construes the term 'formed' to mean legally incorporated in accordance with registration procedures, then in theory, s.51 could be applicable to a situation where a company sought to change its name and subsequently entered into a contract under its new name but in error of the fact that the new name had not been properly registered. However, notwithstanding the potential merit of such a theory, the judicial interpretation of s.51 specifically restricts the provision's applicability and relevance to a situation involving a pure pre-incorporation contract, a fact illustrated by three decisions of the Court of Appeal: *Badgerhill Properties Ltd* v. *Cottrell* [1991] BCLC 805, *Cotronic (UK) Ltd* v. *Dezonie* [1991] BCLC 721 and *Oshkosh B'Gosh Inc* v. *Dan Marbel Ltd* [1989] BCLC 507. In the *Oshkosh* case, an off-the-shelf company was acquired under the name of Egormight Ltd. In 1980, the company passed a resolution to alter its name to Dan Marbel Inc Ltd. As a result of an administrative oversight by the company, a certificate confirming the company's new name was not issued until 1985. Yet, from 1980 onwards, the company (the first defendants) traded as Dan Marbel Inc Ltd. The plaintiff, a creditor of Egormight/Dan Marbel, commenced an action against the second defendant, a director of Egormight/Dan Marbel, for the non-payment of debts on the premise that ECA 1972, s.9(2) was applicable (now CA 2006, s.51). The plaintiff contended that he had entered into contracts (on which the debts arose) with the second defendant, who acted on behalf of a company (Dan Marbel Inc Ltd), at a time when that company had not been formed. Strictly speaking, that assertion was correct as Dan Marbel Inc Ltd had not been legally incorporated until 1985.

Nevertheless, the Court of Appeal concluded that s.9(2) of the 1972 Act was not applicable to this case because the company with which the plaintiff traded had been formed and was not merely in the process of formation. The Court of Appeal could not appreciate how s.9(2) of the 1972 Act could be pleaded successfully unless the company, as under its first name, was a completely different entity from the company under its second name.

2.2 THE REGISTRATION PROCEDURE

A company must be incorporated in accordance with the registration procedures specified by the companies legislation. Prior to the passing of CA 2006, the registration of a company involved the delivery of two principal constitutional documents to the registrar of companies, namely: (i) the company's memorandum of association; and (ii) the company's articles of association (signed by the subscriber(s) named in the memorandum). Further, a statement of compliance was required.

For companies registered after the implementation of CA 2006, the registration procedure is dealt with by CA 2006, ss.8–16. Companies incorporated under CA 2006, on or after 1 October 2009, are required to submit a memorandum of association and articles of association (although, as discussed below, the memorandum is now of much reduced significance). Further, all limited companies, regardless of when they are incorporated, are required to submit an 'application to register', to include a statement of capital and shareholdings or statement of guarantee.

2.2.1 The memorandum and application for registration

In accordance with CA 2006, s.8, a memorandum of association must state that the subscribers:

(a)   wish to form a company under this Act, and
(b)   agree to become members of the company and, in the case of a company that is to have a share capital, to take at least one share each.

The memorandum must be in the prescribed form, in accordance with the Companies (Registration) Regulations 2008, SI 2008/3014 and must be authenticated by each subscriber. The memorandum of association of a company having a share capital must be in the form set out in Sched.1 to the regulations and the memorandum of association of a company not having a share capital must be set out as in Sched.2. It is to be noted that, as from 1 October 2009, those parts of the memorandum of an existing company that are deemed additional to that of the new-style memorandum requirements will be automatically deemed to be part of the company's articles of association.

17

The effect of CA 2006 weakens greatly the previous significance of the memorandum to the extent that, as from 1 October 2009, the memorandum is no longer of any real legal relevance to the constitutional structure of a company. For example, a company is no longer obliged to maintain an objects clause within its memorandum, the purpose of which was to spell out and bind the company in respect of its intended business purposes (discussed further in **Chapter 16**). In effect, for companies incorporated in accordance with CA 2006, a company's constitutional framework will now be determined by the company's articles of association.

2.2.2 The articles of association (articles)

If a company requires 'bespoke' articles, these must be filed with the registration application. In circumstances where bespoke articles of association are not included with the application for registration, the statutory model of articles prescribed for the specific type of company in question will be deemed to take effect. The current three sets of model articles (for a private company limited by shares, a public company and a private company limited by guarantee) are to be found in the Companies (Model Articles) Regulations 2008, SI 2008/3229. (The significance and relevance of the articles of association is discussed in **Chapter 6**.) It is important to note that, in relation to the model set of articles that (may) govern a company, the model set of articles in place at the date of the company's incorporation will ordinarily be the articles that govern the company. Therefore, a company incorporated after 1948 but before 1985 will be governed by the model articles prescribed by the Companies Act 1948 and likewise a company incorporated between 1985 and the implementation of CA 2006 is likely to be governed by the articles prescribed by the Companies Act 1985. A company incorporated prior to the implementation of the 2006 Act may, however, alter its articles (by special resolution) to adopt the model articles prescribed by CA 2006.

2.2.3 Application to register

Specific information relevant to a company's registration that was an obligatory requirement of the memorandum (in accordance with CA 1985) is, following the implementation of CA 2006, now deemed an obligatory requirement of the 'application to register'. Therefore, the following information must be included in the 'application to register' (see CA 2006, s.9):

(a)   the company's proposed name;
(b)   if the company's registered office is to be situated in England and Wales (or specifically in Wales), in Scotland or in Northern Ireland;
(c)   whether the liability of the members of the company is to be limited, and if so whether it is to be limited by shares or by guarantee; and
(d)   if the company is to be a private or a public company.

The application must also contain:

(a)   in the case of a company with a share capital:

    (i)   a statement of initial shareholdings; and

    (ii)   a statement of capital;

(b)   in relation to a company that is to be limited by guarantee, a statement of guarantee;

(c)   a statement of the company's proposed officers;

(d)   a statement of the intended address of the company's registered office; and

(e)   a copy of any proposed articles of association (to the extent that these are not supplied by the default application of the model articles).

2.2.4   Statement of initial shareholdings

For the purposes of CA 2006, s.10(3), the statement of initial shareholdings must contain the names and addresses of the subscribers to the memorandum of association and must state, with respect to each subscriber to the memorandum:

(a)   the number and nominal value of the shares to be taken by the subscriber on formation; and

(b)   the amount (if any) payable in respect of each share on formation, whether on account of the nominal value or by way of a premium.

2.2.5   Statement of share capital

CA 2006, s.10(3) provides that the statement of capital must contain the name and address of each subscriber to the memorandum of association. The statement must state, with respect to the company's share capital on formation:

(a)   the total number of shares;

(b)   the aggregate nominal value of those shares;

(c)   for each class of shares:

    (i)   prescribed particulars of the rights attached to the shares;

    (ii)   the total number of shares of that class; and

    (iii) the aggregate nominal value of shares of that class; and

(d)   the amount paid up and the amount (if any) unpaid on each share (whether on account of the nominal value of the share or by way of premium).

2.2.6   Statement of guarantee

In accordance with CA 2006, s.11(3), for a company limited by guarantee the statement of guarantee must contain the names and addresses of the subscribers to the memorandum and must state that each member undertakes that, if the company is wound up while he or she is a member, or within one year after ceasing to be a member, he or she will contribute to the assets of the company such amount as may be required for:

(a)   payment of the debts and liabilities of the company contracted before ceasing to be a member;
(b)   payment of the costs, charges and expenses of winding up; and
(c)   adjustment of the rights of the contributories among themselves, not exceeding a specified limit.

2.2.7   Statement of proposed officers

The statement of the company's proposed officers must contain the required particulars of:

(a)   the person who is or persons who are to be the first director or directors of the company;
(b)   in the case of a company that is to be a public company, the person who is (or the persons who are) to be the first secretary (or joint secretaries) of the company.

The required particulars must be stated in the company's register of directors or register of secretaries. The statement must also contain the consent of each of the persons named as a director, as secretary or as one of the joint secretaries, to act in the relevant capacity. If all the partners in a firm are to be joint secretaries, consent may be given by one partner on behalf of all of them.

2.2.8   Statement of compliance

The application must be accompanied by a statement of compliance (a statutory declaration by a solicitor engaged in the formation of the company or a person named as a director or secretary of the company) to the effect that the statutory requirements of registration have been complied with. If the company is a public company the declaration must provide that the nominal value of the allotted share capital is not less than £50,000 and that the amount paid up on the allotted share capital is equal to not less than one-quarter of its aggregate nominal value.

2.2.9   Delivery of application

The application, memorandum and bespoke articles (if necessary) must be delivered:

(a)   to the registrar of companies for England and Wales, if the registered office of the company is to be situated in England and Wales (or specifically in Wales);
(b)   to the registrar of companies for Scotland, if the registered office of the company is to be situated in Scotland;

(c)   to the registrar of companies for Northern Ireland, if the registered office of the company is to be situated in Northern Ireland.

If the application is delivered by a person as agent for the subscribers to the memorandum of association, the application must specify the agent's name and address.

2.3   THE CERTIFICATE OF INCORPORATION

On the registration of a company, the registrar of companies will issue a certificate to the effect that the company is incorporated (CA 2006, s.15). The certificate must be signed by the registrar or authenticated by the registrar's official seal. The certificate of incorporation must state:

- The name and registered number of the company.
- The date of its incorporation.
- Whether the company is a limited or unlimited company. If the company is limited, whether it is limited by shares or limited by guarantee.
- Whether the company is a private or a public company.
- Whether the company's registered office is situated in England and Wales (or specifically in Wales), in Scotland or in Northern Ireland.

The certificate is conclusive evidence that the statutory requirements for registration have been complied with and that the company:

(a)   is duly registered under CA 2006; and
(b)   where relevant, is duly registered as a limited company or public company.

2.3.1   Membership and officer requirements

Prior to CA 2006, a public company had to be incorporated with at least two members. However, following the implementation of the 2006 Act, it is now possible to incorporate a single member public company. CA 2006 does not distinguish between private and public companies in respect of a 'membership' qualification (CA 2006, s.123). However, a public company will require two directors, whereas a private company requires only one director. For both private and public companies, at least one of the registered directors of the company must be a natural person (CA 2006, s.155). (For the major differences between a public and private company, see CA 2006, Part 20.) A public company must also be incorporated with a named secretary. Under CA 1985, this 'secretary' requirement was also applicable to a private company; however, this requirement is no longer applicable under CA 2006 (CA 2006, s.270). In the case of a single member public company, the single member cannot be appointed as the company's secretary. It is the duty of the directors of a public company to take all reasonable steps to ensure that the secretary (or each joint secretary) of the company is a person who appears to

21

them to have the requisite knowledge and experience to discharge the functions of secretary of the company. CA 2006, s.273(2) provides that a secretary must have one or more of the following qualifications, namely:

(a) he or she has held the office as a secretary of a public company for at least three of the five years immediately preceding his appointment as secretary;

(b) he or she is a member of any of the bodies specified in subsection (3) (see below);

(c) he or she is a barrister, an advocate or a solicitor called or admitted in any part of the UK;

(d) he or she is a person who, by virtue of his holding or having held any other position or his being a member of any other body, appears to the directors to be capable of discharging the functions required of a company secretary.

The bodies referred to in s.273(3) are:

(a) the Institute of Chartered Accountants in England and Wales;
(b) the Institute of Chartered Accountants of Scotland;
(c) the Association of Chartered Certified Accountants;
(d) the Institute of Chartered Accountants in Ireland;
(e) the Institute of Chartered Secretaries and Administrators;
(f) the Chartered Institute of Management Accountants;
(g) the Chartered Institute of Public Finance and Accountancy.

2.3.2 The refusal to register a company

Prior to the issue of a registration certificate, the registrar of companies must be satisfied that the requirements of the statutory registration procedure have been complied with (CA 2006, s.14). The registrar may refuse to register a company if its proposed activities are illegal or contrary to public policy. For example, in *R* v. *Registrar of Companies, ex parte More* [1931] 2 KB 197, the registrar refused to register a company because its objective was to sell lottery tickets in England, on behalf of an Irish lottery. At that time it was illegal to sell lottery tickets in England. The decision of the registrar to refuse to register a company is, however, subject to judicial review and the registrar's decision may be reversed (see, e.g. *R* v. *Registrar of Companies, ex parte Bowen* [1914] 3 KB 1161).

2.3.3 Incorporation

A company is legally incorporated upon the issue of a certificate of incorporation (CA 2006, s.15). The certificate of incorporation identifies the company registered by its name and allotted serial number and is conclusive of the fact that all the requirements of the statutory registration procedures have been complied with. The certificate is also conclusive of the status of the company registered, i.e. if the certificate provides that a company is registered as a public limited company, then the certificate is conclusive of that fact.

A private company, having obtained a certificate of incorporation is permitted, from the date of the certificate, to enter into business activities as a registered company. For example, in *Jubilee Cotton Mills Ltd* v. *Lewis* [1924] AC 958, a company's certificate of incorporation was incorrectly dated 6 January 1920. The certificate had not been signed by the registrar until 8 January 1920. Nevertheless, the House of Lords held that an issue of shares made by the company on 6 January remained valid. Although a mistake was made in respect of the date of the company's incorporation, the certificate's date was, in law, conclusive proof of the fact that the company's incorporation took effect from 6 January 1920. A public limited company must, prior to the commencement of its business, wait until it receives a trading certificate (CA 2006, s.761). Where a public company commences business prior to receipt of a trading certificate, any party with whom the company dealt will nevertheless be protected and the contract will not be set aside. However, the company and any officer in default of the provision will be liable to a fine.

Once the certificate of incorporation is issued, the legal existence of a company cannot be challenged, save in a case where the Crown sought to challenge the legality of a company's business. The Crown may challenge and rescind the incorporation of a company in circumstances deemed necessary to protect the public interest; for example, the Crown would seek to implement its power where the business of the company was associated with an illegal or morally objectionable scheme. For example, in *R* v. *Registrar of Companies, ex parte Attorney General* [1991] BCLC 476, a company had been incorporated with an objective of establishing a prostitution business. Although the registrar had previously refused to register the company under the names of 'Prostitute Ltd', 'Hookers Ltd' and 'French Lessons Ltd', the company was finally granted its registration under the name of Lindi St Clair (Personal Services) Ltd. Despite the fact that the company had overcome all the procedural requirements for registration, its objectives were clearly contrary to the public interest. As such, the court held that the registrar had erred in granting the registration certificate and accordingly the company was struck off the companies register. Where, in such circumstances, the Crown successfully commences proceedings to strike a company off the companies register, the company's existence is retrospectively denied. In law, the company will be regarded as an enterprise which never achieved incorporation in accordance with the provisions of the companies legislation. As such, any outstanding contractual obligations incurred by the business, while it was on the companies register, will be rendered void. It is to be noted that the Crown's ability to commence proceedings to strike a company off the register may be harmful to creditors and the practice must be questionable, especially when an alternative course of action is available under IA 1986, s.122(1)(g). In accordance with s.122(1)(g), a company that was registered for an illegal purpose may be wound up on just and equitable grounds. Winding the company up under s.122(1)(g) provides the company's creditors with an opportunity to make a claim against the company's assets. (IA 1986, s.122(1)(g) is discussed further in **Chapter 19**.)

2.3.4 'Off-the-shelf' companies

A registered company may be purchased from an agency specialising in the sale of 'off-the-shelf' companies. An off-the-shelf company is one that has been incorporated in accordance with the registration provisions of CA 2006, normally having a minimal share capital. The ultimate purpose for its incorporation is its subsequent sale. The advantage to a prospective purchaser of an off-the-shelf company is the speed, relatively low cost and ease by which a business can attain a corporate form. On the payment of a fee (to the agency supplying the off-the-shelf company) the relevant transfers of shares and company's registers will be conveyed to the purchasers of the company. Notification of the change of address of the company's registered office, company directors and secretary, will then be made. If they so wish, the new shareholders of the company may, in accordance with the relevant statutory procedures, change the company's name and make any other amendment to the company's constitution, for example, by altering the company's articles.

2.3.5 Electronic communications

Following the introduction of the Electronic Communications Act 2000, companies have been permitted to submit registration documents electronically. Electronic incorporation is basically a process of registration via email with appropriate attachments (the memorandum and articles and other registration forms, etc.) being sent to and processed electronically by Companies House. A document that is required to be signed by the registrar or authenticated by the registrar's seal will, if sent by electronic means, be authenticated in a manner specified by registrar's rules (CA 2006, s.1115(2)). Companies may also communicate annual general meeting (AGM) notices and the contents of their annual report and accounts to shareholders by electronic means. Indeed, unless otherwise provided for, companies may use hard copy or electronic communications (or both) in the communication of dealings between the company and others.

2.4 THE COMPANY NAME

A company's name must be stated in its application for registration. The name of a company may be changed subsequently by a special resolution or by other means provided for by the company's articles (CA 2006, s.77). In the case of an existing or transitional company, the company's articles are deemed to contain a statement of its name by virtue of CA 2006, s.28 (the provisions of the memorandum are treated as provisions of the articles). In such a case where the company subsequently changes its name (by any means) on or after 1 October 2009, the company is not required to amend its articles in order to effect the change of name. Accordingly, the company is not required to send a copy of its articles to the registrar in accordance with CA 2006, s.26 (see the Companies Act 2006 (Consequential Amendments, Transitional Provisions and Savings) Order 2009, SI 2009/1941).

In accordance with CA 2006, s.1099, the registrar must keep an index of the names of companies (and other specific bodies to which the section applies). The index of company names applies to:

- UK-registered companies.
- Any body to which any provision of the Companies Acts applies by virtue of regulations under CA 2006, s.1043 (unregistered companies).
- Overseas companies that have registered particulars with the registrar under CA 2006, s.1046, other than companies that the registrar considers should not be required to do so.
- Limited partnerships registered in the UK.
- Limited liability partnerships incorporated in the UK.
- European Economic Interest Groupings registered in the UK.
- Open-ended investment companies authorised in the UK.
- Societies registered under the Industrial and Provident Societies Act 1965.

The registrar of companies is not responsible for checking the companies name index prior to the registration of a company; the responsibility for that task falls on the person in control of the company's promotion process. Any person may inspect the registrar's index of company names (CA 2006, s.1100). The name with which a company is registered must not be one already included in the index of registered company names (CA 2006, s.66). However, the Company and Business Names (Miscellaneous Provisions) Regulations 2009, SI 2009/1085, reg.8 provides circumstances in which a company or other body can consent to the proposed registration of a name that would otherwise be considered the same as the existing registered name.

2.4.1 General restrictions on the use of a company name

Prior to CA 2006, any business was restricted from adopting a name governed by the terms of the Business Names Act 1985. In the context of companies, CA 2006, ss.1192–1199 replace the Business Names Act 1985. In relation to individuals and partnerships CA 2006, ss.1200–1228 replace the Business Names Act 1985. The restrictions contained in ss.1192–1199 apply also to any company which trades under a name other than that under which it is registered. The restrictions apply to any partnership where its members include a company.

A list of characters that may or may not be used in the name of a company and restrictions on the use of certain words, expressions and abbreviations (or words, expressions and abbreviations specified as similar) is set out in the Company and Business Names (Miscellaneous Provisions) Regulations 2009, SI 2009/1085.

A company or limited liability partnership (LLP) (discussed in **Chapter 3**) must not be registered with a name which in the opinion of the Secretary of State would constitute an offence or which would otherwise be offensive (CA 2006, s.53). The approval of the Secretary of State must be obtained by a company or LLP that intends to adopt a name that implies a connection with Her Majesty's Government, a local authority, a specified public authority or where the intended company name includes a word or an expression specified in regulations made by the Secretary of State (CA 2006, ss.54 and 55). Sections 56 and 1195 of CA 2006 also give the Secretary of State the power to require that in connection with an application for the use of a sensitive word or an expression, the applicant must seek the view of a specified government department or other body. In respect of specified 'words or expressions', see the Company, Limited Liability Partnership and Business Names (Sensitive Words and Expressions) Regulations 2009, SI 2009/2615.

The name of a limited company that is a public company must end with 'public limited company' or 'plc' (or Welsh equivalents) (CA 2006, ss.58–59). Subject to exceptions under CA 2006, s.60, the name of a limited company registered as a private company must end with 'limited' or 'Ltd' (or Welsh equivalents) (CA 2006, s.59). Here, providing certain conditions are met, private companies limited by guarantee may be exempt from the s.59 requirement; see the Company and Business Names (Miscellaneous Provisions) Regulations 2009, SI 2009/1085.

2.4.2 Disclosure of name and other matters

In accordance with the Companies (Trading Disclosures) Regulations 2008, SI 2008/495 a company (other than one which has been dormant since its incorporation) must display its registered name at its registered office and any inspection place. Further, other than where the location is primarily used for living accommodation the company must display its registered name at any other location at which it carries on business. In displaying its registered name, the name must be positioned in a manner whereby it may be easily seen by any visitor. The registered name must be displayed continuously but where a company shares its office, place or location with five or more companies, it is only required to display its registered name for at least 15 continuous seconds at least once in every three minutes.

A company must disclose its registered name on its websites and:

(a) its business letters, notices and other official publications;
(b) bills of exchange, promissory notes, endorsements and order forms;
(c) cheques purporting to be signed by or on behalf of the company;
(d) orders for money, goods or services purporting to be signed by or on behalf of the company;
(e) bills, invoices and other demands for payment, receipts and letters of credit;
(f) applications for licences to carry on a trade or activity; and
(g) all other forms of its business correspondence and documentation.

In relation to a company's business letters, if the business letter includes the name of a director of the company, other than in the text or as a signatory, the letter must disclose the name of every other director of that company. In respect of business letters, order forms and its websites, the company must also disclose:

(a) the part of the UK in which the company is registered;

(b) the company's registered number;

(c) the address of the company's registered office;

(d) where a limited company is exempt from the obligation to use the word 'limited' as part of its registered name, the fact that it is a limited company;

(e) in the case of a community interest company which is not a public company, the fact that it is a limited company; and

(f) if the company operates as an investment company within the meaning of CA 2006, s.833, the fact that it is such a company.

In addition, if a company with a share capital discloses the amount of its share capital on its business letters, order forms or its websites, the disclosure must relate to the paid-up share capital.

Finally, a company must comply with a written request, made by any person who deals with it in the course of business, for the address of its registered office or any inspection place and the type of company records which are kept at that office or place. The information must be supplied by the company in writing, within five working days of the receipt of the request. A company commits an offence where it fails, without reasonable excuse, to comply with any requirement in the regulations. An offence is committed by the company and every officer of the company who is in default. For the purposes of this regulation, a shadow director is treated as an officer of the company.

It is to be noted that the previous regulation of such matters (CA 1985, ss.349(1) and 348) was repealed from 1 October 2008 by the Companies Act 2006 (Commencement No.5, Transitional Provisions and Savings) Order 2007, SI 2007/3495.

2.4.3 Repeal of CA 1985, s.349(4) – personal liability of a director

CA 1985, s.349(4) was also repealed as from 1 October 2008 by the Companies Act 2006 (Commencement No.5, Transitional Provisions and Savings) Order 2007, SI 2007/3495. There is no corresponding provision within CA 2006. Although CA 1985, s.349(4) was rarely invoked, the potential consequences of a breach of the provision were severe. CA 1985, s.349(4) provided that:

> If an officer of a company or a person on its behalf signs or authorises to be signed on behalf of the company any bill of exchange, promissory note, endorsement, cheque or order for money or goods in which the company's name is not mentioned as required by [s.349(1)], he is liable to a fine; and he is further personally liable to the holder of the bill of exchange, promissory note, cheque or order for money or goods for the amount of it (unless it is duly paid by the company)

The protection afforded by s.349(4) was one of an assurance to the person receiving a relevant instrument that contained a misdescribed corporate name that if the liability evidenced by the instrument was not met by the debtor company then the person(s) responsible for signing the instrument would be deemed personally liable to discharge that liability. A breach of the provision was also punishable as a fine under the criminal law. In practice, s.349(4) was more likely to be invoked where a company was, itself, unable to meet the terms of the relevant instrument, i.e. where the company became insolvent. In addition, personal liability could be attached to any officer of a company who knowingly authorised the endorsement of an instrument containing a misdescribed form of the company's name unless, in applying a reasonable man test, that officer was unaware (and could not reasonably have been expected to have been aware) that the instrument in question contained a misdescription of the company's name. Despite an occasional authority to the contrary (see, e.g. *Jenice* v. *Dan* [1993] BCLC 1349), motive or intent were factors irrelevant to the operation of the provision (see, e.g. *Lindholst & Co* v. *Fowler* [1988] BCLC 166 and *Fiorentino Comm Giuseppe Srl* v. *Farnesi* [2005] BCC 771).

2.4.4 Change of name due to misleading information or indication of activities

CA 2006, s.75 provides that if misleading information is given for the purpose of a company's registration by a particular name, or an undertaking or assurance is given for that purpose and is not fulfilled, the Secretary of State may direct the company to change its name where the use of the name is likely to cause harm. Any such direction must be given in writing within five years of the company's registration and must specify the period within which the company must change its name.

In accordance with CA 2006, s.76, if the name by which a company is registered gives so misleading an indication of the nature of its activities as to be likely to cause harm to the public, the Secretary of State may direct the company, in writing, to change its name. The direction must be complied with within a period of six weeks from the date of the direction or such longer period as the Secretary of State may determine. The company may, within three weeks of the Secretary of State's direction, apply to the court to set the direction aside. In *Association of Certified Public Accountants of Britain* v. *Secretary of State for Trade and Industry* [1997] 2 BCLC 307, Jacob J held that it is for the Crown to establish that a company's name offends the statute. The learned judge, in formulating a legal test, concluded that:

> … what the court has to do is to decide on the evidence whether the name of the company gives so misleading an indication of the nature of its activities as to be likely to cause harm to the public. It is not sufficient to show that a name is misleading; a likelihood of harm must be shown too. In many cases the latter will follow from the former, but this is not necessarily so: it is difficult to imagine harm, for instance, if a company called Robin Jacob (Fishmongers) Ltd in fact carried on a business of bookbinding. (at p.311)

CA 2006, ss.67 and 68 provide that, within 12 months of a company's registration, the Secretary of State may direct a company to change its name in circumstances where the choice of name was the same as or too similar to the name of a company already listed on the register. Any such direction must specify the period within which the company is to change its name. The Secretary of State may, by a further direction, extend that period. If a company fails to comply with the direction, an offence is committed by (a) the company, and (b) every officer of the company who is in default. For this purpose a shadow director is treated as an officer of the company. A person guilty of an offence under this section is liable on summary conviction to a fine.

CA 2006 also introduces new provisions (CA 2006, ss.69–74) whereby a person (the applicant) may object to a company's registered name on the ground that it is the same as or sufficiently similar to a name associated with the applicant in which he or she has goodwill, whereby the use of the name would be likely to mislead by suggesting a connection between the company and the applicant. The objection must be made by application to a company names adjudicator. The adjudicator may make an order requiring the respondent company to change its name to one that is not an offending name. An appeal lies to the court from any decision of a company names adjudicator to uphold or dismiss an application (CA 2006, s.74). The Company Names Adjudicator Rules 2008, SI 2008/1738 regulate the proceedings before a company names adjudicator.

The economic consequences inherent in a company having to change its name may be serious. For example, after a few years of trading under a specific name, that name may have become associated with the company's product range to such an extent that a change in corporate name may result in a failure by the general public to associate the product with the newly adopted name of the company, a factor which may adversely affect the company's image. Further, if a change in name is ordered costs will be incurred in changing company documents, signs, advertising logos, letterheads, etc.

2.4.5 The passing off action

A company already in existence may, by means of a passing off action, challenge a name adopted by a newly incorporated company on the premise that the reputation of the existing enterprise was exploited by the new enterprise's choice of name and business activity. For incorporated companies, it is probable, following the enactment of CA 2006, ss.69–77, that the passing off action will become impliedly redundant; however, it may still be viewed as an action of the last resort. The passing off action is a common law remedy and may be invoked by an incorporated or unincorporated business in circumstances where a newly formed business adopts the name of an existing enterprise or a name which is similar to the existing enterprise. It should be stressed that in addition to a similarity in the name of the new enterprise, it must also be established that the new enterprise is engaged in a type of business activity similar to that of the claimant (see, e.g. *Ewing* v. *Buttercup Margarine Co Ltd* [1917] 2 Ch 1, *Halifax plc* v. *Halifax Repossessions Ltd* [2004] BCC 281).

CHAPTER 3

The types and classification of companies

3.1 INTRODUCTION

A company registered in accordance with the provisions of the Companies Acts will take one of the following forms:

- a public company limited by shares;
- a private company limited by shares;
- a private company limited by guarantee; or
- a private company that is unlimited.

Prior to 22 December 1980, it was possible to register a fifth type of company, namely, a private or public company limited by guarantee and with a share capital. It is no longer possible to register this type of company (CA 2006, s.5).

In the context of the 'Companies Acts', 'company' means a company formed and registered under CA 2006, or a company that immediately before the commencement of CA 2006 was formed and registered pursuant to CA 1985 or was otherwise an existing company for the purposes of that Act (CA 2006, s.1(1)). CA 2006, s.2 provides that the 'Companies Acts' mean:

- the company law provisions of CA 2006;
- Part 2 of the Companies (Audit, Investigations and Community Enterprise) Act 2004 (community interest companies); and
- the provisions of CA 1985 and the Companies Consolidation (Consequential Provisions) Act 1985 that remain in force.

3.2 TYPES OF COMPANIES

3.2.1 Public companies limited by shares

As from 22 December 1980, a company which proposes to operate as a public company must be specifically registered as a public limited company. Prior to the passing of CA 2006, a public company was required to be registered with at least two shareholders and two directors, whereas the minimum requirement for the registration of a private company was one shareholder and one director. Following the implementation of CA 2006, a public company may now also be registered with one shareholder (CA 2006, s.123) but must still have two directors (CA 2006, s.154). Unlike the position under CA 1985, in relation to both private and public companies, at least one of the registered directors of the company must be a natural person (CA 2006, s.155). Unlike a private company, a public company must also be registered with a company secretary (CA 2006, s.271). Before a public company can trade it must be registered with a minimum share capital, currently £50,000 (CA 2006, s.761). A public company must be identified (at the end of its name) as a public limited company, although the abbreviation 'plc' will suffice (CA 2006, s.58).

In accordance with CA 2006, s.4, any company which is not registered as a public company is construed to be a private company. Unlike a private company, a public company may offer its securities to the general public (CA 2006, s.755). While a public company is entitled to offer its securities to the general public, it is not bound to do so, but where its shares are so offered, it has the option of applying to have them listed for dealing on the stock exchange.

3.2.2 Private companies limited by shares

Private companies limited by shares represent the vast majority (approximately 98 per cent) of all limited companies registered in the UK. Many private limited companies are small concerns and the shareholders of such companies are often the major participants in the management of the enterprise. The Companies (Single Member Private Limited Companies) Regulations 1992, SI 1992/1699 came into force on 15 July 1992 to comply with the EC Twelfth Company Law Directive, which was adopted on 21 December 1989. The regulations gave effect to the birth of the single member private limited company. (However the necessity for the regulations ceased following the implementation of CA 2006 which permits both a private and a public company to be created with just a single member and was repealed by the Companies Act 2006 (Consequential Amendments and Transitional Provisions) Order 2011, SI 2011/1265, art.32.)

The relationship between the shareholders of a small private company may ordinarily be viewed as one built upon mutual trust and confidence, a fact often reflected by the courts' more flexible application of company law to these small enterprises. This flexibility is born from equitable considerations that are closely related to partnership law principles. Although the vast majority of private companies are small concerns, private companies may be large concerns. There is no legal compulsion on the part of a successful private company to re-register itself as a public company. Indeed, the shareholders of a large and successful private company may wish to retain its private limited liability status in order to exert control and influence over the company's destiny, rather than risking the possibility of losing a controlling interest in the company by altering its status to that of a public limited company.

3.2.3 Private companies limited by guarantee

While the vast majority of private limited companies are limited by shares, a private company may be limited by guarantee (CA 2006, s.3). Prior to the passing of CA 2006, the memorandum of a company limited by guarantee would provide that if the company was wound up, the members of the company would be liable to contribute a fixed sum of money, the amount guaranteed (usually a nominal sum, for example, £1) towards the debts of the company. Following the passing of CA 2006, the guarantee contribution must be contained in a statement of guarantee which must be delivered to the registrar as part of the procedure for the company's registration (see CA 2006, s.11). A member's fixed sum liability (guarantee) cannot be altered and continues during the term of the membership of the company or, where the company's liquidation occurs, within a year of the member having left the company (see IA 1986, s.74(2)).

The most appropriate type of company to be registered as a private company limited by guarantee is one with a charitable or non-profit seeking objective, such as a local club or association. As the company will not have shareholders, any profits made by the company will not be distributed as dividend payments. The members' capital (amount of guarantee) will be kept in reserve and may be called upon in the case of the company's liquidation. Unlike the uncalled share capital of a company limited by shares, the sum of money guaranteed is not deemed to be an asset of the company and therefore cannot be used as a means to repay or secure any of the company's debts.

Although a private company must have a name which ends in 'limited' (CA 2006, s.59), a company limited by guarantee was not compelled to include the word 'limited' after its name where it satisfied the terms of CA 1985, s.30. CA 2006, s.62 continues the exemption for companies limited by guarantee but only in circumstances where the company was exempted by virtue of CA 1985, s.30, i.e. the provision only applies to existing companies and will not apply to companies formed pursuant to CA 2006. The s.62 exception applies providing the company does not change its name and the following conditions are met:

- The first condition is that the objects of the company are the promotion of commerce, art, science, education, religion, charity or any profession, and anything incidental or conducive to any of those objects.
- The second condition is that the company's articles:
    (a) require its income to be applied in promoting its objects;
    (b) prohibit the payment of dividends to its members; and
    (c) require all the assets that would otherwise be available to its members generally to be transferred on its winding up either –

        (i)   to another body with objects similar to its own; or
        (ii) to another body the objects of which are the promotion of charity and anything incidental or conducive thereto (whether or not the body is a member of the company).

3.2.4 The community interest company

A new type of company, the 'community interest company' (CIC), was created by the Companies (Audit, Investigations and Community Enterprise) Act 2004 (in combination with the Community Interest Company Regulations 2005, SI 2005/1788 as amended by CA 2006, Sched.15, Part 2) and the Community Interest Company (Amendment) Regulations 2009, SI 2009/1942.

In introducing the CIC, the government's aim was to increase (although not necessarily replace) existing forms of social enterprises, for example, charitable companies and Industrial and Provident Societies, with an ultimate objective of expanding and improving the transparency of the social enterprise sector. The government feared that, without the CIC (to include the flexibility of an attached corporate status), the sector would be unable to achieve sustainable financing for the good of the community.

CICs are regulated by the companies legislation although they are tailored to the needs of non-profit social enterprises. CICs are under the supervisory control of an independent regulator. Social enterprises suited to becoming CICs include those geared to promoting public services, for example, providers of community care services. Part 2 of the 2005 Regulations provides that certain prescribed activities may not be considered suitable activities to be carried on for the benefit of the community; nevertheless; s.35(2) of the Companies (Audit, Investigations and Community Enterprise) Act 2004 seeks to provide a rather general test to determine whether an enterprise satisfies the community interest definition, namely:

> A company satisfies the community interest test if a reasonable person might consider that its activities are being carried on for the benefit of the community.

Section 35(5) goes on to state that 'community' includes a section of the community.

For the purposes of the community interest test, any group of individuals may constitute a 'section of the community' if a reasonable person considers that they share a common characteristic which distinguishes them from other members of the community. (See the Community Interest Company (Amendment) Regulations 2009, SI 2009/1942.)

CICs are formed as limited companies (by shares or guarantee) and take the benefits of a limited liability status. However, as with any other type of limited company CICs will be subject to the disclosure and reporting requirements imposed by the companies legislation. In addition to complying with the usual registration requirements of a limited liability company, a CIC must comply, and continue to comply during its lifetime, with specific 'community interest rules'. For example:

- A CIC must ensure that its profits or financial assets are not ordinarily distributed to its members or investors during its lifetime. However, a CIC may issue shares upon which a capped dividend may be paid, the capped amount to be decided by the CIC Regulator (see Community Interest Company Regulations 2005, regs.17–20).

- Together with the annual accounts, a CIC must submit an annual 'community interest report' to the CIC Regulator. The community interest report must give a detailed account of the activities the company has undertaken in pursuit of its community interest objectives.

However, unlike registered charities, special tax concessions are not afforded to CICs.

3.2.5 The unlimited company

The unlimited company is a separate legal entity; it is formed as a private company and possesses the characteristics of a distinct legal (corporate) entity. While an unlimited company may have a share capital, the members of an unlimited company are without the advantage of a limited liability status. Nevertheless, an unlimited liability company is regulated by the companies legislation, albeit that the regulation is naturally more relaxed than for a limited company. For example, although an unlimited company must, as with limited companies, prepare accounts for the benefit of its members, an unlimited company is not required to file its accounts at Companies House, save in a situation where the company is a subsidiary of a limited liability company (CA 2006, s.448). Further, an unlimited company is not subject to the rules and disclosure requirements in relation to the maintenance of share capital (discussed in **Chapter 10**) in so far as on the winding up of the company, its members are responsible ultimately for the company's debts.

A private unlimited company is similar to a business partnership concern. However, unlike the position with a partnership, the creditors of an unlimited company will not be able to sue the company's individual members for the repayment of business debts (save where the debts have been personally guaranteed) unless the creditors seek an order for the company to be wound up. On the winding up of an unlimited company, the members' contribution towards the repayment of the company's debts will be in accordance with the terms of the company's constitution. Where the constitution fails to specify a procedure for such contributions, calls are made equally upon all the contributories; if a member cannot meet the terms of his or her contribution, the other members of the company will be obliged to make good this loss.

3.3 THE DEREGULATION OF PRIVATE COMPANIES

Government policy has seen a radical departure away from the policy of the 1960s when there was a call for the unification of the rules applicable to both private and public companies. The change of attitude has largely been due to the UK's need to encourage the economic growth of small private enterprises in the wake of a weakening of its once strong industrial base. The desire to expand the population of small private companies has met with a desire to remove certain formal require-ments applicable to all limited liability companies. However, despite the aforemen-tioned change in government policy, CA 2006 regulates both private and public companies irrespective of the size of the enterprise. Nevertheless, in parts, CA 2006 does create a distinguishable split between the regulation of private and public companies with an objective of reducing the administrative burdens placed on the former. Examples related to the deregulation of private companies are alluded to in distinct chapters of this work but include matters pertinent to the role of general meetings and members' resolutions, capital maintenance and the allotment of shares, audit and accounting requirements and the creation of model articles specific to private companies.

While there is an obvious need to encourage the expansion of small business enterprises, an inherent danger with that desire is the incorporation of under-capitalised concerns. If the 'price' to be paid for encouraging under-capitalised concerns prejudices the interests of small trade creditors and customers of poten-tially 'lame' companies, the UK economy will undoubtedly suffer. To safeguard the value of the concept of limited liability it may, for example, be beneficial to increase the registration fee for incorporation (currently only £40; the fee is £15 if registra-tion is by electronic means) and also impose a minimum capital requirement (as for example in Germany) in respect of the incorporation of private limited liability companies. However, given that many of our European counterparts have moved away from a minimum capital requirement, the introduction of a minimum capital requirement in the UK, without a similar requirement being implemented across Europe, would have a negative economic impact; business could be attracted away from the UK to European jurisdictions without the minimum capital requirement. An ability for an individual or a private company based in Europe to incorporate a private company in any European jurisdiction with the objective of escaping a 'home country' requirement (freedom of establishment), such as a minimum capital requirement, was confirmed in the case of *Centros Ltd* v. *Erhvervs-og Selskabssty-relsen* [2000] 2 WLR 1048 (ECJ). (Also see *Uberseering BV* v. *Nordic Construction Co Bauumanagement Gmbh* [2005] 1 WLR 315 (ECJ) and *Cartesio Oktato es Szolgaltato bt* [2008] BCC 745.)

3.4 CHANGING THE STATUS OF A COMPANY

A registered company may change the status with which it was originally regis-tered. For example, in a desire to secure further capital to finance future growth, a private company may wish to offer securities to the general public. In order legitimately to offer securities to the general public, the company must re-register itself as a public company. Conversely, where a public company's issued share capital falls below the minimum requirement of share capital permitted for a public company, the public company must re-register itself as a private company. The following rules provide the statutory framework for a company to alter its registered status.

3.4.1 Private limited company (or private unlimited company) to a public limited company

A private company limited by shares or guarantee may change its status to become a public company by complying with the procedures and conditions for application laid down in CA 2006, ss.90–95 (previously governed by CA 1985, ss.43–48). An unlimited company may also change its status to that of a public company, providing it complies with those procedures and additionally makes such changes to its constitution so as to comply with the fact that the company is to be limited by shares (CA 2006, ss.105–108, discussed below).

The specific procedures for re-registration from a private company to a public company are contained in CA 2006, ss.90–95. First, the general meeting of the company concerned must pass a special resolution to effect the company's re-registration as a public company. In addition, specific conditions must be met. The conditions are summarised below.

Constitutional changes (CA 2006, s.90(3))

The company must make such changes –

(a)   in its name, and
(b)   in its articles,

as are necessary in connection with its becoming a public company.

Share capital requirements (CA 2006, s.91(1))

(1)   The following requirements must be met at the time the special resolution is passed that the company should be re-registered as a public company –

(a)   the nominal value of the company's allotted share capital must be not less than the authorised minimum;

(b)   each of the company's allotted shares must be paid up at least as to one-quarter of the nominal value of that share and the whole of any premium on it;

(c)   if any shares in the company or any premium on them have been fully or partly paid up by an undertaking given by any person that he or another should do work or perform services (whether for the company or any other person), the undertaking must have been performed or otherwise discharged;

(d)   if shares have been allotted as fully or partly paid up as to their nominal value or any premium on them otherwise than in cash, and the consideration for the allotment consists of or includes an undertaking to the company (other than one to which paragraph (c) applies), then either –

(i)   the undertaking must have been performed or otherwise discharged, or

(ii)   there must be a contract between the company and some person pursuant to which the undertaking is to be performed within five years from the time the special resolution is passed.

CA 2006, s.90(2) provides an exception in the context of CA 2006, s.90(1)(b)–(d), namely, shares may be disregarded in respect of an allotment in pursuance of an employees' share scheme or in relation to shares allotted before 22 June 1982. Shares that qualify under this exemption must not amount to more than one-tenth of the nominal value of the company's allotted share capital.

Requirements as to net assets (CA 2006, s.92)

(1)   A company applying to re-register as a public company must obtain –

    (a)   a balance sheet prepared as at a date not more than seven months before the date on which the application is delivered to the registrar,

    (b)   an unqualified report [see CA 2006, s.92(3)] by the company's auditor on that balance sheet, and

    (c)   a written statement by the company's auditor that in his opinion at the balance sheet date the amount of the company's net assets was not less than the aggregate of its called-up share capital and undistributable reserves.

The financial position of the company, so determined by the company's auditor, must not change between the balance sheet date and the date on which the application for re-registration is delivered to the registrar, to the extent that the amount of the company's net assets must not become less than the aggregate of its called-up share capital and undistributable reserves (CA 2006, s.92(2)).

Recent allotment of shares for non-cash consideration (CA 2006, s.93)

Where shares are allotted by the company in the period between the date on which the balance sheet is prepared and the passing of the special resolution to enable the company to re-register as a public company and the shares are allotted as fully or partly paid up as to their nominal value or any premium on them otherwise than in cash, then the registrar shall not entertain the application by the company's re-registration as a public company unless:

(a)   s.93(2)(a): the consideration for the allotment has been valued in accordance with CA 2006, s.593(1) and a report with respect to the value of the consideration has been made to the company during the six months immediately preceding the allotment; or

(b)   s.93(2)(b): the allotment is in connection with:

    (i)   a share exchange, namely the shares are allotted in connection with an arrangement under which the whole or part of the consideration for the shares allotted is provided by the transfer to the company allotting the shares, of shares (or shares of a particular class) in another company, or the cancellation of shares (or shares of a particular class) in another company and the allotment is open to all the holders of the shares of the other company in question (or, where the arrangement applies only to shares of a particular class, to all the holders of the company's shares of that class) to take part in the arrangement in connection with which the shares are allotted; or

(ii) a proposed merger with another company if one of the companies concerned proposes to acquire all the assets and liabilities of the other in exchange for the issue of its shares or other securities to shareholders of the other (whether or not accompanied by a cash payment). Here 'another company' includes any body corporate.

Determining whether a person is a holder of shares for the purpose of a share exchange

In determining whether a person is a holder of shares for the purpose of a share exchange (i.e. CA 2006, s.93(2)(b)(i)), the following will be disregarded:

(a) shares held by a nominee of the company allotting the shares;
(b) shares held by a nominee of the holding company of the company allotting the shares;
(c) a subsidiary of the company allotting the shares, or a subsidiary of the holding company of the company allotting the shares.

The consideration for an allotment is defined to exclude any amount standing to the credit of any of the company's reserve accounts, or of its profit and loss account that has been applied in paying up (to any extent) any of the shares allotted or any premium on those shares. An 'arrangement' means any agreement, scheme or arrangement, including an arrangement sanctioned in accordance with CA 2006, Part 26 or IA 1986, s.110.

The actual application to the registrar for re-registration as a public company (CA 2006, ss.94–96) must contain a statement of the company's proposed name on re-registration and in the case of a company that does not have a secretary, a statement of the company's proposed secretary.

An application must be accompanied by:

(a) a copy of a special resolution to the effect that the company should re-register as a public company;
(b) a copy of the company's articles as proposed to be amended (i.e. to comply with a plc status);
(c) a copy of the balance sheet; and
(d) if there has been a recent allotment of shares for non-cash consideration, a copy of the valuation report (if any).

A statement of compliance must be delivered with the application. A statement of compliance is a statement that provides that the requirements of the re-registration as a public company have been complied with. The registrar may accept the statement of compliance as sufficient evidence that the company is entitled to be re-registered as a public company. If the registrar of companies is satisfied that a private limited company has complied with all the necessary statutory requirements applicable to its re-registration, the company will be issued with a new certificate of incorporation confirming its status as a public limited company. The certificate must state that it is issued on re-registration and the date on which it is issued. The certificate is conclusive evidence that the requirements of the Act (as to re-registration) have been complied with.

3.4.2 Public limited company to a private limited company

In accordance with CA 2006, ss.97–99 (previously CA 1985, ss.53–55), a public company may alter its status to that of a private company limited by shares or guarantee. A public company may be re-registered as a private company where its members in general meeting pass a special resolution to that effect. The company must make necessary changes to its name and articles in connection with becoming a private company limited by shares or guarantee (CA 2006, s.100). An application for re-registration must be delivered to the registrar together with a statement of compliance (a copy of the special resolution must also be forwarded to the registrar: CA 2006, s.100(2)). When the registrar is satisfied that the requirements of the re-registration process have been complied with, the company will be issued with a certificate of incorporation confirming the company's new status as a private company (CA 2006, s.101). The certificate must state that it is issued on re-registration and the date on which it is issued. The certificate is conclusive evidence that the requirements of the Act as to re-registration have been complied with. However, the application may be challenged as follows.

Application to court to cancel a resolution (CA 2006, s.98)

Where a public company is to be re-registered as a private limited company and a special resolution has been passed to effect the change of status, an application to the court for the cancellation of the resolution may be made within 28 days after the passing of the resolution. The application may be made by:

(a) the holders of not less in the aggregate than 5 per cent in nominal value of the company's issued share capital or any class of the company's issued share capital (disregarding any shares held by the company as treasury shares);

(b) not less than 5 per cent of its members if the company is not limited by shares; or

(c) no fewer than 50 of the company's members, but not by a person who has consented to or voted in favour of the resolution.

The ability to challenge the application provides a possible safeguard for shareholders holding shares for investment or speculative reasons, because the loss of the public limited status may severely weaken the shareholders' ability to realise their investment in the company, i.e. the possible market in which shares can be sold will be greatly restricted when the company is re-registered as a private company. On hearing the application the court may make an order either cancelling or confirming the resolution but may make the order on such terms and conditions as it thinks fit. For example, it may compel the company to purchase the shares of the dissentient members.

3.4.3 Limited company to unlimited company

A private or public limited company may seek re-registration as an unlimited company. CA 2006, ss.102–104 provide the procedures to enable a private limited company to re-register as an unlimited company (formerly CA 1985, ss.49–50), whereas CA 2006, ss.109–111 deal with the situation where a public limited company resolves to become an unlimited company. The procedures are very similar. It is to be noted that under CA 1985, a public company could not, as of a direct right, re-register as an unlimited company (CA 1985, s.49(3)). Under CA 1985, if a public company wished to re-register as an unlimited company, it first had to re-register as a private limited company and then subsequently re-register as an unlimited company.

Under CA 2006, s.102, for a private company limited by shares or guarantee to re-register as an unlimited company, the company must not have been previously re-registered as a limited company (i.e. the private company must never have been previously in existence as an unlimited company or a public company). Likewise, in the case of a public company proposing to re-register as an unlimited company, the public company must not have been previously re-registered as a limited or unlimited company (i.e. the company must never have been previously a private company or an unlimited company) (CA 2006, s.109(2)).

To comply with the re-registration formalities, the entire membership of the limited company must assent to the change in status because if, as an unlimited company, the company became insolvent, the membership would be exposed to the risk of having to contribute to the company's debts. The prescribed form of assent to the company's re-registration as an unlimited company (this must be subscribed by or on behalf of all the members of the company) must be delivered to the registrar, together with the application for re-registration and a statement of compliance. The compliance statement must provide that the directors of the company and the persons by whom or on whose behalf the form of assent is subscribed, constitute the whole membership of the company. The registrar may accept the statement of compliance as sufficient evidence that the company is entitled to be re-registered as an unlimited company. The application is subject to additional conditions, summarised below.

The company must make such necessary changes in its name and to its articles in connection with its transformation into an unlimited company (a copy of the company's articles as amended must be delivered to the registrar). The company must deliver a statement of compliance containing a statement by the directors of the company:

(a)   that the persons by whom or on whose behalf the form of assent is authenticated constitute the whole membership of the company; and

(b)   if any of the members have not authenticated that form themselves, that the directors have taken all reasonable steps to satisfy themselves that each person who authenticated it on behalf of a member was lawfully empowered to do so.

Following compliance with the requirements of CA 2006, the registrar will issue the company with a certificate of incorporation confirming the company's new status as unlimited. The certificate must state that it is issued on re-registration and the date on which it is issued. The certificate is conclusive evidence that the requirements of the Act have been complied with.

3.4.4   Unlimited company to private limited company

Provided an unlimited company complies with the statutory requirements contained in CA 2006, ss.105–108 (formerly CA 1985, s.51), it is entitled to re-register as a private limited company. To comply with those procedures, the general meeting of the unlimited company must pass a special resolution to stipulate whether the company wishes to be limited by shares or by guarantee. An unlimited company that previously had an existence as a limited company cannot subsequently be re-registered as a limited company (CA 2006, s.105(2)). In circumstances where an unlimited company re-registers as a private limited company but is then subsequently wound up within three years of its re-registration, then both the present and past members of the company may be personally liable to contribute towards its debts (see IA 1986, s.77).

An application for the re-registration of an unlimited company as a private limited company must be delivered to the registrar together with a statement of compliance. The registrar may accept the statement of compliance as sufficient evidence that the company is entitled to re-register as a private limited company. The application is subject to the following conditions:

• The special resolution (a copy of which must be forwarded to the registrar) must state whether the company is to be limited by shares or by guarantee.

• The company must make such changes in its name and to its articles to equate itself with the status of a company limited by shares or guarantee.

• If the company is to be limited by shares and has not previously had a share capital it must provide:

(i)   a statement of initial shareholdings, and

    (ii) a statement of capital.

- If the company is to be limited by guarantee, it must provide a statement of guarantee and a copy of the company's articles as proposed to be amended.

Following compliance with the requirements of CA 2006, the registrar will issue the company with a certificate of incorporation confirming the company's new status as unlimited. The certificate must state that it is issued on re-registration and the date on which it is issued. The certificate is conclusive evidence that the requirements of the Act have been complied with.

3.5 GROUPS OF COMPANIES

Although a registered company is, as a separate legal entity, responsible in law for its own actions and liable for its own debts, companies may be tied to a group structure: a structure dominated by a holding company. A company which is directly or indirectly dominated by a holding company is termed a 'subsidiary' company. A holding company–subsidiary relationship is legally defined by CA 2006, s.1159. This section provides that a company is a subsidiary of another company, if the other company:

- holds a majority of the voting rights in the company; or
- is a member of the company and has the right to appoint or remove a majority of the company's board of directors; or
- is a member of the company and controls alone or in agreement with other shareholders or members of the company, a majority of the voting rights in the company.

Further, a company (A) will also be classed as a subsidiary of a holding company (B) where company A is a subsidiary of another company (C) and C is a subsidiary of the holding company B.

    For a company to be a subsidiary of another company in respect of the 'member' qualification, the other company must be entered in the register as a member of the subsidiary company (see, e.g. *Enviroco Ltd* v. *Farstad Supply A/S* [2011] 1 WLR 921). A company is classed as a wholly owned subsidiary of another company if its shares are exclusively owned by the holding company and/or other subsidiaries of the holding company, or persons acting on behalf of the holding company and/or its subsidiaries (CA 2006, s.1159(2), previously CA 1985, s.736). CA 2006, Sched.6, para.2 provides that in calculating voting control, the 'voting rights' are those rights held by the shareholders (or members where a company does not have a share capital) in relation to their ability to vote at general meetings on all or substantially all matters. In accordance with CA 2006, Sched.6, para.3(1), the right to appoint or remove a majority of the directors is defined as the right to appoint or remove directors holding the majority of voting rights at board meetings on all or substantially all matters. A company is treated as having the right to appoint a person to a directorship (of the subsidiary) if the appointment necessarily follows from that person's appointment as a director of the company, or where the company itself holds the directorship (CA 2006, Sched.6, para.3(2)). It is to be noted that such rights are deemed to be held by a holding company if they are held by any of its subsidiary companies (CA 2006, Sched.6, para.7).

3.5.1 The membership of a holding company

A subsidiary or a subsidiary's nominee is not permitted to be a member of its holding company and any allotment of shares to the subsidiary (or its nominee) from its holding company will be void (see CA 2006, s.136). However, the general prohibition provided by s.136 is subject to exceptions (previously contained in CA 1985, s.23), namely a subsidiary may continue to be a member of its holding company if:

- It was a member of its holding company before 1 July 1948 (CA 2006, s.137(1)).
- The prohibition in CA 1985, s.23(1) (or any corresponding earlier enactment), as it then had effect, did not apply, or where the prohibition in s.136 does not apply.
- The subsidiary or its nominee holds shares in the holding company in the capacity of a personal representative or trustee. However, this exception will not apply where the holding company or subsidiary has a beneficial interest under the trust (see CA 2006, s.139). An interest in the holding company's shares, held only by way of security for the purposes of a transaction entered into by the holding company or subsidiary in the ordinary course of business, which includes the lending of money, will be disregarded for the purpose of determining whether the holding company or subsidiary is beneficially interested.
- The subsidiary holds shares in the ordinary course of its business as an 'intermediary' (CA 2006, s.141). An intermediary is a person who carries on a bona fide business of dealing in securities and is a member or has access to a regulated market (providing he does not carry on an excluded business – see CA 2006, s.141(3)).

Nevertheless, where a subsidiary company can bring itself within one of the above exceptions, it is denied any right to vote in respect of the shares held in the holding company (CA 2006, s.137(4)).

3.5.2 Accounting purposes

For auditing and accounting matters, the definition of a group of companies is provided by CA 2006, s.1162 and Sched.7 (formerly dealt with by CA 1985, s.258). For accounting purposes a holding company is referred to as a parent company and except for when a parent company qualifies under the small companies regime (CA

2006, s.383) or is exempt by CA 2006, ss.400–402, the parent company must prepare group financial statements in addition to the preparation of individual accounts. The group accounts must be prepared in a consolidated form (CA 2006, ss.399–414). A group relationship is expressed in terms of a parent undertaking–subsidiary undertaking relationship. An undertaking is defined by CA 2006, s.1161 as a body corporate or partnership or an unincorporated association carrying on a trade or business, with or without a view to profit. CA 2006, s.1162 states that an undertaking is a parent undertaking in relation to another undertaking (the subsidiary undertaking), if:

- it (parent) holds a majority of the voting rights in the (subsidiary) undertaking;
- it (parent) is a member of the (subsidiary) undertaking in its own right (or it has a subsidiary that is a member of the undertaking, or shares held in the undertaking are held by a person acting on behalf of it (parent) or any of its subsidiary undertakings) and has the right to appoint or remove a majority of the board of directors of the undertaking;
- it has the right to exercise a dominant influence over the (subsidiary) undertaking by virtue of provisions contained in its articles or by virtue of a control contract; or
- it is a member of the (subsidiary) undertaking (or it has a subsidiary that is a member of the undertaking) and controls alone, pursuant to an agreement with other shareholders or members, a majority of the voting rights in the (subsidiary) undertaking;
- it has the power to exercise, or actually exercises, dominant influence or control over the (subsidiary) undertaking; or
- it and the (subsidiary) undertaking are managed on a unified basis.

A parent–subsidiary undertaking relationship, where an undertaking (parent) is found to have exercised a dominant influence over another undertaking, is defined in CA 2006, Sched.7 as one whereby a dominant undertaking (parent) has the right to give directions which the directors of the other undertaking are required to comply with (in respect of the operating and financial policies of the other undertaking, whether or not they are for the benefit of that other undertaking).

Where a parent–subsidiary undertaking relationship is established the accounts must be composed of a consolidated balance sheet dealing with the state of affairs and the profit and loss accounts of the parent and its subsidiary undertakings. It is to be noted that the statutory requirement for a parent company to prepare consolidated accounts ignores the individual characteristic of the subsidiary company as a distinct and separate legal entity. Therefore, for accounting purposes, a group of companies is treated as a single economic entity.

3.6   OTHER FORMS OF BUSINESS STRUCTURE

3.6.1   Limited liability partnership (LLP)

The limited liability partnership (LLP) is appropriate for a business that wishes to retain the benefits of trading as a partnership but also wishes to take advantage of a limited liability status. Legislation establishing the LLP was enacted by the Limited Liability Partnerships Act (LLPA) 2000 (supplemented by the Limited Liability Partnerships Regulations 2001, SI 2001/1090). The latter regulations were amended by SI 2007/2073 – applying the Companies (Audit, Investigations and Community Enterprise) Act 2004 to LLPs. In taking the benefit of a limited liability status an LLP must comply with the requirements and safeguards of the companies legislation in a manner akin to that of a registered company. The LLP's primary regulatory framework is CA 2006 (see the Limited Liability Partnerships (Application of Companies Act 2006) Regulations 2009, SI 2009/1804). Regulations relating to accounts and audit provisions of the 2006 Act (with modifications for LLPs) were introduced in 2008 (see SI 2008/1911) and apply to accounts for financial years beginning on or after 1 October 2008.

The business form of an LLP is potentially applicable to all business partnerships comprising two or more members. LLPA 2000, s.2 prescribes the documentary requirements for the incorporation of an LLP, including that: 'two or more persons associated for carrying on a lawful business with a view to profit must have subscribed their names to an incorporation document' (s.2(1)(a)). Section 3 provides that the documents delivered under s.2 must be registered with the registrar of companies. Once the documents are registered, the registrar will then issue a certificate of incorporation.

The LLP is a distinct legal entity, a body corporate (LLPA 2000, s.1(2)) and therefore the membership of an LLP will have no personal liability for the acts or obligations of the LLP, except as provided by statute or under the general law. LLPA 2000, s.1(4) provides that the members of an LLP have such liability to contribute to its assets on a winding up as is provided by the Act. In effect, save in circumstances where a member of an LLP agreed previously to contribute a guaranteed amount if the LLP became insolvent, the LLP's assets and not those of its members will be used to discharge its debts. Section 4 deals with the membership of an LLP and provides that on its incorporation its members are the persons who subscribed their names to the incorporation document, although s.4(2) allows for any other person to become a member of an LLP by and in accordance with an agreement with the existing members. In accordance with s.4(3), a person may cease to be a member of an LLP (as well as by death or dissolution) in accordance with an agreement with the other members or, in the absence of agreement with the other members as to cessation of membership, by giving reasonable notice to the other members. Section 4(4) provides that a member of an LLP shall not be regarded for any purpose to be employed by the LLP unless, if he or she and the other members were partners in a partnership, he would be regarded for that purpose to have been employed by the partnership. It should be observed that s.4(4) is somewhat obscure given that in law, a partner (properly established) in a partnership cannot be an employee of the partnership. Basically, the question that will need to be determined is whether, in a partnership, the member of the LLP would legally have been regarded as a partner, or alternatively as a mere employee (see the decision of the Court of Appeal in *Tiffin* v. *Lester Aldridge LLP* [2012] 1 WLR 1887).

The LLP's incorporation document is similar in content to a company's constitutional documents. Although there is no formal set of articles in the manner prescribed for a registered company, the members of an LLP are obliged to enter into an LLP agreement, the purpose of which is to regulate the relationship between the members and the LLP and the rights of the members *inter se* (contrast the position under CA 2006, s.33 in relation to the binding effect of a company's articles). Section 5(1) states that, as far as otherwise provided by this Act or any other enactment, the mutual rights and duties of the members of an LLP, and the mutual rights and duties of an LLP and its members, shall be governed (a) by agreement between the members, or between the limited liability partnership and its members; or (b) in the absence of agreement as to any matter, by any provision made in relation to that matter by regulations under s.15(1).

An LLP has an unlimited capacity to enter into a contract or other transaction (LLPA 2000, s.1(3)). In relation to the authority of members of the LLP to bind the LLP, s.6(2) provides that an LLP is not bound by anything done by a member in dealing with a person if: (a) the member in fact has no authority to act for the LLP by doing that thing; and (b) the person knows that he has no authority or does not know or believe him to be a member of the LLP. In accordance with reg.8 of the Limited Liability Partnership Regulations 2001, SI 2001/1090, a majority of members cannot expel any member of an LLP unless a power to do so has been conferred by express agreement between the members. Minority members of an LLP will be able to avail themselves of the protective provisions of the companies legislation, for example a minority member may petition to protect his or her membership interest in circumstances where the conduct of a company's affairs subjected the interest to conduct of an unfairly prejudicial nature (see, e.g. *Eaton* v. *Caulfield* [2011] EWHC 173 (Ch)). However, it is to be noted that such protective devices may be expressly excluded by the unanimous written agreement of the members of an LLP (see CA 2006, s.994(3); Limited Liability Partnerships (Application of Companies Act 2006) Regulations 2009, SI 2009/1804, reg.48).

An LLP must file financial and other information on a regular basis. For example, an LLP will be obliged to file accounts and an annual return with the registrar of companies and will need to keep a register of charges. Further, the delinquent activities of members of the LLP are subject to similar sanctions to those imposed against company directors in respect of, for example, wrongful and fraudulent trading and disqualification. In respect of wrongful trading it is to be noted that IA 1986, s.214A (introduced by the 2001 Regulations) is specific to an LLP. This provision provides a liquidator with the right to 'claw back' any withdrawals of assets from the LLP which were made by a member(s) within the two years prior to the commencement of liquidation in a situation where the member(s) knew or had reasonable grounds to believe that at the time of withdrawal, or as a consequence of the withdrawal, the LLP was unable to pay its debts and as such the member(s) knew or ought to have concluded that there was no reasonable prospect of the LLP avoiding liquidation.

Although an LLP is primarily regulated by the companies legislation, it is nevertheless taxed as a partnership and its internal structure remains more identifiable with a traditional partnership; for example, it has no share capital and a member's income will not be in the form of dividend payments.

3.6.2 Business partnerships

A business partnership is a contractual relationship, but is subject to equitable principles and the provisions of the Partnership Act (PA) 1890. PA 1890 defines a business partnership as a relationship (an association) between persons carrying on a business in common with a view to profit (PA 1890, s.1). The association may be constituted formally or informally (*Phillips* v. *Symes* [2002] 1 WLR 853). The property of the business belongs to its members and not the actual partnership business. Unlike a registered company, a partnership is not a separate legal entity, although it may sue or be sued using the partnership name. Although the Limited Partnership Act 1907 allows a member of a partnership to attain a limited liability status, a partner with such a status is precluded from taking an active role in the management of the partnership firm and therefore other than for a 'sleeping' partner, the 1907 Act will have little application.

In accordance with PA 1890, s.5, a partnership is contractually bound by an agreement entered into on its behalf in the ordinary course of the firm's business by any of its members other than where a member enters into a contract without the authority of the other members and the 'lack of authority' point is known to the other contracting party. Further, PA 1890, s.10 provides that:

> Where, by any wrongful act or omission of any partner acting in the ordinary course of business of the firm, or with the authority of his co-partners, loss or injury is caused to any person not being a partner in the firm, or any penalty is incurred, the firm is liable therefor to the same extent as the partner so acting or omitting to act.

The vicarious liability principle established by s.10 extends to any wrongful act providing the act in question was undertaken in the ordinary course of the partnership's business. Here, a wrongful act includes an act involving dishonesty (see, e.g. the decision of the House of Lords in *Dubai Aluminium Co Ltd* v. *Salaam* [2003] 2 AC 366).

In contrast to a company, a partnership does not have perpetual succession. A partner's interest in the partnership business is a property right and, while this right may be transferred, the transferee will not be admitted as a member of the partnership firm without first obtaining the consent of the partnership's existing members. In theory, the acceptance of a new member into the partnership will have the effect of dissolving the old partnership, that is, by creating a new one. Where a member leaves a partnership, the retiring member (or his or her estate) must be paid his or her share of the partnership business. Here, again in theory, the partnership will be dissolved, although in practice the partnership will, with the consent of the remaining partners, continue its existence. (On the dissolution of a partnership see, generally, the decision of the House of Lords in *Hurst* v. *Bryk* [2002] 1 AC 185.)

In an attempt to raise finance, a partnership may borrow funds and collectively the partners may give security for loans in the form of the partnership's assets. It must be noted that a partnership's ability to grant security over its assets is subject to statutory restrictions that prevent individuals and partnerships from creating floating charges over fluctuating assets. (The nature of a floating charge is discussed in **Chapter 11**.) Previously, business partnerships were required to have a limit of 20 members (but with exemptions); however, this rule was removed by the Regulatory Reform (Removal of 20 Member Limit in Partnerships etc.) Order 2002, SI 2002/3203. A principal advantage of forming a partnership business is that a partnership business does not have to comply with the many formalities required of a registered company. However, it should be noted that the current trend in legislative policy, aimed towards the deregulation of private companies, may eventually weaken the partnership's advantage in respect of the formality rules.

3.7 EUROPEAN STRUCTURES

3.7.1 The Sócietas Europaea (SE)

As a result of EC Regulation 2157/2001 (and its supplementing Directive (2001/86/EC)), legislation to create a new European Company structure, the Sócietas Europaea (SE), was introduced into the UK by the European Public Limited-Liability Company Regulations 2004, SI 2004/2326, as amended by the European Public Limited-Liability Company (Amendment) Regulations 2009, SI 2009/2400 and the European Public Limited-Liability Company (Employee Involvement) (Great Britain) Regulations 2009, SI 2009/2401.

As a corporate vehicle the SE is available for at least two commercial bodies with operations in more than one Member State. An SE may be created as a European public limited liability company registered in one of the Member States, provided it has a minimum share capital of €120,000. The SE is governed by the terms of the Regulation and more especially the applicable corporate laws of the Member State in which it is registered. If registered in the UK, the SE will therefore be governed by the terms of the Regulation but will primarily be regulated by the UK companies legislation. There are five ways in which an SE may be created:

1. *Merger:* Two or more public limited companies or existing SEs may merge to form an SE provided at least two of them are governed by the laws of different Member States.
2. *A holding SE:* Two or more private or public limited companies (including

49

existing SEs) may form an SE by promoting the formation of a holding SE. The companies promoting the formation must become majority-owned by the SE. At least two of the companies must be governed by the laws of a different Member State, or for two years have had a subsidiary company governed by the laws of another Member State or had a branch in another Member State.

3.   *A subsidiary SE:* Two or more companies, firms or other legal bodies formed under the laws of a Member State may form an SE by subscribing for its shares. At least two of the companies or firms must be governed by the laws of a different Member State or for two years have had a subsidiary company governed by the laws of another Member State or had a branch in another Member State.

4.   *Subsidiary SE formed by another SE:* An existing SE may itself form another SE as a subsidiary company, in which it may be the sole shareholder.

5.   *Plc transforming to become an SE:* An existing plc registered in the UK may transform itself into an SE registered in the UK if the plc has for two years had a subsidiary governed by the laws of another Member State. This process does not involve the winding up of the plc or the creation of a new legal person in the form of an SE.

3.7.2   European Economic Interest Groupings

EC Regulation 2137/85 allows UK businesses, corporate or otherwise, to enter into an agreement of co-operation with a business or businesses in other Member States. The European Economic Interest Grouping Regulations 1989, SI 1989/638 regulate the European Economic Interest Grouping (EEIG) in the context of Great Britain. Both regulations were supplemented by the European Economic Interest Grouping (Amendment) Regulations 2009, SI 2009/2399.

An agreement of this nature creates an EEIG. Set up in much the same way as a company, an EEIG is formed by at least two members with their central administrations or principal activities based in different Member States. A manager(s) must be appointed to operate the EEIG on a day-to-day basis. The members of an EEIG are free, ordinarily, to decide voting procedures so contained within the contract of formation. However, unanimous decisions are required in respect of specific issues that are central to the functioning of the EEIG, for example, an alteration of the number of votes allotted to each member, an alteration to members' contributions to the grouping's financing, an alteration to the formation contract and a transfer of the official address of an EEIG to another Member State.

The purpose in creating the EEIG system was to facilitate co-operation between businesses located in different Member States. The businesses, which together form an EEIG, become its members although an EEIG may not exert control over the business activities of any individual member of its EEIG grouping. An EEIG has a separate legal personality, but unlike a registered company, the members of the EEIG are liable for the EEIG's debts; i.e. it does not possess a limited liability status. An EEIG cannot invite investment from the public. An EEIG must not, in its individual capacity as a separate legal entity, seek to make a profit; it is not required to have a share capital, nor does it need to file annual accounts or reports. Where an EEIG is registered in the UK, the UK companies legislation, in so far as it is applicable to the EEIG, will regulate its affairs.

3.7.3   European Private Company (Societas Privata Europaea (SOPE))

It is to be noted that the European Commission's proposal (draft regulation) for a European Private Company was announced on 25 June 2008. The proposal was expected to be set into a formal regulation on 1 July 2010 but to date the regulation has not materialised. The proposal sought to establish a new corporate form based around the specific needs of small and medium enterprises (SMEs). The objective behind the creation of the SOPE was to ease the legal and administrative barriers encountered by businesses operating across Member States and the costs associated with ensuring that business operations were compliant with the distinct national laws of Member States. The constitutional structure of an SOPE would be akin to that of a UK private company, albeit its shareholders would be permitted to adopt either a two-tier management system (consisting of a management body and a supervisory body) or, as in the UK, a one-tier management system (consisting of only one administrative body). It was intended that the SOPE would be governed by the regulation, and the national law of the country in which the SOPE had its registered office. National company law would be relevant only where specified by the regulation; it was proposed that national law would take effect in matters related to labour law, tax law, accounting, and insolvency. The contractual rights and obligations of the SOPE would also, in part, have been regulated by national law. However, such obligations and rights could have been derived from the articles of association of the SOPE. The rights of minority shareholders would have continued to have been protected in part by national laws although the draft regulation also conferred some protection. The approval of the annual accounts, reduction of capital, transformation or a merger of the SOPE, would have required a resolution passed by at least two-thirds (of the voting rights) of the members of the SOPE.

The registered office and principal place of business of an SOPE was to be located within the European Union, albeit not necessarily in the same Member State. In accordance with the draft regulation, it was intended that an SOPE could be created as an original entity or as a subsidiary of an existing corporate entity or by the merger of existing companies; an SE or another SOPE could also have participated in the formation of an SOPE. However, unlike the SE, there was no cross-border requirement attached to the formation of an SOPE. Under the draft regulation, it was provided that an SOPE should have a nominal minimum share capital of €1. However, it was intended that creditors of an SOPE would be afforded protection in so far as distributions to shareholders could be made only in circumstances where an SOPE's assets would fully cover its liabilities, i.e. after the distribution in question.

CHAPTER 4

The legal consequences of incorporation

4.1 INTRODUCTION

In law, a company is regarded as a distinct legal entity having a separate existence from its membership and management team. The independent legal status of the corporate entity is said to cast a veil between the company and its human constituents, 'the corporate veil'. A company's separate legal existence represents a fundamental and essential characteristic of company law; it is rarely impugned. However, in exceptional circumstances, the corporate veil may be dislodged to impose some degree of liability against the human constituents of the company or its corporate controllers. Nevertheless, in the majority of situations the veil will merely be pierced and not removed completely to the extent that the company's legal status will still be recognised. The corporate veil may be displaced at common law and by statute. In respect of the latter, the majority of statutory provisions that have a capacity to displace the corporate veil seek to penalise the irresponsible conduct of company directors involved in the management of insolvent companies (see **Chapter 5**). After a short discussion around issues relating to the liability of a director for personal undertakings, this chapter will consider the exceptional circumstances sufficient to justify a piercing of the corporate veil at common law.

4.2 THE LIABILITY OF A DIRECTOR FOR PERSONAL UNDERTAKINGS

Where a director acts in accordance with his designated authority, the corporate veil will usually shield the director from the incursion of personal liability. However, a director's immunity from the imposition of personal liability will not be safeguarded where he or she undertook a collateral and personal obligation on behalf of the company, notwithstanding that the undertaking was instigated to benefit the company. For example, in circumstances where the assets of a company are insufficient to secure corporate liabilities, a director may be obliged to enter into a contractual obligation to personally guarantee the repayment of the company's debts. A binding contractual agreement to guarantee a corporate debt may also be found in the guise of a letter of comfort. A letter of comfort may take the form of a personal assurance from a director of a company whereby he or she personally promises that a corporate debt will be met. Where, in reliance on the terms of the letter, its recipient alters his or her position in respect of a right to enforce the debt, that reliance may amount to consideration, thereby in law substantiating the creditor's right to enforce the director's promise that the debt will be met (see, e.g. *Edwards* v. *Skyways* [1964] 1 All ER 494).

4.3 THE CORPORATE VEIL

Although the courts universally accept and vigorously protect the principle of a company as a separate legal entity and as such are reluctant generally to depart from the main principle of law enunciated in *Salomon* v. *A Salomon Ltd* (see **Chapter 1**), in exceptional instances, the courts may consider it necessary to dislodge the corporate veil to prevent an unwarranted exploitation of the corporate form. Specific examples of when the court will displace the corporate veil may be categorised as follows.

4.3.1 Displacing the corporate veil in times of national emergency

When the nation is engaged in a serious political or economic conflict, it may, as a matter of public policy, be expedient for the court to displace the corporate veil to protect the nation's interests. Here, the justification for interfering with the corporate veil is to penalise individuals who have a significant connection with an enemy state. For example, when the nation is in conflict with another state, the corporate veil of a company registered in the UK may be pierced to discover if the shareholders of that company are connected with the enemy state. If the membership of the company is so connected to the enemy state, the company may be viewed as one and the same with its shareholders to the extent that the 'enemy status' of the shareholders will be attributed to the company. For example, in *Daimler* v. *Continental Tyre & Rubber Co* [1916] 2 AC 307, the Continental Tyre Co, a company registered in the UK, sought to enforce a debt owed to it by Daimler, another UK registered company. The membership of the Continental Tyre Co was composed of German nationals. At this period in time the UK was at war with Germany. The House of Lords (reversing the decision of the Court of Appeal) refused to enforce the debt in so far as it would have been contrary to the public interest to enforce the debt owed by a UK company (comprising UK shareholders) to a company, the membership of which was made up of German nationals (see also *The Polzeath* [1916] 32 TLR 674 and *Bank voor Handel en Scheepvaart NV* v. *Slatford* [1953] 1 QB 248).

4.3.2 Piercing the corporate veil in cases of a fraud/sham

The ability to pierce the corporate veil may be justified in cases where the formation or subsequent use of a company is considered a 'facade'. In this context the term 'facade' may be used to describe some form of deceptive cover or front, a mere cloak, fraud or sham, or may also be used to describe an agency type situation (discussed below). A fraud/sham situation will arise in specially defined circumstances, namely, where a company was incorporated or subsequently used by an individual in control of the company to the advancement of an improper and/or illegitimate purpose, namely to impugn an existing obligation or duty that belonged to the individual in control of the company. In such cases the court will recognise the existence of the corporate entity but may nevertheless pierce the corporate veil to prevent the person(s) in control of the company from escaping a liability that would have otherwise been enforceable had the person(s) concerned not sought to hide the liability behind the company's distinct and separate legal status. The courts have generally sought to identify the special circumstances as ones governed and subject to distinct (but narrow) equitable principles. However, while equitable principles may be at play, the concept of a fraud/sham cannot be fully equated with the concept of an equitable fraud in the sense that an equitable fraud may be expected to incorporate a far wider range of conduct of an unconscionably unfair nature, for example, an exploitation of a fiduciary position, undue influence, abuse of confidence and unconscionable bargains (see, e.g. *Nocton* v. *Lord Ashburton* [1914] AC 932). In the context of piercing the corporate veil, the interpretation of a fraud/sham is far more restrained. Further, although it may be contended that the justification for applying equitable rules to the purpose of piercing the corporate veil is derived directly and expressly from the *obiter* judgments of, for example, Lord Halsbury and Lord Macnaghten in *Salomon* v. *A Salomon Ltd* (discussed in **Chapter 1**), such a contention is fundamentally weakened by the absence, generally, of any reference in the case law concerned with piercing the corporate veil to such *obiter* comments. In effect, the fraud/sham exception is a restraint on the concept of an equitable fraud and the exception will only be invoked where the motive for incorporation, or the subsequent use of a corporate structure, was to enable those in control of a company to evade a pre-existing obligation or duty, an obligation or duty entered into by the controllers of the company, dehors the company. To summarise, the fraud/sham exception will only be invoked where X, having committed an impropriety (a breach of an obligation or duty), sought to escape the consequences of that impropriety by hiding it behind a corporate structure, a corporate structure controlled by X.

Gilford Motor Co v. *Horne* [1933] Ch 935 provides the classic example, if not the starting point, for a court's ability to pierce the corporate veil of a company in circumstances where the motive for the incorporation of the company was to hide a fraud/sham of its controlling influence. In this case, Mr Horne (H) entered into a contract with Gilford Motor Co by which he agreed to abide by a restrictive covenant which provided that should he leave Gilford's employment he would not solicit their customers. On leaving Gilford's employment, H, through nominees, formed a company through which he impliedly sought to escape the terms of the restrictive covenant. The court held that the company was a 'sham', an alias of H, and as such an injunction was granted to enforce the covenant. The restrictive covenant was enforced in equity against both H and the company, i.e. the company's corporate existence was not denied although the company's corporate veil was pierced to recognise H's personal culpability for the breach of the restrictive covenant. In effect, H had formed the company (as a fraudulent device) to evade the terms of the restrictive covenant and to escape the terms of the pre-existing contractual obligation that he had entered into with the Gilford Motor Co.

Jones v. *Lipman* [1962] 1 WLR 832 provides a further example of the court's ability to pierce the corporate veil in a situation where the motive for a company's incorporation was designed to permit the controlling influence of the company to evade an existing obligation or duty. Here, Mr Lipman (L) sought to escape specific performance of a contract entered into for the sale of land. L attempted to evade the contract by transferring the land in question to a company that he had recently incorporated. It was held that the incorporation of the company was but a device to evade L's contractual responsibility and as such specific performance of the sale of land was granted against both L and the company. Once again, the company's corporate existence was recognised by the court (in so far as the order was also granted against the company), although the company's veil was pierced to the extent that the court recognised L's personal culpability in relation to this deceit.

Trustor AB v. *Smallbone* [2001] 1 WLR 1177 provides an example of the fraud/sham exception being employed to prevent a person(s) (X) from impugning a pre-existing obligation/duty to a third party in circumstances where X sought to evade the obligation by hiding it behind the corporate veil of a company which X already controlled (i.e. the company already existed, it had been incorporated prior to the time at which X committed the impropriety). In *Trustor*, D, the managing director of a company (T), misappropriated monies from T in breach of his fiduciary duties to T (i.e. the impropriety) transferring the funds to another company (X). D controlled X. T sought the return of the misappropriated monies transferred to X. The corporate veil of X was pierced on the basis that X was a sham, a facade in the sense that it had been used by D as a means to collect the misappropriated funds. The veil was pierced to a conclusion that D was liable in equity to return the funds to T. (Also see, *Gencor ACP Ltd* v. *Dalby* [2000] 2 BCLC 734, *Kensington International Ltd* v. *Republic of the Congo* [2006] 2 BCLC 296 and, more recently, *Anglo German Breweries Ltd (in liquidation)* v. *Chelsea Corp Inc* [2012] 2 BCLC 632.)

4.3.3 Piercing the veil and equitable fraud

While in the context of the fraud/sham exception, the motive for a company's incorporation or subsequent use of a corporate structure may be most relevant in determining whether the corporate veil should be pierced, it does not always follow that an improper or, at the very least, suspect motive, will render the incorporation or use of a corporate structure to be viewed as one constituting a fraud/sham. Other than where the special circumstances apply (i.e. a company must have been incorporated or subsequently used by its controller to evade a pre-existing liability of the controller), the fraud/sham exception will not be invoked even where, in an objective sense, a reasonable person would conclude that in all probability, conscience and as a matter of reality and commercial logic, a controlling shareholder should, for the purpose of incurring a liability, be identified to be one and the same with the company under his or her control. In this sense the fraud/sham exception is narrowly construed and does not really marry with the concept attributed ordinarily to an 'equitable fraud'. For example, in *Yukong Lines Ltd of Korea* v. *Rendsburg Investments* [1998] BCC 870, the defendant company (D) transferred a majority of its funds to another company (L) and on that same day repudiated a charterparty agreement with P which had been entered into by a director (Y) of a firm of brokers (M) on behalf of D. D and L were members of the same corporate group structure. Y held a majority shareholding in D, M and L. The purpose for the transfer of funds was to put D's assets beyond the reach of P. Here, Toulson J held that any improper motive in relation to the transfer of the funds from D to L was not a factor that would justify a piercing of the corporate veil of D. Accordingly, Y, together with L could not be held liable for the repudiation of the agreement. The fraud/sham argument was defeated in so far as the charterparty had not been entered into by D with a view of defeating any pre-existing obligation of its controlling shareholder (Y). Although D had a pre-existing contract (charterparty) with P, and D would have otherwise been liable on that contract, it was not possible to pierce the corporate veil of D to impose that liability on Y or L in so far as Y or L had not, as distinct legal entities, entered into the contract with P (the contract was not dehors D, i.e. the contract had been entered into on behalf of D). Y had not sought to incorporate D to impugn a pre-existing legal obligation nor had L (unlike in *Trustor AB* v. *Smallbone* – see above) been used to hide and evade a pre-existing obligation (of Y) for the benefit of its controlling shareholder (Y). In fact, L had been used by Y to evade the pre-existing obligation of D. However, that said use was not an illegitimate one in the sense that it did not fall within the special circumstances so required to justify a piercing of the corporate veil.

To take another example: in *Ord* v. *Belhaven Pubs Ltd* [1998] 2 BCLC 447 the plaintiffs (P) took a 20-year lease of a public house from the defendant (B); the lease was taken on the basis of a representation by B in relation to the pub's turnover and profitability. B was a subsidiary within a group of companies controlled by Ascot Holdings plc (A). P alleged that B had made serious misrepresentations about the potential profitability of the public house and claimed damages in tort and contract. Prior to the trial of the proceedings the group of companies restructured with the result that B no longer retained any substantial assets (B's assets had been transferred to companies within the A group of companies). Given that B was left with no assets, P applied for leave to substitute B with A – i.e. P sought to pierce (indeed lift) the corporate veil of B to contend that B was part of a single economic entity represented by A. The Court of Appeal (in reversing the first instance decision) refused to recognise the single economic entity argument (discussed below). Further, the Court of Appeal refused to pierce the corporate veil on the basis of the fraud/sham exception in so far as B had not been incorporated to impugn a pre-existing duty or obligation of its controlling shareholder (A). The pre-existing obligation was one that belonged to B (as a distinct legal entity) and not A. (Also see, *Dadourain Group International* v. *Simms* [2004] EWCA Civ 686, *International Ltd* v. *Congo* [2006] 2 BCLC 296 and *Ben Hashem* v. *Ali Shayif* [2009] 1 FLR 115.)

Further, in a holding company–subsidiary relationship, it is considered legiti-mate by the courts for a holding company to eliminate the risk of being held potentially liable for pursuing a future course of conduct by transferring potentially risk-bearing activities to an existing subsidiary company (see the decision of the Court of Appeal in *Adams* v. *Cape Industries* [1990] 2 WLR 657). Following on from this reasoning, it will be legitimate for an individual to incorporate a company with the objective of evading a potential future liability, even if that liability is most likely to occur, providing of course that the potential future liability is unrelated to an obligation that was previously incurred by the individual prior to the company's incorporation.

The strict and narrow interpretation of the fraud/sham exception was confirmed recently by the decision of the Supreme Court in *VTB Capital plc* v. *Nutritek* [2013] UKSC 5 (affirming the decision of the Court of Appeal [2012] 2 BCLC 437). In *VTB Capital*, the claimant bank (C) loaned funds to a Russian company (R). The purpose of the loan was to allow R to fund acquisitions from D1. R and D1 were within the same corporate group of companies; a group structure controlled by an individual, D4. R defaulted on the loan repayments. R obtained the loan as a result of a fraudulent misrepresentation by D1 and although D1 was not a party to the contract with C, C contended that R had been used as a device, a facade (sham/fraud) to conceal the true facts, namely, that R and D1 were members of an economic entity, a group of related companies under the dominant control of an individual (D4). In effect, C contended that, together with the companies within the economic group-ing, the corporate veil of R should be pierced to establish that D4 was responsible ultimately for the breach of the loan agreement. However, in refusing to pierce the corporate veil of R, both the Court of Appeal and the Supreme Court (see, especially, the judgment of Lord Neuberger in the Supreme Court), in upholding the first instance decision of Arnold J, held that in circumstances where a contract had been entered into by a company as a distinct legal entity, the corporate veil could not be pierced to establish a liability for damages against the company's controlling shareholder. The contract belonged properly to the company and not the controlling shareholder and privity of contract rules deemed that the controlling shareholder could not sue (or be sued) on the contract. In this case, although D4 controlled R, R had not (in a technical sense) been used by D4 exclusively for the purpose of evading an existing impropriety (an existing obligation/duty held by D4 or any other company within the group). The obligation/duty properly belonged to R.

In the context of circumstances justifying the piercing of the corporate veil, the decision of the Supreme Court in *VTB Capital* overruled the then recent and contrasting decision of Burton J in *Antonio Gramsci Shipping Corp* v. *Stepanous* [2011] Lloyd's Rep 647, in which it had been held that a remedy for contractual damages could be awarded on the basis of the application of the fraud/sham exception. In *Gramsci* the claimants (C) were ship owners who held shares in a company (LSC); the purpose behind LSC had been to enter into shipping contracts to the benefit of C. S, a senior executive of LSC (together with other executive members of LSC) incorporated distinct companies (V's) with the sole and dishonest objective of diverting corporate opportunities away from LSC. In this respect, V chartered a number of vessels owned by C (through LSC) on charterparties at less than the market rate and subsequently sub-chartered the vessels to third parties at the market rate, thereby depriving LSC (ultimately C) of the difference between the market rate and the charter rates: that is, keeping all the profits. Burton J held that C could obtain restitution of the profits unlawfully diverted as against V (the puppet companies) and/or S (the puppeteer and controlling shareholder). Here, interestingly, it was held that restitution could be obtained against S notwithstanding that the impropriety was not dehors the company (V) – indeed the very objective of V's incorporation was for V to commit the fraud; V was not used (as in *Trustor AB* v. *Smallbone* or incorporated (as in *Gilford Motor Co* v. *Horne*) to hide an existing impropriety that had been committed by its controlling shareholder (S).

The arguments in *Gramsci* and *VTB Capital* were similar in the sense that in both cases the claimant (C) sought to pierce the corporate veil to render a controlling shareholder liable for the contracting company's breach of contract. However, a significant difference between the cases was that in *Gramsci* the company that entered into the contract had been created by its controlling shareholders with the specific purpose of perpetrating a future fraud against the claimant. In *VTB Capital*, the contracting company (R) had some independent purpose; it had not been created exclusively for a fraudulent purpose. Indeed, prior to the Supreme Court's decision in *VTB Capital*, the decision in *Gramsci* had been distinguished but not disputed by Flaux J in *Lisen International Ltd* v. *Humpuss Sea Transport Ltd* [2011] EWCH 2339. In *Lisen*, Flaux J refused to pierce the corporate veil on the basis that unlike in *Gramsci*, the company that entered into the contract had not been created exclusively for the purpose of perpetrating the alleged impropriety. It is suggested that in *VTB Capital*, a factor crucial to the Court of Appeal and Supreme Court's reluctance to accept the outcome in *Gramsci* (in a manner similar to the way *Gramsci* was accepted, albeit distinguished, by Flaux J in *Lisen International Ltd* v. *Humpuss Sea Transport Ltd*) was that the claimant sought a common law remedy in damages. In the Supreme Court in *VTB Capital*, Lord Neuberger stated:

> I doubt that the decision in *Gramsci* can be justified, at least on the basis of piercing the corporate veil. In agreement with the Court of Appeal and Arnold J, I think that the reasoning in that case involved a misinterpretation of the basis of the decisions in Gilford and Jones. It seems to me that the conclusion in *Gramsci* was driven by an understandable desire to ensure that an individual who appears to have been the moving spirit behind a dishonourable (or worse) transaction, action, or receipt, should not be able to avoid liability by relying on the fact that the transaction, action, or receipt was effected through the medium (but not the agency) of a company. But that is not, on any view, enough to justify piercing the corporate veil for the purpose of holding the individual liable for the transaction, action, or receipt, especially where the action is entering into a contract. (at para.147)

Lord Neuberger's analysis in *VTB Capital* in the context of the corporate veil point was shared and agreed to by the other members of the Supreme Court. However, it is interesting to note that Lord Clarke portrayed some degree of reservation in respect of the restrictive nature afforded to the accepted circumstances justifying a piercing of the corporate veil. Lord Clarke opined:

> I agree with Lord Neuberger that this is not a case in which it would be appropriate to pierce the corporate veil on the facts. I would however wish to reserve for future decision the question what is the true scope of the circumstances in which it is permissible to pierce the corporate veil. That includes the question whether *Antonio Gramsci Shipping Corpn* v. *Stepanovs* [2011] EWHC 333 (Comm) was correctly decided. (at para.238)

4.3.4 Displacing the veil to establish a controlling interest/economic entity

Although it should be stressed that an 'economic entity' exception to the *Salomon* principle is now severely eroded as a result of the decision of the Court of Appeal in *Adams* v. *Cape Industries* (discussed below), in exceptional circumstances, involving a holding company–subsidiary relationship (or where a group of companies is under the control of a dominant individual(s)) the group relationship may be viewed as a single economic entity to the extent that the corporate veil of the subservient subsidiary company(ies) may be removed completely to establish the single economic entity. Following *Adams*, the qualifying characteristics necessary to establish a dominant company's control over a subservient entity must now amount to control warranting the finding of an agency relationship (discussed further below). Prior to *Adams* v. *Cape Industries*, an economic entity could be established where the holding company exerted a substantial degree of control over the affairs of the subsidiary company, to the extent that the holding company controlled and dictated the corporate policy of its subsidiary. For example, in *DHN Food Distributors Ltd* v. *Tower Hamlets LBC* [1976] 1 WLR 852, a holding company, DHN, traded from premises owned by its subsidiary company, Bronze Ltd. A third company in the group operated a transport business for the sole benefit of DHN. The land upon which the business premises of the group of three companies was located (land registered to Bronze Ltd) was subsequently made subject to a compulsory purchase order by the council. In accordance with the terms of the order, compensation was payable to the owner of the land (i.e. Bronze Ltd) and for any disturbance to the landowners' business. As Bronze Ltd carried on no independent business, the council refused to pay any compensation for the loss of business. The Court of Appeal unanimously disagreed with the council's decision not to award compensation. Lord Denning opined that the three companies should, for all practical purposes, be treated as one economic entity and that a technical rule of company law, the separate legal identity of each company in the group, could be disregarded, where, as in this case, the ownership and control of corporate policy and strategy of the two subsidiary companies were clearly in the hands of the holding company. (Also see *Holdsworth & Co* v. *Caddies* [1955] 1 WLR 352 and *Scottish Co-op Wholesale Society* v. *Meyer* [1959] AC 324.)

However, following the decision of the Court of Appeal in *Adams* v. *Cape Industries* [1990] Ch 433 (discussed below), a company's (or an individual's) ability to control the overall policy structure of another company is unlikely, of itself, to be sufficient to justify the lifting of the corporate veil. (However, an element of control may establish a liability in tort, see *Chandler* v. *plc* [2012] 1 WLR 3111, discussed below.) To manipulate the corporate veil of a subsidiary and merge it into the holding company to create an economic entity, the courts have demanded that the facts of the case must establish a facade relationship. The requirement to establish a 'facade' emanates from the case of *Woolfson* v. *Strathclyde Regional Council* 1978 SLT 159, in which the House of Lords doubted the correctness of the decision in *DHN Food Distributors Ltd* v. *Tower Hamlets LBC*.

Although the respective cases of *Woolfson* and *DHN* bore many similarities, *Woolfson* was concerned with an individual's control over a group of companies and not a holding company–subsidiary relationship. The individual in question, Mr Woolfson (W), held 99.9 per cent of the shares in Campbell Ltd (C). C carried on a retail business in a chain of shops, three of which were owned by W and the other two by Solfred Ltd (S), a company in which W held two-thirds of the shares. W's wife held the remaining shares in S and the remaining 0.1 per cent of shares in C. The dispute in this case arose when the local council acquired the shop premises in accordance with a compulsory purchase order, the terms of which provided that compensation was payable for disturbance to an occupier or to an owner-occupier but not to an owner who was not an occupier. C occupied the premises and W and S sought further compensation for disturbance on the grounds that together with C they all formed one single economic entity (i.e. they sought compensation as owner-occupiers). However, although the three businesses were associated under the dominant influence of W, unlike in the *DHN* case, the three businesses were not completely controlled by one entity (the House of Lords distinguished the *DHN* case on that basis). In reaching its decision to refuse to merge the three business enterprises into one economic entity, the House of Lords concluded that save where the relationship between a group of enterprises was a facade, the individual companies forming the collective group of companies should not be considered to be a single economic entity. However, the House of Lords did not elaborate upon the meaning to be attributed to the term 'facade'.

In *Adams* v. *Cape Industries* [1990] Ch 433, the Court of Appeal, in following its own decision in *Bank of Tokyo Ltd* v. *Karoon* [1987] AC 45 and the decision of the House of Lords in *Woolfson*, confirmed that a strong economic link between a group of companies could not in itself justify the merging of a group of companies into one economic entity. In *Adams*, an English holding company, Cape Industries plc, pursued its business activities in the asbestos industry. Cape had subsidiaries in the UK, South Africa and the USA. As a result of being exposed to asbestos, employees of the American subsidiary (NAAC) suffered serious illnesses and sought damages (the Tyler 1 action) against NAAC. NAAC was obliged to pay $5.2 million in compensation. Although NAAC was obliged to pay this compensation, in effect, the cost of the action fell on the Cape group. To prevent the incursion of any further future liability in the USA, against the Cape group, NAAC was put into liquidation. Nevertheless, the American marketing base of the Cape group was continued by another company, CPC. CPC was not a subsidiary of Cape, albeit that it had been set up with substantial financial support from the Cape group. CPC operated from the premises previously occupied by NAAC. CPC's managing director, who was also its majority shareholder, had previously been the managing director of NAAC. A Liechtenstein-registered company, AMC, controlled by the Cape group, acted as Cape's agents in the American market; in effect AMC were 'middle men' in the relationship between Cape and CPC.

Shortly after NAAC's liquidation, a second series of actions were commenced successfully in the US by former employees of NAAC (Tyler 2 action). In the UK, the Court of Appeal had to determine whether the judgments in favour of the American employees were enforceable in the UK against Cape, namely, in reality were Cape and NAAC part of a single economic entity? Cape argued that any liability attributable to NAAC had been extinguished following NAAC's liquidation and that Cape itself could not be made party to proceedings in the USA because it no longer had any presence in that jurisdiction. Cape contended that any liability attached to NAAC or for that matter CPC should rest with those companies as distinct and separate legal entities. The plaintiffs contended that NAAC and CPC were part of one economic entity, namely the Cape group, and that Cape was therefore still present in the USA, through CPC.

In finding in favour of Cape, the Court of Appeal denied the validity of the existence of a single economic entity. This denial was understandable in respect of the relationship between Cape and CPC, in so far as CPC was not even a Cape subsidiary. However, the court's finding that NAAC had not been a part of an economic entity with Cape at its head provided a more debatable proposition. The court conceded that Cape controlled the general corporate policy of NAAC and that it determined the subsidiary's expenditure and financial policy. Nevertheless, the court opined that the subsidiary was an independent entity in so far as NAAC was not totally dependent on Cape. NAAC managed the day-to-day running of its own business; for example, it was allowed to enter into business contracts and employ its own staff. In denying the existence of an economic entity, the Court of Appeal considered that the requisite degree of control by a holding company over its subsidiary deemed necessary to justify the recognition of an economic entity required a finding of absolute control in a manner whereby the subsidiary was a facade, a mere alias of the holding company.

In *Adams*, the Court of Appeal gave two independent examples of the existence of a facade. First, in relation to a group of companies, an entity could be described as a facade where it was created on the basis of a lack of any corporate independence of its own, i.e. it was an agent, a mere alias for its master. Secondly, a subservient company could be described as a facade where it was created or used for an improper or illegitimate purpose (akin to piercing the corporate veil under the fraud/sham exception, see above). The Court of Appeal concluded that, save where a particular statute or contractual provision permitted a parent and subsidiary company to be regarded as a single economic entity, the finding of an economic entity would be dependent on establishing the relationship between a holding company and its subsidiary as one that amounted to a facade.

Following the decision of the Court of Appeal in *Adams* v. *Cape Industries*, an agency relationship between a holding company and a subsidiary will facilitate a finding that the holding company (the principal) was responsible and therefore liable for the actions of its subsidiary (the agent). In the context of an agency relationship between corporate entities, agency may be tentatively defined as a relationship which is based upon the express or implied consent of both the subsidiary company and its holding company, whereby the subsidiary company is made subject to the holding company's control and will, to the extent that the subsidiary conducts its business affairs without independence, to the ultimate benefit of the holding company (see, e.g. *Garnac Grain Co Inc* v. *HMF Faure and Fairclough Ltd* [1968] AC 1130 at 1137). As a matter of theory, following a finding of an agency relationship, the court will not be required to lift the corporate veil; rather the principal and agent will be recognised as two distinct entities. However, akin to lifting the corporate veil, the principal will be deemed responsible in law for the activities carried out in the name of its agent. In *Adams* v. *Cape Industries*, Cape's relationship with its subsidiary was not deemed an agency relationship because of a lack of absolute control on the part of Cape over the subsidiary's affairs. The subsidiary employed its own staff, rented its own warehouses, occasionally purchased materials on its own behalf, earned its own profits and paid tax in a foreign jurisdiction (USA). Similarly, in *Kodak* v. *Clark* [1902] 2 KB 450, the court denied the existence of an agency relationship between an English holding company and its overseas subsidiary because the English company, which held 98 per cent of the subsidiary's shares, never attempted to interfere with the management of the subsidiary.

4.3.5 Determining an agency relationship

In *Smith Stone & Knight Ltd* v. *Birmingham Corp* [1939] 4 All ER 116, an agency relationship between a holding company and its wholly owned subsidiary was established on the premise that the holding company had absolute control over the affairs of its subsidiary. Atkinson J considered that on the facts of the case there was in effect an agency relationship because as a matter of reality, the holding company conducted the business operations of its subsidiary. For example, the holding company appointed and instructed the directors of the subsidiary, controlled the subsidiary's corporate policy, decided which contracts it should pursue and received and used, as it thought fit, all the profits made by the subsidiary. In effect, Atkinson J concluded that the subsidiary had no independent existence other than to serve its master, namely, its holding company. (Also see, *Nicholas* v. *Soundcraft Electronics Ltd* [1993] BCLC 360.)

In determining an agency relationship, it must be stressed that it does not necessarily follow that a wholly owned subsidiary will be regarded as the holding company's agent (see, e.g. *Gramophone & Typewriter Ltd* v. *Stanley* [1908] 2 KB 89). Conversely, it does not follow that an agency relationship will not be present in a situation where the subsidiary is not wholly owned. For example, in *Re FG (Films) Ltd* [1953] 1 All ER 615 the court was called upon to determine whether a film made by an English registered company was a British film as defined by the Cinemato-graph Films Act 1938, s.25(1). The English company (FG Films) that claimed to have made the film had a share capital of 100 £1 shares, 90 of which were held on behalf of an American company that financed the film in question. Vaisey J held that the participation of the English company in making the film was so small as to be negligible; it had acted as a nominee of and agent for the American company. The film was therefore deemed not to have been a British film, but one that had been made exclusively under the control of the American company.

4.3.6 Can a 'one-man company' be regarded as the agent of its dominant and controlling shareholder?

If a subsidiary company can be regarded properly as the agent of its holding company, can a 'one-man company' be regarded as the agent of its dominant and controlling shareholder? Although the feasibility of such an agency relationship was rejected in *Salomon* v. *A Salomon Ltd*, in *IRC* v. *Sanson* [1921] 2 KB 492, Lord Sterndale observed that in an appropriate case it may be possible to establish an agency type relationship between a majority shareholder and a 'one-man type company' under his or her absolute control. However, any affirmation of the existence of an agency relationship between an individual and a company under his or her control must be seriously doubted. Indeed, a finding of an agency relationship between a single company and its controlling shareholder would be to challenge the very heart of corporate law. Many small companies are one-man type concerns, the alter ego of the controlling shareholder, having been incorporated on the basis of the perceived incentives provided by the separation of identity and responsibility between the individual and corporate entity. However, it should be noted, in the context of family law cases and in respect of the interpretation of the Matrimonial Causes Act 1973, that a husband, or alternatively, a wife's absolute control over a company has, in some cases, proved to be sufficient grounds to substantiate a finding that the husband or as the case may be, the wife, beneficially owned the company's assets to a conclusion that in divorce proceedings the husband's wife (or alternatively the wife's husband) was entitled to a share of the assets (in reality the company's properties). The Matrimonial Causes Act 1973, s.24(1)(a) provides that:

> On granting a decree of divorce ... the court may make any one or more of the following orders, that is to say – (a) an order that a party to the marriage shall transfer to the other party ... such property as may be so specified, being property to which the first-mentioned party is entitled, either in possession or reversion.

Cases in which a husband's/wife's absolute control over a company's assets resulted in the court concluding that the wife/husband was entitled to share in such assets include, *Mubarak* v. *Mubarak* [2001] 1 FLR 673 and *Kremen* v. *Agrest (No. 2)* [2011] FLR 490. In addition, *obiter* comments from the decision of the Court of Appeal in *Nicholas* v. *Nicholas* [1984] FLR 285 also support that stance. The justification for such a conclusion, the effect of which is to pierce the corporate veil of the 'controlled' company, is that the statutory language of s.24(1)(a) overrides the constraints of the *Salomon* principle. Further justice is served in favour of the wife/husband, namely, why should a husband/wife in absolute control of a company and its assets be allowed to exploit the full advantage of those assets to the detriment of his or her partner?

However, as a controlling shareholder is not, in accordance with the wording of s.24(1)(a), entitled to 'possession or reversion' of a company's assets – a company's assets properly belong to the company and the company alone, it is difficult (other than as a matter of justice) in the light of established corporate law principles, to support any argument that asserts that absolute control of a company's assets will justify a piercing of the corporate veil in a manner advanced by the cases cited above. Other than where an impropriety is alleged, for example, the company in question was formed or subsequently used specifically for the purpose of denying the wife's entitlement to her husband's assets, can it be said that the corporate veil should be pierced. Indeed, this latter conclusion was favoured in *Ben Hashem* v. *Al Shayif* [2009] FLR 115 and more recently by the decision of the Court of Appeal in *Prest* v. *Prest* [2013] 2 WLR 557 (principle affirmed by the Supreme Court [2013] UKSC 34, although the actual decision of the Court of Appeal was reversed on the premise that in the particular circumstances of the case, the company in question held assets on resulting trusts for its controlling shareholder and as such the controlling shareholder and not the company was the beneficial owner of the assets). Accordingly, following the decision in *Prest* v. *Prest*, it would now appear settled that family law and corporate law are aligned in respect of the principles justifying a piercing of the corporate veil.

4.3.7 Disturbing corporate personality by invoking attribution principles

In an expanding number of cases the courts have 'sidestepped' the *Salomon* principle to merge the legal identities of otherwise distinct entities (individuals or corporate persons) on the basis that the overriding control and responsibility for a particular transaction or activity should be vested in but one dominant entity. Here the premise for establishing 'overriding control and responsibility' is akin to the operation of the identification principle, a principle associated ordinarily with the attribution of corporate criminal liability (discussed in **Chapter 20**). Basically, the identification principle attributes an artificial but distinct legal body (the corporate entity) with the mind and will of the directing mind of the company. The directing mind of a company is ordinarily vested in the controlling shareholder and/or director of the company. While the judgments in the 'overriding control and responsibility' cases do not seek expressly to challenge the main *Salomon* principle or directly criticise the arbitrary nature of the exceptions to the principle, it would appear that an implied challenge may be at work. Cases that may be said to sidestep the main *Salomon* principle include the decision of the House of Lords in *Stone & Rolls Ltd* v. *Moore Stephens (a firm)* [2009] 3 WLR 455.

In *Stone & Rolls Ltd* v. *Moore Stephens (a firm)* [2009] 3 WLR 455, the House of Lords held, by a majority of three to two, that a company could not claim damages against its auditors for the latter's negligent failure to detect fraud in circumstances where the controlling shareholder (directing mind of the company) perpetrated the fraud in question. The company was attributed with the fraudulent business activities of its directing mind to the extent that the company was viewed as a primary participant and not a victim of the fraud. Contrary to the accepted interpretation of the *Salomon* principle, and without invoking an accepted exception to that principle, the distinct identities of the directing mind and the company were merged to be treated as one and the same.

A further example is provided by *Coles* v. *Samuel Smith Old Brewery (Tadcaster)* [2008] 2 EGLR 159. Here the Court of Appeal held that a landlord of leasehold property could not avoid the right of tenants to exercise an option to purchase the property. Although the landlord had sold and transferred the property to its subsidiary company, and while the subsidiary company was not bound by the option (as the option had not been registered), the Court of Appeal ordered specific performance against the original landlord, the same having control over the subsidiary company. In effect, although the relationship between the holding company and its subsidiary was not, in law, one of agency and the transfer of property had been for value (although at a much discounted price), the holding company and subsidiary company were merged into, in effect, a single economic entity. The tenant was permitted to exercise the option to purchase. (For further examples of the disturbance of corporate personality by attribution, see, e.g. *Beckett Investment Management Group Ltd* v. *Hall* (2007) *The Times*, 11 July, *KR* v. *Royal & Sun Alliance plc* [2007] Bus LR 139 and *Millam* v. *The Print Factory (London) 1991 Ltd* [2008] BCC 169.)

4.3.8 Justice issues

A court may interfere with a company's distinct legal status where it has been established that there exists a state of national emergency, a fraud/sham or an agency relationship and potentially by invoking attribution principles. It may be argued that those criteria mask the fundamental justification for denying the preservation of the corporate veil, namely, to prevent injustice, a perversion of the corporate form. However, if justice was the fundamental criterion in displacing the corporate veil, it would be expected that much more flexibility would be afforded to the interpretation around the accepted circumstances justifying a disturbance of corporate personality. The boundaries around the accepted circumstances would evolve and expand. However, following the decision in *Adams* v. *Cape Industries*, such flexibility is unlikely and here the Court of Appeal stressed that justice issues should not be given any distinct relevance in determining whether to displace the corporate veil.

Reaffirming the lengthy and powerful comments of the Court of Appeal in *Adams* v. *Cape Industries*, subsequent decisions of the English courts have sought generally to deny that individual issues of justice may facilitate the removal of the corporate veil. For example, in *Ord* v. *Belhaven Pubs Ltd* [1998] 2 BCLC 447, the Court of Appeal condemned the reasoning applied in the first instance decision of *Creasey* v. *Breachwood Motors Ltd* [1992] BCC 639. The Court of Appeal overruled *Creasey*. In *Creasey* an employee (C) of W Ltd (W) claimed unfair dismissal. W carried on business at premises owned by B Ltd (B); the same two individuals controlled both companies. C commenced an action against W for wrongful dismissal. However, before proceedings were commenced against W, the company ceased trading. B took over all of W's assets and paid off W's trade creditors, with the exception of C's claim for compensation. W was subsequently struck off the companies register for not carrying on any business. As the effect of the order was to end the legal existence of W, C's solicitors successfully applied to have W substituted by B as the defendant to the order made in favour of C. B appealed to the High Court but failed. In removing the corporate veil of W, the court considered that W was but a part of B. Therefore, B could be deemed responsible for the payment of any compensation order in favour of C. In *Creasey*, the corporate veil was pierced for justice's sake.

As stated, *Creasey* was overruled by the Court of Appeal in *Ord* v. *Belhaven Pubs Ltd* and subsequent authorities (see, e.g. the Supreme Court in *VTB Capital plc* v. *Nutritek* [2013] UKSC 5) continue to stress that the justice of a case is not, in itself, relevant to an ability to pierce the corporate veil. In *Creasey*, much emphasis and justification for the recognition of 'justice issues', as being sufficient to warrant a piercing of the corporate veil, emanated from the *obiter* comments found in the judgments of Lord Denning. Lord Denning advocated that a court's power to lift the corporate veil should be viewed as a discretionary power as opposed to a tool which could only be employed in set defined circumstances (see, e.g. Lord Denning's judgments in *Littlewoods Mail Order Stores Ltd* v. *IRC* [1969] 1 WLR 1241 and *Wallensteiner* v. *Moir* [1974] 1 WLR 991). In the *Littlewoods* case, Lord Denning stated:

> The doctrine laid down in *Salomon*'s case has to be watched very carefully. It has often been supposed to cast a veil over the personality of a limited company through which the courts cannot see. But that is not true. The courts can and often do draw aside the veil. They can, and often do, pull off the mask. They look to see what really lies behind. (at p.1254)

4.4   LIABILITY IN TORT – A DISTORTION OF CORPORATE PERSONALITY

Where a director of a limited liability company causes the company to be involved in a tortious act, then, in accordance with agency principles, liability will ordinarily be imposed on the principal (the company) and not the agent (the individual officer) (see, e.g. *Rainham Chemical Works Ltd* v. *Belvedere Fish Guano Ltd* [1921] 2 AC 465). However, where the tort in question involves fraud, a director will not be permitted to escape the consequences of his or her own fraudulent conduct, a position affirmed by the House of Lords in *Standard Chartered Bank* v. *Pakistan National Shipping Corporation* [2002] 3 WLR 1547. (Also see, *Contex Drouzhba Ltd* v. *Wiseman* [2008] BCC 301 and *Barclay Pharmaceuticals Ltd* v. *Waypharm LP* [2012] EWHC 306 (Comm).) Here the director's liability will arise from the simple fact that he or she committed fraud, not by virtue of his position as a director. As Lord Hoffmann remarked in *Standard Chartered Bank*:

> No one can escape liability for his fraud by saying 'I wish to make it clear that I am committing this fraud on behalf of someone else and I am not to be personally liable'. (at p.1554)

In exceptional cases, a director as an agent of the company may be deemed personally liable for a tort other than the tort of deceit in circumstances where it can be established that the director exhibited a personal as opposed to a corporate competence for directing or procuring the wrongful act in question. In cases involving a tort of a negligent character, the ability to establish a director's personal liability will be dependent upon complying with the principles of law invoked by the House of Lords in *Hedley Byrne* v. *Heller & Partners Ltd* [1964] AC 465 and *Caparo Industries plc* v. *Dickman* [1992] 2 AC 605, i.e. it will be necessary to establish a special relationship between the plaintiff and tortfeasor (director) and the fact that the director assumed a personal responsibility for the negligent act. Further, to establish liability, the plaintiff must have relied on the director's assumption of responsibility. For example, in *Fairline Shipping Corp* v. *Adamson* [1975] 2 QB 180, although the plaintiff entered into a contract with a company, a director of that company was held to be personally liable for the performance of a negligent act in so far as the director conducted the negotiations with the plaintiff on a personal as opposed to a corporate footing, for example, by personally writing to the plaintiff, as opposed to writing *qua* director on company note paper. The court held that the director had created a clear impression that he was to be personally responsible for carrying out the performance of the contract with the plaintiff.

The evidence to substantiate a claim that a company director should be made personally responsible for the company's commission of the negligent act must be little short of overwhelming, a fact illustrated by the decision of the House of Lords in *Williams* v. *Natural Life Health Ltd* [1998] 1 BCLC 689. In *Williams*, the plaintiffs entered into a franchise scheme operated by Natural Life Health Ltd (N). The plaintiffs were, in part, induced into entering into the scheme by the company's marketing brochure that contained misleading statements falsely alluding to the company's expertise in, for example, product knowledge, finance, management techniques and marketing. However, and of more relevance to the claim, the plaintiffs relied upon projected figures which had been drawn up by the company and which had misleadingly projected a profit of £30,000 for the first 18 months of trading. In reality, the plaintiffs made a loss of £38,600 for that period. Following the commencement of proceedings, N, originally the sole defendant to the action, was put into liquidation. Thereafter, the plaintiffs' claim was pursued against the company's managing director (M) and its majority shareholder. M's role in the franchise agreement, albeit of an indirect nature, had been a considerable one. Indeed, the company's own purported expertise in franchising was exclusively based upon M's own personal experience of the franchise business. The plaintiffs had relied upon the projected figures for their franchise as a result of M's personal proficiency in the franchise business. M was clearly the principal driving force behind the company.

Following the first instance judgment of Langley J ([1996] 1 BCLC 288), the Court of Appeal concluded that a director could only incur personal liability in special and exceptional circumstances. However, the circumstances of this case were such that M was held personally liable. Hirst LJ, in delivering the leading judgment of the Court of Appeal, analysed the legal principles derived from the decisions of the House of Lords in *Hedley Byrne* v. *Heller & Partners Ltd* [1964] AC 465 and *Henderson* v. *Merrett Syndicates Ltd* [1995] 2 AC 145. In harmony with the views expressed by Langley J, Hirst LJ asserted that the ability to establish an assumption of responsibility was devoid of any necessity to ascertain any form of personal dealings between the parties. Accordingly, Hirst LJ observed that personal liability could be imposed against a director for a negligent act where it was evident that he or she was an instrumental figure in the ordinance of the wrongful act, albeit that his or her involvement and relationship with the plaintiff was of an implied as opposed to an express nature. M's role in the franchise agreement had been a considerable one and as such it was held that there had been, on M's part, an implied assumption of personal responsibility, a responsibility that extended beyond his capacity as a director of the company.

On appeal to the House of Lords, the decision of the Court of Appeal was reversed, notwithstanding that the House accepted that it was patently evident that the respondents relied upon negligent advice. The House found that the responsibility for the negligent act resided in the company and not in M and resolved that the Court of Appeal had misapplied the principles enunciated in *Hedley Byrne & Co* v. *Heller & Partners Ltd* and *Henderson* v. *Merrett Syndicates Ltd*. Lord Steyn, in giving the judgment of the House, stressed that the internal arrangements between a director and his company could never be the foundation of a director's personal liability in tort. Although the company had relied almost exclusively on M's personal expertise, such expertise was never marketed or advanced otherwise than under the company's corporate umbrella. While M viewed and impliedly approved the financial projections for P's franchise business, M never sought to play an active role in their preparation, nor had he ever expressly held himself out as having done so. Further, in dealings with the company, the respondents had not identified M, other than as a part of the company.

Lord Steyn concluded that, in so far as M had held himself out at all times as the managing director of a limited company, it followed that there had never been an assumption on his part of personal responsibility (also see, *European International Reinsurance Co Ltd* v. *Curzon Insurance Ltd* [2003] Lloyd's Rep IR 793).

In accordance with the common law's strict desire to uphold the independent legal status of a corporate entity, the decision of the House of Lords in *Williams* v. *Natural Life Health Ltd* is, to say the least, of a conforming nature. The decision confirms that a company director's personal liability in tort may never be presumed on the premise that the director held a dominant position in, or was an integral part of the company's directing mind. Further, the decision of the House of Lords expounds the principle that notwithstanding that a director may be portrayed by his company as the instrumental figure in respect of any given business venture, the director will not be presumed to have assumed any personal responsibility for that venture other than where he himself expressly or impliedly affirms an assumption of personal responsibility.

4.4.1 Circumstances in which a director's personal responsibility may be assumed

Although case examples establishing a director's assumption of personal responsibility will be rare, *D Wetherspoon plc* v. *Van de Berg & Co Ltd* [2009] EWHC 639 (Ch) provides an example of the circumstances in which a director's personal responsibility may be assumed. The case involved a company (W) that operated a number of public houses. W employed a company (V) as a property finder to locate suitable properties that W would run subsequently as public houses. T was the chairman and major shareholder of W. C was the sole director of V. W claimed that V (through C) had wrongly, and in breach of trust, introduced properties to B, a rival of W. In relation to those transactions W contended that C was in breach of duty to W directly. Much of the outside business world considered that V was virtually part of W and over the years, a strong personal relationship had developed between C and T. In reality, W's property acquisitions were decided on by T following C's advice. W (in particular T) conducted business with V (C in particular) for over a decade on the basis of mutual trust. C well understood that T placed great reliance on him in their business relationship. In considering the relationships between W and V, Peter Smith J held that the evidence pointed to a truly special relationship of trust and confidence between T and C. V was C's vehicle for the purpose of discharging the close personal relationship he had with T and as such C owed a direct duty to W.

4.4.2 Groups of companies – liability in tort

Recent case law and in particular the decision of the Court of Appeal in *Chandler* v. *Cape plc* [2012] 1 WLR 3111, affirming the decision of Wyn Williams J ([2011]

EWHC 951 (QB)), asserts that a holding company may be held responsible for a negligent act committed by its subsidiary company. (Also see *Connolly* v. *The RTZ Corporation plc* [1999] CLC 533 and the decision of the Court of Appeal in *Lubbe* v. *Cape* [2000] 1 WLR 1545.)

In *Chandler*, the claimant (R) sought compensation after contracting asbestosis following his exposure to asbestos dust in the workplace. R had been employed by Cape Building Products Ltd (SC), a wholly owned subsidiary of Cape plc (H). H dictated the corporate policy of SC, albeit that SC exerted control over some of its own activities and as such could not, in accordance with the precedent set by *Adams* v. *Cape Industries*, be properly construed as an agent of H. The asbestosis contracted by R occurred as a result of the negligent management practices employed by SC. During R's employment with SC, both the chief medical officer and scientific officer of H directed the health and safety policy of SC and as a consequence of this control, R claimed that the inadequate health and safety policies of SC should be attributed to H. The question before the court was whether H owed R a duty of care.

In seeking to answer this question, the test formulated by the House of Lords in *Caparo Industries plc* v. *Dickman* [1992] 2 AC 605 was applied, namely that the court had to consider whether it had been established that there was a foreseeable risk and a sufficient degree of proximity and, finally, whether it was just to impose the duty. H admitted that working with asbestos gave rise to a foreseeable risk of injury to R and other employees of SC. However, in relation to the proximity issue and in accordance with the decision of the House of Lords in *Smith (Maloco)* v. *Littlewoods Organisation Ltd* [1987] AC 241, H contended that as a distinct legal entity it had no general duty to prevent an independent third party (SC) from causing harm to R. However, in Littlewoods, Lord Goff had identified exceptional circumstances in which the principle alluded to by H could be overturned, one of which provided that proximity could be established if the defendant controlled the activity (of the independent party) that resulted in harm being caused to the claimant. Given that H controlled the health and safety polices of SC, Wyn Williams J held that the *Chandler* case fell within the exceptional circumstances outlined by Lord Goff. H had, or ought to have had, superior knowledge on aspects of health and safety and H knew, or ought to have known that SC's system of work was unsafe. H should have foreseen that SC would rely on H's superior knowledge in the context of health and safety policy. Accordingly, a sufficient degree of proximity could be established between the parties and H was liable to R for a breach of a duty of care.

In the Court of Appeal, Arden LJ, in delivering the leading judgment of the court, concurred with the findings of Wyn Williams LJ. Here, Arden LJ summarised the position in the following manner:

> In summary, this case demonstrates that in appropriate circumstances the law may impose on a parent company responsibility for the health and safety of its subsidiary's employees. Those circumstances include a situation where, as in the present case, (1) the businesses of the parent and subsidiary are in a relevant respect the same; (2) the parent has, or ought to have, superior knowledge on some relevant aspect of health and safety in the particular

industry; (3) the subsidiary's system of work is unsafe as the parent company knew, or ought to have known; and (4) the parent knew or ought to have foreseen that the subsidiary or its employees would rely on its using that superior knowledge for the employees' protection. For the purposes of (4) it is not necessary to show that the parent is in the practice of intervening in the health and safety policies of the subsidiary. The court will look at the relationship between the companies more widely. The court may find that element (4) is established where the evidence shows that the parent has a practice of intervening in the trading operations of the subsidiary, for example production and funding issues. (at p.3131)

In one respect the decision in the *Chandler* case is startling because, if Lord Goff's *dicta* and the approach adopted by Arden LJ (above) had been applied in *Adams* v. *Cape Industries*, then in that case the consideration and reliance on the corporate veil point may have proved irrelevant. The *Adams* case might have had a very different outcome if it could have been established (as is likely) that Cape controlled or exercised superior skill and knowledge in respect of the health and safety policies of NAAC.

In *Chandler*, in establishing the holding company's liability it should be stressed that the outcome of the case had nothing to do with issues related to piercing the corporate veil of the subsidiary with the result of creating an economic entity. However, the effect of establishing that the holding company owed a duty of care is of a similar outcome, namely the holding company was deemed responsible for the actions of its subsidiary.

4.5   THE CORPORATE VEIL – CONTRACTS OF EMPLOYMENT

Although a person occupying the dual position of a shareholder and director of a company may be regarded ordinarily as an employee of the company and as such distinct from the corporate entity (being, for example, entitled as an individual, to benefits under a contract of insurance (see, e.g. *Lee* v. *Lee's Air Farming Ltd* [1961] AC 12)), on occasions, that norm may be overturned. For example, in *Buchan* v. *Secretary of State for Employment* and *Ivey* v. *Secretary of State for Employment* [1997] BCC 145 (joined cases), Buchan (B) a joint director (sole director from 1993) and shareholder (with a 50 per cent holding) of a private company (C), having been paid an annual salary and having paid income tax and national insurance contributions in a manner consistent with that of a full-time employee of the company (but without a written contract of employment) was, following C's receivership in October 1994, denied a claim for a redundancy payment and arrears of wages. The Employment Appeal Tribunal (EAT), affirming the decision of the industrial tribunal, concluded that B could not be classed as an employee in accordance with the Employment Protection (Consolidation) Act (EPA) 1978. The EPA 1978 (now superseded by the Employment Rights Act (ERA) 1996) defined an employee as:

an individual who has entered into or works under (or, where the employment has ceased, worked under) a contract of employment.

Here a contract of employment is defined as a contract of service or apprenticeship, whether express or implied, and (if it is express) whether oral or in writing.

In *Buchan*, the EAT held that the extent of B's shareholding in the company resulted in his ability to effectively control his employer (the company). Accordingly, the EAT found that B could not be dismissed from the company other than through the unlikely process of self-dismissal, i.e. this was unlikely because B could block any ordinary resolution to dismiss him. On the basis of B's control over the company, the EAT concluded that B could not be considered a full-time employee of the company and as such could not be said to have worked under a contract of employment. As B was not an employee before the receivership of the company, he could not become an employee by reason of that appointment of a receiver.

However, by contrast, in *Secretary of State* v. *Bottrill* [2000] 2 BCLC 448, the Court of Appeal, upholding a decision of the EAT, held that B, the sole shareholder and joint director of a company (M), was an employee of M for the purposes of recovering redundancy payments under ERA 1996, ss.166–182. Here, B had entered into a formal three-year contract of employment with the company, a contract specifying his duties, working hours and entitlement to remuneration, holiday and sick pay. B paid tax and national insurance contributions as if he was an employee. Although B was the sole shareholder of the company, it had, from the date of M's incorporation, been intended that an American group which supplied M with all items for sale would hold 80 per cent of the shares in the company. A draft shareholders' agreement describing the proposed relationship between the American group and M had been prepared, although prior to the execution of the agreement, M was declared insolvent and put into receivership. M was put into receivership two years after B had entered into the contract of employment.

While accepting that each case had to be decided on its own merits, the Court of Appeal disapproved of the reasoning applied in *Buchan*. The court refused to accept that the validity of a test to determine the employment status of a director should be based exclusively on whether the claimant was the 'controlling shareholder' of the company (approving the decision of the Inner House of the Court of Session in *Fleming* v. *Secretary of State for Trade and Industry* [1997] IRLR 682). The Court of Appeal held that the crux of determining the status of an employee was to ascertain if there had been a genuine contractual relationship between the director/shareholder and the company. In this context, it was necessary to examine how and for what reasons a contract of employment had come into existence. For example, if the contract came into existence at a time when the company was insolvent or close to approaching a state of insolvency, then the most probable conclusion would be that the contract was a sham. Other than where the contract was a sham, the court opined that it was necessary to consider whether the contract actually gave rise to a real employer–employee relationship. In ascertaining this matter, the court accepted that the degree of control exercised by a company over a shareholder/ employee would be an important factor. In *Bottrill*, although B controlled M (as a consequence of his shareholding interest), in effect, de facto control was held by the American Group.

4.5.1 Clarification of the definition of an employee/contract of employment under ERA 1996, s.182

More recently, in *Secretary of State for Business, Enterprise and Regulatory Reform* v. *Neufeld & Howe* [2009] BCC 687, the Court of Appeal sought to clarify the definition of an employee/contract of employment under ERA 1996, s.182. However, while disapproving of the approach applied in *Buchan*, the court modified its previous stance in *Bottrill*. As a starting point, the Court of Appeal stated that providing a purported contract of employment was not a fraud/sham, evidence as to its validity had to be established by the putative employee, the evidence thereafter to be judged by a tribunal as a question of fact. As a matter of evidence the court held that although the economic interest of a controlling shareholder/director of a company meant that in practice he or she was to be properly regarded as the company's 'owner', this fact alone could not defeat a claim that he or she was an employee of the company. Although the degree of control exerted by a shareholder/ director formed a part of the backdrop against which any assessment would be made in relation to the conduct of a director under a putative written or oral employment contract, 'control' was not of any special relevance in determining, ordinarily, the validity of the contract. Accordingly, the fact that the shareholder/director had substantial capital invested in the company, or provided loans to it, or personally guaranteed its obligations, or acted in a manner consistent with an 'owner' of a business (including the fact that he or she could not be dismissed from his employment except with his consent) was not vital ordinarily to the question of whether he or she was an employee. According to the Court of Appeal, the crucial factor in determining the validity of the putative contract of employment was to consider how the parties conducted themselves under the terms of the contract. Here, matters to be considered would include how the director was paid, for example, by a salary, pointing towards employment, or by way of director's fees, pointing away from an employment contract. The court opined that other matters to determine the employee status question included an investigation into the director's tasks and obligations as a putative employee. Rimmer LJ observed (at [84]–[85]):

> In a case in which no allegation of sham is raised, or in which the claimant proves that no question of sham arises, the question (or further question) for the court or tribunal will be whether the claimed contract amounts to a true contract of employment . . . it will or may be necessary to inquire into what has been done under the claimed contract: there will or may therefore need to be the like inquiry as in cases in which an allegation of sham is made. In order for the employee to make good his case, it may well be insufficient merely to place reliance on a written contract made, say, five years earlier. The tribunal will want to know that the claimed contract, perhaps as subsequently varied, was still in place at the

time of the insolvency. In a case in which the alleged contract is not in writing, or is only in brief form, it is obvious that it will usually be necessary to inquire into how the parties have conducted themselves under it . . . In some cases there will be a formal service agreement. Failing that, there may be a minute of a board meeting or a memorandum dealing with the matter. But in many cases involving small companies, with their control being in the hands of perhaps just one or two director/shareholders, the handling of such matters may have been dealt with informally and it may be a difficult question as to whether or not the correct inference from the facts is that the putative employee was, as claimed, truly an employee. In particular, a director of a company is the holder of an office and will not, merely by virtue of such office, be an employee: the putative employee will have to prove more than his appointment as a director.

The above judgment was subsequently applied in *Ashby* v. *Monterry Designs Ltd* [2009] Appeal No.UKEAT/0226/08/CEA and *Kennedy* v. *Ormonde Terrace Ltd* [2009] Appeal No.UKEATPA/0477/09/RN.

CHAPTER 5

The personal liability of a director – statutory provisions disturbing the corporate veil

5.1 INTRODUCTION

In exceptional circumstances a director may, by the operation of a statutory provision, be held personally liable for wrongs that were committed in the company's name. For liability to accrue, the statutory provision must be clear and unambiguous in its intention to displace the corporate veil (see the comments of Lord Diplock in *Dimbleby & Sons Ltd* v. *NUJ* [1984] 1 All ER 751 at 758).

In the context of statutory provisions that may impose personal liability on a director, in the main, the statutory provisions are targeted to penalise the delinquent activities of directors involved in the management of companies that have fallen into an irreversible state of insolvency.

5.1.1 Insolvency

The term 'insolvency' is often used to describe a company which is 'unable to pay its debts'. IA 1986, s.123 states that a company's 'inability to pay its debts' may be proved by showing either that the company is unable to pay its debts as they fall due ('cash flow' insolvency) or that the value of the company's assets is less than the amount of its liabilities ('balance sheet' insolvency). 'Cash flow' insolvency may be proved by a creditor who is owed an unsecured debt exceeding £750. The creditor will serve a statutory demand on the company requiring payment within three weeks. If the creditor does not receive payment or some other form of reasonable satisfaction within that time, there is a presumption the company cannot pay its debts. 'Balance sheet' insolvency may, in practice, be difficult to prove. Until recently it was considered that to establish balance sheet insolvency the court required evidence, not merely that the company's liabilities outweighed its assets but that the company has reached the 'point of no return'. However, following the decision of the Supreme Court in *BNY Corporate Trustee Services* v. *Eurosail* [2013] 1 W.L.R. 1408, the 'point of no return' test is now discredited. The Supreme Court held that the ability of a company to meet its liabilities, both prospective and contingent, was to be determined on the balance of probabilities with the burden of proof on the party asserting 'balance-sheet insolvency'.

5.2 MISFEASANCE PROCEEDINGS

IA 1986, s.212, commonly referred to as the misfeasance provision, is applicable at a time when an insolvent company is placed into liquidation. (Liquidation and other insolvency procedures are discussed in **Chapter 22**.) The section provides, by way of a summary remedy, that persons who, prior to the company's liquidation, were involved in the management of the company, may be held accountable for any breach of duty or other act of misfeasance. Under s.212, where a company is in the course of being wound up, the court may examine the conduct of any person who is, or who acted as, a promoter, officer, liquidator, administrator or administrative receiver of the company, i.e. where it is suspected that that person misapplied or retained, or became accountable for any money or other property of the company or was guilty of any misfeasance or breach of any fiduciary or other duty in relation to the company (see, e.g. *Re International Championship Management Ltd* [2007] BCC 95). An application under s.212(3) may be made by the official receiver, liquidator or any creditor or contributory of the company (see, e.g. *Re Paycheck Services 3 Ltd* [2009] BCC 37). Here it is bizarre, perhaps, that the wording of s.212(3) was not subsequently amended because it would appear to preclude an application by an administrator; so confirmed by the decision of the Court of Appeal in *Irwin* v. *Lynch* [2011] 1 WLR 1364.

In law, the term 'misfeasance' is employed in a generic sense to describe conduct which results in any breach of duty, conflict of interest or breach of trust, where the consequence of the wrongful act is an improper application of the company's assets or property. Under IA 1986, s.212, misfeasance proceedings may be commenced where, for example, a director is in breach of any of his corporate duties. Following the decision in *Re D'Jan of London Ltd* [1993] BCC 646, the term 'any duty' is indicative of the provision's applicability to both a breach of fiduciary duty and a breach of a director's duty of care. Proceedings under s.212 may only be pursued where, prior to a company's liquidation, the misconduct which formed the subject matter of the misfeasance claim could have been made the subject of an action by the company. Accordingly, the wrong that forms the basis of the proceedings must have been perpetrated against the company and not specifically in violation of the interests of an individual shareholder or individual creditor (see, e.g. *Re Hills Waterfall Estate & Gold Mining Co* [1896] 1 Ch 947).

As a prerequisite to pursuing a misfeasance claim, the applicant must establish that the breach of duty or other act of misfeasance resulted in a pecuniary loss to the company. Pecuniary loss is, however, defined in terms whereby misfeasance proceedings may be sustained notwithstanding that a company's financial loss is not of a quantifiable nature. For example, misfeasance proceedings may still be invoked against a director where the director exploits his or her fiduciary position to obtain a personal secret profit, irrespective of the fact that the company did not suffer any accountable financial loss. In such a case the secret profit will be recoverable on the premise that, in equity, it belongs to the company (see, e.g. *Regal Hastings Ltd* v. *Gulliver* [1967] 2 AC 134).

A potential difficulty in implementing IA 1986, s.212 may arise in circumstances where, prior to a company's liquidation, a breach of duty or other act of misfeasance was ratified by the company's general meeting. Other than where the director's wrongful act results in an ability to pursue a statutory derivative action (see Companies Act (CA) 2006, s.260 – discussed in **Chapter 19**), ratification will ordinarily absolve the delinquent director from any personal liability incurred as a consequence of the wrongful act. As s.212 is a procedural device only, permitting a previous wrong (breach of duty to the company) to be enforced against a delinquent director, the implementation of s.212 would, *prima facie*, appear to be inappropriate in circumstances where the alleged misfeasance was previously ratified by the general meeting.

However, where the ratification of the breach of duty or other act of misfeasance occurred at a time when the company was insolvent or in a situation where the company was being defrauded by its directors to the ultimate prejudice of its creditors, the effectiveness of ratification may be doubted (see, e.g. *Ostrich Farming Corp Ltd* v. *Wallstreet LLC* [2009] EWHC 2501 (Ch)). Indeed, in situations where a company is insolvent or being driven into a state of insolvency, the interests of the company's creditors should effectively override the interests of its shareholders in so far as the latter's financial interest in the company will be superseded by the former's expectation of participating in the liquidation of the company's assets. The effectiveness of the ratification of a wrongful act by the members of a company will be dubious particularly in a situation where the company's liquidation was an inescapable certainty (see, e.g. *West Mercia Safetywear Ltd* v. *Dodd* [1988] BCLC 250).

5.2.1 The extent and nature of the liability

Although in the course of misfeasance proceedings, an applicant may be successful in establishing a director's breach of duty or other act of misfeasance, the court, in accordance with IA 1986, s.212(3), is not compelled to make an order against the delinquent director to account for, to return or to compensate the company in respect of property or monies that were misapplied as a result of the misfeasance. Section 212(3) provides that:

> The court may, on the application of the official receiver or the liquidator, or of any creditor or contributory, examine . . . the conduct of the person falling within subsection (1) and compel him –
>
> (a) to repay, restore or account for the money or property or any part of it, with interest at such rate as the court thinks just, or
> (b) to contribute such sum to the company's assets by way of compensation in respect of the misfeasance or breach of fiduciary or other duty as the court thinks just.

(See, e.g. *Re Morecambe Bowling Ltd* [1969] 1 All ER 753.)

While the court may exercise its discretion in not compelling a director to make some form of restitution for a breach of duty or other act of misfeasance, in the majority of cases it is unlikely that the court's discretion will be applied in this manner. Ordinarily, restitution will reflect the deficiency occasioned by the delinquent director's conduct. However, a possible example of where the discretion could be employed, so absolving a director's responsibility, would be in a situation where a restitutionary order would have the effect of affording the company an unjust or undeserved benefit. For example, in *Re Derek Randall Enterprises Ltd* [1990] BCC 749, a director of a company made secret profits (retention of commissions), but subsequently used the profits to guarantee the company's overdraft. Following a decline in the company's fortunes, the company's bankers demanded the repayment of the overdraft and called in the sum guaranteed. Although the retention of the commissions amounted to an abuse of the director's fiduciary position, the Court of Appeal held that the director was not liable to compensate the company in so far as the company had benefited from the funds represented by the guarantee. In effect, the director's potential liability to the company under s.212 was set off against the sum representing the guarantee.

In accordance with IA 1986, s.212(3), where a director (or promoter, other officer, liquidator, administrator or administrative receiver of the company) is ordered to restore or account for money or property or to contribute to the company's assets, the extent of the liability may not necessarily correspond with the extent of the actual loss sustained by the company. Following the company's liquidation, the calculation of the liability may, in part, depend upon the company's liability to its corporate creditors. For example, where a director's potential liability for the misfeasance is of a greater monetary value than the company's debt to its creditors, then a s.212(3) order may reflect this fact, to the extent that the amount of the order, while at a sufficient level to compensate creditor interests, may be of a sum which falls short of the actual loss sustained by the company (see, e.g. *Re VGM Holdings Ltd* [1942] Ch 235, *Re Home & Colonial Insurance Co Ltd* [1930] 1 Ch 102 and *Re Loquitur Ltd* [2003] 2 BCLC 442).

As the purpose of pursuing proceedings under IA 1986, s.212 is to enforce a pre-existing right of the company, it follows that an ability to pursue misfeasance proceedings is a property right of the company and that any proceeds obtained as a consequence of the proceedings will form part of the company's general assets. Accordingly, the ability of the company's unsecured creditors to participate in the fruits of the s.212 proceedings will be subject to the prior claims of the holder of any secured interest. In relation to an interest secured as a floating charge, the charge must be capable, on crystallisation, of attaching itself to the company's general assets.

5.2.2   Limitation periods

In relation to limitation periods, a claim under IA 1986, s.212 must be initiated in accordance with the six-year limitation period prescribed by the Limitation Act 1980, i.e. from the date a company suffered damage as a result of the breach of duty. It is to be noted that the limitation period does not run from the commencement of the liquidation (see, e.g. *Re Eurocruit Europe Ltd* [2007] 2 BCLC 598).

5.2.3   Shadow directors

Although a shadow director of a company (discussed further in **Chapter 14**) may be liable to account under IA 1986, ss.213–216 (discussed below), it is most unlikely, if one follows the reasoning of *obiter* comments advanced by the Supreme Court in *Revenue and Customs Commissioners* v. *Holland* [2010] 1 WLR 2793, that a shadow director is capable of attracting liability under IA 1986, s.212. This position appears bizarre, given that prior to a company's liquidation a shadow director may be held potentially liable in the context of a breach of duty (the prerequisite for establishing liability under s.212). In *Holland*, the Supreme Court considered that, as s.212 made no specific reference to a shadow director's liability for misfeasance, that omission was conclusive of the fact that a shadow director could not be found liable under the provision. Section 212 specifically provides that the court may examine the conduct of any officer of the company but in accordance with IA 1986, s.251, an officer of a company does not include a shadow director. An officer is defined to include a director, manager or secretary (the term 'director' would include a de jure director or a de facto director – see *Burke* v. *Morrison* [2012] BCC 315). Although case law prior to *Holland* appears vague around the question of whether a shadow director could fall within the scope of the s.212 provision, in some cases (contrary to the reasoning in *Holland*) a shadow director would appear to have attracted liability under s.212 (see, e.g. *QEB Metallics Ltd* v. *Peerzada* [2009] EWHC 3348 (Ch) and *Yukong Line Ltd* v. *Rendsburg Investments Corp (No.2)* [1998] 1 WLR 294).

5.3   FRAUDULENT TRADING

Although fraudulent trading constitutes a breach of the civil law, it is also punishable as a distinct criminal offence. The constituent elements of liability for fraudulent trading, under both civil law and criminal law, are virtually identical. Civil liability for fraudulent trading is dealt with by IA 1986, s.213, whereas criminal liability is dealt with by CA 2006, s.993. IA 1986, s.213 provides:

(1)   If in the course of the winding up of a company it appears that any business of the company has been carried on with intent to defraud creditors of the company or creditors of any other person, or for any fraudulent purpose, the following has effect.

(2)   The court, on the application of the liquidator may declare that any persons who

were knowingly parties to the carrying on of the business in the manner above-mentioned are to be liable to make such contributions (if any) to the company's assets as the court thinks proper.

CA 2006, s.993 provides:

If any business of a company is carried on with intent to defraud creditors of the company or creditors of any other person, or for any fraudulent purpose, every person who is knowingly a party to the carrying on of the business in that manner commits an offence.

The procedural differences between IA 1986, s.213 and CA 2006, s.993 are as follows:

- The burden of proof in civil proceedings (IA 1986, s.213) should, as with any other civil action, be established on a balance of probabilities. The burden of proof under CA 2006, s.993 must be established beyond reasonable doubt.
- A criminal prosecution, unlike a civil action, may be commenced irrespective of whether a company has been put into liquidation.
- In a civil action, the only party who may make an application to commence proceedings is the company's liquidator. In criminal proceedings, the applicant will be the Crown.

5.3.1 Protection afforded by the fraudulent trading provisions

Both IA 1986, s.213 and CA 2006, s.993 are applicable in circumstances where a person knowingly participated in the carrying on of a company's business with intent to defraud creditors of the company or creditors of any other person, or for any fraudulent purpose. The carrying on of a business may include a single transaction designed to defraud a single creditor (e.g. *Re Gerald Cooper Chemicals Ltd* [1978] Ch 262).

5.3.2 Carrying on the company's business

Section 213 is applicable only where the 'business of the company' was carried on with an intention to defraud. However, not every fraudulent act or misrepresentation perpetrated by a company will be classified as an act of carrying on trade in satisfaction of the company's business. For example, in *Morphitis* v. *Bernasconi* [2003] Ch 552, the Court of Appeal (overturning the decision of the High Court ([2001] 2 BCLC 1)), declined to invoke s.213 in circumstances where the alleged fraudulent trading involved a company (C1) making an intentional decision to avoid discharging a debt to X in respect of rent due on a lease that C1 had taken over commercial property. Over a 12-month period, C1 delayed paying the full amount of rent owed to X as part of a complex but 'ingenious' scheme engineered in favour of C1's former directors. In accordance with the scheme, the directors resigned at the start of the 12-month period and formed another company (C2). C2 was incorporated with a very similar name to C1. C1 carried on its usual business until company C2 was ready to trade, at which point C1 ceased to trade in its previous guise as a road haulier but instead re-invented itself as a lessor of trailers. The trailers were leased only to C2. In effect, C1, in the course of the 12-month period and save for its business with C2, was trading as a shell. The ultimate objective of C1's continued existence was to avoid the full payment of the lease debt for a period of 12 months: the 12-month period was crucial in so far as it would have permitted C2's directors to avoid liability under IA 1986, s.216 (discussed below). After the 12-month period was at an end, the objective of the scheme was to put C1 into liquidation (i.e. abandon ship, having sold C1's shares and assets to associated companies, leaving X's lease debt unpaid).

In *Morphitis* it was explained that for liability to be established under the s.213 provision it was necessary to show that 'any business of the company had been carried on with intent to defraud creditors of the company'. In effect it had to be established that by physically carrying on the business of the company, a creditor had been intentionally misled. Therefore, in relation to the construction of s.213, the Court of Appeal's interpretation of 'carrying on business' would permit a company and its directors to act as a vehicle or catalyst in respect of a fraudulent act, providing the sum of that fraud could not be said to involve carrying on a trading activity in relation to the business purposes of the company.

However, it is to be noted that case law suggests that a company which ceases to trade but continues to exist for the purpose of collecting and distributing its assets may be deemed to be carrying on its business, and in the pursuit of that business, may be liable for fraudulent trading (see, e.g. *Re Sarflax Ltd* [1979] 1 Ch 592 and *Carman* v. *The Cronos Group SA* [2006] BCC 451). Similarly, where, for example, a company fraudulently obtains a licence to operate its business, the fraudulent act, although unrelated to the company's physical trading activities, may, in so far as it fundamentally affects the company's capacity to 'carry on its business', give rise to a potential liability for fraudulent trading (see, e.g. *Philippou* (1989) 89 Cr App R 290).

5.3.3   Fraud

In civil cases, the most obvious example of establishing that a company was allowed to continue to trade fraudulently will be where the company continues to trade and incur liabilities, portraying itself (by its continued trading) to be solvent, when in reality it is insolvent, having little or no prospect of repaying its creditors and avoiding liquidation. In *Re William C Leitch Bros Ltd* [1932] 2 Ch 71, Maugham J observed that:

> If a company continues to carry on business and to incur debts at a time when there is to the knowledge of the directors no reasonable prospect of the creditors ever receiving payment of those debts, it is, in general, a proper inference that the company is carrying on business with intent to defraud. (at p.77)

To determine whether a company perpetrated a fraud, the court will assess the nature and degree of the alleged fraudulent conduct in respect of the company's present and future potential to repay its debts. In addition to the non-payment of trade creditors, a company's evasion of Crown debts, for example, the non-payment of corporation tax, value added tax (VAT) and national insurance contributions, may also amount to fraudulent trading (see, e.g. *Re L Todd (Swanscombe) Ltd* [1990] BCLC 454).

5.3.4 Establishing liability

For an individual to incur liability for fraudulent trading under IA 1986, s.213, first it must be established that the defendant was knowingly a party to the carrying on of the company's business. The courts have construed this requirement as indicative of a person's active involvement in the commission of an act of fraudulent trading. For example, in *Re Maidstone Buildings Ltd* [1971] 1 WLR 1085, the administrative tasks of a company secretary were held not to be comparable with a person's active involvement in the fraudulent affairs of a company. Further, it was held that an officer of a company would not incur liability for fraudulent trading notwithstanding that he was in breach of his duty of care and aware of the company's insolvent state and had also failed to take positive steps to prevent the company's incursion of further trade debts. Here the judgment of Penncuick V-C affirmed the view that liability for fraudulent trading would only arise where a person's participation in a company's trading activities was of a dominant and significant nature, a participation which was directly related to the physical commission of the fraudulent act.

Although fraudulent trading may be committed by any person who was actively involved in the commission of the fraud, in practice, liability will ordinarily fall on a person who is construed to have been a part of a company's 'directing mind' (see, e.g. *Miles* [1992] Cr LR 657). A person who acts as a part of a company's directing mind will be actively involved in the management of the company's affairs. As such, executive directors will be the most probable candidates to incur liability for acts of fraudulent trading. However, it is most probable that a shadow director will be capable of attracting a potential liability under IA 1986, s.213. Although s.213 (unlike IA 1986, ss.214 and 216) fails to provide expressly that a shadow director may attract a liability, s.213 does provide that any person (i.e., not only a de jure or de facto director) may be liable under s.213. Indeed, liability may fall on any legal person. For example, in *Morris* v. *Bank of India* [2005] 2 BCLC 328, the Bank of India (B) was deemed liable for fraudulent trading in connection with systematic and widespread fraud at the Bank of Credit and Commerce International (BCCI). BCCI had entered into a number of transactions with B, the purpose of which (from BCCI's point of view) had been to use receipts from B to credit overdrawn accounts to give the false impression that those accounts were being serviced and the indebtedness being repaid by the customers. The liquidator commenced proceedings against B alleging that the employees of B knew that they were dishonestly assisting BCCI to perpetrate a fraud on its creditors. The Court of Appeal held that a company (here, B) was capable of being made liable under s.213 in circumstances where an employee of the company had authority to deal in matters that resulted in the fraudulent conduct. It was irrelevant that an employee acted in breach of his or her duty to the company and that the company was unaware of the fraudulent activities. The employee's knowledge of the fraudulent activities of BCCI was sufficient to fix B with liability under s.213.

5.3.5 Intention

Further, to establish a person's liability for fraudulent trading it must be shown that the 'individual' intended to defraud creditors of the company, or creditors of any other person. In seeking to prove that a person intended to commit the fraudulent act, it is unnecessary to establish that, as a consequence of the fraud, the victim of the fraudulent trading suffered any actual economic loss (see, e.g. *R* v. *Grantham* [1984] QB 675). The essential requirement of the provision is, quite simply, to establish that there was an intention to perpetrate the fraudulent act; it must be established that the defendant acted dishonestly. In accordance with IA 1986, s.213, a person's dishonesty will be measured in accordance with the notions of ordinary decent business people (see, e.g. *Re Patrick Lyon Ltd* [1933] Ch 786). In effect, dishonesty will be ascertained on the basis of whether, at the time the corporate debt was incurred, the defendant was aware that the debt would not be met on the date it was due, or shortly after that date (see, e.g. *R* v. *Grantham* [1984] QB 675). Here the courts employ a subjective test to determine the state of mind of the respondent at the time of the alleged fraudulent trading (see, e.g. *Aktieselskabet Dansk* v. *Brothers* [2001] 2 BCLC 324). However, although the court's perception of whether a person intended to defraud will be measured in a subjective sense, it would be very misleading to suggest that objective considerations are ignored completely in the court's assessment. Realistically, a person's subjective perception of having being unaware that he or she actively participated in a company's fraudulent trading must be viewed in the light of the circumstances surrounding the alleged acts of fraudulent trading. For example, although a person accused of fraudulent trading may genuinely believe that the company in which he or she was involved would soon escape from an insolvent state, that belief may have been without any reasonable foundation. Accordingly, where a company is privy to fraudulent trading, it would be most difficult to discount a person's active involvement in the perpetration of the fraudulent conduct unless he or she honestly and reasonably believed that he or she was not participating in the fraudulent conduct (see, e.g. *Re Augustus Barnett & Son Ltd* [1986] BCLC 170). In *Barlow Clowes International Ltd (in liq)* v. *Eurotrust International Ltd* [2006] 1 WLR 1476, Lord Hoffmann emphasised the significance of the objective element. His Lordship stated:

> Although a dishonest state of mind is a subjective mental state, the standard by which the law determines whether it is dishonest is objective. If by ordinary standards a defendant's mental state would be characterised as dishonest, it is irrelevant that the defendant judges by different standards ... The reference to 'what he knows ...' meant only that his

knowledge of the transaction had to be such as to render his participation contrary to normally acceptable standards of honest conduct. It did not require that he should have had reflections about what those normally acceptable standards were. (at para.10–15)

5.3.6 No reasonable prospect of the creditor being paid

In determining whether a person, for example, a director(s) had knowledge of the fact that there was no reasonable prospect of the company's creditor(s) being paid, knowledge may be assumed in circumstances where the director(s) deliberately ignored the obvious, that is, by deliberately shutting his or her eyes to the obvious. Here, whether a matter was 'obvious' will be determined by asking whether a reasonably diligent person would, given all the circumstances of the case, consider the matter to be obvious (see, e.g. *Re Bank of Credit and Commerce International SA (in liq) (No.14)* [2004] 2 BCLC 236)). In *Manifest Shipping Co Ltd* v. *Uni-Polaris Shipping Co Ltd* [2003] 1 AC 469, the House of Lords identified the essential constituents of the 'blind-eye' knowledge test, namely, blind-eye knowledge required a strong suspicion that the relevant facts did exist and that there was a deliberate decision taken to fail to confirm their existence. Lord Scott opined:

> … blind-eye knowledge requires … a suspicion that the relevant facts do exist and a deliberate decision to avoid confirming that they exist. But a warning should be sounded. Suspicion is a word that can be used to describe a state of mind that may, at one extreme, be no more than a vague feeling of unease and, at the other extreme, reflect a firm belief in the existence of the relevant facts. In my opinion, in order for there to be blind-eye knowledge the suspicion must be firmly grounded and targeted on specific facts. The deliberate decision must be a decision to avoid obtaining confirmation of facts in whose existence the individual has good reason to believe. To allow blind-eye knowledge to be constituted by a decision not to inquire into an untargeted or speculative suspicion would be to allow negligence, albeit gross, to be the basis of a finding of privity. (at para.116)

5.3.7 The nature and extent of the liability

Where a person is found liable under IA 1986, s.213, that person may be subject to make such contributions (if any) to the company's assets as the court thinks proper. The court's declaration will primarily be of a compensatory nature and will take account of the company's trading loss during the period of fraudulent trading. However, the declaration may impliedly include a punitive element and accordingly the contribution may exceed the totality of debts owed to creditors affected during the period of the company's fraudulent trading (see, e.g. *Re a Company (No.001418 of 1988)* [1991] BCLC 197). However, it is to be noted that in *Morphitis* v. *Bernasconi* [2003] Ch 552, the Court of Appeal opined that the court had no power or authority to include a punitive element in the amount of any contribution under s.213.

Notwithstanding that the fraudulent trading activities of a company may have predominantly caused damage to a specific individual creditor, any contribution which the court orders to be paid will be allocated to discharge the collective debts of the company's unsecured creditors because unlike IA 1986, s.212, any contribution ordered is not classed as 'the property of the company' at the time of liquidation and as such the contribution is not subject to the claims of secured creditors (see IA 1986, s.115). The fairness of this approach may be doubted but is rooted in the fact that, under s.213, only a liquidator may commence proceedings for fraudulent trading. Prior to IA 1986, s.213 and under the corresponding provision of the Companies Act 1948, s.332, an individual creditor had a right to apply to the court and on such an application the creditor could be paid in priority to the company's other creditors. In accordance with s.213, the reasoning for excluding applications from individual creditors is to prevent the possibility of multiple actions in individual cases. However, in practice, this reasoning is difficult to comprehend, especially in those cases where the fraudulent trading activities of a company are concentrated around a single or small group of creditors. Further, the cost of commencing proceedings under s.213 would clearly discourage a swarm of individual applications.

Finally, it should be noted that the six-year limitation period for commencing an application under s.213 runs from the date of the making of the winding-up order and not the date on which the presentation of the winding-up petition is made or the appointment of the provisional liquidator (see *Re Overnight Ltd* [2009] Bus LR 1141). In accordance with the Company Directors Disqualification Act 1986, s.10, on establishing a director's liability under s.213, the court may impose a disqualification order against the director for a period of up to a maximum of 15 years. (Disqualification is discussed in **Chapter 17**.)

5.4 WRONGFUL TRADING

The difficulties encountered in seeking to establish 'an intent to defraud,' (i.e. to establish a case of fraudulent trading) led the Cork Committee 1982 (Cmnd 8558) to recommend the introduction of a new provision under which civil liability would arise in a much broader context. In part, the recommendations of the Cork Committee were enacted in the guise of IA 1986, s.214.

As with IA 1986, s.213 (the fraudulent trading provision), s.214 only applies where a company is in liquidation. However, unlike IA 1986, s.213, s.214 purports only to impose liability on company directors (to include de facto directors and shadow directors (IA 1986, s.214(7))). IA 1986, s.214 seeks to curb and deter the irresponsible/negligent conduct of directors who have prejudiced the interests of corporate creditors in a manner that abuses the privilege of limited liability. The essential requirements for determining a person's liability for wrongful trading are contained in IA 1986, s.214(1)–(3). The remaining subsections of the wrongful trading provision, namely, s.214(4)–(8), are relevant to the interpretation of s.214(1)–(3). Section 214(1) provides that:

Subject to subsection (3) below, if in the course of the winding up of a company it appears that subsection (2) of this section applies in relation to a person who is or has been a director of the company, the court, on the application of the liquidator, may declare that person is to be liable to make such contribution (if any) to the company's assets as the court thinks proper.

Section 214(2) provides that:

This subsection applies in relation to a person if –

(a)   the company has gone into insolvent liquidation,
(b)   at some time before the commencement of the winding up of the company, that person knew or ought to have concluded that there was no reasonable prospect that the company would avoid going into insolvent liquidation, and
(c)   that person was a director of the company at that time;

but the court shall not make a declaration under this section in any case where the time mentioned in paragraph (b) above was before 28th April 1986.

Section 214(3) limits the ability of the court to make a declaration in the following circumstances:

The court shall not make a declaration under this section with respect to any person if it is satisfied that after the condition specified in subsection (2)(b) was first satisfied in relation to him that person took every step with a view to minimising the potential loss to the company's creditors as (assuming him to have known that there was no reasonable prospect that the company would avoid going into insolvent liquidation) he ought to have taken.

Therefore, in accordance with s.214(1) and (2), liability under the wrongful trading provision will arise in circumstances where a company is in insolvent liquidation and where a person who was acting, or who had previously acted, as a director of the company, knew, or ought to have concluded at some time before the commencement of the winding up of the company, that there was no reasonable prospect that the company would avoid going into insolvent liquidation. On hearing an application under s.214, the court may declare (other than where the s.214(3) defence applies) that a director is to be made liable to make such a contribution (if any) to the company's assets, as the court thinks proper.

5.4.1   Conduct giving rise to an action under IA 1986, s.214

In the absence of any specific statutory guidance as to the type of conduct that will give rise to the implementation of the provision, the scope of IA 1986, s.214 would appear very wide and applicable to any situation whereby a director is responsible for misconduct in carrying on the affairs of a company at a time when he or she knew or ought to have concluded that there was no reasonable prospect that the company would avoid going into insolvent liquidation. However, the scope of the provision is impliedly limited by reference to the nature of a director's potential liability. As the nature of that liability is a personal contribution to the company's assets, it is logical to assume that the type of misconduct which the provision was intended to govern is conduct, the effect of which a director knew or ought to have known would, at a time prior to the commencement of the winding up of the company, deplete the available assets against which creditors could lay claim. The width of the provision is such that it will be applicable to any type of conduct that had the effect of depleting a company's distributable assets. Examples of such conduct would, during a period in which a company was insolvent, include over-generous dividend payments, excessive payments of directors' remuneration and the sale of corporate assets at an undervalue. In relation to this latter example, see *Re Bangla Television Ltd* [2009] EWHC 1632 (Ch).

5.4.2   Establishing liability – the reasonable diligent person test

In determining liability, IA 1986, s.214(4) provides that:

> . . . the facts which a director of a company ought to know or ascertain, the conclusions which he ought to reach and the steps which he ought to take are those which would be known or ascertained, or reached or taken, by a reasonably diligent person having both:
>
> (a)   the general knowledge, skill and experience that may reasonably be expected of a person carrying out the same functions as those which were carried out by that director in relation to the company, and
> (b)   the general knowledge, skill and experience that that director has.

In ascertaining whether to proceed with an action under s.214, the liquidator is required to undertake a retrospective consideration of the financial state of the company. In his pleadings, the liquidator must select a relevant date which he deems conclusive of a finding that the respondent director should have been aware or ought to have been aware that the company had no reasonable prospect of avoiding liquidation. A failure to select the correct date may be detrimental to the liquidator's cause. For example, in *Re Sherborne Associates Ltd* [1995] BCC 40, His Honour Jack QC, sitting as a High Court judge, dismissed an action under s.214 on the basis that, while it was probable that the date chosen by the liquidator was a date indicative of a time which to establish the company's insolvent state, that date was not conclusive in representing a date on which the company's liquidation had become inevitable. As such, at the date pleaded by the liquidator there was still a reasonable prospect (to which the directors had addressed their minds), that the company could be saved from liquidation. The judge concluded that a reasonable assumption of the inevitability of the company's liquidation could only have been made three months after the date chosen by the liquidator. The learned judge refused to allow the liquidator to substitute new dates for the ones pleaded on the basis that the substitution of dates would have prejudiced the preparation of the respondent's defence. However, to alleviate such difficulty, it would appear possible for the liquidator to plead more than one date (i.e. alternative dates). For example, in *Earp*

v. *Stevenson* [2011] EWHC 1436 (Ch), the alternative dates pleaded were either 28 March or 18 May 2006. The court considered that it was acceptable to plead the alternative dates.

In seeking to establish a director's liability, the liquidator must show that the director's expectation of the company's ability to halt its decline into liquidation was unreasonable. Accordingly, a director's expectation of the company's future survival, based solely upon business instinct and which is speculative in nature will be viewed with much caution (see, e.g. *Singla* v. *Hedman* [2010] BCC 684). However, an expectation based upon factual evidence and professional advice, indicative of a possible reversal in the company's fortunes, will be more apt in convincing the court that the company had a reasonable prospect of avoiding liquidation (see, e.g. *Re Uno plc, Secretary of State for Trade and Industry* v. *Gill* [2006] BCC 725). Determining the state of a company's financial health will be gauged by, for example, examining the company's profit and loss accounts, its purchase and sales figures, its order books and its banking accounts (see, e.g. *Re Purpoint Ltd* [1991] BCC 121). In respect of ascertaining whether, at a specified date, a director ought to have concluded that there was no reasonable prospect of the company avoiding liquidation, the court will be mindful of evidence to include:

- corporate creditors pressing for judgment orders in respect of outstanding debts;
- the withdrawal, suspension or reduction of financial support from the company's bankers;
- the withdrawal of support from the company's holding company;
- the resignation of directors, in an attempt to divorce themselves from any potential liability following the collapse of the company;
- the loss of contracts, or the inability to attain new contracts;
- the non-payment of Crown debts;
- an unrealistic forecast of expected profits; and
- an inadequate or non-existent business plan.

Section 214(4)(b) creates a flexible standard against which a director's awareness of a company's pending liquidation should be measured. The particular level of skill, knowledge and experience attributable to any given director must be viewed through the eyes of and in accordance with the expectations of the reasonably diligent person (see, e.g. *Rubin* v. *Gunner* [2004] 2 BCLC 110).

As the competence of a director is measured in the context of the standard of a reasonably diligent person, a level of skill, experience or general knowledge which falls below that objective standard will be ignored in relation to the subjective part of the assessment. However, in some circumstances, the subjective part of s.214(4)(b) allows for different levels of competency against which the standards of company directors will be measured. For example, the subjective element will be particularly relevant where the director in question possesses skills which are beyond those ordinarily expected of a reasonably diligent director. Accordingly, if the director in question is, for example, a qualified solicitor or accountant, such skills may be relevant in determining whether the actions of the director were reasonable (see, e.g. *Roberts* v. *Frohlich* [2011] 2 BCLC 625, [2011] EWHC 257. Similarly, a director involved in the management of a small private company may be considered to have less competence than a director of a large plc (see, e.g. *Re Produce Marketing Consortium Ltd* [1989] 5 BCC 569) and a director with many years of business experience more competence than a director with limited business experience (see, e.g. *Earp* v. *Stevenson* [2011] EWHC 1436 (Ch)).

5.4.3 The benefit of hindsight

While, prior to its liquidation, a company may, to the knowledge of its directors, have traded in an insolvent state, it does not necessarily follow that such knowledge will automatically imply that the directors should have been in a position to conclude that there was no reasonable prospect of the company avoiding liquidation. In determining liability under IA 1986, s.214, the courts will be mindful that their assessment of the alleged wrongful trading will be made with the benefit of hindsight. Accordingly, a director's judgment in allowing a company to continue to trade while in an insolvent state must be assessed in relation to the circumstances prevailing at the time that decision was made (see, e.g. *Re Sherborne Associates Ltd* [1995] BCC 40). In *Re Hawkes Hill Publishing Co Ltd* [2007] BCC 937, in considering the question of whether a director should perceive liquidation to have been inevitable, Lewison J answered as follows:

> . . . this question does not depend on a snapshot of the company's financial position at any given time; it depends on rational expectations of what the future might hold. But directors are not clairvoyant and the fact that they fail to see what eventually comes to pass does not mean that they are guilty of wrongful trading.

The creditability of such a conclusion may be more apt in the early years of a company's existence, as business reality dictates that costs incurred in setting up a company may initially extinguish its prospects of profitability. In considering whether liquidation should have been perceived as inevitable, the court will be mindful of evidence which portrays a creditable and realistic attempt to reverse the fortunes of the company. For example, if a company was in serious financial difficulty but attracted a potential investor who objectively was perceived as reliable and willing to inject funds into the company, the expectation that the company would be able to avoid liquidation may be realistic and justify the conclusion that there was a reasonable prospect the company would avoid liquidation. However, that expectation will be tainted and rendered redundant where, for example, over a period of time it became apparent (to any reasonably diligent person) that the investor was going to default on his promise to inject funds into the company (see, e.g. *Re The Rod Gunner Organisation Ltd* [2004] 2 BCLC 110).

Evidence which portrays a creditable and realistic attempt to reverse the fortunes of a declining company may include the following:

- an injection of share capital which significantly reduces the level of the company's indebtedness;
- a review of the levels of directors' and employees' remuneration and in appropriate circumstances a reduction in them;
- the employment of cost-cutting measures to reduce corporate expenditure;
- support from the company's creditors in respect of the company's continued trading;
- holding regular board meetings and the constant review and monitoring of corporate policy;
- the production of up-to-date accounts and a detailed and realistic business plan;
- a reorganisation or restructuring of the day-to-day management of the company;
- a reasonable expectation of securing a new and lucrative contract, the effect of which would seek to reverse the company's dire financial position; and
- professional advice, supportive of the company's continued trading.

5.4.4 The 'every step' defence (IA 1986, s.214(3))

The IA 1986, s.214(3) defence will be established where the court is convinced that a director, after first becoming aware that there was no reasonable prospect of the company avoiding liquidation, took every step possible with a view to minimising the potential loss to company creditors. In deciding whether s.214(3) is applicable, the director will be assessed by applying the reasonably diligent person test (see s.214(4), discussed above). Therefore, to satisfy the s.214(3) defence, the court must be persuaded that a reasonably diligent person, imputed with the director's own skill, experience and knowledge and in seeking to minimise loss to corporate creditors would not have been expected to take any further steps than those actually taken by the director in question, i.e. following the director's realisation that there was no reasonable prospect of the company avoiding liquidation. The defence, in requiring that 'every step' must be taken with a view to minimising the potential loss to the company's creditors, sets a daunting standard which, if construed literally, may, save in the most exceptional cases, render its application to be most improbable.

In the absence of any detailed judicial pronouncements on the scope and the requirements necessary to establish the s.214(3) defence, its potential application remains uncertain. However, in seeking to establish the defence, a director would be advised to attend all board meetings, ensuring that his or her opinions were recorded in the board minutes. In addition, a director should seek to ensure that the company's accounts are kept up to date and where necessary he or she should be an active player in instigating meetings with the company's creditors. It is also important for the company's creditors to be kept aware of and support the company's proposed methods for minimising losses, because following the company's slide into insolvency, the creditors will, in effect, become the beneficial owners of the company's assets and as such the company's directors will have a duty to safeguard their interests (see, e.g. *West Mercia Safetywear Ltd* v. *Dodd* [1988] BCLC 250). Although evidence which supports a director's claim to have taken every step to safeguard creditors' interests will be more readily found from the director's continued and active participation in the affairs of the company, in exceptional cases it may be possible to establish that a director's resignation from office was the final and only step available for the director to take; for example, in circumstances where the resignation followed a prolonged but unsuccessful attempt on the part of the director to convince the board of its folly in pursuing a particular course of action. However, in the majority of cases, resignation will probably be viewed as indicative of the fact that the director failed to take every step to minimise the potential loss to creditors. Clearly, evidence which supports a director's claim to have taken every step to safeguard creditors' interests will be more readily found from the director's continued and active participation in the affairs of the company. Indeed, the resignation of a director may be viewed as a step designed to protect the interests and integrity of the individual director, rather than one which sought to benefit the company in its quest to minimise a potential loss to its creditors.

5.4.5 Liability and the beneficiaries of a contribution order

Where the court finds that a director was a party to wrongful trading, the court may order the director to contribute towards the assets of the company (as under IA 1986, s.213). In circumstances where a court finds a director liable under IA 1986, s.214, the contribution order (if any) must be paid into the general assets of the company. The extent of a director's liability will be determined at the discretion of the court. However, it is to be expected that the extent (if any) of a director's liability under s.214 will be calculated by considering the adverse effect the director's conduct had on the extent of the company's losses as from the date that the director should have reasonably concluded that the company had no reasonable prospect of avoiding liquidation (see, e.g. *Re Purpoint Ltd* [1990] BCC 121).

In accordance with the decision of the Court of Appeal in *Re Oasis Merchandising Services Ltd* [1997] 1 WLR 764 (also see, *Re M C Bacon Ltd (No.2)* [1991] Ch 127 and *Re Ayala Holdings (No.2)* [1996] 1 BCLC 467), the potential beneficiaries of the contribution order will be the company's unsecured creditors. In *Re Oasis Merchandising Services Ltd*, the Court of Appeal held that the fruits of a s.214 action (the sum of a contribution order) could not to be regarded as a property right of a company and therefore the sum of any contribution order was incapable of being made the subject of a secured charge.

5.4.6 Financing an application under IA 1986, s.214

IA 1986, s.115 provides that all the expenses incurred in the winding up of a company must be payable out of the company's assets in priority to all other claims. The expenses in question relate to the realising or getting in of any of the assets of the company. However, in respect of proceedings under IA 1986, s.214 (and IA 1986, s.213), such an action will not be regarded as an attempt to realise or get in an asset of the company. Although a s.214 action may result in a contribution being made to the company's assets, that contribution (assets) will have had no existence at the time when the action was commenced (Insolvency Rules 1996, rule 4.218(1)(a)). However, as from 1 January 2003, rule 4.218(1)(a) was amended so that litigation costs in respect of legal proceedings which the liquidator has the power to bring or defend (i.e. ss.213 and 214 proceedings) are now included as winding-up expenses. It should be observed that the limitation period for a s.214 claim is six years (see Limitation Act 1980, s.9(1)). The limitation period begins to run from the date the company enters into liquidation. Once a liquidator commences an action under s.214, it must be prosecuted without inexcusable delay (see, e.g. *Re Farmizer (Products) Ltd* [1995] BCC 926). Finally, it should be observed that the court, in establishing a director's liability under s.214, may, in accordance with the Company Directors Disqualification Act 1986, s.10, impose a disqualification order against the director for a period up to a maximum of 15 years (see, e.g. *Re Brian D Pierson (Contractors) Ltd* [1999] BCC 26). (Disqualification is discussed in **Chapter 17**.)

5.4.7   A concurrent action under IA, s.212 and s.214

In a situation where liability is incurred under s.214, a director may also be made subject to a misfeasance claim under IA 1986, s.212. Conduct justifying an action under s.214 will ordinarily result in a breach of duty (attracting the ambit of s.212) in relation to the interests of corporate creditors (see, e.g. *Roberts* v. *Frohlich* [2012] BCC 407) in so far as where a company is insolvent or approaching an insolvent state, corporate creditors will be regarded as a constituent part of the company to whom duties are owed (see, e.g. West Mercia *Safetywear Ltd* v. *Dodd* [1988] BCLC 250). Where a liquidator makes successful applications under both ss.214 and 212, the extent of a director's liability will be calculated on a concurrent basis (see, e.g. *Earp* v. *Stevenson* [2011] EWHC 1436 (Ch), *Re Idessa (UK) Ltd* [2012] BCC 315). In such circumstances, the total sum of a director's liability under s.214 may be satisfied in circumstances where his or her liability under s.212 was equal to, or in excess of the amount of a contribution order under s.214.

5.5   THE PHOENIX SYNDROME

IA 1986, ss.216 and 217 seek to constrain and penalise directors who, having liquidated a debt-ridden company, subsequently wish to form a new company (the successor company) with the intention of carrying on business activities previously associated with the liquidated company. This scenario is commonly referred to as the 'phoenix syndrome'. The potentially prejudicial effect of the phoenix syndrome is most evident where, prior to the liquidation of the failed company, the company's assets are purchased by its controllers at a significant undervalue, and then the same assets are employed for the benefit of the successor company. The prejudicial effect is compounded where the successor company adopts a name which is the same as or closely associated with the name of the liquidated company, i.e. in an attempt to benefit from any goodwill associated with the name of the liquidated company. IA 1986, s.216 provides that:

(1) This section applies to a person where a company ('the liquidating company') has gone into insolvent liquidation on or after the appointed day and he was a director or shadow director of the company at any time in the period of 12 months ending with the day before it went into liquidation.

(2) For the purposes of this section, a name is a prohibited name in relation to such a person if –

   (a) it is a name by which the liquidating company was known at any time in that period of 12 months, or
   (b) it is a name which is so similar to a name falling within paragraph (a) as to suggest an association with that company.

(3) Except with leave of the court or in such circumstances as may be prescribed, a person to whom this section applies shall not at any time in the period of 5 years beginning with the day on which the liquidating company went into liquidation –

   (a) be a director of any other company that is known by a prohibited name, or
   (b) in any way, whether directly or indirectly, be concerned or take part in the promotion, formation or management of any such company, or
   (c) in any way, whether directly or indirectly, be concerned or take part in the carrying on of a business carried on (otherwise than by a company) under a prohibited name.

(4) If a person acts in contravention of this section, he is liable to imprisonment or a fine, or both.

Therefore, s.216 prohibits a director or shadow director of a company which is in liquidation (the section applies to a director who had held office up to 12 months before the company's liquidation) from being directly or indirectly involved in the promotion, formation or management of a successor company or business, the name of which was the same as that of the first company, or so similar to the name of the first company so as to indicate an association with that company (see, e.g. *IRC* v. *Nash* [2004] BCC 150). References to a name by which a company is known are references to the name of the company at that time or to any name under which the company carries on business at that time. The company's 'name' is not restricted to the company's registered name, but also applies to any business name which it goes or went under (IA 1986, s.216(6); see, e.g. *Griffin* v. *Richmond Magistrates' Court* [2008] BCC 575). The defendant's involvement in the successor company, which may be a newly incorporated company, or a company which has altered its name to the prohibited name, must have occurred within a period of five years from the date of the first company's liquidation. In so far as s.216 imposes a criminal sanction, a defendant's liability must be established beyond reasonable doubt. Section 216 is an offence of strict liability (but note the leave exceptions – see below). In *Thorne* v. *Silverleaf* [1994] BCC 109, Peter Gibson LJ said –

> However in the absence of an application under s.216(3) for leave, the court is left with no discretion on the application of the sections, and so long as the statutory provisions remain unaltered a creditor of a company is entitled to take advantage of them, if they can be shown to be applicable. (at p.113)

5.5.1 Limitations of IA 1986, s.216

Although in some instances, the scope of IA 1986, s.216 may extend to a wider set of circumstances than in the case of a person attempting to exploit the goodwill of a previous insolvent company, it must also be observed that s.216 fails to eradicate completely the phoenix syndrome, in so far as it is only applicable where the successor company adopts a name which is the same as or very similar to the liquidated company. The provision also fails completely to regulate the practice whereby controllers of an insolvent company purchase that company's assets at a significant undervalue for the ultimate benefit of a successor company. However, in an attempt to curb the prejudice suffered by creditors as a consequence of the phoenix syndrome, specific provisions of IA 1986 (ss.98, 99, 114, 166 and 388) restrict the ease by which the directors of a company in liquidation are allowed to purchase the company's assets at an undervalue, a practice known as 'centrebinding', so called after the case of *Re Centrebind Ltd* [1967] 1 WLR 377. In addition, other than where approved by the general meeting, CA 2006, s.190 (discussed in **Chapter 15**) prohibits a company from entering into an arrangement whereby a director or connected person acquires, or is to acquire, one or more non-cash assets of the requisite value from the company. However, here s.190 may be of little worth, given that a party with an interest in the transaction (i.e. a director) is not precluded specifically from casting his or her vote at the general meeting that may ultimately sanction the arrangement.

5.5.2 Prohibition as to name

In determining whether the name of the successor company is sufficiently similar to that of the liquidated company, the court employs an objective test to ascertain whether the name of the successor company is sufficiently similar to the name of the first company, to the extent that the name indicates an association with the liquidated company, To establish liability there must be an obvious and definite linguistic link between the name of the successor company and the original (liquidated) company. For example, in *Archer Structures Ltd* v. *Griffiths* [2004] BCC 156, Kirkham J found that it was patently obvious that the name of a successor company 'MPJ Contractors Ltd' was so similar to that of the liquidated company, 'MPJ Construction Ltd', as to suggest an association between the two enterprises. However, following the decision of the Court of Appeal in *Ricketts* v. *Ad Valorem*

Factors Ltd [2004] BCC 164, in circumstances where there is doubt as to the linguistic similarity between the corporate names of a liquidated company and its successor company, the court may take into consideration (in establishing an association between the two entities), any similarity in (a) the products dealt in by the respective companies, (b) the locations of the business, (c) the types of customers dealing with the respective companies, and (d) those involved in the management of the two companies. In *Ricketts* v. *Ad Valorem Factors Ltd*, after an examination of the aforementioned factors, the Court of Appeal held that the name of the liquidated company 'Air Component Co Ltd' was sufficiently similar to the successor company, 'Air Equipment Co Ltd'. Here, Mummery LJ stated:

> In my judgment, the [district] judge was entitled to find that the name of Air Equipment was so similar to the name of Air Component as to suggest an association with it. I have reached the same conclusion. It is necessary, of course, to make a comparison of the names of the two companies in the context of all the circumstances in which they were actually used or likely to be used: the types of product dealt in, the locations of the business, the types of customers dealing with the companies and those involved in the operation of the two companies. When viewed in that context I have no doubt that the name of Air Equipment suggests an association with Air Component. Once that conclusion has been reached the court has no discretion in the matter of the personal liability of Mr Ricketts. The case falls within ss.216 and 217 even in the absence of proof that there has been any express misrepresentation or that anyone has actually been deceived or confused into thinking that there was an association. (at para.22)

Likewise, in *First Independent Factors & Finance Ltd* v. *Mountford* [2008] BCC 598, Lewison J held that the company name 'Classic Conservatories & Windows Ltd' was so similar to the name 'Classic Roofs Ltd', to suggest an association between the two companies. Lewison J applied an objective test, namely: would a reasonable person dealing or proposing to deal with Classic Conservatories & Windows Ltd consider that there was an association between Classic Roofs Ltd and Classic Conservatories & Windows Ltd. In answering the question in the affirmative, the court was influenced significantly by the fact that both companies operated in similar fields, both companies traded in the same area and location, both adopted the same trading logo and both companies were controlled by the same person. (Also see *Attorney General for Scotland* v. *Reilly* [2011] CSOH 141.)

5.5.3 Exceptions

Although s.216 is a strict liability offence (see, e.g. *Cole, Lees & Birch* [1998] BCC 87), the prohibitive effect of s.216 may be excluded where, in accordance with s.216(3), one of the exceptions prescribed by rules 4.226–4.230 of the Insolvency Rules (IR) 1986 are applicable.

5.5.4   IR 1986, rule 4.226

IR 1986, rule 4.226 provides the court with a discretionary authority to grant leave to enable a person involved in the management of a liquidated company to become associated with the management of a successor company (or business) which adopts a prohibited name. Where the court exercises this discretionary power the applicant will be exempted from the prohibitive effect of IA 1986, s.216. In accordance with s.216(5) the Secretary of State may appear and call the court's attention to any matters which may have a bearing on the application. The court may call on the liquidator (or former liquidator) of the liquidated company for a report into the circumstances surrounding the liquidated company's insolvency and the extent by which the applicant's conduct may have contributed to the company's demise (see IR 1986, rule 4.227).

In the first reported case in which an application for leave was considered, *Re Bonus Breaks Ltd* [1991] BCC 546, although the liquidated company's insolvent state had been substantial (a deficiency of £343,917 in relation to the claims of the company's unsecured creditors), the liquidator's report concluded that there was no evidence to suggest that the applicant had ever conducted the affairs of the liquidated company in a dishonest manner. However, had the applicant not relied upon the advice of two professional advisers, the company's auditor and the company's bank manager, it would have been probable that the applicant would have been subject to a claim for wrongful trading under IA 1986, s.214, having allowed the company to trade for almost two years after it had fallen into a state of insolvency. In respect of the successor company, it was to have a paid-up share capital of £50,000, divided into 1,000 £1 ordinary shares and 49,000 £1 redeemable shares. The applicant was to be one of the company's two directors, the other director being a man of considerable commercial and financial experience; the fact that the second director had expertise in financial matters was relevant in so far as the applicant had been inept in financial matters in the context of the management of the liquidated company. In seeking leave, it is to be noted that the applicant had the support of two of the liquidated company's major creditors. In determining the leave application, Morritt J considered that it was most necessary for the court to consider the successor company's ability to avoid the pitfalls which had resulted in the liquidated company's demise. While Morritt J welcomed the appointment of the second director, he was particularly anxious about the manner in which the successor company's share capital had been structured, in so far as it comprised 98 per cent redeemable shares. Morritt J feared that if such shares were redeemed within a short period, then the company would be left undercapitalised and heavily dependent upon bank borrowings. However, Morritt J granted the leave application in so far as the applicant was willing to undertake that save in a situation where the company appointed a third and independent director and that director approved a reduction in the company's capital, the company would not redeem shares for a period of two years, or, alternatively, purchase its own shares out of distributable profits during that two-year period.

However, in considering subsequent leave applications the courts have adopted guidelines more favourable to the applicant. In both *Penrose* v. *Official Receiver* [1996] 1 WLR 482 and *Re Lightning Electrical Contractors Ltd* [1996] BCC 950, the leave application was not determined exclusively by an examination of the manner in which the successor company was structured or its potential to avoid the pitfalls that had befallen the liquidated company. Rather, the courts opined that an investigation into the applicants' competence to conduct the affairs of a limited company and the business merits of the successor company was not warranted in circumstances where the applicants' participation in the management of the liquidated company had never been called into question on the basis that its management was of an unfit standard, a standard justifying the attention of Company Directors Disqualification Act 1986, s.6 (discussed in **Chapter 17**). In *Penrose* v. *Official Receiver*, Chadwick J noted that although similarities existed between the leave procedure in accordance with IR 1986, rule 4.226 and the leave procedure under the Company Directors Disqualification Act (CDDA) 1986, s.17, under the latter the court would be compelled to instigate a thorough investigation of the applicant and the affairs of the company in which he sought leave to act, because the applicant in seeking leave would be doing so in a situation where his previous conduct of the affairs of a company had already been adjudged to have been of an unfit standard. Accordingly, Chadwick J concluded that the court should only refuse an application for leave under rule 4.226 in circumstances where the applicant's conduct in the affairs of the liquidated company would have warranted the attention of CDDA 1986. Chadwick J observed that the fact that the applicants' involvement in a subsequent corporate venture would carry a degree of commercial risk was irrelevant because the creation of any corporate enterprise always entailed an element of risk. Chadwick J concluded that a leave application under rule 4.226 did not seek to prohibit the incorporation of undercapitalised companies nor did it seek to prohibit inexperienced persons from becoming involved in the management of a company. However, it is suggested that this judicial approach can be criticised in that it fails to recognise that there may be circumstances in which the public interest may be prejudiced by the successor company even where an applicant's conduct does not justify the imposition of a disqualification order.

5.5.5   IR 1986, rule 4.228

IR 1986, rule 4.228 applies in a situation where a person who would otherwise be caught by the s.216 provision wishes to be associated with the management of a successor company which acquires the whole or substantially the whole of the business of the insolvent company under arrangements made by an insolvency practitioner. The successor company is required to give 28 days' notice from the completion of the arrangements to all the creditors of the insolvent company of whose addresses the successor company is aware. The notice must specify:

(i)   the name and registered number of the insolvent company and the circum-
        stances by which its business was acquired by the successor company;

(ii)   the name which the successor company has assumed, or proposes to assume
        for the purpose of carrying on its business, if the name is, or will be, a
        prohibited name under s.216;

(iii)   any change of name which it has made or proposes to make for that purpose;
        and

(iv)   the name of the person to whom s.216 may apply and the nature and duration
        of that person's directorship in respect of the insolvent company.

Where the notice requirements are met, the person may be associated with the
successor company without the need to apply to the court for leave to so act.
However, rule 4.228 notice may only be given in respect of a person who, prior to
the giving of the notice, was not a director or otherwise involved in the management
of the successor company, i.e. notice may not be given retrospectively by a person
who is already acting as a director of the successor company. Accordingly, a person
already acting as a director of a successor company cannot give rule 4.228 notice to
relieve a liability that has already arisen under s.216, i.e. by reason of that person
having acted as a director of the successor company (see, e.g. *Churchill* v. *First
Independent Factors and Finance Ltd* [2007] BCC 45).

5.5.6   IR 1986, rule 4.229

IR 1986, rule 4.229 operates as a temporary exception the purpose of which is to
provide a transient period during which a person will be allowed to continue to be
associated with a successor company. The exception operates where, in accordance
with IA 1986, s.216(3), an application for leave is made not later than seven days
from the date on which the company went into liquidation. The transient period
commences from the beginning of the day on which the company went into
liquidation and ends either on the day falling six weeks after that date, or on the day
on which the court disposes of the application for leave, whichever of those days
occurs first.

5.5.7   IR 1986, rule 4.230

IR 1986, rule 4.230 provides that the court's leave is not required if a successor
company, although known by a prohibited name, was known by that name for the
whole of the period of 12 months ending with the day before the liquidating
company went into liquidation and was not at any time dormant in that period.
However, here it must be noted that rule 4.230 does not apply where the prohibited
name relates to a personal business; the prohibited name must have been attached to
a limited company (see, e.g. *First Independent Factors & Finance Ltd* v. *Mountford*
[2008] BCC 598). The application of this exception is most apt in a situation where a
group of associated companies are known by similar names and one company in the

group is placed into liquidation. In this situation and other than for rule 4.230, the directors of the liquidated company would be potentially liable under s.216 if they remained directors of one or more of the other companies in the group.

5.5.8 IA 1986, s.217 – personal liability

In accordance with IA 1986, s.217, a person who acts in contravention of IA 1986, s.216, or a person who knowingly assists a person who acted in contravention of s.216, may be made personally liable for the debts and liabilities of the successor company (see, e.g. *Glasgow City Council* v. *Craig* [2010] BCC 235). Section 217 defines the extent and nature of a person's potential personal liability. In accordance with s.217(1)(a), a person will be personally responsible for all the relevant debts of a successor company where, in being involved in the management of that company, he or she acts in contravention of the terms of s.216. Liability is not dependent upon an actual conviction under s.216. Further, s.217(1)(b) extends the imposition of personal liability for the relevant debts of the successor company to any person who, being involved in the management of the successor company, acted or was willing to act on the instructions (without the leave of the court) of his principal, being aware that the principal was, in relation to his involvement in the successor company, acting in contravention of s.216. Section 216(2) provides that a name is a prohibited in relation to such a person if:

(a)   it is a name by which the liquidating company was known at any time in that period of 12 months, or

(b)   it is a name which is so similar to a name falling within paragraph (a) as to suggest an association with that company.

A person who is deemed to be personally responsible for the relevant debts of a company will be jointly and severally liable in respect of those debts with the company and any other person who is deemed to have been liable under s.217, or otherwise. A creditor of a successor company will not be precluded from pursuing an action under s.217, even in circumstances where the creditor was aware of and possibly aided and abetted the commission of the s.216 offence (see, e.g. the decision of the Court of Appeal in *Thorne* v. *Silverleaf* [1994] BCC 109).

Finally, it must be noted that, in addition to the imposition of personal liability, a contravention of s.216 may also be regarded as cogent evidence of a director's unfit conduct for the purposes of disqualification under CDDA 1986, s.6.

CHAPTER 6

A company's constitution

6.1 INTRODUCTION

Prior to the implementation of the Companies Act (CA) 2006, a company's constitutional structure was governed by the terms of the memorandum of association and the articles of association. The primary constitutional function of the memorandum was concerned with the regulation and external appearance of the company in its dealings with third parties. For example, the memorandum contained compulsory clauses (Companies Act (CA) 1985, s.2) to the following effect:

- to provide and regulate the name of the company;
- specifying whether the company's registered office was situated in England and Wales, or specifically, Wales or Scotland;
- the objects clause of the company, stating the business or other activities for which the company was incorporated;
- stating that the liability of the company's membership was limited and if so whether the company was a public limited company;
- in the case of a company with a share capital, stating the amount of share capital with which it proposed to be registered and the manner by which the share capital was to be divided into shares of a fixed amount.

Under CA 1985, the articles of association were concerned with matters related to the internal affairs of the company, for example, clauses governing the regulation of general meetings, the appointment, regulation and powers of company directors, and the class rights attached to shares, share capital and dividends.

Following the implementation of CA 2006, although companies must register both a memorandum and articles, the former will be devoid of any significance in respect of the constitutional framework of a company, being relegated to the status of a procedural registration document (discussed in **Chapter 1**). The effect of CA 2006 is that the company's articles will become the primary source of a company's constitutional structure. For companies incorporated prior to CA 2006, the contents of the memorandum are deemed (in respect of the constitutional functions attached to the same), to have effect as if they had been incorporated into the company's articles (see CA 2006, s.28).

Under CA 2006, a company's constitution comprises the company's articles of association and any resolutions and agreements that affect the company's constitution under CA 2006, Part 3, Chapter 3. In effect, Part 3 is defined by CA 2006, s.29. Section 29 applies to the following resolutions and agreements:

(a)   any special resolution;
(b)   any resolution or agreement agreed to by all the members of a company that, if not so agreed to, would not have been effective for its purpose unless passed as a special resolution;
(c)   any resolution or agreement agreed to by all the members of a class of shareholders that, if not so agreed to, would not have been effective for its purpose unless passed by some particular majority or otherwise in some particular manner;
(d)   any resolution or agreement that effectively binds all members of a class of shareholders though not agreed to by all those members;
(e)   any other resolution or agreement to which this Chapter applies by virtue of any enactment.

A copy of every resolution or agreement that affects a company's constitution and to which CA 2006, s.29 applies must be forwarded to the registrar within 15 days after it was passed or made and a failure to do so constitutes an offence by the company and every officer of it who is in default (CA 2006, s.30). While the practical effect of a membership agreement (discussed below at **6.7**) may affect the constitutional functioning of a company, a company cannot be party to a membership agreement and as such a membership agreement cannot be viewed as a constitutional document for the purpose of s.29.

6.1.1   Members

In accordance with CA 2006, s.32, a company must, following the request of any of its members, send to that member any or all of the following documents:

(a)   an up-to-date copy of the company's articles;
(b)   a copy of any resolution or agreement relating to the company to which CA 2006, s.29 applies (resolutions and agreements affecting a company's constitution) and that is for the time being in force;
(c)   a copy of any document required to be sent to the registrar under:

   (i)   s.34(2) (notice where company's constitution altered by enactment); or
   (ii)   s.35(2)(a) (notice where order of court or other authority alters company's constitution);

(d)   a copy of any court order under s.899 (order sanctioning compromise or arrangement) or s.900 (order facilitating reconstruction or amalgamation);
(e)   a copy of any court order under s.996 (protection of members against unfair prejudice: powers of the court) that alters the company's constitution;
(f)   a copy of the company's current certificate of incorporation, and of any past certificates of incorporation;

(g) in the case of a company with a share capital, a current statement of capital. The statement of capital required is a statement of:

   (i)   the total number of shares of the company;
   (ii) the aggregate nominal value of those shares.

and for each class of shares:

   (i)   prescribed particulars of the rights attached to the shares;
   (ii) the total number of shares of that class; and
   (iii) the aggregate nominal value of shares of that class; and
   (iv) the amount paid up and the amount (if any) unpaid on each share (whether on account of the nominal value of the share or by way of premium).

(h) in the case of a company limited by guarantee, a copy of the statement of guarantee.

If a company makes default in complying with s.32, an offence is committed by every officer of the company who is a party to the default.

6.2 THE ARTICLES OF ASSOCIATION

In accordance with CA 2006, s.18, a company must have articles of association prescribing regulations for the company. A company may register its own distinct set of articles (CA 2006, s.18(2)) and will have the freedom to include regulations to govern the company's internal affairs in any manner it sees fit, subject to the qualification that if a company's articles contain a regulation that is contrary to a provision of the companies legislation, or a regulation contrary to the general law, then the offending regulation will have no effect. Where a company declines to register a distinct set of articles, the company's articles will be determined by reference to the relevant model form of articles in place at the time of the company's registration (CA 2006, s.19). However, where a company registers its own distinct form of articles and the same do not exclude or modify the relevant model articles, then the model articles will automatically take effect in relation to any matter that is not covered by the company's own distinct set of articles (CA 2006, s.20). It is important to note that, in relation to the model set of articles that (may) govern a company, the model set of articles in place at the date of the company's incorporation will ordinarily be the articles that govern the company. Therefore, a company incorporated after 1948 but before the enactment of the 1985 Act will be governed by the model articles prescribed by the Companies Act 1948 and likewise a company incorporated between 1985 and the implementation of the 2006 Act model articles is likely to be governed by the articles prescribed by the Companies Act 1985. A company incorporated prior to the enactment of the model articles prescribed by the 2006 Act (i.e., incorporated prior to 1 October 2009) may, however, alter its articles (by special resolution (CA 2006, s.21)) to adopt the model articles prescribed by CA 2006 (see the Companies (Model Articles) Regulations 2008, SI 2008/3229). For companies registered in compliance with CA 2006, the applicable form of model articles will be dependent on the type of company in question. The three sets of model articles (for a private company limited by shares, a private company limited by guarantee and a public company) are available electronically on the Companies House website at **www.companieshouse.gov.uk**.

From 1 October 2009, when any company makes amendments to its articles of association (by special resolution) it must file an up-to-date copy of the entire set of articles not later than 15 days after the amendment takes effect. Failure to do this is an offence by the company and its officers, which carries a civil penalty. However, where a limited company formed on or after 1 October 2009 adopts the 2006 Act model articles without amendment, it need not file its articles at Companies House. However, it must do so if it subsequently makes an amendment to the model articles. For companies registered prior to October 2009, but after the introduction of CA 1985, the model form of articles is found in Table A of the Companies (Tables A–F) Regulations 1985, SI 1985/805. (The Table A articles were amended to accommodate specific provisions of CA 2006 by SI 2007/2826.)

6.2.1 The contractual nature of the articles (CA 2006, s.33)

In accordance with CA 2006, s.33 (replacing and amending CA 1985, s.14):

> The provisions of a company's constitution bind the company and its members to the same extent as if there were covenants on the part of the company and of each member to observe those provisions.

Despite the 'contractual intent' of s.33, and although the courts construe a company's constitutional documents as a commercial/business document (see, e.g. *Tett v. Phoenix Property Ltd* [1986] BCLC 149), a company's written constitution is unlikely to be set aside on grounds of misrepresentation, mistake, undue influence or duress. As with any instrument, be it a contract, a statute or the articles of association, the court has power to construe the instrument but cannot improve upon the instrument. A court cannot introduce terms to alter the meaning of the instrument and is concerned only to discover what the instrument actually means. The plain and ordinary meaning of words in the articles must be given effect and should only be displaced if they produce a commercial absurdity (see the decision of the Privy Council in *Thompson v. Goblin Hill Hotels Ltd* [2011] 1 BCLC 587). Therefore, terms may only be implied into the instrument to provide meaning and clarity in circumstances where the meaning is blurred to a point whereby it is confused and uncertain. As such, the courts may interpret and imply terms into the articles where the express terms of a company's articles are construed to be so vague as to necessitate 'interpretation', i.e. to give them sense and clarity (see, e.g. *Folkes Group plc v. Alexander* [2002] 2 BCLC 254). Terms may only be implied in line with the intentions of the parties so determined by the expectations of a reasonable person having all the background knowledge which would reasonably be available to an audience to whom the instrument is addressed. In deciding whether to imply a term into an instrument the court must consider whether the implied term would add clarity and sense to what that instrument, read against the relevant background, would reasonably be understood to mean (see the judgment of the Privy Council in *Attorney General of Belize* v. *Belize Telecom Ltd* [2009] 1 WLR 1988). For example, in *Cream Holdings Ltd* v. *Davenport* [2012] 1 BCLC 365, the articles of a company provided that following the removal of a director (D) from office, any shares held by the director were to be subject to a transfer at fair value under a right of pre-emption. The fair value of the shares was to be determined by an accountant, the appointment of the same to be agreed by the company (C) and the transferor. Despite the fact that an 'independent' accountant was identified, D and C could not agree on the terms of engagement of the accountant. The Court of Appeal considered that D had acted in an unreasonable manner and held that a term should be implied into the company's articles to the effect that a transferor of shares should not unreasonably withhold his consent to the appointment of an accountant for the purpose of determining the fair value of his shareholding. Such a term was necessary to give business efficacy to the articles.

However, the courts will not imply terms into the articles in circumstances where an implied term introduces extrinsic facts which were known only to some of the people involved in the formation of the company. For example, in *Bratton Seymour Service Co Ltd* v. *Oxborough* [1992] BCC 471, a company was formed to acquire and manage a property divided into flats which also included 'amenity areas' (tennis courts, swimming pool, gardens). The company contended that the articles should be rectified to incorporate an implied term, namely that each flat owner/ member was under an obligation to contribute to the expenses of maintaining the amenity areas. The necessity of incorporating the implied term was said to be derived from the circumstances in which the property was acquired and the terms of the conveyance to the company. The Court of Appeal refused to imply the term on the basis that background facts were not admissible in respect of the construction of the articles. The articles had to be interpreted in accordance with their actual wording. Dillon LJ stated that:

> ... the articles of association of a company differ very considerably from a normal contract ... It is thus a consequence as was held by this court in *Scott* v. *Frank F. Scott (London) Ltd* [1940] Ch 794, that the court has no jurisdiction to rectify the articles of association of a company, even if those articles do not accord with what is proved to have been the concurrent intention of the signatories of the memorandum at the moment of signature. (at p.474)

In denying the possibility of admitting intrinsic evidence to the objective of varying the terms of a company's articles, Sir Christopher Slade commented thus:

> If it were to be admissible, this would place the potential shareholders in a limited company, who wished to ascertain their potential obligations to the company, in an intolerable position. They are in my judgment entitled to rely on the meaning of the

language of the memorandum and articles of association, as such meaning appears from the language used. (at p.476)

6.2.2   Enforcing the terms of the articles

In accordance with a literal interpretation of CA 2006, s.33 (see above) and in the absence of any historical allegiance to the interpretation afforded previously to CA 1985, s.14, CA 2006, s.33 may significantly, albeit perhaps unwittingly, alter the contractual effect of a company's constitution. The wording of CA 1985, s.14 may be traced back to the Companies Act of 1856. Prior to the Companies Act 1985, the Companies Act 1948, s.20 adopted the exact same language found in s.14. Section 14 provided:

> Subject to the provisions of the [Companies] Act the memorandum and articles, when registered, bind the company and its members to the same extent as if they respectively had been signed and sealed by each member, and contained covenants on the part of each member to observe all the provisions of the memorandum and of the articles.

In a contractual sense, CA 1985, s.14 provided that a company's constitution was binding between the company and its members but only to the same extent as if it 'had been signed and sealed by each member'. Section 14 made no mention of the fact that as a distinct legal entity, a company was bound as if it had signed and sealed the constitution. Although in many instances the courts were content to construe s.14 (and its statutory predecessors) in a manner where, in addition to the binding effect of the company's constitution on its members, the terms of the constitution also bound the company in its dealings with its members (as if a contract), in some cases, the absence in s.14 of an express statement that a company was so bound by the provision resulted in confusion and uncertainty, giving rise to much academic debate on whether in fact a company, as a distinct legal entity, was bound by the terms of its constitution. Here, it is interesting to note that the amendment made to s.14 to produce the present format of CA 2006, s.33 was introduced into the House of Lords debates on the Companies Bill, by Lord Wedderburn. As an academic author, Lord Wedderburn sought to contend that s.14 should be interpreted in a manner to afford the members of a company (but suing only in their capacity as members) with full contractual rights in respect of enforcing all the terms of a company's constitution against the company (other than in instances involving procedural irregularities).

6.2.3   Section 33 and obligations enforceable by the company against the membership

As under CA 1985, s.14, in relation to CA 2006, s.33, obligations regulating the relationship between the company and its membership will be enforceable by the company against its membership. Those obligations have full contractual effect. For example, in *Kerr* v. *John Mottram Ltd* [1940] Ch 657, a member of a company sought specific performance against the company for the sale of shares, a sale which had apparently been agreed at an extraordinary meeting of the company. Nevertheless, as the minutes of the meeting failed to verify such an agreement, it was held that the existence of the contract could be denied. This decision was justified on the basis that the articles of the company provided that the minutes of any company meeting would be conclusive evidence of the business of that meeting.

A further and oft-quoted example of a company's ability to enforce obligations against its membership is provided by *Hickman* v. *Kent and Romney Sheepbreeders Association* [1915] 1 Ch 881. Here the articles were subject to the requirement that members should submit first to arbitration before pursuing litigation against the association. It was held that the arbitration clause was enforceable. Indeed, ordinarily, but save where an arbitration agreement is expressly overridden by the terms or intent of a statutory provision, effect must be given to a provision in the articles (or shareholder agreement) which stipulates the arbitration route, other than where the resolution of the dispute by means of the arbitration process would be contrary to public interest considerations (see the Arbitration Act (AA) 1996, s.1(b)). AA 1996, s.9(4) provides specifically that unless an arbitration agreement is null and void, inoperative or incapable of being performed, then in circumstances where a member of a company seeks to resolve a dispute by way of court proceedings, the company may apply to stay the court proceedings. Save for where an arbitration agreement is null and void, etc., it is a mandatory requirement for the court to stay the proceedings (see AA 1996, s.9; this represents a significant change from the Arbitration Act 1975, under which the court had a discretion whether or not to stay the proceedings).

However, until recently and as a qualification to the *Hickman* case, a requirement on the part of a member to abide by an arbitration clause contained in the company's articles (or contained within a distinct shareholders/membership agreement), may have been unenforceable where the effect of the clause was overridden by the right of a member to present a petition for unfairly prejudicial conduct under CA 1985, s.459 (now CA 2006, s.994 – discussed in **Chapter 19**) (see *Exeter City AFC Ltd* v. *The Football Conference Ltd and Anor Ltd* [2004] BCC 498). However, the effect of the decision in *Exeter City AFC Ltd* v. *The Football Conference Ltd and Anor Ltd* is now overruled following the decision of the Court of Appeal in *Re The Football Association Premier League Ltd; Fulham Football Club (1987) Ltd* v. *Richards* [2011] BCC 910. In *Fulham Football Club (1987) Ltd* v. *Richards*, Fulham FC, as a member of the Football Association, petitioned under CA 2006, s.994, albeit that the rules of the association provided that all disputes between the association and its members should be resolved by arbitration. The association sought a stay of the s.994 proceedings under AA 1996, s.9. The Court of Appeal held that where a dispute between a company and one of its members was governed by the terms of an arbitration agreement and the arbitration process was capable of providing a remedy to the dispute of a type and nature that could otherwise have been obtained (for the particular dispute in question) by means of a petition under s.994, then in such circumstances, the dispute had to be referred to arbitration. In such a case the court would stay any court proceedings that attempted to remove the primacy of AA 1996. Further, in *obiter* comments, the Court of Appeal asserted the primacy of AA 1996 in relation to all disputes governed by the terms of an arbitration agreement (other than disputes that fell within the narrow ambit of AA 1996, s.9(4)). The intent of these *obiter* comments was that any dispute governed by a binding arbitration agreement must first be referred to the arbitration process irrespective of whether or not the nature of the dispute may otherwise have been made subject to a s.994 petition (or for that matter a petition for a just and equitable winding-up order under IA 1986, s.122(1)(g) – discussed in **Chapter 19**). As to the nature of an appropriate remedy, the Court of Appeal opined that if necessary, at the stage of the arbitration procedure, it could be decided that the matter of remedy should be referred to and be determined by the court.

6.2.4 Section 33 and obligations enforceable by the membership against the company

Much of the controversy associated with the interpretation of CA 1985, s.14 related to the extent to which obligations contained within a company's articles could be enforced by the members of a company, against the company. Although, as a matter of historical precedent, that controversy may still prevail, in the context of a literal interpretation of the wording of CA 2006, s.33, all obligations within a company's constitution should be enforceable where a member seeks enforcement, suing as a member and not in some other capacity. It is to be noted that, under CA 1985, the courts permitted only one class of obligation as definitely enforceable, namely an obligation often described as a pure membership or insider right. Such rights were common to and shared by all the members of any given class of shares. Examples of insider rights included the following:

- The right of a member to insist that, once a company has declared a dividend, the dividend should be paid in accordance with the terms of the articles (see, e.g. *Wood* v. *Odessa Waterworks Co* (1889) 42 Ch D 639).
- The ability of a member to enforce a right to a share certificate (see, e.g. *Burdett* v. *Standard Exploration* (1899) 16 TLR 112).
- On the winding up of a company, after the company has paid its creditors, a member's right to a return of capital (see, e.g. *Griffith* v. *Paget* (1877) 6 Ch D 511; note that preferential shareholders may have a preferential right to a return of capital over other shareholders: see **Chapter 11**).
- On a valid transfer of shares, the right of a member to have his or her name entered in the register of members (see, e.g. *Re British Sugar Refining Co* (1857) 3 K & J 408).
- The right of a member to insist that an organ or a constituent part of an organ of the company (the board of directors or general meeting) is allowed to exercise its functions in accordance with the terms of the company's constitution. For

example, in *Quinn & Axtens* v. *Salmon* [1909] AC 442, a member and managing director of a company successfully enforced a term of the company's articles associated with the exercise of rights attached to the office of the company's joint managing directors. The facts of the case were as follows. The company's articles provided that any one of the two appointed managing directors of the company could, in certain circumstances, veto a decision of the company's board of directors. In accordance with the terms of this provision, the plaintiff sought to exercise his right of veto. The veto was ignored by the company and the plaintiff sought an injunction to prevent the company from acting otherwise than in accordance with its articles. The managing director pursued the matter as a member of the company (*qua* member) and succeeded in obtaining the injunction. The House of Lords, affirming the decision of the Court of Appeal, held that the company, in seeking to discard the obligation, was in effect attempting to bypass rules on the decision-making process of the company in a manner which would have had the effect of altering its articles contrary to the statutory procedure (i.e. by the passing of a special resolution).

A member holding voting shares in a company is entitled to exercise his or her vote at a company meeting in any way and for whatever purpose he or she so decides (see, e.g. *Pender* v. *Lushington* (1870) 6 Ch D 70). However, a member's entitlement to enforce a right to vote may be lost where a resolution to which the vote relates is concerned with a matter of internal procedure as opposed to a substantive issue affecting the constitutional rights of the membership. For example, in *MacDougall* v. *Gardiner* (1875) 1 Ch D 13, a company meeting was held with a view to the plaintiff proposing a motion to dismiss the company's chairman. The company's deputy chairman presided over the meeting and accepted a vote on the show of hands (one vote per member) to have the meeting adjourned. As a result of the proposed adjournment, the plaintiff demanded a poll vote (recorded vote entitling votes to be cast in accordance with the number of shares held). Although the plaintiff demanded the poll in accordance with the terms of the company's articles, the poll vote was refused. Here, the Court of Appeal emphasised that the plaintiff's action was concerned with an internal procedural irregularity of the company. The procedural wrong (decision to refuse a poll vote) was a wrong committed against the company and not an infringement of the plaintiff's personal rights of membership. The court considered the action as ill conceived, Baggallay LJ remarked:

> I apprehend that it is not the practice of the court to make declarations of so utterly useless a character as is here asked. (at p.27)

Although the Court of Appeal clearly rejected the plaintiff's claims, in doing so, it surely ignored the underlying principle at issue in the case, namely, the ability to enforce the right to vote in accordance with the terms of a company's articles. Had the poll vote been concerned with the actual motion to dismiss the chairman, as opposed to a motion to adjourn the company meeting, it is most likely that the outcome of the case would have been different. The decision in *MacDougall* v.

Gardiner may be a dangerous precedent to follow in that it most certainly distorts the protection of a basic membership right, the right to vote (but note that the decision in *MacDougall* was followed in *Cotter* v. *National Union of Seamen* [1929] 2 Ch 58). Perhaps an even more exceptional example of the court's ability to refuse a member's entitlement to vote is to be found in *Standard Chartered Bank* v. *Walker* [1992] BCLC 603. In that case the court was asked to grant an injunction to restrain a member (W), from exercising his right to vote on a motion that had two linked purposes. The member held a substantial but nevertheless minority holding in a public limited company. The first purpose of the motion was to enable a consortium of banks to instigate a rescue package on behalf of the company; the second sought to remove W from his directorship of the company. The two purposes were advanced as one motion; therefore if the first purpose failed the second would also and vice versa. Given that W would have used his votes to block the ordinary resolution required to pass the two-part motion, the court, casting off its normal reluctance to involve itself in the internal management of a company, granted an injunction to prevent W from exercising his right to vote. While the court's decision may be defended on the premise that the grant of an injunction served to protect the very existence of the company, for without the rescue package the continued existence of the company would have been unlikely, it is difficult, if not impossible to reconcile the decision with the principles enunciated in *Pender* v. *Lushington*.

6.2.5 Unenforceable membership rights under CA 1985, s.14 and the corresponding position under CA 2006, s.33

Although insider right obligations were considered to be enforceable under CA 1985, s.14, other obligations, commonly referred to as 'outsider rights' were deemed unenforceable. An 'outsider right' was an obligation other than one corresponding to the collective constitutional rights of any given class of shareholder. The acceptance of the generally held view that an 'outsider right' was not enforceable in accordance with s.14 owed much to the reliance on the *dicta* of Astbury J in *Hickman* v. *Kent and Romney Sheepbreeders Association Ltd* [1915] 1 Ch 881. Astbury J laid down the following three principles of law which he considered governed the provision:

> First that no articles can constitute a contract between the company and a third person; secondly, that no right purporting to be given by an article to a person, whether a member or not, in a capacity other than that of a member, as for instance a solicitor, promoter, director, can be enforced against the company; and thirdly, that articles regulating the rights and obligations of the members generally as such do create rights and obligations between them and the company respectively. (at p.900)

These principles were quoted with approval in many subsequent cases related to the inability to enforce 'outsider rights' (see, e.g. the Court of Appeal's application of the principles in *Beattie* v. *E & F Beattie Ltd* [1938] Ch 708 at 714). The justification for advancing the principles may be found in the prior cases of *Eley* v. *Positive*

Government Security Life Insurance (1876) 1 Ex D 88 and *Browne* v. *La Trinidad* (1877) 37 Ch D 1. In *Eley*, the articles of the company provided that the plaintiff (E) was to be appointed as the company's solicitor for the duration of his life. E was also a member of the company. The Court of Appeal held that E could not enforce the right to lifelong employment as the company's solicitor because that obligation was unrelated to rights commonly held by the members of the company and as such did not affect the constitutional rights of the shareholding body. In *Browne* v. *La Trinidad*, the plaintiff (B) entered into an agreement with the company (incorporated into the company's articles) whereby, in consideration for the sale of property to the company, B would become a member of the company and would also be appointed as a director of the company for a minimum period of four years. Although B was appointed to a directorship in the company (B never became a member of the company), B was removed from his directorship before the minimum specified period had expired. The Court of Appeal held that even if B had become a member of the company, the right to hold a directorship was not a right common to the membership, rather it was an outsider right and as such was unenforceable (see also *Re Tavarone Mining Co (Pritchard's case)* (1873) 8 Ch App 956).

Following the enactment of CA 2006, s.33, the position in the above cases may have been reversed, providing of course the right in question is enforced as a membership right and not as a right held in some other capacity. Here much will depend on the court's interpretation of the contractual effect of s.33. For example, if the courts interpret CA 2006, s.33 in a literal sense, whereby obligations between members and the company are equally enforceable, then applying such an interpretation to, for example, the facts of the *Eley* case, E's right to be maintained as a solicitor of the company for life may be enforceable where E (or any other member of the company) sought to enforce the right *qua* member, i.e. as a member of the company, in so far as s.33 provides that the terms of a company's constitution bind both the company and its members to the same extent.

6.2.6 Section 33 and obligations enforceable between members *inter se*

As with CA 1985, s.14, CA 2006, s.33 makes no mention of whether obligations contained within the articles are directly enforceable between members *inter se*. As such, and as a matter of contract law theory, it would appear that such obligations should be enforceable only through the company in accordance with the internal management principle associated with the rule in *Foss* v. *Harbottle* (see **Chapter 19**), that is, a member wishing to enforce a regulation in the articles that governs an obligation with a fellow member would need to persuade the company to pursue the action (see, e.g. *MacDougall* v. *Gardiner* (1875) 1 Ch D 13). Accordingly, the wrong would only be corrected where the board of directors or a majority of the membership decided that the company should enforce the right. Support for the view that a member cannot directly enforce obligations against a fellow member is to be found in the *obiter* comments of Lord Herschell in *Welton* v. *Safferey* [1897] AC 299. His Lordship remarked:

> It is quite true that the articles constitute a contract between each member and the company, and that there is no contract in terms between individual members of the company; but the articles do not any less, in my opinion regulate their rights *inter se*. Such rights can only be enforced through the company. (at p.315)

Despite such comments, case law indicates that in specific circumstances a member may be able to enforce obligations directly against a fellow member without the need to pursue the action through the company. The principal justification for allowing a membership action is that the company should not become involved in what would essentially be a dispute between its members; namely, the company should not be involved in unnecessary litigation. Support for this view may be found in cases where pre-emption rights have been enforced between members of a company, that is, rights contained within a company's articles which provide that if a member wishes or is compelled to sell his shares, he or she must first offer them to existing members of the company. For example, in *Rayfield* v. *Hands* [1960] Ch 1 Vaisey J held that a member of a company was allowed to enforce a provision of the company's articles that compelled the directors of the company to purchase the member's shares. Vaisey J held that the directors, as members of the company, were bound by the provision of the articles. However, membership disputes that are regulated by the articles and which are personal in nature with no connection to the constitutional functioning of a company and involve obligations created entirely outside the framework of the internal corporate relationship are (as under CA 1985, s.14) unlikely to be enforceable under CA 2006, s.33. For example, an obligation within the articles relating to a trading transaction between two members of the company is unlikely to be so enforceable (see, e.g. *London Sack & Bag Co Ltd* v. *Dixon & Lugton Ltd* [1943] 2 All ER 767).

6.3 DIRECTORS' SERVICE CONTRACTS AND OTHER INDEPENDENT CONTRACTUAL RIGHTS

Although under CA 1985, s.14 an 'outsider right' was not directly enforceable, it may have been indirectly enforceable where it was supported by an independent contract. Accordingly, a member of a company (or indeed a non-member) was capable of entering into a separate enforceable contractual agreement with the company, an agreement that would have been rendered unenforceable had it been contained within the company's constitution. A typical example of such a contractual agreement was a director's service contract. However, in accordance with the contractual nature of CA 2006, s.33, it is possible (depending on the court's construction of s.33) that a service contract contained within a company's constitution may now be enforceable by the director in question (suing *qua* member) or by any other member of the company (suing *qua* member). However, despite this potential contractual effect of CA 2006, s.33, it is most probable that service contracts will continue to be held as independent contracts given the practical flexibility of a distinct contract and the need potentially to update and alter the terms of the contract (if the contract was contained within the articles, terms could only be changed by altering the articles, i.e. by passing a special resolution (unless possibly entrenched)). It should be noted that where a director's service contract is silent as to a specific matter, for example, the length of the service contract, the relevant term may be implied into the independent service contract where it is included within the terms of a company's articles (e.g. *Re New British Iron Co, exparte Beckwith* (1898) 1 Ch 324 and *Read* v. *Astoria Garage (Streatham) Ltd* [1952] Ch 637). It must also be observed that the appointment of a person to a directorship is not, in itself, evidence of an independent contract between the director and company (e.g. *Newtherapeutics Ltd* v. *Katz* [1991] Ch 226), although upon being appointed to a directorship, a director will be bound by the provisions of the company's constitution even in circumstances where the director is not a member of the company (e.g. *Re Anglo Austrian Printing & Publishing Union* [1892] 2 Ch 158).

6.3.1 Remedies following a breach of an independent contract

Other than where a statutory power provides specifically that its effect cannot in any way be impugned by the articles or otherwise, it would appear legitimate for an independent contractual agreement entered into between a company and a third party to include a provision which seeks to restrain the company's ability to exercise a statutory power. For example, within an independent contractual agreement, a third party could legitimately seek to prohibit a company from altering a term of its articles (see, e.g. *Punt* v. *Symons & Co Ltd* [1903] 2 Ch 506). However, if after entering into such a contract, the company breached the agreement by reasserting its right to alter its articles, would the breach give rise to the usual remedies associated with a breach of contract? Would it be possible for the third party to obtain an injunction to restrain the company from breaching the terms of the contract? In *Punt* v. *Symons & Co Ltd*, it was held that the remedy for the breach of the agreement should be restricted to a claim for damages. Nevertheless, in *Baily* v. *British Equitable Assurance Co* [1904] 1 Ch 374, the Court of Appeal, in distinguishing *Punt* v. *Symons & Co Ltd*, implied that the remedy for a breach of such an agreement should not be so restricted. Although the actual decision of the Court of Appeal was overturned subsequently by the House of Lords ([1906] AC 35) the House of Lords did not seek to challenge the findings of the Court of Appeal in respect of its conclusions relating to the effect and consequences of a breach of the independent contract. Indeed, in *British Murac Syndicate* v. *Alperton Rubber Ltd* [1915] 2 Ch 168, an injunction was granted to prevent a proposed alteration of a company's articles in circumstances where the alteration would have resulted in a breach of an independent contract. However, in *Southern Foundries Ltd* v. *Shirlaw* [1940] AC 701, the House of Lords came to the conclusion (albeit in *obiter* comments) that an injunction should not be granted to prevent a company from altering its articles, irrespective of the fact that the company would have been in breach of an independent contract by acting on its new amended articles. However, here it was stated that the breach could have been remedied by an award of damages. It is submitted that the latter approach (an award of damages), is the correct approach because a company should not be prohibited from acting in accordance with a statutory power in circumstances where the other contracting party is deemed to be aware (by constructive notice) of the potential use of the statutory power.

6.4 ALTERING A COMPANY'S ARTICLES

Except where the effect of the alteration of a company's articles would be inconsistent with a provision of the companies legislation or other than where a regulation in a company's articles is entrenched (discussed below), a company may alter a regulation in its articles by passing a special resolution, namely by a three-quarters majority vote of those members who attend and are entitled to vote at a general meeting (CA 2006, s.21). However, a member of a company is not bound (unless he or she otherwise agrees in writing) by an alteration to the company's articles after the date on which he or she became a member in circumstances where the effect of the alteration is to require him or her to take or subscribe for more shares in the company or in any way to increase his or her liability to contribute to the company's share capital or otherwise to pay monies to the company (CA 2006, s.25).

A company commits an offence where it alters its articles and fails to send a copy of the amended articles to the registrar (not later than 15 days after the amendment takes place). The offence is committed by the company and any officer in default (CA 2006, s.26). Where a company's constitution is altered by an order of the court or other authority, or by an enactment, other than an enactment amending the general law, the company must give notice to the registrar of the alteration not less than 15 days after the alteration takes effect or the enactment comes into force (CA 2006, ss.34–35).

6.4.1 Assessing a valid alteration

Although an alteration of a company's articles may be challenged under CA 2006, s.994, i.e. on the basis that in relation to the petitioner's membership interest, the alteration amounted to conduct of an unfairly prejudicial nature (discussed further in **Chapter 19**) an alteration of the articles may also be challenged at common law. Here the requirements to assess the validity of an alteration of a company's articles are (akin to CA 2006, s.994) primarily for the purpose of safeguarding minority interests. An alteration of a company's articles must be made *bona fide* for the benefit of the company as a whole. This rule seeks to assess the benefit of an alteration in respect of the company's commercial interests but in so far as the benefit must be assessed in relation to the 'company as a whole', the rule extends to encompass an assessment of the interests of the company's human constituents, more especially its members. Therefore, the rule will be employed to prevent a three-quarters majority of the membership altering the articles in circumstances where the alteration would exploit and discriminate against the interests of a minority shareholder(s). To determine whether an alteration of a company's articles is *bona fide* for the benefit of the company, the courts adopt generally a two-part test. The first part of the test is subjective and seeks to determine whether a three-quarters majority of shareholders altered the articles in the honest belief that the alteration would benefit the company as a whole (benefit the shareholders as a whole). The second, objective part of the test, requires the court to consider whether the alteration of the company's articles was undertaken in good faith absent any intention to discriminate against minority interests. As the courts portray generally a reluctance to interfere in the business decisions of a company, the decided cases emphasise ordinarily the importance and predominance of the subjective element of the test (see, e.g. *Shuttleworth* v. *Cox Bros & Co Ltd* [1927] 2 KB 9 and *Rights & Issues Investment Trust Ltd* v. *Stylo Shoes Ltd* [1965] 1 Ch 250, and the more recent decision of the Privy Council in *Citco Banking Corporation* v. *Pusser Ltd* [2007] 2 BCLC 483). Therefore, the fact that an alteration of a company's articles causes some disadvantage to the interests of a minority will not in itself invalidate an alteration of its articles (see, e.g. *Allen* v. *Gold Reef* [1900] 1 Ch 656). For an alteration of a company's articles to be declared invalid, the effect and intent of the terms of the alteration must be perceived, by an obvious objective measure, to have had a prejudicial and discriminatory on the interests of a minority. For example, in *Dafen Tin Plate* v. *Llanelly Steel Ltd* [1920] 2 Ch 124, a company altered its articles to bestow on majority shareholders an absolute right to purchase the shares of any minority shareholder. Here, the reason for the alteration was to prevent a minority shareholder, who had transferred business interests to one of the company's competitors, from retaining his membership in the company. Although the motive behind the alteration may have been for the benefit of the commercial entity, the terms of the actual alteration were too wide. The alteration had the effect of permitting members holding a majority stake to expel a minority shareholder without valid excuse. The nature of the alteration was prejudicial and discriminatory to the interests of the minority. However, in all probability, the alteration would have been declared valid had its terms specifically allowed for the share purchase in circumstances where a member sought to transfer business interests to a competitor of the company (see, e.g. *Sidebotham* v. *Kershaw, Leese & Co* [1920] 1 Ch 154).

Finally, it should be observed that an alteration of a company's articles must not be retrospective in its effect. For example, in *Swaeby* v. *Port Darwin Mining Co* (1899) 1 Meg 385, the Court of Appeal held that the directors of a company could not, by a subsequent alteration of the articles, be deprived of fees that they had already earned under the terms of the company's original articles.

6.4.2 Altering the articles in respect of a director's service contract

In circumstances where a director has a separate service contract and the terms of the company's articles are to be impliedly incorporated into the service contract, to govern the same, a valid alteration of the company's articles will also alter the terms of the service contract. Therefore, following an alteration of the articles, the new terms of the articles will be impliedly incorporated into the director's service contract. For example, in *Shuttleworth* v. *Cox Brothers & Co Ltd* [1927] 2 KB 9, the company's articles provided that its directors were appointed for life unless they were disqualified from holding office in any one of six prescribed ways. The company's articles were subsequently altered by adding a seventh and more general discretionary power of removal. A director, to whom the seventh condition was applied, sought a declaration that the alteration was invalid in so far as it had a retrospective effect on the terms under which he was appointed to hold office. However, in upholding the company's ability to invoke the seventh condition and thereby dismiss the director, the Court of Appeal concluded that the new condition had been validly introduced to alter the articles (by special resolution) and therefore governed the terms of the director's service contract; as such the director had no grounds for complaint. While giving the appearance of a retrospective alteration, here the alteration had not (in contrast, for example, to *Swaeby* v. *Port Darwin Mining Co*) been made with the intention of depriving the director of an existing and specified right but rather the aim was to expand upon the pre-existing conditions for the dismissal of any of the company's directors.

However, it should be noted that where a director's service contract contains express terms which are mirrored by terms within a company's articles, an alteration of the articles will not have the effect of altering the express terms of the director's service contract. In such a case the terms of the service contract remain separate and severable from those contained within the altered articles.

6.5 ENTRENCHED ARTICLES

Prior to the passing of CA 2006, a company was unable to entrench regulations within its articles. However, CA 2006, s.22 now provides that a company's articles may contain a general provision to the effect that specified regulations may be amended or repealed only if specific conditions or procedures are complied with.

The conditions or procedures for altering entrenched articles will be more restrictive than the normal procedure to alter a company's articles, i.e. alteration of the entrenched article will require something more than the passing of a special resolution. In accordance with s.22(2), a general provision for entrenchment could only be made in the articles on the company's formation, or by an amendment to the company's articles agreed to by all the members of the company. However, it is to be noted that the implementation of s.22(2) was cancelled in accordance with the Companies Act 2006 and Limited Liability Partnerships (Transitional Provisions and Savings) (Amendment) Regulations 2009, SI 2009/2476. The cancellation of s.22(2) related to a potential conflict with rules governing the variation of the class rights attached to shares (discussed in **Chapter 8**). As class rights are usually subject to a variation procedure (ordinarily contained in the articles) and require a resolution in excess of 75 per cent of the class members, articles relating to the variation of class rights may have been caught under the definition of an entrenched article. Therefore, had s.22(2) been brought into force it may have restricted the creation of class right clauses in the articles, other than where such rights were created in accordance with the specific terms of s.22(2).

For a company to entrench articles, the company must give notice to the registrar of the inclusion of a power to entrench regulations within the articles (CA 2006, s.23). Where a company seeks to alter the terms of its articles to include a general provision for entrenchment it must send to the registrar any document making or evidencing the alteration and must also deliver a statement of compliance certifying that the alteration has been made in accordance with the terms of the company's articles (CA 2006, s.24).

It is to be noted, however, that a company cannot attempt to entrench regulations in its articles by providing that the entrenched regulations cannot, in any circumstances, be removed. CA 2006, s.22 is implicit of a requirement whereby the method for entrenchment must be linked to a procedure to permit for the removal of the entrenchment power. It will, however, be possible to create a very restrictive power of entrenchment, for example, by providing that an entrenched regulation may only be altered by means of the unanimous written consent of the membership.

A company may amend its articles to remove its general capacity to entrench regulations contained therein, but may do so only with the agreement of its entire membership (CA 2006, s.22(3)). Finally, it should be noted that entrenchment does not affect any power of a court or other authority to alter a company's articles.

6.6 STATEMENT OF A COMPANY'S OBJECTS

Section 31 of CA 2006 provides that a company's objects will be unrestricted unless the company's articles specifically restrict the objects. As such, a company is not tied to the pursuit of specified business purposes. Indeed, even before CA 2006, s.31, the significance of a company's objects clause was one steeped in redundancy (discussed further in **Chapter 16**). Where a company chooses to restrict its objects, i.e. where a company's objects are specifically listed, the effect of the restriction will not affect the ability of a third party to enforce a contract where the purpose of that contract falls outside the terms of the objects. However, in a case where the company purports to act outside the terms of its objects this will give rise to a potential breach of the articles (the internal contract between a company and its membership) and as such it may be possible for a member to obtain an injunction to restrain the intended breach. However, following the execution of a binding legal agreement between a company and a third party, a member will not be able to prevent the proposed transaction, notwithstanding that the agreement would, when enacted, be in breach of the company's objects (discussed further in **Chapter 16**).

6.7 THE WEIGHTED VOTING CLAUSE

A provision(s) contained in a company's articles, the intent of which is to override a statutory provision, will be invalid. However, a company may insert a clause into its articles (a weighted voting clause) the practical effect of which may limit or preclude the company's ability to pass a resolution in a manner consistent with the terms of a statutory provision. A weighted voting clause will enhance the voting rights of any member for which the clause is applicable. The concept of the weighted voting clause was approved by the House of Lords in *Bushell* v. *Faith* [1970] 1 All ER 53. This case involved a small domestic family company in which a brother and two sisters each held 100 shares. After a series of disagreements between the members, an extraordinary general meeting was called whereupon it was proposed to remove the brother from his directorship of the company. After the meeting, the sisters claimed that the brother had been validly removed by an ordinary resolution that had polled 200 votes for dismissal as against 100. The brother disagreed on the basis that the articles of the company included a clause (art.9), which provided:

> In the event of a resolution being proposed at any general meeting of the company for the removal from office of any director, any shares held by that director shall on a poll in respect of such resolution carry the right to three votes per share ...

Applying art.9, the brother claimed that his sisters had failed to secure an appropriate number of votes to dismiss him from office. At first instance, Ungoed-Thomas J found that the brother had been validly removed by the resolution. Ungoed-Thomas J took the view that art.9 was invalid, because it infringed the statutory power to remove a director by an ordinary resolution (a vote passed by a bare majority). However, both the Court of Appeal and House of Lords (Lord Morris of Borth-y-Gest dissenting) overruled the learned judge; the validity of art.9 was upheld. In giving its approval to the weighted voting clause the House of Lords emphasised that as the clause was concerned solely with the allocation of a company's voting rights and Parliament had never sought to fetter the right of a company to issue a share with special rights or restrictions, it would be wrong for the courts to interfere in this matter.

Therefore, although a weighted voting clause may, in a practical sense, have the effect of restricting the ability of a company to pass a particular type of resolution, the weighted voting clause does not offend against the terms of the companies legislation; a company's ability to exercise any statutory power by passing a resolution remains unfettered. Theoretically, the company may still, by a requisite majority (by either ordinary or special resolution) pass the necessary resolution.

Yet, the theory is overridden by the practical effect of the weighted voting clause because the nature of the clause prevents the requisite majority of votes being cast to pass the resolution.

6.8 MEMBERSHIP/SHAREHOLDER AGREEMENTS

In addition to those terms of a company's articles which purport to regulate the relationship of members *inter se*, the shareholders of a company may lawfully bind themselves by way of an independent membership agreement (a contractual agreement), to act or vote in a specific way on issues governed by the terms of the agreement. A membership agreement is a common feature in small private companies and usually purports to bind the entire, or a substantial majority of the, existing membership of the company. The agreement seeks to regulate matters of internal management with the effect that members who are a party to the agreement must act and vote on specific issues in a predetermined way (see, e.g. *Breckland Group Holdings Ltd* v. *London & Suffolk Properties* [1989] BCLC 100 and *Euro Brokers Holdings Ltd* v. *Monecor (London) Ltd* [2003] BCC 573).

In relation to an ability to influence the outcome of any given vote, the effectiveness of a membership agreement will depend on the number of members who are bound by its terms. A membership agreement will be more effective if it incorporates a majority of the company's membership, affording a degree of certainty as to the outcome of issues governed by its terms. However, the terms of a membership agreement may prove to be inflexible where, for example, a majority of members who are party to the agreement consider that a specific term contained within the agreement should no longer be pursued, in so far as the term is no longer viewed as beneficial to the company's interests. If a minority of those party to the agreement refuse to accept the majority view and demand compliance with the disputed term by, for example, seeking an injunction to protect the terms of the agreement, then, following the decision of the House of Lords in *Russell* v. *Northern Bank Development Corporation Ltd* [1992] 1 WLR 588, it is probable they will succeed. In *Russell* the House upheld the validity of a membership agreement by which all five (current) members of the company were bound. Here, the company's five shareholders agreed to refrain from voting to increase the company's share capital, save in a situation where all the parties consented in writing to the increase. Subsequently, as the company's circumstances changed, four of the members proposed that the company should increase its issued share capital. However, the fifth member challenged the proposal in so far as it contradicted the terms of the membership agreement. The House of Lords, overruling the decision of the Court of Appeal [1992] BCLC 431, held that the membership agreement was binding. The House of Lords held that an injunction could have been sought to remedy the purported breach (contrast *Southern Foundries Ltd* v. *Shirlaw* [1940] AC 701, discussed above). Although the House recognised that the membership agreement would have been invalid had it been contained in the company's articles, the agreement was separate and distinct from the company's articles and one of a purely personal nature. Lord Jauncey, expressing the unanimous opinion of the House, quoted with approval (at p.593) a passage from Lord Davey's judgment in *Welton* v. *Saffery* [1897] AC 299, namely:

> Of course, individual shareholders may deal with their own interests by contract in such a way as they may think fit. But such contracts, whether made by all or some only of the shareholders, would create personal obligations, or an *exceptio personalis* against themselves only, and would not become a regulation of the company, or be binding on the transferees of the parties to it, or upon new or non-assenting shareholders. (at p.331)

However, in so far as the membership agreement in *Russell* also sought to bind the company (the company was also a signatory to the agreement), the House held the agreement to be as obnoxious as if it had been contained in the company's articles. The company had in effect agreed not to exercise its statutory powers for a period that would last for so long as any of the members who were a party to its terms remained shareholders of the company. Nevertheless, as the membership agreement between the company's shareholders was found to be independent and severable from the purported agreement with the company, the agreement, in so far as it affected the rights of the shareholders *inter se*, was held to be binding.

The significance of the decision of the House of Lords in *Russell* v. *Northern Bank Development Corporation Ltd* should not be underestimated. Although a company or the future membership of the company will not be bound by a membership agreement (however future members could sign up to the agreement), the practical effect of the House of Lords decision is one which restricts the company, through the membership, from acting in accordance with its statutory powers. While the fetter on the company's ability to act in pursuance of a statutory power is of a temporary nature, that is, for so long as those party to the agreement command a sufficient majority of votes, the effect of the obstruction distorts the intention of the relevant companies legislation, a result which shares some similarity with the application of a *Bushell* v. *Faith* weighted voting clause (discussed above). A motion to pass a resolution which is contrary to the terms of a membership agreement should be agreed upon by all who are party to the agreement. However, note that such a resolution may nevertheless succeed without any formal written consent where, in applying the *Duomatic* principle (discussed in **Chapter 18**), all of the members who are party to the agreement informally agree that it should so succeed (see, e.g. *Euro Brokers Holdings Ltd* v. *Monecor (London) Ltd* [2003] BCC 573). Finally, it is submitted that a far more logical, albeit more passive remedy than the pursuit of an injunction for a breach of a membership agreement, would be for an aggrieved shareholder to pursue an action for damages or seek some other form of redress under CA 2006, s.994 (discussed in **Chapter 19**).

CHAPTER 7

The legal nature and characteristics of holding shares in a limited company

7.1 INTRODUCTION

A company limited by shares is founded on an undertaking that its members will contribute capital in consideration for the allotment of shares. A definition of the legal nature of a share was advanced by Farwell J, in *Borland's Trustee* v. *Steel Bros & Co Ltd* [1901] 1 Ch 279. His Lordship stated:

> A share is the interest of a shareholder in the company measured by a sum of money, for the purposes of liability in the first place, and of interest in the second, but also consisting of a series of mutual covenants entered into by all the shareholders *inter se*. (at p.288)

In respect of the above quotation, the 'sum of money' is the price attached to a share. Following the advancement of the full purchase price, a person's liability to contribute capital ceases.

The minimum amount for which a share may be purchased from a company is termed the nominal value (par value) of the share (see, e.g. *Ooregum Gold Mining Co of India* v. *Roper* [1892] AC 125). Where a company offers to sell shares at a price in excess of their nominal value, the monetary difference between the price paid for the shares and the nominal value is termed the 'share premium' and must be placed into the company's share premium account (Companies Act (CA) 2006, s.610). Once share capital is contributed it becomes the property of the company. The company is not classed as a debtor in respect of the repayment or restoration of capital.

The extent of a shareholder's undertaking to contribute capital, and the rights to participate in dividend distributions and vote at general meetings are all matters related to the number and class of shares held in the company. A shareholding interest is composed of all the legal rights of membership contained within a mutual set of covenants within the company's constitution (discussed in **Chapter 6**). However, the exact scope of a membership interest is likely to extend beyond strict legal rights; the extent of a membership interest will be dependent upon the nature and type of shares held. (The scope of a membership interest is discussed further in **Chapter 19**.)

In accordance with CA 2006, s.9(4), unless a company is unlimited or limited by guarantee, the company's 'application for registration' must indicate the manner in which the contributed capital is to be divided into shares of a fixed nominal value (CA 2006, s.10) and the amount to be paid up on the shares. The shares may be denominated in any currency and different classes of shares may be denominated in different currencies (CA 2006, s.542). The total numbers of shares issued and the rights attached to the shares must be specified for each class of share to be issued. In making any future allotment of shares, a company must, within one month of making the allotment, notify the registrar in respect of the company's new capital position (CA 2006, s.555). The total nominal allotted capital of a public company must not be less than £50,000 (CA 2006, s.763), whereas for a private company there is no minimum capital requirement. It is to be noted that a company does not have an authorised share capital limit (prior to CA 2006 a company was not permitted to issue shares beyond its authorised share capital limit).

7.2 IDENTIFYING A MEMBER OF A COMPANY

CA 2006, s.112 provides that the subscribers to a company's memorandum are deemed to have agreed to become members of the company and on the company's registration they become members and must be entered as such in its register of members. Further, every other person who agrees to become a member of a company and whose name is entered in its register of members is deemed to be a member of the company. In effect, a person may become a member of a company in one of four ways:

(a) by subscribing to the memorandum on the incorporation of the company;
(b) by making a successful application to the company for shares allotted by the company;
(c) by purchasing or acquiring the shares of a company from an existing member of the company; or
(d) by acquiring shares as a result of a member's death or bankruptcy.

For a person to assent to become a member of a company it is unnecessary to establish a binding contract between that person and the company. Accordingly, a person's membership of a company will *prima facie* be conclusive where, irrespective of the absence of a binding contract, that person's name (if he or she so assented) is added to the register of members (see, e.g. *Re Nuneaton Borough AFC Ltd* [1989] BCLC, 454). However, it should be noted that in *POW Services Ltd* v. *Clare* [1995] 2 BCLC 435, Jacob J held that while the conditions laid down in CA 1985, s.22 (now CA 2006, s.112) may be met, a person's membership of a company could nevertheless be denied in circumstances where, for example, that person became a member of the company in contravention of a term(s) of the company's articles.

While the terms 'member' and 'shareholder' are often used synonymously, it is nevertheless possible for a person to be a member but not a shareholder of a

121

company. For example, a company limited by guarantee has members, but not shareholders. Conversely, it is possible to be a shareholder but not a member of a company. For example, the holders of 'bearer shares' are classed as shareholders, but although shareholders, they may not necessarily be members of the company. A holder of bearer shares is entitled to specific shares identified in a share warrant. Subject to any contrary intention within the articles, the bearer of a share warrant is entitled to have his or her name entered in the register of members only upon surrendering the share warrant (CA 2006, s.122).

7.2.1 The register of members

CA 2006, s.113 (see generally, CA 2006, Part 8, Chapter 2) provides that every company must keep a register of its members. The contents of the register must record:

(a)   the names and addresses of the members;

(b)   the date on which each person was registered as a member; and

(c)   the date at which any person ceased to be a member.

Where a company has a share capital, the register must include the names and addresses of the members and a statement of:

(a)   the shares held by each member, distinguishing each share:

    (i)   by its number (so long as the share has a number); and

    (ii)   where the company has more than one class of issued shares, by its class; and

(b)   the amount paid or agreed to be considered as paid on the shares of each member.

CA 2006, s.113(5) specifically provides that joint holders of a share fall to be treated as a single member, although both (or more) names must be stated in the register. A company registered with only one member must include a specific statement to this effect in the register of members (CA 2006, s.123). A failure to comply with the aforementioned provisions will result in the company and every officer of the company in default being made liable on summary conviction to a fine.

In accordance with CA 2006, s.114, a company's register of members must be kept available for inspection at its registered office, or at another place in the part of the UK in which the company is registered. The registrar must be notified of the place where the register is kept available for inspection. If for a 14-day period a company fails to comply with the above requirements an offence will be committed by the company, and every officer of the company who is in default. A person guilty of an offence under s.114 is liable on summary conviction to a fine.

In respect of determining whether a corporate entity (Y) is a subsidiary of another corporate entity (X) (in accordance with CA 2006, s.1159) it is essential that X is a registered member of Y. For example, in *Enviroco Ltd* v. *Farstad Supply A/S* [2011]

1 WLR 921, a company named ASCO (A) entered into a deed of pledge with the Bank of Scotland in order to secure certain obligations and liabilities to the bank. A pledged, charged and assigned all its shares in another company Enviroco (E) to the bank until such a time as its relevant liabilities to the bank had been discharged in full. Prior to the assignment, A held the majority shareholding in E and E was a subsidiary of A (in accordance with CA 2006, s.1159). As a result of the security agreement and the relevant jurisdiction (Scotland), A registered the shares held in E in the name of the bank's nominees. The register of members of E was amended to remove the name of A and replace the same with the name of the nominees of the bank. As such, A was no longer a member of E having been replaced in that capacity by the nominees of the bank. Accordingly, the Supreme Court held that E was not a subsidiary of A, irrespective of the fact that in accordance with the terms of the security agreement, A retained effective day-to-day control over E.

7.2.2 Index of members

In addition to keeping a register of members, CA 2006, s.115 provides that a company with more than 50 members must also keep an index of its members, unless the register of members is in such a format that would qualify it to be classed as an index. The index must contain, in respect of each member, a sufficient indication to enable the account of that member to be readily found in the register and the index must at all times be kept available for inspection at the same place as the register of members. The company must make any necessary alteration in the index within 14 days after the date on which any alteration is made to the register of members. A failure to comply with CA 2006, s.115 by a company, or any officer in default, will, on summary conviction, result in the imposition of a fine.

7.2.3 Inspection of the register and index

The register of members, together with any index, must be kept open to inspection by any member of the company or, on the payment of a prescribed fee, by any other person (CA 2006, s.116). CA 2006, s.117 provides that a company must accept or refuse the request for an inspection (or copy of the register) within five working days of its receipt. If the company decides to reject the request, it must defend its decision via an application to the court and must do so on the ground that the request was for an improper purpose. Where the company's objection is upheld, the person having made the request may be held liable to pay, in part or full, the company's costs. Where a company refuses an inspection or copy of the register without making an application to the court the company and every officer of the company who is in default will commit an offence and will be liable on summary conviction to a fine. In the case of any such refusal or default the court may compel an immediate inspection or direct that the copy of the register be sent to the person who requests it (CA 2006, s.118).

7.2.4 Rectification of the register

Where details entered in a company's register of members are incorrect in some material respect, the error may be challenged in accordance with CA 2006, ss.125–128 (previously CA 1985, s.359) and the register may be rectified accordingly. For example, in *Re Thundercrest Ltd* [1994] BCC 857, the company's three shareholders/directors all expressed a willingness to participate in a proposed allotment of a rights issue of shares. However, one of the shareholders, the plaintiff (P) failed to reply to the letter of provisional allotment. As a result of P's failure to reply to the offer letter (although the letter was correctly addressed, P never received the offer letter), the two other shareholders (the defendants) wrongly assumed that P had declined to participate in the rights issue. The shares, provisionally earmarked for P, were allotted between the defendants.

However, the share issue was declared invalid on the premise that the period of notice allowed for the acceptance of the offer had, in accordance with CA 1985, s.90(6) (now governed by CA 2006, s.562(5)), been less than the prescribed 21 days. (Note that in accordance with the Companies (Share Capital and Acquisition by Company of its Own Shares) Regulations 2009, SI 2009/2022, the prescribed period is now 14 days.) Although the offer letter was posted in accordance with the terms of the company's articles and despite the existence of a provision in the company's articles (so permitted by CA 1985, s.91, now governed by CA 2006, s.567) which allowed the notice for the acceptance period to expire after 'a set time period' (the time period for acceptance of this particular rights issue was set at 18 days), Paul Baker J observed that the relevant legislation (then CA 1985, s.90(6)) would apply, unless it was inconsistent with the articles. As the terms of the company's articles did not specifically make mention of a definite expiry period in relation to the acceptance of an allotment offer but merely alluded to the fact that a 'set time period' for acceptance could be provided, the learned judge held that the expiry period should be determined by s.90(6). Accordingly, the 18-day time period was deemed invalid. Further, the learned judge considered the defendants' case had been prejudiced in so far as P's offer letter had been returned by the Post Office to the company's office prior to the allotment of the shares (i.e. the defendants should have been aware that P had not received the letter). Accordingly, the company's register was modified to reflect a cancellation of the rights issue.

For the purpose of rectification there is a 10-year time limit from the date/ omission of an entry. However, an application to challenge the details of the register must be made without unreasonable delay or prejudice to any innocent third party. For example, in *Re ISIS Factors plc* [2004] BCC 359, Blackburne J held that a six-year delay and the undoubted prejudice to a third party who had acquired control of the company in ignorance of the claimant's interest, rendered the provision inapplicable (see also *Re R W Peak (Kings Lynn) Ltd* [1998] BCC 596).

To challenge an entry successfully, it is necessary to establish a legitimate interest in the shares to which the entry relates. A legitimate interest may be defined as one which must not be contrary to the best interests of the company as a whole. For example, in *Re Piccadilly Radio plc* [1989] BCLC 683, the court refused to correct an entry in the register relating to a transfer of shares (to X), albeit that the transfer was in breach of the company's articles. (Ordinarily, one would expect that an application for rectification following a purported transfer of shares in a manner contrary to the terms of a company's articles would succeed, see, e.g *Re Claygreen Ltd* [2006] BCC 440.) In *Re Piccadilly*, rectification of the register was refused because those seeking rectification (Y) sought to prevent the transfer of shares to X on the premise that X opposed an impending takeover bid of the company. In effect, Y sought rectification for a collateral and improper purpose and acted other than in the best interests of the company as a whole.

7.3 ISSUING AND ACQUIRING SHARES

7.3.1 An allotment of shares

CA 2006, s.549(1) governs the allotment of shares providing a general prohibition on the exercise by directors of a power to allot shares other than in circumstances specified by CA 2006, ss.550 and 551. However, CA 2006, s.549(1) does not apply in the case of the allotment of shares in pursuance of an employees' share scheme, or to the grant of a right to subscribe for or to convert any security into shares so allotted (CA 2006, s.549(2), (3), as amended by the Companies Act 2006 (Allotment of Shares and Right of Pre-emption) (Amendment) Regulations 2009, SI 2009/2561).

CA 2006, s.550 provides:

Where a private company has only one class of shares, the directors may exercise any power of the company –

(a)   to allot shares of that class, or
(b)   to grant rights to subscribe for or to convert any security into such shares,

except to the extent that they are prohibited from doing so by the company's articles.

In relation to a private company with more than one class of shares or in the case of a public company (following the previous position under CA 1985, s.80), an issue of shares may be allotted by the directors of a company in accordance with powers contained within the company's articles, or the directors may allot shares with the authority of an ordinary resolution of the company (see CA 2006, s.551). Shares in a company are taken to be allotted when a person acquires an unconditional right to be included in the company's register of members in respect of the allotted shares (CA 2006, s.558).

Under CA 2006, s.551 an authority to allot shares (the maximum number of shares to be allotted must be specified) is set for a maximum of five years. In the case of authorisation contained in the company's articles at the time of its original incorporation, the five-year period runs from the date of incorporation. In any other case, the five-year period runs from the date on which the resolution to authorise the allotment was passed. Authorisation may be given for a particular exercise of the power or for its exercise generally, and may be unconditional or subject to conditions (CA 2006, s.551(2)). Authorisation may be renewed by an ordinary resolution of the company for a further period not exceeding five years and may be revoked or varied at any time by an ordinary resolution of the company. It is interesting to note that authorisation may be given by an ordinary resolution even if its effect would be to contradict the terms of the company's articles.

However, in accordance with CA 2006, s.551(7), the directors of a company may still allot shares, or grant rights to subscribe for or to convert any security into shares, after the expiry date of any authorisation if:

(a) the shares are allotted, or the rights are granted, in pursuance of an offer or agreement made by the company before the authorisation expired, and

(b) the authorisation allowed the company to make an offer or agreement which would or might require shares to be allotted, or rights to be granted, after the authorisation had expired.

A director who knowingly contravenes, or permits or authorises a contravention of CA 2006, s.551 commits an offence and if convicted is liable on conviction on indictment to a fine, or on summary conviction to a fine not exceeding the statutory maximum. However, in such a case the validity of an allotment or other transaction is not affected. Therefore, a person who purchases shares issued without a proper authority will obtain a good title in respect of those shares.

7.3.2 Registering a return of the allotment

A company limited by share capital must, within one month of making an allotment of shares, register a return of the allotment which must be accompanied by a full and up-to-date statement of the nature of the company's share capital at the date on which the return is made (CA 2006, s.555). The information that must be contained in the statement is prescribed by the Companies (Shares and Share Capital) Order 2009, SI 2009/388, namely:

(a) the number of shares allotted;

(b) the amount paid up and the amount (if any) unpaid on each allotted share (whether on account of the nominal value of the share or by way of premium); and

(c) where the shares are allotted as fully or partly paid up (as to their nominal value or any premium on them) otherwise than in cash, the consideration for the allotment.

It is an offence not to comply with s.555 and every officer of the company who is in default is liable to a fine. However, any person liable for the default may apply to the court for relief. The court may grant relief, extending the time period for the delivery of the document in circumstances where it is satisfied that the omission to deliver the document was an accidental one or due to inadvertence, or that it is just and equitable to grant relief.

Following an allotment (or transfer) of shares (other than where shares are in uncertificated form or where the conditions of the share issue provide otherwise), a share certificate must be distributed to the purchaser of the shares; this is not a document of title although it provides *prima facie* evidence of title (CA 2006, s.768). The CREST system (introduced in 1986) applies to public companies listed on the London Stock Exchange. The system allows a person to hold uncertified shares in electronic form, i.e., rather than holding a physical share certificate. The system is regulated by CA 2006, ss.784–790 and by the Uncertificated Securities Regulations 2001, SI 2001/3755, as amended by SI 2009/1889.

7.3.3 The acquisition of a company's own shares

A company may not allot shares to itself (see, e.g. *Trevor* v. *Whitworth* (1887) 12 App Cas 409) and as a general rule must not acquire its own shares, whether by purchase, subscription or otherwise (CA 2006, s.658). However, CA 2006, s.659(2) provides exceptions to s.658, namely, a company may acquire its own shares:

(a) in a reduction of capital duly made,
(b) in pursuance of an order of the court under –

    (i) s.98 (application to court to cancel resolution for re-registration as a private company),
    (ii) s.721(6) (powers of court on objection to redemption or purchase of shares out of capital),
    (iii) s.759 (remedial order in case of breach of prohibition of public offers by private company), or
    (iv) Part 30 (protection of members against unfair prejudice);

(c) in respect of the forfeiture of shares, or the acceptance of shares surrendered in lieu, in pursuance of the company's articles for a failure to pay any sum payable in respect of the shares.

Further, a subsidiary company cannot ordinarily hold shares in its holding company (see CA 2006, s.136).

It should be noted that while a private company may seek offers for its shares from persons other than existing members (but not by way of an offer to the general public), commonly, the articles of a private company will restrict the class of person who will be permitted to hold its shares. For example, the ownership of shares may be restricted to the existing members of the company or their relatives.

7.3.4 Nominee holdings

Shares may be registered in the name of a nominee, whereby the nominee will hold the shares directly or indirectly for the true owner (beneficial owner). However, where shares are issued to a nominee who holds the shares on behalf of a company, the shares are treated as held by the nominee on his or her own account to the extent that the company is not regarded as having a beneficial interest in them (CA 2006, s.660, but subject to the exception provided by s.660(3)).

7.3.5 Share transfers

A share transfer must take place in accordance with the terms of a company's articles (CA 2006, s.554). In accordance with CA 2006, s.770(1), it is unlawful for a company to register a transfer of shares unless 'a proper instrument' of transfer has been delivered to the company (see, e.g. *Nisbet* v. *Shepherd* [1994] BCC 91). A company's power to refuse to register a transfer of shares must be exercised *bona fide* for the benefit of the company (see, e.g. *Tett* v. *Phoenix & Investment Co Ltd* [1984] BCLC 599). Ordinarily, the instrument will follow that prescribed by the Stock Transfer Act 1963, albeit that the Act does not invalidate the adoption of other forms of instruments of transfer. The instrument of transfer may be specified in the articles or be in a form to be approved by the directors of the company. It is to be noted that the phrase 'a proper instrument' does not mean an instrument complying in all respects with statutory requirements, but rather that the instrument must be appropriate or suitable. For example, in *Nisbet* v. *Shepherd* [1994] BCC 91, an omission relating to a statement of consideration did not invalidate the share transfer. The Stock Transfer Act 1963 applies to all types of transferable securities of any company limited by shares other than transfers of partly paid shares. A company may choose to adopt the procedure specified by the Stock Transfer Act instead of the mode of transfer instrument specified within its own articles.

Often the articles of a private company will include a restriction on a member's ability to transfer shares. A common type of restriction on the transfer of shares is one which provides a right of pre-emption, namely, it is common for the articles of a private company to provide that any member who wishes to transfer legal title in shares by way of sale or gift must first offer the shares to existing members of the company. Where a member wishing to sell shares is compelled to sell to an existing member of the company, the company's articles will normally contain a valuation procedure with the valuation ordinarily undertaken by the company's auditor. Other than where the auditor makes a material mistake, for example by valuing the wrong number of shares, or where instances of fraud or gross negligence are alleged, the auditor's valuation will be applied (see, e.g. *Jones* v. *Sherwood Computer Services plc* [1992] 1 WLR 277 and *Doughty Hanson & Co Ltd* v. *Roe* [2009] BCC 126).

A private company's articles may also provide that at the absolute discretion of the directors of the company, the directors may refuse a transfer of shares or only approve the same on specified grounds. Where this power of veto exists or in any other case where a transfer of shares is refused, the company will be required to give notice and an explanation for the refusal to register shares within two months of the presentation of the transfer (CA 2006, s.771). Where such notice has not been given, as in *Re Swaledale Cleaners Ltd* [1968] 1 WLR 1710 and *Re Inverdeck Ltd* [1998]

BCC 256, then, in accordance with CA 2006, s.125, a person to whom the shares have been transferred may be entitled to an order requiring the company to register the transfer of shares. Where a company's articles stipulate that a refusal to transfer shares may only be invoked in specified circumstances, then prior to the company's refusal to register a transfer, the specified circumstances must have been met (see, e.g. *Re Bede Steam Shipping Co Ltd* [1917] 1 Ch 123).

If the company refuses to register the transfer, the transferee may make a request for further information in respect of the refusal, although here the request must, in all circumstances, be reasonable. It is not unreasonable for a company to refuse to include copies of minutes of meetings of directors. If a company fails to comply with CA 2006, s.771, an offence is committed by the company, and by every officer of the company who is in default. The penalty, on summary conviction, is a fine.

7.3.6 The payment for shares

CA 2006, s.580 provides that a company's shares must not be issued at a discount. Further, except in a situation where a company allots bonus shares to its existing members (discussed below), or where it resolves to extinguish any amount owing on shares which at that time were not fully paid up, the payment for any acquisition of the company shares (including any premium) must be by way of a monetary consideration; the shares must be paid for with cash or something to which a monetary value can be attached, to include goodwill and know-how (see CA 2006, s.582). Section 583(3) defines cash consideration and lists the methods of payment and also provides that 'cash consideration' is constituted by payment by any other means giving rise to a present or future entitlement (of the company or a person acting on the company's behalf) to a payment (or credit equivalent to payment) in cash. Cash consideration includes a settlement bank's obligation to make a payment in respect of the allotment or payment of shares under the CREST system. While a private company may accept an undertaking for the future performance of services in consideration for the sale of shares, a public company is prohibited from doing so (CA 2006, s.585). Further, a public company may not allot shares for a considera-tion which includes any other form of undertaking which is to be, or may be performed, more than five years after the allotment of shares (CA 2006, s.587).

Although the full purchase price of a share may be paid in instalments (partly paid shares), a public company may not (other than for shares allotted in pursuance of an employees' share scheme) issue a share unless at least 25 per cent of its nominal value and the whole of any premium payable on it, has been paid up (CA 2006, s.586).

Where the consideration to be provided for the purchase of shares is other than for a cash consideration, there is a potential for an abuse of the rule that provides shares should not be issued at a discount. However, in relation to a private company, the court will rarely enquire into the adequacy of the consideration and will assume that the directors have not issued the shares at a discount (see, e.g. *Re Wragg* [1897] 1 Ch 796). However, the court may intervene where the inadequacy of the consideration is obvious, namely, if it appears that some form of fraud or bad faith was involved in relation to the transaction (see, e.g. *Hong Kong & China Gas Co* v. *Glen* [1914] 1 Ch 527). In the case of a public company, the company must ordinarily obtain a valuation or validation of the value of the consideration to be provided (CA 2006, s.593; see generally, CA 2006, Part 17, Chapter 6).

CHAPTER 8

The types and classes of shares

8.1 INTRODUCTION

A company may create different types of shares, i.e. the legal rights of a particular type of share (referred to as class rights) may vary from other types of shares issued by the company. The legal rights of any given type of share are determined by either the terms of the company's constitution, or by the terms of the particular share issue. The legal rights attached to a share comprise:

- rights as to dividend payments;
- voting rights; and
- rights to the return of capital on an authorised reduction of capital or on the winding up of a company.

8.2 TYPES OF SHARES

8.2.1 Ordinary (equity) shares

An ordinary share is the most common type of share issued by a company and as a genus ordinary shares will make up the greatest part of a company's share capital. Ordinary shares are issued predominantly with class rights of a 'normative' character. Here the class rights attached to the share will normally comprise a right to participate in any declared dividend, the right to vote at general meetings and the right to a return of capital and to participate in surplus assets on the winding up of the company.

Voting rights

Although ordinary shares will usually carry voting rights, a company's articles may provide that the company may issue ordinary shares as non-voting shares, shares with limited voting rights or shares with enhanced voting rights. For example, a company's ordinary shares may be divided into class A ordinary shares and class B ordinary shares. Although both a class A share and a class B share may carry the same rights in respect to dividend payments, the class A share may carry 100 votes per share, whereas the class B share may only carry one vote per share (see, e.g. *Holt* v. *Holt* [1990] 1 WLR 1250). Further, in accordance with the terms of the company's articles where the same include an enhanced voting rights clause, the voting rights attached to the shares held by a director of a company may be increased in circumstances where, for example, the members in general meeting propose to remove that director from office (see, e.g. *Bushell* v. *Faith* [1970] AC 1099 – discussed in **Chapter 6**).

Dividend payments

In relation to dividend payments (when and if declared) the dividend payable on ordinary shares will usually be determined in accordance with the relative economic performance of the company. A share that is issued with class rights which confer some additional or distinctive class right in relation to dividend payments and, as such, are distinctive from the normative dividend right associated with an ordinary share, will be identified as preference shares (discussed below). Dividends payable on ordinary shares will be paid after the payment of dividends to preference shareholders. Where a company issues shares that have specific class rights in relation to dividend payments (i.e. preference shares) any remaining shares issued by the company which do not contain those specific rights as to dividend payments will be construed and classed as ordinary shares.

8.2.2 Preference shares

A preference share is one which possesses specific preferential rights. Although a preference share is absent of any statutory definition, its most common distinctive attribute is the preferential payment of dividends, a payment in priority to ordinary shares. A company may also issue convertible preference shares; this type of preference share may, subject to the terms of the issue, be converted into ordinary shares at the option of the shareholder. The extent of the legal rights attached to a preference share of a company will be dependent on the construction of the company's articles (or the terms of the specific share issue which govern the particular share issue). The terms of the articles (or terms of the share issue) exclusively define the rights attached to a class of shares (see, e.g. *Scottish Insurance Corporation Ltd* v. *Wilsons & Clyde* [1949] AC 462).

Dividend payments

The dividend payment for a preference share is set at a fixed percentage rate and a preference shareholder's entitlement to the fixed payment will, in any given year, be dependent on the company's ability to declare a dividend. The entitlement to a fixed payment may be either cumulative or non-cumulative. Where the payment is of a cumulative nature and the company is unable to pay a fixed payment in any one year, it must make up the shortfall at some future date, namely, when it is able to declare a dividend. If a company is in liquidation, the entitlement of the company's preferential shareholders to any outstanding amount owed in respect of a cumulative dividend payment will be dependent upon whether the company's articles (or the terms of the specific share issue) make provision for such payments. Where a company's articles do not specifically provide for such payments, any arrears owing to preference shareholders will, following prior payment of the company's creditors, be paid out of the company's remaining surplus assets. If a company's articles contain no specific provision of entitlement, it will be assumed that preference shareholders are unable to claim an arrears of dividend (see, e.g. *Re Crichton's Oil Co* [1902] 2 Ch 86).

A preference share may also be of a participating nature, namely one whereby the rate of return is in the form of a fixed payment but with an additional payment to represent a share in the company's profits. In relation to the additional payment, the right of participation will be limited to an entitlement to share in any surplus profits (i.e. to be paid after a dividend has been paid to the company's ordinary shareholders). For a preference share to have been created as a participating preference share, the company's articles (or terms of the share issue) must specify that the preference share was so created (see, e.g. *Will* v. *United Lankart Plantations Co Ltd* [1914] AC 11). Therefore, unless the terms of a preference share issue state otherwise, there is a presumption that a preference share is cumulative but not of a participating nature (see, e.g. *Webb* v. *Earle* (1875) LR 20 Eq 556).

Repayment of capital – participation in surplus assets

Preference shares may also carry a preference over ordinary shares in respect of the repayment of capital and/or the participation in surplus assets in a situation where the company is wound up (i.e. assets that remain after the company's creditors have been paid and after all the company's shareholders have had their initial capital investment in the company returned to them (see, e.g. *Scottish Insurance Corporation* v. *Wilsons & Clyde Coal Co Ltd* [1949] AC 462)). Whether a specific right exists in relation to the return of capital on a winding up, or an ability to participate in surplus assets, is a matter to be determined by construing the company's articles (or the specific terms of the share issue). Where a term of the company's articles provides specifically that preference shareholders have no preferential right to the return of capital or no right to participate in the distribution of surplus assets following the winding up of the company, then effect will be given to such a term. Where the company's regulations simply afford a preferential return of capital on winding up, the company's regulations will be exhaustive of that right, that is, the preference shareholders will take a preference in the return of their capital investment but will not be entitled to participate in a division of any surplus capital on the winding up of the company.

In respect of the entitlement of preference shareholders to participate in the surplus assets of a company, difficulties may arise in circumstances where a company's surplus assets include accumulated income: income which prior to the company's liquidation could, in accordance with the terms of the company's articles, have only been distributed to the company's ordinary shareholders. Following a company's liquidation dividend payments will cease to be made to ordinary shareholders and therefore any accumulated income should, post liquidation, be considered as part of the company's surplus assets. However, in *Re Bridgewater* [1891] 2 Ch 317, the Court of Appeal took a contrary view. The court's decision was founded on the premise that, irrespective of a company's liquidation, certain non-capital assets of the company could retain their character as income and as such the income could only be converted into capital if an intention to that effect had been made clear by the company's articles. While the decision in *Re Bridgewater* avoided the anomaly of income, exclusively earmarked for ordinary shareholders, being distributed to both ordinary and preference shareholders, the decision appeared to impugn the logical assumption that in liquidation the rights of the company's shareholders should no longer be governed by regulations specifically formulated to regulate the company while it was a going concern. Indeed, subsequent cases appear to confirm the view that following a company's liquidation and unless specifically provided for by the company's articles, the rights of the company's shareholders should not be calculated on the basis of their pre-liquidation rights (see, e.g. *Re Isle of Thanet Electricity Supply Co Ltd* [1950] Ch 161 and *Dimbula Valley (Ceylon) Tea Co Ltd* v. *Laurie* [1961] Ch 353).

Where no provision is made within the articles for the distribution of capital or surplus assets, all shareholders of all classes will participate equally (see, e.g. *Birch* v. *Cropper* (1889) 14 App Cas 525). Here, in expressing the unanimous view of the House of Lords, Lord Macnaghten observed:

> Every person who becomes a member of a company limited by shares of equal amount becomes entitled to a proportionate part in the capital of the company, and, unless it be otherwise provided by the regulations of the company, entitled as a necessary consequence, to the same proportionate part in all the property of the company, including its uncalled capital. (at p.543)

However, it is to be noted that where a preference shareholder is afforded a preference in the return of capital on the winding up of the company, that preference will also be applicable in a situation where a solvent company decides to reduce its capital by returning capital to its shareholders. This implied preferential right exists irrespective of the fact that the right is not attached specifically to the preference share (see, e.g. the decision of the House of Lords in *House of Fraser plc* v. *ACGE Investments Ltd* [1987] AC 387).

Voting rights

The voting rights attached to preference shares will be defined ordinarily in a manner whereby preference shareholders have an entitlement to vote only in circumstances where their dividend payments are in arrears, or in a situation where a proposed variation of the rights attached to the preference share is advanced (see, e.g. *Willow International Investments Ltd* v. *Smiths of Smithfield Ltd* [2003] BCC 769). Where the voting rights of preference shareholders are not defined specifically, the principle in *Birch* v. *Cropper* (1889) 14 App Cas 525 will apply, namely, preference shareholders will be accorded the same voting rights as the holders of the company's ordinary shares.

8.2.3 Deferred/management/founders' shares

This type of share may be issued to the founders of a company. The right to a dividend payment is deferred on a founder's share, namely, the dividend payment is held back until a dividend payment has been made to the company's other shareholders; the holders of founder shares are then entitled to the remainder of whatever amount the company has reserved for dividend payments. Founders' shares are now rare to extinct, especially in public companies, where strict Stock Exchange listing requirements curtail their existence. These stricter rules were introduced to curb promoters of public companies from exploiting their positions (i.e. promoters were often able to take founders' shares to a value in excess of the value of their services to the company).

8.2.4 Employee shares

Many companies (usually, but not exclusively public companies) operate a scheme whereby the company's employees are encouraged to take up shares or debentures in the company. Employee share schemes allow the company's workers to participate in the profits that they help generate. In addition to allowing the employees a right to a share of the company's profits, employee share schemes may be seen also as a means of motivating the workforce to attain higher profit levels.

In accordance with CA 2006, s.1166, an employees' share scheme is for the benefit of:

(a)   the bona fide employees or former employees of –

   (i)   the company,
   (ii)   any subsidiary of the company, or
   (iii) the company's holding company or any subsidiary of the company's holding company, or

(b)   the spouses, civil partners, surviving spouses, surviving civil partners, or minor children or step-children of such employees or former employees.

Where shares are offered to the employees of a company, the general pre-emption rules (discussed below) will not be applicable (i.e. a company is not first required to offer shares that have been designated for its employees to existing members of the company (CA 2006, s.556)). However, where a general allotment of shares is proposed, the pre-emption rules operate in favour of the company employees' share scheme, namely a portion of the general issue of shares must be offered first to holders of existing employee shares. (Further, for specific rules dealing with a

135

company's ability to purchase its own shares in furtherance of an employee's share scheme see the Companies Act 2006 (Amendment of Part 18) Regulations 2013, SI 2013/999 – discussed in **Chapter 10**.)

8.2.5 Treasury shares

In accordance with the Companies (Acquisition of Own Shares) (Treasury Shares) Regulations 2003, SI 2003/1116 and No.2, SI 2003/3031, a public company is afforded the option to purchase its own shares (providing the shares satisfy the qualifying conditions – see CA 2006, s.724) without the need to cancel them; the company may then subsequently reissue the shares at a later date (see CA 2006, ss.690–708). Further, following the Companies Act 2006 (Amendment of Part 18) Regulations 2013, SI 2013/999, a private company may also purchase its own shares in furtherance of or pursuant an employee share scheme without the need to cancel them (see **Chapter 10**). Shares held in this manner (in respect of both a public and a private company) are referred to as treasury shares. If treasury shares cease to be classed as qualifying shares, the shares must be cancelled. In relation to a public company's ability to create treasury shares, the company must sanction the purchase of its own shares by means of an ordinary resolution (CA 2006, s.701(1)). Here an authority to buy back shares is limited in duration to a maximum period of five years. Treasury shares will provide public companies with flexibility in the management and adjustment of their share capital and a reissue of treasury shares will be far less expensive than the costs involved in, for example, the issue of new shares. For specific shares of public companies to 'qualify' under the Regulations, the shares will ordinarily be listed on the Main Market or traded on the Alternative Investment Market (AIM) of the London Stock Exchange. The purchase price of the shares must be taken from the company's distributable profits. Treasury shares must be recorded in the company's register of members. During the period in which the treasury shares are held by the company, the shares do not retain any voting rights. Bonus shares may be allotted to treasury shares (in the same way as bonus shares may be issued to other types of qualifying share). Where bonus shares are allotted to treasury shares those bonus shares will also be held as treasury shares. A company may cancel treasury shares at any time without the necessity of having to abide by the statutory rules that govern a reduction of capital. (The rules relating to a reduction of capital are discussed in **Chapter 10**.)

8.3 CLASS RIGHTS

In the majority of cases, the class rights attached to a particular type of share may be determined by examining the contents of a company's articles, the terms of a particular share issue, or the terms of a special resolution related to the grant of a particular class of shares (see, e.g. *Re Old Silkstone Collieries Ltd* [1954] Ch 169). Further, class rights may also be created by the terms contained in a shareholders' agreement. For example, in *Harman* v. *BML Group Ltd* [1994] 2 BCLC 674, the Court of Appeal upheld the validity of a quorum provision that was contained in a shareholders' agreement to which all the members of the company were party. The shareholder agreement provided that the holder of B shares (Z or his proxy) had an absolute right to be present at all shareholder meetings. The capital of the company was divided between the holders of 'A' ordinary shares of which C and D held a majority (X and Y held a minority of the 'A' shares), and the holders of the 'B' ordinary shares (Z held all of this class of shares). The class A and B shares carried equal rights. C and D held the majority of the voting rights. A dispute arose between C and Z, whereby Z alleged that C and D had perpetrated a fraud against the company. As a consequence of this dispute, an extraordinary meeting was convened by Z; the meeting was convened with the intention of passing a motion to dismiss C and D from their directorships. The meeting (lasting for only one minute) resulted in C and D being dismissed from their directorships; the vote was taken by a show of hands. Z, X and Y voted in favour of the motion; the meeting was closed before C and D could seek the right to a poll vote, a vote which they would have won given that they held the majority of the voting shares.

Following their dismissal, C and D sought to convene a meeting of the shareholders to reverse the decision taken at the extraordinary meeting. Z refused to attend the meeting which, in accordance with the shareholder agreement, would, if it had proceeded, been rendered invalid. C and D sought to hold a meeting pursuant to CA 1985, s.371 (now represented by CA 2006, s.306 (discussed further in **Chapter 18**)) which would have allowed them to convene the meeting irrespective of the terms of the shareholder agreement. The Court of Appeal concluded that an order made under s.371 would have overridden Z's class rights and as such would have been inappropriate. While the decision could be viewed as a technical victory for the procedural requirements of the shareholder agreement, it should be noted that the facts of the case would appear indicative of a breach of C and D's right to cast their votes in accordance with CA 2006, s.33 (previously CA 1985, s.14) (see **Chapter 6**).

In addition to being created by a shareholder agreement, class rights may also be created where, by the terms of a company's articles, rights have been conferred on a particular member of the company in that member's capacity as a shareholder. Here, the class rights exist despite the fact that they are not attached to the specific shares held by the member. For example, in *Cumbrian Newspapers Group Ltd* v. *Cumberland & Westmorland Herald Newspaper & Printing Co Ltd* [1987] Ch 1, the plaintiff acquired a 10.67 per cent holding in the defendant company (Cumberland). As a condition of the acquisition, Cumberland's articles were altered to confer the plaintiff with specific rights designed to prevent an outside party from acquiring control of the company. Irrespective of the fact that the rights were not attached to the shares acquired by the plaintiff, Scott J held that such rights were class rights. Therefore, the rights could only be altered pursuant to the statutory procedure laid down by CA 1985, s.125 (now governed by CA 2006, s.630 (discussed below)).

8.3.1 The variation of class rights

The companies legislation provides little guidance in relation to a definition to be afforded to a variation of class rights. In an obvious sense, CA 2006, s.630(5) provides that an alteration of a provision contained in a company's articles to vary the rights of a class of shareholders or the insertion of such a provision into the articles, is to be construed as a variation of class rights. More specific as to a more tangible element of definition, CA 2006, s.630(6) provides that the abrogation of the class rights of a specific class of shareholder is deemed to be a variation of those rights. However, here it must be noted that the cancellation of an entire class of shares will not always be construed as a variation of class rights. For example, if a company decides to reduce its share capital with a preferential right to the return of capital being afforded to its preference shareholders, the company may, in the reduction of capital, cancel all of its preference shares (see, e.g. *Re Saltdean Estate Co Ltd* [1968] 1 WLR 1844). Here, the reduction of the company's capital and the subsequent return of capital to the preference shareholders accords with the class rights of the preference shareholders and as such is not a variation of those rights and thus will not offend the terms of s.630(6). For example, in *Re Hunting plc* [2005] 2 BCLC 211, the court held that a company was perfectly entitled to effect a reduction of capital by cancelling its preference shares when market interest rates were low. The purpose of the cancellation was to effect a replacement of the capital provided by the preference shareholders with capital obtainable commercially on the market at a cheaper rate. It was held that there was no unfairness attached to the cancellation of the preference shares because it had always been a legitimate expectation that preference shares, carrying a high rate of interest, would in specific and necessary circumstances be paid off in full.

However, in all cases it is essential to construe first the company's articles or the terms of the share issue to determine if preference shareholders have been denied a preferential right to a return of capital. For example, following a reduction of share capital, although a company's preference shares will ordinarily be afforded a priority to the return of capital (see, e.g. *House of Fraser plc* v. *ACGE Investments Ltd* [1987] AC 387), the company's articles or the terms of a specific share issue may provide expressly that the rights of any class of shares (to include preference shares) will be varied by any reduction of the share capital paid up on the shares. In such a case, if a company sought to return capital to its preference shareholders with the effect of cancelling preference shares this would amount to a variation of class rights. The variation would be unlawful unless the company sought the consent of its preference shareholders in accordance with CA 2006, s.630. For example, in *Re Northern Engineering Industries plc* [1994] 2 BCLC 704, a proposal was advanced to reduce a company's capital by paying off preference shares and cancelling that class of shares. The company's articles provided that the rights attaching to any class of shares would be varied by a reduction of the capital paid up on the shares. The company contended that its articles did not apply to the proposed cancellation of preference shares because the articles only had effect where there had been a reduction of capital as opposed to an absolute cancellation of the shares. It was held that a cancellation of shares necessarily implied that there was a reduction of share capital. As the variation of the preference shareholders' rights had not been put to a separate meeting of the preference shareholders in accordance with CA 1985, s.125 (now represented by CA 2006, s.630; see below), the court refused to confirm the reduction in capital.

8.3.2 Determining whether a class of shares is subject to a variation of class rights

In determining whether a class of shares is subject to a variation of class rights, as a general rule, the court will draw a distinction between the rights of a class of shareholder and the enjoyment of those rights. An alteration in the enjoyment of class rights will not, in itself, justify the court in concluding that there was a variation of class rights. To establish a variation of class rights, the rights of a class of shareholder must be altered specifically as opposed to being merely affected in an adverse manner. For example, in *Greenhalgh* v. *Arderne Cinemas Ltd* [1946] 1 All ER 512, the company's share capital was divided between two classes of shares: one class of 2s (10p) shares and the other of 10s (50p) shares. Both classes carried one vote per share. An ordinary resolution was passed which had the effect of subdividing the shares valued at 10s each (50p) into shares of 2s each (10p); each new share was to carry one vote. The resolution increased the voting power (5×) of shareholders who had previously held the 10s (50p) shares. The plaintiff, Greenhalgh (G), objected to the subdivision of the 10s (50p) shares on the ground that its effect was to vary his class rights. Prior to the resolution, G, who held the bulk of the 2s (10p) shares, had control of over 40 per cent of the membership votes, whereas after the resolution, his voting powers were reduced to less than 10 per cent of the votes. The court held that a variation of G's 2s (10p) shares had not taken place, as the resolution subdividing the 10s (50p) shares had not specifically altered G's rights. G still had the same quantity of 2s (10p) shares, each share still carried one vote. Although the effect of the resolution resulted in G's loss of control of over 40 per cent of the membership votes, the resolution did not alter the specific nature of the rights attached to the 2s (10p) shares. (Also see, *White* v. *Bristol Aeroplane Co Ltd* [1953] Ch 65 and *Re John Smith's Tadcaster Brewery Co Ltd* [1953] 1 All ER 518.)

It should be noted that in accordance with CA 2006, s.618, unless a company's articles provide otherwise, a company may pass an ordinary resolution to subdivide its existing shares, or any of them, into shares of a smaller nominal amount, or consolidate and divide all or any of its share capital into shares of a larger nominal amount. Where a company exercises such an authority, *prima facie* there will be no variation of class rights.

8.3.3 Examples of actual variation of class rights

All in all, case examples to illustrate an actual variation of class rights are quite rare. However, one such example is *Re Old Silkstone Collieries Ltd* [1954] Ch 169. This case involved a colliery which had been nationalised (i.e. the colliery had been taken over from private ownership by the State-controlled National Coal Board). The company which operated the colliery remained in existence to collect compensation payable as a result of the nationalisation. Although the company had reduced its capital, by returning a part of the preference shareholders' capital investment, the company resolved that all its shareholders should participate in the compensation award. Despite such assurances, a further reduction in capital was proposed, the effect of which would have been to cancel the class of preference shares. The court held that if such a proposal had been implemented it would have amounted to a variation of the class rights of the preference shareholders because the preference shareholders had been promised a right to participate in the compensation payments. The proposed variation was declared unfair and as such the court refused to sanction the further reduction of capital.

Further examples of a variation of class rights would include:

- where there was a proposal whereby one type of share was to be converted into another type of share, for example, where a company sought to convert ordinary shares into preference shares and vice versa;
- where a company sought to alter the voting rights, dividend rights or any other class right attached to a particular class of share;
- where a company sought to alter the pre-emption rights (discussed below) of a class of shareholder (see, e.g. *Willow International Investments Ltd* v. *Smiths of Smithfield Ltd* [2003] BCC 769).

8.3.4 Authorising a variation of class rights

If a company decides to vary the rights attached to a particular class of its issued shares it must follow the procedure contained in CA 2006, s.630. Section 630 simplifies the more complex procedure that was regulated previously under CA 1985, s.125.

CA 2006, s.630

Prior to implementing a variation to the rights of a given class of share, a company must comply with any internal constitutional procedures attached to the variation of the class of share in question. Further, the company must abide by the procedures stipulated by CA 2006, s.630. Following the implementation of CA 2006, the procedure for a variation of class rights is instantly more straightforward given that the memorandum of a company is no longer deemed a relevant constitutional document, i.e. it is no longer necessary, as under CA 1985, to distinguish, in terms of the variation procedure, between whether the class rights and variation procedure were contained in the articles or memorandum. Indeed, in all cases of a proposed variation and in accordance with CA 2006, s.630, the procedure for a variation of class rights will be determined by either:

- the consent in writing from the holders of at least three-quarters in nominal value of the issued shares of the class (excluding treasury shares); or
- a special resolution passed at a separate general meeting of the holders of the class to which the variation applies (here, the majority vote requirement may be greater (but not less) than the 75 per cent requirement, i.e. if the company's constitution so provides).

Finally, it should be noted that nothing in s.630 affects a court's powers under the following provisions:

- CA 2006, s.98 (an application to cancel a resolution for a public company to be re-registered as a private company);
- CA 2006, Part 26 (arrangements or reconstructions); or
- CA 2006, Part 30 (the protection of members against unfair prejudice).

8.3.5 The minority's right to object to a variation of class rights

Where a decision is taken to sanction a proposed variation of class rights under CA 2006, s.630 and a minority of the class to which the variation applies object to the terms of the variation, the minority may, if they hold at least 15 per cent of the shares of the class to be varied and providing they did not consent to or vote in favour of the variation, apply to the court to have the variation cancelled (CA 2006, s.633). An application to the court under s.633 has the effect of suspending the variation of class rights until such a time as the court decides whether or not the variation should be confirmed. The minority must apply to court within 21 days of the decision affirming the terms of the variation. In deciding whether to affirm the variation, the court must consider whether the effect of the variation would be unfairly prejudicial to the class as a whole. In determining the issue the court must consider whether in affirming a variation of the rights of a specified class of shares, the members of the class exercised their power to vote *bona fide* for the purpose of benefiting the class as a whole. However, here a conflict of interest may arise in a situation where a member (X) holds, for example, both class A and class B shares and where a proposed variation of the class A shares, while detrimental to the general interests of the holders of class A shares, would nevertheless benefit the holders of B shares. If the detriment that would fall on X following the variation of the rights of the A shares would be outweighed by the benefit that X would obtain in relation to his or her holding of the B shares, should X be expected to vote for the greater good of the class A shares? This problem arose in *Re Holders Investment Trust Ltd* [1971] 1 WLR 583, which involved a proposed reduction of capital, whereby the company sought to replace the company's existing preference shares with unsecured loan stock. The cancellation of the preference shares would have benefited the holders of the company's ordinary shares in so far as their dividend payments would no longer have been subject to the prior payment of dividends to the preference shareholders. As the majority holders of the company's preference shares also held a majority of the company's ordinary shares they voted in favour of the proposal. The holders of the minority of preference shares opposed the variation. The court, in refusing to sanction the variation, held that when deciding whether to affirm a variation of class rights the principal consideration for a member of the class was the overall benefit of the class and not his or her own personal interests.

8.4 TYPES OF SHARE ISSUES

8.4.1 Rights issue (pre-emption rights)

In accordance with CA 2006, s.561, where a company offers an issue of equity securities (ordinary shares) for cash, it must, in the first instance, make the offer to its existing ordinary shareholders. The minimum period during which the offer may be accepted was previously set at 21 days (CA 2006, s.562(5)). However, s.562(5) was subsequently amended by the Companies (Share Capital and Acquisition by Company of its Own Shares) Regulations 2009, SI 2009/2022, to the extent that the prescribed period is now set at 14 days. A 'rights issue' must be made in direct proportion to the number of shares held by each ordinary shareholder. A contravention of s.561 (subject to the exceptions, see below) will render every officer of the company who knowingly authorised or permitted the contravention to take place, jointly and severally liable to compensate any member of the company to whom an offer of shares should have been made.

The exceptions

- In accordance with CA 2006, s.567, pre-emption rights may be excluded by a specific provision contained in the articles of a private company (but not those of a public company). The exclusion may be a general one in relation to the allotment of equity securities, or may be in relation to allotments of a particular description or to a particular class of ordinary shares (see CA 2006, s.568).
- An existing shareholder's right of pre-emption does not apply in relation to the allotment of bonus shares (CA 2006, s.564).
- An existing shareholder's right of pre-emption does not apply to a particular allotment of equity securities where the securities are to be wholly or partly paid up otherwise than in cash (CA 2006, s.565).
- An existing shareholder's right of pre-emption does not apply to the allotment of equity securities that would, apart from any renunciation or assignment of the right to their allotment, be held under or allotted or transferred pursuant to an employees' share scheme (CA 2006, s.566 as amended by the Companies

Act 2006 (Allotment of Shares and Right of Pre-emption) (Amendment) Regulations, SI 2009/2561).

Disapplication of pre-emption rights

- A private company with only one class of shares (e.g. a private company having issued only one class of ordinary (equity) shares) may, with regard to any future allotment of shares of that class, choose to disapply pre-emption rights or apply pre-emption rights to the future allotment of shares with such modifications as may be determined by the company's directors, providing the authority to disapply is contained in the company's articles or the authority is by means of a special resolution (CA 2006, s.569).
- Where the directors of a company are generally authorised for the purposes of CA 2006, s.551 (power of directors to allot shares, etc.), the directors may be given an authority in the articles, or an authority may be given by a special resolution, to allot equity securities as if a right of pre-emption did not apply to the allotment, or the right of pre-emption applied to the allotment with such modifications as the directors may determine (CA 2006, s.570–571).

In accordance with s.572, when setting out the recommendation to disapply the pre-emption rules, any person who knowingly or recklessly authorised or permitted the inclusion therein of any misleading, false or deceptive material is liable on conviction to imprisonment or a fine or both.

8.4.2   A bonus issue of shares

Shares may be issued as bonus shares to the ordinary shareholders of a company in circumstances where a company uses reserve funds to pay up any unissued shares. Prior to issuing bonus shares, the articles of a company will usually require the company to pass an ordinary resolution to sanction the issue. In relation to accounting and capital maintenance rules (see **Chapter 10**), a bonus issue of shares is not classed as a distribution of a company's assets to its members. A resolution to issue bonus shares as fully paid up to all shareholders will be rendered void for mistake where shares held by a part of the membership were not fully paid up (see, e.g. the decision of the Court of Appeal in *EIC Services* v. *Phipps* [2004] 2 BCLC 589).

8.4.3   Redeemable shares

A share issued under a condition that it may be redeemed by the issuing company at some specified date in the future (the redemption date), at the option of either the company or the shareholder, is referred to as a redeemable share (CA 2006, s.684). Redeemable shares are often issued to facilitate a company's desire to raise short-term capital. Unlike a private company, the ability of a public company to issue redeemable shares is dependent on an authorisation to that effect. If present, the authorisation will be contained in the company's articles (CA 2006, s.684(3)).

A company may issue redeemable shares providing that the issue does not represent the totality of the company's share capital (CA 2006, s.684(4)). Providing redeemable shares are fully paid up, the shares may be redeemed at the option of the company or the shareholder at a date prior to the specified redemption date. A company must redeem the shares out of its distributable profits or out of the proceeds of a new share issue (CA 2006, s.687). However, a private company may redeem the shares from its own capital (discussed in **Chapter 10**). Any premium payable on the redemption of shares must be paid out of the distributable profits of the company. However, if redeemable shares are issued at a premium, any premium payable on their redemption may be paid out of the proceeds of a fresh issue of shares made for the purposes of the redemption, up to an amount equal to whichever is the least of:

(a)   the aggregate of the premiums received by the company on the issue of the shares redeemed; or

(b)   the current amount of the company's share premium account (including any sum transferred to that account in respect of premiums on the new shares).

8.5   THE VALUATION OF SHARES

Although the value of the shares of a public company may often be ascertained in accordance with the share's quoted market price, the valuation of the shares of a private company may be a more difficult task. The valuation of the shares may be undertaken by a person appointed by the company but here much will depend upon whether the company's articles contain a valuation procedure. Ordinarily, articles that contain a valuation procedure will specify that the valuation should be under-taken by the company's auditor or an appointed accountant (see, e.g. *Dashfield* v. *Davidson (No. 2)* [2008] BCC 662, *Cream Holdings Ltd* v. *Davenport* [2009] BCC 183). In cases where the articles of a company are silent in respect of a valuation procedure or where a constitutional valuation procedure is challenged, the valuation will fall to be determined by the court (see, e.g. *Gillatt* v. *Sky Television Ltd* [2000] 1 All ER 461). A valuation of shares by the court may also be necessary for the purpose of determining a person's liability to capital gains tax or inheritance tax. In the context of a valuation in respect of capital gains tax, see the Taxation of Chargeable Gains Act 1992.

Ordinarily, a court valuation of shares will proceed on the premise of applying an objective test to determine a sale as between a willing but not anxious anonymous vendor and a willing but not anxious purchaser. The vendor is assumed to respond to all reasonable enquiries by the purchaser with such reasonable responses as might reasonably have been made (see, e.g. *IRC* v. *Gray* [1994] STC 360, *Grays Timber Products Ltd* v. *Revenue and Customs Commissioners* [2010] 1 WLR 497). In relation to a valuation of a company's shares, confidential information which is known to the directors of the company will be assumed to be available even if the company's articles prohibit the directors from disclosing it and in such a case it is immaterial whether or not the information would prejudice the company's interests, and whether or not the actual directors would have disclosed it (see generally, *Erdal* v. *HMRC* [2011] UKFTT 87 (TC)).

In relation to the court valuation, the purchaser must be considered to act prudently and reasonably, obtaining all relevant information with reasonable foresight but without the benefit of hindsight. However, the characteristics of any actual potential purchaser may be taken into account to reflect the demand for the 'shares/interest' at the relevant time and as such the purchaser will not always be given the anonymous character so afforded to the vendor. For example, in *Walton* v. *IRC* [1996] STC 68, the Court of Appeal was called upon to value a deceased's interest in an agricultural tenancy. The tenancy was held in partnership as between the deceased and his son (J). The freehold was owned by the deceased, his son (J) and another son (F). The Court of Appeal held that the tenancy should be valued on the basis that the deceased retained his identity as a landlord.

8.5.1 Factors determining share valuation

The crucial factors that will determine any share valuation will be the size of the shareholding and the expected dividend and asset realisation of the shares in question. While the valuation of shares is never an exact science (see, e.g. *Holt* v. *Holt* [1990] 1 WLR 1250, *McArthur's Executors* v. *Revenue and Customs Commissioners* [2008] WTLR 1185), the following guidelines may be tentatively employed.

- Where the block of shares to be valued carries enough votes to enforce a winding up of the company (i.e. 75 per cent or more votes), the most likely method of valuation will be by reference to the value of the company's assets. This method of valuation incorporates a valuation of the net corporate assets of the company. The number of shares to be valued is then represented as a percentage of the value of the total net assets to give the pre-liquidation valuation figure, for example, if 80 out of an issued share capital of 100 shares are to be valued and the company in question has net assets to the value of £10,000, the valuation figure would be £8,000, divided by 80 which would equate to £100 per share. Where the company is to be wound up, a deduction in the valuation figure will be made to take account of the liquidation costs (see, e.g. *M'Connel's Trustees* v. *IRC* 1927 SLT 14).
- The asset valuation method may still be employed where the block of shares to be valued falls below 75 per cent. In such cases, a discount on the asset valuation will be made in accordance with the size of the holding. A majority holding of 50 per cent or more will warrant a discount in the region of 5–10 per cent, whereas a minority holding of, for example, 10 per cent, may warrant a

reduction of between 20 to 50 per cent. The percentage reduction may be greater where the circumstances of a particular case justify the court in imposing a heftier reduction.

- An alternative method for the valuation of shares is one calculated according to the earning capacity of the shares to be valued (i.e. the calculation of the potential dividend entitlement of the shares). In assessing the value of dividends it will be necessary for a court to forecast expected profits. In so determining the potential dividend yield of a share, it is seldom practicable to look more than two to three years ahead. Forecasts that the future profits of a company will be markedly different from recently recorded profits will be treated with caution although such forecasts cannot be completely discounted. Where the expected future profits of a company are minimal or perhaps non-existent, the share valuation will normally be reduced to take account of the relative lack of marketability of the shares. As with the asset valuation method, the smaller the shareholding interest, then the greater the reduction in the share valuation. A reduction in the share valuation may also be appropriate where the shares relate to a family controlled company.

It should be noted that when determining the value of shares in cases under CA 2006, s.994, the court may consider matters other than those outlined above (see **Chapter 19**).

CHAPTER 9

Acquiring and dealing in the shares of a public company

9.1 INTRODUCTION

The purpose of this chapter is to provide a general and introductory overview of the regulation of matters related to an ability to acquire and deal in the shares of a public company. As such this chapter will be concerned primarily with the regulation of offers of shares to the general public by way of a prospectus, the financial assistance rules in respect of the purchase of shares in a public company, insider dealing/market abuse and finally, the regulation of takeovers.

Unlike a private limited company, a public limited company (plc) may trade its securities to the general public and may do so (although the majority do not) by trading in a regulated or an exchange regulated market. Securities include shares and debentures and certificates which represent property rights or contractual rights in shares and debentures. Where securities are traded on the principal UK market for security dealings, namely the London Stock Exchange, a public company's securities may be listed or unlisted. Listed securities are securities which have been admitted to listing on the Main London Stock Exchange (LSE) (the most prestigious trading market). Listed securities are traded in a regulated market. The requirements necessary to the creation and regulation of a regulated market are set out in the EC Directive 2004/39/EC. In accordance with the Financial Services and Markets Act (FSMA) 2000, the listing rules of the UK Listing Authority (UKLA), a branch of the Financial Conduct Authority (FCA), regulate the listing of securities in the UK. This task will be taken over by the Financial Conduct Authority (FCA) following the implementation of the Financial Services Act 2012 (implemented 1 April 2013). The LSE's Admission and Disclosure Standards regulate trading on the Main Market. For a company to gain admission on to the Official List (Main Market) of the Stock Exchange, the company must comply with numerous admission and disclosure requirements (regulation is dominated by necessary compliance with EU directives, for example, the Consolidated Admissions Requirements Directive (2001/34/EC). A company must also issue a prospectus prior to admission on to the Official List (discussed below). Equity shares may be listed as 'standard' or 'premium'. A 'premium' listing requires compliance with additional regulatory requirements. In circumstances where there is a breach of the listing rules, the breach will result in the imposition of an appropriate penalty, to be determined by the FCA (FSMA 2000, s.91).

In relation to unlisted securities, in 1980, the London Stock Exchange created the Unlisted Securities Market (USM) in an attempt to encourage trading in the securities of public companies that were not sufficiently established or willing to offer securities on the listed market. In 1995 the USM was replaced by the 'Alternative Investment Market' (AIM). This market is an exchange regulated market; the regulation of this market is more relaxed and is not dominated by the EU directives deemed applicable to the regulated market, i.e. the Main Market of the London Stock Exchange. The vast majority of public companies that trade securities to the general public do so via admission to the AIM. Unlike securities that are to be listed on a regulated market, unlisted securities admitted to the AIM do not first require the publication of a prospectus, save in circumstances where admission to the AIM also involves an issue of shares to the general public (discussed below).

9.2 AN OFFER (ISSUE) OF SHARES TO THE PUBLIC BY WAY OF A PROSPECTUS

A public company may make an offer of its shares to the general public and will do so by advertising its shares for sale within a prospectus. Contrary to the general law of contract, an advertisement to sell securities to the general public is deemed an offer to sell such securities. Here the regulation and disclosure requirements applicable to public offers (FSMA 2000, ss.72–104) is supplemented and influenced significantly by EU directives (see, e.g. the Prospectus Directive 2003/71/EC as amended by Directive 2010/73/EU). It will be unlawful ordinarily to offer shares to the general public without an approved prospectus being first presented to the general public, i.e., before the offer is made (FSMA, s.85). However, it will be unnecessary to prepare a prospectus in specified circumstances, for example, in the case of offers of securities that are in denominations of at least €100,000, or where the total consideration to be achieved by the offer is less than €5 million over a period of 12 months. The Prospectus Directive deals with initial disclosure requirements in respect of securities to be offered to the public (both listed and unlisted securities). The Directive provides that a prospectus must contain specific obligatory information, the content of which will be dependent on the type of issuer and securities involved. The content of the prospectus must enable an investor to make an informed assessment of the assets and liabilities and general financial status of the issuer. A prospectus of a company offering its shares to the general public must be approved by UKLA (FCA) before it is published. The acceptance of an offer takes place when the company gives notice to the applicant that an allotment of shares has been made.

9.2.1 Misleading statements contained within a prospectus

A person who acquires shares made via a public offer of listed or unlisted securities and suffers loss or damage as a consequence of any untrue or misleading statement or omission contained within the prospectus may pursue a claim for compensation (FSMA 2000, s.90). The claim will be pursued primarily against the issuer or the directors of the issuer. A compensation claim is not restricted to the subscribers of the share issue, namely persons who purchase the securities directly from the issuing company, i.e., there is no requirement that the purchaser of the securities was in a contractual relationship with the issuing company. This extends the scope of the remedy beyond other legislative measures that provide a remedy for false and misleading statements. (See, e.g. the Misrepresentation Act 1967, s.2(1), where the misrepresentation must exist within the context of a contractual relationship.) In seeking to establish liability it is unnecessary to establish that the person acquiring the shares placed any actual reliance on the misstatement or omission. Compensation is payable to any person who suffered damage or loss as a result of acquiring securities that were advertised specifically in the prospectus. Any compensation payable will be calculated on tort principles, namely, by attempting to put the plaintiff back in the position he or she was in prior to the untrue or false statement. The correct value of the shares purchased (had they not been subject to a misrepresentation) will be determined on the date of their acquisition.

However, in valuing shares purchased as a result of a fraudulent misrepresentation, the court may consider events that took place prior to the acquisition of the shares. In *Smith New Court Securities Ltd* v. *Scrimgeour Vickers (Asset Management) Ltd* [1996] 4 All ER 769, the plaintiff (S) purchased shares in Ferranti International Signal plc through the defendant (V) who sold the shares as an agent for Citibank NA (C). Shortly after the sale, the price of Ferranti shares fell dramatically. S subsequently sold the shares at a loss of over £11 million. S claimed damages from V and C on the basis that S had been induced to purchase the shares as a consequence of a fraudulent misstatement, i.e., S had been falsely informed by a director of V (acting for C) that two other reputable bidders were willing to purchase the shares. At first instance ([1992] BCLC 1104), Chadwick J held that the fraud had the effect of creating a false market in the shares. In determining the true market value of the shares, the learned judge considered that events prior to the acquisition were relevant to the calculation of the value of the shares, namely that the price of Ferranti shares at the time of S's acquisition had been inflated by a fraudulently misleading preliminary announcement of Ferranti's end of year profits. The consequences attached to the fraudulent announcement, a reduction in the price of a Ferranti share, only became apparent after S's acquisition of the Ferranti shares. The shares, which had been purchased by S at a price of 82.25p per share, had an apparent market value of 78p at the date of their acquisition, albeit taking account of the fraudulent announcement of Ferranti's end of year profits, the true market value would have only been 44p per share. Accordingly, S was awarded damages of 38.25p per share. Although the Court of Appeal ([1994] BCLC 212) agreed that S's claim for damages should be upheld following the fraudulent misrepresentation relating to the 'supposed' additional bidders of the shares, the court strongly disapproved of the valuation method employed by Chadwick J. The Court of Appeal refused to accept that in the valuation process it was correct to consider events (the fraudulent announcement of Ferranti's end of year profits) that were unknown to both parties at the time of the transaction. Accordingly, the Court of Appeal valued the shares in accordance with the ascertainable market value of the shares at the time of the sale. As a result, the amount of damages payable to S was reduced from 38.25p per share to 4.25p per share. In reversing the decision of the Court of Appeal, the House of Lords concluded that in valuing the shares, damages in the tort of deceit could be calculated on the basis of an assessment of any consequential loss suffered by S as a result of acquiring the Ferranti shares. Accordingly, the valuation could take account of the value of the Ferranti shares prior to the inflationary effect on that value that had been caused by the fraudulent announcement of Ferranti's end of year profits. In effect, the House concluded that it was possible to assess the loss flowing directly from the transaction without any reference to the date of the actual transaction. The level of damages that were awarded in favour of S was restored to the level provided at first instance.

9.2.2 Damages in relation to a non-contractual representation

In circumstances where a purchaser is induced by a misleading statement contained in a prospectus to acquire securities in a company but securities other than those that were actually offered in the prospectus, the purchaser will be unable to claim a statutory remedy against the company or its directors. However, a purchaser may be able to obtain a remedy for the misstatement in two distinct situations. First, where it is possible to establish an action in the tort of deceit, namely the purchaser must prove that, as a direct result and reliance on a fraudulent misstatement, he or she was induced to purchase the shares. Any compensation payable will be calculated on tort principles, namely, by attempting to put the plaintiff back in the position he or she was in prior to the untrue or false statement. On this basis, the correct value of the shares purchased (had they not been subject to a fraudulent misstatement) will be determined on the date of their acquisition (however, note the position in *Smith New Court Securities Ltd* v. *Scrimgeour Vickers (Asset Management) Ltd* [1996] 4 All ER 769, discussed above).

Second, the purchaser may be able to commence a common law action for negligent misstatement. Here it must be established that the seller of the securities owed the purchaser a duty of care. In *Hedley Byrne Ltd* v. *Heller Ltd* [1964] AC 465, the House of Lords established that a duty of care would arise in a situation where there was a 'special relationship' between the parties, evidenced by the representee's reasonable reliance upon the misstatement and the fact there was a sufficient degree of proximity between the parties. The potential scope of the proximity test was reviewed subsequently by the House of Lords in *Caparo Industries plc* v. *Dickman* [1990] 2 AC 605. Here, Lord Oliver defined the proximity test:

What can be deduced from the *Hedley Byrne* case, therefore, is that the necessary relationship between the maker of a statement or giver of advice ('the adviser') and the recipient who acts in reliance upon it ('the advisee') may typically be held to exist where (1) the advice is required for a purpose, whether particularly specified or generally described, which is made known, either actually or inferentially, to the adviser at the time when the advice is given; (2) the adviser knows, either actually or inferentially, that his advice will be communicated to the advisee, either specifically or as a member of an ascertainable class, in order that it should be used by the advisee for that purpose; (3) it is known either actually or inferentially, that the advice so communicated is likely to be acted upon by the advisee for that purpose without independent inquiry, and (4) it is so acted upon by the advisee to his detriment. That is not, of course, to suggest that these conditions are either conclusive or exclusive. (at p.638)

This definition of the proximity test may place an onerous burden on the representee in respect of establishing a negligent misstatement. For the purpose of satisfying the proximity test, a representee's detrimental reliance on a misstatement will only be justified where the representee relied upon the misstatement for a purpose that would have been ascertainable and within the representor's reasonable contemplation at the time the misstatement was made. Further, the representor must have been aware that the misstatement would be relied upon by the representee in the manner in which it was then subsequently relied upon. Indeed, in *Al Nakib Investments (Jersey) Ltd* v. *Longcroft* [1990] 1 WLR 1390, it was held that while the directors of a company owed a duty of care to persons who subscribed for shares in reliance on the contents of a specific prospectus, no such duty would be owed to a person who subsequently purchased the company's shares on the open market, irrespective of the fact that the purchase was made in reliance on the strength and contents of that prospectus. In applying the test advanced in *Caparo Industries plc* v. *Dickman* to the facts of the *Al Nakib* case, Mervyn Davies J concluded that a duty of care could not be attached to a statement that had been made for a particular purpose (the offer of shares in a prospectus) in circumstances where the statement was then used for another purpose (the purchase of shares on the open market). (Also see, *Galoo Ltd and Ors* v. *Bright Grahame Murray* [1994] BCC 319 and *Bank of Credit and Commerce International (Overseas) Ltd (in liq) and Ors* v. *Price Waterhouse and Anor* [1998] BCC 617.) However, a more liberal interpretation of the principles derived from *Caparo Industries plc* v. *Dickman* may be implied from the judgment of Lightman J in *Possfund Custodian Trustee* v. *Diamond* [1996] 2 All ER 774. Here, Lightman J opined that a prospectus could have an implied purpose of seeking to encourage the purchase of shares in the market (in addition to its principal purpose of inviting shares in accordance with the terms of the prospectus) and that that implied purpose could be of a sufficient character to establish a duty of care.

9.2.3 Rescission

Where a person acquires securities in reliance on a fraudulent, negligent or innocent misrepresentation (an omission may also be classed as a misrepresentation) proceedings may be taken to rescind the contract. A person may exercise a right of rescission against the company issuing the securities only where the company allotted the securities in question. In other cases, the right to rescind may be exercised against the offeror of the securities. Following a successful rescission, the purchase price of the securities (plus any interest payable) will be returned to the offeree. A person's right to rescind the contract may be lost where:

(i)   after becoming aware of the misrepresentation, the offeree acted in a manner to affirm the contract;

(ii)   there was an unreasonable delay on the part of the offeree in seeking to rescind the contract; or

(iii) the issuing company is in liquidation.

9.3 FINANCIAL ASSISTANCE FOR THE PURCHASE OF A COMPANY'S SHARES

9.3.1 Financial assistance (defined)

The purpose of the financial assistance rules is to protect the creditors and share-holders of a company from any potential financial abuses in respect of the company's role and assistance in a third party's acquisition of the company shares. As a consequence of CA 2006, the financial assistance rules apply to public companies and do not generally apply to the acquisition of shares in private companies (this was not the position prior to CA 2006). The definition and prohibition of financial assistance so provided by CA 2006, s.677 is wide-ranging and covers any type of financial assistance advanced by a company for the purpose of assisting the acquisition of its shares where the effect of the assistance is to reduce the company's net assets by a material extent. Financial assistance also covers a situation where the assistance reduces or discharges a third party's liabilities that were incurred as a result of the acquisition of the company's shares. For the purpose of the rules which prohibit the giving of financial assistance, financial assistance may be given at a date well in advance of the share acquisition, providing that when given, the share acquisition was in the contemplation of the company. Frequently, a breach of the financial assistance rules will also give rise to a breach of a director's fiduciary duty. (Directors' duties are discussed in **Chapter 15**.) However, it should be stressed that liability under CA 2006, s.677 is not dependent on establishing a breach of fiduciary duty and a director may be held liable under the provision notwithstanding the absence of any such breach (see, e.g. the decision of the Court of Appeal in *Chaston* v. *SWP Group plc* [2003] BCLC 675 – discussed further below).

CA 2006, s.677 defines financial assistance as:

(a)   financial assistance given by way of gift,

(b)   financial assistance given–

     (i)   by way of guarantee, security or indemnity (other than an indemnity in respect of the indemnifier's own neglect or default), or

     (ii)   by way of release or waiver,

(c)   financial assistance given–

(i)   by way of a loan or any other agreement under which any of the obligations of the person giving the assistance are to be fulfilled at a time when in accordance with the agreement any obligation of another party to the agreement remains unfulfilled, or

(ii)   by way of the novation of, or the assignment (in Scotland, assignation) of rights arising under, a loan or such other agreement, or

(d)   any other financial assistance given by a company where–

(i)   the net assets of the company are reduced to a material extent by the giving of the assistance, or

(ii)   the company has no net assets.

(2)   'Net assets' here means the aggregate amount of the company's assets less the aggregate amount of its liabilities.

(3)   For this purpose a company's liabilities include–

(a)   where the company draws up Companies Act individual accounts, any provision of a kind specified for the purposes of this subsection by regulations under section 396, and

(b)   where the company draws up IAS individual accounts, any provision made in those accounts.

Therefore, the definition of financial assistance is not, for example, restricted to the obvious (i.e. loans granted to aid a purchase of shares). Accordingly, financial assistance may be by way of gift, guarantee, security or indemnity, release or waiver, loan or any other agreement (see, e.g. *Belmont Finance Corporation* v. *Williams Furniture Ltd (No.2)* [1980] 1 All ER 393, *Charterhouse Investment Trust Ltd* v. *Tempest Diesels Ltd* [1985] 1 BCC 99, 544, *Barclays Bank plc* v. *British & Commonwealth Holdings plc* [1996] 1 BCLC 1 and *MacPherson and Anor* v. *European Strategic Bureau Ltd* [2002] BCC 39).

What may be described as a far-ranging definition of financial assistance may give rise to uncertainty and have a potential to catch innocent transactions. Therefore, where a transaction is alleged to amount to financial assistance the court must examine the commercial realities of the transaction and in doing so reflect on the penal effect (discussed below) of the statute (see the decision of the Court of Appeal in *Anglo Petroleum Ltd* v. *TFB (Mortgages) Ltd* [2008] 1 BCLC 185).

9.3.2   Rules only applicable where alleged financial assistance is related specifically to a share acquisition

The financial assistance rules are only applicable where the alleged financial assistance is related specifically to a share acquisition. For example, in *Dyment* v. *Boyden and Ors* [2005] BCC 79, the alleged financial assistance consisted of the company's payment of an excessive rent for property that it had leased. It was alleged that the excessive rent had been paid to facilitate the purchase of the company's shares by the owners of the leased property. The Court of Appeal held that the leasing agreement (incorporating the high rent payment) could not be described as the giving of any financial assistance in so far as the owners of the premises leased by the company were in a 'market position' to demand a high rent. Further, the actual share acquisition in question had taken place at a time prior to the company's decision to commit itself to the lease agreement.

Likewise, in *MT Realisations Ltd (in liq)* v. *Digital Equipment Co Ltd* [2003] 2 BCLC 117, the Court of Appeal could find no breach of the financial assistance rules. Here, the claimant company M, had been insolvent owing £8 million to its holding company (D). T agreed to purchase M for £1 and pay £6.5 million for an assignment of the sum owed by M to D. A loan agreement between T and D was entered into in relation to the repayment of the £6.5 million. T had difficulty in meeting the payments and a further agreement (the second agreement) was entered into, whereby until such time as the sum of £6.5 million was repaid, any monies owing to M from business transactions between M and D and between M and any of D's subsidiaries, would be retained by D, those sums to be set off against the debt of £6.5 million. In total, under this agreement, approximately £2 million was retained by D and set off against the sum of £6.5 million. The outstanding amount of the loan was subsequently repaid by T one year after the second agreement between T and D (in respect of the loan there is no mention in the law report of any interest charges having been imposed). M subsequently went into liquidation; the liquidator claimed that the set-off agreement between T and D was, in effect, a breach by M of CA 1985, s.151 (now CA 2006, s.677) (i.e., the set-off agreement equated to financial assistance in respect of T's acquisition of M). The Court of Appeal held that having regard to the commercial realities of the agreement, there was no breach of the provision because there had never been any financial assistance. Nothing had been given by M to T which T had not already acquired as its own (i.e. prior to entering into the set-off agreement with D, T had acquired the right to M's assets, to enforce debts owing to M, which could in turn could be used to repay D). T's agreement with D had nothing to do with the purchase of M's shares.

However, it is submitted that despite the apparent logic of the decision, the outcome appears questionable as a matter of commercial reality. The set-off agreement between D and T had never been contemplated, other than after the purchase of M's shares. Further, T incurred a liability (the debt of £6.5 million) as a direct result of the share acquisition in the knowledge that the repayment of the debt was a condition that had been attached to the share purchase. The liability was incurred as part and parcel of and was related to the acquisition of the shares. Therefore, in relation to this liability was there not financial assistance via the terms of the second agreement, that is, an extended repayment period, one possibly devoid of any interest charges?

9.3.3 Prohibition against financial assistance – private and public companies

Private companies

Prior to the passing of CA 2006, CA 1985, s.151 generally prohibited (but with exemptions for private companies: see CA 1985, ss.153–158) both private and public companies from giving financial assistance (whether directly or indirectly: see CA 1985, s.152) to aid a person's acquisition of shares in a company or the company's subsidiary. An act contrary to the general prohibition (subject to the exemptions) was also a criminal offence. Following CA 2006, the general rule prohibiting a private company from providing financial assistance for the acquisition of its own shares is no more.

Public companies

As a general rule, a public company (or any of its subsidiaries to include private companies) is precluded from giving financial assistance to a person who is acquiring, proposing to acquire or who has acquired shares in the company or its holding company (CA 2006, s.678). Likewise, the prohibited assistance applies where a public company provides financial assistance to any person for the purpose of acquiring shares in a private company which operates as the holding company of the said public company (CA 2006, s.679).

However, financial assistance may be given for the purchase of shares in a public company if the company's principal purpose in giving the assistance was not driven by a specific desire to facilitate the acquisition of the company's shares or the giving of assistance was but an incidental part of some larger purpose, the assistance having been given in good faith and in the interests of the company (CA 2006, s.678(2)) (discussed below). Further, in accordance with s.678(4), financial assistance may be given (providing it is given in good faith and in the interests of the company) where the company's principal purpose in giving the assistance is not to reduce or discharge any liability incurred by a person for the purpose of acquiring shares in the company or its holding company, or the reduction or discharge of any such liability was but an incidental part of some larger purpose of the company.

CA 2006, s.681 provides additional exceptions to ss.678–679, namely specific transactions that are not prohibited; these include a lawful divided payment, an allotment of bonus shares and a reduction of capital in accordance with CA 2006. CA 2006, s.682 provides further conditional exceptions that operate providing the company's net assets are not reduced as a result of assistance being given, or to the extent that those assets are reduced, the assistance provided is taken from distributable profits. However, the assistance is only permitted in relation to specific types of transaction. Examples of such transactions include financial assistance in the form of loans where the lending of money is a part of the company's usual business activities and financial assistance for the purchase of the company's shares in respect of an employee share scheme.

9.3.4 The larger purpose exception

Following the decision of the House of Lords in *Brady* v. *Brady* [1989] AC 755, the term 'larger purpose' is not to be construed liberally and is certainly not to be viewed as a 'blank cheque'. The *Brady* case concerned a family-run business carried on by two brothers (J and B). The business had operated successfully as a private limited company (Brady) since 1959; it was also composed of a number of subsidiary companies. J and B were the sole directors of Brady; the company's issued share capital was split between B, who held 46.68 per cent and J, who held 46.66 per cent of the issued share capital. The remaining 6.66 per cent of the issued share capital was held by X Ltd, a private company. Up until 1982 the Brady group flourished, but in that year the group encountered trading difficulties. The group's difficulties were largely expounded by a management deadlock between J and B.

In an attempt to resolve the management deadlock, an agreement was reached whereby the assets of the group would be split between the two brothers. It was decided that the assets would be split without liquidating Brady Ltd. In order to facilitate the reorganisation, the business interests of the group were to be merged and eventually split in equal proportions: between two new companies, M Ltd, which was to be controlled by J, and A Ltd, controlled by B. The reorganisation was planned to take place via the transfer of the assets of Brady Ltd to M Ltd; M Ltd would then issue loan stock to A Ltd, i.e. representing an equal share of the group's assets. The loan stock was to be redeemed by the subsequent transfer of assets from M Ltd to A Ltd. However, before the scheme was completed, B became dissatisfied with the proposed division of assets and as a result refused to abide by the terms of the agreement. As a consequence of B's refusal, J sought an order for specific performance. B claimed (among other matters) that the transfer of assets from Brady to M Ltd, assets that would be used to discharge M Ltd's debt to A Ltd (the redemption of its loan stock) constituted an illegal transaction.

B's assertion that the transaction was illegal rested in part on the premise that Brady Ltd would be providing financial assistance to M Ltd to reduce M Ltd's liability in respect of the acquisition of Brady shares. However, J contended that the transaction was within the ambit of the exception. At first instance, the court found in favour of J and ordered specific performance. However, the Court of Appeal disagreed ([1988] BCLC 20) (Croom-Johnson LJ dissenting). The majority of the Court of Appeal concluded that any financial assistance to M Ltd would not have been in good faith or for the benefit of Brady Ltd because the assistance comprised a gratuitous disposition. On appeal to the House of Lords, the House overturned the Court of Appeal's findings on the 'good faith' point. Lord Oliver, expressing the unanimous opinion of the House opined:

In the circumstances of this case, where failure to implement the final stage of the scheme for the division of the two sides of Brady's business is likely to lead back to the very management deadlock that it was designed to avoid and the probable liquidation of Brady as a result, the proposed transfer is not only something which is properly capable of being perceived by Brady's directors as calculated to advance Brady's corporate and commercial interests and the interests of its employees but is indeed, viewed objectively, in the company's interest. (at pp.777–778)

However, with a 'sting in the tail' the House of Lords (contrary to the findings of both the High Court and Court of Appeal) took the view that Brady's principal purpose in giving financial assistance to M Ltd was not an incidental part of some larger purpose. Lord Oliver feared that the term 'larger purpose', if it was to be construed in a liberal fashion, could be viewed as a 'blank cheque' for the purpose of avoiding the financial assistance rules. Lord Oliver stated:

The purpose and the only purpose of the financial assistance is and remains that of enabling the shares to be acquired, and the financial or commercial advantages flowing from the acquisition, whilst they may form the reason for forming the purpose of providing assistance, are a by-product of it rather than an independent purpose of which the assistance can properly be considered to be an incident. (at p.780)

Accordingly, Lord Oliver viewed the assistance given to M Ltd by Brady Ltd as devoid of a 'larger purpose'. Here it is suggested that Lord Oliver's restrictive interpretation went too far because in *Brady* surely the principal purpose of the assistance was to facilitate the reorganisation of the group (indeed, see the comments of Croom-Johnson LJ, [1988] BCLC 20 at 32). However, while the motive in providing financial assistance was to facilitate a necessary reorganisation of the companies involved, Lord Oliver considered the actual purpose for providing the financial assistance was to enable the acquisition of the company's shares. In *Brady*, although the financial assistance would have been devoid of any meaningful reason had it not been used to facilitate the reorganisation of the companies, the 'meaningful reason' was ignored in the interpretation of the concept of a 'larger purpose'. Basically, the House of Lords sought to distinguish the 'reason' behind the acquisition (i.e. the reorganisation of the companies) from the 'purpose' of the financial assistance, i.e. the acquisition of the shares.

In *Chaston* v. *SWP Group plc* [2003] BCLC 675, the Court of Appeal revisited the decision in *Brady*. In *Chaston*, shares in company X were purchased by A. However, fees incurred by A as a consequence of instructing accountants to prepare a report into the affairs of X were paid for by B. B was the director of a subsidiary of X. The Court of Appeal held that although B's assistance was given in good faith and was given for the ultimate benefit of X, causing the company no detriment, nevertheless it was of a character that constituted financial assistance. The instructions to the accountants had been directly connected with the negotiations for the sale of X's shares. Further, the breach of financial assistance rules (then CA 1985, s.151) could not be excused on the basis that the assistance was given in advance of and not in the actual course of the share acquisition or that the payment of the fees had no impact on the share price. Adopting a 'commercial realities of the transaction' approach, expounded by Hoffmann J in *Charterhouse Investment Trust Ltd* v. *Tempest Diesels Ltd* [1986] BCLC 1 (at pp.10–11), Arden LJ opined:

> As a matter of commercial reality, the fees in question smoothed the path to the acquisition of shares. (at p.688)

The assistance clearly facilitated the share purchase and there was no 'larger purpose' to save the transaction. The approach taken by Lord Oliver in *Brady*, namely, distinguishing between 'reason' and 'purpose' was applied. Here, the reason for the financial assistance may have been to benefit X, but the purpose of the transaction was the acquisition of X's shares. In respect of the transaction, there was no other larger purpose.

9.3.5 Contravention of rules is a criminal offence

If a public company contravenes the financial assistance rules, the company and every officer of the company who is in default commits an offence (CA 2006, s.680). A person guilty of an offence is liable on conviction on indictment, to imprisonment for a term not exceeding two years or a fine (or both) and on summary conviction to imprisonment for a term not exceeding 12 months or to a fine not exceeding the statutory maximum (or both).

9.4 INSIDER DEALING AND MARKET ABUSE

9.4.1 Insider dealing

As a matter of public interest and in an attempt to protect the confidence of investors in respect of dealings on the security markets, insider dealing in securities is an offence regulated under the Criminal Justice Act (CJA) 1993, s.52 (implementing EC Directive (89/592/EC)). The offence is punishable by imprisonment of up to a maximum of seven years and/or a fine (for sentencing guidelines, see *R* v. *McQuoid* [2009] 4 All ER 388). Prosecutions for insider dealing are difficult to establish and to this end successful prosecutions are rare. The primary offence (s.52(1)) is committed where an individual (this does not cover a corporate entity) who has information as an insider, deals in securities that are price-affected by the 'inside' information. The 'insider' must deal on a recognised and regulated market, for example a market regulated by the London Stock Exchange (this would include the Main Market and the AIM of the London Stock Exchange) or act as a professional intermediary, or act in reliance on a professional intermediary in the case of an off market transaction (CJA 1993, s.59). CJA 1993 also applies to securities other than those listed or admitted to any investment exchange within the EU. However, an offence under CJA 1993 may only be committed where the insider acted within the

UK at the time of dealing or alternatively the dealing (which could have been instigated from outside the UK) took place on a UK market.

In attempting to establish an offence of insider dealing, the prosecution have the arduous task of proving (beyond a reasonable doubt) all the elements of the offence. In seeking to establish the elements of the offence, it is necessary to look at relevant securities defined by CJA 1993, Sched.2 to include shares, warrants and debt securities. An individual deals in securities where in accordance with CJA 1993, s.55, he or she acquires or disposes of securities, or where he or she procures an acquisition or disposal of securities by another person (this would include a corporate entity). CJA 1993, s.55 extends to cover cases in which the 'insider' arranges for a nominee or an agent to acquire or dispose of the securities.

The relevant information must be insider information, namely, information which has not been made public (i.e. information not readily available to potential investors) and information concerned specifically with particular securities or a particular issuer and which would be likely to affect significantly the prices of the securities if it was published (CJA 1993, s.56). The relevant information which may be specifically about the company in question or, for example, related to the company's business prospects, must be dealt with by an 'insider', i.e. a person is in possession of insider information only if he or she knows it to be inside information and knows that he or she has acquired it from an inside source (this constitutes the *mens rea* of the offence). An insider must be an individual who obtains insider information through being a director, employee or shareholder of the issuing company or an individual who must have access to that information by virtue of his employment, office or profession; albeit not necessarily as a result of being connected to the issuer (s.57(2)(a)). Alternatively, CJA 1993, s.57(2)(b) provides that an insider may be an individual who knowingly obtained information from any person subject to the s.57(2)(a) definition. The securities must be price-affected, i.e. on publication it is to be expected that the insider information would have a significant effect on the prices or values of the relevant securities (s.56(2)–(3)).

CJA 1993 creates two further sub-offences of insider dealing, namely:

(i)   encouraging another person to deal in securities on the basis of the inside information (s.52(2)(a)); and

(ii)   improperly disclosing insider information to any other person (s.52(2)(b)).

Under s.52(2)(a), an individual, as an insider, will be guilty of the offence if he or she encourages (no actual dealing or disclosure of insider information is required) any other person to deal in the relevant securities. Under s.52(2)(b), an individual, as an insider, will be guilty of this offence where the insider information is disclosed to anyone who had no right to receive it. However, as a defence, s.53(3)(a) provides that the defendant may establish that he/she had no expectation that any person to whom the information was disclosed would actually deal in the securities as a result of his or her disclosure.

9.4.2   General defences to insider dealing

The burden of establishing a defence to any of the insider dealing offences rests with the accused. The accused must establish a defence on the balance of probabilities. Although more specific related defences may apply, three general (but rather vague) defences are set out in CJA 1993, s.53. First, an individual may establish that he or she would have acted as he or she so acted (irrespective of the fact that the act in question constituted an offence) even if he or she had not been in possession of price sensitive information. Second, the individual in question must have had no expectation that the insider dealing would profit him or her. Third, the individual in question must have had reasonable grounds to believe that the information was no longer price sensitive information, i.e. the information had already been disclosed sufficiently (although not necessarily to the general public).

9.4.3   Market abuse

Market abuse may be defined tentatively as conduct which is prejudicial to the public interest and of a type which distorts and undermines the UK financial markets and/or adversely affects the interests of ordinary investors in the market. Market abuse carries both criminal law and/or civil law sanctions.

Criminal law sanctions

Other than where an individual's conduct is caught by the insider dealing offences (see above) market abuse may be made subject to criminal law sanctions in two distinct situations. First, FSMA 2000, s.397(1) prohibits the making of misleading/false statements, forecasts or promises that have a specific objective of inducing investment activity. The offence carries a maximum penalty of seven years' imprisonment and/or a fine. The *mens rea* for this offence requires either knowledge that the statement is misleading/false, or recklessness as to whether it is misleading/false. Further, there must have been an objective of inducing, or being reckless as to the possibility of inducing, any person who relies on the misstatement to enter into an investment agreement or to enter or decline to pursue an opportunity specific to an existing investment.

The second offence is contained in FSMA 2000, s.397(3). This provision prohibits an act or course of conduct which sets out to create a misleading impression of the market or price/value of an investment and which induced a person to acquire, dispose or retain an investment or to exercise (or not) rights related to the investment. In relation to the *mens rea* of the offence, it is sufficient to establish that the accused's purpose in so acting was to create a misleading impression. The offence carries a maximum penalty of seven years' imprisonment and/or a fine. It is a general defence for the accused to establish that he reasonably believed that the impression he or she created was not misleading.

9.4.4 Civil law regulation of market abuse

In addition to the criminal law offences of insider dealing/market abuse (see above) FSMA 2000, s.118 (the original s.118 was redrafted by the Financial Services and Markets Act 2000 (Market Abuse) Regulations 2005, SI 2005/381) contains civil law procedures to combat insider dealing and other forms of market abuse (see e.g., *Massey* v. *Financial Services Authority* [2011] UKUT 49 (TCC)). The provision applies to prescribed markets. A prescribed market includes any market operated by a body recognised by the FCA. Therefore, both the Main Market and the AIM of the London Stock Exchange are covered under the provision. Although the civil law procedures are of a quasi-criminal law nature, a person's liability is established by applying the less arduous balance of probabilities test. Further, as a genus, the civil law procedures do not incorporate a *mens rea* requirement. For example, under the civil law procedure, liability for insider dealing may be established where a person deals with insider information notwithstanding that he or she is unaware of his or her 'insider' status and/or that the information is insider information. Here, by way of a defence, a person may establish that he or she had reasonable grounds to believe that the dealing was not prohibited or that he or she had taken all reasonable precautions and steps to avoid the prohibition. A contravention of the civil law provisions will result in a financial penalty of an amount determined by the FCA (FSMA, s.123(1)). Section 118 requires a territorial connection between the alleged misconduct and the UK or its markets before any prohibitions or sanctions will apply.

In summary, FSMA 2000, s.118 defines market abuse as either:

- an insider, dealing or attempting to deal on the basis of inside information;
- an insider's disclosure of inside information to another person, other than in the proper course of a person's employment, profession or duties;
- the misuse of information not generally available to the markets that by its nature would influence an investor's decision about the terms on which to deal;
- trading, or placing orders to trade, that give a misleading impression of the supply of, or demand for, one or more investments, so affecting the price of the investment to an abnormal or artificial level;
- trading, or placing orders to trade which employed fictitious devices or deceptions;
- providing misleading or false information about an investment or the issuer of an investment knowing the information to be false or misleading; or
- misleading behaviour of a type that is related to either the supply of, or demand for, an investment, or behaviour that would otherwise distort the market in an investment.

In respect of the above list, 'inside information' may be broadly defined in accordance with FSMA 2000, s.118C as comprising precise information which is price sensitive, information that is not generally available, but if available, would have been used by a reasonable investor in reaching investment decisions. Here, a qualifying investment will include shares and other transferable securities. The FSMA 2000, s.118B defines an 'insider' as any person in possession of inside information as a result of:

- their membership of the administrative, management or supervisory body of an issuer of qualifying investments;
- holding capital of an issuer of prescribed investments;
- having access to the information through their employment, profession or duties;
- criminal activities; or
- information obtained by any other means which they would be reasonably expected to know is inside information.

Further, the Code of Market Conduct provides that 'behaviour' may be market abuse where it falls below the standards expected by the 'regular user', namely a reasonable person who deals regularly and understands the workings of the relevant market.

9.5 INVESTIGATIONS AND RESTRICTIONS APPLIED TO SHARE OWNERSHIP IN PUBLIC COMPANIES

CA 1985, s.442 (as amended by CA 1989, s.62) (note that the CA 1985 provisions mentioned here are not consolidated into CA 2006) permits the Secretary of State to appoint inspectors to investigate the share ownership of a public company. Although information relating to share ownership may be obtained ordinarily from a company's share register, a registered shareholder may act as a nominee for a beneficial owner (the true owner). An investigation into the share ownership of a company may be necessary to protect the public interest or to safeguard the interests of a group of existing shareholders in the company (especially in the context of a potential takeover bid – discussed below). Here inspectors must be appointed if an application is made by 200 or more members, or by members holding 10 per cent or more of the company's issued shares, other than where the Secretary of State considers the application vexatious or considers that the alternative and less intrusive type of action under CA 1985, s.444(1) is more appropriate. Section s.444(1) provides that the Secretary of State may require, of any person, information relating to the ownership of shares.

As a result of enquiries undertaken in accordance with CA 1985, s.444 or an investigation under CA 1985, s.442, where necessary, the Secretary of State may impose restrictions on the rights attached to specified shares. The Secretary of State's powers to make such orders are determined in accordance with CA 1985, s.454. Such an order may:

- prevent the shares from being transferred;
- restrain the votes attached to the affected shares from being exercised;

- suspend rights of pre-emption attached to the affected shares; and
- prevent dividends from being paid and capital (except where the company is in liquidation) from being returned to the holders of the shares.

A breach of such an order constitutes a criminal offence (CA 1985, s.455).

It should also be noted that a public company may seek information as to whether at any time within the last three years a person had (or still has) an interest in its voting shares (CA 2006, s.793) (see generally, e.g. *Re Lonrho plc (No.3)* [1989] BCLC 480). Members of the company holding 10 per cent of the company's issued capital (voting shares) may compel the company to so act. Where a person fails to provide the requested information, the company may apply to the court for an order directing that the shares in question be made subject to restrictions. The restrictions are specified by CA 2006, s.797 and are a copy of those provided by CA 1985, s.454 (discussed above). A report must be compiled of the information gleaned from any investigation flowing from a request for information. In accordance with CA 2006, s.805, the report must be made available to the members of the company.

9.5.1 The disclosure directive

In circumstances where a person acquires 3 per cent of the total voting rights in a public company and the company trades in a prescribed market, namely any market operated by a Recognised Investment Exchange (this covers the Main Market and the AIM of the Stock Exchange) a disclosure of that shareholding interest must be made public by the end of the second trading day following the day the obligation to disclosure arose. A further disclosure must also be made every time an additional acquisition (or reduction) of voting rights equates to a 1 per cent increase (or decrease) in an existing holding which is at or above the 3 per cent level. The disclosure requirement is prescribed by the EC Transparency Directive (2004/109/EC), which was implemented into UK law in January 2007 by FSMA 2000, ss.89A–89G. This disclosure requirement is regulated by FCA rules.

9.6 TAKEOVERS

A takeover occurs in a situation where a company (the offeror) successfully bids for shares in another company (the target company, the offeree) and by doing so acquires control of that company. The target company continues in existence as a subsidiary of the offeror company. In a technical sense, a takeover may be contrasted with a merger (albeit a form of takeover) in that a merger relates to business operations of at least two companies being consolidated into a single company. All forms of takeover are regulated by the Takeover Code. Unless specifically provided for by the terms of the Takeover Code, the consideration for the offer of the target company's shares may be made in cash or as an offer of shares in the offeror company or a combination of both of these forms of consideration. A takeover may be agreed to by the management of the companies concerned (friendly approach) or alternatively it may be as a result of a hostile approach (without the approval of the board of the target company). Where the takeover is not in the hostile form, the takeover may proceed by way of a scheme of arrangement (discussed below).

9.6.1 The regulation of takeovers

In the UK, takeovers are regulated by the Takeover Code and the Companies Act 2006 (Parts 26–28). The UK regulation (see CA 2006, Part 28) complies with the terms of the EC Takeover Directive (2004/25/EC). The Takeover Code (available at **www.thetakeoverpanel.org.uk/the-code**) is overseen by an independent body – the Takeover Panel (the panel members of which are ordinarily made up from the financial/accounting/insurance services sector). In accordance with CA 2006, s.943, the Panel (Code Committee of the Panel) is afforded the power to determine, review and when necessary amend the rules governing the conduct of takeovers. In relation to the day-to-day conduct of takeovers, the decision-making role of the Panel is undertaken by the executive of the Panel. The executive provides rulings and guidance in relation to the interpretation of the rules of the Code and in matters related to the conduct of a takeover; those rulings and guidance may be subject to the review of the Hearings Committee (a committee of the Takeover Panel). Appeals from the Hearings Committee may be made to the Takeover Appeal Board (an independent body which will include members with judicial experience). In exceptional circumstances, decisions of the Panel may, as a matter of last resort, also be made subject to judicial review (see, e.g. *R* v. *Panel on Takeovers and Mergers, ex parte Datafin* [1987] 1 All ER 564). However, here it should be emphasised that the Panel is not concerned with the commercial merits or otherwise of a takeover but rather its concern is centred on the proper application of procedures, rules and practices that are to be adopted in a takeover situation. The Code which is updated regularly (since its introduction in 1968) is (in accordance with the Takeover Directive) afforded a statutory basis (see CA 2006, s.942) and applies ordinarily to takeover offers in respect of a public company (the target company) in which securities are traded on a regulated market in the UK, or stock exchange in the Channel islands or the Isle of Man. The Code is also applicable to any other company (for example a company traded on the AIM) which is considered to have its place of central management and control located in the UK. However, it should be noted that the Code will not apply to a company that does not have a registered office in the UK, Channel Islands or the Isle of Man. The Code (in part) may apply in the case of a shared jurisdiction. The Code will become operative when the board of directors of the target company has reason to believe that a *bona fide* takeover offer is imminent.

The Code purports to apply appropriate business standards to the objective of achieving fairness, primarily for the protection of the target company's shareholders. The current Code (2011) is based upon six General Principles around broad and perceived acceptable standards of commercial behaviour. In addition to the General

Principles, the Code contains 38 rules. The interpretation of the rules is made subject to an objective of achieving the underlying purpose of the specific rule in question. In addition to adhering to the terms of the Code and relevant provisions of CA 2006 and insider dealing/market abuse legislation (i.e. in the context of share dealings and transactions) listed companies must, in the context of takeovers, and where relevant, comply with the provisions of the Listing Rules and the disclosure, transparency and prospectus rules of the FCA. The Principles of the Code are as follows:

1. All holders of the securities of a target company of the same class must be afforded equivalent treatment; moreover, if a person acquires control of a company, the other holders of securities must be protected.
2. The holders of the securities of a target company must have sufficient time and information to enable them to reach a properly informed decision on the bid; where the board of the target company advises the holders of the target company's securities it must give its views on the effects of the implementation of the bid on matters related to the employment of staff, conditions of employment and the location of the company's places of business.
3. The board of a target company must act in the interests of the company as a whole and must not deny the holders of its securities the opportunity to decide on the merits of the bid.
4. False markets must not be created in the securities of the target company, of the offeror company or of any other company concerned by the bid in such a way that the rise or fall of the prices of the securities becomes artificial and the normal functioning of the markets is distorted.
5. An offeror must announce a bid only after ensuring that it can fulfil in full any cash consideration, if such is offered, and after taking all reasonable measures to secure the implementation of any other type of consideration.
6. A target company must not be hindered in the conduct of its affairs for longer than is reasonable where there is a bid for its securities.

The rules of the Code incorporate the following objectives.

9.6.2 The nature and consequences of a voluntary offer

The operation of the Code will be activated in circumstances where the offeror or target company announces the likelihood of the offeror's intention to make an offer for the shares of the target company. Following on from such an announcement, the offeror will have four weeks to decide whether or not to pursue the offer (Rule 2). If it is decided that the offer is to be pursued the offeror must first notify a firm intention of the offer to the board of the target company (Rule 1). The shareholders of the target company must be provided with the terms of the formal offer within a maximum of 28 days from the firm intention announcement (Rule 30). The offer must then remain open for acceptances for up to a minimum of 21 days, up to a maximum, ordinarily, of 60 days (Rule 31). Where the terms of an initial offer fail to achieve sufficient acceptances the offer may be revised and if so the improved and revised terms of the offer must be kept open for at least 14 days after delivery of the revised offer document (Rule 32). The board of directors of the target company (other than those with any conflict of interest in respect of the takeover offer) will advise the shareholders on the terms of any offer (and must do so in accordance with their fiduciary duties – see **Chapter 15**). Further, the target company must appoint a competent independent adviser to provide advice to all of its shareholders (Rule 3).

The shareholders of the target company must be provided with the same information in relation to the offer and persons issuing takeover circulars must include statements taking responsibility for the contents of the same. However, the offer to purchase shares in the target company will be a conditional offer in so far as the Code requires that the offer becomes binding only in circumstances where the offeror acquires or agrees to acquire shares (together with shares already held in the target company) representing over 50 per cent of the voting shares (Rule 10). In all probability, the offeror will have already acquired shares in the target company prior to the takeover offer (albeit those shares already purchased must not equate to shares carrying 30 per cent of the voting rights in the target company otherwise this level of purchase will trigger a mandatory bid – discussed below). In addition, the Code provides that the offer will be conditional on any necessary permissions required from a relevant competition authority (Rule 12). Further conditions may be attached to the offer by the offeror although the extent of the conditions attached is constrained by the terms of the Code (Rule 13). The constraints on the ability to impose conditions ensure that only serious offers will go forward for consideration by the target company's shareholders.

9.6.3 Purchase and consideration issues

Where an offeror acquires interests in shares carrying 10 per cent or more of the voting rights of a class of shares of the target company in the offer period and the previous 12 months, all shareholders of that class must, in terms of the formal offer, be paid the highest level of consideration (in cash or its equivalent) that was paid by the offeror for the class of share in question (Rule 11). This equality principle is also applied generally to purchases of the target company's shares to the extent that where an offeror purchases shares of a specific class in a three-month period prior to an initial formal offer and does so at a lower level of consideration than under the terms provided by the formal offer for the class of share in question, then the offeror must pay the higher rate of consideration for the shares purchased prior to the formal offer (Rule 6). This rule also works in reverse, i.e. shares offered in the formal offer at a lower level of consideration than the consideration at which shares were sold within the three-month period prior to the formal offer must be offered at the higher rate of consideration. Where a formal offer is made for the shares of a target company and the shares of that company comprise different classes of equity share then a comparable offer must be made for each class of share (Rule 14). This rule affords an equal opportunity to holders of all classes of equity share to sell their shares and exit the company (the rule applies also to equity shares absent of any voting rights). Further, following a formal offer for the shares of the target company, where the offeror fails to acquire sufficient shares but revises the bid for shares at an increased rate, then, in such circumstances, shareholders who sold shares under the terms of the initial offer (at the lower price) will be entitled to the higher price specified in the revised bid.

In circumstances where a formal offer (to include revised offers within the requisite time period) fails to induce sufficient shareholders of the target company to accept the offeror's bid, the offeror may make a subsequent bid for the target company's shares but must wait 12 months before doing so (other than where the Panel waives this requirement). During the requisite 12-month period, the offeror must not acquire shares in the target company sufficient to trigger the mandatory bid requirement (discussed below) (Rule 35).

Where the offeror is successful (following either the initial or a subsequent offer) in acquiring sufficient shares to complete a takeover of the target company, the shareholders who declined the offeror's bid may not wish to be shareholders of a company controlled by the offeror. In such a case and in accordance with CA 2006, ss.983–986, such shareholders may insist on leaving the company and having their shares purchased by the offeror. Conversely, in circumstances where a takeover is successful and the offeror wishes to acquire 100 per cent control of the target company and the takeover position is such that in relation to the shares subject to the bid, the offeror acquired at least 90 per cent in value of the shares of any specific class of share, or at least 90 per cent of any class of voting shares, then, in accordance with CA 2006, s.979, the offeror may compulsorily acquire the remaining shares of the specific class of shares in question. However, in accordance with CA 2006, s.986, the compulsory acquisition may be subject to an objection and challenge by dissenting shareholders on the premise that the terms of the compulsory offer were unfair (in relation to the interpretation of the Code in respect of a compulsory offer, see, e.g. *Re Diamix plc* [2002] 2 BCLC 123).

9.6.4 Statements that may induce the shareholders of a target company

In relation to the offeror's bid, all documentation, advertisements and statements made in connection with an offer must be accurate and fair (Rule 19). Any documentation that contains profit forecasts and asset valuations must be made to specified standards and must be approved by professional advisers. Where there are any misleading, inaccurate or unsubstantiated statements contained within documents (or reported in the media, etc.) that are relevant to the terms and consequences attached to the offer, such inaccuracies must be publicly corrected immediately (Rules 9, 23–25 and 28).

9.6.5 Statements relevant to employees

In the offer document the offeror must state its plans and intentions in respect of the future business operations of the target company which must include its intentions related to the future deployment of the target company's workforce. Although the target company's employees will have no direct influence (other than where an employee is also a shareholder of the target company) as to whether the bid is accepted or not, the board of directors in presenting its views on the merits or otherwise of the bid (discussed above) must provide its views and reasons for the same in respect of any implications attached to the bid in so far as those implications affect the interests of its employees (Rules 24–25).

9.6.6 Opposition tactics of the target company

Although the board of directors of a target company may oppose a proposed takeover and may seek to persuade its shareholders not to accept the bid or, alternatively, seek to persuade its shareholders as to the merits of any competing takeover bid, the board of the target company should not, during the period in which the Code is in operation, actively seek to frustrate the terms of a takeover offer unless its shareholders approve the 'frustration plans'. Shareholder approval must be given for every specific defensive plan (see Rule 21).

9.6.7 Mandatory bid

In circumstances where an offeror acquires interests in the shares of a target company carrying 30 per cent or more of the voting rights of the target company, the offeror must make a mandatory cash offer (or with a cash alternative) for the equity shares of all the remaining shareholders at the highest price paid in the preceding 12 months (Rule 9). The offer will be conditional on the offeror acquiring a 50 per cent+ control of the voting shares in the target company. However, the rule is subject to the Panel's discretion, for example, the Panel would be unlikely to require a mandatory bid by the offeror where a person or persons holding 50 per cent or more of the voting shares indicate their refusal to accept a bid.

9.6.8 A scheme of arrangement

In the context of a takeover situation a scheme of arrangement involves the supervision of a friendly takeover by the court, albeit the takeover will still be subject to relevant provisions of the Takeover Code. This form of takeover will ordinarily result in a transfer of total control away from the target company to the offeror. The takeover must be friendly in the sense that the offeror must have the approval and co-operation of the board of the target company; on the adoption of the scheme the board will be directed by the court to order a meeting of the holders of those classes of shares to be affected. However, unlike the usual requirements attached to a takeover (see above), under a scheme of arrangement, the purchase process for the target company's shares will only proceed where the offeror acquires approval by at least 75 per cent of any class of shares affected (CA 2006, s.899). Having attained the 75 per cent requirement, the remaining members of the class of shares affected will also be bound by the terms of the scheme. The court will then be asked to sanction the scheme in accordance with CA 2006, s.899.

9.6.9 Sanctions relating to a breach of the Code

- CA 2006, s.952 provides the Panel with the power (if incorporated within the rules of the Code) to exercise disciplinary powers to include financial penalties. The disciplinary powers contained within the current Code are ones of censure (as occurred in the case of the hostile takeover of Cadbury plc by Kraft Foods in 2010) and an ability to report improper conduct to another official body, for example the FCA; that official body may then, at its discretion, decide to take further action against the wrongdoer.
- CA 2006, s.953 imposes criminal liability on any person (punishable by way of a fine) who was aware or reckless of the fact that the offer documentation (including the response documentation of the target company) for a takeover offer (but only in respect of the shares of a company quoted on a regulated market (Main Market of LSE)) was prepared in a manner contrary to the terms of the Code. A defence to this offence may be made out where it is established that the defendant took all reasonable steps to ensure compliance with the terms of the Code.
- CA 2006, s.954 allows the Panel to adopt Code rules the effect of which would be to permit the Panel to order a person who was in breach of a specified rule of the Code to be subject to a requirement to pay monetary compensation in consequence of that breach.
- CA 2006, s.955 affords the Panel with the power to apply to the court with the purpose of securing an enforcement order to obtain compliance with a requirement of the Code.

CHAPTER 10

Share capital and capital maintenance

10.1 INTRODUCTION

Share capital equates to that part of a company's assets which is made up of the monetary consideration provided by its members following the purchase of the company's shares. While a company will have other 'capital assets' – for example, property, realised profits, etc. – the law does not classify this 'other capital' as capital in respect of the balance sheet rules and procedures relating to capital maintenance. Unlike other forms of capital, the sum of share capital must be maintained as a fixed sum on the balance sheet other than where the law permits a reduction in share capital (see below). In an accounting sense, share capital represents a notional liability to the company's shareholders although in reality it is more readily viewed as a protective buffer offering creditors a financial safeguard should the company's fortunes fail, i.e. following the liquidation of a company its creditors will have a claim against this fund in priority to the claims of shareholders.

Therefore, as a matter of theory, share capital may be regarded as a measure with which asset values should correspond, i.e. if a company is valued at £100,000 one might expect the sum of the shares issued in the company to represent the worth (£100,000) of the company. If the sum representing a company's share capital is in excess of the company's net assets, this fact may give rise to a presumption of insolvency. However, in practice, the theoretical worth of share capital as a yardstick measure of a company's financial worth is often a myth, as the value of assets is prone to fluctuation. The yardstick measure of share capital may be false typically in respect of private companies where the law does not prescribe any minimum share capital requirement. However, in the case of a public company, the Companies Act (CA) 2006, s.656 deems that it is an offence punishable by a fine if the company's net assets fall to an amount that is equal to or below half of its called-up share capital and the company fails (within 28 days of that fact becoming known to one of the company's directors) to convene a general meeting for not later than 56 days thereafter, to consider whether any, and if so what steps should be taken to deal with the situation.

Called-up share capital is the total amount of consideration received from shareholders for issued shares, whereas uncalled share capital is the difference between the total nominal value of a company's issued share capital and the value of the company's called-up share capital. Therefore, shares may be issued as partly paid shares, although in the case of a public company, partly paid shares must be paid up to a minimum of 25 per cent of their nominal value.

While a company's share capital is made up of sums received from the issue of shares, for the purpose of the capital maintenance rules, it also includes any sums held in the company's share premium account or other statutory capital reserves. The most common types of capital reserve accounts are as follows:

- The share premium account which equates to the difference in value between a share's nominal value and any premium paid on the share (CA 2006, s.610).
- The capital redemption reserve: if a company is permitted to redeem or purchase its own shares out of distributable profits it must maintain its capital balance by placing an amount equal to the reduction in share capital into its capital redemption reserve (CA 2006, s.733).
- The revaluation reserve equates to an amount equal to an increase in the value of corporate assets. An amount representing this increase should be transferred to the company's revaluation reserve to maintain the notional balance between capital and corporate assets.

Sums in a capital reserve fund cannot be used to pay dividends, although they may be used in financing an issue of bonus shares. A company's capital reserves should be contrasted with its revenue reserves – the latter represent the sum of a company's retained profits. Unlike reserve capital, retained profits may be used to pay dividends.

Although a company's paid-up share capital cannot be returned to shareholders in the form of dividend payments, in specific circumstances the sum of a company's share capital may be reduced (discussed below). Prior to CA 2006, the total nominal value of shares that could be issued by a company was fixed (but subject to alteration by CA 1985, s.121) by its authorised share capital clause (contained in the memorandum). Following the implementation of CA 2006, this once obligatory clause is now rendered redundant, save that a public company is still obliged to maintain a minimum authorised share capital to the value of £50,000.

10.2   REDUCING SHARE CAPITAL

It may be expedient for a company to reduce its share capital. For example, following a hefty fall in the value of the company's assets and a decline in business activity, it may be necessary, given the likelihood of declining profits, to reduce the sum of a company's share capital to enable the company to retain a future capacity to make dividend payments and attract future investment. In this type of situation it is probable that the reduction will be in the form of a cancellation of share capital. A reduction of share capital by the cancellation of share capital will not result in a return of capital to shareholders; rather, a proportion of the paid-up share capital will be written off. The holders of ordinary shares will be the first to be affected by any cancellation of any paid-up share capital; in effect the face value of their holdings will be reduced in proportion to the level of the cancellation. Ordinarily, preference shares will be protected from any cancellation in share capital, in so far as such shares will usually have a preferential right to the return of capital following a reduction of share capital. Conversely, following a reorganisation (downsize) of a company's business and the sale of corporate assets the sum of a company's share capital may exceed the requirements of the company's future viable and profitable business activities to the extent that as a yardstick measure of the company's worth it may be necessary to reduce share capital to an extent whereby it more readily corresponds with the requirements and new asset values of the business. Here a reduction of capital is likely to be affected by the repayment of capital, i.e., returning paid-up share capital to a class of shareholder. In such circumstances where preference shares were issued with a preferential right to the return of capital, it may be expected that preference shareholders will be the first class of shareholder to participate in the return of capital. However, in so far as a reduction of share capital may be prejudicial to the interests of a part of the company's shareholders (see the variation of class rights discussed in **Chapter 8**) or cause anxiety among the company's creditors, CA 2006 provides statutory confirmation of a long established principle of company law (see *Trevor* v. *Whitworth* (1887) 12 App Cas 409), namely that a company may not, as of right, reduce its share capital. For a company to reduce its share capital by a cancellation or repayment of capital, it must comply with the procedures contained in CA 2006, s.641 or alternatively under the court procedure governed by CA 2006, s.645.

In accordance with CA 2006, s.641(4) in particular, a company may:

(a)   extinguish or reduce the liability on any of its shares in respect of share capital not paid up, or

(b)   either with or without extinguishing or reducing liability on any of its shares –

   (i)   cancel any paid-up share capital that is lost or unrepresented by available assets, or

   (ii)   repay any paid-up share capital in excess of the company's wants.

10.2.1   Section 641 procedure (private companies)

CA 2006, s.641(1) states that a private company may reduce its share capital other than where, if, as a result of the reduction, the only remaining shares held by its members are redeemable shares (CA 2006, s.641(2)). A company may reduce its share capital even if the right to do so is not contained in its articles. However, in accordance with CA 2006, s.641(6) a company's articles may restrict or prohibit a reduction in share capital.

In accordance with s.641(1) a private company may reduce share capital providing:

(a)   the company passes a special resolution to sanction the reduction; and

(b)   the directors of the company, in complying with CA 2006, s.642, issue a solvency statement not more than 15 days before the date on which the special resolution is passed.

If the resolution is proposed as a written resolution, a copy of the solvency statement should be sent or submitted to the company's members before or at the time the resolution is forwarded to the registrar. Where the resolution is proposed at a general meeting, a copy of the solvency statement should be made available for inspection by members throughout that meeting. However, non-compliance with the members' right to view the solvency statement will not render the resolution void, although it will constitute an offence committed by every officer of the company who is in default of the requirement.

10.2.2 Solvency statement

The solvency statement required by CA 2006, s.642 must, as of the date of the statement, state that the company was solvent, specifying that there was no ground on which the company could, at that time, be found to be unable to pay (or otherwise discharge) its debts. The solvency statement must provide that if the company was to be wound up within a year from the date of the statement, it would be able to pay its debts in full within 12 months commencing from the date of the winding up, or alternatively that the company would be able to pay (or otherwise discharge) its debts as they fell due within 12 months commencing from the date of the winding up. The directors of the company (all named in the statement) must be of the opinion that the solvency statement is accurate, and any director who is a party to a solvency statement without having reasonable grounds for the opinions and statements expressed therein, is liable to imprisonment for a maximum term of two years or a fine, or both. In compliance with the Companies (Reduction of Share Capital) Order 2008, SI 2008/1915, a solvency statement must be in writing and indicate that it is a solvency statement for the purposes of s.642 and must be signed by all of the directors. A copy of the solvency statement together with a statement of capital must be delivered to the registrar within 15 days of the passing of the resolution (CA 2006, s.643).

In accordance with CA 2006, s.644(2), the statement of capital must, in relation to the company's share capital, as altered by the order, state:

(a)   the total number of shares of the company,
(b)   the aggregate nominal value of those shares,
(c)   for each class of shares –

    (i)   prescribed particulars of the rights attached to the shares,
    (ii)   the total number of shares of that class, and
    (iii)   the aggregate nominal value of shares of that class, and

(d)   the amount paid up and the amount (if any) unpaid on each share (whether on account of the nominal value of the share or by way of premium).

10.2.3 The court procedure (public company and possibly a private company)

A private company may follow an alternative procedure to effect a reduction in capital. This alternative procedure, the court procedure, is the only procedure available for a reduction of capital in respect of a public company. While the court procedure is more expensive and time consuming, a private company's ability to obtain court approval in respect of a reduction in share capital affords a degree of certainty: the reduction is 'rubber stamped' by the court and it is unlikely to be challenged. The court procedure also affords the directors of the company a degree of security in the sense that they are not required personally to issue a solvency statement and accordingly will not be held potentially liable should the company be wound up within the 12-month period so specified under CA 2006, s.642.

Prior to the passing of CA 2006, the court procedure (see CA 1985, s.143) represented the only permissible way to achieve a reduction of share capital in relation to both a private and a public company. The court procedure is now governed by CA 2006, s.645, which provides that:

- the company must pass a special resolution to sanction the reduction in share capital; and
- the company must obtain the court's approval for the reduction.

10.2.4 Creditors' right to object to reduction

If the proposed reduction of capital involves either a diminution of liability in relation to any unpaid share capital of members, or the repayment to members of any paid-up share capital, any creditor of the company has a right to object to the reduction. A list of the company's creditors will be drawn up. To settle a list of creditors entitled to object, the court is required to ascertain, so far as possible without requiring an application from any creditor, the names of the creditors and the nature and amount of their debts or claims. However, where it is established to the satisfaction of the court that it is unnecessary for a list of creditors to be settled, the court will dispense with the requirement to settle a list (which is the norm as creditors' claims/concerns are ordinarily resolved prior to a point in time when it is necessary to draw up a list).

A creditor's objection may be sustained where he or she can establish that there is a 'real likelihood' that the reduction if confirmed would result in the company being unable to discharge his or her debt or claim when it fell due (see CA 2006, s.646(1), as amended by the Companies (Share Capital and Acquisition by Company of its Own Shares) Regulations 2009, SI 2009/2022). In establishing 'a real likelihood' that the reduction 'would' result in an inability to discharge the debt when it becomes due, the creditor must assess a future state of affairs based upon present facts. The assessment must avoid the purely speculative and must cover a period of time, the duration of which will be affected by the nature and extent of the liability in question. Where the event that will trigger the repayment of the debt is more remote in time then it will be more difficult to establish the reality of the 'real likelihood' that a return of capital will itself result in inability to discharge the debt. The term 'real likelihood' requires the objecting creditor to establish 'beyond the possible but short of the probable' that the reduction would result in an inability to discharge the debt in question (see the judgment of Norris J in *Re Liberty International plc* [2011] Bus LR D17).

Where a creditor who is entered on the creditors list does not consent to the reduction of capital, the court may, if it thinks fit, dispense with the consent of that particular creditor but only if the company secures the payment of the debt in question. If an officer of the company intentionally or recklessly conceals the name of a creditor entitled to object to the reduction of capital, or misrepresents the nature or amount of the debt or claim of a creditor, or is knowingly concerned in any such concealment or misrepresentation, he or she commits an offence and is liable on conviction on indictment, to a fine or on summary conviction, to a fine not exceeding the statutory maximum.

10.2.5 Court's decision on reduction of capital

In accordance with CA 2006, s.648, the court may make an order confirming the reduction of capital on such terms and conditions as it thinks fit. However, the court must not confirm the reduction unless it is satisfied, with respect to every creditor of the company who is entitled to object to the reduction of capital, that the consent of the creditor has been obtained or the creditor's debt has been discharged, determined or secured. Where the court confirms the reduction, it may order the company to publish (as the court directs) the reasons for the reduction of capital, or such other information that the court thinks expedient with a view to giving proper information to the public, and (if the court thinks fit) the causes that led to the reduction. Further, the court may make an order directing that the company must, on or at any time after the date of the order, add to its name as its last words the words 'and reduced'. If such an order is made, the words 'and reduced' will be deemed to be part of the company's name until the end of the period specified in the order.

CA 2006, s.649 provides that the order and statement of capital must be registered following the delivery to the registrar of a copy of the order of the court confirming the reduction of a company's share capital and the delivery of a statement of capital (approved by the court). The statement of capital is in the form prescribed by CA 2006, s.649(2). This prescribed form is identical to that provided by CA 2006, s.644(2) (see above).

Where a company reduces its capital under the court procedure and a creditor who was legitimately entitled to object to the reduction did not object because of his or her ignorance of the proceedings, or the effect of the proceedings, or because he or she was not entered on the list of creditors, then, in such circumstances, if, after the reduction, the company is unable to repay that creditor's debt, all the members of the company, as at the date on which the resolution for reducing capital took effect, are deemed liable to contribute to the payment of the debt or claim. The liability is to the extent of an amount not exceeding that which the members would have been liable to contribute had the company commenced to be wound up on the day before that date (CA 2006, s.653).

In determining whether to sanction a company's reduction of share capital, the court's principal concern will be to consider the effect of the reduction on the company's ability to repay its debts (see *Poole* v. *National Bank of China* [1907] AC 229). The court must be satisfied that the effect of the reduction in capital will not leave the company's creditors in a perilous position. In addition to considering the effect of a reduction of capital on the company's creditors, the court may also consider the effect of the reduction upon the various classes of company share-holder (see, e.g. *Re Ratners Group plc* [1988] 4 BCC 293). The court must determine whether the reduction of capital would vary the rights of a class of shareholder and if so, the consent of the affected class of shareholders must be obtained where the proposed reduction of capital would result in a variation of class rights. For example, where preference shareholders are given the right to a repay-ment of capital in preference to ordinary shareholders, upon a reduction of a company's paid-up capital, the preference shareholders should be paid in full, prior to any payment to the ordinary shareholders.

10.2.6 Cancelling share capital

In respect of a reduction of share capital prescribed by CA 2006, s.641(4)(b)(i) (i.e. by cancelling paid-up share capital in response potentially to a loss in the value of corporate assets), it is necessary for the company to prove a loss of capital. In *Re Jupiter House Investments Ltd* [1985] 1 WLR 975, Harman J held that to prove a loss of capital, the loss should be permanent and not a temporary loss in the value of a capital asset. Nevertheless, his Lordship opined that where the loss could not be proved as permanent, the company could, albeit in exceptional circumstances, attain the court's approval for a reduction in circumstances where it had set aside a non-distributable reserve to ensure that if the loss of capital was subsequently recovered, the same would not be distributed in the form of dividend payments. However, it should be noted that in *Re Grosvenor Press plc* [1985] 1 WLR 980, a contrary view was taken, whereby the court held that although a fall in the value of a capital asset may only be of a temporary nature, there was no compelling reason for the court to require a reserve to be set aside. However, in such circumstances, the company would be obliged to give an undertaking that if any of the capital was recovered it would be set aside in a special reserve to protect the interests of the company's existing creditors. It is to be noted that any reserve arising from the reduction of a company's share capital is non-distributable, although this rule may be subject to exceptions provided by secondary legislation (CA 2006, s.654).

10.3 THE PURCHASE OF A COMPANY'S OWN SHARES

A company may wish to purchase its own shares without the principal objective of reducing capital and in such circumstances may do so without the necessity of having to comply with the statutory procedure related to a reduction of capital. A company may wish to purchase its own shares but maintain capital reserves where, for example, it wishes to boost dividend payments on its remaining shares or to purchase a specific class of shares to enhance the rights of another class of its shares. (This will be subject to a variation of class rights, see **Chapter 8**.) Subject to any restriction contained in its articles, a company may purchase its own shares (providing they are fully paid up at the date of purchase), irrespective of whether the shares were issued as redeemable or non-redeemable shares (see CA 2006, ss.690–691 (previously CA 1985, s.162)). Other than where a private limited company is purchasing shares for the purposes of or pursuant to an employees' share scheme, shares purchased must be paid for in full on the date of purchase (see CA 2006, s.691(2), as amended by the Companies Act 2006 (Amendment of Part 18) Regulations 2013, SI 2013/999, reg.3).

A method of payment is not specified by CA 2006 and while payment will ordinarily be in cash, a non-cash consideration may be acceptable (see, e.g. *BDG Roof-Bond Ltd* v. *Douglas* [2000] BCLC 402). However, a limited company may not purchase its own shares if, as a result of the purchase, it would no longer have any issued shares other than redeemable shares or shares held as treasury shares.

10.3.1 Purchase by private and public companies

For both a private and a public company the purchase of its own shares will be made, where applicable, out of distributable profits or from the proceeds of a new issue of shares, the new issue having been specifically created for the purpose of purchasing the company's existing shares. However, in accordance with CA 2006, s.692 (as amended by the Companies Act 2006 (Amendment of Part 18) Regulations 2013 (reg.4), a private limited company may also expend capital (but only up to the permissible capital payment limit) to purchase its own shares (discussed below) or alternatively may purchase its own shares with cash (if authorised to do so by its articles) up to an amount in a financial year not exceeding the lower of (i) £15,000, or (ii) the value of 5 per cent of its share capital.

Where shares are purchased (or redeemed) wholly or partly out of profits then a transfer of funds must be made to the capital redemption reserve with an objective of preserving the sum of the share capital prior to the share purchase, i.e. thus avoiding a reduction in share capital. Where shares are purchased (or redeemed) from the proceeds of a new issue of shares and the value of the shares redeemed or purchased is greater than the value of the new issue of shares, then again a transfer of funds must be made to the capital redemption reserve with an objective of preserving the sum of the share capital prior to the purchase, i.e. thus avoiding a reduction in share capital. Accordingly, a purchase/redemption of shares will not constitute a reduction of share capital in the context of the capital maintenance rules providing the capital reserves of the company are maintained at the level prior to the company's purchase of its shares. Any premium payable on the shares must normally be paid out of profits. However, if a company's shares were initially issued at a premium, any premium attached to the shares as of the date on which the company purchases the shares may be paid out of the proceeds of an issue of new shares up to an amount not exceeding the lesser of:

- the total amount of premium obtained from the shares when they were first issued; and
- the amount standing to the credit of the share premium account at the time of issue (this amount includes any premium obtained on the new issue).

The amount of the company's share premium account must be reduced by a sum corresponding (or by sums in the aggregate corresponding) to the amount of any payment.

A limited company may only purchase its own shares in the manner prescribed by CA 2006, albeit that the case of *Acatos & Hutcheson plc* v. *Watson* [1995] BCC 450 would appear to paint a contradictory picture. In *Acatos & Hutcheson plc* v. *Watson* the court was asked to determine whether a company (A) in purchasing the entire issued share capital of another company (B) had infringed capital maintenance rules in so far as B's sole asset comprised a holding of 29.4 per cent of the issued share capital in A. Therefore, A's purchase of the entire issued share capital of B would result in the purchase of its own shares (i.e. B's 29.4 per cent stake in A). The background to this case was as follows. B had been used by specific members of A as an indirect means of acquiring shares in A, with the intention that those members of A would, through B, eventually make a takeover bid for A. However, the takeover objective was abandoned and B's holding in A created an adverse effect on the level of trading in A's shares. Although in this case the most obvious solution would have been to place B into liquidation with its holding in A returned to B's shareholders (B had no outstanding creditors), that solution would have attracted a substantial tax burden. Accordingly, an alternative method was advanced, whereby A proposed to purchase the entire share capital of B in exchange for an issue of its own shares to the effect that B would become a wholly owned subsidiary of A. In addition, A proposed to alter the rights attached to the shares B held in A, to the extent that the shares would carry no votes or rights to dividend payments. Basically, while B would technically continue to exist, it would do so in a 'paper state' with no power, in terms of voting rights, to influence the affairs of its newly adopted holding company.

In sanctioning the validity of the proposed agreement, the court held that A had not intended to purchase its own shares but rather it had sought to purchase shares in B. Although the purchase of B's shares would impliedly result in A acquiring its own shares, the court viewed that acquisition other than as one amounting to a direct or express purchase of A's own shares. The court's decision served the interests of all the parties concerned (with the exception of the Inland Revenue).

10.3.2 Purchase procedures

CA 2006, s.693 (as amended by the Companies Act 2006 (Amendment of Part 18) Regulations 2013, reg.6) provides that a company may purchase its own shares by means of either an off-market purchase authorised in accordance with s.693A (for an employees' share scheme) or in pursuance of a contract approved in advance in accordance with CA 2006, s.694 (discussed below), or alternatively by a market purchase (CA 2006, s.701) (discussed below). In respect of s.693A (introduced by the Companies Act 2006 (Amendment of Part 18) Regulations 2013, SI 2013/999, reg.7), a company may make an off-market purchase of its own shares for the purposes of or pursuant to an employees' share scheme if the purchase was authorised by an ordinary resolution of the company. The authority may be general or limited to the purchase of shares of a particular class or description, and may be unconditional or subject to conditions. The authority must specify the maximum number of shares authorised to be acquired, and determine both the maximum and minimum prices that may be paid for the shares. The authority may be varied, revoked or from time to time renewed by an ordinary resolution of the company. A resolution conferring, varying or renewing authority must specify a date on which it is to expire, which must not be later than five years after the date on which the resolution is passed. However, a company may make a purchase of its own shares after the expiry of the time limit specified if the contract of purchase was concluded before the authority expired, and the terms of the authority permitted the company to make a contract of purchase that would or might be executed wholly or partly after its expiration.

An off-market purchase ordinarily describes a purchase of shares otherwise than on a recognised UK investment exchange but the purchase may still be described as off-market if the shares purchased on a recognised investment exchange are not subject to a marketing arrangement on the exchange (CA 2006, s.693(2)). A market purchase (other than one that is not subject to a marketing arrangement) is one made on a recognised investment exchange (CA 2006, s.693(4)).

An off-market transaction can only be executed by means of a private contract between a company and an existing shareholder and must be approved by an ordinary resolution (CA 2006, s.694(2), as amended by the Companies Act 2006 (Amendment of Part 18) Regulations 2013 (reg.5) – prior to the amendment a special resolution was required). It is to be noted that a copy of the proposed purchase contract (or memorandum detailing the terms of the contract) should be made available for inspection by the company's membership at least 15 days prior to the meeting at which the proposed resolution is to be considered (or in the case of a written resolution, by being sent or submitted to every eligible member at or before the time at which the proposed resolution is sent or submitted) (CA 2006, s.696(2)). The member of the company with whom the contract for sale is made is not permitted to vote on the resolution where the effect of that vote permits the resolution to be passed (CA 2006, s.695). If passed, the resolution will be invalid if the above requirements of CA 2006 are not met. Where the company is a public company, the authority contained in the resolution will last no longer than a period of five years (CA 2006, s.694(5), as amended by the Companies (Share Capital and Acquisition by Company of its Own Shares) Regulations 2009, SI 2009/2022 – previously the time limit had been set at 18 months).

A contract of purchase may be contingent giving either the company or the member, or both, an option to purchase (CA 2006, s.694(3)). A payment made by a company in consideration of acquiring any right with respect to the purchase of its own shares in pursuance of any contingent purchase contract must be made from its distributable profits (see CA 2006, s.705).

In making either an off-market purchase or a market purchase of shares, the company must deliver a return to the registrar which must notify the details of the transaction to the registrar and be delivered no later than 28 days from the date of purchase (CA 2006, s.707). Where a company purchases its own shares, the shares will be treated as cancelled. Accordingly, the shares cannot be kept in reserve and resold at a later date (other than if the shares are held as treasury shares) (CA 2006, s.706). A copy of the purchase contract must be kept at the company's registered office (CA 2006, s.702(2)). In the case of a public company, the return to the registrar must specify the aggregate amount paid for the shares, together with details of the maximum and minimum prices paid for each class of share purchased (CA 2006, s.707(4)).

Public company

A market purchase of a company's shares is relevant only in circumstances where a public company purchases its own shares. The purchase will be made on a recognised UK investment exchange. A public company may authorise a market purchase by means of an ordinary resolution (CA 2006, s.701). In addition, the resolution granting the authority to purchase must specify a maximum number of shares to be acquired and the maximum and minimum price to be paid for the shares. The resolution must also specify a date when the authority will expire; the maximum duration for the authority is 18 months after the date on which the resolution was passed.

10.4 PAYMENT OUT OF CAPITAL (PRIVATE COMPANIES ONLY)

A private company may redeem or purchase its own shares by expending capital providing it is authorised to do so by its articles (CA 2006, s.709). However, a private company may only expend capital (the permissible capital payment) to purchase its own shares if, together, any available profits and the proceeds of any new issue of shares made specifically for the purpose of the redemption or purchase are of an insufficient value to facilitate the redemption or purchase. The availability of distributable profits is determined in accordance with the steps provided under CA 2006, s.712. Here, the company must examine its relevant accounts for the relevant period. Relevant accounts are any accounts that are prepared as at a date within the relevant period, and are such as to enable a reasonable judgment to be made of the calculated amounts. The relevant period means the period of three months ending with the date on which the directors' statement (see **10.4.1**) is made. In seeking to determine the availability of distributable profits the first step is to calculate gross profits. The second step is to reduce the calculated amount by reference to:

(a)   any distribution lawfully made by the company; and

(b)   any other relevant payment lawfully made by the company out of distributable profits, after the date of the relevant accounts and before the end of the relevant period. For this purpose 'other relevant payment lawfully made' includes:

- financial assistance lawfully given out of distributable profits;
- payments lawfully made out of distributable profits in respect of the purchase by the company of any shares in the company; and
- payments of any description specified in CA 2006, s.705 (payments other than purchase price to be made out of distributable profits) lawfully made by the company.

The resulting figure is the sum of the available distributable profits. Where the sum required to facilitate a company's purchase or redemption of shares falls short of the sum of any available distributable profits and any sum received from a new issue of shares, any expenditure from capital will be unlawful unless the company complies with the prescribed procedures (discussed below). Although in a technical sense capital expenditure for the purchase of a company's shares would trigger the capital maintenance rules (CA 2006, s.641, a reduction in share capital), those rules do not apply to this situation. Instead, distinct but very similar regulations are applicable (described below).

10.4.1   Directors' statement and auditor's report

A private company that intends to expend capital for the purpose of purchasing its own shares will, in accordance with CA 2006, s.714, require a statement from the company's directors specifying the amount of the permissible capital payment for the shares in question. The statement must state that immediately following the date on which the payment out of capital is proposed to be made and for the year immediately following that date, the directors hold the opinion that there will be no grounds on which the company will be unable to pay its debts. The statement must also include an annexed report from the company's auditor confirming the company's financial viability. Further, the permissible capital payment for the shares in question must be specified. It is an offence for the directors to make a statement under s.714 without having reasonable grounds for the opinion expressed therein. A person found to be guilty of the offence is liable on conviction on indictment to imprisonment for a term not exceeding two years or a fine (or both) and on summary conviction to imprisonment for a term not exceeding 12 months or a fine not exceeding the statutory maximum (or both). The directors' statement must be in the prescribed form and must comply with the Companies (Shares and Share Capital) Order 2009, SI 2009/388; namely it must be in writing; indicate that it is a directors' statement made under that section; and be signed by each of the company's directors. Where the company's business includes that of a banking company or an insurance company, the same must be included in the statement.

Further, in accordance with IA 1986, s.76, where a company redeems or purchases its shares out of capital, but within a year immediately following the capital expenditure, falls into liquidation and cannot pay its debts, the directors of the company having made the declaration of solvency, together with the person from whom the shares were redeemed or purchased, will be liable, at the discretion of the court, to contribute to the assets of the company. A director may escape liability if he or she had reasonable grounds to believe in the accuracy of the statement.

10.4.2 Payment approved by special resolution

A private company that intends to expend capital to purchase its own shares will require the general meeting to authorise the expenditure by means of a special resolution (CA 2006, s.716). The resolution must be passed on, or within the week immediately following, the date on which the directors make the statement required by s.714. In order to consider the resolution, a copy of the directors' statement and auditor's report must be made available to members (CA 2006, s.718(2)). Where the resolution is passed at a meeting of the company, it will not be effective if any member holding shares to which the resolution relates, voted on the resolution and without those votes, the resolution would not have been passed (CA 2006, s.717). Where the resolution is proposed as a written resolution, a member who holds any shares to which the resolution to purchase relates, will not be considered as an eligible member for the purpose of passing the resolution.

In accordance with CA 2006, s.719, a private limited company that makes a payment out of capital for the redemption or purchase of its own shares must, within the week immediately following the date of the resolution under s.716:

- publish details of the expenditure of capital to include a statement providing that any creditor of the company may apply to the court within five weeks of the resolution for an order preventing the payment out of capital;
- publish said notice in the *Gazette*. It must also be published in an appropriate national newspaper or alternatively, notification of the same must be given in writing to each of the company's creditors;
- deliver to the registrar a copy of the directors' statement and auditor's report.

10.4.3 Exception

In accordance with CA 2006, s.720A (introduced by the Companies Act 2006 (Amendment of Part 18) Regulations 2013, reg.12), reduced requirements exist in respect of a payment out of capital for the purchase of a company's own shares for the purposes of or pursuant to an employees' share scheme, The exception provides that full compliance with CA 2006, ss.714, 716, 719 and 720 (the latter provision concerns the directors' statement and auditor's report to be made available for inspection) will not apply to this type of purchase for the purposes of or pursuant to an employees' share scheme in circumstances where the purchase was approved by special resolution and supported by a solvency statement.

10.4.4 Objection to expending capital

Any member of the company who did not vote in favour of the resolution, or any creditor of the company, may, within five weeks from the date of the special resolution sanctioning the expenditure of capital, apply to the court for an order to prohibit the payment (CA 2006, s.721). The applicant must give immediate notification to the registrar and the company (upon receipt of the notice of the application). On hearing the application the court may either adjourn the proceedings to enable the company to enter into an arrangement to compensate the dissentient member(s) or the claims of the dissentient creditors, and/or make an order either confirming or cancelling the resolution for the purchase or redemption of the company's own shares on such terms and conditions as it thinks fit. Where the court confirms the resolution, it may also order that the company should purchase the shares of any other member and order a reduction of the company's capital. Within 15 days of the making of the order (or a longer period if the court so directs) the company must deliver a copy of the order to the registrar.

10.5 DIVIDEND PAYMENTS AND OTHER DISTRIBUTIONS

A distribution may be defined as an allocation of some portion of the company's assets (but not capital assets) to its members, an allocation made either in cash or otherwise. The most common form of distribution made by a company will be a dividend payment. A dividend payment may be seen as the return on a shareholder's investment for the purchase of shares in a company, namely, dividend payments represent a share in the company profits. A dividend is usually payable to a shareholder in proportion to the nominal value of the shares held in the company. To protect the interests of creditors a dividend cannot be paid from a company's capital assets. A dividend payment must only be made out of available profits, a sum to be determined by the company's accounts (CA 2006, s.830). Profits available for distribution are specified by CA 2006, s.830(2) as accumulated realised profits which have not been previously utilised by distribution or capitalisation, minus any accumulated realised losses which have not been previously written off in a reduction or reorganisation of capital. Therefore, a company may not pay a dividend on the premise of one good year's trading if its overall (present and past) profits (accumulated profits) are of a lesser value than its accumulated losses. Further, a dividend cannot be declared unless the profits are realised. However, it is to be noted that bonus shares may still be paid out of unrealised profits (CA 2006, s.829(2)).

10.5.1 Procedure for payment of dividends

The procedure for the payment of dividends is ordinarily provided by the company's articles and it is common (and specified in the model articles for both private and public companies) for the articles to provide that a company may by ordinary resolution declare a dividend, but that no dividend shall exceed an amount recommended by the company's directors. In deciding whether to recommend the payment of a dividend, the directors must act in accordance with their fiduciary duties (discussed in **Chapter 15**).

When a dividend is declared, it represents a debt due from the company to its shareholders. Although a company is not bound to declare a dividend, it should be noted that if the company is capable of doing so, a failure to declare a dividend may unfairly prejudice the interests of its members, thus giving rise to the possibility of an action under CA 2006, s.994 (see, e.g. *Re Sam Weller & Sons Ltd* [1990] BCLC 80).

Public companies are subject to additional and more stringent restrictions. CA 2006, s.831 provides that a public company may only make a distribution out of its profits if, after the distribution, the amount of its net assets is not less than the total sum of its called-up share capital and any undistributable reserves.

Where the directors of any type of company decide that a dividend should not be declared (or decide to declare a reduced dividend), the company may retain its profits in the business; indeed, most companies retain at least a proportion of their profits to inject back into future business projects. The directors of a company may create reserves (taken from what would have been distributable profits) and such reserves may be capitalised and used to allocate bonus shares. Unless the contrary is specifically provided for in the company articles, dividend payments must be paid in cash.

CA 2006, s.847 provides that where a dividend is declared in contravention of s.830 (or in the case of a public company, in contravention of s.831), any member who was aware or had reasonable grounds for believing that there had been a contravention of the statutory procedures will be liable to repay the dividend payment to the company (see, e.g. *Precision Dippings Ltd* v. *Precision Dippings Marketing Ltd* [1986] Ch 447 and *It's a Wrap (UK) Ltd* v. *Gula* [2006] 2 BCLC 634). Further, in such a case, the directors of the company, by declaring the dividend, may have acted in breach of their fiduciary duty and in abuse of their powers and accordingly will *prima facie* be liable to make good any loss incurred by the company.

In accordance with CA 2006, s.851, the statutory rules made applicable to distributions do not overturn the common law rule that provides that a company is not permitted to return capital to its shareholders unless it is authorised to do so by a statutory provision (i.e. by way of a dividend, by a reduction of capital or in a winding up) (see, e.g. *Aveling Barford* v. *Perion Ltd* [1989] BCLC 627).

10.5.2   An unlawful distribution

Whether a distribution of a company's assets is unlawful is a matter to be determined by looking at the substance rather than the outward appearance of the transaction. For example, in *Re Halt Garage* [1982] 3 All ER 1016, the court had to determine whether the members and directors of a company (a husband and wife team) in authorising remuneration payments to themselves as directors, had awarded payments which were gratuitous distributions out of capital, dressed up as remuneration. The company, which had been put into liquidation, sought, through its liquidator, the return of remuneration payments. In determining whether the shareholders had authorised remuneration payments in a manner consistent with a proper exercise of their powers, Oliver J formulated the following test:

> ... I think that in circumstances such as exist in this case where payments are made under the authority of a general meeting acting pursuant to an express power, the matter falls to be tested by reference to the genuineness and honesty of the transaction rather than reference to some abstract standard of benefit ... As it seems to me, the submission of counsel for the respondents involves the notion that where there is a purported exercise of an express power by a general meeting the court is a slave to whatever form of words the members may have chosen to use in the resolution which they may pass. I do not think that can be so. I agree with counsel for the liquidator that it cannot be right that shareholder directors acting in unison can draw any sum they like out of the company's capital and leave the liquidator and the company's creditors without remedy in the absence of proof of intent to defraud because they choose to dignify the drawing with a particular description ... the court is not, in my judgment, precluded from examining the true nature of the payments merely because the members choose to call them remuneration. (at p.1043)

In applying this test, Oliver J concluded that while there was no evidence that the husband's level of takings had been excessive or unreasonable, the level of takings paid to the wife had been unreasonably high. The wife had ceased to be active in the employment of the company and therefore was not entitled to a remuneration payment. Oliver J opined that the awards made to the wife were so out of proportion to any possible value to be attributed to her holding office that it was not possible to consider them as genuine payments of remuneration but, rather, they were dressed-up dividends out of capital. Accordingly, it was held that the payments to the wife were invalid. While there was no evidence of any intent/motive on the part of the wife to defraud the company and its creditors, Oliver J remarked that:

> ... the court must, I think, look at the matter objectively and apply the standard of reasonableness. (at p.1044)

However, in some circumstances it may be possible to consider the state of mind and intentions of the person(s) involved in the transaction. For example, in *Progress Property Co Ltd* v. *Moore* [2011] 1 WLR 1, the Supreme Court had to determine whether a company (Y) had been sold at a gross undervaluation by its holding company (P) to company M. A was the controlling shareholder of companies Y, P and M. A sold P to B but prior to the sale, P sold its subsidiary company (Y) to M for a price of £63,000 – a sum which was a substantial undervaluation of Y (the true value of Y was £4 million). Therefore, A (through M) made a substantial gain and B (through P) a substantial loss. The valuation and subsequent sale of Y had been overseen by an employee of A who acted as a director of both P and Y. Following B's acquisition of P, P contended that the sale of Y to M had resulted in an unauthorised distribution/return of capital assets to A. However, the Supreme Court was satisfied on the evidence of the case that the valuation of Y had been conducted in all honesty, the valuation was an honest mistake as opposed to being an intentional attempt to benefit A. Therefore, the Supreme Court held that although the transaction appeared suspicious, that nevertheless it was a genuine transaction (albeit mistaken in respect of the valuation of Y). Accordingly, the sale was a genuine commercial sale in so far as it was conducted absent of any intention to defraud B or the creditors of P or Y.

CHAPTER 11

Loan capital and the registration of charges

11.1 INTRODUCTION

A company's ability to obtain loan funds or other forms of credit is often essential to the survival and future prosperity of the enterprise. Creditors may demand security to counter the potential risk of default and this will often take the form of a charge on the assets of the debtor company. In the context of the enforcement of security interests and the priority of the same, the law was subject to substantial reform in the guise of EA 2002.

11.2 THE DEBENTURE

A document which purports to acknowledge a credit arrangement between a company and its creditor(s) is commonly referred to as a 'debenture'. There is no precise legal definition of a debenture (see, e.g. the judgment of Bowen LJ in *English & Scottish Mercantile Investment Trust* v. *Brunton* [1892] 2 QB 700). CA 2006 does not define a debenture, although CA 2006, s.738 provides that a debenture includes debenture stock, bonds and any other securities of a company, irrespective of whether it constitutes a charge on the assets of the company. In accordance with the terms of a debenture, a debenture holder is entitled to obtain payment of the sums due to him, whether principal or interest. The prescribed rate of interest, as stipulated in the debenture, must be paid to the debenture holder irrespective of whether the debtor company is in profit.

Many of the statutory rules that regulate an issue of shares are equally applicable to an issue of debentures. However, unlike an issue of shares, a company may offer debentures at a discounted price providing the debentures do not confer an immediate right of conversion into shares (see, e.g. *Campbell's case* (1876) 4 Ch D 470). A debenture may be offered on the basis that it may be converted into shares at a future date (CA 2006, s.551). In the context of public companies, convertible debentures must first be offered to existing shareholders or debenture holders before being offered to the general public (CA 2006, s.561).

Following an allotment of a debenture(s) the company must, within two months after the date of the allotment, register the same with the registrar of companies (CA 2006, s.741). A failure to register the debenture(s) will result in the company, and every officer of the company in default, being made subject to a fine. Where a company elects to keep a register of debenture holders (there is no statutory requirement to the effect that a register must be kept by the company) the register must be kept available for inspection at the company's registered office or at another place in the part of the UK in which the company is registered (CA 2006, s.743). In accordance with CA 2006, s.744, a register of debenture holders must, except when duly closed, be open to the inspection (without charge) of a registered debenture holder or any shareholder of the company and (subject to the payment of a fee) to any other person as may be prescribed (note that an inspection request may be challenged by the company by an application to the court on the ground that the request was not for a proper purpose). A register is 'duly closed' if it is closed in accordance with a provision contained in the articles or in the relevant debentures. The total period for which a register is closed in any one year must not exceed 30 days.

CA 2006, s.739 provides that a debenture(s), or a deed for securing a debenture(s), may be issued whereby the debenture is made irredeemable, or redeemable only on the happening of a contingency (however remote), or on the expiration of a specified period (however long). Unless otherwise provided for by a company's articles, where a company redeems previously issued debentures, the company may reissue the debentures, either by reissuing the same debentures or by issuing new debentures in their place. On a reissue of redeemed debentures the person entitled to the debentures has (and is deemed always to have had) the same priorities as if the debentures had never been redeemed.

11.2.1 Debenture stock

As with a company share, a debenture is transferable; it may be sold on by its original holder. Nevertheless, a debenture may only be transferred in its original form (i.e. a debenture with a face value of £200 cannot be sold off in units of £10; it may only be sold as a £200 debenture). However, an issue of debentures can be made in the form of debenture stock. This will take the form of a loan fund, the sum of which is advanced to the company by trustees (usually a bank or other financial institution). The purpose of this trust relationship is to confer on the trustee the power to enforce the conditions laid down in the debenture in favour of the holders of the stock, namely, the beneficiaries of the trust agreement. Individual investors (the stock holders) subscribe for a portion of the stock. For example, if debenture stock to the sum of £50,000 is issued, a holder of the stock may obtain £5,000 worth of the loan fund (debenture stock). The holder of the £5,000 loan stock is then able to transfer units of whatever minimum denomination is attached to the particular debenture stock issue. Where debenture stock is issued, holders of the stock will, in terms of priority of repayment of the funds invested in the stock, take equally, i.e. *pari passu*.

11.3 SECURITY INTERESTS

In circumstances where a company is required to raise finance, especially long-term finance, it will almost inevitably be obliged to give security for the sum it wishes to borrow. An action by a secured creditor to realise a security interest will not normally be possible until the debtor company fails to meet its obligations under the terms of the debenture contract. However, where a company borrows money by way of an overdraft facility, the overdraft may be expressed to be repayable on demand.

11.3.1 The mortgage/legal charge

As a security interest a mortgage comprises a conveyance of an interest in property with a provision for redemption. Following the enactment of the Law of Property Act 1925, a legal mortgage is ordinarily created by way of a charge by deed expressed to be by way of legal mortgage; this is often referred to as a legal charge. A mortgage may also be of an equitable character, for example, where a mortgage of land is created in writing other than by deed. The available remedies for enforcing a legal or equitable mortgage include possession, foreclosure and sale.

11.3.2 The equitable fixed/specific charge

A fixed charge (alternatively referred to as a specific charge) is equitable in character but, unlike a mortgage, does not involve a conveyance of any interest in the assets that form the subject matter of the security; the fixed charge merely gives the chargee certain rights over the charged property. The precise rights of the chargee will be contained within the debenture creating the charge. However, subject to the requirements of registration (discussed below), a fixed charge will confer an immediate security over the charged property, giving the chargee a right, in accordance with the terms of the debenture, to enforce the sale of the charged assets to discharge the secured debt. Having created a fixed charge over its property, the company cannot sell or deal with the charged asset without obtaining first the permission of the fixed charge holder. It is inconsistent with the nature of a specific charge for the chargor to be at liberty to deal with the charged property. In order to create a fixed charge over a corporate asset, the asset in question must be identifiable and be of a permanent nature, for example a factory. However, the physical subject matter of the fixed charge need not be in existence at the time the charge was created (i.e. a fixed charge may attach to future property). In *Re Yorkshire Woolcombers* [1903] 2 Ch 284, Vaughan Williams LJ stressed that it was quite inconsistent with

189

the nature of a specific charge for the chargor to be at liberty to deal with the relevant property as he or she pleased. His Lordship stated:

> I do not think that for a 'specific security' you need have a security of a subject matter which is then in existence. I mean by 'then' at the time of the execution of the security; but what you do require to make a specific security is that the security whenever it has once come into existence, and been identified or appropriated as a security, shall never thereafter at the will of the mortgagor cease to be a security. If at the will of the mortgagor he can dispose of it and prevent its being any longer a security, although something else may be substituted more or less for it, that is not a specific security. (at p.294)

Property which is subject to a fixed charge and which is sold on to a third party without the chargee's consent will remain subject to the charge unless the third party is a *bona fide* purchaser without notice of the existence of the charge. However, providing the charge is registered, a third party will be deemed to have constructive notice of its existence.

11.3.3   The floating charge

While it may be advisable for a creditor, when loaning funds to a company, to secure the funds by means of a fixed charge or mortgage, priority issues and the nature of the property to be charged may require the creditor to secure his or her interest by means of a floating charge. For example, the company (chargor) may have already created a fixed charge (F) over a particular asset (A) over which a subsequent creditor (C) wishes to secure his loan. Here the merit of C taking a second fixed charge over A may depend upon the value of the asset in relation to the amount of credit secured by F (F as first created over A will have priority over subsequent fixed charges taken over A). If the value of A is only sufficient to meet the debt attached to F, there would be little point in C taking a further fixed charge over A. Where circumstances render the creation of a subsequent fixed charge to be ineffectual, a creditor may secure his or her loan by means of a floating charge (however, note there are other advantages in taking a floating charge – discussed below).

The floating charge is a device that can be given only as a security for a debt incurred by a limited company, a device created by the Court of Chancery (see the *Panama* case (1870) 5 Ch App 318). The nature of a floating charge is that the charge (unlike a fixed charge) does not attach itself to a specific corporate asset until the happening of a specified event; this event triggers the 'crystallisation' of the charge (discussed below). The floating charge will be created over a class of assets which, by their very nature, are of a constantly changing character. Property to which a floating charge is likely to attach will include stock, plant, tools, book debts and other transient assets of a company. However, it is common practice for a floating charge to be expressed to encompass 'the whole of the company's undertaking' (i.e. following its crystallisation, the charge will be intended to take priority over all corporate assets other than those subject to a prior fixed charge or mortgage).

In effect, the floating charge is created over assets of a shifting nature and the sale of such assets will be one of the means by which the company will earn income by which it can meet its obligations under the terms of the debenture that created the floating charge. However, a practical disadvantage of the floating charge is that the security interest is dependent upon a class of assets which, in terms of their volume and therefore value, may depreciate, even to a level which falls below the amount of the loan secured by the charge. Nevertheless, given that assets subject to a floating charge are of a changing nature so preventing them being readily identified (in a quantifiable specific sense), any attempt to create a fixed charge over such assets would be impracticable given that the holder of the fixed charge would need to be continually renewing the terms of his charge so as to keep pace with the changing nature of the assets. In addition, if such assets were made subject to a fixed charge, the company would be put in the most difficult position of having to notify and seek the permission of the holder of the fixed charge whenever it wished to dispose of an asset forming part of the chargee's security.

11.4 CHARACTERISTICS AND NATURE OF THE FLOATING CHARGE

In *Re Yorkshire Woolcombers Association Ltd* [1903] 2 Ch 284 (sub nom. *Illingworth* v. *Houldsworth* (HL)), Romer LJ tentatively identified the floating charge as possessing the following characteristics:

- a charge on all of a class of assets of the company present and future;
- a charge on a class of assets which in the ordinary course of a company's business would be changing from time to time;
- a charge which would allow the company to carry on its business in the ordinary way (i.e. the company would have the ability to trade in the assets which were subject to the floating charge).

Further, it is normal practice in a contract of floating charge to include within its terms express clauses which stipulate (a) that the company will not deal with its assets otherwise than in the normal course of its business and (b) that the company will not grant a further charge over the charged asset which would rank, in terms of priority, ahead of the floating charge (the negative pledge clause). The validity of the negative pledge clause has remained unchallenged and is now regarded as a standard and unexceptional term of most floating charge contracts.

11.4.1 Crystallisation of the floating charge

A company may continue to deal with the assets which form the subject matter of a floating charge right up until the time the charge crystallises (see, e.g. *Re Borax* [1901] Ch 326). Following crystallisation, the class of assets that were subject to the floating charge will be rendered identifiable and as such the floating charge will crystallise into an equitable fixed charge (see, e.g. *Re Griffin Hotel* [1941] Ch 129).

191

A floating charge will crystallise in circumstances where a creditor takes action to realise the security following the happening of a specified event (i.e. the specified event will be provided for within the debenture document, for example, non-payment of interest). Prior to the implementation of EA 2002 (in force from 15 September 2003 and therefore only applicable to charges created after that date), the creditor's 'action to realise the security' would have occurred where he or she sought the appointment of an administrative receiver. However, a floating charge may have crystallised in other circumstances, namely:

- On the happening of a specified event stipulated in the debenture which automatically crystallises the charge. Here, the charge would crystallise into a fixed charge without the need for the chargee to appoint an administrative receiver (discussed below).
- Where the crystallisation of the charge was triggered by an event implied by law – for example, where the company was subject to the appointment of a liquidator, the appointment of a receiver (by another secured creditor) or the cessation of the company's business (or an inability to carry on business in the usual way) (see, e.g. *Re Woodroffes (Musical Instruments) Ltd* [1985] BCLC 227 and *Re The Real Meat Co Ltd* [1996] BCC 254).

Following the enactment of EA 2002 and in respect of floating charges created after 15 September 2003, the floating charge will still crystallise by an event implied by law (see above) or in circumstances where the charge is subject to an automatic crystallisation clause. However, as ordinarily a floating charge will no longer be subject to the appointment of a receiver (i.e. in respect of floating charges created after 15 September 2003) the charge can no longer crystallise on the happening of that event. Following the enactment of EA 2002, the administrative receiver's role is replaced by the role now played by an administrator. (The respective roles of an administrative receiver and an administrator are examined in **Chapter 22**.) However, it is unclear whether a floating charge will now crystallise immediately following the appointment of an administrator (or at some time later) in a way it would previously have done following the appointment of a receiver, especially as an administrator's primary role is to rescue the company and act generally in the interests of all of the company's creditors. Nevertheless, given that a floating charge 'floats' until the company ceases to carry on business in the usual way, the appointment of an administrator will imply, in an obvious sense, that the business of the company is not to be carried on in the usual way which therefore may point to the conclusion that the floating charge will, indeed, crystallise on the appointment of an administrator.

11.4.2 Automatic crystallisation

A clause in a debenture contract that provides that a floating charge will crystallise into an equitable fixed charge on the happening of a specified event without the need for the chargee to make claim to the assets subject to the charge (previously by, for example, the appointment of a receiver) is termed an automatic crystallisation clause. The judicial acceptance of automatic crystallisation clauses was a gradual one. In *Re Brightlife Ltd* [1986] BCLC 418, Hoffmann J opined that automatic crystallisation clauses would be effective in circumstances where very clear language was used to create a term of the debenture giving effect to the process of automatic crystallisation. Hoffmann J interpreted the decision of the House of Lords in *Government Stock & Other Securities Investment Co Ltd* v. *Manila Rly Co Ltd* [1897] AC 81 as indicative of the view that the validity of an automatic crystallisation clause should be sought by the construction of the term purporting to create it. Hoffmann J supported the decision of the New Zealand court in *Re Manurewa Transport Ltd* [1971] NZLR 909, which gave effect to the contracting party's freedom to include a term within a debenture which permitted the automatic crystallisation of the floating charge. The judicial acceptance of the automatic crystallisation clause is now well established (see, e.g. *Griffiths* v. *Yorkshire Bank plc* [1994] 1 WLR 1427).

The principal criticism levied against the concept of automatic crystallisation is one based upon public policy issues, namely, as an automatic crystallisation clause is not subject to the registration procedure, the effect of an automatic crystallisation clause within a floating charge may usurp the priority rights of a floating charge created prior in time (see priority interests – discussed below).

11.4.3 Appointment of receiver/administrator

Where a floating charge was created prior to the implementation of EA 2002 (i.e. pre-15 September 2003) the holder of the charge may appoint an administrative receiver (defined by the IA 1986, s.29(2)) to realise the security interest. An administrative receiver acts as an agent of the chargee and seeks to protect the interests expressed in the charge; the position carries extensive powers (see IA 1986, Sched.1 – discussed further in **Chapter 22**). However, following the implementation of EA 2002, the holder of a floating charge (created after 15 September 2003) will now be obliged to appoint an administrator to (eventually) realise the security (discussed further in **Chapter 22**). (This applies except in exceptional and well-defined circumstances, relating to larger corporate lending agreements, for example, capital market investments of a minimum of £50 million – in such cases a receiver may still be appointed.)

The objective of the new administration system is, where possible, to promote corporate rescue. However, where corporate rescue is deemed to be impossible, the administrator must seek to benefit the interests of the company's creditors as a whole. A holder of one or more qualifying floating charge(s) may appoint an administrator (IA 1986, Sched.B1, para.14). A qualifying charge is defined as an instrument which expressly stipulates that para.14 is to apply or alternatively, a charge which, on its own or taken with other securities, extends to the whole or substantially the whole of the company's property. Where there is more than one qualifying floating charge, the holder of a charge (charge B) may not appoint an administrator if charge A was created prior to B's charge; unless the following conditions are satisfied (IA 1986, Sched.B1, para.15(1)):

- the holder of charge B gives at least two business days' written notice to the holder of any prior floating charge A; or
- the holder of any prior floating charge A consents in writing to the appointment of the administrator (by the holder of charge B).

Schedule B1, para.15(2) provides that a qualifying floating charge is prior to another floating charge if it is either prior in time or if it is to be treated as having priority in accordance with an inter-creditor agreement. An inter-creditor agreement is one whereby a creditor with a charge over corporate property (the first chargee) transfers his or her priority interest in favour of another creditor, the other creditor having previously held an inferior ranking charge. In practice, a contractual agreement between the first and second chargees to effect such an alteration in the priority position may afford some commercial advantage to the first chargee. The first chargee's priority rights may be transferred without the need to seek the approval of the company that created the charge (see, e.g. *Cheah Theam Swee* v. *Equiticorp Finance Group Ltd* [1992] BCC 98, *Re Portbase (Clothing) Ltd* [1993] BCC 96).

11.4.4   Appointment of an administrator (Sched.B1)

In fulfilment of Sched.B1, para.15(2), a holder of a floating charge may appoint an administrator by simply filing a notice of appointment at court, i.e. without the requirement of a court application or hearing, or without demonstrating that the company was or is likely to become unable to pay its debts. The appointment of the administrator takes effect from the date of the filing of the notice of appointment. However, in rare cases (especially those relating to cross-border cases) an administrator may be appointed by the court. It is to be noted that it will be unnecessary to seek the court's approval in relation to the appointment of a receiver where a floating charge was created prior to 15 September 2003. Further, the appointment of an administrative receiver will prevent the subsequent appointment of an administrator, i.e. unless the receiver consents to the subsequent appointment of an administrator.

An administrator may also be appointed without the involvement of the court by the chargor company (by a members' resolution in general meeting or a resolution of the company's directors (IA 1986, Sched.B1, para.22)). However, this type of appointment may be overturned by a debenture holder who, within a five-day period from the company giving notice of its intention to appoint an administrator, may appoint his or her own administrator (or administrative receiver if the charge was created prior to 15 September 2003).

In accordance with IA 1986, Sched.B1, paras.43–44 and following an application to appoint an administrator, creditors will be ordinarily precluded (unless authorised by the administrator or by the court) from enforcing their legal rights relating to the enforcement of a security interest or debt against the company. This moratorium period covers hire purchase agreements, conditional sale agreements, chattel leasing agreements and retention of title agreements. The moratorium allows the administrator to consider and plan suitable options in respect of achieving a corporate rescue and/or the realisation of the company's assets. Once a company has entered administration, the moratorium also prevents a winding-up order being sought or made against the company.

11.4.5   Avoidance of floating charges

In accordance with IA 1986, s.245, a floating charge may be invalidated if it was created in the period of 12 months prior to the onset of the company's insolvency, where, at the time of its creation, the company was unable to pay its debts or, as a result of the transaction creating the charge, the company became unable to pay its debts. An exception to this rule is where the charge was created in consideration for money paid at the same time as or after its creation. However, in respect of a charge created in favour of a connected person, unless it was created in consideration for money paid at the same time as or after its creation, the charge will be deemed invalid where it was created two years prior to the company's insolvency. A connected person is defined by IA 1986, s.249 as a person who is a director or shadow director of the company or an associate of the director/shadow director. An associate is defined by IA 1986, s.435 as a husband or wife, relative, or husband or wife of a relative. Where a charge is invalidated, the property over which the charge was created may be realised to the benefit of the company's unsecured creditors.

11.5   A FIXED OR FLOATING CHARGE?

In some instances (most notably cases in which a charge is created over book debts) it may be difficult to distinguish between whether the charge was created as a fixed or floating charge. In seeking to distinguish between a fixed and floating charge it is important to stress that it would be most incorrect to attempt to distinguish the nature of a charge on the basis that the asset over which the charge operates was one that could be employed in a company's ordinary course of business. Assets over which either a fixed or floating charge is placed will always be used in the pursuit of a company's business activities. In reality the fundamental and distinguishing characteristic between a fixed and floating charge relates to the capacity of the chargor to dispose of or deal with the charged asset. In respect of a floating charge, up until the time the charge crystallises, the chargor may dispose or deal with the assets made subject to the charge without any form of substantive restriction (see, e.g. *Re G E Tunbridge Ltd* [1994] BCC 563, *Re Cosslett Contractors Ltd* [1998] Ch 495). By contrast, if assets over which a charge is taken cannot readily be disposed of or dealt with by the chargor, i.e. without the chargee's permission, the charge will be classed as a fixed charge. In *Re Cosslett (Contractors) Ltd* [1997] BCC 724, the

Court of Appeal held that in considering the nature of a charge, it was essential to determine whether the company (chargor) retained control over the charged assets and not necessarily whether the chargor had an absolute freedom to employ the charged assets in the ordinary course of its business. Where control was retained the charge would be floating in nature. As Millett LJ observed:

> The essence of a floating charge is that it is a charge, not on any particular asset, but on a fluctuating body of assets which remain under the management and control of the chargor, and which the chargor has the right to withdraw from the security despite the existence of the charge. The essence of a fixed charge is that the charge is on a particular asset or class of assets that the chargor cannot deal with free from the charge without the consent of the chargee. The question is not whether the chargor has complete freedom to carry on his business as he chooses, but whether the chargee is in control of the charged assets. (at p.734)

Although the priority position of a fixed charge is superior to that of a floating charge, creditors in purporting to secure a loan by way of a fixed charge have often fallen short of achieving their purpose, even where the debenture specifies, in terms of language, that the security interest is to be created as a fixed charge. Therefore, if a charge is identified within a debenture to be one created as a fixed charge but in reality the characteristics of the charge are more akin to a floating charge, the charge will be construed to have been created as a floating charge (see, e.g. *Royal Trust Bank* v. *National Westminster Bank plc* [1996] 2 BCLC 682). Likewise, a charge described within a debenture contract as one created as a floating charge may, from its characteristics, be held to have been created as a fixed charge (see, e.g. *The Russell Cooke Trust Company Ltd* v. *Elliott* [2007] 2 BCLC 637).

11.5.1 Construction of the charge

The decision of Hoffmann J in *Re Brightlife* [1987] Ch 200 provides a classic example of a charge being construed by the court as a floating charge, notwithstanding that the written terms of the charge had purported to create a fixed charge. The charge was created over a company's book debts. A charge over a company's book debts represents a security interest in both the uncollected debts owed to the company and the realised proceeds of such debts. Although a charge over book debts cannot attach itself to the proceeds part of the secured asset until such a time as the debts are realised, a security interest in acquired property operates as a present interest where it is intended to take immediate effect, subject only to its acquisition by the debtor. Therefore, as from the date of its creation, a charge over book debts is of a continuous nature and will apply to both the unrealised book debt and the realised proceeds part of the book debt. When book debts are realised, the asset over which the charge was originally taken (the unrealised debt) will be substituted by the proceeds of the book debt. To return to the case of *Re Brightlife*, here the terms of the charge prohibited Brightlife Ltd (B) from selling, factoring or discounting its book debts and from dealing with the same otherwise than in the ordinary course of getting in and realising the debts. As the chargor was prohibited from dealing with the unrealised debts, the effect of the charge over uncollected book debts appeared to be that of a fixed charge. However, as the charge failed to restrict B from disposing of the proceeds of its book debts in the ordinary course of its business, here, the nature of the charge appeared to more akin to a floating charge. Indeed, notwithstanding the restrictions placed upon the chargor's ability to sell, factor or discount the unrealised debts and given the ability of the chargor to freely dispose of the realised assets, the overall nature of the charge was held to be a floating charge. Hoffmann J sought to explain this finding on the premise that the nature of a floating charge allowed some form of restriction to be placed on the company's ability to deal with the charged assets, albeit that the usual form of restriction was a negative pledge clause (discussed above) (see also *Re Armagh Shoes Ltd* [1982] NI 59, *Norgard* v. *DFCT* [1987] ACLR 527).

By contrast, in *Siebe Gorman & Co Ltd* v. *Barclays Bank* [1979] 2 Lloyd's Rep 142, Slade J construed a debenture, similar in content to the one found in *Re Brightlife*, as one that had created a specific charge over the present and future book debts of the company. The *Siebe Gorman* case concerned a debenture contract which purported to create a specific charge over the present and future book debts of a company named RH McDonald Ltd (M), the charge having been created in favour of Barclays Bank. The debenture contract prohibited M from selling, factoring or discounting its book debts and from dealing with the same otherwise than in the ordinary course of getting in and realising the debts. M was obliged to pay the proceeds received from all present and future book debts into its account (current account) held at Barclays Bank and that subject to the prior consent of the bank in writing, the company would not charge or assign the 'same' in favour of any other person. Although the company's current account was associated with its day-to-day business expenditure, Slade J considered that the bank's general lien and rights over the funds in the current account (in operation until the charge had been extinguished) enabled it to control and restrict the account, even if in credit, thus removing any contention that the company had a freedom to draw on the account at its absolute will. The charge was construed to be a fixed charge notwithstanding that it must have been contemplated by the parties that while in credit to the bank, the company would be at liberty to draw on its current account (which in practice it did to satisfy its everyday commercial commitments) without having to obtain the permission of the chargee. (Note that in subsequent cases, it may be argued that the courts exhibited an even more liberal approach to the acceptance of a charge as a specific charge notwithstanding that it more readily exhibited the characteristics of a floating charge – see, e.g. the Court of Appeal's decision in *Re Atlantic Computer Systems plc* [1990] BCC 859 and the decision of Vinelott J in *Re Atlantic Medical* [1992] BCC 653.)

11.5.2 *National Westminster Bank* v. *Spectrum Plus Ltd*

Although in terms of an authority, *Siebe Gorman* was followed for over 25 years, the precedent of this decision was finally overruled by the House of Lords in *National*

Westminster Bank v. *Spectrum Plus Ltd* [2005] 2 AC 680 (overturning the decision of the Court of Appeal [2004] 3 WLR 503). The facts of *National Westminster Bank* v. *Spectrum Plus Ltd* gave rise to issues almost identical to those found in the *Siebe Gorman* case. The bank (NW) had purported to create a fixed charge over the book debts of Spectrum (S) with the charge in question providing, *inter alia*, that the company had to pay proceeds arising from its realised book debts into its bank account which was held with NW. The charge contained *Siebe Gorman* type restrictions in respect of the disposal of the unrealised debts but, in respect of the realised proceeds, these were to be paid into a trading account that S could (subject to NW's contractual right to decline to release funds) employ in the ordinary course of its business. The House of Lords held that the security could not be classified as a fixed charge because the terms of the debenture, in allowing S (unless NW intervened) to use the proceeds of the realised book debts in the ordinary course of its business, rendered the charge inconsistent with the characteristics associated with a fixed charge.

11.5.3 Creating a fixed charge over book debts?

A more satisfactory and acceptable method of creating a fixed charge over book debts may be found within the debenture considered by the Supreme Court of Ireland in *Re Keenan Bros Ltd* (1986) 2 BCC 98, 970 (a method approved by the House of Lords in the *Spectrum* case). Here the terms of the charge specified that the chargor could not, without the prior consent of the chargee, waive, assign or otherwise deal with the book debts in favour of any other person. The charge also obliged the company to pay all monies received from realised book debts into a designated account held with the chargee, an account specific for the purpose of collecting the proceeds of the book debts and one which could not be used as a current account. Therefore, once realised, the proceeds of the book debts were paid into a special account and as such were isolated and identifiable as separate funds.

It should be noted, following *obiter* comments by the House of Lords in *National Westminster* v. *Spectrum Plus Ltd* [2005] 2 AC 680, that it is most improbable that a debenture purporting to deal with book debts as divisible between a fixed charge and a floating charge, whereby the fixed charge is attached to the unrealised proceeds part of the book debts and the floating charge applied to the realised proceeds part of the book debts, will be upheld as anything other than an all-embracing floating charge (however, note *Re Harmony Care Homes* [2010] BCC 358 (discussed below)). At one time, following the decision of the Court of Appeal in *Re New Bullas Trading Ltd* [1994] 1 BCLC 485, it was considered that a charge could be construed in a divisible manner. In *Re New Bullas* administrative receivers sought the order of priority by which payments should be made to secured creditors. The sums available for distribution comprised the realised proceeds of the company's book debts, the debts having been uncollected prior to the appointment of the administrative receivers. A creditor holding a charge over the company's book debts sought priority in the repayment of the monies. The terms of the charge prohibited the company from selling, factoring or discounting the book debts and provided that all outstanding book debts were to be the subject of a specific charge, the proceeds of which were to be paid into a nominated account. The charge further provided that on the realisation of the debts, the proceeds were to be dealt with in accordance with the chargee's instructions, albeit in the absence of any such instructions, sums paid into the account were to be released from the specific charge to become subject to a floating charge.

In reversing the decision of Knox J, the Court of Appeal held that the security interest had been intended to operate as a specific charge in relation to the unrealised book debts and a floating charge in respect of the proceeds of the debts. The court's acceptance of the divisible nature of the charge and its application to the uncollected debts (fixed charge) and the proceeds of the debts (floating charge) necessitated the recognition of a procedure by which the assets secured by the specific charge would be transferred to the floating charge and to this end the court gave weight to the contractual intentions of the parties in relation to how the transfer of assets would be achieved. Accordingly, the intention to create a charge which purported to split itself to create a fixed charge over uncollected debts and a floating charge over the proceeds of the debts had to be specifically spelt out within the terms of the debenture, otherwise it would fail to create the divisible charge (see, e.g. *Re Westmaze Ltd* [1999] BCC 441). In *Re New Bullas* the Court of Appeal accepted the validity of the divisible charge on the premise that a fixed charge over uncollected book debts and a floating charge over the proceeds of the debts appeared to equate to a natural and logical division of the distinct elements of a book debt. Further, the Court of Appeal accepted that the parties to the debenture had contractual freedom to agree to the precise moment in time when the fixed charge would convert into a floating charge.

Although the decision in *Re New Bullas* portrayed much commercial logic in its identification of the distinct and split characteristics of book debt assets and sought also to champion the principle of freedom of contract, the decision was subsequently disapproved of by the Privy Council in *Agnew* v. *Commissioner of Inland Revenue (Re Brumark)* [2001] 2 AC 710. In *Agnew* the charge was drafted in almost identical terms to the charge in *Re New Bullas*. Indeed, the only difference between the two charges (which the Privy Council considered to be immaterial) was that in *Re New Bullas* the proceeds of the book debts were not released from the fixed charge until they were actually paid into the company's bank account, whereas in *Agnew* the book debts were released from the fixed charge as soon as they were received by the company. Accordingly, in *Agnew* the parties' intention was that other than if the chargee intervened, the chargor would be able to collect the proceeds of the book debts, whereupon the proceeds would become subject to a floating charge. As such, the proceeds of the book debts would be used in the ordinary course of the company's business unless there was a contrary direction from the chargee directing that the proceeds or a part of the proceeds be paid into a nominated account (in which case the proceeds paid into the nominated account would remain subject to the fixed charge). In *Agnew*, the Privy Council's criticism of *Re New Bullas* was directed at the methodology applied by the Court of Appeal in relation to the construction of the charge in *Re New Bullas*, as one of a divisible nature. In *Agnew*, Lord Millett explained the two-stage process to determine whether a charge was fixed or floating. The first stage was to construe the debenture to gather the intentions of the parties (albeit that that construction could not be considered as the key to determining the nature of the charge). The second and crucial stage was to construe the legal consequences that had been attached to the parties' intentions. In *Agnew*, as in *Re New Bullas*, the intention of the parties was to create a fixed charge over the uncollected book debts, which would convert to a floating charge in respect of the realised debts. However, according to Lord Millett, that intention could not marry with its desired effect in so far as the freedom afforded to the chargor to purportedly divert the realised assets away from the fixed charge – to be made subject then to a floating charge was, in essence, destructive of the very nature of a fixed charge, i.e., if a charge was to be construed as a fixed charge then by its very nature the fixed charge required the chargee to retain absolute control over the charged assets. Although the chargee had an express power (within the debenture) to intervene, at will, to prevent the disposal of the realised debts in the ordinary course of the company's business the Privy Council considered this to be an inadequate method of control to otherwise substantiate the charge being construed as one created as fixed/specific in nature.

Therefore, an authority afforded by the chargee to the chargor to permit the latter to dispose of assets in the ordinary course of its business (as in *Agnew* and *Re New Bullas*) must now be viewed as being inconsistent with the existence of a fixed charge, notwithstanding that the charge allows the possibility of notice being given by the chargee to reverse that position to the intention of converting the floating charge (expressed over the proceeds) back into a fixed charge. For the unrealised debts and proceeds of book debts to be construed to be subject to an all-embracing fixed charge, the chargee must have near to absolute control of the charged assets (see the approach taken in *Re Keenan Bros Ltd*).

However, in *Re Harmony Care Homes* [2010] BCC 358, a debenture purporting to create a divisible security interest (on the face of it one similar to the New Bullas type charge) was held to have created a fixed charge security. Here the security was *prima facie* expressed to be by way of a fixed charge over uncollected book debts and a floating charge over the proceeds of the debts. The proceeds of the uncollected debts were to be paid into a designated account and in the absence of any directions from the chargee, the terms of the debenture created a floating charge over the proceeds of the debts. However, in construing the exact nature of the charge, Susan Prevezer QC, sitting as a deputy High Court judge, concluded that the evidence of the case was that all the collected book debts were subject to the chargee's absolute control, to the extent that from the outset, the status of the security was specific and ascertained. Funds paid into the designated account had not been realised by the chargor nor could they have been without the express permission of the chargee. The effect and intent of the debenture was to disentitle the company from using the proceeds of the book debts as a source of its cash flow. Although in *Re Harmony*

Care Homes the terms of the charge gave the chargor an opportunity to dispose of the proceeds of the book debts in the ordinary course of its business, that option could only be realised with the permission of the chargee. Nevertheless, although the chargor did not activate that option, the fact that the option existed may have suggested that the nature of the charge was not, in an absolute sense, specific. However, in defence of the decision taken in *Re Harmony Care Homes*, to the conclusion that the charge was specific in nature, if one, for example, follows the *dicta* of Romer LJ in *Re Yorkshire Woolcombers Association Ltd* [1903] 2 Ch 284, the effect of the charge did not allow the company to carry on its business in the ordinary way, in so far as the charge restricted severely the company's ability to use the funds from the book debts in the ordinary course of its business.

11.6 THE REGISTRATION OF CHARGES

A company will rarely give up physical possession of the assets made subject to a charge. Accordingly, future creditors may be duped into believing that the property remains unencumbered, with the result that a creditor may advance funds to a company on the strength of an apparent but nevertheless illusionary wealth. To prevent the potential for such abuse, government-administered registers have been devised for the purpose of recording non-possessory charges. In addition to the government registration requirements, a non-possessory charge on almost any kind of property belonging to a registered company will require further registration with the registrar of companies (see the Companies Act 2006 (Amendment of Part 25) Regulations 2013, SI 2013/600). This statutory instrument applies to charges created on or after 6 April 2013. The statutory instrument inserts new ss.859A–859Q into CA 2006. For charges created prior to 6 April 2013, the previous provisions under CA 2006, Part 25, Chapter 1 will still apply (see Companies Act 2006 (Amendment of Part 25) Regulations 2013, reg.6)). In creating a charge, a company must deliver to the registrar of companies the prescribed particulars of the charge, together with the instrument (if any) by which the charge is created or evidenced. A charge is defined to include a mortgage (see CA 2006, s.859A(7)). The prescribed particulars are specified by CA 2006, s.859D and include, *inter alia*, whether the charge is expressed to be a floating charge and whether it contains a negative pledge clause.

The time period for delivery of the same is 21 days, beginning with the day after the day on which the charge is created (CA 2006, s.859A(4)). For guidance in relation to the dates when charges of specified categories are deemed to have been created for the purposes of the 21-day limit, see CA 2006, s.859E.

11.6.1 Charges requiring registration

Prior to the Companies Act 2006 (Amendment of Part 25) Regulations 2013, SI 2013/600 charges that required registration were listed in CA 2006, s.860(7) (there was no change in content from the previous list, i.e. CA 1985, s.396(1)). That list (see below) no longer applies in the case of charges created from the commencement of the Companies Act 2006 (Amendment of Part 25) Regulations 2013, SI 2013/600. SI 3013/600 came into force from 6 April 2013. The list (applicable only to charges created prior to 6 April 2013) was as follows:

(a)   a charge on land or any interest in land other than a charge for rent or any other periodical payment;
(b)   a charge created or evidenced by an instrument, which, if executed by an individual, would require registration as a bill of sale;
(c)   a charge for the purpose of securing an issue of debentures;
(d)   a charge on uncalled share capital of the company;
(e)   a charge on calls made but not paid;
(f)   a charge on book debts of the company;
(g)   a floating charge on the company's undertaking or property;
(h)   a charge on a ship or aircraft, or any share in a ship;
(i)   a charge on goodwill, trademarks, patents, copyright, etc.

In accordance with CA 2006, s.859A(6) (inserted by the Companies Act 2006 (Amendment of Part 25) Regulations 2013) all charges created after 6 April 2013 will require registration other than:

- a charge in favour of a landlord on a cash deposit given as security in connection with the lease of land;
- a charge created by a member of Lloyd's to secure its obligations in connection with its underwriting business at Lloyd's; and
- a charge excluded by or under any other Act.

11.6.2   The registration certificate

In registering a charge it is necessary to include specific information, for example, the date of the creation of the charge, the amount secured by the charge, short particulars of the property charged and the persons entitled to the charge. The registration certificate is deemed to be conclusive evidence that, in terms of registration, the requirements of the Companies Act have been satisfied. The registrar will have the ultimate responsibility for checking the contents of the particulars. It is for the registrar to decide what charges have been created; the registrar will allocate a unique reference code to the charge (CA 2006, s.859I). The registrar may be liable for any loss suffered as a consequence of a mistake in such matters. Prior to the Companies Act 2006 (Amendment of Part 25) Regulations 2013, for failing to register a charge, a company and any officer of the company in default, would be punishable by way of a fine. The failure to register could also be taken into account in any disqualification proceedings instigated against a director. As a result of the Companies Act 2006 (Amendment of Part 25) Regulations 2013, for charges created after 6 April, that criminal liability is no more. A charge that is not registered within the requisite period will be void against a liquidator, administrator and any creditor of the company, although the obligation to repay the money secured by the charge will not be invalidated by a failure to register; indeed, it becomes immediately repayable upon demand (CA 2006, s.859H).

11.6.3 Rectification

The certificate of registration is conclusive, although errors in the filed particulars of a charge will not prevent enforcement of the rights contained therein (see, e.g. *Re Nye* [1971] Ch 1052). However, CA 2006, s.859F permits rectification of the register in circumstances where, for example, the court is satisfied that:

* an omission or misstatement of any particular was accidental;
* an omission or misstatement was due to inadvertence or to some other sufficient cause;
* the omission or misstatement was of a nature to prejudice the position of creditors or shareholders of the company; and
* it is just and equitable to grant relief on other grounds.

Rectification will not be permitted where, for example, the subject matter of a claim is not concerned with the particulars which the registrar is required to enter on to the register of charges. For example, in *Igroup Ltd* v. *Owen* [2004] 2 BCLC 61 rectification was not permitted in a situation where Igroup Ltd sought to remove schedules within the filed particulars that contained personal information about its customers. Igroup sought to remove the schedules on the ground that disclosure of such information could amount to a breach of its duty of confidence.

11.6.4 Late delivery

The only method of registering particulars after the elapse of the 21-day period is by a court order, via an application under CA 2006, s.859F (see, e.g. *Registrar of Companies, ex parte Central Bank of India* [1986] 2 QB 1114). In considering an application under s.859F, the court must find evidence that would justify a decision to allow registration out of time; the court must consider whether it is equitable to grant relief and in doing so must consider the effect of allowing late registration in respect of the interests of other creditors who may be prejudiced as a result of the late registration of the particulars (see, e.g. *Re Telomatic Ltd* [1993] BCC 404).

11.6.5 The company register

In accordance with CA 2006, s.859Q a company must keep a copy of every instrument creating a charge, irrespective of whether the charge is required to be registered in accordance with CA 2006. Copies must be kept at the company's registered office and the copies must be open to inspection. However, a company is no longer required to keep a register of its charges (CA 2006, s.876 is now repealed).

11.7   EXAMPLES OF NON-REGISTRABLE INTERESTS

11.7.1   Hire purchase agreements

Where a company has acquired goods on hire purchase (HP) terms, ownership in those goods will not pass to the company until it has fulfilled all of its obligations under the HP agreement. A company cannot create a charge over goods subject to an ongoing HP agreement because, quite simply, the company is not the legal owner of the goods.

11.7.2   The retention of title clause

A retention/reservation of title clause, sometimes also referred to as a *Romalpa* clause (after the decision of the Court of Appeal in *Aluminium Industrie Vaasen BV* v. *Romalpa Aluminium Ltd* [1976] 2 All ER 552), is a contractual provision inserted into a contract of sale which purports to allow the seller to retain title in the goods he or she sells. The seller reserves title in the goods until such a time as the buyer has fulfilled certain conditions contained within the contract of sale. In terms of priority interests, a supplier of goods with a valid retention of title clause will, in the event of a company being placed into administration or liquidation, be paid monies owing to him or her in priority to a creditor whose interest is secured by a registered charge. Where a seller successfully reserves the right of ownership in goods, the buyer will be unable to create a charge over the goods (i.e. it is impossible for the buyer to create a charge over something that he or she does not legally own). The legal effect of a valid retention of title clause is therefore similar to an HP contract, save that under an HP contract the prospective buyer of the property has no legal right to pass title in the goods. By contrast, in a contract containing a valid retention of title clause, a term is implied into the clause to the effect that the prospective buyer of the goods is to be afforded the legal right to pass title in the goods (see, e.g. *Four Point Garage Ltd* v. *Carter* [1985] 3 All ER 12, *Fairfax Gerrard Holdings Ltd and Ors* v. *Capital Bank plc* [2008] 1 Lloyd's Rep 297 and *Re BA Peters plc (in administration)* [2008] BPIR 1180).

In relation to priority issues, the principal criticism of the retention of title clause is that the law does not impose a legal requirement to register such a clause. Accordingly, without the registration of the clause, a creditor wishing to take a charge over corporate assets will be unable to establish whether the assets have already been made the subject matter of a retention of title clause.

In terms of determining the validity of a retention of title clause, a retention of title clause that does no more than to retain the legal ownership in goods until such a time as the full purchase price of the goods is paid, will be upheld as reserving title in the property (see, e.g. *Clough Mill* v. *Martin* [1984] 3 All ER 982). Further, a retention of title clause may be upheld where it seeks to retain ownership in goods which have already been paid for by the buyer. For example, a contract for the sale of goods may consist of the consignment of goods: A, B, C and D. The buyer may have paid in full, for goods A and B but not for goods C and D. In this given example, the effect of an 'all monies restriction' would be that the seller would retain ownership in goods A, B, C and D until payment for all four goods had been met (see, e.g. the decision of the House of Lords in *Armour and Anor* v. *Thyssen Edelstahlweke AG* [1990] BCC 929). However, a retention of title clause that purports to retain equitable and beneficial ownership in property will not be upheld (see, e.g. *Re Bond Worth* [1980] Ch 228). The same negative conclusion will apply to a retention of title clause that purports to retain title in manufactured items that have been produced from goods supplied under the contract of sale. Here, goods supplied by the seller, having been through the manufacturing process, inevitably lose their original identity, to the extent that the manufactured goods can no longer be identified as those over which the retention of title clause was placed (see, e.g. *Clough Mill* v. *Martin* [1984] 3 All ER 982). Finally, a retention of title clause that purports to restrict the buyer's ability to deal with the proceeds of sale from the goods supplied (i.e. by allowing the seller to trace the proceeds of sale) is unlikely to be upheld. Save for the decision in *Aluminium Industrie Vaasen BV* v. *Romalpa Ltd* [1976] 1 WLR 676, there is no authority in which a restriction of this nature has been accepted, otherwise than by creating a charge on the goods (see, e.g. *Re Bond Worth* [1979] 3 All ER 919 and *Modelboard Ltd* v. *Outer Box Ltd* [1992] BCC 945).

Where the validity of a retention of title is not upheld, the seller's interest will be deemed to be an interest by way of charge that will be rendered void as a consequence of its non-registration.

11.7.3 The trust device

As a general rule, a creditor who invests funds into a company will not be deemed to have become the beneficiary of any trust relationship with the company. Nevertheless, in exceptional circumstances the courts have recognised the possibility of the inclusion of a trust device into a contract, the effect of which is to create a trustee–beneficiary relationship between the contracting parties. The validity of a trust device will afford a creditor (beneficiary) a priority in the funds governed by the trust, ahead of other creditors who may seek to lay claim to the 'trust' funds. The creation of a trust requires certainty of intention, certainty of subject matter and certainty of object. In relation to an intention to create a trust, the test to be applied is an objective one. Therefore, if a company enters into arrangements which have the effect of creating a trust, it is not necessary that it should actually appreciate that it has created a trust (see, e.g. *Twinsectra* v. *Yardley* [2002] 2 AC 164). The payment of the funds (to be subject to the trust) into a separate bank account is a positive (although not necessarily conclusive) indication of an intention to create a trust. For example, in *Re Kayford* [1975] 1 WLR 279, a mail order company took the commendable step of attempting to protect customers' funds by establishing a special trust fund into which advance payment for goods was to be deposited. The mail order company went into liquidation. The question which the court had to decide was whether this purported trust fund had the effect of protecting the company's customers' interests or whether such funds should be included as part of the assets available for distribution to the general body of the company's creditors. Megarry J found in favour of upholding the validity of the trust device, although it is to be noted that the learned judge made special mention of the fact that in this case, the creditors in question were ordinary members of the public, as opposed to trade creditors. Megarry J stated that:

> Different considerations may perhaps arise in relation to trade creditors but here I am concerned only with members of the public, some of whom can ill afford to exchange their money for a claim to a dividend in the liquidation. (at p.282)

In circumstances where a purported arrangement is found not to have achieved its purpose of creating a trust device, the arrangement will be treated as one that purported to create a charge, an arrangement that will be void for non-registration of the charge. For example, in *Gray* v. *G-T-P Group Ltd* [2011] BCC 869, a company (T) (the purported trustee) supplying store debit card services sought to enter into a trust agreement with a company (B) (the purported beneficiary) whereby sums paid by B's customers who used T's debit card would be paid into a bank account maintained by T. Under the trust agreement balances in the account would be held by T to the benefit of B and T would pay out funds (owed to B) at the will of B. Clause 3 of the trust agreement provided for specified events that would enable T to withdraw funds from the trust account, namely, (i) if B failed to pay sums due in respect of the service agreement between T and B and (ii) if B became insolvent. In effect, the account was used as medium through which monies paid by B's customers would flow to T and then on to B. B went into administration and the service agreement with T was cancelled. B was subsequently placed into liquidation and the liquidators sought the recovery of the balance in the bank account (held by T to the benefit of B) on the premise that the trust was void as constituting an unregistered floating charge in favour of T. (The purported charge was over the moneys held by T in its bank account – the charge would in effect crystalise on the happening of a stipulated specified event in clause 3 (see above).) Vos J held that the trust agreement failed in its purpose and did purport to create a floating charge (unregistered). The learned judge concluded that until one of the specified events occurred B (the chargor) could freely dispose of the funds in the account to the extent that the degree of control exerted over the bank account by T was negligible (therefore this could not be an unregistered fixed charge). The arrangement was not of a trustee–beneficiary relationship because in essence clause 3 secured the sums that may in the future have become due to T from B. As such it was a charge (unregistered) on the assets of B.

11.8 PRIORITY RIGHTS

Where a receiver, administrator (under the rules post-15 September 2003) or liquidator of a company is entrusted with the responsibility of selling a corporate asset(s) to discharge the debts of a company, the realisation of such an asset(s) may be insufficient to discharge the full amount of the debt owed to the individual creditors of the company. To determine whether a particular creditor is entitled to a priority in the repayment of his or her debt it is necessary to examine the rules governing the priority interests of competing charge holders.

11.8.1 Priority between fixed charges

A legal charge or a fixed/specific equitable charge, acquired *bona fide* for value will, subject to compliance with the registration procedure, take priority over a subsequently created and registered legal charge/fixed equitable charge because any subsequent chargee, having taken security over the same assets, will be deemed to have constructive notice of the earlier charge. However, if the prior created charge is not duly registered, the holder of the subsequently created and registered charge will take priority over the first created charge.

11.8.2 Priority between fixed and floating charges

A fixed charge created over a particular asset (an asset to which a floating charge may later become attached following its crystallisation – for example where the floating charge is taken over the company's entire undertaking) will, if it is duly registered, take priority over a prior created floating charge (see, e.g. *Re Hamilton Windsor Ironworks Co Ltd* (1879) 12 Ch D 707). A fixed charge will take priority over a prior created floating charge (for example, a floating charge taken over the company's undertaking which necessarily includes fixed assets), even if the floating charge expressly includes a covenant (negative pledge clause) on the part of the company not to create a charge ranking in priority or *pari passu* with the floating charge (i.e. provided that the subsequent fixed charge was created without notice of the content of the covenant (see, e.g. *English & Scottish Mercantile Investment Trust* v. *Brunton* [1892] 12 Ch D 707)). However, note that following the introduction of the Companies Act 2006 (Amendment of Part 25) Regulations 2013, a subsequent charge holder (the fixed charge holder) will be deemed to have constructive notice of both the earlier created floating charge and a negative pledge clause (if the clause is specified in the particulars of registration). Note also CA 2006, s.859O, introduced by the Companies Act 2006 (Amendment of Part 25) Regulations 2013. Finally, it should be noted that a fixed charge will not take priority over a floating charge where the floating charge crystallised prior to the creation and registration of the fixed charge.

11.8.3 Priority in relation to competing floating charges

Where a company creates more than one floating charge over a class of assets, the floating charge that was the first in time (if duly registered) will ordinarily take priority. This priority rule applies notwithstanding that the first in time floating charge did not contain a negative pledge clause (see, e.g. *Re Benjamin Cope & Sons Ltd* [1914] Ch 800). However, in accordance with *Griffiths* v. *Yorkshire Bank plc* [1994] 1 WLR 1427, where a subsequently registered floating charge crystallises prior to an earlier created registered floating charge (i.e. because the subsequent charge contains an automatic crystallisation clause), the subsequent charge will take priority because following its automatic crystallisation the charge becomes fixed in its nature, outranking the floating charge created first in time. It should also be noted that where a company creates a first floating charge and that charge contains a registered negative pledge clause expressed to govern a specific and defined class of assets, then a subsequent floating charge may still take priority over the first floating charge but only in respect of the class of assets that were absent from the terms of the negative pledge clause (see, e.g. *Re Automatic Bottle Markers Ltd* [1926] Ch 412).

11.8.4 Preferential creditors

The preferential debts of a company are listed in IA 1986, Sched.6. Preferential debts rank equally among themselves. Prior to the implementation of EA 2002, preferential debts were categorised as:

- debts due to the Inland Revenue (now Her Majesty's Revenue and Customs (HMRC));
- debts due to Customs and Excise (now HMRC);
- sums owed in respect of social security contributions, contributions to occupational pension schemes, remuneration of employees; and finally
- sums owed in respect of levies on coal and steel production.

However, following the implementation of EA 2002, the Crown's preferential rights have been abolished to the extent that debts due to HMRC and debts due in respect of social security contributions are no longer deemed preferential debts and as such are no longer contained within IA 1986, Sched.6. Therefore, preferential debts now comprise sums owed in respect of contributions to occupational pension schemes, the remuneration of employees and levies on coal and steel production.

In a situation where a company is not in the course of being wound up, the priority position of preferential creditors in relation to the holder of a floating charge is such that preferential debts are to be paid out of the assets coming into the hands of the receiver (administrator) in priority to any claims for principal or interest in respect of the floating charge, irrespective of whether the floating charge had crystallised prior to the appointment of the receiver (IA 1986, s.40 applies where an administrative receiver is appointed (pre-15 September 2003 debenture) and CA 2006, s.767 applies in the case of administration (post-15 September 2003 debenture)).

IA 1986, s.175 concerns the priority position of preferential debts when a company is in the process of being wound up. Where a company is in the course of being wound up, the preferential debts are also paid in priority to debts expressed to be secured by means of a floating charge (see, e.g. *Re Oval 1742 Ltd (in liq);*

Customs & Excise Commissioners v. *Royal Bank of Scotland plc* [2007] BCC 567 (Ch)). Prior to the decision of the House of Lords in *Buchler* v. *Talbot* [2004] 2 WLR 582, s.175 was interpreted in a manner whereby liquidation expenses were paid in priority (out of the realised assets of the company) to the claims of both preferential creditors and the holder of a floating charge (see *Re Barleycorn Enterprises Ltd* [1970] Ch 465). However, in overruling *Barleycorn*, the *Buchler* case held that liquidation expenses could not to be taken ahead of the claims for principal and interest owing to the holder of a floating charge. The position post-*Buchler* equated to a dramatic change in the application of the law having serious consequences in relation to a liquidator's planned expenditure following the realisation of assets. However, following the implementation of CA 2006, IA 1986, s.176 is made subject to an amendment, the effect of which is to reverse the decision in the *Buchler* case. The 2006 Act introduces a new IA 1986, s.176ZA, which provides that winding-up expenses take priority over any claims by preferential creditors, or to property comprised in or subject to any floating charge created by the company.

11.8.5 The effect of the Enterprise Act 2002

As a consequence of the implementation of EA 2002, the priority position of creditors was altered (see the Enterprise Act 2002 (Transitional Provisions) (Insolvency) Order 2003, SI 2003/2332) with the objective of improving the position of unsecured creditors. To effect a more equitable distribution of assets, EA 2002 abolished the Crown's preferential rights by removing paras.1 and 2 (debts due to Inland Revenue, now HMRC), paras.3–5C (debts due to Customs and Excise, now HMRC) and paras.6 and 7 (social security contributions) from IA 1986, Sched.6. The preferential status of other contributions in Sched.6 is retained and here the newly defined preferential creditors will still take in priority to the holder of a floating charge (CA 2006, s.767).

To ensure that the funds (which other than for the passing of the 2002 Act, would have first been distributed to Crown preferential creditors) are made available for unsecured creditors, EA 2002 provides for a prescribed portion (reserve fund) of the net property (i.e. calculated after the payment of holders of fixed charges and liquidation/administration fees) to be set aside specifically for unsecured creditors (see below). Other than where the administration of the reserve fund would be too expensive to administer (for example, the cost in terms of the administration of the fund was in excess of the size of the fund), unsecured creditors will take the prescribed portion of the available assets in priority to the holder of a floating charge. However, save for the prescribed portion, a holder of a floating charge climbs the priority tree at the expense of the Crown's preferential rights, which are now relegated to the position of unsecured debts. It should be noted that for floating charges created prior to 15 September 2003, there is an additional bonus, in so far as the distribution here will be absent any reduction in respect of the prescribed portion. The rules relating to the prescribed portion do not apply retrospectively to floating charges created prior to 15 September 2003.

The prescribed part of the company's net property available for the repayment of the company's unsecured debts will be calculated in accordance with IA 1986, s.176A, namely:

- Where the value of the company's net property is no more than £10,000, then 50 per cent of that property is reserved to the prescribed part.
- Where the company's net property exceeds £10,000 in value, then 50 per cent of the first £10,000 in value will be set aside for the prescribed part; and 20 per cent of any sum in excess of the £10,000 will be set aside for the prescribed part.
- However, the value of the prescribed part to be made available for the satisfaction of unsecured debts of the company cannot exceed £600,000.

Following the decision of Patten J in *Re Airbase (UK Ltd)* [2008] 1 BCLC 437, where there is a shortfall in funds available to the repayment of debts secured by a charge, the shortfall cannot be made up by permitting the holder of the charge to participate in the distribution of the prescribed part. The only exception to this rule is where the sum representing the prescribed part is in excess of the sum that is necessary to discharge all of the debts of the company's unsecured creditors. However, it should be noted that a holder of a floating charge who elects to surrender his security after the commencement of the administration or liquidation of a company and as such adopts the status of an unsecured creditor, may be treated as such and therefore be allowed to participate in the distribution of the prescribed part (see e.g. *Re PAL SC Realisations 2007 Ltd* [2011] BCC 93, *Kelly* v. *Inflexion Fund 2 Ltd* [2011] BCC 93, *Re J T Frith Ltd* [2012] BCC 634).

11.8.6 The revised priority position (order of ranking after the enactment of the Enterprise Act 2002)

(1st) Legal charge/mortgage (the chargee/mortgagee having a right to sell the property made subject to the legal charge).

(2nd) Fixed/Specific equitable charge (charge holder has first call on the sum raised from the sale of the asset over which the fixed charge was taken).

Following the payment of (1) and (2), the realisation of the remaining assets will be applied as follows:

(3rd) Liquidation/administration expenses.

(4th) Preferential creditors (but *not* Crown debts).

(5th) Floating charge (minus the sum representing the prescribed part, i.e. the reserve fund for unsecured creditors).

(6th) Unsecured creditors (this now includes Crown debts).

CHAPTER 12

Accounts and reporting structures

12.1 INTRODUCTION

In the nineteenth century incorporation of companies by entry on the register became the standard method for the formation of companies, largely replacing the formation of corporations by charter or Private Act of Parliament.

The watershed in this development was the introduction of limited liability companies in 1855. The price which companies had to pay for the privilege of being able to create a separate legal person with limited liability was the requirement to produce accounts which conformed to company law and were public documents. These provided the essential safeguard for investors in and creditors of the company, that the facility of incorporation with limited liability would not be abused or be made an instrument of fraud.

The Companies Act 1844, s.XLII required an annual balance sheet signed by the directors. The Companies Act 1856 required a balance sheet and an income and expenditure account. Such accounts had to be drawn up on the basis of double entry bookkeeping. It also gave the directors power to create reserves. The 1856 Act also contained a standard accounts format, which companies were required to adopt. The Companies Act 1929 introduced the requirement for group accounts. The Companies Act 1948, s.149(1) introduced the requirement that the company accounts must give a true and fair view.

Thus, company accounting requirements, including the format, layout and content of company accounts, are the product of and driven by corporate law.

The policy aim of preventing the misuse of corporate personality by the requirement to produce company accounts also profoundly affected the nature of the accounting system. One reason why the safeguarding function of accounts has only been imperfectly realised in practice is that accounts are historic documents, more useful for conducting a post-mortem of a dead patient than a diagnosis of a living one. With the aim of providing current information for investors, Anglo-Saxon accounting placed investor protection above creditor protection, by requiring transparency in accounts. This also reflected the fact that, in the United States and United Kingdom, stock markets played a far more important role in raising finance for business than on continental Europe, which instead developed creditor-friendly accounting systems.

12.2 THE CURRENT REGIME

The accounting provisions of the Companies Act (CA) 2006 came into force on 6 April 2008. The main legislation comprises CA 2006, ss.380–539 and two sets of regulations, namely:

- Small Companies and Groups (Accounts and Directors' Report) Regulations 2008, SI 2008/409.
- Large and Medium-sized Companies and Groups (Accounts and Reports) Regulations 2008, SI 2008/410.

These two sets of regulations are substantially the same, and may be referred to together as the 'Accounts Regulations'.

The general changes in the accounting environment which this legislation reflects have the following features:

1. A dualism is established whereby International Accounting Standards (IAS) now apply alongside UK Generally Accepted Accounting Practice (GAAP).
2. UK GAAP has been substantially reconstructed so as to converge with IAS.
3. Quoted companies must use IAS for their group accounts.
4. The age-old rivalry of investor-friendly v. creditor-friendly accounting systems has been resolved in favour of the former.
5. Law has become increasingly prescriptive about what should appear in accounts, notes to accounts and directors' reports.
6. Accounting standards for their part have become increasingly formalised, detailed and extensive. The aim is to exclude subjective judgment based on professional and commercial experience. Instead, accounting decisions are imposed by standard setters on a centralised basis.
7. As a counterweight to these trends, the same accounting rules are not applied to all companies. Accounting and audit standards have been simplified and abbreviated for small and medium enterprises (SMEs).

The same approach is found in the Tax Acts. In the Tax Acts 'generally accepted accounting practice' means:

(a) where accounts are drawn up using IAS, IAS;
(b) in any other case, UK GAAP.

'UK GAAP' in turn comprises 'old UK GAAP' and 'new UK GAAP'. New UK GAAP differs from old UK GAAP in adopting a number of accounting standards, in particular FRS 25, which implement International Financial Reporting Standards (IFRS), but whose use is not generally required in the UK (Corporation Tax Act 2010, s.1127).

UK GAAP is due to be replaced from 1 January 2015 onwards by a single, comprehensive financial reporting standard, FRS 102. This is intended to produce the same results as IAS.

All companies in a group have to produce individual accounts. Additionally, the principal company of the group must produce consolidated (group) accounts, unless exempt from this requirement.

For accounting periods beginning on or after 1 January 2005, all consolidated accounts of EU listed companies have to be based on IFRS. The use of IFRS has spread to individual company (entity) accounts.

Hence CA 2006 distinguishes between:

- small, medium-sized and large companies;
- Companies Act individual accounts;
- Companies Act group accounts;
- IAS individual accounts;
- IAS group accounts.

12.3 DEFINITIONS

In its accounting and auditing requirements the companies legislation imposes a simplified and lighter regime for small and medium enterprises (SMEs). For accounting purposes the distinction is between small companies, on the one hand, and medium-sized and large companies on the other. For auditing purposes small, medium-sized and large companies are distinguished.

The definitions of small company and small groups are set out in CA 2006, ss.381–384. The definition of medium-sized company and medium-sized groups is found in ss.465–467. For accounting periods beginning on or after 31 December 2006, a small company remains eligible for the small companies regime whether its individual accounts are Companies Act accounts or IAS accounts. A company qualifies as a small or medium-sized company if for the financial year in question and the previous financial year it meets two out of three criteria relating to maximum:

- turnover;
- assets;
- number of employees.

Table 12.1 Maximum figures with effect from 6 April 2008

Maximum (two out of three)	Small companies	Small parent companies	
		Net	Gross
Turnover £	6,500,000	6,500,000	7,800,000
Assets £	3,260,000	3,260,000	3,900,000
Employees	50	50	50

Maximum (two out of three)	Medium-sized companies	Medium-sized parent companies	
		Net	Gross
Turnover £	25,900,000	25,900,000	31,100,000
Assets £	12,900,000	12,900,000	15,500,000
Employees	250	250	250

Net = with adjustments for intra-group transactions

Gross = without adjustments for intra-group transactions

Depending upon the accounting format used, the balance sheet for these purposes comprises either:

(a) called-up share capital not paid, fixed assets, current assets, prepayments and accrued income; or simply

(b) assets.

These definitions are derived from Commission Recommendation of 6 May 2003 (2003/361/EC).

'Quoted companies' are companies whose securities are listed on a European Economic Area (EEA) recognised exchange, the New York Stock Exchange or Nasdaq (CA 2006, s.385). An unquoted company is a company whose securities are not so listed.

A small company cannot apply the small companies regime if it is a public company, an insurance company or a member of an ineligible group (CA 2006, s.384(1), (2)).

12.4 THE ACCOUNTS OBLIGATION

A company's 'statutory accounts' are the accounts for a financial year which the company is required to file with the registrar of companies under CA 2006, s.441 (CA 2006, s.434(3)).

'Annual accounts' are defined in CA 2006, s.471 by reference to the financial year as meaning the company's individual accounts and any group accounts made up for that year. A reference to the accounts includes a reference to the notes to the accounts (CA 2006, s.472). 'International accounting standards' are defined in CA 2006, s.474.

CA 2006 applies to 'UK-registered companies', as defined by s.1158, i.e. companies registered under the UK companies legislation. Companies are artificial persons. Unlike natural persons, they are required to maintain and produce annual accounts. This is a condition imposed for the enjoyment of the privilege of incorporation.

12.4.1   The purpose of accounts

Accounts serve four purposes:

1. They provide information to creditors and other lenders who may deal with the company.
2. They provide information to investors who hold or may acquire shares in the company.
3. They provide a record of the directors' stewardship for stakeholders, i.e. shareholders, employees, suppliers, customers and the public interest.
4. They provide a means of supervising and regulating the operation of companies in the public interest.

12.4.2   The duty to prepare accounts

The obligations imposed by CA 2006 with regard to accounts are essentially threefold, and apply alike to all companies:

- companies must prepare accounts which give a true and fair view;
- the accounts must be filed with the registrar of companies;
- the accounts must be circulated to members.

The duty to prepare annual accounts applies to *all* UK-registered companies. Such company accounts are called 'individual accounts' (previously referred to as 'entity accounts'). The basic duty is set out in CA 2006, s.394:

> The directors of every company must prepare accounts for the company for each of its financial years unless the company is exempt from that requirement under section 394A. Those accounts are referred to as the company's 'individual accounts'.

Company law allows a company to prepare its financial statements either under IAS or under UK GAAP: individual accounts can be Companies Act individual accounts or IAS individual accounts (CA 2006, s.395(1)). A charity can only prepare Companies Act individual accounts (s.395(2)). Once IAS accounts are adopted, IAS must be retained for five years. A company may change between accounting frameworks once every five years (CA 2006, s.395(3)–(5)).

12.4.3   What accounts must comprise

Companies Act individual accounts must comprise (CA 2006, s.396):

- a balance sheet which gives a true and fair view of the state of affairs of the company at the end of the financial year;
- a profit and loss account which gives a true and fair view of the profit or loss of the company for the financial year; and
- notes.

Accounting standards additionally require:

- a Statement of Total Reported Gains and Losses (STRGL);
- a cash flow statement;
- additional notes.

The function of the STRGL is to ensure that the income statement and the balance sheet reconcile by taking the surplus (or loss) for the year in the income statement, and adding to that figure (or deducting from it) changes in balance sheet figures which do not go through the income statement, for example asset revaluations, and changes in pension scheme deficits. IAS individual accounts comprise (CA 2006, ss.397, 474):

- an income statement;
- a balance sheet;
- Statement of Changes in Equity (SOCIE);
- cash flow statement;
- notes.

Such accounts must state that they have been prepared in accordance with IAS.

12.4.4 Nature and extent of the accounts obligation

The nature and extent of the accounts obligation depends upon the type of company. Where provisions do not apply to all companies, the legislation sets out the provisions in the order:

- small companies;
- public companies;
- quoted companies.

The normal currency of account will be sterling. However, companies may draw up accounts which also give the accounts figures in euros (CA 2006, s.469). In *Re Scandinavian Bank Corp plc* [1987] BCLC 220, it was held that a company may have a multi-currency share capital, provided that in the case of a public company it has allotted share capital of not less than the authorised minimum denomination in sterling.

12.4.5 Accounting reference date

Every company must have an accounting reference date, to determine its accounting reference period, i.e. the period for which it makes up its accounts (CA 2006, s.391). The financial year begins at the start of the accounting reference period, and ends on the last day of the period, or up to seven days either side for companies which make up accounts for 52- or 53-week periods (CA 2006, s.390).

The accounting reference date will normally be:

(a)   for companies incorporated before 1 April 1996, the date specified by notice to the registrar of companies; and

(b) in other cases the last day of the month in which the anniversary of the incorporation of the company falls (CA 2006, s.391).

A company can alter its accounting reference date by notice to the registrar, provided that (CA 2006, s.392):

(a) the time for filing accounts and reports has not expired;
(b) the effect of the notice does not extend an accounting reference period beyond 18 months;
(c) the company has not extended its accounting reference period in the previous five years.

12.4.6 Approval of accounts

Accounts must be approved by the board of directors and signed on behalf of the board by a director signing the balance sheet. The balance sheet and other reports must state the name of the director who has signed (CA 2006, s.433). If the accounts do not comply with the requirements of the Act, every director who knew that they did not comply, or was reckless as to their compliance, and does not take reasonable steps to secure compliance, commits an offence (CA 2006, s.414).

12.4.7 Publication of accounts and reports

Every company must send a copy of the annual accounts and reports for each financial year to every member of the company, every debenture holder and every person who is entitled to receive notice of the annual general meeting, where an annual general meeting is required (CA 2006, s.423). Private companies no longer need to hold an annual general meeting, and the accounts must be sent out by the filing date, i.e. within nine months of the end of the financial year (CA 2006, s.424). A public company must send out the accounts at least 21 days before the annual general meeting. A public company must hold an annual general meeting within six months of its accounting reference date (CA 2006, s.336(1)).

Instead of sending out the full accounts and reports, companies can send out summary financial statements, provided that they comply with regulations, and are in the forms prescribed for unquoted companies and quoted companies respectively and other provisions of the Act (CA 2006, ss.426–428).

A quoted company must ensure that its accounts and reports are available on its website (CA 2006, s.430).

Where a company publishes its accounts, they must be accompanied by the auditor's report, unless the company is exempt from audit and the directors have taken advantage of that exemption (CA 2006, s.434(1)).

If a company publishes a balance sheet or profit and loss account otherwise than as part of its annual accounts, these must be identified as 'non-statutory accounts' (CA 2006, s.435).

12.4.8 Filing accounts

Table 12.2 Filing obligations for each type of company

Type of company	CA 2006 section
Small companies	444
Medium-sized companies	445
Unquoted companies	446
Quoted companies	447
Unlimited companies	448

The time limits for filing are set out for all companies in CA 2006, s.442. Public companies have to file their accounts within six months of the accounting year end. This coincides with the requirement to hold the annual general meeting within six months of the accounting reference date. Private companies must file within nine months (CA 2006, s.442). There are provisions for calculating periods of time in CA 2006, s.443.

In the case of private companies there is no need to hold an annual general meeting (discussed at **12.11.1**) and so there is no longer a need to lay the accounts before such a meeting. Instead, the accounts, directors' report and (if applicable) auditor's report must be circulated to members within the period in which they must be filed with the registrar of companies.

Unlimited companies are exempt from the obligation to file accounts with the registrar, provided that the company has not been the subsidiary undertaking of a limited company or the parent of a limited company, and is not a banking or insurance company (CA 2006, s.448).

12.5 DIRECTORS' REPORT

The directors must prepare a report for each financial year, stating the names of the directors and the principal activities of the company. Unless the company comes within the small companies regime, the directors' report must include a business review. This must include 'an analysis using key performance indicators', i.e. 'factors by reference to which the development, performance or position of the company's business can be measured effectively' (CA 2006, s.417(6)). These requirements are relaxed in the case of medium-sized companies. In the case of quoted companies the directors must report on the main trends and factors likely to influence the business's future development, performance and position, as well as providing information about environmental matters, the impact of the company's business on the environment and 'social and community issues' (CA 2006, s.417(5)). Unless the company is exempt from the audit requirement and the directors have taken advantage of that exemption, the report must include a statement from the directors that there is no relevant audit information which has not been made available to the company's auditors (CA 2006, s.418). Except in the case of companies subject to the small companies regime, the directors' report must state the amount of any proposed dividends (CA 2006, s.416(3)). The directors' report must be approved by the directors and signed on their behalf by a director or the company secretary (CA 2006, s.419).

Quoted companies must prepare a directors' remuneration report, containing additional information about the pay of directors, in accordance with regulations (CA 2006, s.421). Prior to the accounts meeting, the company must give notice to those entitled to attend the meeting of the intention to move at the meeting by way of ordinary resolution a resolution approving the report (CA 2006, s.439).

The directors' report must state the amount of any dividends declared, but this requirement does not apply to companies subject to the small companies regime.

12.6 THE SME REGIME

The great majority of companies qualify as SMEs. Where a small or medium-sized company prepares Companies Act accounts, the directors may deliver a balance sheet and a profit and loss account with items specified in regulations omitted. These are called 'abbreviated accounts' (CA 2006, ss.444(3), 445(3)). If abbreviated accounts are delivered, then the obligation to deliver the auditor's report is replaced by the obligation to deliver the auditor's special report in accordance with CA 2006, s.449 (CA 2006, ss.444(4), 445(4)).

Where the directors propose to deliver abbreviated accounts to the registrar, they must include, in a prominent position above the director's signature on the balance sheet, a statement that the abbreviated accounts are prepared in accordance with the SME regime. The ability to file abbreviated accounts does not apply where the directors have taken advantage of the audit exemption (CA 2006, s.477). If a small group company prepares group accounts, it cannot use simpler form accounts for its individual accounts.

Where abbreviated accounts are delivered, but the company is not exempt from audit (or the directors have not taken advantage of the exemption), the accounts must be accompanied by a special auditor's report, confirming the company's entitlement to deliver abbreviated accounts (CA 2006, ss.449–450).

A parent company of a group that qualifies as an SME may take advantage of an exemption from applying group accounts if the group aggregated as a whole meet the SME requirements.

Small companies, instead of using UK GAAP, may use the Financial Reporting Standard for Smaller Entities (FRSSE) or its IAS-equivalent. The accounting treatment required by the FRSSE is intended to be the same as that required by accounting standards or a simplified version of the same. If the FRSSE is used, this must be disclosed on the balance sheet.

The exemptions and simplifications from which small companies can benefit include (CA 2006, ss.444, 444A):

(a)   use of FRSSE;
(b)   omission of disclosures relating to directors' remuneration;
(c)   use of small companies accounting formats;
(d)   simplified directors' report (CA 2006, s.415A);
(e)   simplified information relating to employee numbers and costs, financial year of subsidiary undertakings, shares and debentures held by subsidiary undertakings (CA 2006, s.411);
(f)   audit exemption;
(g)   ability to file abbreviated accounts with the registrar of companies;
(h)   small group companies need not prepare group accounts.

If accounts are prepared in accordance with the provisions applicable to companies subject to the small companies regime, the balance sheet must contain a statement to that effect in a prominent position above the director's signature (CA 2006, s.414(3)).

The following companies are excluded from the small companies regime:

• public companies;
• authorised insurance companies, banking companies, collective investment scheme management companies;
• companies that belong to groups whose securities are admitted to trading on any regulated EEA market (CA 2006, s.384(2)(a)).

The filing obligations for medium-sized companies are set out in CA 2006, s.445. These are very similar to the requirements for small companies set out in ss.444–444A. Medium-sized companies cannot deliver abbreviated accounts to the registrar of companies if they prepare IAS individual accounts. Likewise, a medium-sized company cannot benefit from relaxations for such companies if it is a public company, is carrying on a regulated activity under the Financial Services and Markets Act 2000, is carrying on an insurance activity or belongs to a group containing a member which falls into any of these categories (CA 2006, s.467).

12.7   THE 'TRUE AND FAIR' REQUIREMENT

The cardinal principle is that all accounts prepared by all companies subject to CA 2006 must give a 'true and fair view'. Directive 78/660/EEC, art.2(3) requires that the annual accounts of a company 'shall give a true and fair view'.

In UK law this principle is set out in CA 2006, s.393(1):

(1)   The directors of a company must not approve accounts . . . unless they are satisfied that they give a true and fair view of the assets, liabilities, financial position and profit or loss –

    (a)   in the case of the company's individual accounts, of the company;

(b)   in the case of the company's group accounts, of the undertakings included in the consolidation as a whole, so far as concerns members of the company.

This principle is restated for individual accounts in CA 2006, s.396, and for group accounts in s.404. Likewise, the auditor's report must state whether the accounts give a true and fair view (CA 2006, s.495(3)).

'True and fair' is not defined in the Directive or by statute. In 1983, 1984 and 1993 the opinion of counsel (Leonard Hoffmann QC and Mary Arden QC, as they then were) was sought on the significance of the concept. The view expressed was that:

(a)   'true and fair' was a statutory requirement;
(b)   in interpreting that concept the courts would be unlikely to find that accounts would give a true and fair view, unless they had been drawn up in accordance with the relevant accounting standards;
(c)   accordingly, while accounting standards had no direct legal effect as such, being simply rules of professional conduct for accountants, they were given indirect legal effect through the true and fair concept;
(d)   in short, 'true and fair' means 'drawn up in accordance with accounting standards': compliance with accounting standards is essential.

The Statement of Principles for Financial Reporting issued by the Accounting Standards Board (ASB) deals with the true and fair concept in paras.10–13 and says:

> The concept of a true and fair view lies at the heart of financial reporting in the UK . . . It is the ultimate test for financial statements.

The form and content of accounts, the additional information to be provided, details of any departure from accounting standards in order to give a true and fair view ('the true and fair override') and reasons for such departure must accord with regulations to be issued by the Secretary of State (CA 2006, s.396(3)–(5)). The regulations governing the format of accounts are the two Accounts Regulations (see **12.9**).

The true and fair requirement is linked with the audit requirement, because the main function of the auditor's report is to certify that the accounts give a true and fair view (CA 2006, s.495(3)).

12.8   ACCOUNTING STANDARDS

'Accounting standards' are defined in CA 2006, s.464 as statements of standard accounting practice issued by a body prescribed by regulations. The current regulations are the Statutory Auditors (Amendment of Companies Act 2006 and Delegation of Functions etc) Order 2012, SI 2012/1741. The designated body is the Financial Reporting Council (FRC). This body has oversight regulation of all accounting and audit matters in the UK. It issues Financial Reporting Standards (FRS), which replaced Statements of Standard Accounting Practice (SSAP).

Also under the FRC is the Urgent Issues Task Force (UITF), which was established in March 1991, to produce abstracts on the interpretation of particular accounting standards, for example UITF 40 on income recognition for professional work in progress. Designated trade bodies produce Statements of Recommended Practice (SORP) for particular sectors, where the body in question is recognised by the FRC as a SORP-making body, for example the British Banker's Association SORP on Advances; the Charity Commission's SORP 'Accounting by Charities'. Since 2004 the FRC regulates auditing activities through the Auditing Practice Board (APB).

Listed companies are required to observe the Listing Rules (FCA Sourcebook) and Guidance Manual issued by the FCA. Companies whose shares are listed on the Alternative Investment Market (AIM) have to observe the AIM Rules issued by the Stock Exchange.

The International Accounting Standards Board (IASB) issues International Financial Reporting Standards (IFRS), which are referred to generically as International Accounting Standards (IAS). The International Financial Reporting Standard Interpreting Committee (IFRSIC) plays much the same role as UITF in relation to UK accounting standards.

For adoption within the EU, IFRS have to be 'endorsed' as suitable for use by the European Commission. This process involves consideration by the Accounting Regulatory Committee (ARC) and the European Financial Reporting Advisory Group (EFRAG).

In 2012 and 2013 the FRC issued three new financial reporting standards, designed to replace almost all existing standards:

- FRS 100 Application of Financial Reporting Requirements;
- FRS 101 Reduced Disclosure Framework;
- FRS 102 Financial Reporting Standard applicable in the UK and Ireland.

These are intended to be largely consistent with EU-adopted IFRS. The new standard will apply for accounting periods beginning on or after 1 January 2015. Thereafter, companies will prepare their accounts using FRS 102, unless they prepare accounts using:

- IFRS;
- FRS 101; or
- FRSSE.

12.9 ACCOUNTS FORMATS

The Accounts Regulations prescribe the 'Required Formats for Accounts', the notes which are to form part of the accounts and the accounting policies to be followed. There are two sets of regulations, one governing small companies, the other governing medium-sized and large companies.

Table 12.3 The accounting formats

Companies Act 2006 sections	Type of company	Regulation	Type of accounts
426–429	All companies	SI 2008/374	Summary financial statements
394–396	General company (small company)	SI 2008/409, reg.3, Sched.1, Part 1, Section B	Companies Act individual accounts
396, 409, 410	General company (small company with related under-takings)	SI 2008/409, reg.4, Sched.2	Companies Act or IAS individual accounts
398, 404, 408	General company (small group)	SI 2008/409, reg.8(1), 10, Sched.6	Companies Act small group accounts
444	General company (small company)	SI 2008/409, reg.6(1), Sched.4	Companies Act abbreviated accounts
394–396	General company (medium-sized or large)	SI 2008/410, regs.1, 2, Sched.1	Companies Act individual accounts
394–396	Banking company	SI 2008/410, reg.5, Sched.2; SI 2008/567	Companies Act individual accounts
394–396	Insurance com-pany	SI 2008/410, reg.6, Sched.3; SI 2008/565	Companies Act individual accounts
399; also EC Regulation 2002/1606/EC	General company (medium-sized or large with related undertakings)	SI 2008/410, reg.7, Sched.4	Companies Act or IAS individual or group accounts
39, 403–406	General company (medium-sized or large group)	SI 2008/410, reg.8, Sched.6, Part 1	Companies Act group accounts
39, 403–406	Banking company (medium-sized or large group)	SI 2008/410, reg.8, Sched.6, Part 2	Companies Act group accounts
39, 403–406	Insurance com-pany (medium-sized or large group)	SI 2008/410, reg.8, Sched.6, Part 3	Companies Act group accounts
397	All companies	IAS 1	IAS individual accounts

Companies Act 2006 sections	Type of company	Regulation	Type of accounts
1210, 1242	Partnerships consisting solely of companies	SI 2008/569	Partnership accounts

12.9.1 Accounting principles

Sched.1, Part 2 of both sets of Accounts Regulations deals with Accounting Principles. These are (paras.11–15):

- consistency;
- prudence;
- only profits realised at balance sheet date may be recognised;
- all liabilities must be recognised including those arising between the end of the accounting period and the signing of the accounts (post-balance sheet adjusting events);
- all income and charges relating to the financial year must be brought into account ('matching');
- in determining individual items set-off is not allowed.

Section B sets out Historical Cost Accounting Rules. Section C contains Alternative Accounting Rules, providing for alternative valuation and depreciation rules. Section D contains rules for Fair Value Accounting. While para.36(1) allows financial instruments to be fair valued, para.36(2) excludes fair value accounting for financial liabilities. Part 3 deals with the Notes to the Accounts.

12.9.2 Information to be given in notes to the accounts

In the case of a company not subject to the small companies regime, the notes to the accounts must contain information about the average number of employees in the financial year, and the number of persons employed in each category of employee. The notes must also state the aggregate amounts of wages and salaries, social security costs and pension costs (CA 2006, s.411). Information must also be given in accordance with regulations about directors' remuneration and benefits (CA 2006, ss.412–413). Off-balance sheet arrangements must be disclosed, where they involve material risks and benefits (CA 2006, s.410A). There is a duty to prepare a directors' remuneration report (CA 2006, s.420).

12.9.3 Failure to file

Penalties for failure to file are set out in CA 2006, ss.451–453. If there is default in filing accounts and reports, all directors of such a company will commit an offence, subject to a 'reasonable steps' defence. If the directors fail to make good the default within 14 days of notification, the court can on application make a direction to the directors to remedy the default (CA 2006, s.452).

12.9.4 Defective accounts

After accounts have been filed, directors may find that there is an accounting error, for example sales have been overstated or an equity instrument classified as such when accounting standards required it to be treated as debt. In that case the directors can amend the accounts (CA 2006, s.454). Regulations are set out in the Companies (Revision of Defective Accounts and Reports) Regulations 2008, SI 2008/373. The Financial Reporting Review Panel (FRRP) has power to direct that defective accounts should be remedied.

The Secretary of State can also give notice to the directors of a company requiring explanation of the matters specified in the notice (CA 2006, s.455).

The Secretary of State or a person authorised by him (i.e. an accounting regulatory body) can apply to the court for a declaration that the accounts fail to conform to accounting standards (CA 2006, ss.456, 457).

12.9.5 Accounting records

A company must maintain adequate accounting records, and retain them for three years in the case of private companies and six years in the case of public companies. Officers but not members are entitled to access to the accounting records. In particular the records must account for receipts and payments of money on a day-to-day basis, and provide a record of the assets and liabilities of the company (CA 2006, s.386(2)). In the case of a company dealing in goods, the accounting records must record the stocks, and (except in the case of ordinary retail sales) provide means of identifying suppliers and customers (CA 2006, ss.386–389).

12.10 GROUP ACCOUNTS

In order to give a true and fair view company accounts need to reflect the real economic situation of a company at the accounting reference date. The purpose of group accounts is to present the activities of related companies and undertakings as a single economic entity. The key issue in group accounts is what entities should be included within the scope of the consolidation. The UK, following EU law, takes a broad definition of subsidiary for this purpose, based on both legal control and economic control.

On consolidation the assets, liabilities and turnover of all entities included in the consolidation will be amalgamated with intra-group payments, and intra-group assets, liabilities and payments will be eliminated.

CA 2006, ss.380, 398, 399 distinguish between the following situations:

(a)   companies subject to the small companies regime;
(b)   companies outside the small companies regime and not quoted;
(c)   companies outside the small companies regime and quoted;
(d)   companies subject to the small companies regime which are the parent companies of a group;
(e)   companies outside the small companies regime which are the parent companies of a group.

Parent companies not subject to the small companies regime are required to prepare group accounts as well as individual accounts. A company which at the end of the financial year is a parent company must prepare consolidated accounts, unless (broadly speaking) it is itself a subsidiary undertaking (CA 2006, s.399).

The provisions in CA 2006, ss.399–408, Sched.7 give effect to the requirements of the Seventh Company Law Directive on consolidated accounts (83/349/EEC) and the applicable accounting standards (FRS 2 and IAS 27).

The obligation to prepare group accounts is laid down in s.399. Section 404 sets out the scope of the obligation. Where a parent company prepares Companies Act group accounts, all the subsidiary undertakings of the company must be included in the consolidation, subject to limited exceptions. 'Subsidiary undertakings' means a body corporate, partnership or unincorporated association carrying on a trade or business, with or without a view to profit (CA 2006, s.1161).

'Parent undertaking' and 'subsidiary undertaking' are defined in CA 2006, s.1162 and Sched.7. An undertaking is a parent undertaking in relation to a subsidiary undertaking if it:

(a)   holds the majority of voting rights;
(b)   has the right to appoint or remove directors;
(c)   has the right to exert dominant influence by virtue of the articles or a control contract;
(d)   controls a majority of voting rights;
(e)   has power to exercise or actually exercises a dominant influence;
(f)   is managed on a unified basis with the subsidiary.

Criteria (e) and (f) are set out in CA 2006, s.1162(4) and Sched.7, para.4. The terms 'dominant influence' and 'managed on a unified basis' are also defined in FRS 2 'Accounting for Subsidiary Undertakings'. The test based on factual control is more important in practice than the tests based on legal control, because it restricts attempts to avoid the consolidation obligation.

12.10.1   Exemptions

There are three exemptions:

1.   The first case is for companies whose accounting figures are included in IAS group accounts of an EEA parent undertaking, where the immediate parent company (a) owns all the shares in the subsidiary, or (b) owns more than 50

per cent of the shares and no notice requesting group accounts has been served by shareholders. The securities of the subsidiary must not be traded on an EEA exchange (CA 2006, s.400).

2. The second case is for companies whose accounting figures are included in the group accounts of a parent undertaking established outside the EEA, where the immediate parent company (a) owns all the shares in the subsidiary, or (b) owns more than 50 per cent of the shares and no notice requesting group accounts has been served by shareholders. The securities of the subsidiary must not be traded on an EEA exchange. The company must state in its individual accounts the name of the parent undertaking, and the fact that it is exempt from the requirement to draw up group accounts.

3. The third case is where a parent company prepares Companies Act group accounts and all the subsidiary undertakings of the parent are included in the consolidation (CA 2006, ss.401, 405).

12.10.2 Composition of group accounts

Companies Act group accounts comprise (CA 2006, s.404):

- a consolidated profit and loss account;
- a consolidated balance sheet;
- notes.

Parent companies that are charities must use UK GAAP (CA 2006, s.403(3)).

All subsidiary undertakings must be included in the consolidation, unless such consolidation is not material for the purpose of giving a true and fair view or the parent company is subject to long-term restrictions over the exercise of its powers (CA 2006, s.405).

IAS group accounts must state that they have been drawn up in accordance with IAS (CA 2006, s.406).

Financial reporting in a group should be made on a consistent basis, i.e. 'using the same financial reporting framework' (CA 2006, s.407(1)(a)). This does not apply if both the group and the individual accounts are prepared using IAS.

12.10.3 Accounting basis for group accounts

For accounting periods beginning on or after 1 January 2005, all companies governed by the law of an EU Member State were required to adopt endorsed IAS for their consolidated (group) accounts, if their securities were listed on an exchange in a Member State (Regulation 2002/1606/EC). As this was a Regulation, it did not require implementation in Member States to take effect as a legal obligation.

The Regulation left individual Member States free to decide whether to allow or require listed companies to adopt IAS for individual company accounts within the group, or to continue with national generally accepted accounting practice.

Under the UK regulations:

(a) companies subject to the small companies regime which are the parent companies of a group and ordinary limited companies may adopt either IAS or UK GAAP;

(b) parent companies of listed groups must require group companies to adopt either IAS or UK GAAP, unless there are good reasons not to do so;

(c) in general, the decision as to accounting standards, once made, cannot be reversed.

(Companies Act 1985 (International Accounting Standards and Other Accounting Amendments) Regulations 2004, SI 2004/2947; CA 2006, ss.395, 396.)

'UK GAAP' in turn embraces both 'old UK GAAP' and 'new UK GAAP'. This is because some FRS (replacing previous SSAPs or FRS) apply only to particular types of company. For example, until 2009 FRS 25 and FRS 26 only applied to listed companies, but other companies could voluntarily adopt them.

A parent company preparing group accounts need not include an individual profit and loss account in its statutory accounts, provided that this information is contained in the notes to the accounts (CA 2006, s.408).

12.11 THE AUDIT REQUIREMENT

A company's annual accounts must be audited in accordance with the Act, unless the company is exempt from audit (CA 2006, s.475). A company may be exempt from audit under:

- s.477 (small companies);
- ss.479A–479C (subsidiary undertakings);
- s.480 (dormant companies);
- ss.482–484 (non-profit-making companies subject to public sector audit).

A company is not entitled to the exemption unless it claims the exemption and its balance sheet contains a statement to that effect, above the director's signature.

If a company is eligible to apply for the small companies regime under ss.382–384, it may also claim the exemption from audit. For a group company, both the company and the group must qualify as small for the exemption to be available (s.479).

The members of a company otherwise entitled to audit exemption can require an audit (CA 2006, s.476).

A subsidiary undertaking (as defined in s.1159) of a parent established in an EEA state may claim audit exemption where:

(a)   a financial guarantee is given by the parent undertaking;

(b)   all members agree to the exemption from audit; and

(c)   the subsidiary is included in the group accounts.

Dormant subsidiaries of parents established in an EEA state may claim exemption from the audit requirement and from preparing and submitting financial statements.

Non-profit-making companies subject to public sector audit are exempt from audit under ss.482–484 if they are, in England, subject to audit by the Comptroller and Auditor General under the Government Resources and Accounts Act 2000, s.25(6), or equivalent provisions in other parts of the UK.

12.11.1 Appointment of auditors for private companies

Auditors for private companies must be appointed each year (CA 2006, s.485). Because an annual general meeting is not required under the Act, in the first year the auditor will be appointed by the directors. Thereafter the auditor must be appointed by the members by ordinary resolution. The 'period for appointing auditors' is the period of 28 days beginning with the time by which the accounts and report are required to be circulated to members under ss.423–424, or beginning from the date of sending out the accounts and report, if earlier. If no auditor is appointed, the existing auditor is deemed to be reappointed (CA 2006, s.487(2)). If a casual vacancy arises, the directors have power to appoint an auditor.

Auditors of private companies hold office for the term of their appointment, and cannot take office until the previous auditors have ceased to hold office. They cease to hold office at the end of the next 'period for appointing auditors' unless reappointed (CA 2006, s.487).

12.11.2 Appointment of auditors for public companies

In the case of public companies, the auditor is initially appointed by the directors and thereafter by the members by ordinary resolution at the 'accounts meeting' (CA 2006, s.489). The accounts meeting is 'a general meeting of the company at which the company's annual accounts and reports are . . . laid' (CA 2006, s.437(3)). The directors have power to fill a casual vacancy. In default of appointment under s.489, the Secretary of State has a default power of appointment (CA 2006, s.490).

Auditors of public companies hold office for the term of their appointment, and cannot take office until the previous auditors have ceased to hold office. They cease to hold office at the end of the next accounts meeting unless reappointed (CA 2006, s.491).

12.11.3 Statutory auditor

A 'statutory auditor' is an auditor appointed under the Companies Act. An auditor must hold an appropriate professional qualification, belong to a recognised supervisory body and be qualified to act as auditor under the rules of that body (CA 2006, ss.1212–1264, Scheds.10, 11). Where a company incorporated outside the EEA has transferable securities which are listed on a UK regulated market, its accounts may be audited by a 'registered third country auditor', i.e. an auditor qualified and appointed under approved arrangements in non-EEA countries (CA 2006, s.1241).

Where the auditor is appointed by the members, his remuneration is fixed by ordinary resolution (CA 2006, s.492).

12.11.4 Function of auditor's report

The prime function of the auditor's report is to say whether or not in the auditor's opinion the accounts give a true and fair view of the company's financial affairs for the financial year to which they relate (CA 2006, s.495(3)).

The auditor's report must be unqualified or qualified (CA 2006, s.495(4)(a)).

The auditor's report must state whether the directors' report is consistent with the accounts (s.496). In the case of quoted companies the auditor's report must also state whether the auditable part of the directors' remuneration report has been compiled in accordance with the Act. The auditor's report must be sent out with the annual accounts and directors' report (CA 2006, s.495(1)). The auditor's report should also include a separate corporate governance statement (CA 2006, ss.472A, 497A, 498A).

12.11.5 Duties of the auditor

The duties of the auditor are (CA 2006, s.498):

- to be satisfied as to the adequacy of the company's accounting records and procedures;
- to obtain all the information and explanations which, to the best of his knowledge and belief, are necessary for the purposes of the audit.

The auditor has extensive rights to information relating to the company's financial affairs and it is an offence to withhold information from the auditor or provide misleading information (CA 2006, ss.499–502).

If the auditor is an individual, the auditor's report must be signed by that individual. If the auditor is a firm, the auditor's report must be signed by the 'senior statutory auditor', i.e. the professionally qualified auditor named by the firm as responsible for the audit (CA 2006, s.504).

The auditor can be removed at any time by ordinary resolution (CA 2006, s.510).

The auditor can resign and require the directors to convene a general meeting at which the auditor can explain the circumstances connected with this resignation (CA 2006, s.516). Where an auditor ceases for any reason to hold office, in unquoted companies the auditor must in all cases make a statement, whether of the circumstances or to say that none were relevant (CA 2006, s.519(1), (2)). In quoted companies the auditor must outline the circumstances (CA 2006, s.519(3)).

Any provisions for exempting the auditor from liability for breach of duty or for indemnification of the auditor by the company for breach of duty are void, except as provided by CA 2006, s.533 (indemnification by company for costs of successfully defending proceedings) and ss.534–536 (limitation of liability agreements). Such agreements may not limit liability to 'less than such amount as is fair and reasonable in all the circumstances' (CA 2006, s.537). There is provision for the issue of regulations to specify what matters can and cannot be included in such agreements (CA 2006, s.535(2)). The regulations are in the Companies (Disclosure of Auditor Remuneration and Liability Limitation Agreements) Regulations 2008, SI 2008/489.

CHAPTER 13

Taxation of companies

13.1 INTRODUCTION

A company is essentially a legal vehicle for raising funds to carry on business. Companies are artificial persons. Only real persons can suffer the economic burden of taxation. The best tax is a tax which someone else pays. Corporate profits are taxed as a surrogate for individual taxation of the proprietors of the company. There are three main reasons why companies are taxed:

1. It is a way of taxing corporate profits as they accrue: otherwise companies could simply accumulate untaxed profits for subsequent distribution.
2. It is a way of taxing non-resident investors on UK source profits.
3. It is a way of taxing economic rents, i.e. profits over and above the costs of earning them.

Globalisation has since 1970 caused a fundamental change in the way in which companies carry on business. Even small enterprises now have international operations, and large multinational groups are no longer organised along national lines. With wide international markets branding and intellectual property rights have become more important in economic terms and as a source of profit.

These developments have brought corporate taxation into acute controversy in recent years. There are three main approaches to corporate taxation:

1. Unitary taxation: the worldwide profits of a group are computed on a unitary basis, and then allocated to the jurisdiction where the profits are earned. This requires a formula for apportioning profits on a global basis, and a high degree of international co-operation.
2. The arm's length principle: for tax purposes prices charged on transactions between related entities in different jurisdictions are adjusted to a hypothetical arm's length standard, i.e. the prices which would be charged between unrelated parties: see **13.14**.
3. Entity basis: an entity which only carries on business in one jurisdiction is taxed on the profits earned in that jurisdiction.

The difficulty about approach 1 and, to a lesser extent, approach 2 is that states face conflicting demands to protect the national tax base, to maximise tax revenues and to attract and retain investment. Approach 3 is only appropriate for companies carrying on business in a single jurisdiction.

13.2 CORPORATION TAX

The basis of corporate taxation is the separate existence of a company as a legal person. As legal persons, companies are liable to taxation by analogy with the taxation of individuals. Individuals pay income tax and capital gains tax. Companies pay corporation tax on income and capital gains. The scope of corporation tax is extended by including in the term 'companies' bodies of persons which are not companies. 'Company' means 'any body corporate or unincorporated association'. However, a 'company' does not include 'a partnership, a local authority or a local authority association' (Income Tax Act 2007, s.992; see also Corporation Tax Act 2010, s.1121).

The main legislation on corporation tax is now contained in:

- Taxation of Chargeable Gains Act (TCGA) 1992.
- Corporation Tax Act (CTA) 2009.
- Corporation Tax Act (CTA) 2010.
- Taxation (International and Other Provisions) Act (TIOPA) 2010.

Companies are liable to corporation tax on their 'profits'. 'Profits' comprise two components: income and capital gains (CTA 2009, s.2(2)).

A separate corporation tax was introduced in 1965. However, it was grafted on to income tax (which had existed continuously since 1842) and capital gains tax (which was also introduced in 1965, to tax gains which would escape income tax). Originally, the income and capital gains of companies were classified and computed in much the same way as the income and capital gains of individuals, but then charged to corporation tax. Hence, the income of companies is computed in accordance with income tax principles, and the capital gains of companies are computed in accordance with capital gains principles. In both cases, however, these principles only apply to the extent that they are not modified by law. Increasingly, corporation tax has become based on rules which are quite distinct from those which apply for income tax and capital gains tax. An important factor in this process has been the increasing importance of the principle that taxable profits should follow the commercial computation of profits, and the increasing elaboration and formalisation of accounting standards.

Corporate profits are for tax purposes measured in four ways, set out below, which partly overlap with the measurement of taxable profits and gains of an individual or non-corporate.

13.2.1 Trade profits

As explained in **Chapter 12**, unlike individuals who are not carrying on a trade, companies are required to maintain accounts which give a true and fair view of the company's assets, liabilities, financial position and profit and loss. Trading profits are measured on an accounts basis, using the commercial accounting measurement of profit as the starting point. The profits of a trade must be calculated in accordance with GAAP, subject to statutory modifications (CTA 2009, s.46). Hence companies are broadly taxed in accordance with their accounts, and pay corporation tax on income and capital gains. Individuals who carry on a trade are, like companies, required to compute their profits for tax purposes in accordance with generally accepted accounting practice (Income Tax (Trading and Other Income) Act (ITTOIA) 2005, s.25).

13.2.2 Notional trade profits

Property income is investment income, not trading income, but is computed as if it were trading income (CTA 2009, s.210). The same rule applies for income tax purposes (ITTOIA 2005, s.373).

13.2.3 All income profits

Profits on loan relationships, derivative contracts and intangible fixed assets are taxed on an 'all income' basis for corporation tax purposes, which has no equivalent in the taxation of individuals and non-corporates.

13.2.4 Other income and gains

Other constituents of corporate profits are taxed in accordance with the general rules for the taxation of income and capital gains, which apply to individuals and companies alike, i.e. on a cash (realisations) basis.

Corporation tax applies *instead* of income tax or capital gains tax. If corporation tax does not apply, the charge to income tax or capital gains tax is reinstated. For example, a non-UK-resident investment company pays income tax on its UK source income, not corporation tax.

13.3 LEGISLATION

The principal taxing statutes have been noted at **13.2**. The legislation imposing corporation tax is based on a number of legislative sources:

1. Corporation tax is an annual tax, which is renewed by annual Finance Acts.
2. CTA 2009 imposes a charge to corporation tax on companies which have profits or losses arising from: (a) trading income; (b) property income; (c)

loan relationships; (d) derivative contracts; (e) intangible fixed assets; (f) know-how and patents; (g) dividends; and (h) miscellaneous income. These categories replace the various schedules and cases which formerly appertained to income tax. CTA 2009 also has rules relating to accounting periods, various special forms of relief (such as research and development expenditure) and investment companies.

3. CTA 2010 deals with calculation of profits, foreign currency rules, distributions, small companies rate, loss relief, group relief, leasing, special types of company such as close companies, real estate investment trusts, authorised unit trusts and changes in company ownership.

4. TIOPA 2010 consists of provisions with an international aspect, double taxation, the worldwide debt cap and transfer pricing.

5. TCGA 1992 contains the rules for the computation of capital gains, which in the case of a UK-resident company are charged to corporation tax on capital gains.

6. The Capital Allowances Act (CAA) 2001 contains the rules governing capital allowances, which take the place for tax purposes of the depreciation charge which has to be included in the commercial accounts. This equally applies to unincorporated businesses.

7. Annual Finance Acts contain numerous special rules for corporation tax. These are largely being incorporated into the new Corporation Tax Acts, but some rules remain in separate Finance Acts.

8. The administrative provisions for corporation tax are set out in Finance Act 1998, Sched.18 and the Taxes Management Act (TMA) 1970. These also contain the rules for tax appeals and reviews.

9. There are numerous statutory instruments relating to corporation tax, for example the Corporation Tax (Instalment Payments) Regulations 1998, SI 1998/3175.

10. As noted in **Chapter 12**, Financial Reporting Standards (FRS) are issued by the Financial Reporting Council, while International Financial Reporting Standards (IFRS) are issued by the International Accounting Standards Board. While not legislation, they are given statutory recognition by the Companies Act (CA 2006, s.464).

13.4 PROFITS

Corporation tax is charged on the 'profits' of companies, which comprise 'income' and 'chargeable gains' (CTA 2009, s.2(2)).

Where a company has trading income, the general rule is that trading profits are a matter of fact to be determined by the application of the ordinary principles of commercial accountancy, subject to such adjustments as are required by law. The classic formulation of this method is by Pennycuick V-C in *Odeon Associated*

Theatres Ltd v. *Jones* (1971) 48 TC 257 at 273 and is now codified for corporation tax purposes in CTA 2009, s.46(1), which states:

> (1) The profits of a trade must be calculated in accordance with generally accepted accounting practice, subject to any adjustment required or authorised by law in calculating profits for corporation tax purposes.

Accounting used to be judgmental in that a significant discretion was left to the accountant in drawing up accounts on a pragmatic basis, the correctness or otherwise of the result being judged by whether or not it conformed with good professional practice. Accounting has now become largely prescriptive, the test of correctness being compliance with detailed accounting standards.

Where an 'all income' treatment applies, profits are ascertained in accordance with the commercial accounts, in the usual way, but the taxable profit is then regarded solely as income and not as gains. The areas where the all income treatment applies are:

1. *Loan relationships*: 'Loan relationships' are types of corporate debt defined in CTA 2009, s.302. Profits and gains on loan relationships include interest, capital accruals, expenses, fluctuations in capital values, foreign exchange differences and losses.

2. *Derivative contracts*: 'Derivative contracts' are defined in CTA 2009, ss.576–583, and are contracts for differences, futures and options. However, gains on certain notional derivative contracts are treated as capital gains for corporation tax purposes (CTA 2009, ss.639–673).

3. *Intangible fixed assets*: 'Intangibles' are defined in CTA 2009, s.713. The definition follows the accounting definition in FRS 10 but expressly includes intellectual property. Patents, copyrights, trademarks, registered designs, design rights and goodwill all fall under this concept.

Capital gains for companies are computed by deducting the base cost of the asset from the proceeds of sale. The base cost is increased by index-linking (TCGA 1992, s.53).

Companies can also deduct charges on income from total profits. This is confined to qualifying donations to charity (CTA 2010, s.189).

13.4.1 Trading and investment companies

CTA 2009, s.35 says: 'The charge to corporation tax in income applies to the profits of a trade.' A trading company is a company whose business consists wholly or mainly in carrying on a trade. A trade is an activity carried on on a systematic basis with a view to making a profit. Investment companies derive the bulk of their income from activities other than trading, and in particular from holding investments, being companies whose business consists wholly or partly of making investments (CTA 2009, s.1218(1)). Non-trade profits will be taxable under the various other heads of charge in CTA 2009. Property income is calculated on the same basis as trading profits.

From total profits received from those sources and capital gains a company with investment business deducts expenses of management, by reference to the accounting period in which they are charged against profits (CTA 2009, ss.1219–1223). These will include reasonable directors' fees, interest and office and administrative expenses. Capital expenditure is excluded.

13.4.2 Receipt of distributions

The corporation tax treatment of dividends has been radically modified to conform to EU law. In principle, no distinction is made between distributions received from UK-resident and non-UK-resident companies.

A UK company with a foreign permanent establishment will be subject to foreign tax in respect of the trading profits of the foreign branch. At the same time it will be subject to UK tax on its worldwide income. Double taxation relief is conferred by one of two methods:

1. *Exemption method*: Profits which have borne foreign tax are exempt from domestic tax.
2. *Foreign tax credit (FTC) method*: Foreign income is subject to domestic tax, but credit is allowed against domestic tax for the foreign tax suffered.

The UK gives relief by the exemption method in the case of most dividends received by companies from resident and non-resident companies alike, provided that the dividend is classified as an exempt distribution (CTA 2009, s.931A). In other words, the exemption method has been extended from distributions paid by UK-resident companies to distributions paid by non-UK-resident companies. In practice, the great majority of distributions received by a company, whether the paying company is UK-resident or non-resident, are exempt. Distributions made by UK-resident companies are in general exempt distributions because they are paid out of taxed profits (CTA 2009, ss.931B(a), 931D–931Q). Distributions paid by non-resident companies are exempt if:

(a)   the recipient controls the payer;
(b)   the distribution is in respect of non-redeemable ordinary shares; or
(c)   the distribution is made in respect of a portfolio holding (<10 per cent).

There are different rules for small companies and companies which are not small.

13.4.3 Losses

Losses may be revenue losses or capital losses. Revenue losses in turn may be trading losses or non-trading losses. Trading losses can be set against capital gains of the same or the previous accounting period, but capital gains cannot be set against trading losses. Losses on other forms of income can in general only be carried forward and set against income from the same source. Capital losses can likewise be carried forward and set against future capital gains. The rules are that trading losses may be (CTA 2010, ss.37–47):

(a)   used for set-off against the profits (including chargeable gains) of the same accounting period ('sideways relief'); or

(b)   used to carry back the loss against the profits (including chargeable gains) for a period of 12 months prior to the period in which the loss occurred ('carry back relief'); or

(c)   carried forward against trading income from the same trade ('carry forward relief'); or

(d)   made available for group relief.

Hence, a trading loss may be set off against other profits, including chargeable gains of the same accounting period. Claims must be made within two years of the end of the accounting period in which the loss is made, or such longer period as Her Majesty's Revenue and Customs (HMRC) may allow. The balance of loss unrelieved by a claim for the year in which the loss occurred may be carried back to be set against profits of preceding accounting periods for a period of 12 months ending immediately before the loss period, provided that the trade was carried on in that period. The balance of trading losses not relieved in an earlier period may be carried forward so set against income of the same trade (CTA 2010, s.45).

13.5   COMPANY RESIDENCE

The connecting factor for corporation tax purposes is residence. UK legislation is limited in territorial scope to persons or subject matter which come within the scope of its jurisdiction. There are two tests of company residence, a statutory test and a common law test. The statutory test is that all companies incorporated in the UK are UK-resident (CTA 2009, s.14(1)). The common law test is that a company is resident in the country where its central management and control is exercised (*De Beers Consolidated Gold Mines* v. *Howe* (1906) 5 TC 198; CTA 2009, ss.13(2), 15).

Double tax treaties, which may override domestic law, use a 'place of effective management' test. In the great majority of cases the statutory test will settle questions of company residence.

The case law concept of 'central management and control' is broadly directed to the highest level of control of the business of the company concerned. It has to be distinguished from the place where the main operations of the business are to be found, although of course the two places may often coincide. Moreover, the exercise of control does not necessarily demand any minimum standard of active involvement: it may in some cases be exercised tacitly through passive oversight.

HMRC has indicated that where there are doubts about a particular company's residence status it adopts the following approach.

1. HMRC first tries to ascertain *whether* the directors of the company in fact exercise 'central management and control'.
2. If so, HMRC seeks to determine *where* the directors exercise this central management and control (which is not necessarily where they meet).
3. In cases where the directors apparently do *not* exercise central management and control of the company, HMRC will look to establish where and by whom it is exercised.

The common law test has been reviewed in *Wood* v. *Holden* [2006] STC 443. In the High Court, Park J observed ([2005] STC 789 at 824–5):

> In all normal cases the central control and management is identified with the control which a company's board of directors has over its business and affairs, so that the principle almost always followed is that a company is resident in the jurisdiction where its board of directors meets . . .

There is a difference between, on the one hand, exercising management and control and, on the other, being able to influence those who exercise management and control.

The key issue is where the constitutional organs of the company perform their functions, provided that their authority is not usurped by another body. If the constitutional organs simply do not function, but one dominant individual controls the company, the company will be resident where those control activities are carried on (*Laerstate BV* v. *Revenue and Customs Commissioners* [2009] SFTD 551).

13.5.1   UK-resident companies

A UK-resident company is liable to corporation tax on an unlimited basis, i.e. by reference to its worldwide profits (CTA 2009, s.5(1)).

13.5.2   Non-UK-resident companies

A non-UK-resident company is liable to corporation tax on a limited basis, i.e. by reference to the profits of a permanent establishment in the UK, considered as a distinct and separate enterprise (CTA 2009, ss.19–21).

If a non-resident company is carrying on a trade in the UK through a permanent establishment, it is liable to corporation tax by reference to the profits of the permanent establishment. There are two forms of permanent establishment: 'fixed place of business' permanent establishment, and 'dependent agent' permanent establishment. 'Permanent establishment' is defined as (CTA 2010, s.1141):

(a)   . . . a fixed place of business . . . through which the business of the company is wholly or partly carried on; or
(b)   an agent acting on behalf of the company [who] has and habitually exercises their authority to do business on behalf of the company.

'Fixed place of business' includes a place of management, a branch, an office, a factory or a building site. In double taxation agreements a building or construction site will normally constitute a permanent establishment 'only if it lasts more than twelve months': OECD Model Convention, art.6(3). A representative office is not a permanent establishment.

A non-resident company may arrange its affairs so as not to have a UK permanent establishment. In that case its profits will remain liable to taxation in its country of residence.

13.6　CLOSE COMPANIES

The close company has no counterpart in company law. There are numerous special tax rules which apply only to close companies. Broadly, a close company is defined as one which is controlled by five or fewer participators or is controlled by participators (of whatever number) who are directors (CTA 2010, s.439).

Control is widely defined in terms of (CTA 2010, ss.450, 451):

(a)　ownership of majority voting control or ownership of the greater part of the share capital;

(b)　being entitled on a winding up to receive the greater part of the assets available for distribution through ownership of either ordinary or redeemable share capital;

(c)　ownership of sufficient share capital to ensure that the greater part of the whole income of the company if distributed would be received by the owner.

Two or more persons jointly together possessing 'control' are taken to have control.

The definition of 'participator' proceeds in the same way as the definitions of control. A person is a 'participator' if he falls under any of these headings:

(a)　a person who owns share capital in that company;

(b)　a person who has voting rights in that company;

(c)　any loan creditor of that company except where the loan is made in the ordinary course of banking;

(d)　any person who has a right to receive 'distributions' or amounts payable to loan creditors by way of premium on redemption of a loan; or

(e)　any person entitled to secure that income or assets of that company, whether present or future, will be applied directly or indirectly for his benefit.

In general, entitlement rather than actual possession is sufficient.

The powers of an associate or any number of associates may be added to those of a participator in order to determine whether a company is a close company. Associates are, briefly, close relations and partners of a participator, trustees of a settlement of which the participator or any close relation of his is a settlor, co-beneficiaries of any trust or under any will who possess some interest in 'shares or obligations' of a company along with the participator. The second addition is that any person who exercises the function of a director, for example, a shareholder with a preponderant controlling shareholding who could bring pressure to bear on directors, is counted as a director. A person who does not own shares and is not a loan creditor cannot be a participator nor have associates.

If at least 35 per cent of the shares in a company (excluding preference shares or other shares with a fixed dividend) carrying voting power are owned by the public, then the company is not a close company. A subsidiary of a close company will itself be close.

Where a close company, otherwise than in the ordinary course of a business which includes lending money, makes a loan to a 'participator' or 'associate', the company is obliged to pay corporation tax at the rate of 25 per cent of the amount of the loan (CTA 2010, s.455).

If such a loan is written off or released, the borrower is treated as receiving by way of income the amount written off or released, grossed up at the lower rate of income tax and carrying a non-repayable tax credit of the corresponding amount. If the loan is repaid, the corporation tax is refunded.

13.7 CHARGE TO CORPORATION TAX

Corporation tax is fixed for financial years, which begin on 1 April (as opposed to 6 April for individuals). 'The financial year 2013' means the period 1 April 2013 to 31 March 2014. As noted at **13.5**, UK-resident companies are chargeable to corporation tax on all profits wherever arising. Companies not resident in the UK are only chargeable to corporation tax if they carry on a trade in the UK through a permanent establishment, by reference to the trading income arising directly to the company through the permanent establishment.

The full rate of corporation tax for the financial year 2013 is 23 per cent, and it is planned to reduce it to 20 per cent by the financial year 2015. This full rate applies to companies whose profits exceed £1.5 million. Reduced rates apply for 'small companies' whose profits are under £1.5 million. 'Profits' for these purposes includes franked investment income, i.e. dividends plus the associated tax credit, but excluding dividends from 51 per cent subsidiaries.

Profits up to the 'lower relevant maximum amount' (LRMA) are charged to corporation tax at the 'small profits rate' of 20 per cent. Profits between the LRMA and the 'higher relevant maximum amount' (HRMA), attract marginal relief, i.e. the company is charged to tax at the full rate, but the tax payable is then reduced by the marginal relief fraction of an amount produced by applying a formula (CTA 2010, ss.18–24).

The marginal relief fraction is:
(Full rate – small profits rate)
= 400.

So the marginal relief fraction for 2013 is 3/400.

The formula for calculating small companies marginal relief is:

$(M - P) \times I/P \times F$

Where:
M = upper relevant maximum amount
P = profits
I = basic profits (i.e. profits chargeable to tax)
F = marginal relief fraction

The lower and higher amounts are:
Lower relevant maximum amount (LRMA) £300,000
Higher relevant maximum amount (HRMA) £1,500,000

The upper and lower units are reduced where a company has 'associated companies', by dividing the amount in question by one plus the number of associates. A is an associate of B if either: (i) B controls A, or (ii) A and B are under common control (CTA 2010, ss.2530). 'Control' means possession or entitlement, direct or indirect, of up to 51 per cent of the share capital, voting power, income distributions or assets on a winding up. Where a person is not a 'participator', the rights and powers of his associates are not to be attributed to him, so as to make one company 'associated' with another.

A 'close investment-holding company' is a close company which is an investment company other than a property investment company. A close investment-holding company pays corporation tax at the full rate and cannot claim the small profits rate (CTA 2010, s.34).

The distinction between the full rate and the small profits rate will disappear from 1 April 2015 onwards.

13.7.1 Accounting periods

Companies pay corporation tax by reference to accounting periods, which will normally be the period for which the company makes up its annual accounts, i.e. the 12 months ending on the accounting reference date (CTA 2009, s.9). An accounting period begins:

(a)   when a company becomes UK-resident; or
(b)   when it acquires a source of income, for example by commencing a business; or
(c)   when a previous accounting period comes to an end, without the company ceasing to be within the charge to corporation tax.

An accounting period ends on the first occurrence of any of the following:

(a)   the expiration of 12 months from the beginning of the accounting period;
(b)   the occurrence of the company's accounting reference date;
(c)   the company's beginning or ceasing to trade;
(d)   the company's beginning or ceasing to be resident in the UK;
(e)   the company's ceasing to be within the charge to corporation tax.

An accounting period may not exceed 12 months. Corporation tax rates are fixed by reference to financial years. Where an accounting period straddles a change in corporation tax rates, the profits will be apportioned on a time basis between the financial years which overlap the accounting period.

Example

Trading company with no associated companies

Accounting period: 1 April 2013–31 March 2014

Basic profits:	£440,000
Franked investment income: 90,000 × 10/9	100,000
Profits:	540,000
Corporation tax: 23% × 440,000	101,200
Less: marginal relief	
3/400 × (1,500,000 – 540,000) × (440,000/540,000)	5,866
Tax payable	95,334

13.8   ADMINISTRATION AND PAYMENT OF CORPORATION TAX

Corporation tax self-assessment (CTSA) requires companies to file a corporation tax return and pay the corporation tax shown to be due in it. 'Large companies' (i.e. companies with profits of at least £1.5 million a year including franked investment income and which accordingly pay the main rate of corporation tax) are required to pay corporation tax by quarterly instalments (Corporation Tax (Instalment Payments) Regulations 1998, SI 1998/3175, reg.5. The instalments fall in months seven, 10, 13 and 16 after the start of the accounting period to which they relate. The quarterly instalments are based on the anticipated corporation tax liability for the accounting period, net of all reliefs and set-offs (such as income tax suffered by deduction). Payments are based on current estimated tax liabilities, with interest payable on underpayments and receivable on overpayments. Interest charged will be deductible in computing profits, and interest received will be taxable.

In establishing whether or not a company is 'large', and so required to pay quarterly instalments, the taxable profits limit of £1.5 million has to be split between associated companies, in the same way as is used to determine whether or not a company qualifies for small profits relief.

Other companies are required to pay corporation tax nine months after the end of the accounting period (TMA 1970, s.59D).

The company's tax return is to be filed before a specified filing date, which is usually 12 months from the end of the accounting period. While an amendment is possible, no amendment can be made more than 12 months after the filing date. HMRC can amend the return to correct obvious errors or omissions up to nine months after the filing date. If a company does not make a self-assessment in response to a notice requiring the company to make such a return, HMRC may determine to the best of their information and belief the amount of tax payable by the company. This determination has effect as if it were a self-assessment and no appeal is possible. The determination can only be displaced by filing a return within 12 months of the determination and five years of the filing date.

13.9 INTEREST AND DISTRIBUTIONS

13.9.1 Withholding tax

There is a general obligation on a company to deduct income tax from certain categories of interest payment which it makes (Income Tax Act 2007, ss.847, 874). All quoted Eurobond interest can be paid gross. The definition of 'quoted Eurobond' means any security that (i) is issued by a company, (ii) is listed on a recognised stock exchange, and (iii) carries a right to interest (Income Tax Act 2007, ss.882, 987).Where companies make or receive payments from which income tax has to be or has been deducted, such payments are accounted for on a quarterly return under which the company accounts to HMRC for the net income tax due.

13.9.2 Distributions

Where the company's business is continuing, all payments by a company to its shareholders in respect of their shares will be income distributions, paid from current year taxed profits and distributable reserves, save where capital is returned to shareholders. All payments to shareholders in respect of share capital on a winding up are capital distributions, because once the winding-up resolution is passed, the undistributable reserves of the company become distributable to the extent that they exceed the liabilities of the company. In particular circumstances, a distribution may be accorded a capital gains tax treatment (demergers; redemption of redeemable shares; purchase of own shares).

Tax law expands the company law definition of distribution, so that certain transactions which would not for company law purposes be distributions are such for tax purposes; for example:

(a) a payment of interest in excess of a 'reasonable commercial return' for the use of the principal advanced is a distribution (CTA 2010, ss.1000(1)E, 1005 – 'non-commercial securities');

(b) a payment of interest by reference to the profits of the business, in so far as it exceeds a reasonable commercial return for the principal is treated as a distribution (CTA 2010, ss.1000(1)F, 1015(4) – 'special securities');

(c) a purchase of own shares will ordinarily be a distribution, even if paid for out of capital.

The normal form of distribution will be a cash dividend, though dividends in specie also occur. Distributions are an application of profits, not a charge on profits, and so are non-deductible for accounting and tax purposes.

Distributions are classified as qualifying or non-qualifying (CTA 2010, s.1136). Qualifying distributions carry tax credits, non-qualifying do not. Distributions resulting in an immediate distribution out of the reserves of the company in respect of shares are qualifying. Distributions causing a potential claim on reserves are non-qualifying. Hence all distributions are qualifying distributions, apart from two exceptions:

(a) issue of bonus redeemable shares and bonus securities;

(b) issue of any share capital or security which the company making the distribution has directly or indirectly received from another company in the form of bonus redeemable shares or securities.

A payment by a company to its shareholders is excluded from the qualifying distribution treatment if and to the extent that it represents a repayment of capital on the shares or if and to the extent that 'new consideration' is received by the company making the distribution. Consideration is new if it is external to the company, i.e. it is not provided directly or indirectly by the company itself (CTA 2010, s.1115). A bonus issue is not a distribution because there is no cost to the company. A rights issue where the rights are exercised is not a distribution because the consideration is new. A purchase of own shares from the shareholder direct is a distribution, but a purchase in the open market is not.

Rules on the re-characterisation of interest as a distribution do not apply where the payment is from one UK-resident company to another, except for the rule that interest in excess of a reasonable commercial return for the use of the principal will be regarded as a dividend (CTA 2010, s.1032).

Dividends are treated as paid on the date when they become due and payable. Unless the memorandum or articles provide otherwise a dividend is not payable until it has been declared. Final dividends are declared by the annual general meeting. The articles may give the directors power to pay interim dividends. An interim dividend is paid on account of the final dividend. An interim dividend is due only when actually paid by the company. A final dividend is due when it is sanctioned by the annual general meeting, i.e. it then becomes a debt immediately due from the company to shareholders.

13.9.3 Stock dividends

An option conferred on a shareholder to take additional share capital as the alternative to a dividend is a 'stock dividend' (CTA 2010, ss.1049–1064). Although they may be declared out of distributable profits, stock dividends can also be paid out of share premium account, thus leaving distributable reserves unaffected.

Where the shareholder who is liable to income tax has an option to take shares instead of a cash dividend, the stock dividend is treated as an income distribution (CTA 2010, s.1049; ITTOIA 2005, s.410). The shareholder who opts for a stock dividend instead of cash is treated as receiving a dividend of the 'appropriate amount in cash' plus the 'tax-credit fraction', while for capital gains tax purposes he acquires the shares for 'the appropriate amount in cash'. The amount of the distribution is the tax credit plus 'the appropriate amount in cash'. The 'appropriate amount in cash' is either:

(a)   the amount of the cash dividend which the shareholder would have received, unless the market value of the shares received is significantly different on the date of first dealing from the cash dividend, i.e. varies by more than 15 per cent; or

(b)   if the 'significantly different proviso applies', because the value of the shares has risen or fallen sharply since the declaration of the dividend, the 'appropriate amount in cash' is the market value of the shares. In that case, the amount of the notional tax dividend has to be correspondingly adjusted.

13.9.4 Purchase of own shares

For tax purposes a purchase of own shares is a hybrid transaction, comprising in part a return of capital and in part a distribution. The proceeds of sale must be divided into two parts:

1.   The part (if any) which corresponds to whatever amount of value was received by the company upon the issue of the shares in question. This part is always treated as capital for tax purposes.

2.   The balance ('the income element'), if any. The shareholder receives income of an amount which is ten-ninths of the distribution, which carries a non-repayable tax credit of 10 per cent.

On a purchase of own shares, CA 2006, s.706(b) provides that the shares redeemed or repurchased are to be cancelled on redemption. The nominal value of shares purchased or redeemed has to be carried to a capital redemption reserve. Thus, if 20 £1 shares are to be repurchased at £20 per share, £200 of distributable profits will be required for this purpose. Reserves will be reduced by £200 and share capital by £20. This £20 has to be taken to capital redemption reserve, otherwise non-distributable reserves will be reduced.

Example

A company has an issued share capital of 10,000 £1 ordinary shares. Its capital and reserves are:

Share capital	10,000
Reserves	10,000
	20,000

The company decides to purchase 2,000 ordinary shares at par. The accounting entries are:

	Dr	Cr
Share capital	2,000	
Cash		2,000
Reserves	2,000	
Capital redemption reserve		2,000

After the transaction, the capital and reserves are:

Share capital	8,000
Capital redemption reserve	2,000
Reserves	8,000
	18,000

Where unquoted trading companies (or holding companies of trading groups) purchase their own shares, the transaction may be treated as giving rise to a capital gain rather than an income receipt. Where the purchase is made to benefit the trade carried on by the acquiring company, the vendor is resident and ordinarily resident in the UK and has owned the shares or stock for five years, the income element of the purchase will not be treated as a distribution, but will instead be subject to capital gains tax treatment (CTA 2010, ss.1033–1043).

The operation of the relief is subject to two restrictions:

1. The holding of the shareholder must be 'substantially reduced' after the acquisition, so that not more than 75 per cent of his former interest is retained.
2. The vendor must not be 'connected' with the acquiring company or any other company in its group after the purchase. This term is specially defined, so that a person will be connected if he directly or indirectly possesses or is entitled to acquire more than 30 per cent of the issued ordinary shares, loan capital and issued shares, or votes of a company.

Because capital gains tax is charged at a maximum rate of 28 per cent (as opposed to 45 per cent for income in 2013/2014), and because entrepreneurs' relief may reduce the rate of tax to 10 per cent, the capital gains tax treatment is generally more advantageous for individuals.

13.9.5 Imputation system

In the hands of a UK-resident shareholder a dividend paid by a company is liable to income tax (for 2013–2014 onwards) at the dividend ordinary rate (10 per cent), the dividend upper rate (32.5 per cent) or the higher upper rate (37.50 per cent). A dividend carries with it a tax credit of one-ninth of the dividends. This tax credit franks the dividend from ordinary dividend rate taxation of 10 per cent on the sum of the dividend and the tax credit. Thus, part of the corporation tax paid by the company is imputed to the shareholder, and treated as tax paid by the company on behalf of shareholders (ITTOIA 2005, s.397).

If the taxpayer is liable to higher rate tax, he is subject to dividend upper rate tax at 32.5 per cent. If he is liable to the additional rate, the dividend higher upper rate of 37.50 per cent will apply. In either case additional tax is payable, after giving relief for the 10 per cent tax credit. If the taxpayer is exempt (e.g. a pension fund) or not liable to tax, the tax credit is non-repayable (ITTOIA 2005, s.397(2), (3)).

Example

	Ordinary Rate	Upper rate	Higher upper rate
Dividend	90.0	90.0	90.0
Tax credit	10.0	10.0	10.0
Income	100.0	100.0	100.0
Tax at 10/32.5/37.5%	10.0	32.5	37.5
Tax credit	(10.0)	(10.0)	(10.0)
Additional tax		22.5	27.5

13.10 GROUPS OF COMPANIES

There are extensive special tax rules for groups of companies. The principal reliefs relate to:

(a)   surrender of losses within a group ('group relief');
(b)   transfer of assets within a group.

There are also rules which extend group relief to consortium companies.

A group consists of a parent and one or more subsidiaries. Group relationships are defined in terms of ownership 'directly or indirectly' by the parent of the given percentage (or more) of the 'ordinary share capital' of the subsidiary. 'Ordinary share capital' is defined as meaning 'all the company's issued share capital (however described), other than capital the holders of which have a right to a dividend at a fixed rate but have no other right to share in the company's profits' (CTA 2010, ss.160, 1119).

For group relief purposes, a group consists of a parent company and its 75 per cent subsidiaries (CTA 2010, s.152). Two companies are members of a group for group relief purposes if one is the 75 per cent subsidiary of the other, or both are 75 per cent subsidiaries of a third company. The parent must have 75 per cent of the ordinary share capital of the subsidiary. CTA 2010, ss.165, 166 and 1154 set out in great detail two additional tests which a parent must satisfy if another company is to be regarded as its 75 per cent subsidiary:

(a)   the parent must be beneficially entitled to 75 per cent of any profits available for distribution to equity holders of the subsidiary ('profit distribution' test); and

(b)   the parent must be entitled to at least 75 per cent of any assets of the subsidiary available for distribution to equity holders on a winding up 'notional winding up' test).

Trading losses of one company (the surrendering company) can be transferred to another company (the claimant company) to be allowed to the claimant company by way of relief from corporation tax (group relief) (CTA 2010, s.137). Group relief is only available when the surrendering company and claimant company are members of the same group. Where the conditions for group relief are satisfied, trading losses for the current year can be surrendered to other group companies. Within a group, losses can be surrendered upwards, downwards or sideways.

If the conditions are satisfied in respect of part of an accounting period, but not in respect of another part, the subsidiary will be treated as part of the group during that part of the period in which both conditions are satisfied. The subsidiary's loss would be apportioned between the two parts of the accounting period. The effect of group relief is simply to transfer the use of loss to another company that has an immediate use for it. The company receiving the surrender of losses may make a payment to the surrendering company not exceeding the amount surrendered, and such a payment is left out of account in computing the profits and losses for corporation tax of both parties.

Following decisions of the European Court of Justice, the scope of group relief has been extended where there is an international element. The decisions which have led to these changes are:

• *Imperial Chemical Industries plc* v. *Colmer* (Case C-264/96) [1998] STC 874;
• *Marks & Spencer plc* v. *Halsey* (Case C-446/03) [2006] STC 237.

Group membership can be traced through a non-UK-resident parent. A permanent establishment of a non-resident company will be treated as a UK-resident company for these purposes. Further, a subsidiary resident in the EEA which has suffered trading losses that cannot be utilised in the country of residence can surrender these losses to a UK parent. The qualifying loss conditions restrict claims to those which cannot be given qualifying loss relief for any period, past, current or future in the territory where the loss has occurred, nor have been otherwise relieved outside the

UK. This confines the cross-border loss relief to terminal losses (i.e. losses remain unrelieved when a subsidiary in another EU Member State is wound up).

13.10.1 Consortium relief

A consortium consists of at least two and not more than 20 companies which together own 75 per cent or more of the ordinary share capital of a company (a consortium company) and each of them owns separately at least 5 per cent of the ordinary share capital. A consortium company is a company *owned* by a consortium, not a company which belongs to a consortium.

Within a consortium, losses can be surrendered between the consortium company to the members of the consortium (CTA 2010, ss.132, 133). Each member of a consortium can claim a share of a consortium company's losses which corresponds to its percentage ownership of the consortium company.

A member's share in a consortium in relation to an accounting period of the surrendering company is whichever is the *lowest* of the following percentages:

(a) the percentage of ordinary share capital beneficially owned by the member;
(b) the percentage to which the member is beneficially entitled of any profits available to equity holders; and
(c) the percentage to which the member would be beneficially entitled of any assets available to equity holders on a winding up.

13.10.2 Intra-group transfers of assets

For capital gains tax purposes, groups are defined differently from the way in which they are defined for group relief. There are two limbs to the definition of a capital gains tax group (TCGA 1992, s.170):

1. A group consists of a principal company and 75 per cent subsidiaries and sub-subsidiaries.
2. All members of a group must be effective 51 per cent subsidiaries of the principal company, and satisfy the profit distribution and notional winding-up tests.

For capital gains tax purposes, disposals between connected persons are transactions 'otherwise than by way of a bargain made at arm's length', which are deemed to take place at market value (TCGA 1992, ss.17(1), 18). Members of a group are 'connected persons' (TCGA 1992, s.286). Where *capital* assets are transferred within a capital gains tax group, there is a disposal on a no gain/no loss disposal, instead of a disposal at market value (TCGA 1992, s.171(1)). Hence, if a capital gains tax group exists, when one member of the group disposes of an asset to another member of the group, no corporation tax on capital gains arises at that point. The deemed consideration is taken to be equal to the transferor's indexed base cost.

Example

P, a non-resident company, owns all the share capital of A and B, which are both UK-resident companies. A holds land acquired for £0.2 million. When its market value is £1 million, it sells the land to B for £0.6 million. The indexation factor is 0.287.

B's acquisition cost is:		£200,000
Indexation allowance:	£200,000 × 0.287	£57,400
		£257,400

13.10.3 Notional transfers

Where A and B are members of the same capital gains tax group, and A disposes of an asset to a third company C, which is not a member of the group, A and B may jointly elect that the disposal may be treated as having been made by B rather than A, and that A may be treated as having transferred the asset intra-group to B immediately before the disposal (TCGA 1992, s.171A). Thus, if B has capital losses brought forward, a gain on the disposal of the asset can be set against B's losses, without the need for an actual transfer of the asset to B prior to sale.

13.10.4 Degrouping

Where the company leaving a group owns an asset acquired from another group member within the previous six years, a degrouping charge is imposed. Where s.179 applies, the legislation seeks to charge the gain or loss inherent in the asset at the time of the intra-group transfer. The gain or loss arises on the disposal of the shares in the transferee company which brings about the degrouping (TCGA 1992, s.179(3A)). The effect of s.179 is to treat the acquired asset as having been sold for market value at the time of the transfer. This is the primary degrouping charge (TCGA 1992, s.179(1)–(3)).

There is a secondary degrouping charge which applies where, on a takeover, a company in the acquired group does not become a member of the new enlarged group and, within six years of having acquired the asset intra-group, ceases to be either a 75 per cent or a 51 per cent subsidiary of companies in the new group (TCGA 1992, s.179(5)–(8)).

The notional disposal rules do not apply in a number of situations:

(a) where a company leaves a group in consequence of another company 'ceasing to exist', for example subsidiary transfers asset to parent, subsidiary is liquidated, and the parent has no other subsidiary;

(b) where two companies cease to be members of the group at the same time, and one acquired the asset from the other, provided that both companies are 75 per cent subsidiaries and effective 51 per cent subsidiaries of a third company, or one is a 75 per cent subsidiary and effective 51 per cent subsidiary of the other,

251

both at the time of the original transfer and at the time when the two companies leave the group (TCGA, s.179(2ZB); *Johnston Publishing (North) Ltd* v. *Revenue and Customs Commissioners* [2007] STC 3116);

(c) where the transferee company leaves the group on a demerger (TCGA, s.192(2));

(d) where the transferee company leave the group on a merger (TCGA, s.181(1)–(3)).

13.11 ALL INCOME TREATMENT

Loans of companies and securities representing the indebtedness of companies (e.g. loan notes) are classified as 'loan relationships' for tax purposes, and are subject to a special set of rules. The definition of 'loan relationship' covers all debts arising from transactions for the lending of money, and all securities, payments on which are not distributions for tax purposes. A loan relationship may be a debt arising from a transaction for the lending of money (CTA 2009, s.302(1)) or a debt arising from a 'relevant non-trading relationship', being a debt in respect of which the company has issued a security (CTA 2009, ss.303(3), 479). Only companies can have loan relationships.

The legislation requires a company to bring into account as revenue items all profits and gains and losses on loan relationships, whether or not of a capital nature, i.e. all interest receivable, premiums and discounts received plus fluctuations in the value of loan relationships, including all foreign exchange differences on loan relationships and trade debts.

Expenses are deducted from receipts and the balance charged to corporation tax (or made allowable as a loss).

For tax purposes, positive items (income, an increase in an asset, a decrease in a liability) are called 'credits', while negative items (expenditure, decreases in an asset, and increase in a liability) are called 'debits'.

If the company is party to a loan relationship for the purposes of a trade, profits and losses arising from the loan relationship are included in computation of trading profits as receipts or expenses of that trade (CTA 2009, ss.297–298). If the company is party to a loan relationship other than for the purposes of a trade, profits and losses arising from the loan relationship are brought into account in computing non-trading profits (CTA 2009, ss.299–301). The amounts to be taxed or relieved are determined in accordance with the accounts, depending upon whether the company uses an amortised cost or fair value basis for the financial instrument in question, subject to various statutory overrides.

Trading losses arising from loan relationships will be available in the same way as trading losses generally: see **13.4.3**. Non-trading deficits on loan relationships are pooled with non-trading losses in respect of derivative contracts.

Non-trading deficits on loan relationships (thus augmented) may be used as follows (CTA 2009, ss.456–463):

(a)   treated as trading losses and surrendered by way of group relief;
(b)   set off against any profits for the deficit period;
(c)   carried back to set against non-trading profits from loan relationships for 12 months immediately preceding the deficit period;
(d)   carried forward against non-trading profits (including capital gains) for subsequent accounting periods.

A carried forward deficit is not available for relief under (a) to (c). If non-trading loan relationship losses are utilised for group relief, relief is granted as if they were a trading loss.

Where companies are connected, a number of special rules apply. 'Connection' is defined in terms of control. Control is defined in terms of the ability to control through the holding of shares, voting power or powers in the articles as to how a company's affairs are conducted (CTA 2009, ss.348, 466). The principal rules for connected company loan relationships are (CTA 2009, ss.354, 358):

(a)   if the creditor company releases the debt, the debtor company does not have to bring in a credit;
(b)   if the debtor company cannot repay the loan or interest, the creditor company cannot bring in a debit and so gets no impairment relief.

13.11.1   Derivative contracts

Profits and losses on derivative contracts are taxed under special rules (CTA 2009, s.570). Derivative contracts are 'relevant contracts' which are classified for accounting purposes as 'derivative financial instruments'. A relevant contract is a future, an option or a contract for differences. A derivative contract is a relevant contract which is treated as a 'derivative financial instrument' for accounting purposes (CTA 2009, ss.576–583).

The same terminology of 'credits' and debits' is applied as is used in the loan relationship rules. Under accounting standards, all derivative contracts are required to be taken to the balance sheet at fair value, with changes in value going through the income statement. For tax purposes credits and debits on equity derivatives, property derivatives and embedded derivatives which are share options are treated as capital gains and losses.

13.11.2   Intangible fixed assets

The taxation of intangibles acquired or created after 1 April 2002 is also subject to special rules in CTA 2009, ss.711–906. The rules apply to copyright, patents, trademarks, registered designs, know-how, secret knowledge, goodwill. An 'all income' approach is to be adopted, using the 'credits' and 'debits' terminology. 'Intangible asset' has the meaning which it has for accounting purposes. Goodwill, as defined for accounting purposes, is included in intangible property and when held by companies ceases to be an asset which qualifies for rollover relief. Relief for expenditure on intangibles is to be given as a revenue deduction, based on the amortisation rate used in a company's accounts. Tax broadly follows. The same trading/non-trading distinction is used as in the case of loan relationships and derivative contracts.

There is an option to adopt a 4 per cent straight-line amortisation rate.

Profits on the sale of assets are also taxed as income, subject to rollover relief if the company invests in newly acquired intangibles. The rollover relief will operate by reducing the amortisation relief that can be claimed on replacement assets. The new rollover relief will apply to items acquired after commencement date.

With certain exceptions the rules do not apply to acquisitions of intangibles from related companies. A definition of group is introduced based on the capital gains tax definition of group. Transfers of intangibles intra-group are on a no gain/no loss basis.

13.12   THE PATENT BOX

For accounting periods beginning on or after 1 April 2013, a special regime applies to patent income. Qualifying companies which opt into the scheme are granted an additional tax deduction which reduces the rate of corporation tax to 10 per cent (CTA 2010, ss.357A–357GE). A company is a qualifying company if it is a trading company holding IP rights or an exclusive licence in respect of IP rights. The company must have been actively engaged in the development of the patents, and actively manage their commercial exploitation.

13.13   TRANSFER PRICING

Transfer pricing is a technique to shift profits from one enterprise to another related enterprise by charging 'transfer prices', i.e. prices which do not conform to an arm's length standard. If both enterprises are resident in the same jurisdiction, the overall result is likely to be neutral on profits and tax consolidation. If the two enterprises are resident in different jurisdictions, the result will be to move profits from one jurisdiction to the other. The transfer pricing rules only apply where (a) there are 'arrangements' between two enterprises which do not meet the arm's length standard; (b) one of the enterprises is UK resident and derives a UK tax advantage from the arrangements; and (c) the 'participation condition' is met directly or indirectly as regards the two enterprises: TIOPA, s 147(1)(b); TIOPA, ss.147–163.

For accounting periods beginning on or after 1 April 2004, the transfer pricing rules, including the thin capitalisation rules, apply to arrangements between related UK companies and arrangements between related UK and non-UK companies alike. In domestic situations, transfer pricing situations will arise where one company loans money on non-commercial terms to another group member, or intra-group supplies are made on favourable terms.

In a thin capitalisation situation, one company provides debt finance to a related company in circumstances where a commercial lender would not make a loan at all, or a loan of a smaller amount, or would make the loan on different terms. Where transfer pricing arrangements or thin capitalisation exist, the company which gains a UK tax advantage because a non-arm's length price has been used has to adjust its accounts to conform to an arm's length standard of pricing and calculate its taxable profits accordingly (TIOPA 2010, s.147(5)).

To mitigate the effect of applying the transfer pricing rules in domestic situations, there are a number of broad exclusions, for example for small or medium-sized enterprises. A company qualifies as an SME if it meets two out of three tests (see **Chapter 12**):

(a)   turnover not more than £11.2 million;
(b)   balance sheet total not more than £5.6 million;
(c)   not more than 250 employees.

13.14   CAPITAL ALLOWANCES

Commercial accounts must provide for depreciation of fixed assets, i.e. the reduction in value of fixed assets arising from their use in the business. Depreciation is not an allowable deduction for tax purposes. Instead, uniform capital allowances are granted by statute – principally the Capital Allowances Act (CAA) 2001.

From 2008–2009 the rate of writing-down allowances for plant and machinery is 20 per cent. The main feature of the system is that all expenditure on machinery or plant is pooled. If the total expenditure carried forward from previous periods exceeds the value of any plant or machinery sold or disposed of in that period, the owner obtains a writing-down allowance on the excess. In the converse instance, where the value of the machinery sold or disposed of exceeds the expenditure carried forward, then the owner suffers a balancing charge on the excess.

In the case of short-life assets, an option can be made to write down their values individually (depooling). In that case a balancing allowance (or charge) arises when they are disposed of. If after four years they have not been disposed of, they are transferred to the general pool at their tax written-down value (CAA 2001, ss.83–89).

Long-life assets, i.e. assets with a useful economic life of more than 25 years, are separately pooled and qualify for writing-down allowances of 6 per cent per year on a straight-line basis (CAA 2001, ss.91–104).

From 1 January 2013, companies are entitled to an annual investment allowance (AIA) of £250,000 in respect of plant and machinery expenditure. This gives immediate relief of 100 per cent for the expenditure, up to the limit. A group of companies has one AIA (CAA 2001, ss.51A–51N). The effect is that all the tax allowances are claimed in the first year, and nothing is transferred to the plant and machinery pool.

13.15   SUBSTANTIAL SHAREHOLDING EXEMPTION

A company which is a trading company or a member of a trading group can dispose of shares in a subsidiary free of corporation tax on capital gains, if the qualifying conditions are met. This is the 'substantial shareholding exemption' set out in TCGA 1992, Sched.7AC. The investing company must have held the shares for at least twelve months in the two year period preceding the disposal. The investing company must hold at least 10 per cent of the ordinary shares of the investee company, be entitled to 10 per cent of the profits available for distribution and be entitled to 10 per cent of the assets available for distribution to equity holders on a notional winding up, in order for the shareholding to qualify for the exemption on disposal. The investee company in turn must be a trading company or the holding company of a trading group or sub-group. By the same token losses on a disposal of a 'substantial shareholding' are not allowable. The exemption is automatic and does not need to be claimed. Where the investee company ceases to trade on being put into liquidation, disposals by the investing company can continue to qualify for substantial shareholding exemption for a further period of two years.

CHAPTER 14

Directors and the management of a company

14.1 INTRODUCTION

The management of a company's affairs will reside ordinarily in persons specifically appointed to hold office as company directors. Collectively, persons appointed to act as company directors will be members of the company's board of directors. In addition to a formally appointed director, the law may also class a person as a director of a company in circumstances where the degree of his or her responsibility and authority in the management of a company's affairs equates to the position of either a de facto or shadow director. The significance of a person being labelled as a director will be particularly pertinent in circumstances where the law imposes a personal liability against directors in respect of delinquent conduct, for example, a breach of duty or in relation to acts of fraudulent trading (IA 1986, s.213), wrongful trading (IA 1986, s.214) and disqualification (Company Directors Disqualification Act 1986, s.6).

Where a person is found to be a de facto director, that person will be subject to the responsibilities and liabilities of a formally appointed director. A person classed as a shadow director will be subject to the responsibilities and liabilities of a formally appointed director in circumstances specified by the companies legislation.

14.2 IDENTIFYING COMPANY DIRECTORS

CA 2006 provides little assistance in defining the managerial characteristics of a company director. Section 250 of CA 2006 (affording no change from the previous position under CA 1985, s.741(1)) states that the term 'director' includes:

... any person occupying the position of director, by whatever name called.

Accordingly, a person may be classified as a director where that person is formally appointed to hold office (a de jure director) or in a situation where a person, in the absence of any formal appointment, performs tasks and duties ordinarily associated with the office of a director (a de facto director). A person may also be classed as a shadow director. Section 251 of CA 2006 (again affording no change from the position under CA 1985, s.741(2)) defines a 'shadow director' as:

> ... a person in accordance with whose directions or instructions the directors of the company are accustomed to act ... A person is not to be regarded as a shadow director by reason only that the directors act on advice given by him in a professional capacity.

However, it is to be noted that a body corporate is not to be regarded as a shadow director of any of its subsidiary companies by reason only that the directors of the subsidiary are accustomed to act in accordance with the directions or instructions of its holding company.

14.3   THE DE JURE DIRECTOR

Unless a company's constitution provides otherwise, a de jure director will be formally appointed by the passing of an ordinary resolution or by the decision of the directors (see the Companies (Model Articles) Regulations 2008, SI 2008/3229, Sched.1, article 17 of the model articles for private companies and Sched.3, article 20 for public companies). Following a person's appointment as a director, the person's authority to act in the capacity of a director and his or her ability to bind the company will, in accordance with CA 2006, s.161, be valid for the period during which the office is held, notwithstanding any defect in the appointment process or the fact that he or she had been disqualified from holding office. Further, the validity of a corporate act may not be impugned even in a situation where a director voted on a matter that he or she was not entitled to vote on.

CA 2006, s.154 stipulates that a private company must have at least one director, whereas a public company must have at least two directors. Section 155 of CA 2006 provides that a company must have at least one director who is a natural person, although this requirement is met if the office of director is held by a natural person as a corporation sole or otherwise by virtue of an office. This provision overturns the previous law, i.e. under CA 1985, any legal entity could be formally appointed as a director of another company irrespective of whether the company appointed a natural person to act as a fellow director. Where a company fails to satisfy the ss.154 and 155 requirements, the Secretary of State may give the company a direction under s.156(4) to make the necessary appointment or appointments.

Although CA 2006 stipulates that the ss.154 and 155 requirements must be met in relation to the *appointment* of a director, it is to be assumed that a de facto or shadow director will not be counted in relation to satisfying the numerical and status requirements (i.e. both a de facto and shadow director will not be appointed to hold office).

The details of a person appointed to hold office as a director must be entered into the register of directors (CA 2006, s.162). Every company must keep a register of its directors to contain the required particulars of every person so appointed. The register must be kept available for inspection at the company's registered office. The required particulars must, *inter alia*, include:

- the director's name;
- any name by which the individual was formerly known for business purposes;
- a service address;
- the country or state (or part of the UK) in which the director is usually resident;
- nationality;
- business occupation (if any);
- date of birth.

The register must be open to inspection by any member of the company without charge, and any other person, on payment of such a fee as may be prescribed. It is to be noted that the previous requirement (under CA 1985, s.289) for a director to provide details of any other directorships held or directorships held within the preceding five years, is no longer a prescribed requirement of CA 2006. In respect of the requirement for a company to keep a register of the residential addresses of its directors (CA 2006, s.165) a company must, within the period of 14 days from the occurrence of any change in the constitution of its directors, or any change in the particulars contained in its register of directors or its register of directors' residential addresses, give notice to the registrar of the change and of the date on which it occurred (CA 2006, s.167). Given the imprecise nature of the definition and identification of a person occupying the position of a shadow director (discussed below), a shadow director is nevertheless treated as an officer of the company in the context of a person who may incur liability for non-compliance with procedures relating to CA 2006, s.162 (register of directors) and s.165 (register of directors' residential addresses).

14.3.1 Qualifications

Other than where a company's constitution provides specifically that a person must hold a specified number of shares before his or her appointment as a director of the company (a share qualification), a person may be appointed to a directorship without the necessity of having attained any specific qualifications for the post. Prior to the passing of CA 2006, it was even possible for an infant to hold office as a director, notwithstanding a minor's legal incapacity to contractually bind a company (see, e.g. *Marquis of Bute's case* [1892] 2 Ch 100). As a consequence of CA 2006, s.157, a person must be at least 16 years old before he or she can hold office as a director. This provision applies retrospectively to persons under 16 years of age who held office prior to the implementation of s.157. However, a minor may be provisionally appointed to a directorship at any age on the understanding that he or she does not legally hold office until attaining the age of 16. However, it is to be noted that s.157 is subject to a peculiar exemption in the form of s.158, namely the latter permits the Secretary of State to make provision by regulations to permit the appointment of a person as a director notwithstanding that the said person has not attained the age of 16. An appointment made in contravention of s.157 (but subject to s.158) is deemed void. A person who acts in contravention of s.157 remains liable for any breach of the companies legislation during the period in which he or she purported to act as a director.

14.3.2 Types of de jure directors

The executive director

An executive director will normally be a full-time officer of the company, employed under a contract of employment. A company's articles will normally specify that the company may appoint one or more directors to hold office as an executive director. An obvious example of a person holding an executive office will be where that person is appointed to the post of managing director/chief executive. A managing director is normally appointed to oversee the day-to-day running of a company. The terms of an executive director's service contract (discussed below) and the specific powers delegated to the office held, will be determined by the collective board of directors.

The non-executive director

A person who is appointed to hold the post of a non-executive director will ordinarily be devoid of any contract of employment and as such will not be a salaried employee of the company. Nevertheless, a non-executive director may be held liable for a breach of corporate duty or other statutory obligation in a manner akin to that of an executive director. Once appointed, a non-executive director will hold office for a period determined by the company's articles. However, in public companies, following the trend of recent corporate governance initiatives, the role of a non-executive director takes on a far more important position in management structures. In public companies, the role of a non-executive director has been elevated to a position akin to that of an independent protector of the company and the public interest. In public companies, non-executive directors will be expected to contribute to the development of corporate strategy by, for example, scrutinising the performance of executive directors and by satisfying themselves that financial controls and systems of risk management are robust and defensible (discussed further in **Chapter 21**).

The company chairman

The company chairman is an appointed director of the company with responsibilities of a supervisory nature. The chairman presides over meetings of the board of directors. The chairman of the board will ordinarily preside over general meetings of the company. Although a company chairman will normally have no special powers, where a vote at a meeting of the board or general meeting is tied, he or she may ordinarily, but subject to the terms of the company's articles, be entitled to a second or casting vote.

The alternate director

Where a director is to be absent from board meetings, he or she may appoint a nominee, an alternate person, to act in his or her place. A person appointed to act as an alternate director may be an existing director of the company or any other person. An authority to appoint an alternate director must be provided for in a company's articles and the appointment must be approved by the board of directors. Although an alternate director acts in effect as a replacement, he or she is not an agent for the absent director. Accordingly, an alternate director may act and vote according to his or her own conscience and as such is responsible for his or her own acts.

14.3.3 Retirement

Prior to CA 2006, a director of a public company was obliged to retire at the age of 70, unless he or she continued to hold office with the approval of the company's general meeting (previously CA 1985, s.293(1)). CA 2006 provides no compulsory retirement age for a director.

14.4 THE DE FACTO DIRECTOR

A person may be deemed to act as a de facto director where that person performs managerial tasks properly associated with the office of a director. The tasks performed by that person must exceed those of a mere employee; they must extend to an authority in matters related to the administration and management of the company's affairs in a manner associated with those performed by a de jure director (see, e.g. *Re Red Label Fashions Ltd* [1999] BCC 308). Although a company director will stand in a fiduciary relationship to the company in which he or she holds office, an employee does not assume fiduciary obligations to his employer unless fiduciary obligations may be said to arise from the specific terms of the employee's contract of employment (see, e.g. *University of Nottingham* v. *Fishel* [2000] ICR 1462 and, more recently, *Ranson* v. *Customer Systems plc* [2012] EWCA Civ 841).

While the courts have attempted to define the nature and degree of control considered necessary to identify a person as a de facto director, formal guidelines have not always been of a uniform nature. Historically, two tests emerged to determine the character of a de facto director, namely the 'equal footing test' and 'the holding out test'. The former test, first advanced by Lloyd J in *Re Richborough Furniture* [1996] 1 BCLC 507, considered a de facto director to be identifiable, where there was –

... clear evidence that he had been either the sole person directing the affairs of the company (or acting with others all equally lacking in a valid appointment ...) or, if there were others who were true directors, that he was acting on an equal footing with the others in directing the affairs of the company. (at p.524)

The characteristics of the equal footing test were revised following the decisions of Judge Cooke in *Secretary of State for Trade and Industry* v. *Elms* (16 January 1997, unreported) and Jacob J in *Secretary of State* v. *Tjolle* [1998] BCLC 333. In *Secretary of State* v. *Tjolle*, Jacob J quoted with approval the following passage taken from the judgment of Judge Cooke in *Secretary of State for Trade and Industry* v. *Elms*:

> At the forefront of the test I think I have to go on to consider by way of further analysis what Lloyd J meant by 'on an equal footing'. As to one, it seems to me clear that this cannot be limited simply to statutory functions and to my mind it would mean and include any one or more of the following: directing others, putting it very compendiously, committing the company to major obligations, and thirdly (really I think what we are concerned with here) taking part in an equally based collective decision process at board level, i.e. at the level of a director in effect with a foot in the board room. As to Lloyd J's test, I think it is very much on the lines of that third test to which I have just referred. It is not I think in any way a question of equality of power but equality of ability to participate in the notional boardroom. Is he somebody who is simply advising and, as it were, withdrawing having advised, or somebody who joins the other directors, de facto or de jure, in decisions which affect the future of the company?

By contrast, in *Re Hydrodam (Corby) Ltd* [1994] 2 BCLC 180, Millet J defined a de facto director by applying an alternative test – 'the holding out test'. The learned judge opined:

> A de facto director is a person who assumes to act as a director. He is held out as a director by the company, and claims and purports to be a director, although never actually or validly appointed as such. To establish that a person was a de facto director of a company it is necessary to plead and prove that he undertook functions in relation to the company which could properly be discharged only by a director. It is not sufficient to show that he was concerned in the management of the company's affairs or undertook tasks in relation to its business which can properly be performed by a manager below board level. (at p.183)

However, irrespective of any formula or test, a decision as to whether a person acted as a de facto director will ultimately be a question of fact to be determined from the circumstances of each individual case. Indeed, in *Re Kaytech International plc. Portier* v. *Secretary of State for Trade and Industry* [1999] BCC 390, the first ever case to reach the Court of Appeal on the interpretation of a 'de facto' director, the court approved a statement (at p.402) taken from the judgment of Jacob J in *Secretary of State* v. *Tjolle*, namely:

> ... it may be difficult to postulate any one decisive test. I think what is involved is very much a question of degree. The court takes into account all the relevant factors. Those factors include at least whether or not there was a holding out by the company of the

individual as a director, whether the individual used the title, whether the individual had proper information (e.g. management accounts) on which to base decisions, and whether the individual has to make major decisions and so on. Taking all these factors into account, one asks 'was this individual part of the corporate governing structure?', answering it as a kind of jury question.

Accordingly, to determine whether a person acted as a de facto director, one cannot apply a single decisive test. Matters pertinent to the equal footing test and the holding out test will be relevant, but such matters cannot be decisive in any prescribed formula. However, in seeking to determine what is ultimately a 'jury question', the court will consider specific factors, to include:

- whether there was a holding out by the company of the individual as a director;
- if the individual used the title 'director';
- whether the individual had proper information (e.g. management accounts) on which to base decisions;
- if the individual had or exercised a capacity to exercise control, make or take part in major decision-making; and
- whether the individual contributed management skills in the running of the company.

Taking the above factors into account, the court must determine ultimately whether the individual was a part of the governing structure of the company (see, e.g. *Secretary of State for Trade and Industry* v. *Hollier* [2007] BCC 11). Obviously there will be a strong presumption that a person acts as a de facto director where that person contributes skills and knowledge to the internal management of a company and being concerned with its affairs, portrays to the outside world an obvious understanding and relationship with functions associated ordinarily with and exercised by a de jure director.

It is to be noted that the directors of a company (X) which acts as a corporate director of a company (Y), may not by virtue of the fact that they are directors of X be considered to be de facto directors of company Y. A director of X will only be regarded as a de facto director (or possibly shadow director) of Y in circumstances where 'something more' is established (see *Re Hydrodam (Corby) Ltd* [1994] 2 BCLC 180), namely where the director of X steps outside the confines of his or her role as a member of the board of X to act directly in the affairs of Y (see, e.g. *Secretary of State for Trade & Industry* v. *Hall* [2009] BCC 190 and, more recently, the decision of the Supreme Court in *Revenue and Customs Commissioners* v. *Holland* [2010] 1 WLR 2793). Indeed, in such circumstances, an ability to establish a person's role as a de facto director of Y (other than from evidence of his or her active participation in Y), will be most problematic. As a distinct legal entity, X will carry the ultimate responsibility for managing the affairs of Y and although an individual may dominate the business activities of X, as a matter of law, X will be regarded as the legal entity that directs the policy of Y. Accordingly, in order to find that an individual director of X acted as a de facto director of Y it will be necessary to pierce the corporate veil of X to establish that the individual and not X, directed the policy of Y. (Piercing the corporate veil is discussed in **Chapter 4**.) However, such a finding is most unlikely. In *Revenue and Customs Commissioners* v. *Holland* [2010] 1 WLR 2793, Lord Hope observed:

> So long as the relevant acts are done by the individual entirely within the ambit of the discharge of his duties and responsibilities as a director of the corporate director, it is to that capacity that his acts must be attributed. (at p.2812)

14.5 THE SHADOW DIRECTOR

In contrast to a de facto director, a shadow director will rarely be held out as an officer of a company (albeit this assumption may be questioned in the context of ss.162–165 (see above)). The need to attach a level of responsibility to a person who directs and influences corporate activity through a formally appointed board of directors is patently obvious. A person who exerts influence over a company's affairs must be regulated and be made subject to duties and responsibilities associated ordinarily with the company's appointed directors. Although CA 2006, s.251 would appear expressly to exempt a person from being construed as a shadow director where that person acts in a professional capacity, the exemption is limited and will not cover a situation where, for example, a professional offers advice beyond the reasonable scope of advice one would normally expect from a person occupying a similar professional status. For example, a bank manager, an accountant or a solicitor may be classed as a shadow director by exercising a degree of control over a company's affairs in a manner to suggest real influence as opposed to the provision of a reasonable and expected level of professional advice. For example, in *Re Tasbian Ltd (No.3)* [1992] BCC 358, an accountant, Mr Nixon (N), was employed by a finance company, Castle Finance Ltd (C), to act as financial consultant to Tasbian Ltd (T), a subsidiary of C. The Court of Appeal held that, to justify a finding that N acted as a shadow director of T, it was necessary to establish that N exercised a degree of control over the company's affairs which went far beyond the influence expected from an accountant offering financial advice. In concluding that there was sufficient evidence to establish a finding that N had acted as a shadow director of T, Balcombe LJ stated:

> Mr Nixon decided which cheques drawn by the company could and which could not be submitted to the bank. This meant that he was concerned with which of the company's creditors were paid and in which order, and to that extent it would appear – I say no more than that, that he was able to control the company's affairs. (at p.364)

The court's finding was strengthened by the fact that N manipulated the management functions of the company's appointed directors (see also, *Re a Company (No. 005009 of 1987)* (1988) 4 BCC 424, in which Knox J refused to hold, on a preliminary point of law, that a company's bank was incapable of acting as the company's shadow director).

14.5.1 Changing definitions of shadow director

Prior to the decision of the Court of Appeal in *Secretary of State* v. *Deverell* [2001] Ch 340, case law identified a shadow director as any person who, from outside formal management structures, exerted a dominant and controlling influence over the company's affairs, i.e. a person, for example, a dominant shareholder, who was responsible for engineering and directing corporate activity through what may be described as a 'puppet' board of directors. However, following the decision of *Secretary of State* v. *Deverell*, this former definition can no longer be viewed to be conclusive of establishing a person as a shadow director. In accordance with the decision in *Deverell*, establishing a controlling, dominant and hidden influence in the affairs of a company may now be regarded as an exaggeration of the level and degree of involvement deemed necessary to identify a shadow director.

In *Deverell* the Secretary of State sought to impose a disqualification order against D and H in accordance with s.6 of the Company Directors Disqualification Act 1986. (The disqualification of directors is dealt with in **Chapter 17**.) It was contended that both had acted as shadow directors of the company (E). In defending the proceedings, D and H argued that their involvement in E had been as management consultants and not as directors. In relation to D, he had been involved in the management of the company from the time of its incorporation although he had never been formally appointed as a company director. As one of the signatories to the company's bank account, D was an active player and influential in the accounting and financial structures of the company and was its principal negotiator in business dealings. D's involvement in and attachment to the company was substantial to the extent that he had personally guaranteed a loan entered into by the company. H's involvement in the internal management structures of E was less transparent. H was subject to a bankruptcy order and was precluded from any involvement in the company's formal management structures. Nevertheless, irrespective of H's inability to actively involve himself in the internal affairs of the company, his informal participation and influence in management issues was considerable, especially in the context of advising the company on its future direction. For example, notwithstanding the company's insolvent position and concerns expressed by the company's board of directors in respect of the company's financial state, H had instructed the company's de jure directors to continue to trade, an instruction which was obeyed.

The Court of Appeal held that both D and H had acted as shadow directors of E. In reaching this decision, Morritt LJ, delivering the leading judgment of the court, held that, in seeking to substantiate a person's role as a shadow director, it was unnecessary to establish a subservient relationship between that person and the board of directors. His Lordship reached this conclusion on the premise that the use of the term 'accustomed to act' in CA 1985, s.741(2) (now CA 2006, s.251) should not be interpreted to be conclusive of a requirement that the board of directors must always be compelled to obey the guidance of a shadow director. Accordingly, a person was capable of acting as a shadow director even if the board of directors had a capacity to exercise independent judgment. In relation to the giving of a 'direction' or 'instruction', Morritt LJ considered that the giving of advice, if given on a regular and consistent basis, could be considered in the same vein as a direction or instruction because a direction, instruction, or the giving of advice all shared the common characteristic of an act of guidance. Therefore, according to his Lordship, having established that there was a sufficient degree of guidance, the court would then be in a position to ascertain whether the direction, instruction or advice so relied and acted upon by the board of directors carried real influence in relation to the business activities of the company. However, Morritt LJ found that if 'real influence' was established, it was immaterial whether or not the guidance would always be followed and adhered to by the board of directors. Further, according to Morritt LJ, it was unnecessary to establish that the 'real influence' extended over the whole of the company's business operations. Finally, Morritt LJ considered that a shadow director could be identified as a person involved in either the internal management structure of the company or as an external contributor to a company's affairs.

Therefore, following the judgment of the Court of Appeal in *Deverell*, a shadow director may be identified in the following manner, namely, as a person who customarily tenders advice, instructions or directions to the company's board of a type which, as an act of guidance, carries real influence in relation to a part or the whole of the company's business affairs. While the company's board will normally follow the guidance tendered by a shadow director, it is not essential that it is habitually followed or that there is any expectation that it will be followed. A shadow director may be independent from or form a part of the internal management structures of the company. This reformulated definition now casts a wide net into which a person may be caught and labelled as having acted as a shadow director.

14.5.2   Problems with reformulated definition of shadow director

Although the revamped definition of a shadow director may be applauded in the sense that it increases the pool of persons who, as shadow directors, may be held personally accountable following a company's demise, affording greater protection to the interests of creditors and the general public, the credibility of the reformulated definition may be doubted. First, can mere advice be equated with a direction or instruction? While a direction, instruction or the giving of advice may all share the common characteristic of an act of guidance, a direction or instruction, as an act of guidance, implicitly carries an expectation of obedience. In contrast, 'advice' is, as an act of guidance, couched more in the form of a suggested course of action and therefore is absent of an expectation that it must ordinarily be followed. Secondly, in *Deverell*, Morritt LJ interpreted the term 'accustomed to act' in a passive sense by indicating that it was unnecessary to establish that a shadow director dominated the company's de jure directors, thereby casting the board of directors in a subservient role. However, with respect, although the term 'accustomed to act' may be interpreted in a manner whereby a company's board need not always act in accordance with a direction or instruction, the term nevertheless implies that it would not be the norm for a direction or instruction to be ignored. Surely the question of whether a board of directors is 'accustomed to act' will rest upon a case-by-case analysis of whether a person in directing or instructing the board of directors was obeyed on a regular basis, and more specifically, whether that person's directions or instructions were ordinarily obeyed in relation to decisions crucial to the governance, direction and pursuit of the company's internal, external and financial affairs. Finally, following *Deverell*, a shadow director may be identified as a person involved in either the internal management structure of the company or as an external contributor to a company's affairs despite the fact that the expression 'shadow' suggests an exertion of influence over corporate affairs from outside formal management structures. Indeed, would not a person exerting influence from inside management structures be more aptly described as a de facto director?

14.6 THE DISTINCTION BETWEEN A DE FACTO AND A SHADOW DIRECTOR

Although, in a practical sense, the ability to distinguish between a person's activities as either a de facto director or shadow director may, in the majority of cases, be irrelevant in calculating a person's potential liability as a director, the ability to distinguish between these types of directorship will be most relevant in respect of a person's potential liability under IA 1986, s.212 (discussed in **Chapter 5**). The s.212 provision is applicable only in the case of 'an officer of a company' and, in accordance with IA 1986, s.251, an officer of a company is defined to include a director, manager or secretary but there is no specific reference to a shadow director. Therefore, because a shadow director is not classified as an 'officer of a company', apparently a shadow director cannot incur liability under IA 1986, s.212.

Post *Deverell*, the hallmarks of a shadow director have been modified to such an extent that any distinction between a shadow and a de facto director is now blurred significantly. For example, following *Deverell*, a person's classification as a shadow director may, in common with that of a de facto director, be established without proof of a controlling influence. Secondly, prior to *Deverell*, a shadow director would have been defined as a person detached from the company's internal management, operating in a hidden capacity; post *Deverell*, a person may now be classed as a shadow director where he wields influence over a company's affairs irrespective of whether that influence is as a part of the company's internal management structure. Finally, prior to *Deverell*, a shadow director would have been expected to be in a position to give directions or instructions that would be obeyed by the company's board. Following *Deverell*, the giving of advice is now equated with directions or instructions to the extent that a shadow director is in effect on an 'equal footing' with the company's de jure directors in a sense previously construed as relevant only to the identification of a de facto director. The fact that there is little if any distinction between the identification of a de facto director and a shadow director was echoed in the judgments of the Supreme Court in

Revenue and Customs Commissioners v. *Holland* [2010] 1 WLR 2793. Indeed, following *Deverell*, the only real and significant distinction between the character-istics associated with the definition of a de facto director and those associated with a shadow director is that where a person performs managerial tasks from outside the internal management structures of the company that person will not be labelled as a de facto director albeit the said person could still qualify to be identified as a shadow director of the company. However, this distinction may still prove crucial. For example, while in attempting to establish that an individual director (D) of X acted also as a de facto director of Y (a subsidiary of X) it will be necessary to disturb the corporate veil of X to assert that D and not X was ultimately responsible for the management of X, by contrast, where D acts and operates outside the internal management structures of X, D's liability as a shadow director of Y may be established in circumstances where, by CA 2006, s.251, the individual is 'a person in accordance with whose directions or instructions the directors of the company are accustomed to act'. In cases concerned with the identification of a shadow director of Y, it will not be a prerequisite to lift the corporate veil of X to arrive at a conclusion that D acted as a shadow director of X.

14.7 THE BOARD OF DIRECTORS

A company's board of directors will comprise the individually appointed de jure directors of the company. The scope of a board's management powers is determined by the company's constitution. A company's articles will ordinarily confer the general management powers of a company to the company's board (expressed as the general meeting of directors), albeit specific powers may be retained by the general meeting. For example, the general meeting may be afforded a power by the articles (usually by means of a special resolution) to challenge the decisions of the board of directors (discussed further in **Chapter 18**).

An individual director's management functions are delegated to him or her by the board. The directors can pursue and authorise any corporate act in relation to third-party dealings even in a situation where the corporate act is outside the company's own contractual capacity (discussed further in **Chapter 16**).

14.7.1 Board meetings

The regulation of the meetings held by a board of directors is determined by the company's constitution and by specified requirements attached to the recording of the minutes of the meeting (see CA 2006, ss.248–249). The ability to call and regulate board meetings will be ordinarily decided upon by the directors. Usually, any director of the company will be permitted to call a board meeting. Unless the directors of a company decide otherwise, or unless the company is composed of a sole director, a board meeting must have a quorum of two directors. It is to be noted that a director cannot invalidate a properly summoned board meeting by refusing to attend the meeting (see, e.g. *Smith* v. *Paringa Mines Ltd* [1906] 2 Ch 193 and *Colin Gwyer & Associates Ltd* v. *London Wharf* [2003] 2 BCLC 153). It is for a director who contends that a board meeting was not duly held and convened to prove that contention. Further, the onus of establishing that the minutes of a board meeting are inaccurate in recording the proceedings of the meeting will rest with the person seeking to establish the inaccuracy. However, where proceedings/minutes and therefore matters decided at a board meeting are deemed invalid and are not otherwise saved by the provisions of CA 2006 or by the terms of the company's articles, the invalidity of the proceedings/matters (i.e. matters decided at the invalid meeting) as recorded in the minutes of that meeting, may be subsequently rendered valid in circumstances where those minutes and the content therein (i.e. of the 'invalid' meeting) are ratified at a subsequent validly called meeting (see, e.g. in *Re Portuguese Consolidated Copper Mines Ltd* (1890) LR 45 Ch D 16 and, more recently, *Sneddon* v. *MacCall* [2011] CSOH 59).

Unless otherwise provided for by the terms of a company's articles, at a convened meeting of the board of directors, each director will be entitled to one vote on any particular resolution. A formal resolution will be passed by a simple majority of directors; where there is an equality of votes the resolution will be lost (see, e.g. *Re Hackney Pavilion Ltd* [1924] 1 Ch 276). To avoid the possibility of a deadlock situation, a company's articles may afford the company's chairman a casting vote. However, where all the directors agree on the outcome of a proposed motion, then in accordance with a unanimous informal agreement, the resolution may be passed without a formal board meeting.

14.7.2 Notice requirements

Subject to a contrary indication in a company's articles and except for directors who are absent from the UK, ordinarily, notice of board meetings must be given to all the members of the board. The notice of the meeting need not contain specific details of the business to be discussed at the meeting, even if that business is in any way 'extraordinary' (see, e.g. *La Compagnie de Mayville* v. *Whitley* [1896] 1 Ch 788). Although a director may have been absent from the UK and therefore not entitled to notice of the meeting, a resolution passed by a remaining director in the absence of the absent director will be invalid where it impugns the quorum requirement (see, e.g. *Globalink Telecommunications Ltd* v. *Wilmbury Ltd and Ors* [2002] BCC 958). Nevertheless, a company may be estopped from denying the validity of a resolution in circumstances where the terms of the resolution were acted on by the company and where to subsequently deny its validity would be unconscionable (see, e.g. *Hood Sailmakers Ltd* v. *Axford* [1997] 1 WLR 625).

In determining a time period that amounts to an appropriate period of notice, the court will be influenced by whether, in all the circumstances of the case, it was reasonable to expect a director to attend a particular meeting given the specific period of notice in question. For example, in *Bentley-Stevens* v. *Jones* [1974] 1 WLR 638, inadequate notice of a meeting was found in a situation where a letter was sent to a director on a Sunday, convening a meeting of the board for the morning of the next day (Monday). The director in question had been on a weekend holiday and did not discover the letter until the Monday evening, by which time the board meeting had taken place. However, despite the fact that the notice period was inadequate, Plowman J concluded that the director's absence would not have altered the outcome of the board meeting and therefore the resolution as passed at the meeting was allowed to stand. Plowman J quoted with approval the judgment of Lindley LJ in *Browne* v. *La Trinidad* (1887) 37 Ch D 1, Lindley LJ stated:

> I think it is most important that the court should hold fast to the rule upon which it has always acted, not to interfere for the purpose of forcing companies to conduct their business according to the strictest rules, where the irregularity complained of can be set right at any moment. (at p.17)

Indeed, where a board meeting is called and a director's non-attendance would not affect the outcome of any vote taken at the meeting it would appear logical for the court not to set aside the meeting on the basis that it was called at short notice. However, in some situations this apparent logic may be misplaced, especially where, for example, had an individual director attended a meeting, he or she may have been able to influence other members of the board to vote in a manner contrary to the actual outcome of the final vote. A director who claims to have received inadequate notice of a board meeting must state his objection as soon as is reasonably possible, i.e. after discovering that the meeting has taken place (see, e.g. *Browne* v. *La Trinidad* (1887) 37 Ch D 1).

14.7.3 Delegation of the board's powers to individual directors

It is commonplace for a company's constitution to empower its board to appoint committees of one or more of its directors to exercise powers normally reserved to the board. The necessity for permitting the board of directors to delegate its powers arises from the practical difficulties that occur in the day-to-day management of a corporate enterprise. Obviously, a company would cease to function if all senior managerial decisions could only be justified on the basis of a resolution of the company's board.

14.8 SERVICE CONTRACTS AND DIRECTORS' REMUNERATION

14.8.1 Remuneration

A director's remuneration is a payment received by a director for services provided to the company in which he holds office. The method of remuneration may be in cash or other financial incentives, for example, share options. It should be noted that a director is not entitled, as of right, to any remuneration other than in a situation where the director holds a service contract under which a level of remuneration representing an annual salary package is included as a contractual term of the contract. The articles of a company will normally provide that directors are entitled to receive such remuneration as the company by ordinary resolution determines (this will not apply to the determination of the level of salary in respect of a director's service contract). A remuneration award may be paid to a director in addition to his or her annual salary. As the power to grant remuneration is ordinarily vested in the general meeting, the board has no authority to delegate this power to individual directors or a committee of directors. However, a company's constitution may provide that remuneration awards should be determined by the board of directors. For example, in *Guinness* v. *Saunders* [1990] 2 AC 663, Guinness's (G) articles provided that G's board could determine directors' remuneration up to £100,000; anything in excess of that amount was to be determined by the general meeting. G's articles provided further that the board was responsible for fixing any special remuneration payable to a director who served on a committee. A committee of three directors with full authority from G's board was appointed to facilitate a takeover bid. W, a member of the committee, undertook successful negotiations which resulted in the takeover of the target company. W was paid, in accordance with the committee's instructions, remuneration to the sum of 0.2 per cent of the estimated value of the takeover. The validity of this payment was later challenged by G on the ground that the committee had no authority to authorise the remuneration award. In addition to the relevant articles of G (noted above) G's articles also contained a regulation which defined the board of directors as: 'The directors of the company for the time being ... or any committee authorised to act on its behalf.' The House of Lords found in G's favour. In delivering the leading judgment, Lord Templeman considered that the company's articles were incompatible with a finding that a committee could be regarded as 'the board.' His Lordship held that the intention behind the wording of the article providing that 'the board was responsible for fixing the remuneration of a director who served on a special committee', would have been meaningless if a committee itself had the capacity to award remuneration to its own members (i.e. a committee of directors could not be regarded as the board of directors). His Lordship remarked:

> It cannot have been intended that any committee should be able to grant special remuneration to any director ... The board must compare the work of an individual director with the ordinary duties of a director. The board must decide whether special remuneration shall be paid in addition to or in substitution for the annual remuneration determined by the board ... These decisions could only be made by the board surveying the work and remuneration of each and every director. (at p.687)

Nevertheless, despite the commonsense wisdom of Lord Templeman's words, it is submitted that a literal construction of G's articles implied that the committee of three directors was indeed capable of awarding one of its number special remuneration. The articles clearly permitted a duly appointed committee to undertake the functions of the board, functions which included the power to award remuneration. Indeed, although Lord Templeman's interpretation may appear to be one born of a practical logic, the interpretation may nevertheless be criticised given that it was based on an 'assumed' interpretation of the company's articles rather than an interpretation of the actual literal wording and meaning of those articles.

14.8.2 Service contracts

The majority of company directors appointed to executive posts will hold service contracts. The salary package for the services of such directors may often be negotiable on an annual basis. The terms of a director's service contract will be determined in accordance with any procedure specified in the company's articles, albeit the salary package for the services of executive directors will usually be determined by the board of directors. A director is prohibited from voting on the terms of his or her own service contract, nor can a director be counted as part of the quorum for the meeting at which his or her service contract is to be considered. Other than where CA 2006, s.188 applies (discussed below), the terms of a director's service contract will not require the approval of the general meeting, although CA 2006, s.229 provides that a director's service contract must be made available for inspection by the general meeting. Following the introduction of the Directors' Remuneration Report Regulations 2002, SI 2002/1986 (see CA 2006, s.420), quoted companies are required to publish a directors' remuneration report as part of their annual reporting cycle and to file a copy at Companies House. The remuneration report must disclose details of the directors' pay packages, details of how the board determined directors' pay, the membership of the remuneration committee; the names of any remuneration consultants used, a statement of the company's policy on directors' remuneration, an explanation of how the remuneration packages relate to performance, together with details and an explanation of policy on contract and notice periods and a performance graph providing information on the company's performance in comparison with an appropriate share market index. A shareholder vote must be held on the report at the company's annual general meeting. However, if the report is not approved by the general meeting, the company is not obliged by law to adhere to the wishes of the general meeting.

In accordance with CA 2006, s.227, a director's 'service contract' is a contract under which:

- a director of the company undertakes personally to perform services (as director or otherwise) for the company, or for a subsidiary of the company; or
- services (as director or otherwise) that a director of the company undertakes personally to perform are made available by a third party to the company, or to a subsidiary of the company.

CA 2006, s.228 provides that a company must make available a copy of every director's service contract (or a variation of the contract) with the company or with a subsidiary of the company or, if the contract is not in writing, a written memorandum setting out the terms of the contract. The copy of the service contract (or written memorandum) must be open to inspection (without charge) by any member of the company. The service contract (or written memorandum) must be kept available for inspection at the company's registered office and must be retained by the company for at least one year from the date of termination or expiry of the contract; during this retention period it must be kept available for inspection. The company must give notice to the registrar of the place at which the contracts are kept available for inspection, and of any change in that place. If default is made in complying with the notice requirement, an offence is committed by every officer of the company in default and a person guilty of this offence is liable on summary conviction to a fine. Although a director's service contract will not normally require the approval of the general meeting, the general meeting's approval will be required (other than where the company is a wholly owned subsidiary of another company) in circumstances where the service contract is to operate in excess of a guaranteed period. The prescribed guaranteed period is defined by CA 2006, s.188 as a period in excess of two years (previously the duration period was set to a maximum of five years; see CA 1985, s.319) if the contract contains a term under which the company cannot terminate the employment by notice (or, if giving notice, the notice period would, on its own, or together with the duration of the contract, be for a period in excess of two years). CA 2006, s.188 is also applicable where, for the guaranteed period, a term(s) of the contract restricts the company's ability to terminate a director's employment in 'specified circumstances'. Here the Act is somewhat vague as it fails to attribute any meaning to the term 'specified circumstances'. Where the approval of the general meeting is required in respect of the service contract, other than seeking a formal resolution to approve the contract, approval may also be made by way of a written resolution. Further, it is probable that the contract could also be approved informally by the entire body of shareholders (see, e.g. *Atlas Wright (Europe) Ltd* v. *Wright* [1999] BCC 163).

It is to be noted that in the case of an existing service contract in excess of two years, it will be unnecessary for a company to seek the subsequent approval of shareholders if it intends to extend that existing service contract for a further period in excess of two years. However, this applies only if the ability to so extend the contract was included within the terms of the existing contract. In all other cases, if, more than six months before the end of the guaranteed term of a director's employment, the company enters into a further service contract, the company must comply with CA 2006, s.188 where the unexpired period of the guaranteed term, when added to the guaranteed term of the new contract, is in excess of the two-year period. A contravention of s.188 will render the offending provision of the contract void and thereafter the company may terminate the contract at any time by giving the director reasonable notice of its intention.

14.9 THE REMOVAL OF DIRECTORS

It is commonplace for a company's articles to contain conditions which regulate the circumstances in which directors can be removed from office. For example, a director may be obliged to cease to hold office if he or she resigns, is prohibited by law from holding office, becomes bankrupt, or is absent from board meetings without due excuse for a period of six months. It is also commonplace to find that the articles of a public company will provide that a director may be removed from office by a simple resolution of the board of directors.

In accordance with CA 2006, s.168, a company may, by ordinary resolution, remove a director before the expiration of his or her period of office, notwithstanding anything in any agreement between the company and the director (but note the possibility of a weighted voting clause (discussed in **Chapter 6**) or a clause that is contained within a membership agreement restricting a director's removal (discussed in **Chapter 6**)). CA 2006, s.168 replaces the previous provision governing the removal of directors, namely CA 1985, s.303(1). At first sight, the wording of CA 2006, s.168 is similar to that of CA 1985, s.303. However, unlike its predecessor, CA 2006, s.168 fails to specify that its terms cannot in any manner be overridden by a contrary provision within the company's articles, although it is suggested that such a term is likely to be implied. In introducing a motion to dismiss a director, special notice (28 days) must be given to the company (CA 2006, s.168(2)). A director must be given a copy of the form of motion together with the opportunity (even if he or she is not a member of the company) to present representations at the meeting at which the motion is to be heard. A copy of a written form of the representations may, if requested by the director (and providing the representation is of a reasonable length), be distributed to members, providing the delivery would be practicable, given the date on which the representations were delivered by the director to the company and the proposed date of the meeting. If a copy of a director's representations is received too late or because of the company's default, the director may (without prejudice to his or her right to have his representations heard orally) require the representations be read out at the meeting (CA 2006, s.169). An exception to a director's right to present representations is provided by CA 2006, s.169(5), namely, in a situation where, on the application of either the company or of any other person who claims to be aggrieved, the court is satisfied that the rights conferred by s.169 are being abused. This extends the ambit of the exemption beyond the previous law where, under CA 1985, s.304, the director's 'abuse' had to be for the purpose of securing needless publicity for a defamatory matter.

14.9.1 Payments for loss of office

CA 2006, s.168(5) provides that the power of the general meeting to dismiss a director will not, however, deprive the director of a claim to compensation or damages for a breach of his or her service contract (see, e.g. *Southern Foundries Ltd* v. *Shirlaw* [1940] AC 701). A payment made to a director or past director of a company by way of compensation for loss of office must be approved by an ordinary resolution of the members of the company (CA 2006, s.217). A resolution approving a payment must not be passed unless a memorandum setting out the particulars of the proposed payment (including the amount of the payment) is made available to the members of the company under the following conditions:

- in the case of a written resolution, by being sent or submitted to every eligible member at or before the time at which the proposed resolution is sent or submitted to him or her;
- in the case of a resolution at a meeting, by being made available for inspection by the members both at the company's registered office for not less than 15 days ending with the date of the meeting, and at the meeting itself.

However, approval is not required under s.217 for a payment made in good faith:

- in discharge of an existing legal obligation that was not entered into in connection with, or in consequence of, the event giving rise to the payment for loss of office, or by way of damages for breach of such an obligation;
- by way of settlement or compromise of any claim arising in connection with the termination of a person's office or employment;
- by way of pension in respect of past services; or
- where the value of the payment made by the company does not exceed £200.

If a payment is made in contravention of s.217, then the payment must be held on trust for the company. Any director who authorised the payment is jointly and severally liable to indemnify the company for any loss that may result from the payment having been made (CA 2006, s.222).

14.10   THE COMPANY SECRETARY

A company secretary's responsibilities are primarily of an administrative, as opposed to a managerial nature. However, the role of a company secretary may be vital to the proper functioning of the corporate entity. The specific responsibilities of a company secretary will naturally depend upon the size and nature of the company in which office is held. However, tasks common to all company secretaries will include:

- maintaining the company's registers;
- sending relevant details to the registrar of companies;
- preparing share certificates;
- making arrangements for board meetings;
- drafting the minutes of such meetings;
- keeping the company's documentation in order;
- keeping up to date with the relevant companies legislation in so far as it affects the running and administration of the company.

As a company secretary's responsibilities are geared to the administration of the company's affairs, the post may carry an authority to bind the company in contracts related to the ambit of a particular secretary's actual or ostensible authority (see, e.g. *Panorama Developments Ltd* v. *Fidelis Furnishing Fabrics Ltd* [1971] 2 QB 711).

14.10.1   Private companies

Previously, under CA 1985, s.283(1), every company (private or public) was required to appoint a company secretary. However, following the implementation of CA 2006, s.12(1), private companies are no longer obliged to appoint a company secretary. The change in the law recognises that, in respect of private companies, the obligatory requirement of appointing a company secretary was often an unnecessary burden. Indeed, in small private companies the requirement of having to appoint a company secretary was often complied with via the 'artificial' appointment of a secretary, for example, the appointment of a family member or friend.

14.10.2   Public companies

A public company is obliged to appoint a company secretary. A secretary is appointed by the directors of the company on such terms as they may determine. The power to remove the secretary is vested in the directors. A company must keep details of its company secretary at its registered office (CA 2006, s.275). It must also send relevant details of its secretary to the registrar who must, when necessary, be notified of any change in the person to be appointed as company secretary. The company secretary must be a suitably qualified person, that is, he or she must have the necessary experience to perform the functions attributable to the post and/or must have a professionally recognised qualification. The suitability issue is determined by the board of directors.

A director of the company may be authorised by the board of directors to act in the place of a formally appointed company secretary; the director may act as a secretary providing a task which requires the consent or authorisation of both the company secretary and a company director is not performed by the same person acting in the capacity of both a director and company secretary (CA 2006, s.280). A company may also act as the secretary of another company.

14.11   THE AUDITOR

An auditor holds office (CA 2006, s.487), but the nature of an auditor's office cannot be equated with that held by a director or company secretary. An auditor is not a member of a company's general management team; the auditor is an independent contractor. An auditor is appointed by the directors or by an ordinary resolution of the general meeting (CA 2006, s.485 (private company) and s.489 (public company)). If a company fails to appoint an auditor in accordance with s.485 or s.489, the Secretary of State may appoint one or more persons to fill the vacancy. CA 2006, s.492 provides that the remuneration of an auditor appointed by the members of a company must be fixed by the members by ordinary resolution or in such manner as the members may by ordinary resolution determine. The remuneration of an auditor appointed by the directors of a company must be fixed by the directors.

The statutory audit aims to provide an independent, external professional opinion of a company's accounts and financial returns. An auditor's task is primarily to advise the shareholding body in respect of the financial affairs of the company. CA 2006, s.495(2) prescribes that the auditor's report must include:

(a) an introduction to identify the annual accounts that are the subject matter of the audit together with the financial reporting framework that was applied in their preparation; and,

(b) a description of the scope of the audit identifying the auditing standards in accordance with which the audit was conducted.

The report must have been properly prepared in accordance with the relevant financial reporting framework and statutory rules and must state clearly whether, in the auditor's opinion, the annual accounts give a true and fair view (CA 2006, s.495(3)(a)) of the following:

(i) in the case of an individual balance sheet, of the state of affairs of the company as at the end of the financial year;

(ii) in the case of an individual profit and loss account, of the profit or loss of the company for the financial year;

(iii) in the case of group accounts, of the state of affairs as at the end of the financial year and of the profit or loss for the financial year of the undertakings included in the consolidation as a whole, so far as concerns members of the company.

The auditor's report may be either unqualified or qualified, and must include a reference to any matters to which the auditor wishes to draw attention by way of emphasis. In relation to the report on the company's annual accounts, the auditor must state whether in his or her opinion the information given in the directors' report for the financial year for which the accounts were prepared was consistent with those accounts. Where the company is a quoted company, the auditor, in his or her report on the company's annual accounts, must report to the company's members on the auditable part of the directors' remuneration report (see CA 2006, s.421), and state whether in his or her opinion that part of the directors' remuneration report was properly prepared in accordance with CA 2006.

14.11.1 Removal of an auditor

Notwithstanding any form of agreement between a company and its auditor, an auditor may be removed by the general meeting by an ordinary resolution. Nevertheless, the dismissal of an auditor will not preclude the auditor from seeking compensation for a breach of any service contract. Where there is a motion to remove an auditor and the removal would take place prior to the expiration of the auditor's term of office, then in such circumstances those proposing the motion to dismiss the auditor must give at least 28 days' special notice to the company prior to the date of the meeting at which the motion is to be heard (CA 2006, s.511). An auditor who is subject to a proposed resolution to remove him or her may make written representations to the company (in a like manner to a director) and such representations must be distributed to the company's members.

(The role of an auditor is discussed further in **Chapter 12**.)

CHAPTER 15

Directors' duties

15.1 INTRODUCTION

In an attempt to eradicate potential abuses of the powers afforded to the board of directors and persons expressly or impliedly authorised to act on the board's behalf, the regulation of company law incorporates a series of statutory, common law and compliance rules, designed to provide a mechanism for both the internal and external governance of company directors. The rules and duties relating to the internal governance of directors are ultimately concerned with a company's ability to prevent, curb and penalise the delinquent conduct of directors. Prior to the passing of the Companies Act (CA) 2006, the said rules and duties were largely, albeit not exclusively, prescribed by the common law and equitable principles. In CA 2006, the legislature sought to codify the common law/equitable rules and duties. However, in accordance with CA 2006, the codified rules and duties will, where appropriate, be interpreted and applied in the same way as the common law rules and equitable principles (CA 2006, s.170(4)).

The rules of 'external governance' which comprise voluntary codes of best practice and which are also tied to Stock Exchange listing requirements are essentially concerned with the regulation of public companies. (These rules are examined in **Chapter 21**.)

15.2 THE DUTIES

Directors (de jure and de facto directors) and other authorised company officers owe duties to the company in which they hold office. However, it is unclear to what extent shadow directors owe duties to a company for which they act. CA 2006, s.170 provides that the governing provisions in relation to directors' duties apply to shadow directors. However, by way of qualification, s.170 further provides that the provisions only apply to shadow directors to the extent that corresponding common law rules or equitable principles apply. Here, s.170 is couched in uncertainty because the corresponding common law rules, etc. are, as a genus, sparse and vague with regard to identifying when liability should be attached to a shadow director. However, it is to be observed that in *Ultraframe (UK) Ltd* v. *Fielding* [2005] EWHC 1638 (Ch), Lewison J opined that directors' fiduciary duties did not apply to shadow directors on the premise that unlike a de jure or de facto director, a shadow director directs or instructs those who, themselves, owe a fiduciary duty to the company. Nevertheless, with respect to the learned judge, it is submitted that a shadow director does assume a fiduciary position by the very nature of the activities which define his position and role in the management of a company.

The most common analogy of the duties owed by a director of a company is that of a trust and/or agency relationship. In relation to a trust relationship, in *Re Lands Allotment Co* [1894] 1 Ch 616, Lindley LJ opined:

> Although directors are not properly speaking trustees, yet they have always been considered and treated as trustees of money which comes to their hands or which is actually under their control; and ever since joint stock companies were invented, directors have been held liable to make good moneys which they have misapplied upon the same footings as if they were trustees. (at p.631)

The basis for a comparison between directors' duties and the duties arising from a trustee–beneficiary relationship can be traced back to the early part of the nineteenth century. Prior to the passing of the Joint Stock Companies Act 1844, unincorporated companies vested the property of the company in trustee directors. However, in today's corporate world the analogy between trustees and directors seems less likely. Although directors may be regarded as occupying the status of a trustee in a situation where they are responsible for the management of corporate funds and property (see, e.g. *Bairstow* v. *Queens Moat Houses plc* [2001] 2 BCLC 531), perhaps a more apt analogy of the general relationship between a director and company is that of agency. As agents, the directors stand in a fiduciary relationship to the principal, i.e. the company. A fiduciary may be defined as a person who undertakes to act for or on behalf of another in a particular matter in circumstances which give rise to a relationship of trust and confidence. The distinguishing obligation of a fiduciary is the obligation of loyalty. In *Bristol & West Building Society* v. *Mothew* [1998] Ch 1, Millett LJ defined a fiduciary in the following terms:

> A fiduciary is someone who has undertaken to act for or on behalf of another in a particular matter in circumstances which give rise to a relationship of trust and confidence. The distinguishing obligation of a fiduciary is the obligation of loyalty. The principal is entitled to the single-minded loyalty of his fiduciary. This core liability has several facets. A fiduciary must act in good faith; he must not make a profit out of his trust; he must not place himself in a position where his duty and his interest may conflict; he may not act for his own benefit or the benefit of a third person without the informed consent of his principal ... (at p.18)

15.3 THE STATUTORY LIST OF DUTIES

CA 2006 codifies and in some respects expands the previous common law/ equitable duties of company directors. The process of codification is an attempt to clarify and simplify what, by many, was often perceived as regulation by a complex and uncertain set of common law and equitable rules. The codification of the general duties has effect subject to any rule of law enabling the company to give authority, specifically or generally, for anything to be done (or omitted) by the directors (or any of them), that would otherwise be a breach of duty.

The codified duties which are cumulative (so that more than one duty may apply to a particular state of affairs) are as follows.

15.3.1   The duty to act for a proper purpose (CA 2006, s.171)

CA 2006, s.171 provides that:

A director of a company must –

(a)   act in accordance with the company's constitution, and
(b)   only exercise powers for the purposes for which they are conferred.

Although a director may honestly believe that in entering into a transaction he or she acted in the best interests of the company as a whole, the director will nevertheless be held to be in breach of a fiduciary duty if, objectively, his or her conduct was outside or in abuse of the director's allocated powers (see, e.g. *Hogg* v. *Cramphorn* [1967] Ch 254). The duty amounts to one whereby a director must act for a proper purpose in the exercise of his or her powers and that proper purpose must be the dominant purpose for the act in question. For example, if a director exercises a power to issue unissued shares with a principal objective of manipulating the voting control of the company (notwithstanding that a subsidiary purpose for the issue may be to raise additional capital), the director's dominant purpose in issuing the shares will be viewed objectively as having been for an improper purpose, i.e. the proper purpose attached to an issue of shares is to raise capital and not to manipulate voting control. For example, in *Howard Smith Ltd* v. *Ampol Petroleum Ltd* [1974] AC 821, Ampol (A) controlled 54 per cent of the issued share capital in a company (X) and unsuccessfully submitted a bid for X's remaining shares. Howard Smith Ltd (H) then submitted a rival bid for the remaining shares but that bid was also rejected (A, X's majority shareholder rejected the bid). X's board of directors favoured H's offer and to overcome the problem of A's majority control in X, the board allotted unissued shares to H. The purpose of the allotment was to provide needy capital as well as relegating A to the position of a minority shareholder (i.e. following the allotment, A's shareholding in X would have fallen below the 50 per cent mark). A objected to the allotment of the new share issue on the ground that it had not been for a proper purpose. X's directors argued that the allotment had been in the best interests of the company as a whole (i.e. that they had not been motivated by self-interest but had genuinely believed that the company's best interests would be served if H was in a position to secure majority control in X). The Privy Council, in giving judgment in favour of A, held that X's power to allot shares had not been used for a proper purpose. Lord Wilberforce opined that in order to decide whether the allotment was for a proper purpose the court should consider first the *bona fide*

281

intentions of the directors. However, even if the directors honestly believed that they had acted for the benefit of the company, the *bona fide* test could not be viewed in isolation. The court then had to consider, in an objective sense, whether the underlying purpose for the allotment had been a proper purpose. In applying an objective test, the Privy Council concluded that although X would have benefited from the capital raised from the sale of shares to H, the dominant purpose behind the share allotment had been an improper one, namely the allotment had, as its primary purpose, the aim of manipulating voting control in favour of H. Lord Wilberforce stated:

> Just as it is established that directors, within their management powers, may take decisions against the wishes of the majority of shareholders, and indeed that the majority of shareholders cannot control them in the exercise of these powers while they remain in office ... so it must be unconstitutional for directors to use their fiduciary powers over the shares in the company purely for the purpose of destroying an existing majority, or creating a new majority which did not previously exist. To do so is to interfere with that element of the company's constitution which is separate from and set against their powers. (at p.837)

The reasoning adopted by the Privy Council in *Howard Smith Ltd* v. *Ampol Petroleum Ltd* to the view that the court must seek out the dominant purpose behind a power use to determine whether the proper purpose duty is infringed, is a view universally adopted and applied. For example, in *Mutual Life Insurance Co* v. *The Rank Organisation Ltd* [1985] BCLC 11, a company decided to issue further shares, a proportion of which were to be made available to its existing shareholders. However, the company resolved not to make the offer of the issue available to shareholders situated in the USA and Canada. Although the company's decision may *prima facie* have suggested a form of discrimination, Goulding J held that the dominant purpose behind this share allocation did not purport to discriminate against the shareholders situated in the USA and Canada. The learned judge held that the company's decision was based upon the practical commercial reality of avoiding the considerable expense involved in complying with the share issue procedures in the USA and Canada. The decision not to offer the shares to members in those countries was a legitimate exercise of the board of directors' discretion to consider the best interests of the company as a whole.

However, it is to be noted that while the directors of a company may not ordinarily use their powers to issue shares for the purpose of manipulating voting control, an exception may be made where, with a view to resisting a takeover bid, the exercise of the power is objectively viewed as one essential and proper to the company's survival as a going concern. For example, if A Ltd and B Ltd are in competition and B seeks to destroy A's share of the marketplace by obtaining a controlling interest in A to the purpose of running down A to obtain a greater share of the marketplace for itself, then the directors of A may be justified in issuing further shares in A to a purpose of maintaining their control over the company. Here the dominant and legitimate purpose of the power use would be to prevent the demise of A Ltd (see, e.g. *Cayne* v. *Global Natural Resources plc* [1984] 1 All ER 225).

In all cases the court must seek out the dominant purpose in relation to the use of a power with the objective of determining whether the proper purpose duty has been infringed. For example, in *Lee Panavision Ltd* v. *Lee Lighting Ltd* [1992] BCLC 22, Panavision Ltd (P) had been given an option to purchase the share capital of Lee Lighting Ltd (L). During the option period, P was given a proxy over the voting shares of L and under a management agreement, the right to appoint the directors of L. However, when P decided that it would not exercise the option to purchase the share capital of L, a majority of the directors of L (appointed by P), aware that they would be removed from office when the option period ended, voted in favour of extending the management agreement with P. The decision went against the wishes of L's majority shareholder. A dominant and ancillary reason why P wished to exert influence in the management of L was that L had entered into a loan agreement with one of P's associated companies. By controlling L's board of directors, P could ensure that L paid sums due under the loan agreement. Although the Court of Appeal considered that it was for the directors of L to decide if it was in the company's best interests to continue the management agreement with P, the court concluded that, in determining that issue, the directors should have taken into account the views of the general body of shareholders as opposed to the artificial interests of the commercial entity. The Court of Appeal held that it was unconstitutional for the directors of L, knowing that the general body of the shareholders of L were proposing to end the management agreement with P, to, in effect, commit the management powers of L to P, thus fettering the powers of L's future board of directors. The dominant purpose behind the vote, to retain P's domination over the management functions of L, was an improper purpose, namely, to secure L's payment of an outstanding debt to P's associated company.

15.3.2 The duty to act *bona fide* in good faith in the interests of the company (CA 2006, s.172)

CA 2006, s.172 states that:

(1)   A director of a company must act in the way he considers, in good faith, would be most likely to promote the success of the company for the benefit of its members as a whole, and in doing so have regard (amongst other matters) to –

   (a)   the likely consequences of any decision in the long term,
   (b)   the interests of the company's employees,
   (c)   the need to foster the company's business relationships with suppliers, customers and others,
   (d)   the impact of the company's operations on the community and the environment,
   (e)   the desirability of the company maintaining a reputation for high standards of business conduct, and
   (f)   the need to act fairly as between members of the company.

(2)   Where or to the extent that the purposes of the company consist of or include purposes other than the benefit of its members, subsection (1) has effect as if the

reference to promoting the success of the company for the benefit of its members were to achieving those purposes.

(3)   The duty imposed by this section has effect subject to any enactment or rule of law requiring directors, in certain circumstances, to consider or act in the interests of creditors of the company.

In accordance with CA 2006, s.172, in conducting the business of a company, a director must act to promote the success of the company for the benefit of its members as a whole and not for some other collateral purpose (see, e.g. *Re Smith & Fawcett Ltd* [1942] Ch 304 and *Fusion Interactive Communication Solutions Ltd* v. *Venture Investment Placement Ltd* [2006] BCC 187). In considering whether a director is in breach of this duty the court must determine the matter by applying a subjective test (see, e.g. *Extrasure Travel Insurances Ltd* v. *Scattergood* [2003] 1 BCLC 598). As the test is subjective, it may be passed even in circumstances where the court considers the actions of a director to have been unreasonable, that is, providing the court is of the opinion that the director honestly believed that he or she was acting to promote the success of the company for the benefit of its members as a whole. Therefore, to a large extent, in determining the issue, the director's state of mind will be of great relevance. Accordingly, in the majority of cases, the subjective nature of the test will favour the director and it may be difficult to establish a breach of the duty. For example, in *Regentcrest plc* v. *Cohen* [2001] BCC 494, a company (R) contended that one of its director's (A) had acted in breach of his fiduciary duty in voting to allow R to waive the clawback of certain sums due to the company. The background to the case was as follows. R acquired all the issued shares in a company (G), the sole asset of which comprised development land. The consideration for the sale of G's shares had been an allotment of shares in R. The vendors of the G shares included two directors of R (Y&Z). The sale agreement contained, *inter alia*, a clause providing that if after the sale the value of the development land fell, the vendors (Y&Z) would be liable to repay any shortfall to R (the clawback agreement). R subsequently encountered serious financial difficulties notwithstanding that two of its directors, A and B (who were not directors in G) injected some £5 million of their own money into the company. The value of the development site declined, giving rise to a shortfall of £1.5 million, an amount the vendors were liable to pay under the clawback agreement. However, R agreed to waive any claim under the agreement in return for Y&Z's future free services as directors of R. Less than a year later, R was subject to a compulsory winding-up order. R's liquidators claimed damages against A for breach of fiduciary duty, alleging that in voting in favour of the resolution to waive the clawback claim he had acted other than in the best interests of the company. In dismissing the claim, Jonathan Parker J considered the scope of the subjective test to determine whether A had been in breach of his fiduciary duty. R was insolvent when the clawback claim was waived but A and B remained willing to support the company as evidenced by the injection of £5 million of their own funds in an attempt to ensure its survival. The learned judge concluded that A and B had genuinely believed that there was a real chance of rescuing the company. Further, there were viable commercial reasons for releasing the claim against Y&Z who were also directors of R, that is, to retain their services and enable the board to present a united front. R's chances of survival would have been impaired if it had commenced contested proceedings against two of its own directors. Further, A and B knew that it was doubtful whether Y&Z could meet any judgment against them. In all the circumstances, the learned judge came to the conclusion that A honestly believed that waiving the clawback claim was in the best interests of R. In relation to the application of the subjective test Jonathan Parker J opined:

> The duty imposed on directors to act bona fide in the interests of the company is a subjective one ... The question is not whether, viewed objectively by the court, the particular act or omission which is challenged was in fact in the interests of the company; still less is the question whether the court, had it been in the position of the director at the relevant time, might have acted differently. Rather, the question is whether the director honestly believed that his act or omission was in the interests of the company. The issue is as to the director's state of mind. No doubt, where it is clear that the act or omission under challenge resulted in substantial detriment to the company, the director will have a harder task persuading the court that he honestly believed it to be in the company's interest; but that does not detract from the subjective nature of the test. (At para.120)

Establishing a breach of CA 2006, s.172

However, despite the subjective nature of the test to determine a breach of the CA 2006, s.172 duty, there may be cases in which it is patently obvious that the director's intention could not have been to promote the success of the company for the benefit of its members as a whole. For example, in *Re W & M Roith Ltd* [1967] 1 WLR 432, a director, who was in very poor health, entered into a new service agreement with the company, an agreement which included provision for a generous pension to be paid to his widow in the event of his death. The director, who failed to disclose his poor health, died shortly after entering into the agreement. His widow claimed the benefit of the pension. As the deceased director's service agreement had been entered into with the object of enabling his wife to make a claim upon the company's assets (in the form of the pension payments) in excess of an amount that might otherwise have been considered appropriate by the company had it been aware of the seriousness of the undisclosed illness, the court held that the director had acted contrary to the interests of the company. The director's sole intention was to benefit his wife. (Also see, *Odyssey Entertainment Ltd (In Liquidation)* v. *Kamp* [2012] EWHC 2316 (Ch).)

In determining the subjective test, evidence as to whether a director actually gave any thought to the question of any accruing benefit to the company will also be a relevant consideration. For example, in *Dryburgh* v. *Scotts Media Tax Ltd* [2011] CSOH 147, the directors of a company were found to be in breach of the s.172 duty in circumstances where they had paid themselves excessive bonuses, payments that the company could ill afford. Although the directors believed that they deserved the bonus payments, they had given no consideration to the potential dire consequences of their conduct in relation to the interests of the company. Therefore, where objectively, a director's conduct is considered to be totally unreasonable, the extent and degree of that unreasonable behaviour may, in extreme cases, be so out of line with all perceptions of expected conduct that the director's actual conduct cannot, in any logical sense, be viewed as promoting the success of the company for the benefit of its members as a whole. To take a hypothetical – if not extreme – example, if a director of a company sold a corporate asset that had been independently valued at £200,000 for a price of £2,000, honestly believing the sale to be beneficial to the company, it is most probable that the director's belief would be viewed as totally unreasonable and with much suspicion, thereby negating any suggestion that his or her conduct should be perceived as having any legitimate degree of benefit to the company.

CA 2006, s.172(1) specifies that in purporting to act in good faith, a director must act in a manner most likely to promote the success of the company for the benefit of its members as a whole. Accordingly, a director owes his or her duty to the company (in the form of the shareholders as a collective body) in which he or she holds office and does not, for example, owe duties to a specific individual shareholder or any other individual (see, e.g. *Percival* v. *Wright* [1902] 2 Ch 421). In relation to the interests of the collective body of shareholders, in *Heron International* v. *Lord Grade* [1983] BCLC 244, the Court of Appeal suggested that when considering competing takeover bids, the directors of a company were under a duty to ensure that they did not exercise their powers to prevent shareholders obtaining the best possible price available for their shares. However, it should be noted, following the decision of the Court of Appeal in *Peskin* v. *Anderson* [2001] BCC 874, that directors will not be in breach of their fiduciary duty in circumstances where they fail to disclose to the membership that they are in the process of considering (but without any actual commitment) plans to invite offers for the sale of the business.

In the context of establishing a breach of s.172, a breach of duty may also be found impliedly in a situation where a director fails to reveal his own wrongdoing. In *Item Software (UK) Ltd* v. *Fassihi* [2004] BCC 994, Arden LJ (with whom Mummery LJ and Holman J expressed agreement) held that although a director does not owe a separate and independent duty to disclose misconduct, nevertheless a director's duty to act in what he or she considers to be in good faith in the best interests of his company, may, in terms of a duty of loyalty, be interpreted as meaning that a director must disclose misconduct on his part. (Also see, *British Midland Tool Ltd* v. *Midland International Tooling Ltd* [2003] 2 BCLC 523, *Shepherds Investments Ltd* v. *Walters* [2007] 2 BCLC 202 and *GHLM Trading Ltd* v. *Maroo* [2012] 2 BCLC 369.) In *Item Software (UK) Ltd* v. *Fassihi*, Arden LJ opined:

> For my part, I do not consider that it is correct to infer from the cases to which I have referred that a fiduciary owes a separate and independent duty to disclose his own misconduct to his principal or more generally information of relevance and concern to it. So to hold would lead to a proliferation of duties and arguments about their breadth. I prefer to base my conclusion in this case on the fundamental duty to which a director is

subject, that is the duty to act in what he in good faith considers to be the best interests of his company. (at p.1004)

15.3.3 CA 2006, s.172(1)(a)–(f)

Although a director must seek to promote the success of the company for the benefit of its members as a whole, CA 2006, s.172(1)(a)–(f) does provide that in seeking to achieve corporate success, directors must act fairly between members and further take into account the interests of employees, suppliers and customers, etc. Indeed, in the context of defining the success of a 'company', the view that a company can have a separate and distinct interest in any given project which is independent from the interests of the company's human constituents and players, is, in reality, a myth. A company's interest is, in effect, dominated by a collection of parties, all of which may be said to have a stake in the success of the company. Directors must also take account of the interests of affected communities and the environment. However, here the intent of the legislation is vague and in part confusing because if, to the detriment of generating profits, a director takes account of the interests of communities and the environment or, for example, the interests of suppliers or customers, may this not prejudice the company's shareholders and other parties with a financial interest in the company? Further, will a shareholder in a company which pursues a policy of building a reputation for high standards of business conduct view that policy as a benefit when, in achieving such high standards by considerable expenditure, the company may be unable to declare a favourable dividend? Will a company, through its shareholders, really enforce such third-party obligations and interests to the potential detriment of securing profits?

As the principal duty under s.172 is owed to the members of the company and the success of a company will, in relation to the interests of members, be predominantly concerned with the company's ability to generate sustainable profits, it is most unlikely that the matters mentioned in the statutory list (CA 2006, s.172(1)(a)–(f)) will be afforded the attention that they may merit in determining whether a director(s) breached the s.172 duty. Although s.172 provides that the statutory list must be considered by a director(s), namely the directors must have regard among other matters to the list, here consideration/regard could simply amount to a note of record in the board minutes that all matters provided by s.172(1)(a)–(f) were considered (almost as a tick box exercise). Section 172 does not provide that a director(s) must ensure that matters mentioned in the statutory list may, in any way, override or be considered equally with matters that are deemed beneficial to the members' financial interests.

Finally, in construing the *bona fide* duty, it must also be observed that even if a director is not in breach of this particular duty, his or her conduct may still be viewed to be contrary to the proper purpose duty (CA 2006, s.171 – see above). It is to be observed that the proper purpose duty overrides the *bona fide* duty, so, if a director passes the *bona fide* duty test but fails the proper purpose duty test the director in question will be found to be in breach of his or her fiduciary duty (see, e.g. *Bishopsgate Investment Management Ltd* v. *Maxwell* [1993] BCC 120).

15.3.4 A creditor's interest (CA 2006, s.172(3))

The scope of a director's duty does not ordinarily extend to a consideration of the interests of a company's creditors (see, e.g. *Multinational Gas & Petrochemical Co* v. *Multinational Gas & Petrochemical Services Ltd* [1983] Ch 258). This view can be supported on the basis that a company's objective is ordinarily geared to maximise profits to enable it to pay dividends to its shareholders. Therefore, the interests of the shareholding body outweigh considerations relating to the payment of company creditors. Nevertheless, in a situation where a company continues trading, having reached a state of insolvency (a state of insolvency is discussed further in **Chapter 22**) there will be a substantial risk that the company may be unable to discharge its debts. Here the common law recognised that following a company's slide into an insolvent state, it became logical to surmise that the interests of creditors were paramount, to the extent that the company's directors would owe a duty to creditors in respect of the maintenance of corporate assets. Indeed, the interests of creditors could take hold prior to a 'technical insolvency,' that is, in circumstances where the company's dire financial position placed the creditors at imminent risk (see, e.g. *West Mercia Safetywear Ltd* v. *Dodd* [1988] BCLC 250, *Whalley (Liquidator of MDA Investment Management Ltd)* v. *Doney* [2004] BPIR 75, *Singer* v. *Beckett* [2007] 2 BCLC 287 and *Eastford Ltd* v. *Gillespie* [2012] BCC 303). As such, CA 2006, s.172(3) seeks to give statutory force to the previous common law protection of corporate creditors to the extent that given a company's actual or imminent state of insolvency, its directors may no longer be expected to owe a primary duty to the company's shareholders in respect of the maintenance of corporate assets, rather, the primary duty will be owed to its creditors.

15.3.5 The duty to act with independent judgment (CA 2006, s.173)

CA 2006, s.173 provides that:

(1)   A director of a company must exercise independent judgment.
(2)   This duty is not infringed by his acting –

(a)   in accordance with an agreement duly entered into by the company that restricts the future exercise of discretion by its directors, or
(b)   in a way authorised by the company's constitution.

A director of a company must exercise independent judgment and should not be subject to considerations or influences that would deter him or her from acting otherwise than in the best interests of the company as a whole. Accordingly, a director should not allow himself or herself to be unduly influenced to act in a manner inconsistent with his or her own belief and reasoning. However, this duty will not be infringed where a director acts in accordance with the terms of the company's constitution or in respect of an agreement duly entered into by the company restricting the future exercise of discretion by its directors.

Although a director will exercise corporate powers in a fiduciary capacity and as such it may be assumed that he or she may not, by a contractual agreement or otherwise, fetter the future exercise of such powers, commercial reality dictates that it may be necessary for a director to bind the company to a specific course of future conduct. The case of *Fulham Football Club Ltd* v. *Cabra Estates plc* [1992] BCC 863 validates this point of view. Here, the directors of Fulham Football Club (F) undertook to support, in preference to a plan proposed by the local authority, a planning application by the football ground's owners (Cabra Estates plc (C)) for the future development of 'Craven Cottage' (the football ground). At the time of giving the undertaking, given in return for substantial financial support by C to the football club, the directors believed that their decision had been taken in the best interests of the company. However, subsequent events resulted in the directors and shareholders of F changing their minds. It was considered that the undertaking could no longer be construed as beneficial to F. The Court of Appeal held that F was bound by the terms of its agreement with C. F had obtained a substantial benefit at the time of entering into the agreement and it had been permissible for the directors of F to act to bind the company to an agreed future course of conduct.

15.3.6 The duty of care (CA 2006, s.174)

CA 2006, s.174 states that:

(1)   A director of a company must exercise reasonable care, skill and diligence.

(2)   This means the care, skill and diligence that would be exercised by a reasonably diligent person with –

      (a)   the general knowledge, skill and experience that may reasonably be expected of a person carrying out the functions carried out by the director in relation to the company, and

      (b)   the general knowledge, skill and experience that the director has.

In accordance with cases such as *Lister* v. *Romford Ice & Cold Storage Ltd* [1957] AC 555, *Norman* v. *Theodore Goddard* [1991] BCLC 1028 and *Re D'Jan of London Ltd* [1993] BCC 646, a director need not exhibit in the performance of his or her duties any greater degree of skill than could be expected from a reasonable diligent person in circumstances where the diligent person is imputed with the general knowledge, skill and experience that may reasonably be expected of the holder of the position in question. The standard of care required of a director is not measured by a universal professional standard applicable to directors as a class, but, in part, is dependent upon the abilities and qualifications of the individual director in question. For example, a director who is qualified in a particular business-related area will be expected to exhibit a reasonable standard of skill appropriate to that area of expertise. However, where, for example, the knowledge, skill and experience of a director falls below the standard expected of a reasonable diligent person, the director cannot rely on his or her poor standards in an attempt to argue that he or she did not breach the duty of care. The test to determine a breach of a duty of care is therefore comparable to the one used to determine wrongful trading under IA 1986, s.214 (discussed in **Chapter 5**).

Although the standard of care expected from executive directors may be ordinarily of a higher standard than that for non-executive directors, the expectation may be displaced where, for example, non-executive directors are entrusted with specific business matters or deal with matters in which they have a personal expertise. For example, in *Dorchester Finance Co Ltd* v. *Stebbing* [1989] BCLC 498, a company successfully commenced an action against two non-executive directors for a breach of their duty of care. One of those directors was a chartered accountant, while the other had considerable accounting experience. The company commenced the action because the two directors had been in the practice of signing blank cheques relating to the company's bank account. As experienced accountants, the directors should have known better.

Although a director is expected to exhibit a reasonable degree of care in the performance of his or her duties, it is nevertheless essential to the promotion of an enterprise culture that the expectation of due care is balanced against the potential benefit of risk. In entering into a business transaction, a director may be placed in a position where he or she is aware that the particular venture carries a risk of failure. A commercial gamble may be necessary to secure economic stability and/or growth. Therefore, mere errors of judgment or acts of imprudence will rarely equate to a breach of a duty of care. Accordingly, although a director will be expected to exhibit a reasonable degree of care in the performance of his duties, it is clear that the standard and extent of care will be far less onerous than, for example, what is expected of a trustee. However, to comply with the duty of care, a director must pay diligent attention to the business affairs of the company in which he or she holds office (see, e.g. *Re Barings plc* [1999] 1 BCLC 433 and *Re Westmid Packing Services Ltd* [1988] BCC 836). Accordingly, the failure of a director to act in a specific matter, when it would have been reasonable in the circumstances for him to so act, will not afford a defence to a claim that he or she breached a duty of care. For example, in *Lexi Holdings plc* v. *Luqman* [2009] BCC 716, S, an executive director of a company (C) caused C to enter into a fraudulent loan arrangement. M and Z, the two non-executive directors of C, believed the loan account to be genuine and made no attempt to challenge its legitimacy. However, M and Z were aware of S's previous convictions for dishonesty and as such should have enquired into the legitimacy of the loan account. M and Z should have been on guard in relation to any explanations that were advanced by S. Had M and Z made reasonable enquiries into the legitimacy of the loan account and the explanations advanced by S, they would not have been satisfied that the account was genuine. As such, the Court of Appeal held that M and Z were in breach of their duty of care. Likewise, in *Re Duomatic* [1969] 2 Ch 365, a director who failed to seek specialist help or guidance (in this case from the general body of shareholders), when it was reasonable in the circumstances for him to do so, was found to be in breach of his duty of care. Here it should also be noted that a relevant and important factor in determining the existence of a breach of the duty of care may be to consider whether a director failed to take professional advice, when, in the circumstances it was reasonable and appropriate for him to so (see, e.g. *Re Ortega Associates Ltd* [2008] BCC 256).

15.3.7 The conflict of interest duty (CA 2006, s.175)

CA 2006, s.175 provides that:

(1) A director of a company must avoid a situation in which he has, or can have, a direct or indirect interest that conflicts, or possibly may conflict, with the interests of the company.

(2) This applies in particular to the exploitation of any property, information or opportunity (and it is immaterial whether the company could take advantage of the property, information or opportunity).

(3) This duty does not apply to a conflict of interest arising in relation to a transaction or arrangement with the company.

(4) This duty is not infringed –

    (a) if the situation cannot reasonably be regarded as likely to give rise to a conflict of interest; or

    (b) if the matter has been authorised by the directors.

(5) Authorisation may be given by the directors –

    (a) where the company is a private company and nothing in the company's constitution invalidates such authorisation, by the matter being proposed to and authorised by the directors; or

    (b) where the company is a public company and its constitution includes provision enabling the directors to authorise the matter, by the matter being proposed to and authorised by them in accordance with the constitution.

(6) The authorisation is effective only if –

    (a) any requirement as to the quorum at the meeting at which the matter is considered is met without counting the director in question or any other interested director, and

    (b) the matter was agreed to without their voting or would have been agreed to if their votes had not been counted.

(7) Any reference in this section to a conflict of interest includes a conflict of interest and duty and a conflict of duties.

Prior to the introduction of CA 2006, s.175, the prohibition against a director's involvement in a transaction involving a conflict of interest was regulated not as a specific fiduciary duty but rather as a rule of equity (see, e.g. *Movitex Ltd* v. *Bulfield and Ors* [1986] 2 BCC 99). Although the rule of equity is akin to a fiduciary duty, a transaction in breach of the equitable rule, involving a potential or real conflict of interest would, unlike a breach of a fiduciary duty, be set aside without enquiry as to whether any harm was inflicted on the company to the extent that there would be no consideration of whether the disputed conduct in question was performed *bona fide* in the interests of the company. In *Aberdeen Railway Co* v. *Blaikie Bros* (1854) 1 Macq 461, Lord Cranworth proposed that this rule of equity involved –

> … a rule of universal application that no one, having … duties to discharge, shall be allowed to enter into engagements in which he has, or can have, a personal interest conflicting, or which may possibly conflict, with the interests of those whom he is bound to protect. (at p.471)

However, in *Boardman and Anor* v. *Phipps* [1967] AC 46, Lord Upjohn suggested that Lord Cranworth's remarks relating to the 'possibility of conflict' should be construed to mean:

> … the reasonable man looking at the relevant facts and circumstances of the particular case would think that there was a real sensible possibility of conflict. (at p.124)

Accordingly, while the effect of the conflict of interest rule was strict, the nature of the conflict giving rise to the operation of the rule required more than a trivial interest, that is, there must have been a real and viable possibility of the existence of a conflict. Prior to *Boardman and Anor* v. *Phipps,* in *Boulting* v. *ACTAT* [1963] 2 QB 606, Lord Upjohn remarked that the conflict of interest rule should be applied in the following manner:

> … a broad rule like this must be applied with common sense and with an appreciation of the sort of circumstances in which over the last 200 years and more it has been applied and thrived. It must be applied realistically to a state of affairs which discloses a real conflict of duty and interest and not to some theoretical or rhetorical contract. (at p.637)

In effect, the conflict of interest duty specified in CA 2006, s.175 codifies the conflict of interest rule and transforms it into a statutory fiduciary duty. The statutory duty, in its simplest form, may be described as a duty of loyalty and fidelity which prohibits a company director from exploiting or potentially exploiting his or her position in respect of a corporate opportunity, corporate property or infor-mation. In effect, a director of a company will be in breach of the conflict of interest duty where, by virtue of his or her fiduciary position, he or she uses to his or her own advantage information or an opportunity which came into his or her hands while holding office: information or an opportunity in which the company had, or potentially had, an interest (see, e.g. *Bhullar* v. *Bhullar* [2003] 2 BCLC 241). A director's liability for a breach of the conflict of interest duty is not dependent on proof of fault or proof that a conflict of interest caused the company any form of loss.

A director will be in breach of the conflict of interest duty even in circumstances where the company in which he or she holds (or has held) office could not in relation to its ordinary business activities have been expected to use or benefit from the information or opportunity in question. Therefore, in determining whether there was a breach of the conflict of interest duty it is irrelevant to consider if the company could or was able to take up the opportunity giving rise to the potential conflict. If the opportunity is presented to the company, it is the company's opportunity and the company must come to an affirmative conclusion whether or not it wishes to pursue it. For example, in *O'Donnell* v. *Shanahan* [2009] BCC 822, the appellant (O) and the two respondents (S and L) were shareholders in a quasi-partnership company that specialised in the provision of financial services. O presented a petition under CA 1985, s.459 (now CA 2006, s.994), the substance of which was that S and L had exploited a business opportunity that had been presented to the company: in effect that both S and L had breached the conflict of interest duty. The opportunity in question involved the sale of a property to a client of the company; however, the company had never previously been involved in any estate agency business. The sale benefited S and L but not O or the company. In defending the petition, S and L admitted that the opportunity to acquire the property in question had come to them in their capacity as directors of the company but, given that property investment was outside the scope of the company's ordinary business activities, the exploitation of the opportunity did not give rise to a breach of duty. In the High Court, the deputy judge dismissed the petition. However, in reversing that judgment, the Court of Appeal held that in circumstances where a business opportunity came to a director in his capacity as a director of the company, the director could not take up the opportunity for his own benefit, other than in circumstances where the company had waived its right to pursue the opportunity in question. In *O'Donnell* v. *Shanahan*, it was possible that the company may have decided to engage in property investment and as such the director's failure to involve the company in respect of the sale of the property amounted to a breach of duty. Therefore, in such a case the defence of 'no real possibility of conflict' will not be applicable other than where the business opportunity was considered and rejected by the company.

The conflict of interest duty is strict also in the sense that it fails to distinguish between, on the one hand, directors who have purposely set out to exploit a corporate opportunity for their own benefit and profit (an intentional or reckless abuse of the duty) and, on the other hand, directors who personally profit from a corporate opportunity in circumstances where the company was, at the time of the opportunity, unable or unwilling to act upon it. For example, in *Regal (Hastings) Ltd* v. *Gulliver* [1942] 1 All ER 378, a company (R) was the owner of a cinema. The directors of R wished to obtain two more cinemas with a view to eventually selling the company as a going concern. R formed a subsidiary company (A) for the purpose of obtaining a leasing agreement for the two other cinemas in question. In order to secure the leasing agreement the subsidiary company was required to raise £5,000. However, R was unable to meet this requirement. R's directors injected their own personal funds (£3,000) to finance the balance between R's contribution and the total amount required. The directors subsequently sold their shares in both A and R, making a substantial profit in the process. The new controllers of R sought to recover the profit from the sale of the shares in A on the premise that the directors had made that profit as a result of an exploitation of a corporate opportunity. The House of Lords held unanimously that the directors were liable to account for the profits made from the sale of the shares. Notwithstanding the directors' honest and well-informed intentions, their liability resulted from the mere fact of a profit having been made.

In common with the conflict of interest rule in equity, the CA 2006, s.175 duty is a strict duty, albeit in the interpretation of the provision, the courts may apply some element of 'common sense' to perhaps temper the otherwise arbitrary nature of the duty. Indeed, in effect, s.175(4) provides that the duty is not to be considered as having been infringed in circumstances where, in applying a test of reasonableness to the situation in question, the court arrives at a conclusion that the conduct in question is unlikely to give rise to a conflict of interest. The circumstances of each individual case should be examined carefully to discover whether a fiduciary relationship exists in relation to the matter of complaint. In this respect the strict application of the conflict of interest duty may be subject to some leniency.

In *Plus Group Ltd* v. *Pyke* [2003] BCC 332, the business relationship between P and X, the directors of a company (C) deteriorated to the point whereby in practice, P was excluded generally from participating in the management of the company's affairs. P incorporated a new company (Z) through which he competed and procured a lucrative contract with one of C's principal customers. The Court of Appeal held that although P was a director of C, his duty to C had been diminished by his inability to participate in the company's affairs. In effect, P had no real influence in the company. P had been effectively expelled from the company prior to the incorporation of Z and prior to obtaining the lucrative contract. Further, P had not used any of C's property or any confidential information that came to him *qua* director of C. In such circumstances the court found that P had not been in breach of the conflict of interest duty. However, despite this 'common sense' or 'reasonableness' consideration in determining whether a conflict of interest exists, in the vast majority of cases the duty will be applied in a strict sense to the extent that if the situation in question portrays a possibility of a conflict of interest that possibility will generally override any likelihood of the supposed conflict of interest being viewed as too remote to warrant the application of CA 2006, s.175.

For example, in *Towers* v. *Premier Waste Management Ltd* [2012] BCC 72, a director (D) of a company (C) borrowed some equipment (digging machinery) from a customer (X). The loan agreement was arranged through (F), a colleague of D. F was an employee of C but not a director of the company. At the time of the agreement for the equipment, X had not sought any payment from D. The equipment was used by D to develop his personal property. The agreement between D and X took place without the knowledge or consent of C. From the facts of the case, C suffered no loss nor would it have benefited from the subject matter of the agreement. Indeed, the agreement appeared to be of a purely personal nature as between D and X and it is probable that it would have remained that way had it not been for X's subsequent decision to seek to charge C for the loan of the equipment. As a consequence of X's payment demand, C sought to recover the sum from D. Here the Court of Appeal held that the no conflict of interest duty prevented D from depriving C of the ability to consider whether or not it objected to the diversion of an opportunity that had been presented by X, who was a customer of C. D had obtained an advantage, a secret profit from the agreement with X, without consulting or seeking the consent of C. According to the court, the absence of any finding of bad faith on the part of D, the reasonableness of the reliance by D on X that X would not seek a fee for the loan of the equipment, the lack of direct contact between D and X, and the absence of any quantifiable loss by C or the negligible profit to D, were factors that were insufficient to justify finding that D had not breached the conflict of interest duty.

The prohibition against a director benefiting from a corporate opportunity is operative for the duration of a director's term of office. The conflict of interest duty may also be enforced against a director following his or her departure from the company, albeit that an ex-director will not be precluded from using his or her general fund of skill and knowledge, or his personal connections, to compete with his or her former company. Accordingly, a director of company X may resign his or her position to set up business in competition with X providing he or she does not have any plan or immediate intention to engage in any competitive activity with X at a time prior to his or her resignation. For example, in *Foster Bryant Surveying Ltd* v. *Bryant* [2007] BCC 804, a director (D) of a company (F) resigned his directorship but during his notice period agreed to undertake work for C. C had initially offered to share the work in question between F and D but F had declined the offer. F commenced a claim against D for breach of duty. The Court of Appeal held that D had not resigned his directorship for the purpose of exploiting a corporate opportunity although by agreeing, while still a director of F, to work for C after he ceased to be a director, it was arguable that he had obtained a business opportunity in conflict with his fiduciary duty to the company. Nevertheless, in the context of retiring directors, the court adopted a pragmatic approach and in this case, the court concluded that there had been no breach of duty in so far as D had been excluded from his role as a director of F immediately following his resignation. D agreed to undertake the work for C only after his resignation became effective.

Nevertheless, a potential liability of an ex-director may arise (after resignation or dismissal) in circumstances where he or she exploits information or an opportunity which is directed towards the company in which he or she held office and which came to his or her attention during the period in which office was held. For example, liability may arise where a director of a company resigns from the company with an objective of diverting a maturing business opportunity of the company to a new business venture in which he or she is involved (see, e.g. *Industrial Development Consultants Ltd* v. *Cooley* [1972] 1 WLR 443 and *Island Export Finance Ltd* v. *Umunna* [1986] BCLC 460). In circumstances where a director exploits a corporate opportunity for the benefit of another company which then takes advantage of that opportunity, then both the director and the new company will be liable to account having both jointly participated in a breach of trust (see, e.g. *CMS Dolphin Ltd* v. *Simonet* [2002] BCC 600 and *Quarter Master UK* v. *Pyke* [2005] 1 BCLC 245).

However, in relation to the exploitation of a business opportunity, a director of a company (or an ex-director) will not be in breach of the duty where the company itself successfully exploits a business opportunity and as a result of that exploitation the director obtains an ancillary benefit. A director may accrue an ancillary benefit from a business opportunity that falls to the company providing the benefit was obtained without prejudice to the company's interests (see, e.g. *Framlington Group plc* v. *Anderson* [1995] BCC 611). For example, if company A decides to sell a part of its business (G) to company B, and X, a director of A and previously the head of G, resigns his position with A to take up a directorship with B, to the purpose of managing G for B, X will not be in breach of any duty to A, providing X obtained no undue advantage at the expense of A. Here, in this situation, A exploits the corporate opportunity and not X. Further, and running with the previous scenario, X would not be in breach of duty where, on becoming a director of B, he or she receives an additional payment from B in consideration of his or her continued management of G. However, in this instance the payment to X must obviously be made as a genuine incentive to X and not as a 'back handed' payment to reward X for a misappropriation of information, etc. in respect of the business transaction between A and B.

15.3.8   Duty not to accept any benefits from a third party (CA 2006, s.176)

CA 2006, s.176 states that:

(1)   A director of a company must not accept a benefit from a third party conferred by reason of –

(a)   his being a director, or

(b)   his doing (or not doing) anything as director.

(2)   A 'third party' means a person other than the company, an associated body corporate or a person acting on behalf of the company or an associated body corporate.

(3)   Benefits received by a director from a person by whom his services (as a director or otherwise) are provided to the company are not regarded as conferred by a third party.

(4)   This duty is not infringed if the acceptance of the benefit cannot reasonably be regarded as likely to give rise to a conflict of interest.

(5)   Any reference in this section to a conflict of interest includes a conflict of interest and duty and a conflict of duties.

CA 2006, s.176 expands the definition of a conflict of interest to encompass a situation whereby a director of a company is precluded from benefiting personally from the provision of a service or information to a third party, a benefit conferred on the basis of the director's office. A service may be equated with non-activity on the part of a director, for example, where the director is, by receiving a benefit, influenced by a third party to abstain from voting on a specific matter in his or her capacity as a director. The s.176 duty covers any inducement or incentive type of payment to a director but may also cover a situation where, for example, a director is 'wined and dined' or provided with some other type of non-monetary type inducement by a third party.

15.3.9 Disclosure and the waiver of the conflict of interest duty (CA 2006, s.177)

Where a director of a company is, in any way, directly or indirectly interested in a proposed transaction or arrangement between the company and a third party or has in any other way a conflict of interest, the conflict of interest may be excused in accordance with CA 2006, s.180 where it is disclosed to the directors of the company. CA 2006, s.177 provides that:

(1) If a director of a company is in any way, directly or indirectly, interested in a proposed transaction or arrangement with the company, he must declare the nature and extent of that interest to the other directors.

(2) The declaration may (but need not) be made –

(a) at a meeting of the directors, or
(b) by notice to the directors in accordance with –

(i) section 184 (notice in writing), or
(ii) section 185 (general notice).

(3) If a declaration of interest under this section proves to be, or becomes, inaccurate or incomplete, a further declaration must be made.

(4) Any declaration required by this section must be made before the company enters into the transaction or arrangement.

(5) This section does not require a declaration of an interest of which the director is not aware or where the director is not aware of the transaction or arrangement in question.

For this purpose a director is treated as being aware of matters of which he ought reasonably to be aware.

(6) A director need not declare an interest –

(a) if it cannot reasonably be regarded as likely to give rise to a conflict of interest;
(b) if, or to the extent that, the other directors are already aware of it (and for this purpose the other directors are treated as aware of anything of which they ought reasonably to be aware); or
(c) if, or to the extent that, it concerns terms of his service contract that have been or are to be considered –

(i) by a meeting of the directors, or
(ii) by a committee of the directors appointed for the purpose under the company's constitution.

Following the decision of the Court of Appeal in *Lee Panavision Ltd* v. *Lee Lighting Ltd* [1992] BCLC 22, disclosure of an interest may be given informally without any need for it to be declared at a formal board meeting (also see *Runciman* v. *Walker Runciman plc* [1992] BCLC 1084). The disclosure must specify the nature and extent of the conflict of interest. However, a sole director of a company is not subject to the formal disclosure requirement and here the effect of CA 2006 overturns the decision of Lightman J in *Neptune (Vehicle Washing Equipment) Ltd* v. *Fitzgerald* [1995] BCC 474.

The board of directors (i.e. members of the board who are independent of the conflict) may vote to waive any potential conflict of interest, other than where the company's constitution prohibits waiver. However, it is to be noted that in the case of a public company, the company's constitution must specifically allow for a waiver of the conflict of interest (in effect, this duplicates the previous position under the Companies Act (CA) 1985, i.e. Table A, art.85). Further, in respect of both a public and a private company, a transaction giving rise to a conflict of interest that is not waived by the directors may, as with any breach of duty, be waived by the general meeting (albeit the director with the conflict of interest will not be allowed to vote on the matter (i.e. as a member of the company)).

It is to be noted that, as CA 2006 now classifies a conflict of interest as a duty (previously a conflict of interest was deemed a distinct rule of equity and was not strictly speaking a fiduciary duty), a potential problem may have arisen in respect of the operation and application of CA 2006, s.232 (previously CA 1985, s.310), i.e. this provision prohibits a company's ability to waive a breach of duty. Previously, a conflict of interest (because it was classified not as a duty but rather as a rule of equity) could be waived without disturbing the effect of CA 1985, s.310 (see, e.g. *Movitex Ltd* v. *Bulfield* [1988] BCLC 104). However, in respect of CA 2006, this potential problem is eradicated, i.e. a company's ability to waive a breach of the conflict of interest duty is, in accordance with CA 2006, s.180(4), not defeated by the effect of CA 2006, s.232.

15.3.10 Competing directorships

Although there is no specific statutory provision or common law principle which prohibits a person from holding a directorship in two or more companies (see, e.g. *London & Mashonaland Exploration Co Ltd* v. *New Mashonaland Exploration Co Ltd* [1891] WN 165), the test to determine a breach of the conflict of interest duty may, in theory, be indicative of a finding of conflict in cases of competing directorships, especially in circumstances (as, for example, in the *Mashonaland* case) where a director holds office in two distinct companies which, by virtue of their business purposes, may be viewed to be in direct competition with each other. The potential conflict is apparent. How, for example, can a director who holds office in company A, ignore information, projects, dealings or potential contracts in relation to that company when, in also acting as a director of company B, he or she is considering business matters, projects, dealings and potential contracts of a type which are equally relevant to company A? How in such circumstances can a director act in the best interests of both companies? (See the *obiter* comments of Sedley LJ in *In Plus Group Ltd and Ors* v. *Pyke* [2003] BCC 332.)

15.3.11 Consequences of non-compliance with the conflict of interest duty

While the non-disclosure of a conflict of interest will not, in itself, invalidate the proposed transaction in which a director has an interest (see, e.g. *Coleman Taymar*

Ltd v. *Oakes* [2001] 2 BCLC 749), the resulting transaction will become voidable and may be avoided by the company in general meeting (see, e.g. *Hely Hutchinson* v. *Brayhead Ltd* [1968] 1 QB 549). In circumstances where a director fails to declare a conflict of interest and the subsequent breach of duty is not ratified by the general meeting, the director must reimburse the company for any benefit gained or loss sustained as a result of entering into the transaction. A dishonest agreement between a company's directors to impede the exercise of the company's right to recover any benefit gained as a result of a director entering into a transaction involving a conflict of interest will constitute a conspiracy to defraud (see, e.g. *Adams* v. *R* [1995] BCC 376 (PC)).

15.3.12 A conflict of interest in respect of an existing transaction or arrangement (CA 2006, s.182) (criminal liability)

In a situation where a director fails to declare an interest in a proposed transaction or arrangement (and so acts in breach of duty – see CA 2006, s.177) and the proposed transaction/arrangement materialises into an existing transaction/arrangement, then providing the director is deemed to be directly or indirectly aware of the interest in the existing transaction or arrangement, the director must, in accordance with CA 2006, s.182, declare the nature and extent of the interest to the company's board of directors. CA 2006, s.182 would appear also to be operative where a director is deemed to have an interest in an existing transaction without having had a prior interest in the transaction, i.e. before it materialised into an existing transaction. This latter scenario will be rare, but may, for example, arise in a situation where a person is appointed to a directorship at a time after a contract was concluded, a contract in which the newly appointed director had an interest.

A failure to declare the conflict of interest is deemed an offence punishable by way of a fine (note, however, that disclosure under CA 2006, s.177 will satisfy the disclosure requirements under s.182). A director is deemed to be aware of an interest if, by the application of an objective test, he or she is considered to have been aware of matters of which he or she ought reasonably to be aware. Ordinarily, disclosure should be made at a meeting of the directors (but may also be made by notice in writing or by general notice). A breach of CA 2006, s.182 results in the imposition of criminal liability and as such the effect of s.182 is akin to the previous law represented by CA 1985, s.317. However, where an interest is disclosed in accordance with CA 2006, s.182, the interest cannot (in relation to the civil consequences of the breach) be subject to a right of waiver by the board of directors, i.e., in the sense that the directors are not afforded a power to waive a breach of duty unless permitted to do so by a statutory provision (CA 2006, s.232). Unlike CA 2006, s.175, s.182 is absent of the directors' ability to waive a breach of duty. However, the breach could still be ratified by a resolution of the general meeting but only in relation to the civil consequences of that breach.

15.3.13 The consequences attached to any breach of duty

Where a director is discovered to be contemplating the pursuit of a transaction that would, if completed, amount to a breach of duty, the company may apply for an injunction to restrain the commission of the breach. In circumstances where a breach of duty has actually occurred, the director in breach may be liable to account for any profit made or loss sustained as a result of his or her transgression. It is to be noted that an account of profits can be awarded even in circumstances where the company has suffered no loss (see, e.g. *Regal Hastings Ltd* v. *Gulliver* [1967] 2 AC 134). However, save possibly in a situation where a breach of duty results in a fraud on the minority or is otherwise unfairly prejudicial to minority interests (discussed in **Chapter 19**), the company may legitimately excuse the breach by the passing of an ordinary resolution. However, in an equitable and logical change to the previous law (which was silent on the issue) it is to be noted that any director who is in breach of a duty (or connected person), will not (if he or she is a member of the company) be permitted to vote at the general meeting (or take part in a written resolution) where the motion to excuse the breach is to be considered (CA 2006, s.239). However, nothing in s.239 affects the validity of a decision taken by unanimous consent of the members of the company, or any power of the directors to agree not to sue, or to settle or release a claim made by them on behalf of the company.

15.3.14 Relief available from the court

In accordance with CA 2006, s.1157 (formerly CA 1985, s.727), the court may relieve, partly or wholly, the liability of any officer of the company (or auditor) in proceedings involving negligence, default, breach of duty or breach of trust. Liability may be relieved on such terms as the court sees fit. A director (or auditor) may apply for relief under s.1157 in the course of proceedings taken against him or her (see, e.g. *Re Kirby's Coaches Ltd* [1991] BCC 130) or he or she may make an anticipatory application.

Notwithstanding that the applicant's conduct amounted to a breach of a duty, the court's jurisdiction under CA 2006, s.1157 arises where the court considers that the applicant acted in an honest and reasonable manner. The provision permits the court to take account of the economic realities of a case in seeking to do justice between a variety of interests, including the interests of creditors (see, e.g. *Re Loquitur Ltd* [2003] 2 BCLC 442). The burden of satisfying the s.1157 defence lies upon the applicant who must persuade the court that he or she did not intend to harm the interests of the company as a whole. Even where the court is satisfied that an applicant acted honestly and reasonably, the court may still decide to decline relief, under its general discretion (see, e.g. *Coleman Taymar Ltd* v. *Oakes* [2001] 2 BCLC 749). Following the decision of Hoffmann LJ in *Re D'Jan of London* [1993] BCC 646, s.1157 may even prove an appropriate defence in circumstances where a negligent breach of duty is alleged, notwithstanding that a negligent act necessarily equates to an unreasonable act. Here, although in an objective sense an applicant's conduct may be considered negligent and unreasonable, Hoffmann LJ opined that CA 1985, s.727 (now CA 2006, s.1157) lends itself to a subjective consideration of the applicant's conduct and while negligent conduct cannot be ignored, an applicant's error of judgment may, in a particular case, be viewed with some understanding (in *Re D'Jan*, the applicant was negligent in the completion of an insurance document). However, it is suggested that the decision of Hoffmann LJ should be viewed with caution because, in *Re D'Jan of London*, the s.727 defence was construed with a more than generous leaning towards a subjective consideration of events. A director's honesty should, in itself, be insufficient in circumstances where the breach of duty is deemed an unreasonable act; that is, the s.1157 provision requires a director to have acted both honestly and reasonably in all the circumstances of the case (see, e.g. *Dryburgh* v. *Scots Media Tax Ltd* [2011] CSOH 147). Indeed, although the provision allows relief in circumstances where a director was negligent, other than where a director's negligence was induced by his or her reliance on a reasonable but false perception of events, for example, where the director relied on inept professional advice, it is very difficult to conceive of a situation in which a director's negligent act should be excused on the basis that the director acted in a reasonable way (see, e.g. *Re MDA Investment Management Ltd; Whalley (liquidator of MDA Investment Management Ltd)* v. *Doney* [2005] BCC 783).

15.4 PROTECTION FOR DIRECTORS – INDEMNITIES

Provisions relevant to indemnifying (but not exempting) company directors against liability in specified circumstances were introduced by the Companies (Audit, Investigations and Community Enterprise) Act 2004. These matters are now dealt with under CA 2006, ss.232–238. As a starting point, a company is precluded generally from providing any form of indemnity for a director of the company or an associated company in respect of any negligence, default, and breach of duty or breach of trust on the part of the director (CA 2006, s.232). However, a company may purchase insurance for a director in respect of the consequences of a director's negligence, default, breach of duty or breach of trust (CA 2006, s.233). Further, an indemnity may be provided in specific instances, namely in cases involving qualifying third-party proceedings (CA 2006, s.234) and in relation to qualifying pension scheme indemnity provisions (CA 2006, s.235). The details of all qualifying indemnity provisions must be disclosed in the directors' report and if a provision is in force for the benefit of one or more of the directors (to include former directors within the financial year) of the company (or an associated company) the directors' report must specify that fact (CA 2006, s.236). Copies of all qualifying indemnity provisions must be kept by the company (for at least one year from the expiry date of the provision) at either the company's registered office, the place where its register of members is kept, or its principal place of business; the nominated place must be notified to the registrar. A company commits an offence in respect of a failure to comply with this latter requirement (CA 2006, s.238(1)). Further it commits an offence in respect of s.238(2) where it fails to allow an entitled member, on request and on payment of such fee as may be prescribed, to be provided with a copy of any indemnity provision.

15.4.1 Third-party indemnities (CA 2006, s.234)

CA 2006, s.234 defines a 'qualifying third party indemnity provision', to include any indemnity, other than where:

- the director's liability is incurred directly to the company or an associated company;
- liability is in the form of a fine imposed in criminal proceedings or a sum payable to a regulatory authority (e.g. the FCA) by way of a penalty;
- a director incurs liability in defending criminal proceedings in which he or she is convicted, or civil proceedings brought by the company or an associated company in which judgment is made against him or her; and
- the court refuses a director relief in an application under CA 2006, s.1157 (formerly CA 1985, s.727).

15.5 THE CONSTRUCTIVE TRUSTEE

15.5.1 Knowing receipt

Where a corporate asset is transferred to a person following and as result of a breach of a director's fiduciary duty, the company as a beneficiary to a trust type relationship (see, e.g. *In re Lands Allotment Co* [1894] 1 Ch 616 and *Re Duckwari* [1999] Ch 253) may be able to recover the asset or the value of the same from its recipient where the recipient is viewed as a constructive trustee. If a property right exists in an asset, the person entitled to that property right may enforce it until the asset passes into the hands of a purchaser in good faith for value without notice. The value of the proprietary interest may also be traced into identifiable substitutes for the original asset, unless the substitute passes to a purchaser in good faith for value without notice. Any legal person may be viewed as a constructive trustee in circumstances where that person 'received and became charged with trust property' (knowing receipt). To establish 'knowing receipt' the recipient's knowledge of the breach of fiduciary duty must make it unconscionable for him or her to retain the benefit of the asset (see, e.g. the decision of the Court of Appeal in *Bank of Credit and Commerce International (Overseas) Ltd* v. *Akindele* [2001] Ch 437). The test to determine a recipient's state of knowledge as unconscionable may be satisfied without the necessity of establishing any fraud or dishonest intent on the part of the recipient. The test to determine unconscionable behaviour is purely an objective test.

15.5.2 Knowing assistance

Here it is possible for a third party, a stranger to the trust who has never had possession of the trust property, to be made liable as a constructive trustee (i.e. as an accessory to the breach of trust). In such circumstances it is not necessary that, in addition, the trustee or fiduciary (knowing receipt) was acting dishonestly. Here, the criteria to establish a third party's responsibility and liability as a constructive trustee take their roots from the *dictum* of Lord Selborne LC in *Barnes* v. *Addy* (1874) LR 9 Ch App 244. Lord Selborne opined that the liability of third parties may exist:

> ... if they are found ... actually participating in any fraudulent conduct of the trustee to the injury of the *cestui que trust*. But ... strangers are not to be made constructive trustees merely because they act as the agents of trustees in transactions within their legal powers, transactions, perhaps of which a Court of Equity may disapprove, unless those agents receive and become chargeable with some part of the trust property, or unless they assist with knowledge in a dishonest and fraudulent design on the part of trustees.

However, the nature of the conduct and state of mind necessary to establish a person's liability as a constructive trustee, based upon a knowing assistance, is to some degree marred by uncertainty in the form of judicial terminology. Following the decision of Ungoed-Thomas J in *Selangor United Rubber Estates Ltd* v. *Cradock and Ors (No.3)* [1968] 1 WLR 1555, knowing assistance may be established where the circumstances of a case indicate that a person who had no actual or obvious knowledge relating to the illegality of the transaction was in a position to have been reasonably suspicious of the possibility of the illegality to the extent that he or she should have sought to act on those suspicions. Accordingly, a person's recklessness/negligence in failing to so act may suffice to satisfy the requirement of 'knowing assistance'. This interpretation was followed, in part, in *Lipkin Gorman* v. *Karpnale Ltd* [1989] 1 WLR 402 and *Baden Delvaux & Lecuit* v. *Société Générale pour Favoriser le Développement du Commerce et de l'Industrie en France SA* [1983] BCLC 325 (affirmed by the Court of Appeal [1985] BCLC 258).

Nevertheless, subsequent cases related to the interpretation of 'knowing assistance' have sought to adopt a reformulated test with an emphasis upon the need to prove an objective element of dishonesty in respect of a third party's assistance in the breach of trust (see, e.g. *Re Montague's Settlement Trusts* [1987] Ch 264 and *Polly Peck International* v. *Nadir (No.2)* [1992] 4 All ER 769). Indeed, the decision of the Privy Council in *Royal Brunei Airlines Sdn Bhd* v. *Tan Kok Ming* [1985] 2 AC 378, confirmed the importance to be attached to establishing the dishonesty element in an objective sense. In *Royal Brunei Airlines Sdn Bhd*, the Privy Council stressed that dishonesty should not be interpreted in the context of a person's subjective perception of the conduct in question but rather dishonesty should measure a person's conduct against the standard of honesty one would reasonably expect a person to display in the circumstances of any given case, taking into account the personal attributes of that person, such as his or her experience and intelligence (see also, *Cowan de Groot Properties Ltd* v. *Eagle Trust plc* [1992] 4 All ER 700). In

Royal Brunei, Lord Nicholls explained the meaning of dishonesty in the context of 'knowing assistance'. His Lordship opined:

> Before considering this issue further it will be helpful to define the terms being used by looking more closely at what dishonesty means in this context. Whatever may be the position in some criminal or other contexts (see, for instance, *Rv Ghosh* [1982] QB 1053), in the context of the accessory liability principle, acting dishonestly, or with a lack of probity, which is synonymous, means simply not acting as an honest person would in the circumstances. This is an objective standard. (at p.389)

15.5.3 Knowing assistance – subjective element in dishonesty test

However, more recently in *Twinsectra Ltd* v. *Yardley* [2002] 2 AC 164, the House of Lords have injected a subjective element into the dishonesty test. While the House of Lords accepted that the test to determine dishonesty should measure a person's conduct against the standard of honesty one would reasonably expect a person to display in the circumstances of any given case, taking into account the personal attributes of that person, such as his or her experience and intelligence, the House added a further requirement (Lord Millett dissented on this point), of a subjective nature, being that the third party must himself or herself have appreciated that the conduct giving rise to a claim of 'knowing assistance' was dishonest according to the standards of honesty one would expect a person to reasonably display in the circumstances of any given case. In the words of Lord Hoffmann:

> A finding by a judge that a defendant has been dishonest is a grave finding, and it is particularly grave against a professional man, such as a solicitor. Notwithstanding that the issue arises in equity law and not in a criminal context, I think that it would be less than just for the law to permit a finding that a defendant had been 'dishonest' in assisting in a breach of trust where he knew of the facts which created the trust and its breach but had not been aware that what he was doing would be regarded by honest men as being dishonest. (at p.174)

Although in the majority of situations the additional subjective element may not necessarily hamper the court in arriving at a conclusion that the third party was dishonest, in a minority of situations the subjective element may be obstructive to a conclusion that the third party's conduct was dishonest. For example, where, for whatever reason, the third party was unable to appreciate that the conduct giving rise to the alleged 'knowing assistance' was, in an objective sense, dishonest, it would not, in such circumstances, appear (in respect of Lord Hoffmann's observations – see above) to matter that the third party's appreciation of the nature of the conduct fell below the standard of appreciation to be expected of, in the circumstances of any given case, any reasonable diligent person. Further, the subjective qualification may also be applicable in a situation where the third party failed to actually consider whether the conduct was dishonest, that is he or she took a blinkered approach, or buried his head in the sand and in effect did not consider the possibility that the conduct was dishonest. It is submitted that the subjective element so constructed by the House of Lords in *Twinsectra Ltd* should at the very least have been linked to the perception of a reasonable diligent person (as, for example, in cases of wrongful trading (see IA 1986, s.214), discussed in **Chapter 5**). Unfortunately, the subjective element may, in its present form, be a potential licence for a third party to attempt to escape liability for 'knowing assistance' by alleging that their appreciation of the nature of the conduct fell below an appreciation that, in reality, should have been expected of a reasonable diligent person or, alternatively, liability could be escaped on the premise of the third party alleging that they had never even contemplated the possibility of the conduct being considered objectively, as conduct of a dishonest nature.

15.6 OTHER STATUTORY DUTIES AND OBLIGATIONS

15.6.1 Substantial property transactions

In accordance with CA 2006, s.190 (previously regulated under CA 1985, s.320), a company is prohibited from entering into an arrangement whereby a director of the company or a director of its holding company, or a connected person of such a director, acquires, or is to acquire, directly or indirectly, a substantial non-cash asset(s) of the requisite value from the company. However, the arrangement may be approved by an ordinary resolution (or may be validated conditional on the approval being obtained). In addition, s.190 prohibits an arrangement whereby the company (directly or indirectly) acquires or is to acquire a substantial non-cash asset(s) of the requisite value from a director or director of its holding company or connected person of such a director. As the s.190 provision prohibits 'corporate conduct', as opposed to the conduct of individual directors, regrettably there would appear to be no restriction on an 'interested' director voting on the matter, i.e. where the director has an interest in the transaction he or she may still be permitted to vote on any resolution to approve the substantial property transaction. Accordingly, CA 2006, s.239 (discussed above) may be inapplicable in relation to s.190. However, note that the transaction may involve a distinct breach of the conflict of interest duty (discussed above), in which case an 'interested' director will be precluded from taking part in a vote to sanction the conflict of interest.

Where an arrangement involving a substantial property transaction with a director or connected person has not been approved by the general meeting of the company, the transaction may be avoided (CA 2006, s.195). However, a company will lose its right to avoid the transaction where restitution of the subject matter is no longer possible or where the company is indemnified by any other person for the loss or damage that it has suffered, or where rights to the property have been acquired by a *bona fide* third party for value without actual notice of the contravention. Regardless of whether the transaction is (or can be) avoided, the director or connected person in breach of CA 2006, s.190 (and any other director who authorised the transaction) will be liable to account to the company for any profit or loss sustained as a result of the breach of the provision (the loss sustained may be measured in relation to any depreciation in value of the asset(s) acquired in contravention of s.190) (see, e.g. *Re Duckwari plc (No.2)* [1998] 2 BCLC 315 and *Re Duckwari plc (No.3)* [1999] 1 BCLC 168). However, where the breach of s.190 was committed by a connected person, the director with whom the person is connected will not be liable if he or she can prove that all reasonable steps had been taken to secure the company's compliance with s.190. The connected person and any authorising director may also escape liability if they can establish that at the time of the transaction they were unaware of the relevant circumstances giving rise to the contravention of s.190.

15.6.2 Requisite value

The requisite value of a substantial asset is currently set at £100,000 or 10 per cent of the company's net assets (transactions of less than £5,000 are not included). Asset value is measured (at the time of the arrangement) by the company's most recent statutory accounts or if no statutory accounts have been prepared, the amount of the company's called-up share capital (CA 2006, s.191).

15.6.3 Connected person

A connected person is defined by CA 2006, ss.252–255 to include, *inter alia*, the director's spouse, child or step-child and a company with which the director is associated, i.e. if the director and the persons connected with him or her hold at least one-fifth of the associated company's share capital, or are entitled to exercise or control the exercise of more than one-fifth of the voting power at any general meeting of that body.

15.6.4 Exceptions to CA 2006, s.190

There are the following exceptions to CA 2006, s.190:

- *Group transactions*: CA 2006, s.192 permits holding companies to acquire or transfer assets from or to their wholly owned subsidiaries. The section also permits wholly owned subsidiaries of the same holding company to acquire or transfer assets between each other.
- *Members*: CA 2006, s.192 provides that a person may acquire an asset from the company in which he or she is a member providing the arrangement is made with that person in his character as a member and not in any other capacity.
- *Winding up or administration*: Approval is not required where a company in administration or in the course of being wound up (other than by means of a members voluntary winding-up order) enters into an arrangement for the acquisition of a non-cash asset (CA 2006, s.193).

- *Transactions on a recognised investment exchange*: Membership approval is not required where the transaction is on a recognised investment exchange and is executed by a director or a person connected to the director through the agency of a person who in relation to the transaction acts as an independent broker (CA 2006, s.194).

15.6.5 Contracts for loans and guarantees

The statutory rules (see CA 2006, s.197 *et seq*) alter the previous regulatory regime (see CA 1985, s.330 *et seq*). Under the terms of CA 1985, a company was generally prohibited from entering into a loan agreement to the benefit of one or more of its directors. The position under CA 2006, s.197 is now that a company may enter into loan agreements with directors and connected persons providing the transaction in question is approved by an ordinary resolution (approval may take place within a reasonable period after the transaction, see CA 2006, s.203). A resolution approving the transaction must not be passed unless a memorandum setting out the nature and amount of the transaction and the extent of the company's liability under any transaction connected with the loan, etc. has first been made available to the members (CA 2006, s.197(3)). Additional rules exist in the case of relevant companies (public companies). These additional rules (not applicable to private companies other than where the private company is connected via a group relationship with a public company) are concerned with quasi-loans and other credit transactions. Therefore, in the case of relevant companies, the following also require shareholder approval:

- *Quasi-loans (CA 2006, s.198)*: A 'quasi-loan' is defined by CA 2006, s.199 as an arrangement under which a company meets a financial obligation of a director, a connected person, or its holding company on terms that the director, etc. will reimburse the company. Shareholder approval will also be required in the case of guarantees entered into by a relevant company in respect of a quasi-loan made by a third party for the benefit of a director, connected person or holding company.
- *Credit transactions (CA 2006, s.201)*: A credit transaction is a transaction under which one party (the creditor) supplies, hires or leases goods or sells land under a hire purchase contract, or for periodical payments, or otherwise disposes of land or supplies goods or services on the understanding that payment (whether in lump sum or instalments or by way of periodical payment) is to be deferred (CA 2006, s.202). A credit transaction entered into by a relevant company for the benefit of a director, connected person or holding company must be approved by a resolution of the members. The same is true of a guarantee given by the company in respect of a credit transaction between a director, connected person or holding company and third party.
- *Related arrangements (CA 2006, s.203)*: Shareholder approval is required where a relevant company takes part in an arrangement under which another

person enters into a transaction and in doing so obtains a benefit from the company or an associated company in circumstances where, if the transaction had been entered into by the company, the company would have been subject to CA 2006, ss.198 or 200.

15.6.6   General exceptions to CA 2006, s.197

CA 2006 provides exceptions to the requirement that shareholder approval must be sought in respect of loan transactions. The exceptions are as follows.

- Shareholder approval is not required in respect of loan funds, etc. made available (maximum amount of £50,000) to a director of the company or holding company (or connected person) to facilitate the performance of the director's duties (CA 2006, s.204). Likewise, shareholder approval is not required where a company provides a director (or a director of its holding company) with loan funds, etc. (here no maximum amount is specified) to meet expenditure incurred in defending any criminal or civil proceedings in connection with any alleged negligence, default, breach of duty or breach of trust (CA 2006, s.205). Loan funds may be given providing the director repays those funds in circumstances where judgment is given against him or her. Further, shareholder approval is not required where a company provides loan funds, etc. (no maximum amount specified) for a director or a director of its holding company to meet any expenditure incurred in relation to defending an investigation by a regulatory body (CA 2006, s.206).
- CA 2006, s.207 provides that shareholder approval is not required in respect of an arrangement that does not exceed £10,000 in respect of a loan or quasi-loan (£15,000 in respect of a credit transaction). Likewise, CA 2006, s.208 states that a loan, quasi-loan, credit transaction or guarantee or security made in respect of an associated company is not subject to shareholder approval.
- Finally, CA 2006, s.209 provides wide exceptions in relation to a company that pursues a money lending business, i.e. one whose ordinary business includes the making or guaranteeing of loans or quasi-loans. Any loan, quasi-loan or guarantee made by a money lending company is permissible without shareholder approval providing it is made within the ordinary course of business on terms which the company might reasonably have afforded to an unconnected person of the same financial standing. A loan made to a director or an employee of the company or a director of the company's holding company enabling the director/employee to purchase or improve his or her main residence is permissible without shareholder approval, providing loans are ordinarily made by the company to employees and the terms of the loan in question are no more favourable than the loans that are ordinarily made.

15.6.7 Civil penalties

CA 2006, s.213 provides that a transaction in breach of CA 2006, ss.197, 198, 200, 201 or 203 will be voidable (see, e.g. *Re Ciro Citterio Menswear plc* v. *Thakrar* [2002] 1 BCLC 672, decided under CA 1985, s.330). The company may (although it is not obliged to) avoid the transaction by ordinary resolution. However, although a transaction may be avoided, the following persons (listed in CA 2006, s.213(4)) will remain liable to account (whether jointly or severally) to the company for any gain or loss sustained as a consequence of the transaction:

(a) any director of the company or of its holding company with whom the company entered into the transaction or arrangement in contravention of section 197, 198, 201 or 203,

(b) any person with whom the company entered into the transaction or arrangement in contravention of any of those sections who is connected with a director of the company or of its holding company,

(c) the director of the company or of its holding company with whom any such person is connected, and

(d) any other director of the company who authorised the transaction or arrangement.

In the case of a transaction or an arrangement entered into by a company (in contravention of ss.200, 201 or 203) with a person connected with a director of the company or of its holding company, the director in question is not liable by virtue of CA 2006, s.213(4)(c) in circumstances where he or she establishes that all reasonable steps were taken to secure the company's compliance with the section concerned.

It should be noted that a transaction may not be avoided:

(i)   if restitution of its subject matter is no longer possible;

(ii) in circumstances where the company has been indemnified for the loss resulting from the transaction; or

(iii) where the rights acquired by a third party, having been acquired in good faith, for value and without actual notice of the contravention, would be affected by an avoidance.

15.6.8 Removal of criminal sanctions

Previously, under CA 1985, s.342, the directors of relevant companies were also subject to criminal sanctions by way of imprisonment or fine in circumstances indicative of an intentional or reckless contravention of the provisions relating to loans and guarantees (see CA 1985, s.330). The relevant company was also subject to a fine although it could escape liability where it was established that at the time of entering into the transaction or arrangement, it did not know (i.e. the company's directing mind did not know) of the relevant circumstances giving rise to the contravention. As a result of CA 2006, criminal liability is removed from the provisions dealing with loans, etc., albeit that CA 2006, s.213 provides that nothing in s.213 shall be read as excluding any other legal rule which may be brought into operation by a contravention of CA 2006, ss.198, 202 or 220 (i.e. the other legal rule in question may result in a criminal sanction; for example, the loan transaction may incorporate a fraudulent act which may itself be made subject to the criminal law).

CHAPTER 16

Directors' authority and the validity of corporate transactions

16.1 INTRODUCTION

The ability of a company to enter into a transaction or other obligation with a third party will be dependent upon the company's contractual capacity and issues relating to whether a director or other authorised agent of the company is authorised to bind the company in respect of the transaction/obligation in question. In a historical context, a company's contractual capacity was at one time determined by the *ultra vires* rule. During the twentieth century the significance of the *ultra vires* rule declined to a point whereby it now plays no part in issues related to the contractual capacity of a company. In effect, the abrogation of the *ultra vires* rule provides companies with an unrestricted contractual capacity to enter into any type of legal transaction or other legal obligation. However, despite this unrestricted corporate capacity, a transaction or other obligation that is entered into on behalf of a company may still be deemed voidable in circumstances where the transaction or other obligation in question was of an unauthorised nature. Here, issues related to the authority of a company's directors are highly relevant in respect of an ability to bind, or authorise others to bind, the company to a particular type of transaction.

16.2 CORPORATE CAPACITY – THE HISTORICAL DEVELOPMENT AND DEMISE OF THE *ULTRA VIRES* RULE

Historically, a company's capacity to enter into a contractual obligation was dominated by the *ultra vires* rule. In the context of limited liability companies the origin of the *ultra vires* rule may be traced back to cases involving statutory companies, many of these companies having been formed to construct public utilities, for example, railways and canals. Statutory companies were restricted in the pursuit of legitimate business activities by the particular statute that granted them a corporate status. Any act by a statutory company which contravened a limitation placed upon its capacity would be deemed *ultra vires* and void (see, e.g. the decision of the House of Lords in *Eastern Counties Rly* v. *Hawkes* (1855) 5 HLC 331). In 1855, following the introduction of a limited liability status for joint stock companies, the legislature considered it necessary to offer some means of protection for corporate creditors to curb the potential danger of investment in enterprises which, as a consequence of their limited liability status, offered only minimal protection should they become insolvent (i.e. the limited liability status of companies precluded the personal resources of a company's membership from being used to repay corporate debts). Accordingly, the legislature introduced provisions into the Companies Act 1856, whereby companies were obliged to register an objects clause, the said clause to be included in the company's memorandum. The objects clause specified a company's intended business purposes. Therefore, prior to entering into a credit agreement with a company, a creditor could inspect the company's objects clause to discover its business purposes, an inspection which could influence potentially a creditor's decision to advance loan funds or offer other forms of credit.

In *Ashbury Railway Carriage and Iron Co* v. *Riche* (1875) LR 7 HL 653, the House of Lords construed the Companies Act 1862 (which replaced the 1856 Act) in a restrictive manner, to hold that any business purpose that was not authorised expressly or impliedly by a company's objects clause would be beyond the contractual capacity of the company. This strict interpretation of the 1862 Act was subject further to the *eiusdem generis* rule of construction. This latter rule limited the scope of any of the company's stated objects, namely all stated objects had to be construed in conjunction with the company's specified main object. Therefore, in *Ashbury*, an object which permitted the company to act as 'general contractors' could not be read as indicative of the company's ability to engage in a business as finance agents, although arguably, the term 'general contractors' may have covered such an activity. Applying the *eiusdem generis* rule, the object which permitted the company to act as general contractors was construed in relation to the company's main object, namely, the company's principal business purpose of mechanical engineering. Therefore, the company could only act as general contractors in connection with the business of mechanical engineering. By acting as general finance agents, the company acted *ultra vires* and the transaction was deemed void.

The justification for the House of Lords' strict interpretation of the Companies Act 1862, and indeed the rationale for the *ultra vires* rule, was couched in terms of both shareholder and creditor protection. The *ultra vires* rule protected shareholders in so far as they could seek an injunction to restrain the company from entering into an *ultra vires* transaction, or if a company's main object (substratum) had failed, they could petition the court for a winding-up order (see, e.g. *Re German Date Coffee* (1882) 20 Ch D 169). Alternatively, where a company acted beyond its capacity, the members of the company, by passing an ordinary resolution on the matter, could avoid the contract and seek the return of the subject matter of the contract, or where that was not possible, seek compensation from the party (the constructive trustee) with whom the contract had been made. Unlike company shareholders, a company's unsecured creditors had no ability to enforce the *ultra vires* rule, although a secured creditor, having taken a charge over the company's property, had the right to seek an injunction to restrain the company from entering into an *ultra vires* transaction (see, e.g. *Cross* v. *Imperial Continental Gas Association* [1923] 2 Ch 553).

Where a contractual transaction exceeded a company's corporate capacity, the transaction would be deemed void to the extent that not even the unanimous consent of the company's shareholders could validate the transaction (see, e.g. *Ashbury Railway Carriage and Iron Co* v. *Riche* (1875) LR 7 HL 653). While giving some form of protection to both shareholders and creditors, the *ultra vires* rule was not conducive to the efficient conduct of commercial business. Given that the objects clause was contained within the memorandum, a document available for public inspection, a person contracting with a company was deemed to have constructive notice of its contents, irrespective of whether any actual inspection of the document had actually taken place. Therefore, a person who dealt with a company could not complain if a transaction to which he was a party conflicted with the company's objects clause; the company could avoid the transaction. (It should be noted that at first instance in *Bell Houses Ltd* v. *City Wall Properties* (1966) 1 QB 207, Mocatta J suggested that a third party could also invoke the *ultra vires* rule against a company. However, in subsequent cases this suggestion was never accepted. On appeal, the decision of Mocatta J was overturned, but on different grounds.)

In an attempt to rectify the restrictive nature of the *ultra vires* rule, in cases subsequent to *Ashbury,* the courts sought to weaken the rule. For example, in *A-G* v. *The Great Eastern Railway Co Ltd* (1880) 5 App Cas 473, the House of Lords held that a company could pursue a course of business which was reasonably connected to its stated objects or, for that matter, could employ a power, for example, the power to borrow money, where the power use was necessary to the fulfilment of the company's objects irrespective of whether the particular power use was contained within the company's objects clause. (The powers of a company were often contained within the objects clause and were tools to be employed to assist in the fulfilment of stated objects.)

16.2.1 The weakening of the *ultra vires* rule

In 1904 came one of the most significant decisions in connection with the weakening of the *ultra vires* rule, namely *Re David Payne & Co Ltd* [1904] 2 Ch 608. Here the Court of Appeal, in affirming the decision of Buckley J, inflicted what should have been a fatal blow to the *Ashbury* interpretation of the rule. Prior to *Re David Payne*, in circumstances where a company employed a legitimate power but for a purpose outside its stated objects, the exercise of the power would be deemed *ultra vires* and void. In *Re David Payne*, that view was discarded on the premise that the question of whether the use of a corporate power was valid had to be determined by asking the following questions.

1. Was the power use in question capable of being used to pursue the corporate objects?
2. Did the capacity to employ the power expressly or impliedly exist?

The Court of Appeal in answering those two questions held that if a company was legitimately capable of exercising a corporate power, the use of that power would be valid (*intra vires*) even if ultimately the purpose for its use was for an activity outside the company's objects clause.

In *Cotman* v. *Broughman* [1918] AC 514, the House of Lords (albeit reluctantly) struck another nail into the coffin of the *ultra vires* rule by refusing to invalidate an objects clause, the effect of which removed the main objects (or substratum) rule enunciated in the *Ashbury* case. In *Cotman* every stated object of the company was given an equal status thereby precluding the need to link an ancillary object to the main object of the company. The *Cotman* type clause became a regular feature in the objects clauses of companies. As a result of the removal of the substratum rule (main objects rule) companies began to include a multitude of business objects within their objects clauses to expand their corporate capacity and prevent a transaction being challenged on the basis of the *ultra vires* rule. However, it should be noted that in respect of companies absent of a *Cotman* type clause, the power of a shareholder to petition for the winding up of a company on the basis that the company's main object had failed remained, albeit in *Re Kitson & Co Ltd* [1946] 1 All ER 435, the Court of Appeal diluted the substratum rule by providing that a company could have more than one main object. In *Bell Houses Ltd* v. *City Wall Properties* [1966] 2 QB 656, the scope of a company's objects clause was further extended by the approval of a clause which authorised the company to carry on any business whatsoever which, in the opinion of the directors, could be advantageously carried out by the company in conjunction with or ancillary to any of the ventures specified in the objects clause.

16.2.2 The confusion between *ultra vires* and an abuse of powers

In relation to the issue of corporate capacity, although a transaction may not have been *ultra vires*, it may have been entered into as a result of an abuse of the powers afforded to the company's directors. The legal consequences flowing from the latter type of transaction were explained in *Re David Payne*, namely, a transaction within the capacity of a company would nevertheless be voidable where the third party had actual notice of the transaction being used to pursue something which constituted an abuse of a director's power. However, unfortunately, the correct rationale of *Re David Payne* became confused with the concept of *ultra vires*. The confusion between *ultra vires* transactions and those which had taken place as a result of an abuse of directors' powers became commonplace. For example, in *Re Lee Behrens & Co Ltd* [1932] 2 Ch 46, a case concerned with an implied power to grant pension policies to employees and their spouses, Eve J, in considering whether the issue of a particular pension policy had been beyond the capacity of the company, declared that two questions had to be asked and answered in the affirmative before the transaction could escape the consequences of the *ultra vires* rule, namely, was the transaction *bona fide*? Secondly, was the power used for the benefit and to promote the prosperity of the company? In reality, those questions had no relevance to the issue of capacity (*ultra vires*) but were instead concerned with whether a director of the company had abused his or her powers in allowing a particular transaction to proceed. Therefore, in declaring the pension policy in *Re Lee Behrens & Co Ltd* to be void on the premise that negative answers had been supplied to the two questions, Eve J clearly erred in his construction of the determination of a company's corporate capacity. The investigation into corporate capacity should not have been concerned with the state of mind of the officers of the company. In *Re Lee Behrens* the implied power was capable of being used to pursue the objects of the company and as such should not have been declared *ultra vires*. Regrettably, the decision in *Re Lee Behrens* became widely accepted as an authority for determining whether the use of a corporate power rendered the power use *ultra vires*. The judgment of Eve J was applied in cases such as *Re Jon Beauforte Ltd* [1953] Ch 131, *Parke* v. *Daily News Ltd* [1962] Ch 927, *Re Ward M Roith Ltd* [1967] 1 WLR 432 and *Introductions* v. *National Provincial Bank* [1970] Ch 199.

The correct principles of the *Re David Payne* case were to remain clouded with confusion until the decision of Pennycuick J in *Charterbridge Corporation Ltd* v. *Lloyds Bank* [1970] 1 Ch 62. Here, the ability of a company (Castleford Ltd) to mortgage its property was called into question on the grounds of capacity. Castleford sought a mortgage from a bank to secure the indebtedness of a group of other companies to which Castleford belonged. Castleford, having taken a mortgage over its property, subsequently sold the property to the Charterbridge Corporation but did so prior to repaying the mortgage that it owed to the bank. As the mortgage remained unpaid, the bank claimed the property in accordance with its mortgage terms. Charterbridge, which had been unaware of the existence of the mortgage, contended that notwithstanding that the power to mortgage property had been contained within Castleford's objects clause, the mortgage transaction should be viewed as *ultra vires* because it had been entered into not for the benefit of Castleford, but merely to support other companies in the group of companies to which Castleford belonged. Here, Pennycuick J had to determine whether the mortgage, in relation to its benefit to Castleford, was an issue of any relevance to the determination of an *ultra vires* transaction. Pennycuick J held that as the power to mortgage was one which was capable of being used to pursue Castleford's objects, the use of the power could not be *ultra vires*. In other words, Eve J's benefit test had no application to the determination of whether the transaction was *ultra vires*. The confirmation of the correctness of Pennycuick J's decision was provided in subsequent cases, namely, *Re Halt Garages* [1982] 3 All ER 1016, *Re Horsley & Weight* [1982] Ch 442 and *Rolled Steel Products Ltd* v. *British Steel Corporation* [1986] Ch 264. In this latter case, the Court of Appeal finally put to death any confusion that may have remained in relation to directors' powers and the *ultra vires* rule. The Court of Appeal killed off any suggestion that the doctrine of *ultra vires* was interwoven with issues relating to directors' powers. Accordingly, transactions which involved a dispute over a director's authority to exercise delegated powers or a director's duty to exercise powers *bona fide* and for a proper purpose, had no place in determining whether the transaction in question was *ultra vires*.

16.3   THE STATUTORY REFORM OF THE *ULTRA VIRES* RULE

While the courts sought to curtail the severity of the *ultra vires* rule, in contrast, the legislature was slow in the reform of the rule. The first statutory intervention was introduced by the Companies Act 1948, following the recommendations of the Cohen Committee Report in 1945 (Cmnd 6659). The intervention permitted a company to alter its objects clause by the passing of a special resolution. This statutory reform allowed companies a greater degree of flexibility in altering the direction of their corporate purposes. If, however, the Cohen Committee recommendations had been enacted in full, then in relation to third-party transactions, companies would have had the powers of a natural person in effect, the *ultra vires* rule would have been abolished in respect of third-party transactions. In 1962, the Jenkins Committee Report (Cmnd 1749) proposed that the doctrine of constructive notice should be abolished. However, the committee's recommendations were not heeded. The statutory overhaul of the *ultra vires* rule was to remain dormant until the UK entered the European Community. Here the legislature was press-ganged into action in order to comply with the requirements of art.9 of the EC First Company Law Directive. As a consequence of the directive, ECA 1972, s.9 was introduced. The basic intent of the reform, which subsequently became CA 1985, s.35(1), was to accept the validity of any transaction between a company and a third party where the third party dealt with the company in good faith and in circumstances where the transaction in question had been authorised by the directors of the company. CA 1985, s.35(2) sought, in compliance with art.9(2), to abrogate the constructive notice rule in circumstances where the conditions laid down in s.35(1) had been satisfied. However, the language of s.35(1) failed fully to achieve its objective (see, e.g. *International Sales and Agencies Ltd* v. *Marcus* [1982] 3 All ER 551 and *Barclays Bank Ltd* v. *TOSG* [1984] BCLC 1). As a result of the problems associated with the wording of s.35, the ghost of the *ultra vires* rule remained and while the threat of the *ultra vires* rule prevailed, companies, in drawing up object clauses, continued to create elaborate and well-defined clauses. Further reform was advanced by the Companies Act (CA) 1989, s.110. In amending CA 1985, s.35, the effect of s.110 finally abolished the *ultra vires* rule in relation to a company's dealings with third parties, Section 35(1) (as amended by CA 1989) provided that:

> The validity of an act done by a company shall not be called into question on the ground of lack of capacity by reason of anything in the company's memorandum.

Although the provision did not afford a company the capacity of a natural person, corporate capacity was nevertheless unrestricted by the contents of the objects clause within the memorandum. Although CA 1989 did not remove the need for an objects clause, it sought to avoid the practice of prolonged clauses and did so by introducing an optional standard type of objects clause (CA 1985, s.3A, inserted by CA 1989). The standard clause allowed companies to pursue any activity within a commercial context. It should be noted that if a company adopted an objects clause in line with s.3A, but wished to place a limitation on a power to exercise the general commercial objects (express limitations on the exercise of objects were to be found in cases decided pre-Companies Act 1989; see, e.g. *Simmonds* v. *Heffer* [1983] BCLC 298 and *Rosemary Simmons Memorial Housing Association Ltd* v. *UDT Ltd* [1986] 1 WLR 1440), then in such cases the limitation had to be provided for separately as an 'additional extra' to the '3A type' objects clause. Nevertheless, even where a limitation on the '3A type' objects was included, such a limitation could not defeat the commercial capacity of a company in its dealings with third parties; the wording of s.35(1) prevented this from happening. However, limitations so attached to an objects clause, while not limiting corporate capacity, would have the effect of regulating the powers of the board of directors and a transaction falling foul of a stipulated limitation, albeit not void (i.e. not *ultra vires* a third party), would render any director who acted contrary to the limitation in question, liable to contribute personally to any loss that the company sustained as a consequence of entering into the transaction. However, in such cases a director could escape personal liability in circumstances where the general meeting ratified the transaction by the passing of a special resolution (see CA 1985, s.35(3)).

By retaining the concept of an objects clause, CA 1989 maintained one of the initial justifications for the *ultra vires* rule, namely, shareholder protection. Indeed, CA 1985, s.35(2) specifically afforded a shareholder with the ability to prevent the company from pursuing a transaction that would have fallen outside its objects clause. However, the practical effect of s.35(2) was to place a severe limitation on a shareholder's ability to intervene, in so far as intervention was prohibited if the company had acted in furtherance of an existing legal obligation. Therefore, a commercial transaction which went beyond a company's capacity would, in so far as it was subject to a prior contractual agreement, be outside the ambit of shareholder control, i.e. following the agreement relating to the transaction, a legal obligation would have been created, thereby negating the effect of CA 1985, s.35(2).

16.3.1 Political donations

Corporate powers outside the ambit of the CA 1985, s.3A definition but which the company wished to include additionally within its objects clause had to be expressly provided for; such powers included the ability to make charitable or political donations. However, it is to be noted that in respect of the latter and following the Political Parties, Elections and Referendums Act 2000, a company, if it wished to make a political donation, could do so, providing it obtained the approval of the general meeting by the passing of an ordinary resolution.

16.3.2 CA 2006

CA 2006 no longer compels a company to register an objects clause and as such a company's objects may be unrestricted. However, a company may include an objects clause within its articles (note, the objects clause will no longer be contained in the memorandum as the memorandum ceases to have any constitutional effect).

CA 2006, s.31 provides that:

(1)   Unless a company's articles specifically restrict the objects of the company, its objects are unrestricted.

(2)   Where a company amends its articles so as to add, remove or alter a statement of the company's objects –

    (a)   it must give notice to the registrar,

    (b)   on receipt of the notice, the registrar shall register it, and

    (c)   the amendment is not effective until entry of that notice on the register.

Although a company may (where it chooses to adopt an objects clause) restrict the scope of its objects, the restriction will have no consequence in relation to third-party dealings; these are afforded absolute security in accordance with CA 2006, s.39(1). However, as under the previous legislation (discussed above) the restriction may operate as an internal fetter to limit the powers of the directors. Therefore, in effect, the significance of an objects clause will only affect the relationship between the membership and its directors. CA 2006, s.39(1) provides that:

> The validity of an act done by a company shall not be called into question on the ground of lack of capacity by reason of anything in the company's constitution.

It is to be noted that CA 2006 contains no specific provision (unlike CA 1985, s.35(2)) in respect of a shareholder's ability to challenge a proposed transaction which, if pursued, would fall foul of the company's objects clause (i.e. if an objects clause was to be contained in the articles).

16.3.3 Political donations

Political donations are now governed by CA 2006, ss.362–379. Again, under CA 2006, an ordinary resolution is required to confer on a company an authorisation to make a political donation where the donation exceeds £5,000 in the period of 12 months ending with the date on which the donation is made. Any authorisation has effect for a period of four years beginning with the date on which it was passed, unless the directors determine otherwise, or the articles require that it should have effect for a shorter period. The power of the directors to propose a political donation is subject to any provision of the articles that prevents them from doing so. If the directors breach this requirement they will be collectively liable to repay to the company the amount of the donation. The holders of not less than 5 per cent of the company's issued share capital may, with the leave of the court, enforce this right in the company's name against the directors.

Finally it should be noted that the threshold for the disclosure (to be contained within the annual directors' report) for political donations and expenditure and charitable donations for a company that is not the wholly owned subsidiary of a company incorporated in the UK is (per financial year) now set at a figure of £2,000 (see the Small Companies and Groups (Accounts and Directors' Report) Regulations 2008, SI 2008/409, Sched.5 and the Large and Medium-sized Companies and Groups (Accounts and Reports) Regulations 2008, SI 2008/410, Sched.7, para.3).

16.4 THE AUTHORITY OF DIRECTORS AND OTHERS TO BIND THE COMPANY

16.4.1 The agency relationship

The rules of agency determine whether a director or other authorised person is afforded an authority to bind the company in a contractual relationship with a third party. Here the term 'other authorised person' may refer to a mere employee of the company but for the employee to bind the company, the employee's authority must be derived from and be traceable through the internal command structure of the company, i.e. the employee's authority must ultimately be traceable to a director of the company who himself must have been authorised to act by the company's directors (as a collective). There are two principal forms of valid authority: actual authority – which may be express, implied or usual (real); and second, ostensible (apparent) authority (see *Criterion Properties plc* v. *Stratford UK Properties LLC* [2004] 1 WLR 1846).

16.4.2 Actual authority

The directors of a company, acting as a collective body, are invested with the powers of the company; the company is the principal in the agency relationship. Subject to a contrary intention within a company's articles, an actual authority to exercise the powers of the directors or part of those powers may be delegated to individual directors, a committee of directors or to directors occupying an executive position. The delegation of actual authority follows a resolution passed by the directors to appoint a director or committee of directors to take charge of specific corporate powers. A delegation of actual authority in any matter is termed an express actual authority. The delegation of actual authority may also be implied. For example, where a director is appointed to a particular executive position or permitted by the company's other directors to act as if he had been appointed to that position, the director concerned will have an implied authority to bind the company in a manner consistent with the powers associated with that position, that is, he or she will have a usual (real) authority. An oft quoted case example of the operation of implied actual authority is *Hely Hutchinson* v. *Brayhead Ltd* [1968] 1 QB 549. This case concerned the extent of an authority vested in a company chairman to bind a company to a contractual relationship in circumstances where the chairman had not sought the prior approval of the company's board in respect of the approval of the contract in question. The Court of Appeal found that as the chairman was accustomed to commit the company to similar type contracts, his actions were akin to those of a de facto managing director. Given that in the chairman's previous dealings, the remaining members of the board of directors had not sought to curb the chairman's powers, the court held that the chairman's authority to contractually bind the company could be implied from the executive position he was permitted to occupy, namely, he acted as the company's de facto managing director.

An executive position to which an implied actual authority is attached may be subject to express or implied restrictions, imposed by either the collective will of the directors or the company's articles. In such circumstances the implied authority granted to the executive position may be more restrictive than the usual authority ordinarily associated with the position in question. For example, in *Smith* v. *Butler* [2012] BCC 645, the Court of Appeal was called upon to determine whether the powers of a managing director (B) (B was a minority shareholder) entitled him to suspend the respondent majority shareholder (S) from his office as the company's executive chairman. B and S were the company's only shareholders. S had expressed dissatisfaction about the way B was running the company and intended to use his powers as the majority shareholder to remove B from his office. In reliance on his authority as managing director, B informed S that he was suspending him from his office as chairman. B also excluded him from the company's premises. The company's articles enabled the board of directors to appoint a managing director and to delegate any of their powers to the managing director. However, in this case there had been no express delegation of any specific powers by the board to B.

S sought to requisition a meeting of the company with the objective of seeking a resolution to remove B, but B made it clear that he would not attend the meeting. S applied to the court for an order under CA 2006, s.306, namely, to the purpose of convening a meeting of the company with a reduced quorum of one to consider a resolution to remove B as a company director. B caused the company to oppose the application. At first instance it was held that B's purported suspension of S from his office as chairman was outside his powers as the company's managing director and the court made an order under s.306. The court further held that B should indemnify the company for the substantial costs that it had incurred in resisting S's application. In denying B's appeal the Court of Appeal held that B had not been expressly delegated the power to usurp the powers afforded to the company's board of directors. In relation to B's implied powers as a managing director, those powers extended only to carrying out those functions of a managing director which did not require specific directions from the board of directors. In this particular case, any potential suspension of S from his role as the company's executive chairman was a matter for the board, and not for B acting alone. B had no implied authority to suspend S and no power to cause the company to support his actions by resisting S's application. Accordingly, B was liable for the costs incurred by the company in accordance with the application under s.306.

However, in the context of CA 2006, s.40 (discussed below) it should be observed that where an implied authority is subject to express restrictions imposed by the company's articles (as opposed to a restriction placed on the authority by the collective body of the company's directors), the effect of those restrictions will be irrelevant in relation to determining the validity of a corporate transaction with an independent third party acting in good faith.

16.4.3 Ostensible authority

Ostensible authority (apparent authority) operates in accordance with a representation made by the company (the principal) to a person (third party) to the effect that a specific agent/employee of the company possesses the necessary authority to bind the company in respect of the transaction in question. In all instances of an alleged ostensible authority, the third party must have altered his position as a consequence of relying upon a representation of authority from the company. An agent of a company who possesses ostensible authority will in effect be absent of any actual authority to perform the act to which the ostensible authority relates. A representation which affords an agent an ostensible authority to act on behalf of the company may be an express or implied representation (i.e., the latter by conduct or acquiescence) and must emanate from the directors (as a collective) or a director duly authorised by the directors. The representation will acknowledge the right of the company's agent (albeit the agent will have no actual authority) to bind the company in a particular transaction. An oft-quoted case example of ostensible authority is *Freeman & Lockyer* v. *Buckhurst Park Properties Ltd* [1964] 2 QB 480. Here, Kapoor (K), a director of the defendant company (C) entered into a contract with the plaintiffs (P) without first seeking the approval of the three other members of C's board. The board subsequently refused to honour the terms of the contract on the premise that K had no actual authority to enter into the contract. The Court of Appeal held that, although K had never been appointed to a position which carried an actual authority to bind the company in the contractual relationship with P, nevertheless the board of directors had been aware of K's managerial activities: K had been left in charge of the day-to-day management of the company. As such, P was justified in relying on K's ability to bind the company. The company by its conduct (or by its acquiescence in allowing K to so act) had represented to P that K had an authority to act. P had relied upon this representation of authority. It is to be observed that the cases of *Freeman & Lockyer* v. *Buckhurst Park Properties Ltd* and *Hely Hutchinson* v. *Brayhead Ltd* are, in many respects, similar. The distinction between implied authority and ostensible authority may, on occasions, be a very fine one. In seeking to attempt to distinguish the two cases it is suggested that in *Freeman Lockyer* the court was unwilling to find an implied actual authority because K had never formally or impliedly been appointed to a management position consistent with the position of a de facto managing director. The acquiescence of the individual members of the board to K's activities was insufficient to amount to a valid authority that K should manage the day-to-day business of the company in a position akin to that of a managing director. By contrast, in *Hely Hutchinson*, the company chairman was accustomed and was permitted to act in a manner consistent with the position of a managing director.

Where the directors of a company have not provided an agent of the company with an authority to act in a specified manner, and the third party with whom the agent contracts is aware that the agent is absent of that requisite authority, the third party cannot contend subsequently that the agent acted with an ostensible authority, irrespective of the fact that the company's constitution may have afforded the directors an ability to delegate the requisite authority in question. In *Heinl* v. *Jyske Bank (Gibraltar) Ltd* [1999] Lloyd's Rep 511, Nourse LJ summarised the position as follows:

> Where an agent is known by the other party to a purported contract to have no authority to bind his principal, no contract comes into existence. The agent does not purport to contract on his own behalf and the knowledge of the other party unclothes him of ostensible authority to contract on behalf of the principal. (at p.519)

In addition, if a third party, in dealing with a director or an authorised agent, knows or has reason to believe that the transaction is contrary to the commercial interests of the agent's principal, to the extent that the third party must be aware that the agent would never have been afforded an actual authority to so act, it follows that the transaction will not be saved by alleging that the agent had an ostensible authority to act (see the decision of the House of Lords in *Criterion Properties plc* v. *Stratford UK Properties LLC* [2004] 1 WLR 1846). Further, a third party cannot claim that a director or purported authorised agent had an actual or ostensible authority to bind the company to a particular type of transaction in a situation where, to the knowledge of the third party, the purported agent had never been afforded an authority to bind the company and in reality sought to enter into the contract with the third party for the benefit of himself or herself as opposed to the benefit of the company. For example, in *The Lorenz Consultancy Ltd* v. *Fox-Davies Capital Ltd* [2011] EWHC 574 (Ch) the claimant, a property agent (C) entered into an agreement to find new office premises for R. R proposed to purchase a company (D) and sought the new premises with the intention of expanding D's business operations. F, the founding owner of D, had agreed to sell D to R. C found new premises suitable for D, and F (acting on behalf of D) signed the lease agreement for these new premises. Subsequently, F decided not to sell D to R. C sought a fee from D (but surprisingly not from R) for finding D the new premises, claiming that R had either actual or ostensible authority to bind D to the agency agreement with C. Here Kitchin J held that as F had never given any actual authority to R to bind D, it was impossible to contend that D was bound to C. Further, as D had made no representation to C by conduct or otherwise, to the effect that R was acting on behalf of D, it could not be contended that D had given R an ostensible authority to act on its behalf. R had never intended to contract with C on behalf of D but rather R contracted with C on his own behalf. While R intended the premises to be occupied by D he was never in a position to legally bind D with C, given that at the time of the contract with C, R did not control D.

However, a case example which establishes the potential flexibility/applicability of the concept of ostensible authority is *First Energy Ltd* v. *Hungarian International*

Bank Ltd [1993] BCC 533. Here, the Court of Appeal held that a bank's senior manager had, from his position as a senior employee of the bank, an ostensible authority to communicate to the plaintiff that the bank had approved the plaintiff's proposed transaction. The court so held, notwithstanding that the bank had not given its approval to the transaction in question and that the plaintiff was indeed aware that the manager did not have an actual authority to approve the transaction without first seeking the approval of the bank's head office. Although the Court of Appeal accepted that the bank manager would not ordinarily have an ability to self-authorise transactions without the approval of his head office (by analogy, see, e.g. *Armagas Ltd* v. *Mundogas SA* [1986] 2 All ER 385), the court found that in the instant case, the bank's head office (the principal) had clothed its agent (the bank manager) with the trappings of authority in a manner capable of inducing the plaintiff to rely on the existence of an agency relationship (i.e. ostensible authority had been given). The bank had done so by, for example, allowing the bank manager, in previous dealings between the bank and the plaintiff, to instigate negotiations for loans on behalf of the bank and to communicate the bank's acceptance of short-term credit facilities to the plaintiff. The plaintiff relied on the bank manager's ostensible authority in dealings with the bank, the bank manager having been expressly held out as having an accepted power to communicate the bank's acceptance of the type of transaction in question. Indeed, it would have been nonsensical and contrary to commercial reality had the court reached a contrary judgment, because had it done so, it would have resulted in a bizarre conclusion, namely, the plaintiff would have been expected to seek the approval of the bank's head office whenever it sought confirmation of a communication in relation to a proposed transaction, a communication which it had already received from the bank's manager.

Prior to ECA 1972, s.9 the confirmation of an agency relationship so as to bind a company to a third-party transaction was also dependent upon the potential scope of a director's authority to act, so determined by the company's constitutional documents, Therefore, a third party could not rely on an agent's authority to bind a company in circumstances where the authority relied upon was, in accordance with the company's constitution, outside the ambit of the director's actual authority. A third party was deemed to have constructive notice of the contents of the memorandum and articles. However, as a consequence of ECA 1972 and subsequent legislation, the relevance of the company's constitution as the ultimate source of a company's capacity to delegate authority is no longer of significance in relation to third-party transactions.

16.4.4 The effect of the governing legislation (CA 2006, s.40)

In addition to curtailing the *ultra vires* rule, the companies legislation seeks to limit restrictions placed upon the authority of company directors to bind the company and does so in an attempt to produce a commercial climate of contractual freedom. The legislation applicable to directors' authority is aimed at complementing that made in connection with matters relating to the scope of a company's capacity to enter into contractual relationships. Accordingly, providing a third party acts in good faith when entering into a transaction with a company, the power of the directors to bind the company or authorise others to do so is, as a consequence of CA 2006, s.40 (replacing CA 1985, s.35A(1)) deemed free of any limitation that may have been placed on the power of the directors under the company's constitution. Constitutional limitations include those derived from a resolution of the company or of any class of shareholders, or from any agreement between the members of the company or of any class of shareholders.

CA 2006, s.40(1) provides:

> In favour of a person dealing with a company in good faith, the power of the directors to bind the company, or authorise others to do so, is deemed to be free of any limitation under the company's constitution.

In common with its statutory predecessor (CA 1985, s.35A), the effect of CA 2006, s.40 is that the directors of a company will act as the guardians of the principal's (the company's) ability to delegate authority. Section 40 specifically vests this guardianship of authority in the 'directors' although unlike CA 1985, s.35A, the term 'board of directors' is not used. The significance behind the removal of the term 'board of directors' may be considered radical if, as is possible, the term 'directors' is interpreted in a manner which permits an individual director to bind the company as of right even in circumstances where the individual director does not, in seeking to bind the company, have the support or authority of the collective board of directors. However, this 'radical' interpretation must be questionable given that the management powers of a company and the ability to delegate an authority to bind the company are ultimately vested in the directors as a collective body as opposed to being placed in the hands of individual directors. Here it should be observed that although CA 2006, s.40 provides that a third party is not to be deprived of the benefit of an agreement with a company in circumstances where the directors exceed limitations placed on their powers by the company's constitution, any limitations placed on directors' powers will still prevail where the limitations are placed on a director's authority to bind the company in accordance with the rules of agency.

A director must have an authority (determined by the agency rules) to bind the company or to authorise others to bind the company. For example, in *Smith* v. *Henniker-Major & Co* [2003] Ch 182 (decided under CA 1985), an agreement to assign a right of action vesting in the company (C) to a director of the company (S) was concluded at a board meeting but the meeting was inquorate because only one director (S) was in attendance; C's articles required a quorum of two directors. If the assignment was invalid then S had no standing to commence the action to enforce the agreement. S contended that, under CA 1985, s.35A (now CA 2006, s.40), knowing that an act was beyond the powers of the directors did not prevent a person (here, S himself) from seeking to rely on s.35A and further that a person must be presumed to have acted in good faith unless the contrary was proved. S argued that a quorum requirement should, in the context of s.35A, be treated as a 'limitation,' thus extending the prescribed ambit of s.35A to the facts of the instant case. At first instance, Rimer J ([2002] BCC 544) held that a director could not bind a company via s.35A where there had been no delegation of authority from the board of directors. Rimer J pointed out that in this particular case the agreement in question had never, in accordance with s.35A, been authorised by the board. In effect, S sought to ignore the crucial requirement of s.35A, namely, a director's authority to act must originate from the directors as a collective body. Clearly a director (S) who had entered into an agreement that was purportedly authorised by an inquorate board could not attempt to save the validity of the agreement by claiming that the quorum requirement was a limitation on the power of the directors, therefore bringing the transaction within the scope of s.35A.

On appeal, the decision of Rimer J was affirmed in relation to the s.35A point, Carnwarth LJ opined that as the agreement was concluded at an inquorate board meeting, S had no more authority to take a decision in the name of the company than its office boy; the agreement was therefore a nullity. However, his Lordship did qualify this view by adding that in appropriate circumstances an independent third party (i.e. not a director or connected party) may be able to rely on the apparent authority of an agent of the company who represented to the third party (albeit without actual authority) that a transaction had been authorised by the board (by analogy, see *First Energy Ltd* v. *Hungarian International Bank Ltd* [1993] BCC 533, discussed above).

In accordance with CA 2006, s.40(4) (previously CA 1985, s.35A) a member of a company is afforded a limited right to challenge an act of the directors where the act in question is beyond the powers of the directors. This provision is also likely to be relevant where a company retains an objects clause but the directors propose to exceed the stated objects. Section 40(4) states:

> This section does not affect any right of a member of the company to bring proceedings to restrain the doing of an action that is beyond the powers of the directors.
> But no such proceedings lie in respect of an act to be done in fulfilment of a legal obligation arising from a previous act of the company.

Nevertheless, the difficulty with this provision is in its requirement that a member must establish that the 'challenged act' was not subject to an existing legal obligation. For example, a company will inevitably enter into some form of legal obligation with a third party prior to the commencement of an agreed act. While the ability to enter into a legal obligation (i.e. a contract) could theoretically be challenged by a member of the company on the premise that it constituted an infringement of the directors' powers, the subsequent performance of the contract will not be capable of challenge on the basis of s.40(4). The obligation (for example, the contractual agreement), once created, will negate the effect of s.40(4).

For the purposes of CA 2006, s.40(1), a person must deal with the company in good faith. However, a person is presumed to have acted in good faith unless the contrary is proved. The fact that a third party knows that a corporate act went beyond the powers of the directors, so determined by the company's constitution is, in itself, insufficient to establish bad faith and as such this extends the protection afforded by the *Turquand* rule (in so far as it removes the first exception to the *Turquand* rule (discussed below). As with CA 1985, CA 2006 fails to provide a definition of 'bad faith'. Accordingly, it is suggested that bad faith will be limited to circumstances where the court deems it unconscionable for the third party to seek to enforce the contract (see the discussion relating to the interpretation of 'bad faith' in *Ford* v. *Polymer Vision Ltd* [2009] 2 BCLC 160). In the unlikely event that a third party is unable to rely on CA 2006, s.40, a transaction involving a breach of director's authority may nevertheless be ratified by an ordinary resolution of the general meeting (subject to the rights afforded to minority shareholders – see **Chapter 19**). It is to be noted that CA 2006, s.40 does not affect any potential liability incurred by a director(s), or any other person, by reason of a director(s) exceeding his or her powers.

16.4.5   CA 2006, s.41

CA 2006, s.40 (discussed above) permits the directors of a company to bind the company or authorise others to do so free of any limitation under the company's constitution. However, s.40 is subject to an exception in the guise of CA 2006, s.41 (s.41 replaces CA 1985, s.322A). Section 41 provides:

(2)   Where –

    (a)   a company enters into such a transaction, and
    (b)   the parties to the transaction include –

        (i)   a director of the company or of its holding company, or
        (ii)   a person connected with any such director,

    the transaction is voidable at the instance of the company.

(3)   Whether or not it is avoided, any such party to the transaction as is mentioned in subsection (2)(b)(i) or (ii), and any director of the company who authorised the transaction, is liable –

    (a)   to account to the company for any gain he has made directly or indirectly by the transaction, and
    (b)   to indemnify the company for any loss or damage resulting from the transaction.

Therefore, where a company enters into a transaction or other act (which would otherwise have been valid in accordance with s.40) but the person with which the company deals is an insider, i.e. a director of the company or a director of its holding company or a person connected with any such director, then in such circumstances, the transaction will be voidable at the instance of the company (by ordinary resolution) (CA 2006, s.41(2)). Irrespective of whether the transaction is avoided, the insider and any director of the company who authorised the transaction will be liable to account to the company for any gain he or she made directly or indirectly as a result of the transaction and must indemnify the company for any loss or damage resulting from the transaction (CA 2006, s.41(3)). However, an insider, other than a director of the company, is not liable if he or she shows that at the time the transaction was entered into he or she did not know that the directors were exceeding their powers (CA 2006, s.41(5)). Nothing in s.41 is to be read as excluding the operation of any other enactment or rule of law by virtue of which the transaction may be called in question or any liability to the company may arise.

It is to be noted that the transaction will cease to be voidable if, by CA 2006, s.41(4):

(a) restitution of any money or other asset which was the subject matter of the transaction is no longer possible, or

(b) the company is indemnified for any loss or damage resulting from the transaction, or

(c) rights acquired bona fide for value and without actual notice of the directors' exceeding their powers by a person who is not party to the transaction would be affected by the avoidance, or

(d) the transaction is affirmed by the company.

The content of CA 2006, s.41 does not affect the rights of any party to the transaction other than those of a director or insider (i.e. those covered by s.41(2)). Nevertheless, the court may, on the application of the company or any such party, make an order affirming, severing or setting aside the transaction on such terms as appear to the court to be just.

In the context of CA 2006, s.40, the courts' interpretation of CA 2006, s.41 is likely to follow the interpretation of the similar provisions found previously in CA 1985, namely, s.35A (now CA 2006, s.40) and s.322A (now CA 2006, s.41). Indeed, in *Ford* v. *Polymer Vision Ltd* [2009] 2 BCLC 160, the interpretation afforded to the aforementioned provisions of CA 2006 corresponded to the previous interpretation afforded to s.35A and s.322A. In respect of the courts' interpretation of s.35A and s.322A, in *Smith* v. *Henniker-Major & Co* [2003] Ch 182 (discussed above), the Court of Appeal held that a director of a company was unable to take the benefit of s.35A (now CA 2006, s.40), in respect of a purported agreement involving the company and himself. Following on from *Smith* v. *Henniker-Major & Co*, it is to be noted that in *EIC Services* v. *Phipps* [2004] 2 BCLC 589 (see especially the judgment of Peter Gibson LJ at 559–661) the Court of Appeal construed s.35A in a manner whereby a 'person dealing with a company' could not include a member of the company. The court held that, in the context of a company, s.35A naturally referred to persons other than the company and its members. However, it is to be noted that a difficulty with such an interpretation is that, in the context of s.322A (now CA 2006, s.41), a 'member' is not specified as falling within the definition of an 'insider'.

16.5 THE RELEVANCE OF THE INDOOR MANAGEMENT RULE (THE *TURQUAND* RULE)

The indoor management rule, derived from the case of *Royal British Bank* v. *Turquand* (1856) 6 E & B 327, provides that when dealing with a company, a third party acting in good faith is not bound to ensure that all the internal regulations of the company have been complied with in respect of the exercise of an authority to bind the company. The operation of the rule was subject to a number of exceptions, namely:

- A third party with actual knowledge that a transaction is outside the authority conferred by the company's constitution could not plead the rule (see, e.g. *Howard* v. *Patent Ivory Manufacturing Co* (1888) 38 Ch D 156).
- A third party could not rely on the rule in circumstances where he or she was an insider, namely where he or she was an officer of the company (see, e.g. *Morris* v. *Kanssen* [1946] AC 459).
- A third party would not be able to rely on the rule where there were suspicious circumstances surrounding the authorisation of a transaction and the third party should reasonably have been aware of such circumstances (see, e.g. *Underwood* v. *Bank of Liverpool & Martins Ltd* [1924] 1 KB 755).
- The rule would not operate in circumstances where the contractual authorisation was a forgery (see, e.g. *Ruben* v. *Great Fingall Consolidated* [1906] AC 439).
- The rule would apply where an ordinary resolution was required to validate an exercise of authority, however, where the necessary authorisation for a transaction required the passing of a special resolution, a third party would be deemed to have notice of the outcome of the resolution, as a special resolution had to be registered and was therefore open to public inspection (see, e.g. *Irvine* v. *Union Bank of Australia* (1877) 2 App Cas 366).

The indoor management rule is operative in relation to the company's internal procedures. However, under the rule a third party was not entitled to assume that an officer of a company had been given an authority by the directors of the company to act in excess of his or her actual or usual authority. In abolishing the doctrine of constructive notice, the companies legislation has, to a large extent, extinguished the need for the indoor management rule. However, the rule may still be of assistance in matters concerning a directors delegation of authority. For example, where the directors' delegate authority to one of their number (an individual director) but in doing so place internal restrictions (restrictions not contained in the constitution) on the ability of their agent to carry out his or her functions (a matter not covered by the legislation), then, in accordance with the *Turquand* rule, the third party will not, unless he or she acted in bad faith, be deemed to have knowledge of those restrictions; he or she may assume that the director in question acted with a usual authority. A case example which illustrates the relationship between the *Turquand* rule and ostensible authority is *Mahony* v. *East Holyford Mining Company* (1875) LR 7 HL. This involved a claim by a company to the effect that its bank had paid monies from the company's account without due authorisation. The bank, in making payments from the company's account, had done so in the belief that it was following the conditions laid down in the company's articles; the articles prescribed that payments should only be made when cheques had been signed by two directors and then countersigned by the company secretary. The difficulty in this case was that no director or company secretary had actually been appointed by the company. However, the persons who purported to authorise the payments for the company had been allowed to do so by the company. The House of Lords held that the bank was allowed to assume (as it had no actual notice to the contrary) that the internal regulations of the company had been complied with, and that appointments to the positions of corporate responsibility had been made (operation of indoor management rule). The House found that the acquiescence of the company in its failure to deny that the persons acting for the company had an authority to act created a representation upon which the bank could rely (operation of ostensible authority).

CHAPTER 17

The disqualification of company directors

17.1 INTRODUCTION

The disqualification process is governed by the Company Directors Disqualification Act (CDDA) 1986. The objective of a disqualification order is to temporarily remove a director's future capacity to participate in the management activities of a company. Although provisions of CDDA 1986 may be implemented against a person involved in the management of a solvent company, examples of corporate mismanagement giving rise to the imposition of a disqualification order will be most evident following the collapse of a corporate enterprise. While corporate failure may be attributed to factors unrelated to managerial abuse or incompetence, it is often caused (or at least compounded) by managerial error or wrongdoing. During the period in which a person is subject to a disqualification order, the public interest will be protected by the removal of that person's capacity to repeat his or her past misconduct in respect of the future management of another company.

17.2 THE DISQUALIFICATION REGIME

Although CDDA 1986 is permissive of a disqualification order being imposed against any person involved in the management of a company (save for CDDA 1986, ss.6, 8 and 9, where the person must be a director), in the vast majority of cases the person made subject to a disqualification order will have acted in the capacity of a company director. For the purposes of CDDA 1986, the definition of a director is that of 'any person occupying the position of director, by whatever name called' (see CDDA 1986, s.22(4)). This vague definition is the same as that found in the Companies Act 2006 and will therefore include both a de jure and de facto director. A disqualification order may also be imposed against a shadow director. (For further discussion relating to the definition of a director, see **Chapter 14**.) Save for CDDA 1986, ss.6 and 9 the disqualification regime operates on the basis that the imposition of a disqualification order is discretionary, namely a disqualification order may or may not be made in the circumstances of a case and this is left open to the discretion of the court. Disqualification orders imposed under CDDA 1986, s.6 and s.8 are, in the majority, now made under the undertaking procedure (discussed below).

Under CDDA 1986, s.1(1), the effect of a disqualification order is such that the disqualified person shall not, without the leave of the court:

- be a director of a company; or
- act as an insolvency practitioner or administrator of a company; or
- be a receiver or manager of a company's property; or
- in any way, whether directly or indirectly, be concerned or take part in the promotion, formation or management of a company.

The disqualification period takes effect from the date of the order and runs for the duration of the order. During the period in which a disqualification order is operative, and following the judgment of the Court of Appeal in *Re Cannonquest; Official Receiver* v. *Hannan* [1997] BCC 644, s.1(1) will have the effect of disqualifying a person from acting in all the capacities indicated by s.1(1). Accordingly, the court is not permitted to restrict the operation of the order to preclude any of the categories listed in s.1. In accordance with CDDA 1986, s.13, a breach of a disqualification order carries a maximum penalty of two years' imprisonment and a fine. A person in breach of the order will also be made jointly and severally liable (with the company and any other relevant person) for the debts of the company incurred during the period in which the disqualified person acted in breach of the order (CDDA 1986, s.15).

CDDA 1986, s.11 further provides that other than with the leave of the court, it is an offence for a person who is an undischarged bankrupt to act as a director, or take part in (directly or indirectly) or be concerned in, the promotion, formation or management of a company. It is no defence to an action under s.11 for a person to allege that at the time of his relevant involvement in the activities of a company he was under a reasonable but mistakenly held belief that he had been discharged from a bankruptcy order. The offence is one of strict liability (see, e.g. *R* v. *Brockley* [1994] 1 BCLC 606). Where an undischarged bankrupt acts in contravention of s.11, he or she will, in accordance with CDDA 1986, s.15, be made jointly and severally liable for the debts incurred by the company during the period in which he or she was involved in its management. He or she will share this liability with the company and any other person who, whether under s.15 or otherwise, was liable for the company's debts during the requisite period.

17.2.1 The register of disqualification orders

Under CDDA 1986, s.18(2), the Secretary of State is obliged to maintain a register of disqualification orders. The register is open to public inspection on the payment of a small fee. Where the duration of a disqualification order has expired, the Secretary of State must, in accordance with CDDA 1986, s.18(3), remove the entry from the register and all particulars relating to the order.

331

17.3 DISCRETIONARY DISQUALIFICATION ORDERS

In exercising its discretion to impose a disqualification order the court must consider both the necessity of protecting the public interest and the interests of the individual subject to the potential disqualification order. The decision of the Court of Appeal in *R* v. *Holmes* [1991] BCC 394 provides a good example of the court's consideration of such matters. Here, the Court of Appeal quashed a disqualification order made under CDDA 1986, s.2 in circumstances where, in addition to a disqualification order, the director had been ordered to pay a compensation order in the sum of £25,000. The Court of Appeal quashed the disqualification order on the basis that it had been wrong for the trial judge to disqualify a director following the making of the compensation order in circumstances where, once disqualified, the director would have had no obvious financial means to discharge the terms of the compensation order. The Court of Appeal emphasised that in making a compensation order (which in this case the Court of Appeal also quashed), care must be taken to not reduce or inhibit a director's means to pay off the order.

17.3.1 CDDA 1986, s.2

Section 2 permits the court to impose a disqualification order in circumstances where a person is convicted of an indictable offence connected with the promotion, formation, management or liquidation of a company, or with the receivership or management of a company's property. In *R* v. *Austen* (1985) 7 Cr App R 214, the Court of Appeal defined the management of a company as involving the company's internal or external affairs in relation to any activity covering the company's birth, life, or death. The indictable offence must have had some relevant 'factual connection' with the management of a company (see, e.g. *R* v. *Goodman* (1993) 14 Cr App R 147). However, while the nature of the indictable offence must be connected to a person's involvement in the management of a company's affairs, it is unnecessary to establish that the indictable offence was committed in the course of the day-to-day management of the affairs of a company or that the offence was associated with an improper exercise or abuse of the administration of a company's affairs. In *Goodman*, although the Court of Appeal failed to define the exact meaning of the term 'factual situation' it may be implied from the judgments that an offence connected to the management of a company extends beyond one which is associated with an improper exercise or abuse of the administration of a company's affairs. In *Goodman*, the relevant offence was insider dealing, an offence which is not connected to the administration of a company's affairs but one which nevertheless demands a factual connection with the management of a company, that is, the offence is committed as a consequence of the defendant's knowledge of the company's affairs. In *Goodman*, the defendant acquired the requisite inside knowledge in his capacity as the company's chairman, an office which is undoubtedly associated with the management of the company's affairs.

A further and more recent example of the scope of s.2 in relation to its application to an offence 'connected' to a person's involvement in the management of a company's affairs is *R* v. *Creggy* [2008] BCC 323. Here the defendant, a solicitor (S), formed a company for a client. The company became the recipient of dishonestly obtained funds but as it had no bank account S allowed it to use his solicitor's client account as a repository to receive the illegal funds. S was charged and convicted of money laundering in the sum of £916,750. S was disqualified under CDDA 1986, s.2 for a period of seven years. S appealed on the basis that the offence of assisting the retention of criminal property through the client account was not an offence committed in connection with the management of a company. S was not a manager of the company nor was he convicted of operating the company or any other company for the purpose of the fraud. In dismissing S's appeal, the Court of Appeal held that S, in sheltering the criminal proceeds of fraud, was factually connected with the management of the company. The factual connection was with the financial management of the company. S had suspected that the funds had been fraudulently obtained and received them in circumstances where his personal participation was necessary to the disbursement of the funds by those who managed the company's affairs. The Court of Appeal held that it was unnecessary in seeking to impose a disqualification order under s.2 to establish that the defendant had fraudulently used the company as a vehicle with the objective of personally benefiting from the fraud.

For the purposes of s.2, any court with a jurisdiction to wind up a company may impose a disqualification order. Alternatively, s.2(2) provides that the disqualification order may be imposed by the court in which the person was convicted of the indictable offence. The maximum period of disqualification is five years in the case of an order made by a court of summary jurisdiction and 15 years in any other case. It should be noted that a conditional discharge is not to be interpreted as a conviction in relation to the making of a s.2 order (see, e.g. *R* v. *Young* [1990] BCC 549). CDDA 1986, s.16(2) allows an application under CDDA 1986, s.2 to be made by the Secretary of State, the Official Receiver, the liquidator, or any past or present member or creditor of a company that is being wound up.

17.3.2 CDDA 1986, ss.3 and 5

Under CDDA 1986, ss.3 and 5, the court may impose a disqualification order in circumstances where a person is in persistent breach of provisions of the companies legislation that require any return, account or other document to be filed with, delivered, or sent, or notice of any matter to be given to the registrar of companies (see, e.g. *Re Civica Investments Ltd and Ors* [1983] BCLC 456).

CDDA 1986, s.3(2) provides that without prejudice to its proof in any other manner, a person will be conclusively established to have been in persistent default of a relevant provision of the companies legislation where it is shown that in the five years ending with the date of the application, the person was found guilty of three or more defaults of the relevant provisions of the companies legislation. In respect of

CDDA 1986, ss.3 and 5, the disqualification period is set to a maximum period of five years. The difference between ss.3 and 5 is that under the former provision, a disqualification order may be made by a court with a jurisdiction to wind up a company, whereas under s.5, the disqualification order is restricted to the court of summary conviction in which the person was found guilty of the offence relating to a persistent breach of the companies legislation in relation to the return or filing, etc. of relevant documents. It should be noted that in accordance with CDDA 1986, s.16(2) an application under CDDA 1986, s.3 may be made by the Secretary of State, the Official Receiver, the liquidator, or any past or present member or creditor of a company that is being wound up.

17.3.3   CDDA 1986, s.4

Section 4 deals with the disqualification of a person who, during the winding up of a company, was shown to have acted in a fraudulent manner in the conduct of the company's affairs. CDDA 1986, s.16(2) permits an application under CDDA 1986, s.4 to be made by the Secretary of State, the Official Receiver, the liquidator, or any past or present member or creditor of the company being wound up (see, e.g. *Wood* v. *Mistry* [2013] 1 BCLC 389, involving an application by the company's liquidator in respect of the fraudulent conduct of the company's previous liquidator). Here the maximum disqualification period is 15 years. A person is judged to have acted in a fraudulent manner where the court considers that his or her conduct justified a guilty verdict (irrespective of whether that person has actually been convicted of an offence) in respect of a charge of:

(a)   fraudulent trading under CA 2006, s.993 (as this is a criminal offence, a person's 'fraudulent' activities will need to be established in accordance with the criminal standard of proof, i.e. beyond any reasonable doubt); or

(b)   being otherwise guilty while an officer, liquidator, receiver of the company, or administrative receiver, of any fraud connected with the management of the company or any fraud related to any breach of duty to the company (for the purpose of s.4 an 'officer' includes a person who acts as a shadow director – see, CDDA 1986, s.4(2)).

17.3.4   CDDA 1986, s.8

CDDA 1986, s.8 provides that a person may be disqualified as a director of a company following an investigation by the Department for Business, Innovation and Skills (BIS) (formerly the Department for Business, Enterprise and Regulatory Reform (BERR), which in turn was formerly the Department of Trade and Industry (DTI)). As the imposition of a disqualification order under CDDA 1986, s.8 is determined in a like manner to CDDA 1986, s.6, namely on the basis of a director's unfit conduct, it is somewhat peculiar that s.8, unlike s.6, does not incorporate a mandatory period of disqualification. However, it may be possible to explain this apparent lacuna on the basis that a director of a solvent company may be subject to proceedings under s.8 but cannot be subject to proceedings under s.6. In relation to a director of a solvent company, the public interest may be adversely affected by the imposition on that director of a disqualification order in so far as the order may be prejudicial to the interests of the company as a whole. Generally, the approach and principles applied to cases heard under CDDA 1986, s.8 are akin to those applied under CDDA 1986, s.6 (see, e.g. *Secretary of State for Trade and Industry* v. *Hollier* [2007] BCC 11). However, in considering whether to impose a disqualification order under s.8, the court, in its assessment of whether a director was unfit, must take into account the relevant matters set out in CDDA 1986, Sched.1, Part 1 (discussed below). The matters mentioned in Part 1 of Sched.1 are appropriate to the determination of whether a person's conduct as a director or shadow director of a solvent or insolvent company makes him unfit to be concerned in the management of a company. Part 2 of Sched.1 (discussed below) is only relevant to the determination of a director's unfitness to act in the management of a company in a situation where a director acted in the management of an insolvent company. Under CDDA 1986, s.8, the maximum period of disqualification is 15 years.

17.3.5   CDDA 1986, s.10

Where the court finds that a person is liable to make a contribution to a company's assets under IA 1986, s.213 (fraudulent trading) or IA 1986, s.214 (wrongful trading), the court may, of its own volition, make a disqualification order against that person under CDDA 1986, s.10 (see, e.g. *Re Brian D Pierson (Contractors) Ltd* [1999] BCC 26). Here, the maximum period of disqualification is 15 years. Although s.10 offers no guidance on this matter, it may be assumed that the fraudulent or wrongful trading must be confirmed as conduct of an unfit nature of a type that would have established culpability under CDDA 1986, s.6 (discussed below). Given that CDDA 1986, ss.6 and 10 both penalise managerial misconduct in the context of an insolvent company and both carry the same maximum penalty in terms of the disqualification period, it would, it is suggested, be inappropriate for the court to impose a disqualification order under s.10 in circumstances where the delinquent conduct was insufficient to justify a finding of unfitness under s.6. In all probability, conduct deserving of a s.10 order in the context of fraudulent trading will be classed as conduct of an unfit nature. However, in relation to wrongful trading, the delinquent conduct may not always be of a sufficiently serious nature to justify a like comparison with conduct of an unfit nature. (IA 1986, ss.213 and 214 are discussed in **Chapter 5**.)

17.4   MANDATORY DISQUALIFICATION (CDDA 1986, S.6)

CDDA 1986, s.6 carries a mandatory disqualification period. Section 6(4) provides for a mandatory disqualification period of a minimum period of two years. The maximum period of disqualification is 15 years. Under CDDA 1986, s.6(1), the court is under a duty to impose a disqualification order against any person in circumstances where:

(a) that person is or has been a director of a company which has at any time become insolvent (while the person was a director or subsequently). An insolvent company is defined in broad terms by CDDA 1986, s.6(2) as either:

(i)   a company which goes into liquidation at a time when its assets are insufficient for the payment of its debts and other liabilities and the expenses of the winding up;

(ii) where an administration order is made in relation to a company; or

(iii) where an administrative receiver is appointed to the company; and

(b) that person's conduct as a director of the company (either taken alone or taken together with the person's conduct as a director of another company or companies) makes the person unfit to be concerned in the management of a company.

17.4.1 Commencement of proceedings

Where, in accordance with CDDA 1986, s.7(1), the Secretary of State considers it to be in the public interest, an application to impose a disqualification order under CDDA 1986, s.6, may be made:

(a) by the Secretary of State; or

(b) if the Secretary of State so directs in relation to a person who is or has been a director of a company, where the company is being wound up by the court in England and Wales, by the Official Receiver.

The following statement, taken from the judgment of Henry LJ in *Re Grayan Building Services Ltd* [1995] BCC 554, aptly illustrates the purpose of the s.6 provision. His Lordship opined:

> The concept of limited liability and the sophistication of our corporate law offer great privileges and great opportunities for those who wish to trade under that regime. But the corporate environment carries with it the discipline that those who avail themselves of those privileges must accept the standards laid down and abide by the regulatory rules and disciplines in place to protect creditors and shareholders . . . The Parliamentary intention to improve managerial safeguards and standards for the long term good of employees, creditors and investors is clear. Those who fail to reach those standards and whose failure contributes to others losing money will often be plausible and capable of inspiring initial trust, often later regretted. Those attributes may make them attractive witnesses. But as section 6 makes clear, the court's focus should be on their conduct – on the offence rather than the offender. (at p.577)

17.4.2   The prosecution of CDDA 1986, s.6 actions

In accordance with CDDA 1986, s.7(3), insolvency practitioners are under a statutory obligation to report to the BIS any director who is suspected of conducting the affairs of a company in an unfit manner. In submitting a report, the office holder must investigate conduct by reference to guidelines set out in CDDA 1986, Sched.1 (see below). The insolvency practitioner is required to consider matters related to conduct on the basis of information acquired in the course of his or her normal duties and by reference to the books and records available to him or her. An insolvency practitioner is not obliged to undertake an investigation that he or she would not otherwise have considered necessary for the purposes of his or her appointment. The Insolvency Service, a department of the BIS, is, through its Disqualification Unit, responsible for determining whether to commence proceedings under CDDA 1986, s.6.

A failing system

By the late 1990s, the growing number of prosecutions under CDDA 1986, s.6 was such as to endanger an already overburdened court system. For example, for the period 2000–01, 58 per cent of s.6 cases had not been concluded within two years from the commencement of proceedings and as such exceeded the two-year limit specified by CDDA 1986, s.7(2). Indeed, had it not been for the courts' willingness to adopt a summary form of procedure, 'the *Carecraft* procedure' (taking its name from *Re Carecraft Construction Co Ltd* [1994] 1 WLR 172), the strain on the disqualification system would have been even more transparent. In 2000–01 the *Carecraft* summary procedure accounted for approximately 30 per cent of all s.6 cases. The *Carecraft* procedure was applied in circumstances where the facts relating to a director's misconduct were not disputed and where both the Secretary of State and the respondent were willing to allow the case to be dealt with on the understanding that an agreed disqualification order would be made for a period falling within one of the brackets specified in *Re Sevenoaks Stationers (Retail) Ltd* (discussed below).

17.4.3   The Insolvency Act 2000 – the undertaking procedure

Following the implementation of the Insolvency Act (IA) 2000, a statutory undertaking procedure was introduced for the disqualification of directors but only in respect of CDDA 1986, s.6 and s.8 disqualifications (subsequently, it applied to CDDA 1986, s.9A). The purpose of this procedure was to create a more efficient disqualification system. The provisions of IA 2000 that create the undertaking procedure are incorporated into CDDA 1986. The effect and consequences attached to an undertaking are the same as for a disqualification order imposed by the courts.

CDDA 1986, s.1A permits the Secretary of State to accept an undertaking as an alternative to instigating disqualification proceedings through the courts. A director is not obliged to proceed via the undertaking procedure and where a case is contested by a director it will obviously continue to be dealt with by way of a court action. According to the Insolvency Service, approximately 80 per cent of all disqualifications under s.6 now proceed by way of the undertaking procedure. The Secretary of State may accept an undertaking if it appears expedient in the public interest to do so (see CDDA 1986, s.7(2A) in respect of a s.6 type disqualification and s.8(2A) in respect of a s.8 type order). Under the undertaking procedure a defendant will agree to refrain from acting as a director or in any other capacity so specified by CDDA 1986, s.1A(1)(a) and (b) for a predetermined period (i.e. a minimum duration of two years and a maximum duration of 15 years). However, a director who agrees to an undertaking may still seek leave to act as a director under CDDA 1986, s.17 (discussed below).

The expected efficiency of the undertaking procedure should permit the Secretary of State (Insolvency Service) to prosecute disqualification cases with greater speed and in greater numbers, although the fact that only very serious instances of corporate malpractice will justify disqualification under s.6 may inhibit any substantial increase in the overall number of prosecutions. The statutory undertaking procedure advances the *Carecraft* procedure in a logical way albeit extinguishing any future need for disqualification proceedings to be determined by way of the *Carecraft* procedure. However, as delinquent directors will largely be dealt with in the absence of judicial and public scrutiny, the disqualification process has lost significant transparency (evidenced by, for example, a dramatic fall in the number of reported s.6 cases since the introduction of the undertaking procedure). Further, the additional costs and time burdens in respect of managing and administering the undertaking procedure must be added to the disadvantages of the procedure.

Following a defendant's acceptance of the undertaking procedure, the courts will only be called upon to consider the merits or otherwise of a disqualification order in a situation where a defendant applies in accordance with CDDA 1986, s.8A to have the duration of the order reduced or cancelled. For the court to vary the duration of an undertaking the applicant will be required to establish 'special circumstances' which subsequently render the factors surrounding the making of the original disqualification order to be considered unjust or unwarranted (see, e.g. *Re INS Realisations Ltd* v. *Jonkler* [2006] BCC 307).

17.5 DETERMINING WHETHER CONDUCT IS OF AN UNFIT NATURE

The effect of a disqualification order may dramatically infringe upon the commercial liberty of a director in relation to his ability to pursue employment in the management of a company. Therefore, although disqualification proceedings are governed by the civil law, the courts (Secretary of State in respect of undertakings) have adopted a tendency to afford the respondent the benefit of any reasonable doubt in the course of the proceedings. As such there is an unwillingness to impose disqualification orders in situations where the fault element attached to a director's act or omission was attributable to business practices of an improper but neverthe-less naive and imprudent standard or where the consequences of the fault element were not significantly prejudicial to the public interest. Therefore, a disqualification order will not be imposed under CDDA 1986, s.6 where a director's imprudent conduct was undertaken without any form of malice, recklessness or serious neglect. For example, a director's awareness that his or her company is trading while insolvent will not in itself substantiate a finding of unfit conduct. However, if that director was aware or should have been aware that, at the time of trading in an insolvent state, there was no reasonable prospect of the company avoiding insol-vency, then in such circumstances there will be a strong presumption for the finding of unfit conduct (see, e.g. *Re Uno plc; Secretary of State for Trade and Industry* v. *Gill* [2006] BCC 725).

17.5.1 CDDA 1986, s.9

In assessing whether conduct is of an unfit nature in respect of determining a director's culpability under s.6, the court, or the Secretary of State under the undertaking procedure must, in accordance with CDDA 1986, s.9, have particular regard to the matters set out in CDDA 1986, Sched.1, both Parts 1 and 2. However, as s.9 directs the court to have particular regard to the matters contained in Sched.1, as opposed to confining the court to the matters mentioned in Sched.1, conduct giving rise to a finding of unfitness may still be found in circumstances which are not directly governed by the Schedule. Schedule 1, Part 1, lists the following matters for the court to consider in relation to a director subject to a potential disqualifica-tion order.

1. Any misfeasance or breach of any fiduciary or other duty by the director in relation to the company.
2. Any misapplication or retention by the director of, or any conduct by the director giving rise to an obligation to account for, any money or property of the company.
3. The extent of a director's responsibility for the company entering into any transaction liable to be set aside under IA 1986, Part XVI (provisions against debt avoidance).
4. The extent of a director's responsibility for any failure by the company to comply with any of the following provisions of CA 2006, namely:

    (a) ss.113 and 114 – relating to an obligation to keep and make available for inspection the register of members;
    (b) ss.162, 165, 167, 275, and 276 – relating to the register of directors and secretaries and the notification of changes to the register;
    (c) s.386 – relating to the requirement of companies to keep accounting records;
    (d) s.388 – relating to where and for how long accounting records are to be kept;

(e)   s.854 – relating to a duty of the company to make annual returns; and

(f)   ss.860 and 878 – relating to a company's duty to register charges which it creates.

5.   The extent of the director's responsibility for any failure by the directors of the company to comply with the following provisions of CA 2006, namely:

(a)   s.394 or s.399 relating to the duty to prepare annual accounts;

(b)   s.414 or s.450 relating to the approval and signature of abbreviated accounts;

(c)   s.433 relating to the name of signatory to be stated in the published copy of the accounts.

The matters mentioned in Sched.1, Part 2 (relevant when a company is insolvent) are as follows:

1.   The extent of the director's responsibility for the causes of the company becoming insolvent.

2.   The extent of the director's responsibility for any failure by the company to supply any goods or services which have been paid for (in whole or in part).

3.   The extent of the director's responsibility for the company entering into any transaction or giving any preference, being a transaction or preference:

(a)   liable to be set aside under IA 1986, s.127 or ss.238–240, or

(b)   open to challenge under IA 1986, s.242 or s.243 or under any rule of law in Scotland.

4.   The extent of the director's responsibility for any failure by the directors of the company to comply with IA 1986, s.98 (duty to call creditors' meeting in creditors' voluntary winding up);

5.   Any failure by the director to comply with any obligation imposed on him or her by or under any of the following provisions of IA 1986:

(a)   para.47 of Sched.B1 (company's statement of affairs in administration);

(b)   s.47 (statement of affairs to administrative receiver);

(c)   s.66 (statement of affairs in Scottish receivership);

(d)   s.99 (directors' duty to attend meeting, statement of affairs in creditors' voluntary winding up);

(e)   s.131 (statement of affairs in winding up by the court);

(f)   s.234 (duty of anyone with company property to deliver it up);

(g)   s.235 (duty to co-operate with liquidator, etc.).

17.5.2 Seriousness of the conduct and its effect on public interest considerations

In determining whether unfit conduct can be established, it should be stressed that the crucial factor will be the seriousness of the conduct and its effect on public interest considerations and not necessarily the type of conduct in question. In *Re Bath Glass Ltd* [1988] BCLC 329, Peter Gibson J stated that a director's unfitness would be established where:

> a director has been guilty of a serious failure or serious failures, whether deliberately or through incompetence to perform those duties of directors which are attendant on the privilege of trading through companies with limited liability. (at p.333)

In the majority of disqualification cases heard under s.6, it will be rare (although not impossible) to find proceedings which are commenced on the basis of just one count of alleged misconduct. While it is possible to disqualify a director on the premise of one complaint of misconduct, or to indicate that a specific complaint taken from a number of complaints of misconduct was sufficient to justify disqualification, it is more common to find that a director's unfitness was established in relation to a series of delinquent acts. The seriousness of a particular course of conduct will be measured in accordance with its perceived prejudicial effect in relation to public interest considerations. Public interest factors will include the interests of, for example, creditors, shareholders, customers and employees of the company in question.

Whether a director's conduct was of an unfit nature will always be a question of fact, to be determined from the individual circumstances of any given case. Other than where a director conducts the affairs of a company in a fraudulent/dishonest manner, it is impossible to predict with any degree of certainty whether a director's conduct may be properly labelled as amounting to conduct of an unfit nature. In considering the matters mentioned in Sched.1, it must be determined whether, on a balance of probabilities, a director's conduct was sufficiently serious to justify his or her disqualification. The courts have emphasised that misconduct must be established at a level which is considered harmful to the public interest, namely where it conveys a clear exploitation of the privileges attributable to the limited liability status of a company. Such exploitation will ordinarily be exhibited following a deliberate or patently reckless or grossly negligent abuse of creditor interests or a persistent failing to abide by provisions of the companies legislation (see, e.g. *Secretary of State for Trade and Industry* v. *Gray* [1995] 1 BCLC 276).

In *Re Sevenoaks Stationers (Retail) Ltd* [1991] Ch 164, the Court of Appeal stated that a disqualification order should only be made where there was conclusive proof of conduct which established that a director's conduct amounted to commercially culpable behaviour of a type constituting a threat to the commercial community. The ability to label a particular course of business malpractice as one equating to commercially culpable behaviour will be a question of fact dependent upon the circumstances of each individual case (see, e.g. *Re Civica Investments Ltd* [1983] BCLC 456).

17.5.3 Commercial misjudgment

Although conduct which is attributable to an act of mere commercial misjudgment or business folly will not normally result in a finding that the conduct was of an unfit nature, commercial misjudgment or ignorance of commercial reality may still be considered relevant to establishing conduct of an unfit nature in circumstances where the consequences attached to the commercial misjudgment are dire and could reasonably have been avoided by, for example, a director seeking or following professional advice. For example, in *Re GSAR Realisations Ltd* [1993] BCLC 409, a director was disqualified under s.6 for, in effect, wrongful trading, i.e. allowing the company to continue to trade in an insolvent state. Here the director completely ignored the recommendations of a report compiled by a firm of accountants commissioned by the company. The report found the company's financial position to be very fragile but nevertheless recommended that the company's bank (the principal creditor) should, in an attempt to save the company, increase the company's overdraft facility. The director chose to disregard the underlying finding of the report, namely that the company's financial position was in a critical state, and foolishly interpreted the bank's decision to increase the company's overdraft facility as being supportive of his own misconceived belief that the report had been incorrect to conclude that the company's financial stability was precarious. Less than a year after the report had been finalised, the principal creditor was obliged to appoint an administrative receiver. In imposing a disqualification order for a period of three years, Ferris J remarked:

> I have reached the conclusion that Mr Smith's [the director's] conduct . . . in relation to the charge of causing the company to trade after it became insolvent does demonstrate his unfitness to be concerned in the management of a company . . . Mr Smith's treatment of creditors . . . and his failure to accept in full the conclusions of the Hacker Young [the accountants] report manifest, in my judgment, a degree of indifference to his duties which constitutes unfitness . . . In taking this line Mr Smith was, in my view, guilty of significantly more than commercial misjudgment. To my mind he was obstinately and unjustifiably backing his own assessment of the company's position and largely ignoring the assessment made by Hacker Young. (at p.422)

Likewise, in *Re Hitco 2000 Ltd* [1995] 2 BCLC 63, the respondent, the sole director of a company, was disqualified under s.6 for a period of two years, following misconduct which portrayed an obvious failure to acquaint himself with the financial affairs of the company. The respondent, who had been ignorant of the company's true financial position, had allowed the company to trade while it had been in an insolvent state. The respondent admitted that he would have failed to understand all the financial information had it been in his possession. In effect, this admission served to provide evidence of the respondent's neglect in allowing the company to conduct its business affairs without employing a person properly qualified in the administration of the company's financial matters.

In respect of determining whether a director's conduct was of a commercially incompetent nature it is important to distinguish commercial incompetence from conduct exhibiting the hallmarks of mere business folly. For the purpose of justifying a finding of unfit conduct, commercial incompetence will be established where a director's standard of behaviour is, in relation to the circumstances of any given case, objectively determined to be of a standard which is significantly below a standard one would reasonably expect to be exhibited by a company director. In calculating the appropriate standard of behaviour against which a director's behaviour should be measured, the court will also take into account a director's level of skill and experience and the nature and type of company in which he held office. Commercial incompetence substantiating a finding of conduct of an unfit nature may be found in a situation where a director of a company abandons his responsibilities and duties to the company by failing to involve himself in the performance of managerial tasks which he would ordinarily be expected to perform. Where, for example, a director's commercial incompetence results in a failure to keep proper accounting records and such a failure conceals the fact that a company was trading in an insolvent state, the consequences of the negligent conduct may be so prejudicial to the interests of corporate creditors to justify the imposition of a disqualification order (see, e.g. *Re DD.J Matthews (Joinery Design) Ltd and Anor* [1988] BCC 513, *Re City Investment Centres Ltd* [1992] BCLC 956, *Re Burnham Marketing Services Ltd* [1993] BCC 518 and *Secretary of State for Trade & Industry* v. *Arif* [1997] 1 BCLC 34). In *Re Park House Properties Ltd* [1997] 2 BCLC 530, Neuberger J observed that:

> As a matter of principle, it appears to me that it cannot be right that a director of a company involved in activities which justify a disqualification order against the director responsible for those activities can escape liability simply by saying that he knew nothing about what was going on. The court must enquire whether in the circumstances the failure to discover what was going on was attributable to ignorance born of a culpable failure to make enquiries or, where inquiries were made, of culpable failure to consider or appreciate the results of those enquiries: if such culpability is established then the court would have to go on to decide whether, in all the circumstances, the culpability was sufficient to justify the conclusion that the conduct of the person concerned was such as to make him unfit to be concerned in the management of a company. (at p.554)

17.5.4 Crown debts

In considering whether a director's conduct was of an unfit nature, the degree of importance to be attached to a company's non-payment of Crown debts has often been the subject of some controversy. The controversy is centred on the issue of whether a company's inability to repay Crown debts should be viewed to be a more or less serious misdemeanour than a company's inability to repay ordinary trade creditors. The principal point of distinction between trade debts and Crown debts is that the Crown is an involuntary creditor of a company, whereas a trade creditor extends credit facilities to a company on a voluntary basis. A Crown debt incorporates debts by way of taxes (for example, VAT) and monies payable to the state in the form of PAYE and national insurance contributions. The non-payment of Crown debts affects the public purse in so far as the failure to discharge Crown debts diminishes the pool of funds available for state expenditure. In *Re Sevenoaks Stationers (Retail) Ltd* [1991] Ch 164, the Court of Appeal emphasised that the non-payment of Crown debts should not be viewed as evidence of any automatic assumption of a director's unfitness to act in the management of a company, but rather the non-payment of Crown debts should be viewed in a like manner to a company's non-payment of ordinary trade creditors. However, the Court of Appeal did provide an exception: the court stated that where a company chose to pay trade creditors who were pressing for the repayment of their debts ahead of passive creditors (the Crown) then in such circumstances the non-payment of the passive creditor should be viewed as a serious form of misconduct (see *Re Structure Concrete Ltd* [2001] BCC 578). (Also see the judgment of Neuberger J in *Re Verby Print for Advertising Ltd* [1998] 2 BCLC 23.) Likewise, the Court of Appeal concluded that a director who had expended corporate funds which were specifically kept back for the purpose of discharging Crown debts should be presumed to have acted in an unfair and culpable manner (see, e.g. *Re Stanford Services Ltd* [1987] BCLC 607 and, more recently, the decision of the Court of Appeal in *Cathie* v. *Secretary of State for Business Innovation and Skills* [2012] EWCA Civ 739).

17.5.5 Conduct in relation to other companies

CDDA 1986, s.6(1)(b) provides that the court shall impose a disqualification order (or the Secretary of State may accept an undertaking, see s.7(2A)) against a director of an insolvent company where:

> . . . his conduct as a director of that company (either taken alone or taken together with his conduct as a director of any other company or companies) makes him unfit to be concerned in the management of a company.

Therefore, in determining whether a director's conduct was unfit in the management of a company (the lead company), the court may take into account the director's conduct in relation to any other company(ies). Prior to the Court of Appeal's decision in *Re County Farm Inns Ltd; Secretary of State* v. *Ivens* [1997] BCC 801, the interpretation of s.6(1)(b) in the context of establishing a finding of unfitness in relation to the director's misconduct of the lead company was such that the misconduct in the affairs of another company had to be of a type which was the same as or similar in nature to the director's misconduct in relation to his or her management of the lead company (see, e.g. *Re Goodwin Warren Control Systems plc* [1993] BCLC 80). However, following the decision in *Re County Farm Inns Ltd; Secretary of State* v. *Ivens,* it is now clear that any impropriety in relation to the conduct of another company may be advanced to support a finding of unfitness in relation to the director's misconduct in the lead company. Indeed, from the wording of s.6(1)(b) no requirement that the conduct in relation to another company was the same or as similar to that alleged in the lead company is to be inferred. Accordingly, very different types of misconduct may be taken into account and such misconduct may be accumulated in calculating whether a director may be deemed unfit to be concerned in the management of a future company. While for the purpose of s.6, the lead company must be insolvent, it is unnecessary, in respect of s.6(2)(b), for the other company(ies) to have been insolvent.

17.5.6 Civil proceedings and human rights

As a contravention of s.6 invokes no form of criminal liability, the proceedings are regulated by the civil law and as such a person's culpability must be established in accordance with the civil law, namely, the balance of probabilities test (see, e.g. *Secretary of State* v. *Deverell* [2000] 2 All ER 365). However, as allegations made in the course of disqualification proceedings may involve very serious insinuations of misconduct, there may be some reluctance on the part of a court to apply a standard of proof based upon evidence which is indicative but not sufficiently conclusive of a director's culpability. However, given the civil nature of the proceedings, it follows that hearsay evidence and findings of primary and secondary fact will be more readily admissible than had the proceedings been dealt with under the criminal law (see, e.g. *Secretary of State for Trade* v. *Ashcroft* [1997] BCC 634, *Secretary of State for Trade* v. *Baker* [1999] 1 BCLC 433 and *Aaron* v. *Secretary of State for BERR* [2009] BCC 375). Further, as s.6 proceedings are of a regulatory as opposed to criminal nature, art.6 of the European Convention on Human Rights (ECHR) will have limited application. The Human Rights Act 1998 gives effect to the rights and freedoms guaranteed under the ECHR. ECHR, art.6(1) provides:

> In the determination of his civil rights and obligations or of any criminal charge against him, everyone is entitled to a fair and public hearing within a reasonable time by an independent and impartial tribunal established by law.

As disqualification cases are of a civil nature they will not ordinarily be within the jurisdiction of art.6(1) (see, e.g. *Secretary of State for Trade and Industry, ex parte McCormick* [1998] BCC 379, *DC, HS and AD* v. *United Kingdom* [2000] BCC 710 and *Re Westminster Property Management Ltd* [2001] BCC 121). However, a director subject to s.6 proceedings is entitled to a fair hearing (see, e.g. *WGS and MSLS* v. *United Kingdom* [2000] BCC 719) and delays in the prosecution of proceedings under CDDA 1986 may constitute a violation of art.6(1) (see, e.g. *EDC* v. *United Kingdom* [1998] BCC 370 and *Davies* v. *United Kingdom* [2005] BCC 401: however, contrast the decisions in *Re Blackspur Group plc (No.3); Secretary of State for Trade and Industry* v. *Eastaway* [2003] BCC 520).

17.6 THE MANDATORY NATURE OF A DISQUALIFICATION ORDER UNDER CDDA, S.6

Although a director's capacity to act in the future management of a company is the essential yardstick to determine whether, in any given instance, a disqualification order should be imposed under CDDA, s.6, nevertheless the imposition of a disqualification order is mandatory where the court concludes that a director's conduct was of an unfit nature. Accordingly, s.6 prohibits any consideration of a director's ability or potential ability to reform his or her past misconduct in respect of their future involvement in the management of an enterprise. Indeed, in *Secretary of State* v. *Gray* [1995] 1 BCLC 276, the Court of Appeal made it clear that, notwithstanding a director's potential to reform his or her past indiscretions, the court was obliged to impose a disqualification order where it was established that the director's past conduct was of an unfit nature. Although extenuating circumstances may influence any decision in relation to whether a director's past conduct reached an appropriate standard of unfitness, a decision whether to impose a disqualification order must not be influenced by considering a director's capacity to reform his or her past activities. Nevertheless, a director's potential to reform past misconduct, portrayed, for example, by reason of his or her success in the management of another company, may be a significant mitigating factor in determining the length of any disqualification order to be imposed (see, e.g. *Re Pamstock Ltd* [1994] 1 BCLC 716).

17.6.1 The duration of a s.6 order

CDDA 1986, s.6(4) provides that the length of a disqualification order/undertaking must be for a minimum of two years and for a maximum period of 15 years. In determining the length of a disqualification period, the court (or the Secretary of State in respect of the undertaking procedure) must consider the extent and seriousness of a director's misconduct. Where a director's misconduct is founded on dishonest conduct, it is logical to assume that the disqualification period will be for a greater duration than had the misconduct been of a reckless or negligent character (see, e.g. *Re Goodwin Warren Control Systems* [1993] BCLC 80). Further, it is to be assumed that where a director holds a senior executive position, or otherwise has a capacity to dictate a company's operations, the extent of his or her culpability (and the duration of any disqualification order) will be greater than where, for example, the director occupies a more minor position in a corporate structure (see, e.g. *Re Peppermint Park Ltd* [1998] BCC 23).

In *Re Sevenoaks Stationers (Retail) Ltd* [1991] Ch 164, the Court of Appeal advanced guidelines to the lower courts in respect of the duration of disqualification orders. However, notwithstanding the potential benefit of such guidance, in reality, the guidelines amounted to little more than commonsense generalisations. They were as follows:

1.   The top bracket of disqualification for a period of over 10 years should be

reserved for particularly serious cases of commercial abuse. Here, this bracket could also include cases where a director had a past record of being made subject to a disqualification order(s).

2. The middle bracket of disqualification for a period between six and 10 years should apply in serious cases.

3. The minimum bracket of between two and five years should be applied where a director was found to be unfit in the management of a company. However, while unfit, the conduct would not be of a sufficiently serious nature to justify disqualification within the first or second brackets.

17.6.2 Mitigation

In considering the length of any disqualification period or, in respect of CDDA 1986, s.17 (discussed below), whether the court should grant leave to a person made subject to a disqualification order, the court/Secretary of State will be permitted to take account of mitigating factors. The significance and effect of a mitigating factor will be dependent upon issues relating to the justice of an individual case. In considering the justice issue, the court or Secretary of State must attempt to balance the respective interests of the defendant against the seriousness of the unfit conduct and its perceived threat to the public interest. The following factors are examples of circumstances that may be considered in mitigation:

- A director's conduct during the actual course of the disqualification process may, in appropriate circumstances, act as a mitigating factor if, for example, such conduct enables the proceedings to be dealt with in a more efficient manner. Accordingly, co-operation with the liquidator and/or admission of responsibility for the alleged acts of misconduct may result in a director escaping a heftier disqualification period than would otherwise have been the case.

- In at least one reported case, namely, *Re Melcast (Wolverhampton) Ltd* [1991] BCLC 288, the age of a director (he was 75 years old) was, of itself, considered to be a mitigating factor. Here the court imposed a more lenient disqualification period than the nature of the director's misconduct would ordinarily have warranted. However, a director's age may be of more relevance as a mitigating factor where the director also suffers from very poor health. Indeed, there would seem little point in imposing a lengthy disqualification order against a person of advancing years who is physically or mentally incapable of repeating his or her past misconduct.

- A director who is to be disqualified may, in terms of the calculation of the disqualification period to be imposed, also expect to be afforded some leniency where, prior to the collapse of the company, he or she sought to expend, or put at risk, his or her own personal funds, in an attempt to secure the company's financial wellbeing. The director's personal losses may be justified as a mitigating factor in the sense that such funds were voluntarily provided in an attempt to aid the company's financial position. Indeed, as a result of a loss of personal funds the court may consider that the director has, to some extent, already been penalised for his or her misconduct of the company's affairs (see, e.g. *Re Pamstock Ltd* [1994] 1 BCLC 716).

- A director may be afforded a more lenient disqualification period where the conduct of the company's affairs was attributable to his or her reliance on the skill and expertise of a professional adviser (see, e.g. *Re Park Properties Ltd* [1997] 2 BCLC 530).

17.6.3   An application for leave to act (CDDA 1986, s.17)

Although a director must be made subject to a disqualification order when he or she is deemed to have acted in an unfit manner in the context of CDDA 1986, s.6, that director may, at any time during the term of the disqualification order, apply for leave to act in the management of a specified company (CDDA 1986, s.17). A specified company cannot be a company in which the disqualified director's management conduct was judged to be of an unfit nature, nor can a specified company be a future company, i.e. one that the director was not already involved in prior to his or her disqualification. The practical effect of a grant of leave is the creation of a modified type of disqualification order, whereby a director is disqualified in a general sense but is nevertheless allowed to continue in the management of another specified company (or companies), in a manner specified by the terms of the order (see, e.g. *Secretary of State for Trade and Industry* v. *Rosenfield* [1999] BCC 413). The justification for the grant of leave is that the director's involvement in the management of the specified enterprise is considered beneficial to the public interest, for example, beneficial in the sense of protecting the interests of the employees and creditors of the specified company.

As the modified order permits a director with a dubious past history in the management of a company(ies) to, in part, escape the consequences of his or her past indiscretions, the modified order must be applied with caution. In deciding whether to grant a director leave to act in the management a specified company, the court must consider whether the grant of leave would result in a potential risk to the public interest. Obviously, when considering a grant of leave the court must ponder the likelihood of a director 're-offending'. The length of the disqualification order will be a relevant consideration in determining whether leave should be granted (see, e.g. *Hease* v. *Secretary of State for Trade and Industry* [2006] BPIR 425, where the period of disqualification was six years and an application under s.17 was refused). The court must be satisfied of a need to make the modified order and in doing so must always bear in mind that the purpose of a disqualification order is to safeguard the public interest.

Where a s.17 order is made, it will normally be granted subject to specific conditions notwithstanding that neither CDDA 1986, s.1 nor s.17 provide the court with a capacity to grant leave subject to such specific conditions. Those specific conditions may include, for example, that the director provides an undertaking that he or she will set up proper financial controls in respect of the company (in which he or she continues in a management capacity), or that the director must appoint another person (approved by the court) to the company's board of directors, or a qualified accountant or auditor (approved by the court). For example, in *Re Gibson Davies Ltd* [1995] BCC 11, Sir Mervyn Davies upheld an appeal by a director against the dismissal of an application for leave under s.17, but did so only on the understanding that the modified order would be made subject to nine conditions. Those conditions specified, *inter alia*, that the director should give an undertaking that he would set up proper financial controls in respect of the company's financial affairs, that he would restrict his own ability to obtain financial benefits from the company and that he would also be responsible for making proper accounting returns to the registrar of companies.

17.6.4   CDDA 1986, s.9A

A court (the Secretary of State in the case of an undertaking, see CDDA 1986, s.9B) is also obliged to impose a mandatory disqualification order against a director of a company following a breach of competition law by the company. The breach must illustrate that the director is unfit to be concerned in the future management of a company. Here, the maximum disqualification period is 15 years.

CHAPTER 18

The company in general meeting

18.1 INTRODUCTION

Historically, the general meeting was perceived as the ultimate source of corporate power. However, in modern society, the general meeting's position of power has declined in the management of corporate affairs. Nevertheless, the general meeting is still, in the exercise of its inherent powers, properly regarded as an essential organ of the body corporate. Although the general meeting's powers are limited, the effect of such powers may carry real influence in the management of a company's affairs. The powers and procedures attached to the general meeting of a company are a subject area of company law that was significantly reformed following the implementation of the Companies Act (CA) 2006. It is also to be noted that the Companies (Shareholders' Rights) Regulations 2009, SI 2009/1632 apply amending Parts 9 and 13 of CA 2006 in relation to issues surrounding the voting procedures and voting rights of shareholders. In part the regulations are applicable generally to all companies but will be relevant especially to traded/public companies. The regulations, which are detailed and at times complex in the context of their insertion into the relevant parts of CA 2006, seek to advance Directive 2007/36/EC, the effect of which seeks to ensure that a shareholder of a traded company may exercise his or her vote effectively at company meetings, even in a situation where the shareholder is a member of a company registered in another Member State.

18.2 THE HISTORICAL DEVELOPMENT OF THE DIVISION OF CORPORATE POWERS

The origins of the registered company may be traced back to the unincorporated partnership businesses of the nineteenth century (see **Chapter 1**). Accordingly, it is not surprising that the power structure of the registered company was originally determined in a manner compatible with the principles derived from partnership law, whereby the collective will of a company's membership, namely the company in general meeting, was the ultimate source of corporate power. To this end, a company's board of directors was appointed merely to carry out the will of the general meeting. Therefore, conflicts between the board and general meeting were ordinarily resolved to the latter's advantage. For example, in *Isle of Wight Rly Co* v. *Tahourdin* (1883) 25 Ch D 320, Cotton LJ emphasised the ultimate dominance of the general meeting as the company's principal power source. Cotton LJ stated:

> … If a shareholder complains of the conduct of the directors while they keep within their powers, the court says to him, 'If you want to alter the management of the affairs of the company go to the general meeting, and if they agree with you they will pass a resolution obliging the directors to alter their course of proceeding'. (at p.330)

The ability of the general meeting to supervise and, if necessary, determine corporate policy, persisted throughout the nineteenth century. However, the growth and expansion of the corporate form inevitably resulted in the general meeting's decline in matters of dictating corporate policy. In expanding companies, share-holders invested in companies for potential profit rather than the capacity to participate in management decisions. In such companies, the attendance, interest and participation in general meetings all declined. This decline was and still is today particularly prevalent in public companies where commercial reality dictates that the administration of corporate policy demands a consolidation of corporate powers into a centralised body of management, namely the board of directors.

18.2.1 Decline in the importance of the general meeting as the principal corporate power base

The decline in the importance of the general meeting as the principal corporate power base was reflected historically in the reduction of the powers afforded to the general meeting by the company's articles of association. In *Automatic Self-Cleansing Filter Syndicate Co* v. *Cuninghame* [1906] 2 Ch 34, the Court of Appeal recognised that, subject to certain powers reserved to the general meeting by statute, a company's articles were decisive to the extent of powers to be exercised by both the board and general meeting; in effect an acceptance of the quasi-contractual effect of the articles in accordance with what is now CA 2006, s.33 (discussed in **Chapter 6**).

However, prior to the adoption of the model articles for CA 1985, the construc-tion of the standard form model articles was the source of some controversy. The 1948 Companies Act Table A, reg.80 (the Table A articles for earlier enactments of the companies legislation dealing with a division of powers were written in a similar vein to reg.80) provided that:

> The business of the company shall be managed by the directors, who may . . . exercise all such powers of the company as are not by the [Companies legislation] or by these regulations, required to be exercised by the company in general meeting, subject, nevertheless … to such regulations being not inconsistent with the aforesaid regulations or provisions, as may be prescribed by the company in general meeting; but no regulation made by the company in general meeting shall invalidate any prior act of the directors which would have been valid if that regulation had not been made.

The wording of reg.80 (and its statutory predecessors) was ambiguous. In *Marshall's Valve Gear Co Ltd* v. *Manning, Wardle & Co Ltd* [1909] 1 Ch 267, Neville J suggested that the general meeting, by the passing of an ordinary resolution, had, in a situation of conflict, an ultimate authority over the board of directors. This interpretation of the reg.80-type provision suggested that the general meeting had an overriding power, by means of an ordinary resolution, to effect a temporary change to the powers afforded to the board of directors. To effect a permanent change to the directors' powers the company would have been obliged to alter its articles (by special resolution). However, in subsequent cases, the courts were unwilling to accept that in accordance with reg.80, the general meeting had an absolute right to interfere in the board's management powers by the means of passing an ordinary resolution (see, e.g. *Quinn & Axtens* v. *Salmon* [1909] 1 Ch 311, *John Shaw & Sons (Salford) Ltd* v. *Shaw* [1935] 2 KB 113, *Scott* v. *Scott* [1943] 1 All ER 582 and *Gramophone and Typewriter Ltd* v. *Stanley* [1908] 2 KB 89). A more recent example is provided by *Breckland Group Holdings Ltd* v. *London and Suffolk Properties* [1989] BCLC 100. Here a company (C) had two corporate members: company A (the majority shareholder) and company B. The board of C included two directors appointed by A and one director appointed by B. The corporate members agreed by means of a formal shareholders' agreement that should C wish to commence any form of litigation the matter would first require the approval of one director from both A and B. In contravention of the agreement, C commenced litigation without the support of B (the minority shareholder). B moved to restrain the action from being commenced in C's name. In denying that A, as the majority shareholder, had a right to overturn the powers properly vested in the board of C, the court refused to accept that had a general meeting of C been convened to 'rubber stamp' by ordinary resolution A's decision to commence litigation, the general meeting's authorisation would have been capable of overturning the powers properly vested in the board. The court restrained proceedings until a properly held board meeting could determine whether C should commence litigation.

In CA 1985 Table A articles, any surviving confusion that flowed from the construction of the 1948 Table A articles as to the extent of the general meeting's power to override the powers of the board of directors was finally resolved. CA 1985 Table A, reg.70 stated that:

> Subject to the provisions of the Act, the memorandum and the articles and to any directions given by special resolution, the business of the company shall be managed by the directors who may exercise all the powers of the company. No alteration of the memorandum or articles and no such direction shall invalidate any prior act of the directors which would have been valid if that alteration had not been made or that direction had not been given.

Accordingly, the general meeting was afforded a power to effect a temporary change in directors' powers, albeit that the temporary change of power had to be exercised by means of a special resolution.

18.2.2 The general meetings management powers under the articles and CA 2006

Ordinarily, the articles of association of a company will be drafted in a manner whereby they confer the vast bulk of the powers of management to the company's directors. In relation to the ability of the general meeting to intervene to override an exercise of the board of directors' powers, CA 2006 model articles for both a public and private company (reg.4) (affording no change to the position under CA 1985, Table A) provide that:

1. The members may, by special resolution, direct the directors to take, or refrain from taking, specified action.
2. No such special resolution invalidates anything which the directors have done before the passing of the resolution.

In addition to the limited power afforded to the general meeting under reg.4, other powers provided to the general meeting include:

1. A power to elect directors (in relation to a public company incorporated under CA 2006, see, reg.20, for a private company incorporated under CA 2006, see, reg.17).
2. A power to authorise the directors (by ordinary resolution) to capitalise (if the directors so decide) any profits of the company (in relation to a public company incorporated under CA 2006, see, reg.78, for a private company incorporated under CA 2006, see, reg.36).
3. The declaration of dividends up to an amount recommended by the directors (in relation to a public company incorporated under CA 2006, see, reg.23, for a private company incorporated under CA 2006, see, reg.30).
4. Without prejudice to the rights attached to any existing share, the company may issue shares with such rights or restrictions as may be determined by ordinary resolution (in relation to a public company incorporated under CA 2006, see reg.43, for a private company incorporated under CA 2006, see reg.22).

The companies legislation also reserves certain exclusive powers of management to the general meeting. The powers reserved are few, but are nevertheless substantive, being concerned with the constitutional functioning of the company – for example, the power to alter the terms of the company's articles by special resolution and a right to remove a director from office by ordinary resolution. This latter power is of some significance because, where members of a company disagree with the directors' management policy and the members command sufficient support, they may seek to alter the direction of management policy by either threatening the directors with dismissal or, if that tactic fails, actually enforcing the power of removal.

18.3 THE DUTY OF THE GENERAL MEETING TO ACT FOR THE BENEFIT OF THE COMPANY

In exercising its limited powers of management, the general meeting must, in a manner akin to the company's directors, apply its powers in, for example, passing or declining resolutions, for the benefit of the company as a whole. In any given situation the test to determine whether the general meeting acted for the benefit of the company as a whole is dominated by an objective consideration of whether the general meeting's powers were exercised for a proper purpose. However, the interpretation of the test may be clouded in some confusion. This confusion was most evident in *Clemens* v. *Clemens Bros Ltd* [1976] 2 All ER 268. Here, a small domestic type company, Clemens Bros Ltd (C), had a share capital divided between Miss Clemens (M) and her niece (N). M held 55 per cent of the shares and N the remaining 45 per cent. M was one of five directors; the other four directors were not shareholders in the company. The board of directors proposed a new share issue; the substance of the issue was to create an employee share scheme and also to allow the four non-shareholding directors to hold a small minority of the company's shares. The effect of the new share issue would have been to reduce M's shareholding interest in C to below 50 per cent; N's holding would have been reduced to below 25 per cent. M exercised her voting control in a general meeting to pass the new share issue. N objected on the basis that following the new share issue, the income which she derived from dividend payments would be reduced and further, N's new holding would have resulted in the loss of her negative control in C, because she would have been unable to prevent (had she so wished) the passing of a special resolution. The loss of N's negative control was an advantage to M because prior to the new share issue, N and M had experienced a very poor working relationship.

In finding in favour of N's minority action, Foster J held that M's majority voting control should not have been exercised without questioning whether it had been exercised for the benefit of the company as a whole. Foster J considered that M's motive in assenting to the resolution was primarily aimed at removing N's voting influence in the company and not by a desire to benefit the company's employees and four non-voting directors. Therefore, the learned judge concluded that M had acted not for the benefit of the company as a whole but for her own selfish interests. However, it is difficult to decipher the precise principle of law on which the interpretation of the test applied to determine the 'benefit of the company as a whole' was reached. Foster J was content to leave the reasoning for his decision wrapped up in a number of principles, or, as he put it:

> I think that one thing which emerges from the case to which I have referred is that in such a case as the present, Miss Clemens is not entitled to exercise her majority vote in whatever way she pleases. The difficulty is in finding a principle, and obviously expressions such as 'bona fide for the benefit of the company as a whole', 'fraud on a minority' and 'oppressive' do not assist in formulating a principle. (at p.282)

The decision taken in *Clemens* in relation to the 'the benefit of the company as a whole' is difficult to rationalise in terms of anything other than having been decided on purely equitable considerations to the benefit of the niece. However, was justice really served? Was Miss Clemens' act a purely selfish one? If one considers the effect of the new share issue in an objective sense, then had the issue been allowed, M would have lost her majority control in the company. In addition, M's income from dividend payments would also have been reduced. Further, the benefit of the share issue could have benefited the company as a whole in terms of benefiting company employees and the non-shareholding directors. Indeed, in an objective sense, the contention that M acted for her own selfish interests may have been somewhat overstated.

In addition to considering the interests of minority shareholders, a power reserved to the general meeting must not be used where its effect would be to defraud or seriously prejudice creditors (by analogy, in considering the interests of the company as a whole, directors of a company may be obliged to consider the interests of creditors). For example, in *Re Halt Garage* [1982] 3 All ER 1016, the court sought to determine whether a company's membership, which comprised a husband and wife team (both held directorships in the company) had, in authorising remuneration payments to themselves as directors, awarded payments which were in reality gratuitous distributions out of capital dressed up as remuneration (discussed in **Chapter 10**). The company (which had been put into liquidation) sought (through its liquidator) the return of remuneration payments over a period of three years. In determining the matter, the court was called upon to consider what the true nature of the payments had been, in terms of the genuineness and honesty of the transactions, and in doing so reached the conclusion that while there was no evidence that the husband's level of takings had been excessive or unreasonable, the level of takings paid to the wife had been unreasonably high. The wife had ceased to be active in the employment of the company and therefore was not entitled to remuneration during the period to which the complaint related. Although the company's articles included a power to award remuneration for the mere assumption of the office of director, Oliver J opined that the awards made to the wife were so out of proportion to the value attributed to her holding office that the court was justified in treating them not as genuine payments of remuneration but, rather, as dressed-up dividends out of capital. The payments to the wife had been invalidly authorised by the general meeting.

18.4 THE GENERAL MEETING'S ABILITY TO RATIFY AN IRREGULAR ACT OF THE DIRECTORS

Where a company director commits a breach of duty or exceeds his or her authority in exercising a management power, the irregular act will, in most instances, be voidable. The general meeting may ratify the irregular act by an ordinary resolution (although the culpable director, *qua* member, will not be allowed to vote on the resolution – discussed in **Chapter 15**). However, prior to a purported ratification by the general meeting, an irregular act may be challenged by a minority shareholder(s) (i.e. giving rise to a derivative action – discussed in **Chapter 19**). The ratification of an irregular act could also be challenged in circumstances where the general meeting's ratification was deemed not to have been for the benefit of the company as a whole, as evidenced, for example, in the case of *Re Halt Garage* (discussed above).

Although directors are not permitted to exercise powers which, by the terms of a company's articles, are vested in the general meeting, should such a usurpation of a power occur, the general meeting may nevertheless ratify the abuse of power by ordinary resolution, regardless of the fact that the power use would otherwise have required a special resolution (see, e.g. *Grant* v. *United Kingdom Switchback Railways Co* (1888) 40 Ch D 135). While in such a case the general meeting's power to ratify the abuse of power by ordinary resolution would appear contradictory to the manner in which the general meeting could otherwise have exercised the power, in reality, the power to ratify affects the approval of a specific unauthorised act, as opposed to an attempt to usurp the terms of the company's articles; ratification does not confer a future power on the directors to usurp the power use in question, whereas an alteration of the articles would have a permanent effect in relation to the power use.

However, if an ordinary resolution of the general meeting purports to ratify an irregular act and the nature and type of act in question contravene the terms of a company's articles, then in such a case the general meeting's attempted ratification will be invalid. For example, in *Boschoek Proprietary Co Ltd* v. *Fuke* [1906] 1 Ch 148, the directors of a company appointed a managing director at a level of remuneration in excess of the amount prescribed in the company's articles and also in contravention of a share qualification clause. The appointment was purportedly ratified by the general meeting. The court concluded that the general meeting could not, of itself, alter the terms of the appointment in contravention of the articles and as such the purported ratification was invalid. Until and unless altered, the articles bound the membership and the board of directors.

18.5   TYPES OF GENERAL MEETING

18.5.1   The annual general meeting (AGM)

Prior to the introduction of CA 2006 and except in a situation where a private company resolved to dispense with the holding of an annual general meeting (AGM), the Companies Act 1985 provided that a company was required to hold an AGM once every calendar year with no more than 15 months elapsing between each AGM. Following the introduction of CA 2006, the position is now changed for private companies, via the introduction of a prescribed default regime. The effect of this regime is that unless there is a contrary intention within a private company's articles, a private company is no longer required to hold an AGM. However, the

AGM requirement is retained for public companies. Every public company must hold a general meeting as its AGM in each period of six months beginning with the day following its accounting reference date (CA 2006, s.336(1)). In accordance with CA 2006, s.337, a notice calling an AGM of a public company must state that the meeting is to be held as an AGM. If all the members entitled to attend and vote at the meeting agree, the notice required for the AGM may be shorter than that specified by CA 2006, s.307(2) (i.e. 21 days' notice) or shorter than any period specified in the company's articles. The matters dealt with at a company's AGM will be dependent upon the business raised by the board or individual members of the company, although where the holding of an AGM is applicable, prescribed procedural tasks will be addressed. The procedural tasks will include the appointment of an auditor and the adoption of accounts, the receipt of the directors' report, the election of directors and, in appropriate circumstances, the approval of directors' remuneration.

CA 2006, s.338 provides that the members of a public company may require the company to give notice of any proposed resolution (a motion) which may properly be moved and is intended to be moved at the AGM. The request from members must be received by the company not later than:

(a) six weeks before the AGM to which the requests relate; or
(b) if later, the time at which notice is given of that meeting.

A company is required to give notice of a proposed resolution (motion) if it has received requests from either:

1. members representing at least 5 per cent of the total voting rights of all the members who have a right to vote on the resolution at the AGM to which the requests relate (excluding any voting rights attached to any shares in the company held as treasury shares); or
2. at least 100 members who have a right to vote on the resolution at the AGM to which the requests relate and hold shares in the company on which there has been paid up an average sum, per member, of at least £100.

A resolution may properly be moved at an AGM unless:

(a) it would, if passed, be ineffective (whether by reason of inconsistency with any enactment or the company's constitution or otherwise);
(b) it is defamatory of any person; or
(c) it is frivolous or vexatious.

18.5.2 A 'general meeting'

A general meeting other than an AGM is simply referred to by CA 2006 as a 'general meeting' (previously known as an 'extraordinary general meeting' (EGM)). A general meeting may be convened by a company at the will of the company's board of directors. The minimum period of notice for a general meeting to be called by the directors is 14 days. Alternatively, the board may be required to convene a general meeting where, under CA 2006, s.303 (as amended by reg.4 of the Companies (Shareholders' Rights) Regulations 2009, SI 2009/1632), they are requisitioned to do so by members of the company holding not less than 5 per cent of the company's paid-up share capital; here the share capital must carry voting rights. In the case of a company not having a share capital, a general meeting may be requisitioned by members who, together, represent 5 per cent or more of the total voting rights of members entitled to vote.

Where, under CA 2006, s.303, the directors of a company are requisitioned to call a meeting, they must do so, i.e. arrange notice of the meeting, within 21 days of receiving the requisition (see, e.g. *Re Windward Islands (Enterprises Ltd)* (1988) 4 BCC 158). The actual meeting must be called no more than 28 days after the notice to convene the meeting is sent out. By CA 2006, s.305, where, after receiving the requisition, the directors fail to give notice of the meeting within the 21-day period, those seeking the requisition, or any of them representing more than one-half of the total voting rights of all of them, may convene the meeting, providing that the meeting is held before the end of three months after the date on which the directors become subject to the requirement to call the meeting. Any reasonable expenses incurred by the members who requested the meeting must be reimbursed by the company. Any sum reimbursed by the company may be taken out of any sums due (or to become due) from the company to its directors (who were in default) in connection with the payment of fees or other remuneration in respect of the services of those directors. It is to be noted that a purported general meeting of a company and the resolutions passed at the meeting will be invalid where the required notice period is not complied with other than where there is an implied agreement by the shareholders to treat the resolutions passed as valid, i.e. in accordance with the *Duomatic* principle (discussed below – see the decision of the Court of Appeal in *Schofield* v. *Schofield* [2011] EWCA Civ 154).

18.5.3   General meetings of traded companies

A traded company is defined as a company having voting shares, the shares of which are admitted to trading on a regulated market in an EEA state (see CA 2006, s.360C).

CA 2006, s.307A (inserted by Companies (Shareholders' Rights) Regulations 2009, reg.9) requires meetings of traded companies (other than a meeting to decide whether action should be taken to frustrate a takeover) to be called with at least 21 days' notice other than where the articles of the company prescribe a greater period of notice than the said 21 days. The content of the notice is prescribed by s.311(3) (inserted by the Companies (Shareholders' Rights) Regulations 2009, reg.10) and the publication of material relevant to the meeting must be placed on the company's website in advance of the meeting (see CA 2006, s.311A, inserted by the Companies (Shareholders' Rights) Regulations 2009, reg.10). However, the minimum

21-day notice period will not apply in relation to a meeting where all of the following three conditions are met:

- the meeting is not an AGM;
- where the company offers the facility for all members holding voting shares and entitled to vote, to vote by electronic means providing there is a facility, offered by the company and accessible to all such members to appoint a proxy by means of a website; and
- where, at the previous AGM, a special resolution was passed reducing the period of notice for general meetings to 14 days or where at another general meeting subsequent to the previous AGM, a special resolution was passed reducing the period of notice for general meetings to at least 14 days.

In all three cases listed above, the meeting may be held following the giving of at least 14 days' notice (unless the articles of the company require a greater period of notice than 14 days). Adjourned meetings may be called at shorter notice, but where a meeting is adjourned for lack of a quorum; the meeting must be held at least 10 days after the original meeting and must not include any new business (see CA 2006, s.307A).

18.5.4 Electronic meetings and voting

In accordance with CA 2006, s.360A (introduced by reg.8 of the Companies (Shareholders' Rights) Regulations 2009, SI 2009/1632), a company meeting may be held and conducted in a manner whereby persons who are not present together at the same place may by electronic means, attend and speak and vote at the meeting. In the case of a traded company, the use of electronic means for the purpose of enabling members to participate in a general meeting may be made subject only to such requirements and restrictions as are necessary to ensure the identification of those taking part and the security of the electronic communication. Such measures must be proportionate to the achievement of those objectives.

18.6 FORMAL REQUIREMENTS FOR MEETINGS

18.6.1 The quorum requirement

CA 2006, s.318 states that unless a company's articles provide otherwise, two members (or proxies) must be present at a general meeting in order to satisfy the quorum requirement. In the case of single-member companies, one member present in person or by proxy will constitute a quorum. Where, at a general meeting, the quorum requirement is not satisfied, the meeting will be null and void, other than in a situation where the court employs its powers under CA 2006, s.306 (discussed below). (In relation to the formal requirements for meetings, etc., reference should be made to the model set of articles in place at the time of the company's incorporation – in relation to a public company incorporated under CA 2006, see regs.28–33, for a private company incorporated under CA 2006, see regs.37–41.)

18.6.2 The notice requirement

CA 2006, s.308 provides that notice of an intention to call a general meeting of a company must be given in hard copy form and, either in electronic form or by means of a website. Notice of a general meeting of a company must state the time and date of the meeting, and the place of the meeting together with the general nature of the business to be dealt with at the meeting (CA 2006, s.311). Notice of a general meeting must be sent to every member of the company and every director. A previous requirement (contained in CA 1985, s.387), that notice of a general meeting had to be given to the company's auditor, is no longer present within CA 2006. The reference to members includes any person who is entitled to hold a share in consequence of the death or bankruptcy of a member, i.e. providing the company has been notified of their entitlement. In the case of electronic or website communication, notice may be given partly by one such means and partly by another. Where notice is to be posted on a website, notice is not validly given by a company unless, as of the date of notifying a member of the presence of the notice on the website, the notification states that it concerns notice of a company meeting, specifying the place, date and time of the meeting. In the case of a public company, the notification must also state whether the meeting will be an AGM. The notice must be available on the website throughout the period beginning with the date of the notification and ending with the conclusion of the meeting (CA 2006, s.309).

In accordance with CA 2006, s.307, a general meeting (i.e. other than an AGM) of a private or public company (but not an adjourned meeting) must be called by notice of at least 14 days. A provision in a company's articles which seeks to increase the prescribed notice period will be valid although where a provision in the articles declares a shorter time period, the relevant provision will be deemed void, unless, in relation to the proposed meeting, it is agreed to by the holders of 90 per cent of the nominal value of the shares (90 per cent of the said members must have been entitled to attend and vote at the meeting).

Although an accidental failure on the part of a company to give notice to a member will rarely invalidate a meeting (see CA 2006, s.313), a deliberate act or omission on the part of a company that prevents a member from receiving proper and adequate notice of the meeting will render the meeting invalid (see, e.g. *Royal Mutual Benefit Building Society* v. *Sharman* [1963] 1 WLR 581).

18.6.3 Special notice

Where a provision of the companies legislation expressly stipulates a requirement to provide special notice of an intention to pass a resolution (e.g. the removal of a director or auditor), CA 2006, s.312 provides that the motion, if passed, will not be effective as a resolution if its proposers failed to give at least 28 days' notice to the company, before the date of the meeting at which the resolution was moved. On receiving notice, a company must, where practicable, also provide its membership with 28 days' notice of the proposed resolution and must do so at the same time that it gives notice of the meeting at which the resolution is to be heard. Where this is not practicable, the company must give its members at least 14 days' notice before the meeting by way of an advertisement in a newspaper having an appropriate circulation, or in any other manner allowed by the company's articles.

18.6.4 Members' statements

A company may be obliged to circulate to its membership a statement (of not more than 1,000 words) with respect to the content of a proposed motion to be dealt with at a general meeting (CA 2006, s.314). The company is obliged to circulate a statement, providing the request for the issue of the statement is received by the company at least one week before the meeting to which it relates and providing the request is in accordance with s.314(2), from:

(a)   members representing at least 5% of the total voting rights of all the members who have a relevant right to vote (excluding any voting rights attached to any shares in the company held as treasury shares); or

(b)   at least 100 members who have a relevant right to vote and hold shares in the company on which there has been paid up an average sum, per member, of at least £100.

Where a company is required to circulate a statement (under s.314) it must, in accordance with CA 2006, s.315, send a copy of the statement to each member of the company entitled to receive notice of the meeting. It must do so at the same time as, or as soon as reasonably practicable after, it has given notice of the meeting. In the event of non-compliance with s.315, an offence is committed by every officer of the company in default. Here, an officer guilty of the offence is liable, on conviction on indictment, to a fine and on summary conviction, to a fine not exceeding the statutory maximum.

By way of an exception to s.315, CA 2006, s.317 provides that a company is not required to circulate a members' statement if, on an application by the company or another person who claims to be aggrieved, the court is satisfied that the rights conferred by s.314 and s.315 are being abused. In such a case the court may order the members who requested the circulation of the statement to pay the whole or part of the company's costs.

18.6.5 Expenses of circulating members' statement

The expense involved in complying with CA 2006, s.315 need not be incurred by the members who requested the circulation of the statement if:

(a)   the meeting to which the request relates is an AGM of a public company; and

(b)   the requests that are sufficient to require the company to circulate the statement are received before the end of the financial year preceding the meeting.

Otherwise:

(a)   the expense of complying with s.315 must be paid for by the members who requested the circulation of the statement unless the company resolves otherwise; and

(b)   unless the company has previously so resolved, it is not bound to comply with s.315 unless a sum reasonably sufficient to meet its expenses is deposited with or tendered to it, not later than one week before the meeting.

18.6.6   Circulars

When giving notice of a general meeting, a company may issue circulars. The usual purpose of a circular is to inform the membership of the views of the company's board of directors. Although it is possible for dissentient members to issue circulars (e.g. to explain an opposing view to the one taken by the board), the expense of doing so may prove prohibitive. As a company's board is authorised to represent the company's interests, the expense of issuing circulars by the board may be met from the company's funds. However, the board of directors must not issue information for the purpose of personal gain or advantage, nor must the purpose of the circular be to paint a false and misleading picture of a company's affairs. In *CAS (Nominees) Ltd* v. *Nottingham Forest FC plc* [2002] BCC 145, Hart J observed that:

> A circular to shareholders must give a fair, candid, and reasonably full explanation of the purpose for which the meeting is called.

Where, in issuing a circular, a company misrepresents a particular state of affairs and a resolution favoured by those responsible for the misleading circular is passed at the meeting, the resolution may be set aside. The misrepresentation may take the form of an omission to provide accurate information.

18.7   THE COURT'S DISCRETION TO CALL MEETINGS

In accordance with CA 2006, s.306 (previously CA 1985, s.371), if it is impracticable to call or conduct a meeting of a company by a manner prescribed by either the Companies Act or the company's articles, or a shareholders' agreement, the court may, on an application from a director or a member of the company otherwise entitled to attend and vote at the meeting, order a meeting to be called and provide appropriate relief in a manner to be prescribed by the court. Section 306 will be invoked rarely and ordinarily by a majority shareholder in circumstances where a minority shareholder purports to employ quorum tactics to prevent the majority shareholder from exercising the voting rights attached to his or her shares.

Section 306 is a procedural provision and is not designed to affect substantive voting rights or class rights or interfere with the proper constitutional functioning of a company (see, e.g. *Monnington* v. *Easier plc* [2006] 2 BCLC 283). Neither may the provision be used to shift the balance of power between shareholders in circumstances where there is an agreement to share power equally or where a potential deadlock was a matter that must be taken to have been expressly or impliedly foreseen as being relevant for the protection of each of the parties (see, e.g. the decision of the Court of Appeal in *Ross* v. *Telford* [1997] BCC 945, *Harman* v. *BML Group Ltd* [1994] 1 WLR 893 and *Alvona Developments Ltd* v. *The Manhattan Loft Corporation (AC) Ltd* [2006] BCC 119). Further, in deciding whether to grant relief the court will consider other options available to the parties, for example, the right of a minority shareholder to petition under CA 2006, s.994.

An example of the application of the provision is to be found in the case of *Re Opera Photographic* [1989] 5 BCC 601. Here the court directed a meeting to be held to overcome a quorum requirement with the purpose of enabling a resolution to be passed to dismiss a director of the company. The director against which the dismissal was sought had refused to attend a convened meeting of the members (there were only two members). Here, the quorum requirement was prevented from being used as a device to curb the implementation of a statutory power, namely, the ability of the general meeting to pass an ordinary resolution to remove a director from office. A further example of the application of the provision is found in *Union Music Ltd and Anor* v. *Watson and Anor* [2004] BCC 37. Here, the Court of Appeal accepted that CA 1985, s.371 (now CA 2006, s.306) did not permit the court to break a deadlock between two equal shareholders. However, in *Union Music*, the shareholdings were not equal. The issued share capital of the company was held by two shareholders, one holding 49 per cent and the other 51 per cent. Both the shareholders were directors of the company. Although a shareholders' agreement included a clause which provided that 'the company could not without the prior consent of both shareholders hold any meeting or transact any business at such a meeting unless there were present duly authorised representatives or proxies for each shareholder', the court considered that the shareholders' agreement could not be interpreted or designed to ensure that power between the two parties was shared equally. Therefore, the shareholders' agreement could not prevent the court from making an order under s.371 in circumstances where the order was necessary to allow the company to manage its affairs in an effective and proper manner: in this instance, to allow the majority shareholder to remove or appoint a director in accordance with the majority voting power (see also, *Vectone Entertainment Holding Ltd* v. *South Entertainment Ltd* [2004] BCLC 224).

18.8 TYPES OF RESOLUTION

Other than in the case of an informal resolution (discussed below), CA 2006, s.281 specifies that, for a private company, a resolution must be passed as a written resolution or at a meeting of the members, whereas, for a public company a resolution must be passed at a meeting of its members. It should be noted that a clause within a company's articles will be invalid where it purports to alter a resolution requirement provided for by the companies legislation, i.e., in respect of the requisite majority required to pass the resolution in question.

18.8.1 The ordinary resolution

An ordinary resolution is one passed by a simple majority, namely a majority in excess of 50 per cent of the members who are present (or present by proxy) and entitled to attend and vote at a company meeting. Unless the companies legislation or articles deem otherwise, resolutions passed by a company in general meeting will be by means of an ordinary resolution (CA 2006, s.282).

18.8.2 The special resolution

In some instances, the companies legislation or the terms of a company's articles will specify that a resolution may only be passed by not less than a 75 per cent majority of those members present (or present by proxy) and entitled to attend and vote at a company meeting. This type of resolution is a special resolution. Where a resolution is passed at a meeting, the resolution is not a special resolution unless the notice of the meeting included the text of the resolution and specified the intention to propose the resolution as a special resolution (CA 2006, s.283).

It is to be noted that prior to CA 2006, a form of resolution referred to as an extraordinary resolution was also in use. An extraordinary resolution was required in specific instances, for example, to commence a voluntary winding up of a company or to pass a resolution of a class of members where the company proposed to vary the rights of the class. As with a special resolution, an extraordinary resolution would be passed by a 75 per cent majority of those members entitled to attend and vote at a company meeting (CA 1985, s.378(1)). In reality, the effect of an extraordinary resolution was the same as the effect of a special resolution and, as such, its removal from CA 2006 as a defined type of resolution should be no specific consequence.

18.8.3 The written resolution

In the case of private companies, CA 2006, s.288 provides that the passing of a resolution in general meeting or at a separate meeting of a specific class of shareholders may be achieved by means of a written resolution (i.e. it is not necessary to call a formal meeting – the resolution may be passed in writing – the written consent of the requisite majority). The directors or members of the company may instigate the written resolution procedure. Any resolution may properly be moved as a written resolution unless, if passed, it would be ineffective, be defamatory of any person, or it is frivolous or vexatious. Where the members require the company to circulate a motion to pass a written resolution they may also compel the company to circulate a statement of not more than 1,000 words appertaining to the subject matter of the resolution. A company is required to circulate the motion and any accompanying statement if it receives requests to do so from members representing not less than 5 per cent of the total voting rights (or such lower percentage as is specified by the company's articles). Where the directors wish to instigate the written resolution procedure, the company must send or submit a copy of the motion to every member who would have been entitled to vote on the resolution on the circulation date of the motion. In relation to the circulation of any proposed written resolution, the resolution will lapse if it is not passed before the end of the period specified for this purpose in the company's articles, or if no period is specified, the period of 28 days beginning with the circulation date.

The written resolution takes effect as if agreed by the company in a general meeting or by a meeting of the relevant class of members of the company. A written resolution may be passed by the same majority that would be required had the resolution been passed at a formal meeting, although a company may (in the case of a written resolution) by the terms of its articles, adopt a stricter requirement in terms of the required majority. The revised written resolution procedure contained in CA 2006 is a significant change to the position represented under CA 1985: in accordance with CA 1985, s.381A, a written resolution could only be passed where all the members of the company who, as of the date of the resolution would have been entitled to attend and vote at a general meeting of the company, agreed (in writing) to the terms of the resolution.

It should be noted that a written resolution may be invoked to pass any type of resolution other than the exceptions stipulated by CA 2006, s.288(2). The exceptions stipulated by CA 2006, s.288, are as follows:

(a) a resolution under CA 2006, s.168 removing a director before the expiration of his or her period of office;

(b) a resolution under CA 2006, s.510 removing an auditor before the expiration of his or her term of office.

Further, in accordance with CA 2006, s.300, a provision in the articles of a private company will be void where its effect would be to deny a company the ability to propose and pass a written resolution in accordance with a provision of CA 2006 (other than the exceptions noted above).

18.8.4 The informal resolution at common law

Although CA 2006, s.288 requires an informal resolution to be in writing, the common law makes no such demand. An informal resolution which is not in writing may be passed and have the same effect as a formal resolution in circumstances where it is passed by all the members of the company who would have been entitled to vote on the resolution had it been considered at a formal meeting. This common law principle is often referred to as the *Re Duomatic* principle (the principle is taken from the case of that name, *Re Duomatic* [1969] 2 Ch 365, although in reality the origins of the principle pre-date *Re Duomatic* – see, e.g. the decision of the Court of Appeal in *Re Express Engineering Works Ltd* [1920] 1 Ch 466). The *Duomatic* case concerned the validity of payments made for the personal benefit of a company's directors. In relation to those payments no resolution had been passed authorising the directors to receive remuneration, nor were they entitled to remuneration under the company's articles. On the liquidator's application for the repayment of the payments made to the directors, Buckley J held that some of the payments were to be treated as properly authorised because they were made with the full knowledge and consent of all the holders of voting shares in the company at the relevant times. Buckley J formulated the following principle:

> ... I proceed upon the basis that where it can be shown that all shareholders who have a right to attend and vote at a general meeting of the company assent to some matter which a general meeting of the company could carry into effect, that assent is as binding as a resolution in general meeting would be. (at p.373)

Indeed, this common law principle is now recognised by CA 2006, s.281(4) (see, e.g. *Re Oceanrose Investments Ltd* [2009] Bus LR 947).

Given the nature of an informal resolution, it would appear unlikely (the legislation is silent on the matter) that any specified notice requirement of an intention to pass an informal resolution must, as with a formal resolution (or impliedly with a written resolution), be sent to all members of the company. An informal resolution is valid as if the resolution had been passed in a general meeting, irrespective of whether the informal resolution approves a matter that would ordinarily have required a vote from either a simple or a 75 per cent majority vote. For example, in *Cane* v. *Jones* [1980] 1 WLR 1451, the court approved the alteration of a company's articles by the unanimous (but informal) agreement of the company's voting members. The flexibility of the common law approach (the *Re Duomatic* principle) allows members of a company to pass an informal resolution or reach an agreement to waive a formality required by the company's constitution or by law (see, e.g. *Re Bailey, Hay & Co Ltd* [1971] 3 All ER 693, *Re Home Treat Ltd* [1991] BCC 165, *Atlas Wright (Europe) Ltd* v. *Wright and Anor* [1999] BCC 163 and *Euro Brokers Holdings Ltd* v. *Monecor (London) Ltd* [2003] BCC 573). However, the principle will have no application where an informal resolution is passed by the members of an insolvent company (here the creditors' interests override the interests of the shareholders) or where the effect of the resolution is to bring about the company's insolvency (see, e.g. *Lexi Holdings* v. *Luqman* [2009] BCC 716). In addition, the principle will only apply in relation to agreements between the registered shareholders of a company, therefore the principle may not, for example, be relied upon by a beneficial owner of shares. As such, a person who is not listed on the register of members will not be able to rely on the *Re Duomatic* principle (see, e.g. *Domoney* v. *Godinho* [2004] BCLC 15).

18.8.5   Effective operation of the *Re Duomatic* principle

It should be stressed that it is imperative to the effective operation of the *Re Duomatic* principle that the voting members of the company unanimously agree to the matter that is sought to be made subject to the principle. For example, in *Schofield* v. *Schofield* [2011] 2 BCLC 319, the Court of Appeal held that the *Re Duomatic* principle was not applicable in order to treat as valid and effective a purported general meeting (held at short notice and contrary to CA 2006, s.307) at which a director (L) and holder of 0.1 per cent of the company's shares was removed from office. While L attended the meeting, he did so on the basis that it was an informal meeting to discuss a proposed later formal meeting at which a resolution for his removal had been listed as an agenda item. L never sought to treat the meeting that took place as a valid and effective general meeting. The Court of Appeal found that, while L could have agreed to the validity of the meeting expressly or by implication, verbally or by conduct, either at the time the meeting took place or even at a later date, he had never done so. The court held that there was no unqualified, objective agreement by L, *qua* shareholder, in relation to the validity of the purported general meeting. In relation to the necessity to determine the matter on the basis of an objective assessment of L's intentions, the Court of Appeal approved the following statement taken from the judgment of Newey J in *Rolfe* v. *Rolfe* [2010] EWCH 244 (Ch), namely:

> … I do not accept that a shareholder's mere internal decision can of itself constitute assent for Duomatic purposes. I was not referred to any authority in which it had been decided that a mere internal decision would suffice. Further, for a mere internal decision, unaccompanied by outward manifestation or acquiescence, to be enough would, as it seems to me, give rise to unacceptable uncertainty and, potentially, provide opportunities for abuse. A company may change hands or enter into an insolvency procedure; in either event, it is desirable that past decisions should be objectively verifiable. In my judgment, there must be material from which an observer could discern or (as in the case of acquiescence) infer assent. The law applies an objective test in other contexts: for example, when determining whether a contract has been formed. An objective approach must, I think, also have a role with the Duomatic principle.

18.8.6   Operation of the *Re Duomatic* principle by acquiescence

In relation to operation of the *Re Duomatic* principle by acquiescence, in *Re Home Treat Ltd* [1991] BCC 165, Harman J suggested that the informal consent of the membership of a company could be found in the negative; that is in a situation where the members of the company did not positively seek to oppose a proposed course of action. The learned judge opined:

> … acquiescence by shareholders with knowledge of the matter is as good as actual consent. (at p.168)

However, if consent by acquiescence is acceptable it must only suffice where there is, on the part of all the shareholders, actual knowledge of the nature, extent and content of the proposed informal motion or agreement and where there is no evidence of dissent. This is apparent from the judgment of Hoffmann LJ in *Re D'Jan of London Ltd* [1994] 1 BCLC 561. Here his Lordship observed (at 563–4) that the *Re Duomatic* principle:

> requires that the shareholders should have, whether formally or informally, mandated or ratified the act in question. It is not enough that they probably would have ratified it if they had known or thought about it before the liquidation removed their power to do so.

Accordingly, it will be insufficient to show that a shareholder who did not assent to, for example, an informal resolution, would, in all probability have assented to the resolution had he been aware of the full facts (see, e.g. *Vinton* v. *Revenue and Customs Commissioners* [2008] WTLR 1359). However, the assent of a shareholder may be given retrospectively and 'after the event' in the sense that a shareholder, having full knowledge of all the facts may wish to assent and validate a corporate act that had been instigated absent of some required formality, a formality, the absence of which, would otherwise have caused the corporate act to be invalid. In *EIC Services Ltd* v. *Phipps* [2003] 1 WLR 2360, Neuberger J opined:

> The essence of the *Re Duomatic* principle, as I see it, is that, where the articles of a company require a course to be approved by a group of shareholders at a general meeting, that requirement can be avoided if all members of the group, being aware of the relevant facts, either give their approval to that course, or so conduct themselves as to make it inequitable for them to deny that they have given their approval. Whether the approval is given in advance or after the event, whether it is characterised as agreement, ratification, waiver, or estoppel, and whether members of the group give their consent in different ways at different times, does not matter. (at para.122)

It may also be possible for a shareholder agreement to be viewed as an implied mechanism to sanction an informal resolution in circumstances where the subject matter of the resolution is specifically dealt with by the terms of the shareholders' agreement and where the agreement comprises the will of the entire membership of the company. However, a shareholder agreement will not be capable of impliedly sanctioning an informal resolution where the shareholder agreement is absent of some material matter, so specified and required by the terms of the resolution (see, e.g. *Demite Ltd* v. *Protec Health Ltd* [1998] BCC 638).

18.8.7 The *Re Duomatic* principle and a possible conflict with statutory provisions

Where a statutory provision is linked and necessary to the passage of a resolution and the provision specifies an additional requirement other than the formal act of passing the resolution, then in such a case, an informal resolution may be ineffective and if relied upon may be set aside. In such a case, whether the *Re Duomatic* principle can be relied upon will depend on the underlying purpose and effect of the additional requirement(s) of the provision and whether formal compliance, as opposed to informal compliance is deemed absolutely necessary to the proper functioning of the provision. An obvious example of an informal resolution, the validity of which would be most unlikely, would be one that sought to remove a director (or an auditor). Here the legislation specific to, for example, the removal of a director specifies additional requirements other than the mere passing of an ordinary resolution. In such an instance not only must special notice be given of an intention to remove a director but the director must also be given the opportunity to make representations at the meeting at which the resolution to remove him is moved (see CA 2006, ss.168–170). In *Bonham-Carter* v. *Situ Ventures Ltd* [2012] EWHC 230 (Ch), Richard Sheldon QC (sitting as a deputy judge of the High Court) observed that:

> In my view it is plain that the requirements under s.169 are imposed, at least in part, for the benefit of the director(s) whose removal is sought. The heading of s.169 is 'Director's right to protest against removal'. Section 169(1) provides that the notice of the intended resolution 'must' be served on the director concerned. Section 169(2) provides for the director to be entitled to be heard on the resolution at the meeting. Section 169(3) and s.169(4) provide for written representations of the director concerned to be sent to the members in advance of the meeting to consider the resolution or, if received too late, to be read out at the meeting. These requirements to circulate the written representations or read them out at the meeting can be dispensed with if an application is made by certain identified persons to the court and the court 'is satisfied that the rights conferred by this section are being abused'. The last phrase can only mean the rights conferred by the section on the director concerned. In my view, it is clear that s.169 confers rights on the director whose removal is sought and that its provisions afford him an element of substantive protection. (at para.36)

Generally, the courts have adopted a strict approach to ensure that the formal requirements laid down by statutory provisions are complied with. For example, in *Re R W Peak (King's Lynn) Ltd* [1998] BCC 596, a written agreement was entered into between X and the company (X was one of two shareholders in the company) for the sale of X's shares to the company; the agreement was signed for and on behalf of the company by the company's other shareholder (Y) who was also a director of the company. Y subsequently died. X then sought an order to rectify the company's register of members to reinsert his name as the holder of the shares on the basis that the agreement of sale was void being contrary to the terms of the statutory provision governing the sale transaction (CA 1985, s.164 (now CA 2006, s.694)). It was void in the sense that a special resolution had not been passed to authorise the sale contract. The company contended (in accordance with the *Re Duomatic* principle) that the formalities required by the statutory provision could be waived because both of the shareholders had unanimously assented to the transaction. However, Lindsay J held that the *Re Duomatic* principle could not operate to cure a failure to comply with the statutory provision because the provision required specifically that the agreement had to be approved by a special resolution having been passed prior to the agreement having been entered into. It was insufficient to contend that the resolution had been passed simultaneously with or subsequent to the company entering into the agreement because such a contention did not marry with the specific and precise terms of the provision.

In determining whether to sanction the operation of the *Duomatic* principle, much will depend upon the terms and purpose of the actual statutory provision under consideration and the individual circumstances of the case. For example, in *Re Barry Artist Ltd* [1985] BCLC 283, a case concerned with a reduction of a company's capital, the court was reluctant to accept an informal resolution to sanction the reduction of capital because the relevant provision stated that the court had to exercise its discretion in relation to determining whether to approve a special resolution passed in general meeting for the purpose of reducing share capital. In *Re Barry Artist*, an informal resolution sought to sanction the reduction in capital; as such there was no formal special resolution which the court could approve or disapprove. However, the informal resolution was accepted because the court was still able to exercise its discretion (which had not been affected by the informal resolution) in respect of whether or not to permit the reduction of capital. However, as stated, the court's decision was taken with some aversion. Nourse J commented:

> My strong inclination has been to adjourn this petition so that a meeting can be held and a special resolution passed, but it has been represented to me that the company has a good reason, into which I need not go, for having the reduction confirmed before the end of this term. In the circumstances, although with great reluctance, I am prepared to accede to the petition today. I would not be prepared to do so in any similar case in the future. (at pp.284–5)

18.8.8 Copies of resolutions or agreements to be forwarded to registrar

Where a company passes a special resolution or any resolution or agreement agreed to by all the members of a company that, if not so agreed to, would not have been effective for its purpose, then a copy of the resolution or agreement (or a written memorandum setting out its terms) must be forwarded to the registrar within 15 days after it is passed or made (CA 2006, s.30). Where a company fails to comply, it commits an offence, as does every officer (to include a liquidator of the company) who is in default. A person guilty of an offence is liable on summary conviction to a fine.

Section 30 also applies to:

- any resolution or agreement agreed to by all the members of a class of shareholders that, if not so agreed to, would not have been effective for its purpose unless passed by some particular majority or otherwise in some particular manner;
- any resolution or agreement that effectively binds all members of a class of shareholders though not agreed to by all those members;
- any other resolution or agreement by virtue of any enactment.

18.9 VOTING PROCEDURE

At a general meeting the standard procedure for casting votes in favour of or against proposed resolutions is for the members present at the meeting to vote by a show of hands (each member will have one vote irrespective of the number of shares held). In effect, this means that if, for example, a motion is required to be carried by a special resolution and only 50 members out of a total membership of 500 attend the meeting at which the motion is proposed, the resolution may be carried by just 38 members voting in its favour. Indeed, it is not an uncommon feature at company meetings for resolutions to be passed by but a small percentage of the total membership. (On voting procedures, etc., reference should be made to the model set of articles in place at the time of the company's incorporation; in relation to a public company incorporated under CA 2006, see regs.34–42; for a private company incorporated under CA 2006, see regs.42–47.)

However, as an alternative to a vote by a show of hands, a member may demand that a poll vote be taken. A poll vote entitles members to cast votes in proportion to the number of voting shares held; that is, if a member holds 20 shares, each carrying one vote, he or she will be entitled to cast 20 votes. On a poll vote taken at a general meeting of a company, a member entitled to more than one vote need not, if he or she votes, cast all the votes or cast the votes in the same way (CA 2006, s.322). CA 2006, s.321 provides that any provision contained within a company's articles which seeks to exclude the right to demand a poll on any matter other than the election of a chairman or the adjournment of a meeting, will be void. CA 2006, s.321(2) further provides that any provision contained within a company's articles will be void where it prohibits a poll from being demanded by:

- not fewer than five members; or
- a member or members representing not less than 10 per cent of the total voting rights of all the members having the right to vote on the resolution (excluding shares held as treasury shares); or
- a member or members holding voting shares on which an aggregate sum has been paid up equal to not less than 10 per cent of the total sum paid up on all the voting shares (excluding shares held as treasury shares).

In accordance with CA 2006, s.285A (inserted by reg.3 of the Companies (Shareholders' Rights) Regulations 2009, SI 2009/1632), in relation to a resolution required or authorised by an enactment, if a private company's articles provide that a member is to have a different number of votes in relation to a resolution when it is passed as a written resolution as opposed to when it is passed on a poll taken at a meeting the said provision will be deemed void. In such a case a member has the same number of votes in relation to the resolution when it is passed on a poll as the member has when it is passed as a written resolution.

18.9.1 Proxies

A proxy is a person appointed by a member of a company to represent that member's voting interests at a general meeting. However, it is to be noted that a company may provide shareholders with the ability to vote by correspondence in advance (which could be electronic or by post) without appointing a proxy (see CA 2006, s.322A, introduced by the Companies (Shareholders' Rights) Regulations 2009, reg.5).

Section 324 of CA 2006 provides that any member of a company who is entitled to attend and vote at a general meeting may appoint a proxy to attend in his or her place. In the case of a traded company notice of the appointment of a proxy must be notified to the company in writing (see CA 2006, s.327(A1), inserted by the Companies (Shareholders' Rights) Regulations 2009, reg.13). Previously, under CA 1985, a proxy was only allowed to vote on a poll vote, but in accordance with s.324, that restriction is removed. A proxy need not himself be a member of the company and any member of a company entitled to vote at a general meeting is permitted to appoint one or more proxies to attend, speak at, vote, and be counted as a part of the quorum requirement of the meeting (see CA 2006, s.285). In the case of a company with a share capital, a member may appoint more than one proxy in relation to a meeting, provided that each proxy is appointed to exercise the rights attached to a different share or shares held by him, or (as the case may be) to a different £10, or multiple of £10, of stock held by him.

As a member's agent (and in accordance with CA 2006, s.324A, inserted by the Companies (Shareholders' Rights) Regulations 2009), a proxy must vote in accordance with any instructions given by the member by whom the proxy is appointed. However, where a proxy acts contrary to his or her principal's instructions, it is probable that the votes cast may still be counted, other than where perhaps they are considered crucial to the final outcome of the vote (see, e.g. *Oliver* v. *Dalgleish* [1963] 3 All ER 330).

18.9.2 Adjournments

In certain circumstances, it may be necessary for the chairman of a general meeting to adjourn a meeting and, if so, unfinished matters of business will be postponed to a new date. By exercising the power to adjourn a meeting the chairman must act *bona fide* in the best interests of the company. The decision to adjourn a meeting must be a reasonable one to take in the light of all the relevant circumstances. A meeting must not be adjourned as a means to prevent delay, or handicap the will of the company in general meeting. An example of a chairman's decision to adjourn a meeting that attracted judicial disapproval is to be found in *Byng* v. *London Life Association Ltd* [1990] Ch 170. Here, the Court of Appeal considered it impracticable for a chairman to adjourn a meeting for a period of two hours and to a venue located in a different part of London from the one in which the original meeting had taken place on the premise that the meeting hall for the original meeting was too small. The haste with which the adjourned meeting was rearranged meant that many of the members who attended the original meeting were unable to attend the rescheduled meeting. Following the adjournment, a special resolution was passed. The resolution had the support of the board of directors but attracted opposition from a part of the membership; had the original meeting not been adjourned, the outcome of the vote may have been different. The fact that the meeting was rescheduled at such short notice and at a different venue, gave rise to a finding that, in the circumstances of the case, the chairman's decision had been unreasonable. The vote to secure the special resolution in question was declared invalid.

CHAPTER 19

The protection of minority shareholders

19.1 INTRODUCTION

This chapter considers both:

(a)   the remedies available to a minority shareholder in respect of an ability to redress a wrong committed against the company as a result of delinquent management practices or the wrongful act of a third party, and

(b)   the personal rights available to a minority shareholder in relation to remedying corporate conduct which adversely affects a membership interest.

In relation to (a), where a wrong is committed against a company the ability of a shareholder to redress the wrong is regulated by the rule taken from the judgment of Wigram V-C in the case of *Foss* v. *Harbottle* (1843) 2 Hare 461. The rule is generally prohibitive of the availability of any shareholder intervention in the affairs of a company in a situation where the majority of the membership has declined to seek a remedy for a wrong committed against the company by the company's director(s) or an independent third party. In *Foss* v. *Harbottle*, Wigram V-C made clear in his judgment that every individual shareholder must realise that on becoming a member of a company, majority rule prevails. However, given that a wrong committed against a company may have been perpetrated by those in control of the company, by way of an exception to the principal rule in *Foss* v. *Harbottle*, a minority shareholder is afforded a capacity to correct that wrong to the benefit of the company. In such circumstances, a minority shareholder may be able to pursue a derivative action. A minority shareholder's ability to pursue a derivative action is now governed by CA 2006, s.260. The justification for the exception (the ability to proceed by way of a derivative action) was actually advanced by Wigram V-C in *Foss* v. *Harbottle*. His Lordship stated:

> If a case should arise of injury to a corporation by some of its members, for which no adequate remedy remained, except that of a suit by individual corporators in their private characters, and of asking in such a character the protection of those rights to which in their corporate character they were entitled, I cannot but think that the . . . claims of justice would be found superior to any difficulties arising out of technical rules respecting the mode in which corporators are required to sue. (at p.492)

In relation to (b), in circumstances where a company subjects a member (his or her membership interest) to conduct of an unfairly prejudicial nature, a minority shareholder may petition the court under CA 2006, s.994 to pursue a remedy for such conduct (the procedure to petition under s.994 is governed by the Companies (Unfair Prejudice Applications) Proceedings Rules 2009, SI 2009/2469). Unlike a derivative action, where the object of the remedy is to benefit the company, the objective of a petition under s.994 is for the petitioning member to secure a personal remedy. As an alternative to a petition under s.994, and in accordance with IA 1986, s.122(1)(g), a minority shareholder may petition to have the company wound up on a just and equitable ground. This latter remedy is a remedy of last resort.

19.2 THE DERIVATIVE ACTION/CLAIM

Where a wrong is committed against a company, the company, as a distinct legal entity, is the proper claimant to instigate proceedings against the wrongdoer. Therefore, as a general rule, a minority shareholder will be precluded from commencing an action in the company's name unless, in the first instance, he or she secures the support of a majority of the membership in general meeting. Without the support of the general meeting, the proceedings will be struck out by the court and the applicant and his or her solicitor will be personally liable to pay the costs of the litigation. Indeed, even if a minority shareholder obtains the support of the general meeting, the company's board of directors must agree to instigate proceedings in the company's name in so far as the power to instigate litigation on behalf of a company is vested in its directors (see, e.g. *Breckland Group* v. *London & Suffolk Properties* [1989] BCLC 100). However, it is to be noted that if, in this instance, the directors refused to follow the will of the general meeting by refusing to sanction the litigation, it would be open to the general meeting to resolve to remove those directors from office (by ordinary resolution) and replace the same with directors who were willing to commence litigation.

The only exception to the proper claimant rule is where a minority shareholder fulfils the requisite conditions to enable him or her to pursue the complaint in the derivative form. The ability to pursue a derivative action is relevant particularly in relation to companies in which corporate malpractice may be hidden and unwittingly tolerated by a majority of the company's shareholders. It is to be noted that a derivative claim may be commenced by a group of minority shareholders. Here the wrongdoing will affect more than one shareholder. In this situation the appropriate action will be a representative one. The representative claim will be commenced by a shareholder on behalf of himself and all other aggrieved shareholders. Further, a derivative action may be commenced to protect the interests of company X by a shareholder of company Y in circumstances where X is wholly controlled by Y but where C, the controlling influence of Y, refuses to litigate to correct the wrongdoing to X (ordinarily because C is the perpetrator of the wrongdoing to X). Indeed, it would appear this latter type of common law derivative action (known as the multiple derivative action) survives the new statutory derivative claim (discussed below), so held by Briggs J. in *Universal Project Management Services Limited* v. *Fort Gilkicker Limited* [2013] EWHC 348 (Ch).

19.2.1 Regulation of derivative action by common law

Prior to the statutory procedure to determine a minority shareholder's ability to pursue a derivative action (introduced by CA 2006), the derivative action was regulated by the common law. To proceed with an action a minority shareholder was obliged to establish that the wrong, the subject matter of the complaint, constituted 'a fraud on the company' and that the company was unable to bring an action in its own name, namely those persons accused of the alleged wrongdoing were in control of the company and were unwilling to proceed with an action (see, e.g. *Birch* v. *Sullivan* [1957] 1 WLR 1247). The alleged wrongdoers and the company would be made defendants to the action. (The company was made a defendant to enable it to take the benefit of any court order.) The courts were reluctant generally to overturn the wishes of a majority of the membership and would only permit a derivative action in circumstances where the conduct of those in control of the company was inspired by actions other than to promote the best interests of the company as a whole. To permit a derivative action, the wrong in question had to be of a 'serious' nature and the principal motive for pursuing the action must not have been inspired by a minority shareholder's desire to benefit his or her own personal interest. Although under the common law there was no exact definition of 'wrongs' that would equate with the concept of a 'fraud on the company', case law established that the concept of fraud was not to be identified necessarily in a manner that required a dishonest intent or deception. The nature and degree of the wrong and whether it was sufficient to constitute a fraud on the company was determined on a case-by-case basis. Nevertheless, case law examples pertinent to the interpretation of 'fraud' indicated that a 'fraud' would be established in circumstances where:

(a)   The controllers of the company intentionally committed a breach of duty that resulted in a misappropriation of corporate assets (see, e.g. *Cook* v. *Deeks* [1916] 1 AC 554).

(b)   The controllers of the company were party to a negligent and self-serving abuse of corporate power (see, e.g. *Daniels* v. *Daniels* [1978] Ch 406). Here, not every negligent act that resulted in the loss or devaluation of a corporate asset could be classed as a fraud on the company (see, e.g. *Pavlides* v. *Jensen* [1956] Ch 565). The negligent act in question had to be committed by those in control of the company and it had to be established that those controllers attained some personal benefit from the negligent act.

(c)   The controllers of a company committed a discriminatory act against a minority shareholder(s) that resulted in the controllers of the company obtaining an unfair advantage at the expense of the minority. For example, in *Estmanco* v. *Greater London Council* [1982] 1 All ER 437, a company was formed by the Greater London Council (GLC) to manage a block of flats. The company entered into a tenancy agreement which provided that the block of flats (comprising 60 flats) would be sold privately and that each purchaser would acquire one share in the company; the shares of the individual purchasers did not to carry voting rights until all the flats had been sold. After 12 of the flats had been sold, the political constitution of the GLC changed and the newly constituted council altered its policy of selling off the flats: instead of being sold privately, the flats were to be rented to needy council tenants. As the GLC retained 48 of the flats (a figure representing the total number of flats unsold), the GLC was able to prevent the company from taking any action to challenge the policy change (i.e. the purchasers of the 12 flats were in the minority and further had no voting rights). Megarry V-C held that the council (in effect the majority shareholders) had acted otherwise than in the best interests of the company as a whole. The council had gained an unfair advantage by preventing the company from challenging the council's decision to alter its policy in respect of the sale of the council flats.

Although example (c) resembled in some part a finding of an equitable fraud, it must be observed that, following the decision of the Court of Appeal in *Prudential Assurance Co Ltd* v. *Newman Industries (No.2)* [1982] Ch 204, the justice of a particular case was not, in itself, to be regarded as a standard ground to instigate a derivative action.

In circumstances where a 'fraud' was established, ratification of the alleged wrong (by a majority of the membership) would be ineffective other than where, for example, an independent board of directors or a majority of the independent part of the minority shareholders (those not involved in the wrongdoing) resolved to rescind from proceeding with the action in question (see, e.g. *Atwool* v. *Merryweather* (1868) LR 5 Eq 464, *Rights and Issues Investment Trust* v. *Stylo Shoes* [1956] Ch 250, *Smith* v. *Croft (No.2)* [1987] BCLC 206 and *Smith* v. *Croft (No.3)* [1987] BCLC 355).

19.2.2   The statutory derivative claim

Under the common law, the pursuit of a derivative action was a great rarity. The governing characteristics for the common law derivative action were obscure and complex. In creating the statutory derivative claim (with an objective of abrogating the common law derivative action (but note the survival of the multiple type action; see above), CA 2006 may at least be viewed as providing a minority shareholder with a clearer and more certain set of prescribed circumstances that define the method by which to challenge corporate wrongdoing. However, CA 2006 procedure remains prohibitive and is still weighed heavily in favour of the concept of majority rule. The statutory claim is regulated by CA 2006, ss.260–264. Although CA 2006, s.260(2) permits a derivative claim to be brought in pursuance of an order of the court in proceedings under CA 2006, s.994 (discussed below), a distinct procedure for commencing a statutory derivative action is provided by CA 2006, s.260(3). Here, a derivative claim may be commenced by a member of the company (to include a person who is not a member but to whom shares in the company have been transferred or transmitted by operation of law) in respect of a cause of action arising from an actual or proposed act or omission involving negligence, default, breach of duty or breach of trust by a director of the company. The cause of action may be against the director (the definition includes both a former director and a shadow director of the company) or another person (or both) and it is immaterial that the cause of action arose before or after the person seeking to bring or continue the derivative claim became a member of the company. Here it is to be noted that the type of wrongdoing capable of triggering a statutory derivative claim extends generally beyond the type of conduct that would have justified a common law action under the 'fraud on the minority' exception (however, note that the *Estmanco* v. *Greater London Council* exception (at common law) may not necessarily be covered by the s.263 definition – see above).

As proceedings under s.260 will be commenced to protect the interests of the company and obtain a remedy on its behalf, proceedings may only be brought against a third party in circumstances where the company would itself be entitled to bring proceedings against the third party. The proceedings against a third party must be in respect of an act or omission involving a director's breach or threatened breach of duty. As one of the objects of the 2006 Act was to introduce a more flexible criterion than the former 'fraud on the company' exception to the rule in *Foss* v. *Harbottle,* it is also suggested that leave to commence a derivative claim may be given irrespective of whether the director(s) (whose breach of duty is in issue) is/are, and remain in majority control of the company. However, in practice it is likely that most cases will proceed in circumstances where those in control of the company's affairs are the alleged wrongdoers.

Subject to the procedural conditions laid down in CA 2006, s.261, a derivative claim may be commenced in circumstances where the company itself initially sought, but failed, to pursue an action against a director or third party in circumstances where that failure was due to a lack of diligence in the prosecution, or the prosecution otherwise amounted to an abuse of the process of the court (see CA 2006, s.262). Where the court deems it appropriate, the claimant's derivative claim (to include a claim covered under CA 2006, s.262) may also be taken over and pursued by another member (the applicant) in circumstances where the claimant's action failed due to a lack of diligence in respect of its prosecution, or the prosecution otherwise amounted to an abuse of the process of the court. Here, the court procedure for a derivative claim to be pursued by the 'applicant' is provided by CA 2006, s.264(3)–(5). The procedure is identical to that contained in CA 2006, s.261 (detailed below).

19.2.3 Procedure

CA 2006, s.261 provides that in commencing a derivative claim, a member of the company must apply first to the court for permission to continue that action. Under the Civil Procedure Rules, the application is commenced by the issue of a claim form which is accompanied by a separate application for permission to continue the claim. In effect, s.261 creates a two-stage procedure (similar in part to the test for the granting of leave to commence a derivative action prior to the 2006 Act; so advanced by the Court of Appeal in *Prudential Assurance Co Ltd* v. *Newman Industries Ltd (No.2)* [1982] Ch 204 at 221–2). Under the statutory derivative procedure, the application to pursue the claim and the evidence filed in support of it are considered by the court without the company being made a respondent. On hearing the application, the court may give permission for the claimant to continue the claim on such terms as it thinks fit, refuse permission and dismiss the claim or adjourn the proceedings on the application and give such directions as it thinks fit. Where the court considers that a proposed application does not disclose a *prima facie* case, the court in dismissing the application may make any consequential order it considers appropriate. If the claim is allowed to proceed, the court may give directions in respect of the evidence to be provided by the company and may adjourn the proceedings to enable the evidence to be obtained. Where the application is allowed to proceed, the court will order that the company and any other appropriate third party be made a respondent to the application, and will direct service on them of the application notice and claim form. A hearing is then held on the application.

Under the pre-hearing procedure, the court may at any point use a discretionary power to order that the costs of the claimant/applicant be paid for by the company, even in circumstances where the claimant's/applicant's action proves to be unsuccessful (see, e.g. *Wallersteiner* v. *Moir (No.2)* [1975] QB 373). This discretionary power arises as a matter of equity on the premise that is just and equitable that a minority shareholder should (providing he or she had reasonable grounds to commence the action and was acting in good faith) be indemnified against costs incurred in the pursuit of an action which seeks to benefit the company (in a similar manner to an agent or trustee). (Note that derivative claims are currently regulated by rule 19.9 of the Civil Procedure Rules, as amended by the Civil Procedure (Amendment) Rules 2007, SI 2007/2204.)

19.2.4 Deciding whether the application should proceed (CA 2006, s.263(2))

In considering whether to give permission to continue the claim (the first stage of proceedings), the court must have particular regard to whether it should interfere in the management of the company by overriding the decision of those responsible under the company's constitution for the management of its affairs. In deciding whether a derivative claim should proceed, the court must refuse the application if, in accordance with CA 2006, s.263(2), it is satisfied that:

(a) a person acting in accordance with CA 2006, s.172 (duty to promote the success of the company) would not seek to continue the claim; or

(b) if the cause of action arises from an act or omission that is yet to occur, that the said act or omission will be authorised by the company; or

(c) where the cause of action arises from an act or omission that has already occurred, that the act or omission was

    (i) authorised by the company before it occurred, or

    (ii) has been ratified by the company since it occurred.

In respect of (a), the claimant is not required to satisfy the court that a person acting in accordance with s.172 would seek to raise the derivative proceedings, rather the court must refuse the application if it is satisfied that such a person would not seek to raise the proceedings. Here, s.263 will not defeat the claim merely because some, or even most, directors would not seek to continue the claim. In *Iesini* v. *Westrip Holdings Ltd* [2010] BCC 420, Lewison J explained the position as follows:

> . . . s.263(2)(a) will apply only where the court is satisfied that no director acting in accordance with s.172 would seek to continue the claim. If some directors would, and others would not, seek to continue the claim the case is one for the application of s.263(3)(b). (at para.86)

In respect of (b) and (c), it is important to note that a wrongful act that results in a derivative claim may not be effectively ratified in circumstances where ratification is or will be achieved by counting the votes of the perpetrators of the delinquent conduct that gave rise to the derivative claim. Although this requirement is not specifically spelt out in CA 2006, ss.260–264, it is nevertheless applicable in respect of a general meeting's ability to sanction (or otherwise) a director's breach of duty, etc. (see CA 2006, s.239).

19.2.5 Second stage procedure – deciding whether the application should proceed (CA 2006, s.263(3))

However, even if the conditions stated in CA 2006, s.263(2) do not prevent the proceedings from continuing to trial, the court may still refuse its permission to allow the continuance of the action. In deciding whether the claim should proceed to trial, and under the second stage of procedure, the court must take into account the matters specified by CA 2006, s.263(3). (Note, however, that it may be possible for the parties to abandon the two-stage procedure by dealing with the application in its entirety at a single hearing – see, e.g. *Franbar Holdings Ltd* v. *Patel* [2008] BCC 885.) The matters specified by s.263(3) are as follows:

(a) whether the member is acting in good faith in seeking to continue the claim;

(b) the importance that a person acting in accordance with the s.172 duty to promote the success of the company would attach to continuing it;

(c)   where the cause of action results from an act or omission that is yet to occur, whether the act or omission could be, and in the circumstances would be likely to be:

    (i)   authorised by the company before it occurs; or

    (ii) ratified by the company after it occurs;

(d)   where the cause of action arises from an act or omission that has already occurred, whether the act or omission could be, and in the circumstances would likely to be, ratified by the company;

(e)   whether the company has decided not to pursue the claim;

(f)   whether the act or omission in respect of which the claim is brought gives rise to a cause of action that the member could pursue in his own right rather than on behalf of the company.

In relation to point (a), a member must not seek to advance a derivative claim for an improper purpose or to achieve a collateral objective. In relation to point (b), even if, in accordance with CA 2006, s.263(2)(a), the court considers that a hypothetical director would consider the claim worthy of being continued, the court must, in accordance with CA 2006, s.263(3)(b), consider whether the hypothetical director would (in consideration of CA 2006, s.172) attach sufficient importance to continuing the claim. Here a person (in effect a hypothetical director) acting in accordance with CA 2006, s.172 would ordinarily be expected to have regard to a range of factors, including the amount at stake, the apparent strength of the case, the prospects of securing a satisfactory outcome without litigation, the prospects of the successful execution of any judgment, the likely cost of the proceedings, the disruption caused to the company's business and potential risks to reputation and business relationships (see, e.g. *Wishart* v. *Castlecroft Securities Ltd* 2009 SLT 812). However, in relation to the interpretation of CA 2006, s.263(3)(b), the court may be more inclined to favour a liberal and flexible evaluation of any perceived potential advantage in allowing the claim to proceed to trial. For example, in *Stainer* v. *Lee* [2011] BCC 134, Roth J opined:

> In particular, under s.263(3)(b), as regards the hypothetical director acting in accordance with the s.172 duty, if the case seems very strong, it may be appropriate to continue it even if the likely level of recovery is not so large, since such a claim stands a good chance of provoking an early settlement or may indeed qualify for summary judgment. On the other hand, it may be in the interests of the company to continue even a less strong case if the amount of potential recovery is very large. (para.29)

19.2.6   Whether a member can bring proceedings in their own right

In respect of point (f), the nature of the enquiry is whether a member could bring proceedings in his or her own right so as to obtain a remedy in respect of the act or omission in question which forms the subject matter of complaint. Here, the court must take into account the availability of alternative remedies. In relation to a private company the most obvious alternative under which a member could proceed would be to commence a petition under CA 2006, s.994 (discussed below). Indeed, derivative claims have been declined on the premise that s.994 provides an alternative route in the cases of *Franbar Holdings Ltd* v. *Patel* [2008] BCC 885, *Iesini* v. *Westrip Holdings Ltd* [2010] BCC 420 and *Kleanthous* v. *Paphitis* [2012] BCC 676. However, in determining whether the availability of alternative proceedings should defeat a derivative claim, the courts have not merely sought to identify the availability of alternative proceedings but rather have sought to investigate whether alternative proceeding would be more suited to the nature of the claim in question. Although the court may accept the availability of alternative proceedings, it may still permit the action to proceed by way of a derivative claim on the premise that the derivative claim will afford a more appropriate remedy. Accordingly, the theoretical availability to the applicant of proceedings by way of, for example, an unfair prejudice petition under s.994 is not in itself a reason to refuse permission to pursue a derivative claim (see, e.g. *Stainer* v. *Lee* [2011] BCC 134).

In some respects point (f) follows the common law approach to determining the suitability of a derivative action (see, e.g. the decision of the Court of Appeal in *Barrett* v. *Duckett* [1995] 1 BCLC 243). However, contrary to the common law approach, under the statutory procedure the availability of an alternative remedy is not necessarily conclusive in relation to the question of whether or not leave should be granted. For example, an alternative remedy may only provide an indirect means of achieving what could be achieved directly by the derivative proceedings. For example, in *Wishart* v. *Castlecroft Securities Ltd* 2009 SLT 812, the petitioner (P) complained that a director (D) of the company had acted unlawfully in relation to property transactions and had done so with the knowing assistance of a third party (S). P sought relief in a manner whereby the company would be restored to its position prior to D's unlawful act and sought that the properties in question should be declared to be held by S upon a constructive trust for the company. P did not wish to have his shares purchased (i.e. be bought out) and did not wish to pursue an alternative remedy under CA 2006, s.994. The Court of Session (Inner House) allowed the derivative claim to proceed on the basis that issues relevant to the case (D's alleged breach of duty) would be raised more directly by way of a derivative claim and that, further, S would be able to participate (as a third party) in the action and as such could be made accountable to make restitution or pay damages. It is to be noted that in *Kiani* v. *Cooper* [2010] 2 BCLC 427 (the first reported English derivative claim to be allowed to proceed to a trial), alternative proceedings under s.994 were also considered inappropriate, albeit the reasoning for this decision was perhaps less convincing than that advanced in *Wishart* v. *Castlecroft Securities Ltd*. In *Kiani*, the company had two shareholders, K and C; each held 50 per cent of the shares and together they were the company's only directors. K and C were in a deadlock position but while the company had ceased trading it was, on a balance sheet basis, solvent. C had acted in breach of his fiduciary duties and K sought relief on behalf of the company to the sum of £296,000. In allowing the derivative claim to proceed to trial, Proudman J weighed up the merits or otherwise of alternative proceedings under CA 2006, s.994. Although the dispute in question was one concerned primarily around the conflicting interests of the shareholders (K and C and therefore more akin to a s.994 petition) the learned judge concluded that despite the prospect of an alternative remedy under s.994, that prospect alone did not preclude relief by way of a derivative claim. K and the company had been deprived of the opportunity to pursue properly the business of the company and further, K did not wish to exit the company (although it is to be noted that if the matter had proceeded by way of a s.994 petition, the court may have acceded to K's wishes by ordering that C should be obliged to dispose of his shares to K). Importantly, and of much relevance to the decision to permit the matter to proceed by way of a derivative claim, Proudman J concluded that the costs of the claim would not necessarily be disproportionate to the potential claim (i.e. the company would not suffer any great financial hardship if the derivative claim was to proceed). However, as the case involved a dispute between two directors/shareholders and involved no significant claim in respect of the interests of any unsecured creditor the learned judge was only prepared to grant a modified type of *Wallersteiner* order. In effect, K was required to assume part of the risk of the litigation.

Finally, again it is important (in the context of points (c)–(e)) to note that a wrongful act that results in a derivative claim may not effectively be ratified in circumstances where ratification is or will be achieved by counting the votes of the perpetrators of the delinquent conduct giving rise to the derivative claim (see CA 2006, s.239).

19.3 THE UNFAIR PREJUDICE REMEDY

CA 2006, s.994 (previously CA 1985, s.459) provides:

> A member of a company may apply to the court by petition for an order . . . on the ground –
>
> (a) that the company's affairs are being or have been conducted in a manner that is unfairly prejudicial to the interests of members generally or of some part of its members (including at least himself), or
>
> (b) that any actual or proposed act or omission of the company (including an act or omission on its behalf) is or would be so prejudicial.

The s.994 provision affords protection to the legal rights of the membership and also subjects such legal rights to equitable constraints. In respect of subjecting legal rights to equitable constraints, a membership interest will, in respect of the conduct which forms the subject matter of the complaint, be founded on a petitioner's relationship, *qua* shareholder, with the other members of the company. Other than where a member petitions under s.994 to enforce a strict legal right, the ability of a petitioner to protect a membership interest (i.e. an interest of an equitable nature) will require the petitioner to establish that his or her relationship as a member of the company was based on mutual trust and understanding with the company's other members. In *Re Coroin Ltd* [2012] EWHC 2343 (Ch), Richards J opined:

> Equitable considerations, affecting the manner in which legal rights can be exercised, will arise only in those cases where there exist considerations of a personal character between the shareholders which makes it unjust or inequitable to insist on legal rights or to exercise them in particular way. Typically that will be in the case of a company formed by a small number of individuals on the basis of participation by all or some of them in the management of the company. (at para.635)

In effect, a petitioner will be required to show that his or her relationship with the other members was more akin and similar to a partnership type relationship, although it is not essential to establish the quasi-partnership type relationship as one requiring the company to have been entered into, or run, as if it were a legal partnership. Whether the relationship between the members can be considered as one of quasi-partnership will be a matter to be determined by the court by taking into account all the circumstances of the case. For example, in *Re Coroin Ltd,* the court declined to find a quasi-partnership company in circumstances where the company in question had been formed by a group of highly sophisticated and experienced business people and investors, with little or no prior relationship between many of the investors. Further, the complexity of the company's articles and a shareholders agreement clearly pointed to the fact that the company had not been formed or was to be run on the basis of mutual trust and confidence as between its members.

19.3.1   Determining the existence of a quasi-partnership type company

In determining the existence of a quasi-partnership type company, it is not destructive to the petitioner's case that the company was not originally conceived as a quasi-partnership company. The essential point is that, at the time of the alleged unfairly prejudicial conduct, the company was being operated as a quasi-partnership type company (see, e.g. *Croly* v. *Good* [2011] BCC 105). In *Croly* v. *Good*, Cooke J suggested that evidence to support the finding of a quasi-partnership type company may be found where the petitioner participated in the management of the company:

> . . . in the character of someone who was essentially an owner of the business or someone who was acting under the instruction or delegation of the controlling owners. It was not conclusive against his acting in that character that the scope of his management functions was limited or exercised in conjunction with others, as owners of a business may agree to divide or share the management responsibilities they exercised. (at p.107)

In *Croly* v. *Good*, evidence to support the fact that the petitioner participated in a quasi-partnership company could be found from the fact that he acted in the management of the company in the character of an owner rather than an employee in so far as in relation to the dealings with a franchisor, which were the very heart and foundation of the company's business, he was held out and considered to be a 'principal' in the business. Further, the bulk of the petitioner's remuneration was paid by way of dividend payments (paid from profits), a fact which made him personally interested in, and concerned with, the overall running and performance of the company. Accordingly, the petitioner's subsequent expulsion from a directorship in the company was prejudicial to his interests as a member of the company. The expulsion was unfair because his participation in the business was an essential part of the basis on which the quasi-partnership nature of the company had operated.

Although a quasi-partnership company may be an apt description of the type of personal relationship between shareholders in the internal workings of many a private company, it is generally misplaced in the context of a public company or large private company. Accordingly, the CA 2006, s.994 provision will almost exclusively be confined to the protection of a shareholder's membership interest (equitable considerations) in the context of a small sized private company. However, where the conduct of a company's affairs affects exclusively a pure legal right of the membership, here the membership interest may not necessarily, in the context of a s.994 petition, be dependent on establishing a quasi-partnership type company. In such circumstances it may be possible for a shareholder of a public company or large private company to proceed with a petition under s.994. For example, if a shareholder of a public company claimed that the company had breached the terms of its constitution (a breach of a legal right), why should the shareholder be precluded from seeking recourse under s.994 in circumstances where the breach resulted in his or her membership interest (legal right) being made subject to conduct of an unfairly prejudicial nature? Here a petition under CA 2006, s.994 would potentially be less troublesome than if, for example, the shareholder sought to obtain a remedy for the breach under CA 2006, s.33 (discussed in **Chapter 6**).

Although the primary function of CA 2006, s.994 is to afford statutory protection to minority shareholders, the provision does not preclude the possibility (albeit this is rare) of a petition from a majority shareholder (see, e.g. *Re Baltic Real Estate Ltd* [1992] BCC 629, *Re Legal Costs Negotiators Ltd* [1999] BCC 547 and *Re Ravenhart Service (Holdings) Ltd* [2004] 2 BCLC 376). Procedural rules governing a petition under CA 2006, s.994 are provided by the Companies (Unfair Prejudice Applications) Proceedings Rules 2009, SI 2009/2469.

19.3.2 Unfairly prejudicial conduct

The court employs an objective type test to determine whether a particular type of conduct is of an unfairly prejudicial nature. Prejudicial conduct relates to damaging conduct of a commercial nature (see, e.g. *Re Unisoft Group Ltd (No.3)* [1994] 2 BCLC 609) to the extent that if conduct is to be construed to be 'prejudicial' it must ordinarily depreciate or fetter the financial worth of a member's shareholding interest. For example, in *Rock Nominees Ltd* v. *RCO (Holdings Ltd) plc* [2004] 1 BCLC 439, the Court of Appeal held that there could be no unfairly prejudicial conduct in circumstances where the petitioner suffered no financial detriment. The court so held, notwithstanding that the transaction which formed the basis of the complaint amounted to conduct properly described as unfair because it had been entered into by the respondent directors in breach of their fiduciary duties.

However, in one prescribed instance, unfairly prejudicial conduct is deemed to have occurred without any investigation into issues of unfairness or prejudice or whether the conduct resulted in a decline in the financial worth of a membership interest. The instance in question is prescribed by CA 2006, s.994(1A) (introduced by the Statutory Auditors and Third Country Regulations 2007, SI 2007/3494). Section 994(1A) provides:

> (1A) For the purposes of subsection (1)(a), a removal of the company's auditor from office –
>
> (a) on grounds of divergence of opinions on accounting treatments or audit procedures, or
> (b) on any other improper grounds, shall be treated as being unfairly prejudicial to the interests of some part of the company's members.

With the exception of CA 2006, s.994(1A), and to justify the operation of s.994, the prejudicial conduct must be established as unfair. Unfair conduct must be established from the individual facts of any given case. In *Grace* v. *Biagioli* [2006] 2 BCLC 70, Patten J (sitting as a judge in the Court of Appeal) opined:

> The concept of unfairness, although objective in focus, is not to be considered in a vacuum. An assessment that conduct is unfair has to be made against the legal background of the corporate structure under consideration. This will usually take the form of the articles of association and any collateral agreements between shareholders which identify their rights and obligations as members of the company. Both are subject to established equitable principles which may moderate the exercise of strict legal rights when insistence on the enforcement of such rights would be unconscionable. (at p.93)

19.3.3 Establishing unfairness

All in all, a member of a company will be unable to establish unfairness unless there is a breach of the terms on which he or she agreed that the affairs of the company would be conducted. The underlying motive (as perceived by an objective type test) behind the pursuit of a particular course of conduct will be a dominant but not necessarily exclusive factor in construing whether the conduct in question was unfair. In establishing unfairly prejudicial conduct a petitioner will often seek to rely on establishing discriminatory conduct and/or an improper exercise of the company's powers. An example of an improper exercise of a company's powers giving rise to a successful petition under s.994 is found in *Re Sunrise Radio Ltd* [2009] EWHC 2893 (Ch). Here, the petitioner (P) established unfairly prejudicial conduct on the basis (among other allegations) that in issuing a rights issue of shares, the company's directors failed to consider adequately the price at which the shares should be offered for sale to existing shareholders who were willing and able to subscribe. The shares in question were issued at par value; a price that was significantly below their true market value. Although the reason behind the rights issue was a genuine and legitimate need for an injection of cash into the company and not purposely to dilute P's shareholding, the effect of the issue at par value did dilute the value of P's shareholding interest. The court held that a failure to give proper consideration to the true value of the share price amounted to a breach of fiduciary duty to the extent that the allotment of shares at par value amounted to conduct that was unfairly prejudicial to P's membership interest. However, it is to be noted that this decision may be viewed as controversial in the sense that the rights issue was not intended to discriminate against P's interests. While the directors may have expected that P would not wish to take up the issue, the decision of the court was not (unlike, for example, in the case of *Re a Company* [1986] BCLC 362) based specifically on the premise that the directors knew that P did not have sufficient funds to take up the rights issue. In cases where a petitioner cannot rely on an intentional act of discrimination or an intentional but improper exercise of the company's powers, establishing unfairly prejudicial conduct may prove to be a difficult task.

19.3.4 Negligent mismanagement in internal administration and organisation of a company's affairs

Nevertheless, a petition under CA 2006, s.994 may be sustained where, in the context of a quasi-partnership company, negligent mismanagement is concerned with the internal administration and organisation of a company's affairs, or a failure to have proper regard and contemplation in the exercise of corporate powers (see, e.g. *Re Macro (Ipswich) Ltd* [1994] 2 BCLC 354). In *Re Macro (Ipswich) Ltd*, it is interesting to note that Arden J referred to the recommendations of the then leading corporate governance report, namely the Cadbury Committee Report (despite the fact that the report was concerned with public and not private companies) and concluded that the absence of an independent director on the board of a company could, in appropriate circumstances, amount to conduct unfairly prejudicial to the interests of the minority shareholders of the company. By partial analogy, it should be noted that following the decision of Jonathan Parker J in *Re Astec (BSR) plc* [1999] BCC 59, it is unlikely that a public company's non-compliance with corporate governance issues will ever be capable of giving rise to a successful action under s.994. Although Jonathan Parker J held that the shareholders of a public company would rightly have an expectation that rules relating to corporate governance issues should be complied with, he nevertheless opined that such an expectation could not give rise to an equitable constraint on the exercise of legal rights so contained within the company's constitution. Jonathan Parker J justified his belief on the premise that for the legal rights of the membership to be subject to equitable constraints it would be essential to establish a personal relationship (of mutual trust and understanding) as between the petitioner and the company, a relationship that would be misplaced in the context of a public company.

In cases where the internal mismanagement of a company is alleged to have constituted unfairly prejudicial conduct, the mismanagement must be of a very serious nature because the court will not 'second guess' the worth of legitimate management decisions that were taken on reasonable grounds but which subsequently turned out to be decisions running contrary to the interests of the company (see, e.g. *Fisher* v. *Cadman* [2006] 1 BCLC 499). It should be noted that payments of excessive directors' remuneration or the award of over-generous bonus payments may constitute unfairly prejudicial conduct. It may amount to unfairly prejudicial conduct where, for example, in making payment of a dividend payment to a minority shareholder(s) (who does not hold office as a director of the company) the dividend payment had not been increased proportionally in relation to an increase in the directors' remuneration payment/bonus payment (see, e.g. *Re McCarthy Surfacing Ltd* [2009] 1 BCLC 622, *Croly* v. *Good* [2011] BCC 105 and *Re Annacott Holdings Ltd* [2012] EWCA Civ 998).

19.3.5 Corporate misjudgment

It is doubtful whether an act of mere corporate misjudgment, for example, a poor investment decision, etc., will ever enable a member to petition for unfairly prejudicial conduct other than where the matter of misjudgment results in self-serving negligence. For example, in *Re Elgindata Ltd* [1991] BCLC 959, Warner J remarked that:

> ... a shareholder acquires shares in a company knowing that their value will depend in some measure on the competence of the management. He takes the risk that the management may not prove to be of the highest quality. Short of a breach by a director of his duty of skill and care ... there is prima facie no unfairness to a shareholder ... (at p.994)

Section 994 does not seek to penalise commercial gambles. Indeed, it is a natural expectation that the management of a company will engage in commercial gambles.

19.3.6 Conduct of a company's affairs

To petition under CA 2006, s.994 it must be established that the affairs of the company in question have been conducted in an unfairly prejudicial manner or that an act or omission of the company is the cause of the prejudicial conduct. In accordance with the decision of Rattee J in *Re Leeds United Holdings Ltd* [1996] 2 BCLC 545, it is an essential requirement of a s.994 petition to ensure that the membership interest which is central to the petitioner's case is specifically derived and related to the conduct of a company's affairs as opposed to the exercise (or not) of personal rights afforded to the petitioner by, for example, the terms of a shareholder agreement. Rattee J opined that:

> In my judgment, the legitimate expectation which the court has held in other cases can give rise to a claim for relief under s 459 must, having regard to the purpose of the section as expressed in s 459(1), be a legitimate expectation relating to the conduct of the company's affairs, the most obvious and common example being an expectation of being

allowed to participate in decisions as to such conduct. An expectation that a shareholder will not sell his shares without the consent of some other or other shareholders does not relate in any way to the conduct of the company's affairs and, therefore, cannot, in my judgment, fall to be protected by the court under s 459. (at pp.559–60)

As a company's management functions are primarily vested in its board of directors, it is to be expected that the board or individual directors properly authorised to act by the board, will normally be responsible for the conduct of the company's affairs. However, this presumption may be rebutted. For example, in *Nicholas* v. *Soundcraft Electronics Ltd* [1993] BCLC 360, the Court of Appeal found that in a holding company–subsidiary relationship, it would be possible for a holding company to be held responsible for conducting the affairs of its subsidiary (a principle confirmed by the decision of the Court of Appeal in *Gross* v. *Rackind* [2004] 4 All ER 735). The *Nicholas* case concerned an allegation by a minority shareholder of the subsidiary company to the effect that the holding company's policy of withholding payments due to its subsidiary amounted to unfairly prejudicial conduct. While the Court of Appeal concluded that the holding company conducted the affairs of its subsidiary in a prejudicial way, the court nevertheless held that by withholding funds from its subsidiary, the holding company had acted for the greater good of the group (i.e. to secure the survival of the holding company without which the subsidiary company would have perished). As such, it was impossible to contend that the holding company conducted the affairs of its subsidiary in an unfair manner. (Also see *Scottish Co-op Wholesale Society* v. *Meyer* [1959] AC 324.)

Although a CA 2006, s.994 petition may, in appropriate circumstances, be successfully commenced in the context of a holding company–subsidiary relationship (i.e. where the unfairly prejudicial conduct of the subsidiary's affairs was instigated as a consequence of its holding company's de facto control), it is nevertheless, by analogy, improbable to assert that a majority shareholder of a company could, *qua* shareholder (not as a director), ever be found to have conducted the company's affairs (in a manner akin to a holding company) other than where he or she controlled the constitution of the company's board as a shadow director (see, e.g. *Re Astec (BSR) plc* [1999] BCC 59). However, where an allegation under s.994 is founded on conduct emanating from a resolution of the general meeting, it would appear logical to conclude that the responsibility for conducting the company's affairs would fall on the general meeting as an organ of the company, or at the very least the majority of the membership who sanctioned the offending resolution.

19.3.7 The effect of the conduct must be more than trivial

To substantiate a finding of unfairly prejudicial conduct, the petitioner must show that the conduct of the company's affairs resulted in more than a trivial assault on the substance of his or her membership interest (see, e.g. *Re Saul D Harrison & Sons plc* [1994] BCC 475 and *Hawkes* v. *Cuddy* [2009] 2 BCLC 427). Here, the crucial factor is the effect of the conduct in relation to the membership interest. For example, a small and technical breach of a director's duty may cause little harm in relation to the financial standing of a company but nevertheless the breach may result in a loss of trust and confidence in the management of the company. Although the conduct may have been trivial, the effect of that conduct may be very damaging in respect of the relationship between the members of the company to the extent that in such circumstances a petition under s.994 may be sustainable (see, e.g. *Re Baumler (UK)* [2005] 1 BCLC 92).

19.3.8 Unfairly prejudicial conduct must affect a membership interest

Unfairly prejudicial conduct must affect a membership interest or there must be evidence to establish the likelihood of a threatened act (see, e.g. *Re Kenyon Swansea Ltd* [1987] BCLC 514). In the construction of CA 2006, s.994, a membership interest is to be defined as one which bears some relationship to matters pertinent to the proper functioning of a company as opposed to a matter of a purely personal nature. For example, a member of a company who owned land adjacent to a proposed extension of the company's premises would not be able to successfully petition under s.994 in circumstances where the subject matter of the complaint was that the extension would devalue the member's own land. Clearly, this example illustrates a purely personal interest as opposed to a membership interest related to the internal and/or external functioning of the company's affairs.

It is settled law that the phrase 'membership interest' incorporates the strict legal rights of the membership, for example, the legal rights of membership as contained within the company's constitution, membership rights within a membership agreement (although not of a purely personal nature) and legal rights afforded by the companies legislation. However, to what extent does a membership interest extend beyond a strict legal right? In *Re a Company (No.008699 of 1985)* [1986] BCLC 382, Hoffmann J opined that a membership interest encompassed a wider concept than a membership right, and coupled with the word 'unfair', permitted the court to consider the legitimate expectations of the membership of a company. For example, Hoffmann J believed that in a small quasi-partnership type company, a legitimate expectation could exist in a situation where a person became a shareholder on the premise that he or she would be allowed to participate in the management of the company. Indeed, this notion of membership interest encompassing an expectation of participating in the management of a company has been echoed and confirmed by subsequent court decisions (see, e.g. *R & H Electrical Ltd* v. *Haden Bill Electrical Ltd* [1995] BCC 958, *Quinlan* v. *Essex Hinge Co Ltd* [1996] 2 BCLC 417 and *Re Eurofinance Group Ltd* [2001] BCC 551). However, it must be noted that a member's exclusion from management will, in itself, be insufficient to justify a successful petition under CA 2006, s.994; the exclusion must be of an unfairly prejudicial nature. For example, a member's exclusion from management may not be unfair in the sense that it may be justified on the basis that he or she failed to participate in management issues or that he or she was unhelpful or unreasonably hostile to other board members, or that he or she acted in breach of duty (see, e.g. *Re John Reid & Sons (Strucsteel) Ltd* [2003] 2 BCLC 319 and *Grace* v. *Biagioli* [2006] BCC 85).

19.3.9 Dilution of a member's influence as a board member

A petition under CA 2006, s.994 may also be sustained where a member's (X) influence as a board member is diluted significantly by, for example, the appointment of additional directors to the board of the company. Here, much will depend on the nature of the company and whether the company was, as a quasi-partnership type company, run on the assumption that X would be expected to participate as a dominant member of the company's board. In *Re Coroin Ltd* [2012] EWHC 2343 (Ch), the influence of a director, who previously held a dominant position as a member of the board of directors, was significantly reduced following the appointment of further directors to the company's board. The director's position was diluted to the extent that he became a permanent minority on the board of directors. However, here it was held that the company was not of a quasi-partnership type status and as such equitable considerations could not be considered in respect of the legal rights afforded to his position as a member/director. As the director was, in accordance with his legal rights, still afforded the ability to attend and contribute to board meetings, his membership interest (legal rights) could not be said to have been subject to conduct of an unfairly prejudicial nature.

19.3.10 A membership interest extending beyond strict legal rights

In *Re J E Cade & Son Ltd* [1991] BCC 360, Warner J held that a membership interest in a company could not be subject to expectations founded on a general concept of fairness (i.e. expectations that were unrelated to the legal rights of membership). In construing the scope of a membership interest, the learned judge maintained that the interpretation of an 'interest' should be strictly confined to rights or obligations related to strict legal rights, for example, the terms of a company's constitution, a director's service contract or an express shareholder agreement. While Warner J accepted that equitable considerations should be examined, the learned judge believed that considerations unconnected expressly or impliedly to the strict legal rights of membership could not, for the purposes of CA 2006, s.994 (and IA 1986, s.122(1)(g) – see below), found appropriate grounds upon which relief could be sought. Warner J stated that there could be:

> ... no such third tier of rights and obligations. The court, exercising its jurisdiction to wind up a company on the just and equitable ground or jurisdiction conferred by s 459 ... has a very wide discretion, but it does not sit under a palm tree. (at p.372)

The interpretation afforded to a 'membership interest' by Warner J in *Re J E Cade* would now appear settled as the acceptable norm in construing the ambit of the s.994 provision. This view was confirmed by the House of Lords in *O'Neill* v.

Phillips [1999] 1 WLR 1092. In *O'Neill* v. *Phillips*, P owned the company's entire share capital and had acted as its sole director. A company employee (O) proved himself to be invaluable to the company and was rewarded with a gift of a 25 per cent holding of the company's shares, a directorship in the company and half of the company's profits (some of which he left in the company). O subsequently acted as the company's de facto managing director and his personal involvement and commitment to the company was such that he guaranteed the company's bank overdraft; this was secured by a charge over O's principal residence. As a result of O's involvement in the company, P entered into informal negotiations with O (although no formal agreement was ever signed) to the effect that if certain targets were met, O would be given a 50 per cent holding in the company (50 per cent voting rights). Initially, the company prospered but this gave way to a gradual but sustained fall in the company's fortunes, to the extent that P became extremely concerned about the company's performance and O's involvement in the management of its affairs. P's concern was such that he returned to head the management of the company. Subsequently, O was informed that he would no longer be paid 50 per cent of the profits and that he would only be paid his salary and dividends in respect of his 25 per cent holding in the company. O left the employment of the company and petitioned under CA 1985, s.459 (now CA 2006, s.994). O claimed he had a legitimate expectation of acquiring a 50 per cent holding in the company and an expectation of continuing to receive 50 per cent of the company's profits. Further, O claimed that P had been treated him very poorly forcing him to leave the company's employment. In reversing the first instance decision of Judge Paul Baker QC, the Court of Appeal held that, irrespective of the absence of any formal agreement, O did have a legitimate expectation of receiving 50 per cent of the profits and 50 per cent of the shares (i.e. when agreed targets had been met). Nourse LJ stated ([1997] 2 BCLC 739):

> I am, with respect to the judge, unable to accept his assessment of the position. On 29 January 1985, less than two years after he had started to work for the company, Mr O'Neill became both a member and a director of it. It is true that he did not subscribe for his shares and did not bring any capital into the company. But that is immaterial. From the end of January 1985, or at any rate from May of that year when the understanding as to an equal sharing of profits was come to, the company represented an association continued on the basis of a personal relationship involving mutual confidence between Mr Phillips and Mr O'Neill, with an understanding that Mr O'Neill should participate in the conduct of the business and restrictions on share transfers. All three typical elements of a quasi-partnership were present. At all times thereafter Mr O'Neill had a legitimate expectation that he would receive 50 per cent of the profits. By the beginning of 1991 he had a legitimate expectation, subject to meeting the £500,000 and £1,000,000 targets respectively, that he would receive 50 per cent of its voting shares. (at p.769)

However, the House of Lords subsequently overturned the decision of the Court of Appeal. Lord Hoffmann, delivering the leading judgment of the House, emphasised first, that a member of a company would have grounds to complain of unfairly prejudicial conduct where there had been a breach of the legal rules which governed the manner in which the affairs of the company should be conducted. Second and alternatively, but more exceptionally, a member of a company could make complaint in circumstances where a reliance on strict legal rights would be contrary to good faith to the extent that equitable considerations made it necessary to abandon the application of strict legal rights in order to prevent unfairness. Nevertheless, here Lord Hoffmann did express caution in relation to his previous use of the term 'legitimate expectation' as a term best used to describe a membership interest. (Lord Hoffmann first used this term in *Re a Company (No.008699 of 1985)* [1986] BCLC 382 – see above.) Here his Lordship opined that equitable principles should not stand as an indefinite notion of fairness. Lord Hoffmann considered that he had been wrong to use the term 'legitimate expectation' to identify the concept of a membership interest because a membership expectation could be considered to be legitimate even if unrelated to a legal rule or legal right affecting a membership issue. As a matter of protecting legal certainty, Lord Hoffmann emphasised that it was necessary to limit the scope of potentially applicable equitable principles. Lord Hoffmann considered that equitable principles had to be expressly or impliedly related/connected to a legal right afforded to the membership. In relation to the facts found in *O'Neill* v. *Phillips*, Lord Hoffmann held that the petitioner's expectations could not be enforced as a membership interest because such expectations were not subject to any binding agreement or legal right (i.e. a formal agreement covering the distribution of profits or shares simply did not exist). Lord Hoffmann remarked:

> On this point, one runs up against what seems to me the insuperable obstacle of the judge's finding that [P] never agreed to give them. He made no promise on the point. From which it seems to me to follow that there is no basis, consistent with established principles of equity, for a court to hold that [P] was behaving unfairly in withdrawing from the negotiation. This would not be restraining the exercise of legal rights. It would be imposing upon [P] an obligation to which he never agreed. Where, as here, parties enter into negotiations with a view to a transfer of shares on professional advice and subject to a condition that they are not to be bound until a formal document has been executed, I do not think it is possible to say that an obligation has arisen in fairness or equity at an earlier stage. The same reasoning applies to the sharing of profits. The judge found as a fact that [P] made no unconditional promise about the sharing of profits.

Further, according to Lord Hoffmann, there could be no implied right and expectation relating to a share in the company's profits and its shares because the nature and structure of this particular company was not, in respect of the petitioner, a typical quasi-partnership type company, i.e. the petitioner (as a non-founding member of the company) had not become a member of the company on the basis of a position of mutual trust and understanding with the company's other shareholder in respect of the management of the company's affairs.

However, in respect of the identification of a quasi-partnership type company, it should be observed that, contrary perhaps to Lord Hoffmann's observations, a non-founding shareholder has been regarded as part of a quasi-partnership company in circumstances where his or her participation in the company is as one of its 'owners' as opposed to as a mere shareholder or employee, the said participation being built on an understanding of mutual trust and confidence with the company's other dominant shareholder(s) (see *Croly* v. *Good* [2010] EWHC 1 (Ch) and the prior discussion of quasi-partnership type companies, above).

19.3.11 The position post *O'Neill* v. *Phillips*

To summarise the position post *O'Neill* v. *Phillips*, it is to be observed that a CA 2006, s.994 petition will not be available where the alleged membership interest is not expressly or impliedly linked to an enforceable legal rule or right afforded to the membership. In a quasi-partnership type company where a legally binding agreement fails to incorporate a member's expectation, it may be possible to imply the expectation (term) as under the general law of contract, or subject the legally binding agreement to equitable considerations. For example, in *Jones* v. *Jones* [2003] BCC 226, the Court of Appeal held (on a preliminary point) that an informal agreement in relation to the voting structure of the company's board of directors could constitute a membership interest for the purpose of substantiating a petition under CA 1985, s.459 (CA 2006, s.994). Accordingly, where, as in *Jones,* a company's shares were controlled and split equally between two shareholder/ directors and the informal agreement provided that a subsequently appointed director who held no shares in the company would not, at board meetings, be permitted to exercise a casting vote on issues of substance, it was found that the agreement could be enforced as having created a membership interest. A director's right to vote at board meetings (the legal right) was therefore made subject to equitable considerations. Support for this approach may be found in the words of Sir Donald Nicholls V-C in *Re Tottenham Hotspur plc* [1994] 1 BCLC 655, namely:

> In deciding whether and how to exercise its wide powers under s 459, the court will have regard not only to the company's constitution but also to equitable considerations arising from expectations created by the dealings between the members. The court will do what is just and equitable in all the circumstances. (at p.659)

Although the decision of the House of Lords in *O'Neill* v. *Phillips* may be considered restrictive in respect of curtailing the applicability of equitable principles in the construction of a membership interest, nevertheless it does create a substantive degree of certainty in respect of the definition to be afforded to a membership interest. In accordance with the decision in *O'Neill*, equitable considerations would appear to be irrelevant where they are indicative of matters unrelated and detached from any legal right or legal agreement. Therefore, although there may be positive evidence (as in *O'Neill* v. *Phillips*, for example the fact that O personally guaranteed the company's debts) to suggest that as a matter of equity a member's claim was justified in giving rise to a membership interest, such evidence will be immaterial and irrelevant in respect of substantiating a petition under CA 2006, s.994 unless the company is considered as one of a quasi-partnership nature. Further, in a quasi-partnership type company, a petitioner, in seeking to establish a membership interest must convince the court that the membership interest, upon which he or she relies, was one not of a purely individual nature but one that objectively would have been commonly perceived to exist by the entire membership. For example, in *Phoenix Office Supplies Ltd* v. *Larvin* [2003] BCC 11, the petitioner (L), who held one-third of the company's issued share capital, decided to resign his directorship in the company; the resignation was on personal grounds and had nothing to do with the substance of the subsequent CA 1985, s.459 (CA 2006, s.994) petition. The substance of L's petition was that he had been the pivotal force behind the company's success and as such sought a fair valuation for his shareholding, contending that the company's two other shareholders had breached a common understanding, namely that in a quasi-partnership company of this type, a shareholder would, if he left the company, be entitled to one-third of the company's net asset value. The defendants (the company's two other shareholders) offered to purchase L's shares at a discounted rate to reflect L's minority holding. The company's articles contained no right of pre-emption in the event of a shareholder seeking to dispose of his shares. The Court of Appeal rejected L's claim. The valuation procedure, in discounting a minority interest, was not unfair because L had no equitable entitlement to expect more (i.e. there had been no legal right or formal understanding between the parties in respect of an alternative valuation procedure). Although the company was a quasi-partnership concern, it was not, in this case, possible to find any agreement or understanding (an implied expectation/ right) between the shareholders to confirm the existence of a share valuation procedure in accordance with L's own expectations.

19.4 THE REMEDIES AVAILABLE TO A PETITIONER UNDER CA 2006, S.996

Where a petitioner succeeds in a petition under CA 2006, s.994, the court may make an order under CA 2006, s.996. However, it does not follow, even where unfairly prejudicial conduct is established, that the court will always grant relief. In some cases the court may conclude that the unfairly prejudicial conduct was not sufficiently serious to justify the court's intervention, or that intervention should be limited, or that an alternative remedy should be provided for. For example, in *Re Full Cup International Trading Ltd* [1995] BCC 682, Ferris J considered that the petitioner's interest would be better served if the company in question was subject to a winding-up order (a decision subsequently approved by the Court of Appeal [1997] 2 BCLC 419).

In accordance with CA 2006, s.996, the court is afforded a wide discretion in respect of the nature of the relief to be granted, with an ability to make 'such order as it thinks fit'. In granting relief the court may also take into account the interests of the other members and creditors of the company (see, e.g. *Re Neath Rugby Ltd* [2009] EWCA Civ 291). In determining the nature of any relief there is no requirement that a petitioner should come to the court with 'clean hands'. However, any adverse conduct on the part of the petitioner may be taken into account and as such affect the extent of any remedy (see, e.g. *Richardson* v. *Blackmore* [2006] BCC

276). A decision which highlights the power of the courts to exercise discretion in the making of an order under s.996 is *Re Nuneaton Borough AFC Ltd (No.2)* [1991] BCC 44. The unusual facts of the case resulted in a decision to allow a minority shareholder (P) to purchase a controlling interest in the company (from the majority shareholder, R). However, as R had given substantial loans to the company, Harman J declared that it would be inequitable to force R to surrender his majority control without being able to recoup the money loaned to the company. Accordingly, his Lordship ordered that as a condition of the purchase of R's shares, P should also be required to repay the amount of the loan on behalf of the company. The potential scope of the decision may be viewed as extreme, in that the minority shareholder, in whose favour the petition was decided, was ultimately made responsible for the company's debts.

19.4.1 Examples of the types of order available to a petitioner

A non-exhaustive list of examples of the types of order which are available to a petitioner is provided by CA 2006, s.996(2). This section states that without prejudice to the generality of s.996, the court's order may:

(a)   regulate the conduct of the company's affairs in the future;

(b)   require the company to refrain from doing or continuing an act complained of by the petitioner or to do an act which the petitioner has complained it has omitted to do;

(c)   authorise civil proceedings to be brought in the name and on behalf of the company by such person or persons and on such terms as the court may direct;

(d)   require the company not to make any, or any specified, alterations in its articles without the leave of the court;

(e)   provide for the purchase of the shares of any members of the company by other members or by the company itself and, in the case of a purchase by the company itself, authorise the reduction of the company's capital.

The most common type of order sought is the one provided by example (e) above. Although in the majority of cases which involve a share purchase order, the order will be to the effect that the respondent (usually the majority shareholder) purchase the petitioner's shares, it is possible for the court to decide that a minority shareholder should be allowed to purchase the respondent's shareholding (see, e.g. *Re Brenfield Squash Racquets Club* [1996] 2 BCLC 184, *Re Nuneaton Borough AFC Ltd (No.2)* [1991] BCC 44 and *Oak Investment Partners XII Ltd Partnership* v. *Boughtwood* [2009] 1 BCLC 453). However, it is to be noted that in *Re Ringtower Holdings plc* (1989) 5 BCC 82, Peter Gibson J opined that an order for the purchase of the shares of a majority shareholder would be inappropriate where the majority opposed the sale and the minority held less than 5 per cent of the company's share capital.

While the court may make an order affording a petitioner the right to purchase the shares of a majority shareholder, the most common order sought and granted is for the purchase of the petitioner's shares (a minority holding). This latter remedy provides the petitioner with an exit route from the company. The nature of this remedy and the fact it is the most popular remedy sought explains why the s.994 provision is almost exclusively employed in the context of private companies, i.e. in a public company a shareholder may more readily exit the company by selling his or her shares on the open market.

19.4.2 The valuation method

In cases where the example (e) order is sought the valuation of shares will be of paramount importance. The underlying theme in determining the value of shares is one of fairness. The valuation date should be assessed to compensate the petitioner fairly and should be reflective of a date portraying a connection with the commencement of the prejudice that formed the subject matter of the petition (see, e.g. *Re Abbington Hotel Ltd* [2011] EWHC 635 (Ch)). As such, the actual moment in time at which the valuation is to be calculated is apt to vary on a case-by-case basis, being dependent upon the individual circumstances of the case. Accordingly, the valuation of shares may be based upon the share value:

- at a time prior to the petition;
- at the date of the petition; or
- at the conclusion of the hearing (the date of the order for the share purchase).

In *Re London School of Electronics Ltd* [1986] Ch 211, it was stated that the valuation procedure should normally take place following the hearing of the petition (see also *Re D R Chemicals Ltd* (1989) 5 BCC 39) as the valuation at that time would best reflect the value of what the shareholder is actually selling. However, this presumption is rebuttable; for example, the company's financial position may have improved or worsened between the date of the petition and the hearing, rendering the valuation procedure unfair if it was to be calculated at a time following the date of the hearing. Indeed, in *Re London School of Electronics Ltd*, on the facts of the case, the court held that the valuation procedure should be as of the date of the petition, in so far as the company's fortunes had improved in the period between the petition and the hearing. It was considered to be unfair to allow the petitioner to reap the benefit of the company's improved position (also see, e.g. *Profinance Trust SA* v. *Gladstone* [2002] 1 WLR 1024). Much will depend upon the individual circumstances of the case. For example, in *Scottish Co-operative Society* v. *Meyer* [1959] AC 324, the House of Lords valued the company's shares prior to the date of the hearing on the basis that the time of valuation should be at a moment in time prior to the effect that the offending conduct may have had on the value of the shares. In *Re Cumana Ltd* [1986] BCLC 430, Lawton LJ also put forward an example of a situation (also see, *Re OC (Transport) Services* [1984] BCLC 251 and *Croly* v. *Good* [2011] BCC 105) which would warrant the court in valuing shares prior to the commencement of the petition, namely:

If, for example, there is before the court evidence that the majority shareholder deliberately took steps to depreciate the value of shares in anticipation of a petition being presented, it would be permissible to value the shares at a date before such action was taken. (at p.436)

In accordance with *Re Castleburn* [1989] 5 BCC 652, where the articles of association provide a mechanism for a fair and independent valuation of shares, the court should not ordinarily interfere with that procedure save perhaps where the procedure is, itself, considered to be unfair (see, e.g. *Re Abbey Leisure* [1990] BCC 60, *Re a Company (No.00330 of 1991), ex parte Holden* [1991] BCLC 597). Generally, in determining the value of shares, the court will normally discount the value of a minority holding. However, in respect of s.996, there is no universal rule to suggest that a minority holding must be valued at a discounted rate. Indeed, where the petitioner is not at fault, the court will tend to favour an undiscounted valuation (see, e.g. the comments of Lord Hoffmann in *O'Neill* v. *Phillips* [1999] 1 WLR 1092 at 1105–8.) The determining factor for the valuation process is to achieve justice between the parties to the petition. In cases where the petitioner's interest is affected in an extreme and oppressive manner, the court's desire to achieve justice may, in the overall valuation of the shares, incorporate a compensatory award in favour of the petitioner (see, e.g. *Re Bird Precision Bellow* [1986] 1 Ch 658 and *Quinlan* v. *Essex Hinge Co Ltd* [1996] 2 BCLC 417).

In relation to the other types of order, an order under CA 2006, s.996(2)(a) will be rare because of a court's general reluctance to involve itself in issues of dispute concerning the internal management of a company. However, this type of order was used in the case of *Re Harmer Ltd* [1959] 1 WLR 62 to remove the voting control afforded to H, the company's founder and governing director. H, aged 88, had imposed his will in the management of the company contrary to the advice and wishes of the other members of the company. For example, H had entered into contracts without the board's approval. As a result of H's attitude and interference, the company's business suffered. The Court of Appeal ordered that H should be stripped of his control over the company's affairs.

An example of a s.996(2)(b) type order would be where a minority shareholder sought to prevent the company from engaging in an act which, if instigated, would constitute conduct unfairly prejudicial to the interests of a shareholder or shareholders generally (see, e.g. *Re Kenyon Swansea Ltd* (1987) 3 BCC 259). CA 2006, s.996(2)(c) is, in effect, a means to a future remedy, as it affords the petitioner the right to pursue a statutory derivative action (see CA 2006, s.260(1)). Under s.996(2)(c), the court is given a power to order civil proceedings to be commenced in the name and on behalf of the company. The order may be sought where, for example, a petitioner establishes that the company's affairs were conducted in a manner unfairly prejudicial to the interests of the company as a whole (members generally). In *Re a Company (No.005136 of 1986)* [1987] BCLC 82, Hoffmann J suggested that where a derivative claim was brought by way of a s.459 petition (now CA 2006, s.994), the petitioner would be entitled to an indemnity from the company for his or her costs in line with the principle in *Wallersteiner* v. *Moir (No.2)* [1975]

QB 373 (a view impliedly confirmed by the Court of Appeal in *Clark* v. *Cutland* [2003] 2 BCLC 393).

Finally, it should be stressed that the court may make any order as it sees fit under CA 2006, s.996 and as such is not bound to prescribe an order of the type represented by CA 2006, s.996(2)(a)–(e) (see, e.g. *Wilton Davies* v. *Kirk* [1997] BCC 770, where in terms of a remedy, the court ordered the appointment of a receiver to oversee the company's affairs).

19.5 A PERSONAL OR CORPORATE ACTION?

Confusion surrounding whether an action should be of a personal or corporate nature is evident in cases where a shareholder suffers an indirect personal loss as a consequence of a wrong committed against the company, i.e. where there is a depreciation in the value of a member's shares following the wrongful act of a third party, or a breach of directors' duty, the effect of which is to depreciate the value of the company's assets. Here, a shareholder's personal loss may be particularly striking, especially in a situation where, in reality, the company is little more than the alter ego of the shareholder. Nevertheless, although a corporate loss may also result in a personal loss to a shareholder, as such a loss is merely a reflection of the overall corporate loss, it will not be recoverable by the shareholder, as a contrary conclusion would be unjust, giving rise to double recovery against the wrongdoer (see, e.g. *Prudential Assurance Co* v. *Newman Industries* [1982] Ch 204). More recently, in *Johnson* v. *Gore Wood & Co* [2002] 2 AC 1, the House of Lords sought to explain and expand the decision in *Prudential*. Lord Bingham advanced three propositions, namely:

1. Where a company suffers loss caused by a breach of duty owed to it, only the company may sue in respect of that loss. No action lies at the suit of a shareholder suing in that capacity and no other to make good a diminution in the value of the shareholder's shareholding where that merely reflects the loss suffered by the company. A claim will not lie by a shareholder to make good a loss which would be made good if the company's assets were replenished through action against the party responsible for the loss, even if the company, acting through its constitutional organs, has declined or failed to make good that loss.

2. Where a company suffers loss but has no cause of action to sue to recover that loss, the shareholder in the company may sue in respect of it (if the shareholder has a cause of action to do so), even though the loss is a diminution in the value of the shareholding.

3. Where a company suffers loss caused by a breach of duty to it, and a shareholder suffers a loss separate and distinct from that suffered by the company caused by breach of a duty independently owed to the shareholder,

each may sue to recover the loss caused to it by breach of the duty owed to it but neither may recover loss caused to the other by breach of the duty owed to that other.

In accordance with the three propositions, a shareholder will be precluded generally from proceeding with a personal action to recover a loss where the wrong affects adversely (in an economic sense) the company (however, note the possibility of an action under CA 2006, s.994, discussed below). In reality, a shareholder loss, accountable as a reflection of an economic loss to the company, will not be recoverable, other than where the company is, by law, precluded from maintaining the action or alternatively, where the shareholder can establish that the defendant's conduct resulted in a breach of a distinct legal duty that had been owed to the shareholder in a personal capacity, i.e. the defendant's conduct must cause a personal loss which is separate and distinct from any loss suffered by the company.

In cases subsequent to *Johnson* v. *Gore Wood & Co* [2002] 2 AC 1, the Court of Appeal has sought to follow Lord Bingham's propositions to the letter (see, e.g. *Day* v. *Cook* [2002] 1 BCLC 1, *Ellis* v. *Property Leeds (UK) Ltd* [2002] 2 BCLC 175, *Shaker* v. *Al-Bedrawi* [2003] BCC 465, *Floyd and Ors* v. *Fairhurst & Co* [2004] EWCA Civ 604 and *Gardner* v. *Parker* [2005] BCC 46). However, a possible diversion from Lord Bingham's propositions may be found in the Court of Appeal's decision in *Giles* v. *Rhind* [2001] 2 BCLC 582 (decided after *Johnson*). Here, the issued share capital of the company (S) was divided between G and R. G and R were the appointed directors of S. The company refinanced and G and R were left with a combined holding of approximately 20 per cent of the issued share capital. The refinance agreement was subject to a shareholders' agreement to which G and R were parties. The relationship between R and G broke down. R set up a new business, of a type similar to the business pursued by S, and took with him employees of S and a vital contract which had properly belonged to S. R used confidential information to divert the contract away from S and in doing so acted contrary to the shareholders' agreement, i.e. in breach of a contractual duty of confidence. S commenced proceedings against R but before the hearing S was placed into receivership and then liquidation. G issued proceedings against R claiming that R's actions had resulted in personal losses equating to a loss of remuneration and the loss in the value of his shareholding.

In reversing the judgment at first instance, the Court of Appeal sought to distinguish *Johnson* on two distinct grounds. First, in *Giles*, the company was unable to sustain an action against R due to a lack of funds; as such there could be no double recovery against R. (However, note that this first ground would appear to contradict the second proposition advanced in *Johnson*, namely, although the company was unable to pursue the action due to a lack of funds, the company did, nevertheless, have a cause of action.) The second and it is submitted more valid ground related to G's claim for the loss of future remuneration. While the court accepted that G's claim for the loss of accrued earnings would be defeated ordinarily on the basis of the reflective loss principle (i.e. the loss suffered by G as an employee was reflective of the company's own loss), the issue concerning future earnings was a different matter. In this context, the loss suffered by G was not reflective of any loss suffered by the company because the loss flowed from the termination of G's employment. Even if the company had been able to enforce its rights against R, any damages recoverable by the company would, following the collapse of its business, not have compensated G for a loss of future earnings. Also note, *Perry* v. *Day* [2005] 2 BCLC 405, where, albeit reflective of the loss suffered by the company, a shareholder succeeded in a claim for damages on the basis that the company had been disabled from bringing its claim by the defendant's own wrongdoing.

19.6 THE RELATIONSHIP BETWEEN CA 2006, S.994, THE STATUTORY DERIVATIVE ACTION AND THE NO REFLECTIVE LOSS PRINCIPLE

Prior to the introduction of the statutory derivative claim, the rule in *Foss* v. *Harbottle* was rarely overturned. Although the introduction of the statutory derivative claim may alter this position, it is suggested that it is unlikely to do so. Although the new statutory derivative claim may extend the ambit of the type of conduct justifying a derivative claim, the procedural requirements attached to the commencement and hearing of the claim may remain an obstacle to an increase in the deployment of the statutory claim. The popularity of a derivative claim is also likely to be undermined, especially in the context of a private company, given that matters which may substantiate a derivative (or corporate) action may often be pursued as a personal action via CA 2006, s.994 or as a derivative claim (see CA 2006, s.260(2)) in pursuance of an order of the court in proceedings under CA 2006, s.994. Indeed, in respect of a petition under s.994, it may be possible for a remedy to give effect to both a petitioner's interests and the interests of the company as a whole. For example, in *Clark* v. *Cutland* [2003] 2 BCLC 393, the Court of Appeal accepted that the relief sought under CA 1985, s.461 (now CA 2006, s.996) could also be sought for the benefit of the company.

However, where a member of a company petitions under CA 2006, s.994 and the alleged unfairly prejudicial conduct is of a type that would also give rise to a corporate action (i.e. it incorporates a wrong perpetrated against the company), should not the company be the proper plaintiff to the action, or if the company declines to pursue the action, should it not be pursued as a derivative claim (CA 2006, s.261) or alternatively as a derivative claim (see CA 2006, s.260(2)) in pursuance of an order of the court in proceedings under CA 2006, s.994? Following the case of *Johnson* v. *Gore Wood & Co* [2002] 2 AC 1, it would appear that a shareholder is not afforded a personal right of action where the wrong in question adversely affects the company. Here, in effect, this type of wrong should be the substance of a corporate action. However, CA 2006, s.994 is a statutory claim for relief and overrides the common law. Therefore, it is unlikely that the principles enunciated in *Johnson* v. *Gore Wood & Co* will ever be relied upon to defeat the claims of a minority shareholder under CA 2006, s.994 (see, e.g. *Re Brightview Ltd* [2004] BCC 542), irrespective of the fact that in a case involving a corporate wrong the 'membership interest' will not relate to a legal right of the membership but rather will be concerned with a legal right that, in law, is vested in the company as a distinct legal entity. Nevertheless, there are numerous case examples under CA 1985, s.459 and CA 2006, s.994 that proceed on the basis of allowing a petition by a minority shareholder in circumstances where the wrong in question (ordinarily a breach of a director's duty) constitutes a wrong against the company (to name a few, see, e.g. *Re Brightview Ltd* [2004] BCC 542, *Re Macro (Ipswich) Ltd* [1994] 2 BCLC 354, *Anderson* v. *Hogg* [2002] BCC 923, *Re Baumler Ltd* [2005] BCC 181, *Dalby* v. *Bodilly* [2005] BCC 627, *Allmark* v. Burnham [2006] 2 BCLC 437, *Re McCarthy Surfacing Ltd* [2009] 1 BCLC 622 and *O'Donnell* v. *Shanahan* [2009] BCC 517).

19.7   THE JUST AND EQUITABLE WINDING-UP PROVISION

In accordance with IA 1986, s.122(1)(g), a company may be wound up on the premise that its liquidation would provide a just and equitable remedy. IA 1986, s.124 allows any contributory to petition for an equitable winding-up order if the petitioner's shares were either allotted originally to him or her or held by him or her and registered in his or her name for at least six months during the 18 months prior to the presentation of a petition. In all cases, the court will require the petitioner to establish the following:

- *Tangible interest*: The petitioner must establish that the company is solvent and would be solvent after the payment of its debts (see, e.g. *Re Expanded Plugs Ltd* [1966] 1 WLR 514).
- *The qua member requirement*: In a similar vein to CA 2006, s.994, a petitioner must petition in his or her capacity as a member and the interest that he or she seeks to protect must be a membership interest. For example, in *Re JE Cade & Son Ltd* [1991] BCC 360, the petitioner claimed relief under CA 1985, s.459 (now CA 2006, s.994) and in the alternative sought a winding-up order on the just and equitable ground. Warner J refused to grant relief under both heads of the petition. According to the learned judge, the petitioner, albeit a member of the company, pursued the petition to protect the ownership of his land; the land had been occupied by the company; the petitioner's interest was not related to a membership interest but rather was concerned with the ownership of the land.
- *Just and equitable considerations*: As with CA 2006, s.994, a petition under IA 1986, s.122(1)(g), must be based upon an interest which is linked to a legal right afforded to the membership.

In cases where the just and equitable provision is applied, the category of company made subject to a winding-up order will be the quasi-partnership type of company. In order for a petition under IA 1986, s.122(1)(g) to succeed, it will be necessary to establish an 'underlying obligation or agreement between the shareholding parties' (see the judgment of Lord Wilberforce in *Ebrahimi* v. *Westbourne Galleries* [1973] AC 360). In the decided cases this obligation has arisen as a result of:

- an implied agreement on the part of the shareholders to conduct the company's business in a certain manner (see, e.g. *Re Crown Bank Ltd* (1890) 44 Ch D 634 and *Loch* v. *John Blackwood Ltd* [1924] AC 783);
- an implied understanding as to a shareholder's right to participate in the management of the company (see, e.g. *Re A & BC Chewing Gum Ltd* [1975] 1 WLR 579, *Re RA Noble Clothing Ltd* [1983] BCLC 273 and *Re Zinotty Properties Ltd* [1984] 1 WLR 1249);
- an implied duty on the part of the directors to consider the distribution and proper payment of dividends to the company's shareholders (see, e.g. *Re a Company (No.00370 of 1987)* [1988] 1 WLR 1068).

19.8   A COMPARISON BETWEEN CA 2006, S.994 AND IA 1986, S.122(1)(G)

CA 2006, s.994 and IA 1986, s.122(1)(g) are both concerned generally with quasi-partnership companies (although note it may be possible for a member of a non-quasi-partnership company to successfully commence a s.994 petition in a situation where a petitioner seeks relief for a breach of a strict legal right). In relation to a quasi-partnership company both provisions require the petitioner to establish a membership interest as one which may extend beyond the strict legal rights of membership. In respect of IA 1986, s.122(1)(g) the membership interest in question must be subject to inequitable conduct of a type that destroys a previous relationship of mutual trust and confidence and in this respect conduct justifying a petition under CA 2006, s.994 and conduct justifying a winding-up order under IA 1986, s.121(1)(g) will often be indistinguishable, the choice of provision being dependent upon the anticipated remedy. Accordingly, it would appear pointless to plead both CA 2006, s.994 and IA 1986, s.122(1)(g) as alternatives. Indeed, Practice Direction No.1 of 1990 ([1990] 1 WLR 1089) stipulates that IA 1986, s.122(1)(g) should not ordinarily be pleaded as an alternative to a petition under CA 2006, s.994. Given the similarities required to establish a petition under CA 2006, s.994 and IA 1986, s.122(1)(g), the latter will be invoked rarely. In *Hawkes* v. *Cuddy* [2009] EWCA Civ 291, the Court of Appeal, confirming the first instance judgment of Lewison J (*Hawkes* v. *Cuddy (No.2)* [2008] BCC 390), held that:

- Conduct justifying a winding up on the just and equitable ground will almost always amount to unfair prejudice for the purpose of CA 2006, s.994.
- However, exceptionally, conduct not found to be unfair for the purposes of CA 2006, s.994 may be capable of founding a case for a winding-up order on the just and equitable ground.

Indeed, in respect of this latter point, surely Parliament would not have employed disparate language in the two respective provisions if the jurisdictions were intended to cover the exact same ground. For example, in a situation of deadlock between the company's shareholders, a petition under CA 2006, s.994 may be more appropriate where conduct by one party to the quasi-partnership company causes an irrevocable breakdown in the relationship of trust and confidence between the company's shareholders (see, e.g. *Rackind* v. *Gross* [2005] 1 WLR 3505). However, in a deadlock type situation, CA 2006, s.994 may be inappropriate if neither of the deadlocked factions acted in an unfair manner (see, e.g. *Re Jayflex Construction Ltd* [2004] 2 BCLC 145). Here, although the conduct in question may not justify a petition for unfairly prejudicial conduct, why should the conduct, in so far as it results in a breakdown of mutual trust and confidence, not found a petition under IA 1986, s.122(1)(g)? Indeed, in *Re RA Noble & Sons (Clothing) Ltd* [1983] BCLC 273 and *Jesner* v. *Jarrad Properties Ltd* [1992] BCC 807 (a decision of the Court of Session (Inner House)), relief was granted under s.122(1)(g) in circumstances where neither of the deadlocked factions had acted in an unfair manner.

Although in exceptional circumstances a petitioner may be granted a winding-up order on the just and equitable ground in circumstances where there is *prima facie* an alternative remedy under CA 2006, s.994, it should be pointed out that IA 1986, s.125(2) provides that a winding-up order may be struck out if the court considers that the petitioner acted in an unreasonable manner by not pursuing an alternative course of action (see, e.g. *Re Woven Rugs Ltd* [2008] BCC 903). However, in exceptional circumstances IA 1986, s.122(1)(g) may afford the most equitable remedy, for example, in a situation of 'shared deadlock' (discussed above) or where a petitioner contends that a company's conduct and formation was directed at defrauding minority shareholders and the investing public (see, e.g. *Re Millennium Advanced Technology* [2004] 2 BCLC 77). Further, an equitable winding-up order may be a more appropriate remedy in circumstances similar to those evidenced in *Re Abbey Leisure* [1990] BCC 60. Here, there was an implied understanding between the shareholders that the company was to be formed with the sole purpose of acquiring, refurbishing and managing a nightclub. The nightclub in question was acquired but subsequently sold. The petitioner argued that as the principal purpose in forming the company had failed, the company should be wound up. The respondents contended that a petition under CA 1985, s.459 (now CA 2006, s.994) was a more appropriate course of action and that the petitioner should, as a means of remedy, have sought the purchase of his shares in accordance with an independent valuation procedure contained within the company's articles. The Court of Appeal, reversing the first instance judgment of Hoffmann J, held that in the circumstances of the case, a winding-up order was the most appropriate remedy. Relying to a large extent on Lord Wilberforce's comments in *Ebrahimi* v. *Westbourne Galleries* [1973] AC 360, the court opined that the strict legal rights of the petitioner, represented by the valuation procedure in the company's articles, should be made subject to equitable considerations. In so far as the petitioner would gain a greater financial benefit from having the company wound up, as opposed to selling his shares in accordance with the valuation procedure, the court concluded that the just and equitable provision could be employed to override the strict legal rights contained within the company's articles. Here, the circumstances of the case vindicated the application of the just and equitable winding-up order.

CHAPTER 20

The criminal liability of a company

20.1   GENERAL LIABILITY

A company may be liable for the commission of certain torts in its own right, for example, torts where liability is imposed upon it as the occupier of property. As an employer, a company may be held vicariously liable for the tortious acts of its employees even in a situation where an employee acts in a manner inconsistent with the company's instructions, or carries out his or her duties in a dishonest manner. A company may also be held liable for the actions of its servants in a situation where, in the course of his or her employment, the servant commits a tort for which malice is an essential ingredient.

However, other than where a company adopts an unauthorised act, vicarious liability will cease if the employee acts beyond the scope of his or her authority (see, e.g. *Credit Lyonnais Bank Nederland NV* v. *Export Credits Guarantee Department* [1999] 2 WLR 540). Nevertheless, other than in tort, the extent of a company's culpability for an employee's unlawful act (criminal act) will ordinarily be determined (with the obvious exceptions of corporate manslaughter and a specific offence under the Bribery Act 2010, s.7) by ascertaining whether the culpable employee is capable of being identified with the company's directing mind (the identification principle).

20.2   CRIMINAL LIABILITY

20.2.1   The identification principle

The directing mind of a company represents the physical being and will of the corporate body and is found ordinarily in the company's board of directors. However, as the board of directors may delegate some part of their functions of management, giving their delegate full discretion to, in a particular instance, act independently, the directing mind of a company may be found in the authorised delegate. In law, to identify the directing mind with the actions of an employee, the employee must have been authorised to act in a specific manner by the directing mind or by a person to whom powers, ordinarily vested in the directing mind, have been delegated. Where a person commands a position within the company's directing mind, the physical act (*actus reus*) and mental state (*mens rea*) of that person may be imputed to the company for the purpose of establishing corporate liability. The origins of the identification principle may be traced back to *Lennard's Carrying Co Ltd* v. *Asiatic Petroleum Co Ltd* [1915] AC 705. The case concerned a company which ran a business involving the management and maintenance of a ship, a ship that was damaged due to a failure to correct a fault in the ship's boiler system. The failure in question was directly attributable to the company's director. Proceedings were commenced against the company, which sought to defend itself on the premise that the damage to the ship had occurred without the company's actual fault or privity; in effect the state of mind of the company's director could not be attributed to the company. The company failed in its defence. The House of Lords held the company liable under the Merchant Shipping Act 1894, s.502. In the oft-quoted words of Viscount Haldane LC:

> My Lords, a corporation is an abstraction. It has no mind of its own any more than it has a body of its own; its active and directing will must consequently be sought in the person of somebody who for some purposes may be called an agent, but who is really the directing mind and will of the corporation, the very ego and centre of the personality of the corporation. (at p.713)

In small private companies the directing mind of a corporation will often be found in a person who is regarded as the alter ego of a company, i.e. the dominant or sole director of the company (see, e.g. the judgments of Lord Parker in *John Henshall (Quarries) Ltd* v. *Harvey* [1965] 1 All ER 725 at 729 and Denning LJ in *Bolton Engineering Co Ltd* v. *TJ Graham & Sons Ltd* [1957] 1 QB 159 at 172). In large private companies and public companies the directing mind of the company may be one or more members of the board of directors. However, the act of a mere employee of a company may be sufficient to render a company culpable for a criminal offence in circumstances where the employee's authority to act for the company (in committing the offence in question) may be directly traced to an authority emanating in the company's directing mind (by agency rules – discussed in **Chapter 16**). However, in many cases the problem of identifying whether an employee of a company was authorised, ultimately, to act by an individual who represented the company's directing mind may be most problematic. Nevertheless, in, for example, *El Ajou* v. *Dollar Land Holdings plc* [1994] BCC 143, the Court of Appeal held a company liable under the terms of a constructive trust in circumstances where it was doubtful whether the company employee, in knowingly participating in that breach, was, in the strictest sense, traceable to the company's directing mind. The case involved a former director (F) of a company. F had knowingly been a party to the fraudulent receipt of monies acquired as a result of a massive share fraud. The plaintiff (P) in this action sought to trace proceeds from that fraud. The defendant company was controlled by two US citizens but was managed by an appointed agent (S). However, S was not a member of the company's board of directors; the board was composed of three nominees, one of which was F. F acted as the company's chairman. F had been asked by S to find an investor for a proposed building project.

Having found a willing investor (C), F made the necessary arrangements between C and the company. After negotiations had been completed, F played no further part in the subsequent dealings between C and the company; further, shortly after F finalised the negotiations, he ceased to be a director of the company. C's investment in the company's property project, of over £1 million, represented funds fraudulently obtained from P, a fact known to F, but one not known by S or any of the company's other directors. Indeed, the company's board of directors never authorised the negotiations between C and F. The question for the court was whether F could, for the purpose of the transaction with C, be regarded as having bound the company with an authority emanating from the company's directing mind, to the extent that F's knowledge of the fraud could be imputed to the company. The Court of Appeal concluded that F had been given the sole responsibility by S to find and conduct dealings with an investor for the property project, a responsibility which F undertook on behalf of the company. Therefore, the company was liable on F's actions; F's actions were directly attributable to an authority to act which could be traced to the company's directing mind (S).

20.2.2 Determining whether an employee's wrongful act can be attributed to the company

For the purpose of determining whether an employee's wrongful act can be attributed to the company, it must be established that the employee acted as the company's directing mind or had been authorised to act by the directing mind. Here it is often necessary, if not essential, to pierce the corporate veil to examine the company's management structure and chain of command. Such an examination will aid the determination of whether an employee's wrongful act is attributable to the company.

The leading authority on the judicial identification of a company's directing mind is the decision of the House of Lords in *Tesco Supermarkets Ltd* v. *Nattrass* [1972] AC 153. Here, Tesco (T) was charged with an offence under the Trade Descriptions Act (TDA) 1968, s.11(2), namely, for offering to supply goods (in this case a packet of washing powder) at a price higher than the one which had been indicated as applying to the goods in question. (The offence is now regulated by the Consumer Protection Act 1987, s.20.) In seeking to defend the action, T relied upon TDA 1968, s.24(1), which stated that, subject to TDA 1968, s.24(2) (see below), a defence could be established where the accused could prove that:

(a) the commission of the offence was due to the fault of another person or some other cause beyond the accused's control; and

(b) the accused took all reasonable precautions and exercised all due diligence to avoid the commission of the offence, or did so in respect of a person under his control.

TDA 1968, s.24(2) required notification to the prosecutor by the accused of the person who the accused believed was at fault. T complied with s.24(2) by notifying the prosecutor that the fault in question was attributable to the supermarket's manager. The question to be determined by the court was whether the supermarket manager's fault was directly attributable to Tesco.

At first instance, the magistrates took the view that the store manager was not 'another person' but rather a part of the company, so that T's defence under TDA 1968, s.24(1) failed. The Divisional Court overturned the magistrates' finding in respect of the term 'another person', but nevertheless concluded that the company had delegated responsibility for the pricing of its goods to its managers and, as such, the store manager in this case (S) acted with the authority of the company's directing mind; T was therefore guilty of the offence charged. On appeal, the decision of the Divisional Court was overturned by the House of Lords. The House was of the unanimous opinion that S could not be construed to have acted with the authority of T's directing mind. In attempting to define the conceptual boundaries of a company's directing mind, Lord Reid disagreed with the notion that company servants engaged in the 'brain work' of a company could automatically be classed as part of a company's directing mind. Lord Reid opined that only a company's superior officers, those persons who ultimately controlled the overall corporate policy of an enterprise, could be regarded as a part of a company's directing mind. S did not have the capacity to determine T's corporate policy. Nevertheless, Lord Reid did recognise that a board of directors could:

> ... delegate some part of their functions of management, giving to their delegate full discretion to act independently of instructions from them. (at p.171)

In concluding that T was not guilty of the offence charged, the House of Lords found that TDA 1968, s.24(1) did not impose any form of vicarious liability. A store manager who acted in contravention of T's corporate policy could not be said to have acted as the company. Therefore, the delegation of managerial tasks to a company's store manager could not be interpreted as the delegation of an authority in respect of the corporate policy of T so as to deem that S acted with the authority of T's directing mind. Here the House allowed T's defence under s.24(1). The identifiable directing mind of T, the company's board of directors, had set up an effective system to avoid the commission of the offence charged under TDA 1968, s.11(2). The directing mind had not delegated any form of authority in respect of allowing S discretion to act independently of its instructions.

20.2.3 Necessity of case-by-case analysis

However, a company acting through its directing mind may be convicted of a criminal offence irrespective of whether the offence is of a regulatory nature (often an offence of strict liability) or one which involves proof of a guilty mind (*mens rea*). In *Tesco Supermarkets Ltd* v. *Nattrass* [1972] AC 153, Lord Reid opined:

> If the guilty man was in law identifiable with the company then whether his offence was serious or venial his act was the act of the company. (at p.173)

Therefore, the question of whether an employee's actions can be linked to the company's directing mind may only be resolved by a case-by-case analysis and examination of the nature of the employee's act and the position which that servant occupied in the corporate structure. An ability to attribute the mental state of an individual to the directing mind of a company, to establish the criminal liability of a company, is, however, marred by uncertainty in relation to the degree and extent by which a delegation of authority emanating from the 'directing mind' is sufficient to create the necessary level of proximity between the company and the individual responsible for the commission of the criminal act. Indeed, prior to 1944, there had never been a successful conviction against a company in respect of an offence involving a *mens rea* requirement. Yet, in 1944 there were three such convictions. The convictions were sustained in: *DPP* v. *Kent & Sussex Contractors Ltd* [1944] KB 146 on a charge of deception, *ICR Haulage Ltd* [1944] KB 551 on a charge of conspiracy involving a company's transport officer, and *Moore* v. *I Bresler Ltd* [1944] 2 All ER 515 on a charge of fraudulent evasion of tax related to a company's sales manager.

20.2.4 General exceptions to criminal liability

The Interpretation Act 1978, s.5 and Sched.1 provide that a corporate entity may, unless otherwise stated, be construed as a 'person' in terms of being considered culpable for an offence which requires the wrongful act of a person. However, a company cannot be convicted of a crime which is defined in such a way whereby the criminal act must be performed by a human entity. For example, an artificial person cannot be convicted of bigamy, rape or any other sexual offence. Following such logic, a company may be incapable of being convicted of, for example, an offence specifying a requirement that involves a physical ability to drive a vehicle: so held by the Divisional Court in *Richmond-on-Thames BC* v. *Pinn* [1989] RTR 354. Here it was held that a company was incapable of being convicted of driving vehicles without permits in restricted streets during proscribed hours contrary to the Greater London (Restriction of Goods Vehicles) Traffic Order 1985, art.3 and the Road Traffic Regulation Act 1984, s.8(1). However, while it is impossible for a company to drive a vehicle, the logic of this decision may be questioned. Although, in relation to the *actus reus* of the offence, a driving offence will require the performance of a human act by a human entity, the crucial difference between, for example, a sexual offence and a driving offence is that the human act of driving a vehicle may be performed on behalf of and for the benefit of the company as part of the employee's employment. If so performed, the company should, through its employee and the chain of managerial command, be capable of being found responsible, via the identification principle, of committing the criminal offence. For example, if a company does not discourage and/or turns a blind eye to a driver exceeding the speed limit to complete deliveries on time, and a driver of the company so exceeds the speed limit and as a consequence of driving at an excessive speed causes an accident, then in such circumstances, surely the company and the driver should both be capable of prosecution in relation to the 'driving' offence. It is to be noted that in *Richmond-on-Thames BC* v. *Pinn*, Glidewell LJ observed that an ability to impose corporate liability depended on the language of the relevant provision. For example, if the word 'use' or 'permit a vehicle to be so used' is inserted into a provision rather than the word 'drive' the difficulty in establishing corporate liability may disappear.

A company may not be convicted of the offence of conspiracy in circumstances where the company and an officer of the company, one representing its directing mind, are charged with the offence in so far as the offence of conspiracy involves at least two independent minds conspiring together, i.e. a company and its directing mind are one and the same (see, e.g. Road Traffic Regulation Act 1984). However, where a company and a person representing its directing mind are involved in a conspiracy with other persons, the company may be charged with conspiracy (see, e.g. *R* v. *IRC Haulage* [1944] 1 All ER 691). Finally, a company may not be convicted of an offence where the sentence for the offence in question is incapable of being imposed on an artificial entity; for example, a company cannot be charged with the offence of murder because following the conviction for the offence the punishment is a mandatory one of life imprisonment.

20.2.5 Extending corporate liability

In some exceptional cases a company may, itself, be deemed liable for the wrongful act of an employee notwithstanding that the culpable act was performed without the authority of the company's directing mind. Here corporate liability will be determined by reference to the language and interpretation of the specific obligation or rule. Corporate liability will be imposed where the court considers that a failure to impose liability would defeat the very purpose and intent of the legislation in question (see generally the comments of Lord Hoffmann in *Meridian Global Funds Management Asia* v. *Securities Commission* [1995] 2 AC 500). For example, in *Re Supply of Ready Mixed Concrete (No.2)* [1995] 1 AC 456, a company gave an undertaking to the Restrictive Practices Court (in compliance with the Restrictive Trade Practices Act 1976) to refrain from entering into any restrictive arrangement that would amount to a breach of the undertaking. Notwithstanding the undertaking, senior employees of the company, acting within the scope of their employment, entered into a restrictive agreement. The employees acted without the consent of the company's board (directing mind), which had actively encouraged its employees to abide by the terms of the restrictive agreement. In finding that the actions of the employees could be attributed to the company (rendering the company in contempt of court), the House of Lords concluded that an undertaking of this nature would have been worthless had the company been able to avoid liability for the acts of its employees by alleging (even if true) that its board of directors (directing mind) had been unaware of the actions of its employees.

Similarly, in *R* v. *British Steel plc* [1995] 1 WLR 1356, the defendant company was prosecuted under the Health and Safety at Work etc. Act (HSWA) 1974, following the death of a worker; the death, in part, was caused by the ineffective supervision of the worker. The Court of Appeal found a clear breach of the statutory duty so imposed by HSWA 1974, to ensure that persons were not exposed to risk. The company's defence, namely that its directing mind had sought to take reasonable care by implementing safety measures, was deemed irrelevant given the terms and nature of the statute. As the statute, in seeking to protect public health and safety, imposed (subject to the defence of reasonable practicability) absolute criminal liability, it was held that the health and safety legislation would be rendered ineffective if corporate employers were able to avoid criminal liability in circumstances where the wrongful act had been committed other than by or with the authority of the directing mind of the company.

20.3 CORPORATE MANSLAUGHTER

Prosecutions for corporate manslaughter are a recent phenomenon and extremely rare. To date, convictions have been limited to a diminutive pool of small private companies. Indeed, prior to the Corporate Manslaughter and Corporate Homicide Act (CMCHA) 2007, the operation of the identification principle was such that a causal link between the act of an employee and the command structure of the company (the directing mind) could, in all reality, only be established in the case of a small private company. In a small private company the directing mind and the company's employees are often closely aligned or indistinguishable from each other. The first recorded conviction for manslaughter was in the Lyme Bay Canoe case (noted in (1994) *The Times*, 9 December). Here, a group of eight students and their teacher were accompanied by instructors from an outdoor centre on a canoe trip; the group was swept out to sea, and four of the students drowned. Following the conviction of the company's managing director on a charge of involuntary manslaughter, the company, OLL Ltd, was also convicted of manslaughter. The company's managing director was the company's directing mind (the company was a small concern, the managing director was the alter ego of the company). Both the managing director and the company were convicted of manslaughter on the basis of ignoring and not complying with relevant safety standards and procedures.

By contrast, in a large corporation, establishing a causal link between an employee and the directing mind is much more problematic. In a large corporation, corporate policy and the implementation of corporate powers emanating from the directing mind may become misinterpreted, confused or abused by middle management and the general workforce, to the extent that although the wrongful act of an employee may be linked to the instructions of a senior employee, it may nevertheless be devoid of any direct and binding authority emanating from the directing mind. In *Attorney General's Reference (No.2 of 1999)* [2000] 3 WLR 195, the Court of Appeal considered the circumstances in which a company could be convicted of involuntary manslaughter, with specific reference to the offence of manslaughter by gross negligence (i.e. this is the category of manslaughter associated with the prosecution of a company prior to CMCHA 2007). The Court of Appeal's opinion was delivered at the request of the Attorney General and followed the Southall rail disaster of 1997, in which seven train passengers were killed. The court was asked to consider two questions.

- Can a defendant be convicted of manslaughter by gross negligence without the need to establish the defendant's state of mind?
- Can a non-human defendant be convicted of manslaughter by gross negligence in the absence of evidence establishing the guilt of an identified human being for the same crime?

In relation to the first question the court gave an affirmative answer because, following the decision of the House of Lords in *R* v. *Adomako* [1995] 1 AC 171, the definition of manslaughter by gross negligence enabled a defendant's guilt to be established on the basis of the defendant having had an obvious and reckless disregard for human life, recklessness being construed in an objective sense with no prerequisite of having to prove a subjective form of *mens rea*. However, in respect of the second question, the Court of Appeal answered this in the negative. The court held that in seeking to establish a company's guilt it was still necessary to show that in causing death, the act of the employee was an act attributable to the company, via its directing mind. In effect, the identification principle was as relevant to the *actus reus* as it was to the *mens rea* of a criminal offence.

20.3.1 The Corporate Manslaughter and Corporate Homicide Act 2007

Over the last 20 years, proposals to reform the law of corporate manslaughter were given much prominence (see, e.g. the 1994 Law Commission's (Consultation Paper No.135), Legislating the Criminal Code: Involuntary Manslaughter (1996, Consultation Paper 237), Reforming the Law on Involuntary Manslaughter: the Government's Proposals: Home Office report (2000), The joint report of the House of Commons Home Affairs and Work and Pensions Committees (2005)). The prominence may be explained as a consequence of a failure to successfully prosecute larger companies for involuntary manslaughter following high-profile disasters. Such disasters included the sinking of the *Herald of Free Enterprise*, and the Southall, Paddington and Hatfield rail disasters.

With the introduction of CMCHA 2007, the government replaced the identification principle as the principal means of determining a company's liability for manslaughter. The Act came into force on 6 April 2008 and will not be applied retrospectively, i.e. the Act only applies to deaths that occurred after 6 April 2008. Prior to the implementation of the 2007 Act, a company's potential liability for the common law offence of corporate (involuntary) manslaughter centred on the prosecution's ability to establish that an act or omission of a company employee, in causing the death of a person by gross negligence, was attributable ultimately to an officer of the company who acted as the company's directing mind (see, e.g. *Attorney General's Reference (No.2 of 1999)* [2000] 3 WLR 195). Further, it followed that a company could not be convicted of manslaughter unless a distinct conviction for manslaughter could also be sustained against a person who consti-tuted the company's directing mind. CMCHA 2007 abolishes the common law offence of manslaughter by gross negligence in respect of corporations and other relevant organisations in relation to deaths that occurred after 6 April 2008.

20.3.2 CMCHA 2007, s.1

Under CMCHA 2007, s.1(1) a company (or other organisation specified by CMCHA 2007, s.1(2)) will now be guilty of the offence of corporate manslaughter if the way in which its activities are managed or organised causes a person's death and the said management or organisation of those activities amounts to a gross breach of a relevant duty of care owed by the company to the deceased. However, a company will be guilty of the offence of corporate manslaughter only if the way in which its activities are managed or organised by its senior management is a substantial element in the breach of the relevant duty (see CMCHA 2007, s.1(3)). Here the jury will be required to consider the degree of responsibility attached to the senior management failure and must only return a guilty verdict where that responsibility is deemed substantial. But what is meant by the term 'substantial'? Does this term mean something more than trivial or should it be given its more natural meaning, namely something that exceeds the norm? Will the judge hearing a corporate manslaughter case offer a direction on the term? Indeed, without such a direction the jury are more likely to construe the term in its more natural context and as such in defending a charge of corporate manslaughter, it may be possible, especially in the context of a large company with complex tiered management structures, for the senior management of the company to contend that the most relevant management failings took place below the level of senior management. Although, in such an instance, the senior management may still be deemed culpable on the premise that they failed (in a substantial sense) effectively to oversee the activities of the lower tiers of management or mere employees, it may be possible for senior management to deflect culpability on the basis that their failure was a mere contributory factor and not a substantial element in the breach of duty.

In relation to the definition of 'senior management' this term is defined in two distinct ways (a two-part test), see CMCHA 2007, s.1(4)(c). First, senior manage-ment may comprise persons who play a significant role in the making of decisions about how the whole or a substantial part of the company's activities are to be managed or organised. Second, senior management may comprise persons who play a significant role in the actual managing or organising of the whole or a substantial part of those activities. Here, the reference to a 'significant role' is somewhat vague. However, in the context of the second classification, the adoption of the term 'significant' may appear indicative of a level of authority emanating from the company's command structure. If so, a delegation of authority from the company's directors (directing mind) may still be relevant in determining whether an employee's role in the company is capable of being classed as being that of a senior manager.

20.3.3   CMCHA 2007 marks a fundamental change to common law position

However, here CMCHA 2007 does mark a fundamental change to the common law position represented by the identification principle. In accordance with the second classification of 'senior management' in respect of the specific act or omission that culminates in the death of a person, corporate liability will no longer be founded on establishing an agency line of authority between a culpable senior manager and the company's directing mind. Here, in accordance with CMCHA 2007, it will be necessary, in seeking to establish a company's guilt for corporate manslaughter, to assess whether a company's senior manager was responsible for management practices which ultimately led to the breach of the relevant duty of care and to the ultimate death of an individual. At common law, if a senior manager who was outside the definition of the directing mind negligently caused the death of a person by, for example, acting inconsistently with the health and safety legislation and the general policies of the company's directing mind, the company would have escaped liability for corporate manslaughter notwithstanding any failures in the general management or organisation of the company. The company would have escaped liability as the employee acted otherwise than in accordance with the will of the directing mind. However, under CMCHA 2007, a company may be made potentially liable for corporate manslaughter, irrespective of a senior manager's (i.e. a manager below the level of the directing mind) non-compliance with the will of the directing mind. It should also be observed that the use of the term 'senior management' may afford a radical departure from the existing law, given the term's implied support for the aggregation of liability between members of the company's senior management.

While, in any given case, it may be impossible to attribute responsibility for a breach of a relevant duty to an individual senior manager, it may be possible to establish corporate liability through the cumulative conduct of the senior managers of the company. The combined effect of the aggregated conduct of senior managers may equate to a substantial factor in the breach of a relevant duty of care.

20.3.4   CMCHA 2007, s.2

Identifying whether a company owes a duty of care to an individual is a matter of law and as such must be decided by the judge at the criminal proceedings. However, in basic terms, a duty of care may be identified as a duty on the part of the company to exercise such care and skill as is reasonable in the circumstances of the case. CMCHA 2007, s.2(1) requires that the duty of care must be related to specific corporate functions or activities, namely, the company as an employer, the company as an occupier of premises (which is defined to include land), the company as a supplier of goods or services, constructing or maintaining buildings, infrastructure or vehicles, and other activities carried out on a commercial basis. Where the court identifies the existence of a duty of care, the jury's task will be to determine whether there was a breach of the duty and if so whether the breach amounted to gross negligence. Here, the criminal law standard for establishing negligence is akin to the civil law standard.

20.3.5 CMCHA 2007, s.8

In seeking to establish a breach of a company's duty of care as an act of gross negligence, CMCHA 2007, s.8 provides that the jury must consider whether, in relation to the alleged breach of duty, the company failed to comply with any health and safety legislation. The jury must consider the extent of any such failure and how much of a risk of death it posed. Here, problematical questions may arise. For example, what is a reasonable standard in the provision of health and safety matters? Will the reasonable standard be a universal standard applicable to companies of a similar size or companies engaged in a particular industry, or a combination of these considerations? Will economic considerations dictate that smaller and less successful companies maintain a health and safety regime which is perhaps inferior to a well-financed health and safety regime of a larger and successful company?

CMCHA 2007 identifies the concept of gross negligence by stipulating that negligent conduct must fall 'far below' a reasonable standard. In interpreting whether a company's breach of duty of care deviated 'far below' a reasonable standard, the jury is permitted to consider the extent to which the evidence establishes attitudes, policies, systems or accepted practices within the company that were likely to have encouraged or alternatively produced tolerance of the management or organisational failure of the company in respect of the breach. The jury may also have regard to any health and safety guidance that relates to the alleged breach and any other factor that it considers relevant to the case. Accordingly, in relation to corporate conduct resulting in a breach of duty, a company's past and current record of compliance with health and safety matters may become, in relation to the type of breach of duty in question, a paramount and decisive factor in the determination of corporate liability.

20.3.6 Sentencing companies convicted of corporate manslaughter

Where a company is convicted of the crime of corporate manslaughter, it will be liable to an unlimited fine. Guidelines for sentencing companies found guilty of corporate manslaughter were issued by the Sentencing Guidelines Council in February 2010. The guidelines state that, following a conviction for corporate manslaughter, the fine should not fall ordinarily below £500,000 (in comparison to a recommended minimum fine of £100,000 for health and safety offences that are related to the death of an individual (discussed below)).

However, the size of the fine is likely to be variable and will be dependent upon the nature and consequences of the managerial or organisational failure. Further, a guilty plea will be recognised as one which may reduce the size of the fine. The payment of the fine may take the form of a payment in instalments. In reality, the extent of the fine may also be influenced by the size, resources and future commercial potential of the company in question. In accordance with the decision of the Court of Appeal in *Cotswold Geotechnical Holdings Ltd* [2012] 1 Cr App R 26 (an appeal relating to sentence), the fact that the imposition of a fine may propel a company into an insolvent state should not necessarily influence the court's determination of the level of the fine to be imposed. However, in practice this may not necessarily always be the case especially where the court considers other commercial interests such as the interests of shareholders, creditors and employees. It is to be noted that in the three decided cases thus far relating to the offence of corporate manslaughter (see below), the fines imposed have been less than the recommended £500,000 minimum. With some practical sense, the court may also order the convicted company to remedy any failings which led to the gross breach of duty, setting a defined period in which time the remedial steps must be undertaken. A failure to comply will result in the imposition of a fine. Further, CMCHA 2007, s.10 provides the court with a discretionary power to make an order requiring the convicted organisation to publicise in a specified manner the fact that it has been convicted of the offence. However, under the terms of CMCHA 2007, s.18, a company's senior management have no secondary liability following on from a company's conviction for corporate manslaughter.

To date, there have been three convictions under CMCHA 2007 but only one of the same proceeded to the trial process (*R* v. *Cotswold Geotechnical Holdings Ltd* (2011) *The Times*, 20 July). In the other two cases, JMW Farms Ltd (Northern Ireland, May 2012) and Lion Steel Ltd (July 2012), the respective companies pleaded guilty to a charge of corporate manslaughter and in the case of Lion Steel Ltd the company did so following an agreement with the prosecution (and with the agreement of the court) to the effect that the company would plead guilty providing other charges (of involuntary manslaughter) made against the company's directors were not pursued. This form of 'plea bargaining' – agreed between the parties is, to say the very least, questionable, especially when one considers the seriousness of the offence. It is also to be noted that in relation to the three successful prosecutions all were concerned with private companies. Here it is most probable that, had CMCHA 2007 not been in force, those cases would still have resulted in successful prosecutions under the previous common law offence (involuntary manslaughter) in so far as in all cases the culpability of the directing mind of the company was clearly established. As such, the depths and complexities of CMCHA 2007(especially in the context of the extended definition of senior management) are yet to be made the subject of intense judicial/jury scrutiny.

20.4 CORPORATE LIABILITY FOR DEATH UNDER THE HEALTH AND SAFETY LEGISLATION

In circumstances where a company is deemed to be responsible for causing the injury or death of an individual, the company may be charged with an offence under

HSWA 1974. It is to be noted that in relation to causing the death of an individual, CMCHA 2007, s.19, sanctions a company to be charged with the offence of corporate manslaughter and (in the same proceedings) an offence under the health and safety legislation. For a company to be prosecuted under HSWA 1974 there is no requirement to establish the culpability of a senior manager, or to prove the breach of duty amounted to gross negligence. The offence under HSWA 1974 is therefore less arduous to establish than the offence of corporate manslaughter and further the trial and prosecution process will be generally less expensive on the public purse. Given that HSWA 1974 affords the prosecution the more achievable task of establishing a defendant's culpability, it is likely that a decision to prosecute a company for corporate manslaughter, as opposed to an offence under HSWA 1974, will require much consideration. In addition, although in accordance with the Sentencing Guidelines Council (February 2010), a conviction for corporate manslaughter is likely to attract a heftier fine than had the conviction been under HSWA 1974, in reality, the disparity between the level of the fine imposed under CMCHA 2007 and HSWA 1974 may not necessarily justify the cost of proceedings under CMCHA 2007. Indeed, other than if there are clear and poignant public interest issues at play and/or the neglect of the defendant can be established obviously as one of gross negligence, it is, in harsh reality, probable that the DPP will more readily prosecute a company for causing the death of an individual under HSWA 1974 rather than seeking to advance a prosecution under CMCHA 2007.

The provisions of HSWA 1974 which are relevant to a prosecution in respect of the injury or death of an individual are s.2 and s.3.

HSWA 1974, s.2(1) provides that:

> It shall be the duty of every employer to ensure, so far as is reasonably practicable, the health, safety and welfare at work of all his employees.

HSWA 1974, s.3(1) provides:

> It shall be the duty of every employer to conduct his undertaking in such a way as to ensure, so far as is reasonably practicable, that persons not in his employment who may be affected thereby are not exposed to risks to their health or safety.

For a detailed analysis of the constituent elements of these offences, see the decision of the Court of Appeal in *R* v. *Tangerine Confectionery Ltd* [2011] EWCA Crim 2015. In relation to the HSWA offences, an employer is provided with a defence under HSWA 1974, s.40. The defence applies where the accused proves that it was not practicable or not reasonably practicable to do more than was in fact done to satisfy the duty or requirement, or that there was no better practicable means than was in fact used to satisfy the duty or requirement. Here, the accused must establish the defence on a balance of probabilities.

20.4.1 Potential prosecution of culpable senior manager(s)

Although under CMCHA 2007, a senior manager(s) of a company will not attract any criminal liability (although it may still be possible to prosecute him or her under the common law for gross negligent manslaughter), culpable managerial conduct substantiating a company's conviction for corporate manslaughter, or an offence under HSWA 1974, s.2 or s.3 may result in a potential prosecution of the culpable senior manager(s) under HSWA 1974, s.37 (this may also lead to the imposition of a disqualification order under CDDA 1986, s.2 – discussed in **Chapter 17**). A prosecution under HSWA 1974, s.37(1) is dependent upon first establishing that the commission of an offence under HSWA 1974, s.2 or s.3 was undertaken with the consent or connivance of, or was attributable to any neglect on the part of, any director, manager, secretary or other similar officer of the body corporate. In the context of s.37(1), 'consent' and 'connivance' imply both knowledge and a decision made on the basis of such knowledge. Consent requires the defendant to have consented to conduct the company's business in the knowledge that the company was committing an offence. Connivance requires the defendant to have been aware that the conduct of the company's business amounted to an offence notwithstanding that the defendant did not actively participate in, or encourage the commission of the offence (see, e.g. *Attorney General's Reference (No.1 of 1995)* [1996] 2 Cr App R 320). Where the consent or connivance of a senior manager cannot be established, proof of a senior manager's neglect will suffice for the purpose of establishing liability under s.37(1). Although a senior manager's functions and responsibilities will be highly relevant in determining the extent and nature of any duty held, in the context of s.37(1) neglect refers to any neglect of duty, however constituted (see, e.g. *Armour* v. *Skeen* 1977 SLT 71). Therefore, it is unnecessary to establish that a defendant's neglect related to a duty imposed by statute.

20.4.2 Sentencing under HSWA 1974

Where a company is deemed responsible for the death of an individual under HSWA 1974, the company will be liable to a fine which should reflect the seriousness of the offence. Here, in accordance with the Sentencing Guidelines Council (February 2010), the recommended minimum fine is £100,000. However, it is to be noted that, in accordance with the decision of the Court of Appeal in *R* v. *F Howe & Son (Engineers) Ltd* [1999] 2 All ER 249, in setting the level of a fine the court may consider mitigating factors. Here, although the Court of Appeal recognised that the level of the fine should reflect the seriousness of the offence, the court stated that a fine should not be at a level that would propel a company into a state of bankruptcy. The court held that, in determining the seriousness of an offence, it was often useful to consider how far short of the appropriate standard the defendant had fallen, the degree of risk and extent of the danger involved and whether the company had deliberately breached regulations for the purposes of profit. Mitigating factors included an early admission of responsibility and plea of guilty, the taking of action to remedy any breach brought to the company's notice and a good safety record. A court's ability to consider the extent of a fine in relation to a company's financial position was further considered by the Court of Appeal in *R* v. *Deeside Metals Ltd* [2012] 2 Cr App R 29. In this case, the court justified its decision to reduce the level of the original fine of £100,000, to a sum of £50,000, on the premise that the original fine would have destroyed the company's ability to continue trading and as such severely prejudiced the interests of the company's remaining, and entirely innocent, employees.

20.5 THE BRIBERY ACT 2010

The Bribery Act (BA) 2010 was introduced in the wake of the corruption scandal involving Saudi Arabia and the English defence company BAE Systems (the Act received Royal Assent on 8 April 2010 and came into force on 1 July 2011). The scandal was subject to a Serious Fraud Office investigation but the investigation was subsequently halted for diplomatic and political reasons. Following the curtailment of the investigation, public and media disquiet of the failure to persist with the investigation assisted in the advancement of the reform of UK anti-corruption law. The enactment of BA 2010 also met with the UK's need to comply with its obligations under the Economic Co-Operation and Development (OECD) Convention on Combating Bribery of Foreign Public Officials in cross-border commercial and related activities. Previous regulation of the corruption issues, in the guise of the Public Bodies Corrupt Practices Act 1889, the Prevention of Corruption Act 1906 and the Prevention of Corruption Act 1916 were all repealed in respect of offences committed after the coming into force of BA 2010.

The Act is a complex piece of legislation and consists of two general offences (BA 2010, ss.1 and 2), a further offence (BA 2010, s.6) related to the bribery of a foreign public official and finally an offence (BA 2010, s.7) concerned specifically with commercial organisations. The offences provided by ss.1, 2 and 6 may be committed by any person (therefore to include a corporate entity). In respect of corporate liability for the offences specified by ss.1, 2 and 6, liability must be established in accordance with attribution principles, i.e. liability must be established through the company's directing mind (discussed above). Any prosecution under BA 2010 may only take place with the consent of the Director of Public Prosecutions, the Director of the Serious Fraud Office or the Director of Revenue and Customs Prosecutions (BA 2010, s.10). Here an offence will be prosecuted only where there is a realistic prospect of conviction and further the prosecution must be in the public interest. Accordingly, despite a theoretical possibility to the contrary it is most unlikely that a prosecution would ever be commenced where, for example, a 'bribe' related to corporate hospitality, unless the hospitality in question far exceeded an acceptable industry norm. In accordance with BA 2010, s.11, the offences specified in ss.1, 2 and 6 carry a maximum penalty of 10 years' imprisonment and/or an unlimited fine, whereas the offence specified in s.7 carries a maximum penalty of an unlimited fine.

20.5.1 The general offences

BA 2010, s.1 defines the offence of bribery in relation to the person who instigates the bribe, as an offence relating to the offering, promising or giving of financial compensation or any other advantage (to include a gift) with the intention of inducing a person to perform improperly a relevant function or activity, or to reward a person for an improper performance of such a function or activity.

BA 2010, s.2 defines an offence committed by the recipient of a bribe. The offence is committed where a person requests, accepts, or actually receives an advantage, intending that, in consequence, a relevant function or activity should be performed improperly (note here it is necessary to prove the recipient's intention). The offence may be committed in two further instances:

(i)   where a person requests, agrees, or accepts an advantage and the request, agreement or acceptance, in itself, constitutes an improper performance of a relevant function or activity; or

(ii)   in circumstances where a person requests, agrees, or accepts an advantage as a result of performing, or in anticipation of performing improperly, a relevant function or activity.

Section 3 defines a person's 'functions and activities' as:

(i)   any function of a public nature;

(ii)   any other private activity connected with or performed on behalf of a business;

(iii) any activity performed in the course of a person's employment; or

(iv)   any activity performed by or on behalf of a body of persons (whether corporate or unincorporated).

A person is deemed only to be relevant for the purpose of attracting liability only where in performing the function or activity he or she is:

(i)   expected to perform it in good faith;

(ii)   expected to perform it impartially; or

(iii) in a position of trust by virtue of performing it.

BA 2010, s.4 defines the improper exercise of a function or activity. An improper exercise of a function or activity is where it is performed in breach of a relevant expectation (i.e. good faith, impartially, position of trust; defined above in (i), (ii) and (iii)) or where the failure to perform the function or activity is itself a breach of a relevant expectation. In relation to s.3 and s.4, the court will employ an objective test, i.e. what a reasonable person in the UK would expect in relation to the performance of the type of function or activity concerned (BA 2010, s.5).

20.5.2 BA 2010, s.6 offence

BA 2010, s.6 is concerned with the bribery of a foreign public official and provides that it is an offence for a person to intentionally influence a foreign public official with the objective of intentionally obtaining or retaining business or an advantage for his or her business. The bribery will take place in circumstances where the person (either directly or through a third party) offers, promises, or gives financial advantages (or gifts) to the foreign public official or, at the official's request or acquiescence, another person.

20.5.3 The liability of directors/senior managers under BA 2010, ss.1, 2 and 6

Where a company is prosecuted for an offence under BA 2010, ss.1, 2 or 6, then in accordance with BA 2010, s.14, any director or senior officer of the company (senior officer is not defined by BA 2010) who consented to or connived in the activity will also be guilty of the offence. Therefore, where corporate liability is established through the company's directing mind (but note the difficulties associated with the attribution test – discussed above), s.14 liability will fall on the directing mind and in addition may also fall on any other director or senior officer (outside the directing mind) in circumstances where such a person was shown to have consented to or connived in the activity in question.

20.5.4 A specific offence against a relevant commercial organisation

A specific offence targeting relevant commercial organisations is created by BA 2010, s.7. A relevant commercial organisation may be identified in two forms. First, either a partnership formed in the UK (to include an LLP) or a business incorporated in the UK which carries out business activity in the UK or in another jurisdiction. Second, a partnership formed in another jurisdiction or a business incorporated in another jurisdiction which carries out business activity in the UK. Under BA 2010, s.7, a commercial organisation which fails to prevent a bribe for or on its behalf by a person associated with the organisation is guilty of the s.7 offence in circumstances where the associated person intends to obtain or retain business or a business advantage for the organisation. In respect of this provision, an associated person bribes another person if, and only if, the associated person is, or would be, guilty of an offence under BA 2010, ss.1 or 6 (whether or not the associated person was prosecuted for such an offence), or would otherwise have been guilty of such an offence under ss.1 or 6, if BA 2010, s.12(2)(c) and (4) were omitted from consideration. (Here the relevant parts of s.12 are concerned with jurisdiction.)

BA 2010, s.8 provides that an associated person is one who 'performs services' for or on behalf of the organisation. This affords a wide definition of an 'associated person' to include employees, agents or a subsidiary of the commercial organisation in question. Whether or not an associated person is a person who performs services for or on behalf of the organisation is a matter to be determined by reference to all the relevant circumstances and not merely by reference to the nature of the relationship between the associated person and the organisation. However, if the associated person is an employee of the organisation, this will raise the presumption (unless the contrary is established) that the associated person is a person who performs services for or on behalf of the organisation. Nevertheless, although the definition of an 'associated person' is wide it should be remembered that liability under s.7 will only ensue in circumstances where the associated person was or could have been made liable for an offence under BA 2010, ss.1 or 6, to the extent that in respect of a s.1 offence, the associated person must, by implication, have been expected to perform a function or activity for the commercial organisation either (i) in good faith, or (ii) impartially, or (iii) have been in a position of trust by virtue of performing it. While this definition would certainly include, for example, a director or senior manager, it is unclear whether it would apply to a 'mere' employee of the company.

BA 2010, s.7(2) provides a defence to the s.7 offence, namely where the organisation had in place adequate procedures designed to prevent persons associated with it from committing the s.7 offence. BA 2010, s.9 provides that it is the responsibility of the Secretary of State to publish guidance on what amount to 'adequate procedures'. Guidance notes were published in 2011 and, *inter alia*, provided that procedures would be adequate where, for example, they were proportionate to the nature and type of a company's business and derived from regular documented risk assessments which were monitored and periodically revised and supported by senior level management. However, it must be observed that the guidance notes (advanced under s.9) do not have the force of law and ultimately it will be for the courts to decide, on a case-by-case basis, whether or not adequate procedures have been put in place.

CHAPTER 21

Corporate governance issues

21.1 INTRODUCTION

Debate, discussion and government intervention in relation to issues of corporate governance may be viewed as a natural consequence of the economic and social impact of companies and the role companies play in the economic wellbeing of a nation. Corporate governance issues are concerned with the formal and informal regulation of both the internal and external mechanisms under which companies operate. The Cadbury Committee defined corporate governance as 'a system by which companies are directed and controlled' (para.2.5). In effect, all aspects around the regulation of company law fall to be defined by the term 'corporate governance'. However, in the main, the specific purpose of this chapter is to consider corporate governance issues outside the regulation of companies as provided by the companies legislation with particular regard to the governance of management functions and structures. In this context, the purpose of corporate governance is to facilitate effective, entrepreneurial and prudent management that seeks to deliver the long-term success of the company. Here, government intervention in issues of corporate governance is concerned primarily with the regulation of public companies.

21.2 GOVERNANCE AND CORPORATE EFFICIENCY

Business activity is stimulated by the pursuit of profit but the pursuit of profit obviously involves risk taking by the managers of companies, especially in the context of investment decisions and the allocation of corporate resources. Further, the pursuit of profit may result in an abuse of the corporate structure whereby the adverse human desire of greed and ambition to, for example, expand a business enterprise, is sometimes pursued otherwise than by legitimate means. While the pursuit of profit may often be advantageous to the growth and expansion of a corporate enterprise, in some cases inopportune risk taking or pure 'human' greed/ambition may result in corporate failure. While the regulation of risk or human nature is probably not an achievable task, the regulation of excessive and unwarranted risk taking and/or the illegitimate pursuit of business objectives provides an essential purpose behind any corporate governance technique. Corporate governance in action must therefore attempt to alleviate and, if possible, prevent unwarranted risk taking and/or the illegitimate pursuit of business objectives.

In the context of a public company, the companies legislation provides essential tools to the purpose of affording protection and stability for the corporate enterprise, the general economy and the general public interest. However, additional regulatory tools may also be essential for the protection of the public interest. In public companies especially, the shareholders will generally function as investors as opposed to an active 'watchdog' in respect of the necessary regulation of the company's affairs. The protection of the public interest is also paramount in an economic sense, that is, many members of the public will have a financial stake in the affairs of public companies whether as shareholders, employees and/or members of pension schemes, in which employees' contributions will be invested in shares and other securities. In terms of the public interest, the interests of all stakeholders must be protected and the perceived champion for this protection is a regulatory system of corporate governance.

Regulation and government interference into the corporate law field will often, if not always, be ignited by a serious corporate failure or scandal. The interference is driven by both an economic and political desire to rid the corporate infrastructure of systems and practices which may give rise to a potential for future similar failures and scandals. In seeking to clear up a 'corporate mess', a government's objective will be to calm and reassure investors, corporate players and markets, thereby protecting economic stability and the general public interest. Corporate law history is indicative of the introduction of governance measures following major corporate failures and scandals. In the UK probably the earliest example of a corporate scandal giving rise to government intervention was the South Sea 'bubble' episode of the eighteenth century (discussed in **Chapter 1**).

21.3 HISTORICAL SUMMARY OF UK CORPORATE GOVERNANCE MEASURES 1992–2000

In the UK, the current trend of corporate governance initiatives may be traced back to the 1980/90s. The developments followed a number of high profile corporate scandals that included those associated with the following companies, namely, Polly Peck, BCCI, and the Maxwell group of companies. A common theme of such corporate failures was the presence of financial reporting irregularities and inadequate boardroom structures. The latter failures led to the publication of the Cadbury Committee Report in 1992. The report recommended a Code of Best Practice, to be complied with by the boards of listed companies as a condition of continued listing on the Stock Exchange. The Code of Best Practice recognised the significance of the following practices:

- The appointment of independent non-executive directors to the boards of listed companies (although the term 'independent' was not defined).
- Appointments to the post of executive director to be vetted by a nomination committee, the appointees of which were to be principally taken from the ranks of a company's non-executive directors.
- The roles of chief executive and chairman should, where possible, not be held by the same person thereby promoting the independent nature of the board.
- Service contracts in excess of three years should not be granted to executive directors unless approved by the general meeting.
- Executive directors' salaries should be determined by means of a remuneration committee to be made up wholly or principally from the ranks of the non-executive directors.
- The creation of an audit committee to oversee the company's financial matters, the constitution of which should be made up by a majority of non-executive directors.

The Code required all listed companies to include a statement in their annual report acknowledging compliance with its terms or justifying instances of non-compliance. However, the Code had no statutory force and its terms were not implemented as enforceable Listing Rules and, as such, compliance with the terms of the Code was not a prerequisite for listing.

A number of subsequent reports added to the findings of the Cadbury Report. These reports included the Rutteman Report (1994) on internal control and financial reporting, the Greenbury Report (1995) concerning excessive remuneration payments for company directors, and the Hampel Committee Report (1998). The Hampel Report sought to progress and where necessary add to the recommendations of the reports of both the Cadbury Committee and Greenbury Committee. The remit of the Hampel Committee was to review the role of both executive and non-executive directors, consider matters relating to directors' remuneration and further to consider the role of both shareholders and auditors in corporate governance issues. In respect of the management structures of public companies, the conclusions of the Hampel Report were as follows:

- Both executive and non-executive directors should be subject to the same corporate duties. However, directors should be provided with more information and instruction in relation to the performance of such duties.
- Although the report fell short of recommending that executive directors should have some form of recognised qualification, the report considered that persons who held an executive directorship should have the necessary experience to be capable of understanding the nature and extent of the interests of the company in which they held office.
- The majority of non-executive directors in companies of all sizes should be independent and make up at least one-third of the board of directors.
- An individual should not ordinarily occupy the role of both chairman and chief executive.

- All companies should have nomination committees for the purpose of recommending new board appointments. Directors should be obliged to seek re-election at least every three years following their appointment.
- Executive directors' remuneration should not be excessive and should be based upon recommendations from remuneration committees which should be composed of non-executive directors. Remuneration should be related to performance and a general statement on remuneration policy should be included in a company's annual report.
- Directors' contracts should not exceed one year.

The Hampel Committee Report led to the introduction of the Combined Code of Corporate Governance (1998). The Combined Code applied to all listed companies and introduced the concept of 'comply or explain', by which listed companies were obliged to produce a narrative statement detailing the extent to which they had complied with the Code, or alternatively an explanation for why, in any particular instance, they had not complied with its principles. However, it must be stressed that the Combined Code did not have the force of law, albeit the consequence of non-compliance with the Code was that it was possible for a company to be refused listing.

Following the publication of the Combined Code, the content of and principles entrenched in the Code were supplemented and revised in a continuous process of review. The future revision of the Code was influenced by, for example, the Turnbull Committee Report (1999) (which sought to ensure that the board of directors of a listed company had or put in place a system of risk management for identifying and managing key business risks) and the Myners Review (2001), relating to shareholder engagement in matters of corporate governance. In 2003 a Revised Code was issued; this superseded and replaced the Combined Code 1998. With some minor modifications, the Revised Code embraced the recommendations contained in a report by Derek Higgs entitled the 'Review of the role and effectiveness of non-executive directors', DTI (January 2003). The spark which ignited the introduction of the Revised Code had its origins in the infamous American corporate disaster centred around the Enron Corporation.

21.4 THE COLLAPSE OF THE ENRON CORPORATION

In December 2001, the collapse of the Enron Corporation, at the time the largest ever bankruptcy in the US, adversely affected individuals and sectors of the US economy and global markets, causing much economic hardship. More significantly, Enron's collapse may be viewed as the principal catalyst in the large scale revamping of the global corporate governance rules. The underlying cause of Enron's demise was its rapid but unsustainable policy of growth. The corporation pursued an untenable expansionist policy involving the incurring of substantial debt to finance capital expenditure. Initially, its principal business was as an energy supplier; however, during the 1990s, the company's growth and diversification into

427

other business areas took off at a rapid rate. By 1995, Enron was the world's largest trader in natural gas and further had expanded its trading base into a variety of commodities ranging from the supply of water to internet capacity. During the period from 1995 to 1998, up to 40 per cent of the company's earnings were generated from new businesses, non-existent some five years earlier.

As Enron's debt increased, the company sought an alternative method to continue to finance its operations but one whereby it could avoid the declaration of any acceleration in debt, thereby maintaining investor confidence in the company's stock and easing any pressure on its credit ratings. Here an apparent solution was the creation of investment partnerships, a form of limited liability partnership. As distinct legal entities, albeit in effect subsidiaries of Enron, the partnerships had their own legal capacity to borrow funds from lending institutions. Many of the partnerships were structured in the form of special purpose entities (SPEs), which, for accounting purposes, entitled any debts of the SPE to be kept off Enron's balance sheet. In accordance with the US Financial Accounting Standards Board, an SPE could be created where an independent owner(s) of the SPE made a substantial capital investment in the entity (a minimum of 3 per cent of total capital) and where the independent owner(s) took substantial risks and rewards of ownership, exercising ultimate control over the SPE. However, in respect of Enron, those requirements for the creation of SPEs were never met. A number of transactions involving the SPEs were not designed for the purpose of accomplishing *bona fide* economic objectives, but rather were intended to achieve favourable financial statement results for Enron. While in theory, losses could be set off against the SPEs, in reality, the losses remained as debt because the SPEs were but mirror images of the Enron corporation. For example, in 1997, an SPE was created to take over a previously legitimate energy project known as JEDI. The project was in debt and Enron wished to wipe that debt from its balance sheet.

To create JEDI as an SPE, Enron assisted one of its senior employees, a close associate of the company's chief executive, in the formation of a new partnership company named Chewco. However, this partnership company had no financial capacity to acquire a 3 per cent interest in JEDI. In effect, Enron financed Chewco's purchase of the JEDI interest but almost entirely with debt and not equity. Notwithstanding the shortfall in the 3 per cent equity capital requirement, Enron maintained the pretence of Chewco's SPE status and failed to consolidate Chewco (or for that matter JEDI) into its consolidated financial statements.

21.4.1 Enron's 'hedging agreements'

Additional improper transactions involving offsetting losses included, for example, Enron's 'hedging agreements'. Enron performed this particular accounting trick by purporting to insure itself against potential losses resulting from specific transactions. However, instead of entering such hedging agreements with independent third parties, the hedging agreements were with related SPEs, namely the LJM1 and LJM2 partnerships, controlled and managed by senior executives of Enron. The

SPEs were given Enron stock in return for covering the sum of any losses sustained as a result of a specific transaction. While, in theory, the losses could be set off against the SPEs, in reality the losses remained as debt in so far as the SPEs were but mirror images of the Enron Corporation. The hedging agreements involved no substantive transfer of economic risk. In addition, they contained the inherent flaw that, if Enron's stock fell, the hedges would also fail. Indeed, this flaw was to become a reality. However, notwithstanding Enron's use of the SPEs, by the end of 2001 the company was in debt to the sum of approximately £3 billion. Market confidence in the company was destroyed and, in December 2001, Enron filed for relief under Chapter 11 of the United States Bankruptcy Code.

21.4.2 Apportioning responsibility for Enron's demise

In the context of apportioning responsibility for Enron's demise, the greater part of any culpability was attached to the corporation's internal watchdogs, namely its directors, executives and auditors. In the US, the ultimate responsibility for the internal governance of a public company rests on the shoulders of its board of directors. The board is composed of a majority of directors who are devoid of day-to-day managerial responsibilities. Both State and Federal law regulate the directors of a public company, whereby directors are subject to duties of loyalty and care although, in accordance with the US business judgment rule, directors operate under the favourable presumption that in making business decisions they will have acted on an informed basis, in good faith and in the honest belief that the decision was in the best interests of the company. Further, a director's personal liability for a breach of duty may be eliminated or limited by the company's constitution other than where the act or omission giving rise to the breach was instigated in bad faith or where it involved intentional misconduct, a knowing violation of the law, or where it involved a transaction whereby a director gained an improper personal benefit at the expense of the company. Basically, in the US the promotion of corporations is centred on an enterprise culture where risk taking is encouraged to the extent that company directors will escape the imposition of any form of liability other than where they acted in a fraudulent and dishonest manner.

21.4.3 The Powers Report

Although in the US the board is viewed as independent guardian of shareholder interests, in the Enron case the board failed to act in such a capacity. Following the Enron scandal, a special committee of Enron's board of directors was set up to investigate the company's demise. The report of the special committee (the Powers Report) concluded that the board had failed to act with sufficient diligence in its approval of the partnership transactions. For example, in 1999, with board approval, Enron entered into two partnership related transactions (the LJM transactions) for which a senior executive of the corporation was both a manager and investor. While the board considered that the relationship may have given rise to a conflict of interest, it mistakenly believed that any such conflict would be mitigated by board control and oversight. Furthermore, the board considered the creation of the partnerships to be beneficial to Enron. Although the board put various controls in place and directed its audit and compliance committee to conduct annual reviews of the partnership transactions, the rules and practices set up in respect of such reviews were inadequate. This inadequacy was not addressed by the company's management, nor were any of the apparent problems associated with the reviews ever brought to the board's attention.

While the Powers Report acknowledged that the executive management of the company had misled and concealed key facts from the board, the report concluded that information available to the board should, had it properly been scrutinised, have been sufficient for the board to detect the many serious problems associated with the partnership transactions. Accordingly, the Powers Report opined that the board had failed to take adequate care to protect the interests of shareholders and that it had overreached itself in a number of respects. The board failed adequately to monitor the activities of senior management, having only five meetings a year and spending under an hour reviewing even the most complicated transactions. Yet despite this lack of diligence, members of the Enron board enjoyed remuneration packages of twice the national average for a public corporation.

However, although the board of directors of Enron may have been negligent in the performance of their corporate duties, the conduct of the company's executive directors was reckless and, in some instances, fraudulent. In addition to breaches of duty and fraudulent practices, the executive directors of Enron engaged in insider dealing. Further, senior executives withheld key information from the board of directors relating to substantial losses in connection with the related partnership transactions. The executive failed, through their reckless inactivity, to protect the interests of the company and, in intentionally concealing the true financial position of the company, sought to deceive the company's board. The executives manipulated Enron's financial statements in a manner inconsistent with their fiduciary duties and in a manner in excess of any delegated authority from the board of directors. The executives failed to advance a system of effective oversight and controls.

21.4.4 Auditors' independence compromised

In respect of Enron's auditors, their independence was compromised, given that they also acted as financial consultants to the company. This was indeed a common practice across the US. In Enron's case, the company's accounting principles were determined with extensive participation from the company's auditors, who helped structure many of the transactions which Enron used to improve the appearance of its financial statements. In 2000, Enron's auditors earned $52 million in fees from the corporation, more than half of which was made up of consultancy fees, of which $5.7 million was received for advice in connection with the LJM and Chewco partnerships. In addition to the firm's conviction on a charge of obstruction of justice in connection with the shredding of documents relating to Enron's affairs, Enron's auditors performed miserably, exhibiting a lack of independence by failing to properly discharge responsibility in verifying the accuracy of Enron's accounts.

21.4.5 The Sarbanes-Oxley Act 2002

As a result of the collapse of Enron, the US passed the Sarbanes-Oxley Act (SOA) 2002. SOA 2002 applies to companies listed by the Securities and Exchange Commission (SEC) in the United States. SOA 2002 also carries extraterritorial impact in so far as it applies to a large number of non-US incorporated companies whose shares are listed on the New York Stock Exchange. Public and government support for this new legislation was further justified by the collapse of the World-Com Corporation, which filed for bankruptcy a week prior to the passing of the Act. WorldCom overtook Enron as the largest ever corporate bankruptcy in the US.

SOA 2002 purports to protect investors by improving corporate transparency via the accuracy and reliability of corporate disclosure and reporting procedures. The rationale for such regulation may be explained as a necessary prerequisite in regulating the consequences attached to the concept of the limited liability company and a separation between the investors' ownership of a company and the board of directors' power to manage the entity. Problems emanating from the division of ownership and control were identified as early as the eighteenth century by Adam Smith and more recently in the 1930s by the American economists Berle and Means – the latter observed that the separation and fragmentation of ownership (shareholders) from the management of a company resulted in the reduction of effective shareholder intervention in the management and regulation of companies.

SOA 2002 contains criminal, civil and administrative reforms designed to alter accounting, corporate governance and securities industry practices and seeks to expand and exalt the importance of corporate accountability as its principal weapon in a desire to rid the investing public of the evils associated with corporate wrongdoing. In relation to disclosure provisions, the Act introduces a certification procedure whereby the chief executive officer (CEO) and chief financial officer (CFO) of public companies must certify that they evaluated the effectiveness of the company's internal controls and that disclosure to the company's auditors and audit committee took place to include all significant deficiencies in the design or operation of controls relating to the effectiveness of the company's financial reporting. The company's annual report must include an assessment of management's internal controls and procedures relating to financial reporting. The CEO and CFO must certify the report as accurate. The certification applies not only to year-end financial statements, but also to quarterly, unaudited reports. SOA 2002 sets out significant criminal penalties for failure to so certify. Any officer who knowingly makes a false return is liable to a fine of $1 million and imprisonment for up to 10 years, or both. If the violation is deemed wilful then the fine increases to $5 million and the potential term of imprisonment up to 20 years or both. In respect of transparency provisions, the Act seeks to strengthen the role and independence of the audit committee. Audit committees have the sole responsibility for hiring and firing the company's independent auditors and for approving any significant non-audit work. SOA 2002 precludes any person who is affiliated with a major shareholder from being on the audit committee and further requires that an audit committee member must not receive any remuneration from the company other than compensation received in his or her capacity as a director, and that a member of the committee must not be an affiliated person of the issuer or any of its subsidiaries.

Under the Act, at least one member of the audit committee must have accounting or financial experience. Audit committees must be composed only of independent directors. All listed companies are required to have a majority of directors who satisfy a test of independence (prior to SOA 2002, only three independent directors were so required). A director will be classed as independent where he or she has no material relationship with the company directly or as a partner, shareholder or officer of an organisation which has a relationship with the company. SOA 2002 also contains several new reporting requirements for public companies. Significantly, given the facts of the Enron case, the SEC, in compliance with SOA 2002, enacted final rules seeking disclosure of all off-balance sheet transactions, arrangements, obligations and other relationships of the issuer with unconsolidated entries or other persons that have, or are reasonably likely to have, a current or future effect on a company's financial condition. In relation to the regulation of auditors SOA 2002 created the Public Company Accounting Oversight Board, the duty of which is to police the auditing of public companies. In accordance with the latter, auditing firms are precluded from supplying advisory services to companies for which they act as auditors. Further, a principle of auditor rotation is introduced whereby the alternation between companies of independent auditors is made mandatory.

21.5 ENRON AND THE UK'S RESPONSE – THE HIGGS REPORT AND A REVISED CODE

Reforms to the UK system of corporate governance were greatly influenced by the corporate scandals witnessed in the US. In the wake of the Enron scandal, the UK reforms may be best described as an attempt to maintain a competitive edge in the retention of global confidence in the UK markets so as to avert any fear of an Enron-type UK scandal. Following Enron, the proposed UK reforms emanated from the Higgs Report 2003, which was concerned with boardroom structures and the role of non-executive directors and, further, the Smith Report 2003 – a report of the Co-ordinating Group on Audit and Accounting Issues (CGAA). In common with the US reforms, the UK reforms concentrated on attempting to achieve higher standards of transparency, accountability and greater independent representation within the boardroom. However, in contrast to the US, the UK and other European states did not seek reform by way of a legislative approach. Rather, governance reforms were intended to build on the 'comply or explain' approach of the Combined Code.

21.5.1 The Higgs Report

The central theme of the Higgs Report was to ensure that UK boards had an overriding responsibility in setting the company's values, standards and obligations. The report stressed a collective board responsibility in terms of the entrepreneurial leadership within a framework of prudent and effective controls. In relation to boardroom structure, Higgs preferred the existing unitary nature of the board structure adopted in the UK and rejected a form of substantial reform based on the European system, which typically separates managerial responsibility between a management and supervisory board, or the US system, where the board is composed largely of outside directors with a small minority of management executives.

The core proposal of the Higgs Report related to the significance and role of the non-executive directors of public companies, a theme which also played a dominant role in the SOA 2002. Higgs considered that as independent guardians of the interests of investors, non-executive directors should challenge and contribute to the development of corporate strategy by scrutinising the performance of executive directors and management and by satisfying themselves that financial controls and systems of risk management were robust and defensible. Higgs considered that non-executive directors should be viewed as independent and divorced from the interests of persons with large financial or shareholding stakes in the company. In common with the listing requirements in the US, France and emerging commercial nations such as China, Higgs considered that a majority of the board should be composed of independent directors and recommended that the board's composition in a UK public company should be composed of at least 50 per cent independent non-executive directors. The independent non-executive directors were to be led by a senior independent director who would also act as a contact point with shareholders. Higgs sought to define an independent non-executive director as a person who sits on the board free of any potential conflict of interest. Indeed, the striking characteristic of the Higgs Report was the shift in influence and regulatory control away from executive directors to non-executive directors.

Building on the recommendations of the then existing Combined Code, it is apparent that Higgs proposed an increased momentum in the non-executive director's assumption of greater responsibility in the internal structures of the public company. In relation to boardroom structures, Higgs considered that a chairman of a company should lead the company in terms of its organisation and efficiency, ensuring effective communication with shareholders, evaluating the board's performance and that of its committees and facilitating the effective contribution of non-executive directors and general relations between executive and non-executive directors. The report considered that the role of chairman and managing director should be separate and that a division of their responsibilities be set out in writing. Further, a person retiring from his position as managing director should be discouraged from becoming the company's chairman because of the potential conflict between the two roles.

The Higgs Report highlighted the importance of the role of board committees and in wishing to promote the theme of independence provided that independent non-executive directors should dominate in the composition and influence of the board committees. In accordance with the terms of the final report of the CGAA, the Higgs Report sought to amend the Combined Code in respect of audit committees by strengthening the influence and role of the committee in relation to issues of financial accountability. For example, Higgs proposed that the committee should also make recommendations to the board in relation to the appointment and remuneration of the external auditor and have responsibility for reviewing the external auditor's independence and effectiveness. Higgs recommended that the audit committee should comprise at least three directors, all of whom should be independent non-executive directors with at least one member of the committee having had significant recent and relevant financial experience. The report further suggested that the directors should be obliged to include a separate section in their annual report describing the role of the committee and the activities and action that it had taken. In relation to a company's nomination committee, Higgs considered its role to be somewhat undeveloped. Higgs recommended that all listed companies should be obliged to have a nomination committee consisting of a majority of independent non-executive directors, a committee chaired by an independent non-executive director. It was recommended that the procedures and activities of the committee should be included in the company's annual report. With regard to the composition of a company's remuneration committee, Higgs recommended that it should be made up exclusively of non-executive directors who were independent of management and who met the test of independence so prescribed by the report. The report stipulated that the committee should have at least three members. As a minimum responsibility, the report provided that the committee should set the remuneration levels of all executive directors and the chairman. The report also recommended that the committee should consider setting remuneration levels for senior executives. As a consequence of the recommendations of the Higgs Report, key changes (in line with the Higgs recommendations) were incorporated into a revised Combined Code 2003.

21.5.2 Revision of the Combined Code

In 2005, following a review of the implementation of the Combined Code, the FRC consulted on a small number of minor changes to the Code which were subsequently incorporated into an updated version of the Code, published in June 2006. A review of the Code was completed in October 2007 and a revised Combined Code was published in 2008. While the fabric of the 2003 Code remained in place, examples of key principles to be attached to this revised Combined Code were as follows:

- *The board of directors*: Companies should be headed by an effective board, to be made collectively responsible for the success of the company. At the head of the company there should be a clear division of responsibilities between the running of the board (company chairman) and the executive responsibility (chief executive) for the running of the company's business. The board should include a balance of executive and non-executive directors (and, in particular, independent non-executive directors) such that no individual or small group of individuals could dominate the board's decision-making powers. There should be a formal, rigorous and transparent procedure for the appointment of new directors to the board. The board should be supplied in a timely manner with information in a form and of a quality appropriate to enable it to discharge its duties. All directors should receive induction on joining the board and should regularly update and refresh their skills and knowledge. The board should undertake a formal and rigorous annual evaluation of its own performance and that of its committees and individual directors. All directors should be submitted for re-election at regular intervals, subject to continued satisfactory performance. The board should ensure a planned and progressive refreshing of its composition.

- *Remuneration of directors*: Levels of remuneration should be sufficient to attract, retain and motivate directors of the quality required to run the company successfully, but a company should avoid paying more than is necessary for this purpose. A significant proportion of directors' remuneration should be structured so as to link rewards to corporate and individual performance. There should be a formal and transparent procedure for developing policy on executive remuneration and for fixing the remuneration packages of individual directors by the remuneration committee. No director should be involved in deciding his or her own remuneration.

- *Financial reporting*: The board should present a balanced and understandable assessment of the company's financial position and prospects and maintain a sound system of internal control to safeguard shareholders' investment and the company's assets. The board through its audit committee should establish formal and transparent arrangements for considering how they should apply the financial reporting and internal control principles and for maintaining an appropriate relationship with the company's auditors.

- *Relations with institutional shareholders*: There should be a dialogue with shareholders based on the mutual understanding of objectives. The board as a whole had a responsibility for ensuring that a satisfactory dialogue with shareholders took place. The board should use the AGM to communicate with investors and to encourage their participation. In evaluating a company's governance arrangements, particularly those relating to board structure and composition, institutional shareholders should give due weight to all relevant factors drawn to their attention. Institutional shareholders had a responsibility to make considered use of their voting rights.

21.5.3 The role of the non-executive director

The central theme of the Higgs Report so adopted into the Combined Code and its revisions was the significance and role of non-executive directors in the management of a public company. As independent guardians and monitors of the interests of investors, non-executive directors were expected to challenge and contribute to the development of corporate strategy by scrutinising the performance of executive directors and management. Non-executive directors were expected not only to be independent of mind but also to be seen to be independent and divorced from the interests of persons with large financial or shareholding stakes in the company in which they held office (see also, the Tyson Report 2003). The composition of the board of a UK public company was expected to be composed of at least 50 per cent independent non-executive directors. An independent non-executive director was defined as a person who sits on the board free of any potential conflict of interest.

21.6 THE BANKING CRISIS

In 2007–8, large scale problems emerged in the global banking sector. The problems emanated as a result of what had become the accepted policy of banks' lending in the subprime market, namely the banking sector loaned funds at too high a risk, with borrowers unable to repay the loans. Defaulting loans led to liquidity problems in the banks, resulting in a loss of confidence in global markets and the collapse of banking institutions, for example, Lehmans in the US, and Bradford and Bingley in the UK. With an intention of diluting the economic crisis and in attempt to restore confidence in the banking sector, the banking failures led to large scale government intervention. In the UK, leading banks were financially bailed out with government funds and in return the State took shareholding interests in a number of banks, for example an 80 per cent+ share in the Royal Bank of Scotland (RBS). In the case of one bank, Northern Rock plc, the government took the necessary step of completely nationalising the bank (the State became the bank's sole shareholder). Northern Rock plc was nationalised in February 2008 in accordance with the Banking (Special Provisions) Act 2008. Northern Rock was protected as a matter of national interest, namely the government considered that there was a serious risk that other parts of the UK banking system would be destabilised were Northern Rock to suffer a total demise. Further, the government sought to safeguard depositors' funds. Under public ownership, the government planned to take the entire proceeds from any future sale of the business for the benefit of the taxpayer in return for bearing the risk of the bank's perilous position. The demise of the bank is explained as follows.

Northern Rock plc, a former building society, was demutualised in 1997. Northern Rock was a principal mortgage provider in the UK. From its conception, the bank appeared to prosper and, by January 2007, its assets, comprising in the main residential mortgages (which represented 90 per cent of its assets), had grown to over £100 billion. Between 2000 and January 2007, the bank's share price rose by some 325 per cent. Despite its rapid growth, Northern Rock did not encounter an increase in the level of its arrears, which apparently remained about half the industry average. Indeed, in January 2007, the bank appeared to be in good health. However, the growth of the bank was built on risky loan/mortgage provision; for example, it adopted a policy of advancing loans worth up to 125 per cent of home values. As the retail deposits of the bank were relatively low (funds from deposit accounts accounted for about 22 per cent of its total funds) the bank depended heavily upon the availability of inter-bank and wholesale loans from other banks and financial institutions to fund its operations. The bank exhibited ambitious growth plans and to finance its growth Northern Rock was required to borrow heavily from the money markets. In August 2007, following the US subprime housing problems, banks globally eased up their lending to each other for fear of exposure to bad debt and as such Northern Rock's chief source of funding became severely depleted. Northern Rock's problems were compounded by the fact that it lacked sufficient liquidity insurance. The business strategy of Northern Rock, with its reliance on short- and medium-term wholesale funding, was high-risk, reckless, and coupled with an absence of sufficient insurance it was unable to deal with the liquidity pressures placed upon it. In September 2007, Northern Rock announced that the Treasury had authorised the Bank of England to provide emergency financial support in the form of a loan secured against the company's highest quality assets. When Northern Rock's customers became aware of the existence of the support, within a week, over £4.5 billion was withdrawn from depositors' accounts. By the end of September 2007, the bank's share price had fallen to a low of £1.32.

In reviewing the reasons for the collapse of Northern Rock, the Treasury Committee of the UK House of Commons concluded that the executive directors of the bank were to blame, in so far as they had pursued a reckless business model, which was excessively reliant on wholesale funding. Further, the company's non-executive directors had failed to act as guardians of the bank's interests. Blame was also apportioned to the Financial Services Authority for systematically failing in its regulatory duty to ensure that Northern Rock would not pose a systemic risk.

21.6.1 The UK's response

The UK Corporate Governance Code (formerly the Combined Code) was updated in June 2010. The following month, the FRC published the first Stewardship Code for institutional investors (discussed below). The new Codes were published in the wake of the Turner Report (in March 2009) and the Walker Report (November 2009). The former report considered the global reasons for the financial crisis and identified internal risk management as being ineffective and a major cause of the crisis. This report criticised management boards for failing to identify and constrain risk taking and further criticised the policy of management in providing incentives via excessive remuneration for the advancement of short-term gains. The Walker Report was concerned more specifically with the banking problems encountered in the UK. The report called for the remuneration structures of directors and senior managers to be improved to prevent excessive risk taking resulting from short-term payment incentives. The report found that the weakness of company boards was not necessarily the fault of boardroom organisation or structure but rather the weakness was due to the behaviour of individual executives and the lack of any independent challenge to their authority. As such the report recommended that non-executive directors should be afforded greater strength and authority and that executive performance required more frequent monitoring especially in the context of risk management. Further, the report suggested that institutional shareholders should play a more active role in the governance of companies. However, the report concluded that it considered that the 'comply or explain' approach to corporate governance remained a better alternative than seeking to enforce regulation via legislation.

21.6.2   The content of the FRC Governance Code

The FRC Governance Code 2010 made limited but potentially significant changes to the previous Combined Code, with the most striking change being that FTSE 350 companies should put all directors forward for re-election every year. Other significant changes included the requirement for company chairmen to make a personal statement on how the Code's principles were applied in relation to the role and effectiveness of the board and the requirement to incorporate disclosure of the company's business model. The purpose behind the latter change was that an explanation related to a company's ability to generate value over the longer term would enable shareholders and other stakeholders to determine whether the company's strategy would deliver that value, and the extent to which the company understood and was addressing the main risks of its strategy (see the Kay Review 2012).

21.7   THE CORPORATE GOVERNANCE CODE 2012

The 2010 Code was updated in September 2012 and the new Code is summarised below. The 2012 Code introduces some subtle changes to the 2010 Code, although of greater significance is the extension in the role afforded to the audit committee. Obligatory disclosure requirements in respect of the Corporate Governance Code apply to companies registered in the UK with a premium listing. A premium listed company is a company listed on the FTSE UK Index Series. A company with a standard listing (not included in the FTSE index) will be required to comply with the less arduous EU Company Reporting Directive and will not be subject to the Listing Rules. A premium listed company is required to report on how it applied the main principles of the Code and to confirm whether it complied with the Code's provisions. In circumstances where a company does not comply with specific provisions it must provide an explanation for non-compliance. The main principles of the 2012 Code are divided into the following sections:

A.   *Leadership*: A company should be headed by an effective board which is collectively responsible for the long-term success of the company. There should be a clear division of responsibilities at the head of the company between the running of the board and the executive responsibility for the running of the company's business. No one individual should have unfettered powers of decision-making. The chairman is responsible for leadership of the board and ensuring its effectiveness on all aspects of its role. As part of their role as members of a unitary board, non-executive directors should constructively challenge and help develop proposals on strategy.

B.   *Effectiveness*: The board and its committees should have the appropriate balance of skills, experience, independence and knowledge of the company to enable them to discharge their respective duties and responsibilities effectively. There should be a formal, rigorous and transparent procedure for the appointment of new directors to the board. All directors should be able to allocate sufficient time to the company to discharge their responsibilities effectively. All directors should receive induction on joining the board and should regularly update and refresh their skills and knowledge. The board should be supplied in a timely manner with information in a form and of a quality appropriate to enable it to discharge its duties. The board should undertake a formal and rigorous annual evaluation of its own performance and that of its committees and individual directors. All directors should be submitted for re-election at regular intervals, subject to continued satisfactory performance.

C.   *Accountability*: The board should present a fair, balanced and understandable assessment of the company's position and prospects. The board is responsible for determining the nature and extent of the significant risks it is willing to take in achieving its strategic objectives. The board should maintain sound risk management and internal control systems. The board should establish formal and transparent arrangements for considering how they should apply the corporate reporting, risk management and internal control principles and for maintaining an appropriate relationship with the company's auditors.

D.   *Remuneration*: Levels of remuneration should be sufficient to attract, retain and motivate directors of the quality required to run the company successfully, but a company should avoid paying more than is necessary for this purpose. A significant proportion of executive directors' remuneration should be structured so as to link rewards to corporate and individual performance. There should be a formal and transparent procedure for developing policy on executive remuneration and for fixing the remuneration packages of individual directors. No director should be involved in deciding his or her own remuneration.

E.   *Relations with shareholders*: There should be a dialogue with shareholders based on the mutual understanding of objectives. The board as a whole has responsibility for ensuring that a satisfactory dialogue with shareholders takes place. The board should use the AGM to communicate with investors and to encourage their participation.

In summary, the provisions of the new Governance Code (provided, by subject area) are as follows.

21.7.1 Board of directors

- The board should meet sufficiently regularly to discharge its duties effectively; there should be a formal schedule of matters specifically reserved for its decision and a statement of how the board operates should be included within a company's annual report. The statement within the annual report should include a statement of which types of decisions are to be taken by the board and which are to be delegated to management. The statement should also set out the number of meetings of the board and its committees and record individual attendance by directors.
- The roles of 'chairman' and 'chief executive' should not be exercised by the same individual. The division of responsibilities between the chairman and chief executive should be clearly established, set out in writing and agreed by the board. The chairman is responsible for ensuring that the directors receive accurate, timely and clear information. The chairman should ensure effective communication with shareholders. The chairman should on appointment meet the independence criteria (discussed below). A chief executive should not go on to be chairman of the same company. If, exceptionally, a board decides that a chief executive should become the chairman of the company, the board should consult major shareholders in advance and should set out its reasons to shareholders at the time of the appointment and in the next annual report.
- The board should include an appropriate combination of executive and non-executive directors (and, in particular, independent non-executive directors) such that no individual or small group of individuals can dominate the board's decision-taking. In respect of a meeting of the nomination, audit or remuneration committees, only the committee chairman and members of the particular committee in question are entitled to be present at the meeting other than where others attend at the invitation of the committee.
- All directors of FTSE 350 companies should be subject to annual election by shareholders. All other directors should be subject to election by shareholders at the first annual general meeting after their appointment and to re-election thereafter at intervals of no more than three years. Non-executive directors who have served longer than nine years should be subject to annual re-election.
- The board should not agree to a full-time executive director taking on more than one non-executive directorship in a FTSE 100 company nor the chairmanship of such a company. The board should ensure that directors, especially non-executive directors, have access to independent professional advice at the company's expense where they judge it necessary to discharge their responsibilities as directors. Committees should be provided with sufficient resources to undertake their duties.

- The board should state in the annual report how performance evaluation of the board, its committees and its individual directors has been conducted. 'Evaluation of the board of FTSE 350 companies should be externally facilitated at least every three years. The external facilitator should be identified in the annual report and a statement should be made available as to whether they have any other connection with the company. The non-executive directors, led by the senior independent director, should be responsible for performance evaluation of the chairman, taking into account the views of executive directors. Evaluation of the board should consider the balance of skills, experience independence and knowledge of the company on the board, its diversity including gender (see the Davies Review – discussed below) how the board works together as a unit, and other factors relevant to its effectiveness. The board should present a fair, balanced and understandable assessment of the company's position and prospects. The board's responsibility to present a fair, balanced and understandable assessment extends to interim and other price-sensitive public reports and reports to regulators as well as to information required to be presented by statutory obligations. The board should establish arrangements that will enable it to ensure that the information presented is fair, balanced and understandable. The directors should explain in the annual report their responsibility for preparing the annual report and accounts, and state that they consider the report and accounts, taken as a whole, are fair, balanced and understandable and provide the information necessary for shareholders to assess the company's performance, business model and strategy. There should be a statement by the auditor about their reporting responsibilities.

21.7.2 Non-executive directors

- Non-executive directors should scrutinise the performance of management in meeting agreed goals and objectives and monitor the reporting of performance. They should satisfy themselves on the integrity of financial information and that financial controls and systems of risk management are robust and defensible.
- Non-executive directors are responsible for determining the appropriate levels of remuneration of executive directors and have a prime role in appointing and, where necessary, removing executive directors, and in succession planning.
- The board should appoint one of the independent non-executive directors to be the senior independent director to provide a sounding board for the chairman and to serve as an intermediary for the other directors when necessary. The senior independent director should be available to shareholders if they have concerns which contact through the normal channels of chairman, chief executive or other executive directors has failed to resolve or for which such contact is inappropriate.

- The chairman should hold meetings with the non-executive directors without the executives present. Led by the senior independent director, the non-executive directors should meet without the chairman present at least annually to appraise the chairman's performance and on such other occasions as are deemed appropriate. Where directors have concerns which cannot be resolved about the running of the company or a proposed action, they should ensure that their concerns are recorded in the board minutes. On resignation, a non-executive director should provide a written statement to the chairman, for circulation to the board, if they have any such concerns.

- A person cannot be regarded as an independent non-executive director in circumstances where that person:

  (i)   has or has had within the last three years, a material business relationship with the company either directly, or as a partner, shareholder, director or senior employee of a body that has such a relationship with the company;

  (ii) has received or receives additional remuneration from the company apart from a director's fee, participates in the company's share option or a performance-related pay scheme, or is a member of the company's pension scheme;

  (iii) has close family ties with any of the company's advisers, directors or senior employees;

  (iv) holds cross-directorships or has significant links with other directors through involvement in other companies or bodies;

  (v)   represents a significant shareholder; or has served on the board for more than nine years from the date of their first election.

- Except for smaller companies (below the FTSE 350), at least half the board, excluding the chairman, should comprise non-executive directors determined by the board to be independent. A smaller company should have at least two independent non-executive directors. The board should identify in its annual report each non-executive director which it considers to be independent. The board should determine whether the director is independent in character and judgment and whether there are relationships or circumstances which are likely to affect, or could appear to affect, the director's judgment. The board should state its reasons in circumstances where it determines that a director is independent notwithstanding the existence of relationships or circumstances which may appear relevant to its determination.

21.7.3   Appointment to the board – nomination committee

- There should be a nomination committee which should lead the process for board appointments and make recommendations to the board. A majority of members of the nomination committee should be independent non-executive directors. The chairman or an independent non-executive director should chair the committee, but the chairman should not chair the nomination committee when it is dealing with the appointment of a successor to the chairmanship. Non-executive directors should be appointed for specified terms subject to re-election and to statutory provisions relating to the removal of a director. Any term beyond six years for a non-executive director should be subject to particularly rigorous review, and should take into account the need for progressive refreshing of the board. A separate section of the annual report should describe the work of the nomination committee, including the process it has used in relation to board appointments. This section should include a description of the board's policy on diversity, including gender (see the Davies Review – discussed below), any measurable objectives that it has set for implementing the policy, and progress on achieving the objectives.

21.7.4 Accountability – audit committee

- The board should establish an audit committee of at least three or, in the case of smaller companies, two independent non-executive directors. In smaller companies the company chairman may be a member of, but not chair, the committee in addition to the independent non-executive directors, provided he or she was considered independent on appointment as chairman. The board should satisfy itself that at least one member of the audit committee has recent and relevant financial experience. The audit committee should have primary responsibility for making a recommendation on the appointment, reappointment and removal of the external auditors. FTSE 350 companies should put the external audit contract out to tender at least every 10 years. If the board does not accept the audit committee's recommendation, it should include in the annual report, and in any papers recommending appointment or reappointment, a statement from the audit committee explaining the recommendation and should set out reasons why the board has taken a different position.

- A separate section of the annual report should describe the work of the audit committee in discharging its responsibilities. The report should include the significant issues that the committee considered in relation to the financial statements, and how these issues were addressed. The report should provide an explanation of how it has assessed the effectiveness of the external audit process and the approach taken to the appointment or reappointment of the external auditor, and information on the length of tenure of the current audit firm and when a tender was last conducted and, if the external auditor provides non-audit services, an explanation of how auditor objectivity and independence is safeguarded. The audit committee should report to the board on how it has discharged its responsibilities.

- Where requested by the board, the audit committee should provide advice on whether the annual report and accounts, taken as a whole, are fair, balanced and understandable and provide the information necessary for shareholders to assess the company's performance, business model and strategy.

21.7.5 Remuneration committee

- The board should establish a remuneration committee of at least three or, in the case of smaller companies, two, independent non-executive directors. In addition the company chairman may also be a member of, but not chair, the committee if he or she was considered independent on appointment as chairman. The level of remuneration for non-executive directors should reflect the time commitment and responsibilities of the role. Remuneration for non-executive directors should not include share options or other performance-related elements. Where remuneration consultants are appointed, they should be identified in the annual report and a statement made as to whether they have any other connection with the company.
- The remuneration committee should carefully consider what compensation commitments (including pension contributions and all other elements) their directors' terms of appointment would entail in the event of early termination. The aim should be to avoid rewarding poor performance. They should take a robust line on reducing compensation to reflect departing directors' obligations to mitigate loss. Notice or contract periods should be set at one year or less.
- The remuneration committee should have delegated responsibility for setting remuneration for all executive directors and the chairman, including pension rights and any compensation payments. The committee should also recommend and monitor the level and structure of remuneration for senior management. The definition of 'senior management' for this purpose should be determined by the board but should normally include the first layer of management below board level.

21.7.6 Relationship with shareholders

The chairman should ensure that the views of shareholders are communicated to the board as a whole. The chairman should discuss governance and strategy with major shareholders. Non-executive directors should be offered the opportunity to attend scheduled meetings with major shareholders and should expect to attend meetings if requested by major shareholders. The senior independent director should attend sufficient meetings with a range of major shareholders to listen to their views in order to help develop a balanced understanding of the issues and concerns of major shareholders.

21.7.7 Relationship with other stakeholders

While in law the company is primarily accountable to its shareholders, and the relationship between the company and its shareholders is also the main focus of the Code, companies are encouraged to recognise the contribution made by other providers of capital and to confirm the board's interest in listening to the views of such providers in so far as these are relevant to the company's overall approach to governance.

21.7.8 Comply or explain

In complying with the disclosure requirements, a company should aim to illustrate how its actual practices are consistent with the principle to which the particular provision relates, and contribute to good governance and promote delivery of business objectives. It should set out the background, provide a clear rationale for the action it is taking, and describe any mitigating actions taken to address any additional risk and maintain conformity with the relevant principle. A company may choose not to comply with a provision or provisions of the Code (although it must comply with the main and supplementary principles), in which case it must explain why it has not complied with a particular provision. Where deviation from a particular provision is intended to be limited in time, the explanation should indicate when the company expects to conform with the provision.

21.7.9 The directors' report

Companies with a premium listing

The Listing Rules require companies with a premium listing in the UK (to include overseas registered companies) to disclose in their annual report the extent to which they have complied with the UK Corporate Governance Code and in any situation of non-compliance with provisions of the Code, to provide reasons for the same. Where a company fails to comply with these disclosure requirements it will be in breach of the Listing Rules which may render it (and its directors) liable to sanctions.

All companies

In accordance with CA 2006, s.415, for each financial year the directors of any company must prepare a report which states the names of the directors and the principal activities of the company (CA 2006, s.416). A failure to produce the report will render the directors of the company concerned liable to a fine (CA 2006, s.415(5)). The annual directors' report is the principal means of communication between the company and its shareholders, the market and other stakeholders.

Companies outside the small companies regime

Unless the company in question falls within the small companies regime, the directors' report must include a business review (CA 2006, s.417). The business review is intended to inform and help members of the company assess how the directors have performed their duty under CA 2006, s.172: namely whether the directors have promoted the success of the company for the benefit of the members as a whole. (The s.172 duty is discussed in **Chapter 15**.) In accordance with CA 2006, s.417(6), the business review must include a fair analysis using key performance indicators, namely factors by reference to which the development, performance and position of the company's business can be measured effectively. The review must also include a description of the principal risks and uncertainties facing the company. In the case of quoted companies the directors should report on the main trends and factors likely to influence the business's future development, performance and position, as well as providing information about the company's employees and the impact of the company's business on the environment and 'social and community issues' (CA 2006, s.417(5)). The report should include a statement from the directors confirming that there is no relevant audit information which has not been made available to the company's auditors (CA 2006, s.418). Except in the case of companies subject to the small companies regime, the directors' report must state the amount of any proposed dividends (CA 2006, s.416(3)). Other than for a small or medium-sized company the review must include an analysis using key financial performance indicators (CA 2006, s.417(6)).

Quoted company

In the case of a quoted company, the company must also prepare a directors' remuneration report (CA 2006, s.420). A failure to produce the report will render the directors of the company concerned liable to a fine (CA 2006, s.420(3)).

In all cases, the directors' report must be approved by the directors and signed on their behalf by a director or the company secretary (CA 2006, s.419).

21.8 INSTITUTIONAL SHAREHOLDERS AND THE UK STEWARDSHIP CODE

In large public companies shareholdings are dispersed widely among the general public and larger shareholding groups such as financial institutions, pension funds, insurance companies and investment trusts. In addition, since the Cadbury Report was first published, significant changes in patterns of ownership shares in the UK market (an increase in investment from outside the UK) has produced an even more obvious climate of short-term equity investment where investors look to short-term financial gain as opposed to the long-term investment in a company. Here, as shareholders generally invest for short-term financial gain, in times of policy conflict or signs of economic or management failure, investors are more likely to exit a company and re-invest elsewhere than seek to engage with matters of effective corporate governance. Further, even a large institutional shareholder will typically hold only a relatively small percentage of the total shareholding in a large public company and as such the cost and time involved in mobilising other shareholders may prevent generally any concerted challenge to management policies. Accordingly, in the majority of large public companies institutional shareholders are generally passive as opposed to active exponents of the virtues of effective corporate governance.

As a tool of effective corporate governance, the role of institutional shareholders is also weakened by the fact that they are often courted and influenced to vote in a manner prescribed by company directors. The active co-operation of groups of shareholders is also weakened by the fact that they may have conflicts of interest in respect of their respective business interests; the institutional shareholders of a company may be competitors and therefore may find it difficult to communicate with each other or to unite to challenge corporate policy. Further even where there is a united front between institutional shareholders the necessity of obtaining majority shareholder support runs the risk of exposing an opposition strategy to the public, which may result in poor publicity for the particular company and as a result a decline in the value of its shareholdings to the ultimate detriment of the institutional shareholder. Although the Corporate Governance Code seeks to encourage institutional shareholders to engage in and take responsibility for matters of corporate governance by making considered use of their votes and, where practicable, to enter into a dialogue with companies based on the mutual understanding of objectives, all in all, it is rare for groups of institutional shareholders to act together in unison in an attempt to monitor and influence management boards. Effective shareholder intervention in matters of corporate governance is a difficult objective given the necessity of achieving a critical mass of long-term investors that are willing and able to exercise their stewardship responsibilities and hold company boards to account.

The UK Stewardship Code was published in an attempt to promote a more effective culture around shareholder responsibility. The Code was first published in July 2010 and was updated in September 2012. The Code is applied on a 'comply or explain' basis. The Code is addressed at firms of asset managers who manage assets on behalf of institutional shareholders. The objective of the Code is to enhance the quality of engagement between institutional investors and companies to aid an improvement in the long-term returns to shareholders and the efficient exercise of governance responsibilities. However, the success of the Code will be dependent on achieving more stringent stewardship of investee companies by the ultimate beneficiaries (institutional shareholders). Since December 2010, the Financial Services Authority (now the Financial Conduct Authority) has required all firms authorised to manage funds on behalf of others to state whether they apply the Stewardship Code. Those that do so are expected under the terms of the Code to comply with its principles and report on how it has been applied or explain why they have not so complied. The seven principles of the Code are as follows:

Institutional investors should:

1. Publicly disclose their policy on how they will discharge their stewardship responsibilities.

2.   Have a robust policy on managing conflicts of interest in relation to steward-
     ship which should be publicly disclosed.
3.   Monitor their investee companies.
4.   Establish clear guidelines on when and how they will escalate their steward-
     ship activities.
5.   Be willing to act collectively with other investors where appropriate.
6.   Have a clear policy on voting and disclosure of voting activity.
7.   Report periodically on their stewardship and voting activities.

21.9   BOARDROOM STRUCTURES – GENDER DIVERSITY AND THE DAVIES REVIEW

The great majority of directors on the boards of publicly quoted companies are men
and as such, issues around the gender diversity of boardrooms is of some contention. Given the increased proportion of women completing university degrees and
the fact that more women are now entering the corporate world, it is perhaps
surprising that women have not as a genus progressed to the boardroom. In
February 2011, Lord Davies of Abersoch published a government-backed report
entitled *Women on Boards*. The report considered the extent of the diverse gender
composition of boardrooms and the reasons why there were barriers preventing
more women reaching the boardroom. The report found that in 2009/10 only 12.2
per cent of directors of FTSE 100 companies were women and in respect of the
boards of FTSE 250 companies the percentage of women represented at boardroom
level was even lower, at 7.3 per cent. The figures were even more startling in respect
of the number of executive directorships held by women – only 5.5 per cent of FTSE
100 companies had executive directors who were women. Further, over one in five
(21 per cent) of FTSE 100 companies and over half (52.4 per cent) of FTSE 250
companies had no women at all on their boards.

The Davies Review considered that the case for increasing the number of women
on boards of directors was obvious, especially as evidence presented to the review
suggested that companies with a strong female representation at boardroom and top
management level performed better than those without such representation. The
review sought to make recommendations in respect of how the government and the
business world could increase the proportion of women on corporate boards. Given
the massive shortfall in the number of women directors, the Davies Review
considered whether the government should set quota targets for the proportion of
female board members in line with other EU states. For example, in 2007, Spain
introduced a gender-equality law requiring, by 2015, a minimum of 40 per cent of
each sex on the boards of public companies that had more than 250 employees.
However, the Davies Review concluded that it would not recommend a quota
system albeit it did suggest that the government should reserve the right to introduce
prescriptive alternatives if the recommended business-led approach did not achieve
significant change. The recommended business-led approach suggested as follows:

- That targets should be set to increase the number of women directors. For example, that FTSE 100 boards should aim for a minimum of 25 per cent female representation by 2015.
- Quoted companies should be required to disclose each year: the proportion of women on their boards; women in senior executive positions and female employees in the whole organisation.
- The Financial Reporting Council should amend the UK Corporate Governance Code to require listed companies to establish a policy concerning boardroom diversity, including measurable objectives for implementing the policy, and annually disclose a summary of the policy and the progress made in achieving the objectives (implemented in the 2012 Code).
- Chairmen should disclose in the annual report (in connection with the work of the nomination committee), meaningful information about the company's appointment process and how it addressed diversity, including a description of the search and nominations process.
- In advertising non-executive board positions, companies should encourage greater diversity in applications.
- Executive search firms should draw up a voluntary Code of Conduct addressing gender diversity and best practice which covered the relevant search criteria and processes relating to FTSE 350 board appointments.

21.9.1 European response

Following the Davies Review, the UK witnessed a gradual increase in the number of women holding senior corporate management positions and positions at boardroom level (especially in the context of positions as non-executive directors). By the end of 2012, women held around 18 per cent of FTSE 100 directorships and around 13 per cent of FTSE 250 directorships. However, the increase in women board members is marginal and female representation in senior management positions in the UK is, in many cases, less favourable than in other European countries. Indeed, it is probable that the European Commission will seek to produce a Directive aimed at improving gender balance on the boards of listed companies in the European Union and will do so by the imposition of quotas. However, a quota system, if it promotes positive gender discrimination, may itself fall foul of discrimination laws.

21.10 A EUROPEAN RESPONSE TO CORPORATE GOVERNANCE ISSUES

In December 2012, the European Commission announced a major provisional Action Plan for modernising European rules on corporate governance. The Action Plan is the first major European initiative around the reform of European corporate governance issues since 2003 at which time the European Commission announced that it believed it to be unnecessary to compile a European Governance Code.

Instead of adopting a general Code, the Commission favoured the development of future directives and reform in respect of selected core governance issues. Those issues included:

- more effective annual corporate governance statements;
- increased disclosure measures;
- the reform of boardroom structures;
- an increase in the numbers and role of independent directors;
- greater autonomy and significance to be attached to board committees;
- more effective shareholder meetings; and
- a more supportive and effective role for institutional shareholders.

Once again, the Commission's Action Plan 2012 seeks to develop specific key objectives through directives. The key objectives concern the following:

- The role of the non-executive director: The Commission is concerned to strengthen disclosure requirements in relation to board diversity and risk management. Building on its belief that successful corporate governance is enhanced by the effective oversight and supervision of executive directors by non-executive directors, the Commission wishes to promote increased diversity in respect of the independence and appointment of executive directors.
- The Commission is concerned to improve corporate governance reporting. The Commission criticised the current 'comply or explain' approach of national corporate governance codes in the EU. The Commission considered that the current system permits companies to depart from implementing specific parts of the Code without providing sufficient detail and explanation for non-compliance with the same. Therefore, the Commission proposes that the quality of corporate governance reporting should be improved.
- The Commission believes that there should be more transparency in relation to the identity of shareholdings in listed companies. To this end the Commission will consider measures to require additional information to be made available in respect of the ownership of shares.
- Improving and encouraging shareholder engagement (especially in relation to institutional shareholders) and influence in corporate decision-making and governance issues especially in the context of directors' remuneration and related party transactions.

CHAPTER 22

Corporate insolvency procedures

22.1 INTRODUCTION

The worldwide recession has had a significant impact on businesses in the UK. The law of insolvency has, in recent years, moved from being a niche specialist area into the mainstream. Insolvency law was completely overhauled in the mid-1980s with a new emphasis on the so-called 'rescue culture' and has been the subject of several Parliamentary interventions since that time. In particular, the Enterprise Act 2002 introduced significant changes to IA 1986 (the principal statute in the area).

The purpose of this chapter is to provide an outline and introduction to the main UK insolvency law procedures and to explain how they have developed and how they operate. (For a more detailed account of insolvency law, see, e.g. Dennis, *Insolvency Law Handbook* (3rd edn, Law Society, 2013); Keay and Walton, *Insolvency Law Corporate and Personal* (3rd edn, Jordans, 2012).) What may be termed 'non-terminal' procedures such as receivership, administration and company voluntary arrangements, do not necessarily in themselves lead to the demise of a company. The 'terminal' procedure of liquidation or winding up (these two terms may be used interchangeably) will lead to the company ceasing to exist. Often a company will undergo a non-terminal procedure with limited or no success and subsequently proceed into liquidation.

It is frequently the case that it is only once a company enters a formal insolvency procedure that, for example, directors are held accountable for breaches of fiduciary or other statutory duties. Further, a director's conduct may lead to his or her disqualification. In addition to breaches of general company law, once a company enters a formal insolvency procedure (particularly administration or liquidation), other specific causes of action are available to the office holder (the administrator or liquidator), such as rights to reverse transactions at an undervalue and voidable preferences.

This chapter deals with insolvency law in England and Wales. It does not extend to cover matters of international (or cross-border) insolvency.

22.2   A HISTORICAL OUTLINE OF CORPORATE INSOLVENCY LAW

Corporate insolvency law began with the introduction of registered companies in 1844 (by the Joint Stock Companies Act 1844). The Joint Stock Companies Winding-Up Act 1844 was passed to regulate the winding up of such companies. Insolvency is not the only reason for a company to be wound up but it is by far the most common ground. The Winding-Up Act 1844 limited the rights of a company's creditors to look to the assets of the company only, and in general prevented them from seeking repayment of corporate debts directly from the members of the company.

In the latter half of the nineteenth century, companies registered under the Companies Acts became progressively more common. Not just large undertakings were being incorporated. By way of example we have the classic case of *Salomon* v. *Salomon & Co Ltd* [1897] AC 22 (discussed in **Chapter 1**). By the end of the nineteenth century, the practice of small sole trader businesses incorporating became popular. Along with the benefits of limited liability, companies were able to borrow on the strength of executing a floating charge (something individuals and partnerships were legally prevented from doing by the Bills of Sale Act 1882). In the latter part of the nineteenth century, the floating charge became a very common form of secured lending and covered all or substantially all of the company's present and future property (often referred to as its undertaking).

Together with the power to borrow on the security of a floating charge came powers taken by the charge holder to enforce the charge when the company defaulted under the loan agreement. Although it was possible for the charge holder to take possession of the charged assets and realise those assets as a mortgagee in possession, it became common practice for such debenture holders to appoint a receiver instead, to realise the charged assets. The main reason for this seems to have been a fear that debenture holders could incur serious personal liability under the potentially onerous duties owed by mortgagees in possession. At first, debenture holders who wished to enforce their security would ask the court to appoint a receiver who would then realise the assets in order to pay off the lender. As time went by, it became common practice to include in standard form debentures the power to appoint a receiver out of court, which led to cheaper and swifter realisations of companies' charged assets. Court appointed receivers are extremely rare nowadays and are only sought where a particularly difficult legal or other problem has arisen.

The system of debenture holders appointing receivers out of court remained largely undisturbed for about a hundred years. Insolvent companies that had secured their borrowing by way of a floating charge, over all or substantially all of their assets, would often find themselves plunged into receivership and when the receiver had finished realising the charged assets to pay off the debenture holder, a liquidator would be appointed to finish off and dissolve the company. This scenario is still encountered today but, as will be seen below, it is becoming relatively rare and will soon all but disappear. Receivers are appointed by debenture holders to realise assets to pay off the secured loan. Often the company will, during the receivership, also enter liquidation. In such a case, the liquidator will normally take no active steps in the winding up until the receiver has completed the receivership. Once the receivership is completed the liquidator will act as a kind of corporate executioner to kill off the company.

22.2.1 Modern developments

The corporate insolvency landscape became more crowded in the mid-1980s with the introduction of administration and company voluntary arrangements. These procedures were hailed as bringing a new 'rescue culture' to insolvent companies. At this time, the most common form of receivership (where the receiver is appointed under a floating charge over the whole or substantially the whole of the company's undertaking) was renamed 'administrative receivership'. The report of the Insolvency Law Review Committee, *Insolvency Law and Practice* (Cmnd 8558, 1982) (known as the 'Cork Report') marked the beginning of modern insolvency law. The Cork Report's recommendations were, in the main, given effect to by IA 1986. Importantly, this resulted in an attempted change of emphasis away from merely debt enforcement by creditors, to a new system where companies might be rescued, whenever possible.

Under IA 1986, only licensed insolvency practitioners are able to act as administrative receivers, administrators, nominees and supervisors of company voluntary arrangements and liquidators (see IA 1986, s.390). The requirement that office holders be highly qualified and regulated professionals has also influenced other areas of the law such as directors' disqualification where the reports of insolvency practitioners are crucial in proving directors are unfit to be directors of companies (under the Company Directors Disqualification Act 1986 – discussed in **Chapter 17**). IA 1986 has been amended over the years, notably by the Insolvency Act 1994, the Insolvency Act 2000 and, most importantly, the Enterprise Act 2002. Although administration was only introduced in 1986, its ability to initiate widespread company rescue was initially limited and it was, in consequence, substantially re-invented in 2002. The Enterprise Act has also spelled the prospective end to debenture holders being able to enforce their debentures by the appointment of administrative receivers.

22.3 RECEIVERSHIP

IA 1986 contains a number of provisions that regulate receivers generally as well as other provisions which only cover administrative receivers. Administrative receivers may now be viewed as an endangered species, given that the Enterprise Act 2002 has abolished the power to appoint administrative receivers under debentures created on or after 15 September 2003. However, they will still be encountered for some years to come as, for debentures entered into prior to 15 September 2003, debenture holders retain the power to appoint an administrative receiver. The amendments to the power to appoint administrative receivers introduced by the Enterprise Act have no impact on the ability of a secured creditor to appoint a fixed charge or Law of Property Act (LPA) receiver.

A receiver is a person who receives or takes control of property belonging to another. Receivers are encountered in situations other than corporate insolvency. For example, a receiver may be appointed under the Partnership Act 1890 where a partnership is being dissolved, or to take control of a charity where there have been irregularities in the charity's administration. Receivers perform different tasks in different contexts. When a company is placed into receivership, the reason is usually that the company has defaulted under its secured loan agreement with a debenture holder.

Strictly speaking, a receiver appointed under a debenture can only take control of assets subject to the debenture and receive income from those assets, for example rent from a block of flats charged. From the position of the charge holder, this may be sufficient to pay off the loan. As well as any express powers given to the receiver under the terms of the debenture, for example, a power to sell the charged assets, the receiver will also benefit from powers implied by the Law of Property Act 1925. A receiver appointed under a debenture containing only a fixed charge is referred to as a fixed charge or LPA receiver. A fixed charge receiver will rarely have the power to manage the company's business.

When a company borrows money it is usual for it to execute security over all its assets both present and future, not just fixed assets. A common form debenture will create fixed charges over certain specified assets present and future and also a floating charge over the company's 'undertaking'. The important thing to note here is that 'undertaking' includes all the other assets of the company (e.g. stock in trade and goodwill) present and future and the right to carry on the company's business. The consequence of this is that when a receiver is appointed over the company's undertaking, the receiver has the power to run the business of the company and, in realising the charged assets, will have the ability to sell all of the company's assets including the business as a going concern. This is important, because a sale of a company's business as a going concern will invariably realise a greater sale price than would be achieved by a 'fire sale' of all the company's assets piecemeal. This type of receiver is referred to as a 'receiver and manager', due to the management powers associated with his or her position. He or she will usually have powers to take control of the charged assets, manage the business of the company to the exclusion of the directors and to sell assets either individually or as a going concern (see, e.g. Jessel MR in *Re Manchester & Milford Rly Co* (1880) 14 Ch D 645 at 653). Receivers exercising these powers owe certain duties to interested parties. The most commonly encountered type of receiver in an insolvency context is a receiver and manager appointed under a debenture, which includes a floating charge, over the whole or substantially the whole of a company's undertaking. Following the Cork Report's recommendations, IA 1986, s.29(2) reclassified this type of receiver as an 'administrative receiver'.

22.3.1 Appointment of receivers

A debenture holder who decides to appoint a receiver must ensure that the appointment is made consistently with the wording of the debenture. It is usual to list in a debenture a number of default events, for example failure to pay interest owing to the debenture holder within a specified period of it becoming due. If one or more of the specified events has occurred, the debenture will commonly state that the default causes all monies owing to the debenture holder to become payable on demand. The debenture holder will then serve a formal demand on the company for immediate payment of all monies, both capital and interest. If the company fails to pay (as is likely, otherwise it would not have defaulted), the debenture holder can then appoint the receiver. As the money will be payable on demand, the company is afforded no time to allow it to attempt to renegotiate its finances. The company is only given sufficient time to put the 'mechanics of payment' into effect. Accordingly, the company is only given sufficient time to pay as it would take it to go to a convenient place to collect the funds owed. The reality of this is that the company will have no more than an hour or so to pay the money over otherwise the receiver will be appointed to take control of the company's assets (see, e.g. *Cripps (Pharmaceuticals) Ltd* v. *Wickenden* [1973] 1 WLR 944 and *Bank of Baroda Ltd* v. *Panessar* [1987] Ch 335).

There is no statutory form of appointment which needs to be satisfied. The appointment will usually be in writing (prepared ahead of time) but may need to be by deed if so required by the debenture's terms. The appointment will take effect when it is given to the prospective receiver and the receiver has accepted the appointment. The appointment of an administrative receiver is only effective if it accepted before the end of the business day after that on which the instrument of appointment is received. The date of the appointment is backdated to the date of receipt of the instrument of appointment (IA 1986, s.33). All invoices for goods and other business letters of the company must disclose the fact that a receiver has been appointed (IA 1986, s.39).

It should be noted that it is commonly reported in the media that a company has called in the receivers. This is not the case, as it is the debenture holder who will appoint the receiver, although it should be appreciated that frequently companies will inform their bank, the debenture holder, that the company cannot continue and will invite the bank to appoint a receiver. Not all appointments are therefore hostile.

The appointment of an administrative receiver will crystallise any floating charge (if this has not already occurred – discussed in **Chapter 11**), and it will generally prevent the company from entering administration (see IA 1986, Sched.B1, paras.15–17, 25 and 39) although, as mentioned above, it does not prevent the company from entering liquidation. The appointment will not generally terminate contracts of employment as the company as a separate legal entity continues as before but now under the management of the receiver. The appointment of a receiver will not, in itself, affect contracts between the company and third parties, although many such contracts specify that by entering administrative receivership the contract will be brought to an end.

22.3.2 Powers of receivers

A receiver is appointed to realise the charged assets and pay off, as far as possible, the debt of the appointing debenture holder. Although clearly acting on behalf of the debenture holder, a receiver will act as agent of the company. Administrative receivers are deemed to be agents of the company under IA 1986, s.44(1)(a). Fixed charge receivers are deemed to be agents of the company under the Law of Property Act 1925, s.109(2). Other types of receiver will invariably be expressly stated by the debenture to be appointed as agents of the company. This agency is unusual, as the receiver cannot be dismissed by the principal (the company) and the agent's primary duty is owed to the appointing debenture holder and not the company. It is also unusual in that a receiver (unlike other agents) may become personally liable on contracts entered into by the company.

Any well-drafted debenture will list extensive powers which the receiver may exercise, for example to get in and sell company assets. In addition, an administrative receiver has statutory powers implied by IA 1986, ss.42 and 43 and Sched.1. Once appointed, an administrative receiver takes control of the company, usurping the management powers of the directors (see, e.g. *Re Emmadart* [1979] Ch 540). When selling company assets, the receiver may sell as agent of the company but, without an appropriate deed of release from the debenture holder, cannot transfer assets free from the debenture under which the appointment was made (see, e.g. *Re Real Meat Co.* [1996] BCC 254). The alternative to this is for the debenture holder to appoint the receiver as its agent for that particular purpose only, i.e. to give an unencumbered title to the buyer.

22.3.3 Statutory duties of receivers

Administrative receivers owe a duty under IA 1986, s.47 to obtain a statement of affairs from company officers, detailing the company's assets and liabilities. A report must be prepared by the administrative receiver and made available to creditors. The report will explain how the company came to be in receivership and what the receiver is planning to do with the assets. It will also give an indication of how much each secured and preferential creditor is likely to receive (an administrative receiver will not make distributions to unsecured creditors).

An administrative receiver's function is to realise enough of the charged assets to pay off the appointing debenture holder. Even where the business can be sold on as a going concern, there is frequently insufficient money realised by such a sale to pay off the debenture holder. Once the assets have been realised the administrative receiver must distribute the proceeds in an order laid down by IA 1986, namely:

1. Any secured creditor with priority over the debenture under which the administrative receiver is appointed.
2. The administrative receiver's own costs, expenses and remuneration.
3. Fixed charges contained within the debenture under which the administrative receiver is appointed.
4. Debts due to preferential creditors under IA 1986, s.40. Following the abolition of the Crown's preferential status in insolvency by the Enterprise Act 2002, preferential creditors are now essentially limited to certain claims by employees. The maximum amount of remuneration that an employee may claim for the period prior to the receivership is four months' pay with an aggregate maximum of £800. This rather modest right is extended slightly by a right to a redundancy payment from the National Insurance Fund under the Employment Rights Act 1996, s.184, where up to eight weeks' pay (the maximum amount that can be counted for these purposes is currently £450 per week) may be claimed.
5. Debts secured by a floating charge. The top slicing of floating charge assets in favour of unsecured creditors, introduced following the Enterprise Act 2002 by IA 1986, 176A will not usually be deducted in an administrative receivership because the receivership will generally have been commenced under a debenture entered into prior to 15 September 2003 and one consequence of this is that the debenture will not be subject to the top slice.
6. If any money remains, it will be handed back to the company. If, as is commonly the case, the company is by this time in liquidation, the money will be handed over to the liquidator who will then distribute any excess among the remaining unsecured creditors.

22.3.4 Duties owed by receivers at common law or in equity

Although acting as agent of the company, a receiver owes a primary duty to the debenture holder who appoints the receiver. Secondary duties are owed to others who have an interest in the equity of redemption of the charged assets such as the company itself, any guarantors of the secured debt and any prior or subsequent charge holders. If the receiver manages the business negligently or conducts the sale of the business in an incompetent fashion, this may cause the secured assets not to be realised in the most beneficial way. If the sale price is too low, the appointing debenture holder and other secured creditors may not be paid. The debenture holder may have to call in personal guarantees given by third parties. No duty is owed to directors, shareholders or unsecured creditors as they are seen as having no direct interest in the charged assets (see, e.g. *Burgess* v. *Auger* [1998] 2 BCLC 478 and *Medforth* v. *Blake* [1999] BCC 771).

In considering the exact duties owed by receivers, a number of preliminary points need to be made. First, due to the similarity of function between a receiver and a mortgagee in possession, it is common for the case law examining the duties owed by both mortgagees and receivers to use the authorities in one area as authoritative in the other. Secondly, the case law is somewhat contradictory. Thirdly, there is a debate as to whether receivers owe duties of care at common law in the form of normal negligence principles or whether they are only subject to equitable rules. The better view seems to be that the duties are owed only in equity but arguably the distinction is of little, if any, practical importance.

22.3.5 Case law

In the nineteenth century, two lines of case law developed. In one, the courts held that as long as a receiver (or mortgagee in possession) acted within his or her powers and exercised those powers in a *bona fide* manner, the court would not look to impose any liability even where the sale price achieved was low (see, e.g. *Warner* v. *Jacob* (1882) 20 Ch D 220 and *Kennedy* v. *de Trafford* [1897] AC 180). During the same period, a conflicting line of cases held that a receiver (or mortgagee in possession) could be held personally liable if a sale was conducted negligently resulting in the sale price being too low (see, e.g. *Robertson* v. *Norris* (1859) 1 Giff 421 and *Tomlin* v. *Luce* (1889) 43 Ch D 191), or where charged assets were allowed to deteriorate due to negligence and therefore needlessly reduced in value (see, e.g. *McHugh* v. *Union Bank of Canada* [1913] AC 299). In the words of Sir George Jessel MR in *Nash* v. *Eads* (1880) SJ 95 a mortgagee, when exercising a power of sale 'must conduct the sale properly, and must sell at a fair value'.

Until recently, modern case law has shown a similar polarisation of views. The Court of Appeal in *Re B Johnson & Co (Builders) Ltd* [1955] 1 Ch 634 limited the duty owed by receivers to a duty to act in good faith and within their powers. It was explained that there could be no duty to carry on the company's business nor to preserve its goodwill. The receiver is given powers of management not for the benefit of the company but to realise the assets for the debenture holder. By the 1970s, the courts had decided to extend common law negligence principles to a mortgagee in possession. In *Cuckmere Brick Co Ltd* v. *Mutual Finance Ltd* [1971] Ch 949, the duty to act in good faith was extended to include a duty to act with reasonable care to obtain what the members of the court variously described as the 'proper market value' or 'best price' or 'proper price'. There is no duty to choose the best possible time to sell, but once the decision to sell is made, the sale needs to be carried out with reasonable care. The Court of Appeal couched the test in terms of the 'neighbour' principle and discussed the concept of 'proximity'. This extension of common law negligence principles to a previously exclusively equitable domain caused subsequent problems. It became possible, from this extension, to argue a duty should even be owed to unsecured creditors, although in reality this argument has never seriously been considered by any court. The common law formulation of duties was followed in *Standard Chartered Bank* v. *Walker* [1982] 3 All ER 938. In *Palk* v. *Mortgage Services Funding plc* [1993] 2 All ER 481, the court considered the duties owed by a mortgagee to exist both at common law and in equity.

Reasonable care was required in managing the property and in conducting a sale of it.

In what appeared to be a bid to turn back the relentless expansion of common law negligence, the Privy Council, in *Downsview Nominees* v. *First City Corporation* [1993] AC 295, explained that receivers owed a duty in equity only and not at common law. The Privy Council attempted to limit the case of *Cuckmere* and ended up with a somewhat unsatisfactory compromise between different viewpoints. Their Lordships effectively held that the duty owed by a receiver was to act within his or her powers and to act *bona fide* in exercising those powers. This is fairly straight *Re B Johnson* fare. However, the rather strange effect of the Privy Council's decision was to graft on to this restrictive traditional view, a limited view of *Cuckmere*. The ratio of the case is therefore that receivers must act generally within their powers and *bona fide*, but when they exercise their power of sale they have the additional specific duty to take reasonable care to ensure a proper price is achieved.

22.3.6 *Medforth* v. *Blake*

Happily, these difficult issues have now been resolved by the Court of Appeal in *Medforth* v. *Blake* [1999] BCC 771. The court rejected the rather restrictive view of *Downsview* but did not go headlong into a restatement of the law in terms of common law negligence. The case concerned the receivership of a pig farm. The main issue was whether or not the receiver owed a duty of care to the mortgagor in conducting the farming business. The court assessed some of the previous case law and concluded that it was inconsistent in places because equity was by its nature a flexible thing. The court also concluded that whether the matter was viewed as being governed by equity or the common law, the result would be the same and the distinction was not important. Seven propositions were laid down:

1. A receiver owes duties to anyone interested in the equity of redemption of the charged assets.
2. The duties include, but are not necessarily limited to, a duty of good faith.
3. Any additional duty will depend on the facts of a particular case.
4. In exercising powers of management, the receiver's primary duty is to pay off the secured debt.
5. Subject to the primary duty, the receiver owes a duty to manage the property with due diligence.
6. Due diligence does not require the receiver to continue to carry on the business.
7. If the receiver does carry on the business, due diligence requires that reasonable steps be taken to try to do so profitably.

Medforth brought some welcome clarification to the area and suggests that the duty owed to persons with an interest in the equity of redemption is one whereby the receiver should act with due diligence. It would appear that this duty extends to both managing the business and, once a sale has been decided upon, in conducting the sale process. The decision as to when to sell assets is one for the receiver and no duty of care is owed as to the timing of any sale (see, e.g. *Silven Properties Ltd* v. *Royal Bank of Scotland plc* [2004] 4 All ER 484). In assessing what price should reasonably be obtained, the court will assess the market value to see whether the price realised falls within an acceptable margin of error (see, e.g. *Michael* v. *Miller* [2004] EWCA Civ 282). It appears settled now that the duties owed by a receiver are owed in equity and not at common law (see, e.g. *Bell* v. *Long* [2008] BPIR 1211). Receivers cannot delegate their equitable duties and so will not escape liability if they employ negligent agents even if the appointment itself was not negligent. Receivers therefore have a form of strict liability for the negligence of agents they employ. Such receivers can, of course, bring an action against negligent agents if the receivers suffer consequent loss (see, e.g. *Glatt* v. *Sinclair* [2012] BPIR 306).

22.3.7 Contractual liability of administrative receivers

IA 1986, s.44 governs the personal liability of an administrative receiver under contracts entered into by the company. As an agent of the company the administrative receiver may enter into contracts on behalf of the company and will frequently need to do so to keep the business ticking over pending any proposed sale. The administrative receiver will be personally liable on any contracts entered into by the company during the receivership unless (as is common) the contract provides otherwise. If personally liable, the administrative receiver has the benefit of an indemnity from the company's assets (under IA 1986, s.44(1)(c)).

As the administrative receiver acts as agent of the company, normal agency rules apply to contracts entered into by the company prior to the receivership, that is, the company (as principal) remains liable under the contract and the receiver incurs no personal liability (see, e.g. *Hay* v. *Swedish and Norwegian Rly Co* (1892) 8 TLR 775). As agents, receivers incur no personal liability if they cause the company to breach existing contracts. Although the company may be liable for the breach, the receiver is free from any liability (see, e.g. *Airline Airspares* v. *Handley-Page* [1970] Ch 193).

Accordingly, in deciding how best to continue the business of a company, the receiver is given a relatively free hand, i.e. the receiver may decide not to pay certain creditors or may, for example, decide to change suppliers. Although generally free to ignore a third party's contractual rights, a receiver cannot ignore proprietary rights which have already passed under a contract, for example, under a specifically enforceable contract where the equitable interest has already passed to the contracting party (see, e.g. *Freevale* v. *Metrostore Holdings* [1984] Ch 199).

An important issue that faces an administrative receiver on taking office is whether to keep on or dismiss employees. If a sale of the business as a going concern is to be considered, some employees will usually need to be retained. If an administrative receiver causes an employment contract to remain in force by not acting to terminate it within 14 days of taking office, the administrative receiver will be deemed to have adopted the contract. The receiver will be personally liable to pay out under the contract for services rendered after the contract is deemed to be adopted, that is, for services rendered after the 14 days have elapsed (IA 1986, s.44). Again, the receiver has an indemnity from the company assets for this liability. Any liability incurred to employees under s.44 is in addition to any payment which the employee may be entitled to as a preferential creditor or under the Employment Rights Act 1996, s.184.

22.3.8 Termination of receivership

A receivership will normally cease when the receiver completes the task of realising enough of the charged assets to pay off the debenture holder and other creditors who must be paid in priority to the debenture holder. Once the money has been handed over, the receiver informs the registrar of companies that he or she is vacating office. The receivership is then over. As the company itself may, by this point, be an empty shell, due to the sale of all or most of its business and assets, the company will usually be placed into liquidation if it is not already being wound up.

22.3.9 Abolition of administrative receivership

As previously mentioned, the Enterprise Act 2002 has signalled a slow and lingering death for administrative receivership (IA 1986, s.72A). With the exception of certain specific types of company charges, for example, charges created by public private partnerships (see IA 1986, ss.72B–72F for the full list), debentures which constitute a 'qualifying floating charge' (defined under IA 1986, Sched.B1, para.14 as a floating charge over the whole or substantially the whole of the company's property) entered into on or after 15 September 2003 can no longer be enforced by the appointment of an administrative receiver. Instead, the debenture holder is able to appoint an administrator out of court. The main reason for this change is the perception that the interests of unsecured creditors of companies are inadequately protected in administrative receivership because the receiver owes no duties to unsecured creditors. In contrast, an administrator owes a duty to all the company's creditors. The collective nature of administration has therefore been preferred over the regime of administrative receivership (where the primary duty is owed to the appointing debenture holder). Administrative receivership is seen very much as 'old school' insolvency, while administration is seen as a more modern and collective approach. In keeping with this view, holders of debentures which came into existence prior to 15 September 2003 do not have to enforce by the appointment of an administrative receiver but instead have a choice whether to appoint an administrative receiver or an administrator. In practice, debenture holders who have the power to appoint an administrative receiver frequently nowadays prefer to appoint an administrator, thus hastening the eventual demise of administrative receivership further.

22.4 ADMINISTRATION

An original administration procedure was introduced following the Cork Report's recommendations. Together with company voluntary arrangements, it was heralded in the 1980s as the start of the 'rescue culture'. This original administration regime (hereafter referred to as the 'old regime') was brought into effect by IA 1986, Part II. The old regime remains in force for certain types of companies, for example, water companies, railway companies and building societies (see the Enterprise Act 2002, s.249). For other companies, indeed the vast majority of companies registered under the Companies Act, the old regime was replaced following the Enterprise Act 2002, by a new IA 1986, Sched.B1 (hereafter referred to as the 'new regime'). It is the new regime which is gradually replacing administrative receivership as the most common remedy for debenture holders.

Initially, the reason why the Cork Report recommended the introduction of administration was to fill a gap. The gap that was identified was that, in some circumstances, there may be no single debenture holder with the power to appoint an administrative receiver. The Cork Report recommended that such companies should still be able to take advantage of the appointment of a specialist insolvency practitioner, who could work either to save the company or its business or to ensure the company's assets were realised in the most beneficial manner. This was essentially the purpose of the old regime (see IA 1986, s.8 for the purposes for which an administration order may be made under the old regime). The primary purpose under the new regime is to attempt to rescue the company.

The really innovative characteristic of administration under both the new and old regimes is that it creates a moratorium on actions against the company. During administration, creditors' rights are frozen. Creditors cannot enforce their legal rights against the company without leave of the court. This temporary freedom from creditor harassment is designed to allow the administrator some breathing space within which to put a proposal to the creditors in an attempt to rescue the company or achieve some other beneficial realisation of the company's assets.

Under the old regime, the administrator is appointed by the court. This process is expensive and time consuming. Under the new regime, although court appointment is still possible, nearly all administrators are appointed out of court. Administration has taken over from administrative receivership as the only option open to a debenture holder whose debenture was created on or after 15 September 2003.

The main changes made to administration by the new regime deal with how the administrator is appointed, the purpose of the administration and the termination of the administration. Much of the substance of the old regime remains largely intact in Sched.B1. The moratorium on actions and the duties owed by administrators remain largely as before. Those with an interest in the old regime are directed to IA 1986, Part II. We will now concentrate on the new regime.

22.4.1 Appointment of administrators

A company enters administration when an administrator is appointed. An administrator cannot usually be appointed if the company is already in administration, is in liquidation or is subject to an effective administrative receivership. An administrator may be appointed in one of three ways, as described below.

22.4.2 Appointment of administrators by the holder of a 'qualifying floating charge'

Under IA 1986, Sched.B1, para.14, the holder of a qualifying floating charge may appoint an administrator without the involvement of the court. A floating charge is qualifying for these purposes if, either on its own or together with other securities, it relates to the whole or substantially the whole of the company's property (in effect a standard form floating charge). The power to appoint an administrator covers debentures executed both before and after 15 September 2003. A debenture holder may appoint the administrator out of court once the charge has become enforceable under its own terms. If there is another floating charge holder whose debenture was executed first in time (or has priority due to some agreement between the parties), the second floating charge holder must give the prior charge holder at least two business days' notice of an intention to appoint an administrator. The prior floating charge holder may then decide to appoint its own administrator instead.

A person who appoints an administrator under IA 1986, Sched.B1, para.14 must file, *inter alia*, a notice of appointment at the court. The notice will contain the consent of the administrator to act and a statement that the floating charge has become enforceable. The appointment takes effect from the date of the filing of the notice of appointment (see, e.g. *Fliptex Ltd* v. *Hogg* [2004] BCC 870).

22.4.3 Appointment of administrators by the company or its directors

Under IA 1986, Sched.B1, para. 22, either the company (by members' resolution in general meeting) or the directors (including an appointment by a majority of directors) may appoint an administrator without the involvement of the court. However, restrictions are placed upon this power to appoint. For example, no appointment is possible if the company had been in administration during the past 12 months before the intended (new) appointment where the (previous) appointment of the administrator had been made by the company or its directors.

At least five business days' notice of any proposed appointment must be given to any debenture holder who may be entitled to appoint an administrative receiver or administrator. The debenture holder may decide to appoint its own administrative receiver or administrator during this period. Such an appointment has the effect of vetoing the proposed appointment by the company or its directors. Primacy is given to the interests of the secured creditor. Once the five days' notice has expired the appointment may be made. The appointor must file notice of appointment at the court. The appointment takes effect when all the paperwork has been filed at court.

In addition to providing notice to any qualifying debenture holder, the directors or company may also need to give notice to other prescribed parties, such as the company itself, the supervisor of a company voluntary arrangement (if there is one in place) and the FCA if the company carries on a financial services business. Two inconsistent lines of first instance case law have considered whether an appointment under IA 1986, Sched.B1, para.22 which is subject to a procedural defect is totally invalid (see, e.g. *Minmar* v. *Khalastchi* [2011] BCC 485) or can be rectified by correcting the procedural defect subsequently (see, e.g. *Re Ceart Risk Services Ltd* [2012] EWHC 1178 (Ch)). Although a definitive appellate decision is still awaited, the preponderance of opinion seems to favour the latter view, that is, that any procedural defect may be put right subsequently. This will have the effect of retrospectively validating any actions carried out by the administrator between the date of the defective appointment and the date of rectification of the defect.

22.4.4 Appointment of administrators by the court

Due to the ability of various parties to appoint an administrator out of court it is quite rare for the court to be asked to make an administration order under the new regime. The parties who can apply for such an order are essentially the company, its directors or any of creditors (see, IA 1986, Sched.B1, para.12). Attempts by unsecured creditors to obtain an administration order are unlikely to meet with any great success as they are unlikely to know enough about the company's business to be able to draft an extensive and full application (see, e.g. *Re Colt Telecom Group plc (No.2)* [2003] BPIR 324 – a case decided under the old regime and *Re Simco Digital UK Ltd* [2004] 1 BCLC 541 – decided under the new regime). Notice of any application has to be served on any person with the power to appoint an administrator or administrative receiver. A debenture holder with security over the whole of the company's undertaking can effectively veto the application by appointing its own administrator or administrative receiver. Singular facts may lead to a debenture holder preferring the certainty of an administration order where there is some doubt as to the debenture holder's ability to appoint out of court (see, e.g. *Bank of Scotland plc* v. *Targetfollow Properties* [2010] EWHC 3606 (Ch)).

22.4.5 Effect of appointment of administrators

As soon as an administrator is appointed, he or she must notify the company, its creditors and the registrar of companies of the appointment and publish a notice of appointment in the prescribed manner. While the company is in administration, any business document of the company must state the name of the administrator and that the affairs of the company are being managed by the administrator. The administrator must request a statement of affairs from the company's officers.

22.4.6 Purpose of administration

Once an administrator is appointed he or she must act with the purpose of:

- rescuing the company as a going concern; or
- achieving a better result for the company's creditors as a whole than would be likely if the company were wound up (without first being in administration); or
- realising enough property in order to make a distribution to one or more secured or preferential creditors.

These purposes are listed in order of primacy. Only if the administrator thinks that the first purpose is not reasonably practicable can he or she move to consider the second purpose and so on to the final purpose. In practice the first purpose is attempted in only approximately 10 per cent of administrations. The second purpose is the most commonly adopted, with the result that the company's business is sold (usually) as a going concern. The end result of the majority of administrations therefore bears some comparison with what would have happened in the majority of administrative receiverships under the old regime.

22.4.7 Moratorium on actions

In order to assist the administrator in achieving the purpose of the administration, a company in administration is effectively protected by a moratorium against the enforcement of actions by creditors. This moratorium was present under the old regime and has survived into the new regime with only a very slight rewording. The substance of the moratorium has not changed and therefore case law decided under the old regime is still relevant under the new regime. Without the benefit of the moratorium, the whole purpose of the administration may be frustrated. For example, without the moratorium, suppliers of goods could repossess those goods under valid retention of title clauses. Judgment creditors could enforce their judgments by writs of fifa. Landlords could distrain for unpaid rent (seize goods on the tenanted premises without the need for a court order and sell the assets to pay the rent). If these things occurred while the administrator was trying to rescue the company or straighten out its business, it could clearly prevent the administration being effective.

Once the company is in administration, the moratorium prevents any resolution to wind up the company from being passed and no winding-up order may be made. In addition, the following actions are precluded without either leave of the court or the permission of the administrator:

- No step may be taken to enforce any security over the company's property. The term 'security' is defined widely to mean 'any mortgage, charge, lien or other security' (IA 1986, s.248). IA 1986, s.436 defines 'property' to include 'money, goods, things in action, land and every description of property wherever situated and also obligations and every description of interest, whether present or future or vested or contingent, arising out of, or incidental to, property'. For an example of a case where a creditor with a lien over a stock of *La Senza* lingerie, intimate apparel and nightwear was permitted to enforce its security despite the moratorium see *Uniserve Ltd* v. *Croxen* [2012] EWHC 1190 (Ch).

- No step may be taken to repossess goods in the company's possession under a hire purchase agreement. For these purposes, 'hire purchase agreement' includes conditional sale agreements, chattel leasing agreements and retention of title agreements. For an example of how this operated in attempts to repossess computers held under hire purchase and leasing agreements, see the leading case of *Re Atlantic Computer Systems plc* [1992] Ch 505.

- A landlord may not exercise a right of forfeiture by peaceable re-entry in relation to tenanted premises.

- No legal process may be instituted or continued against the company. This includes any legal proceedings, execution (by judgment creditors) and distress (landlords' self-help remedy). This part of the moratorium has, for example, been held to prevent employees bringing actions in an employment tribunal (see, e.g. *Re Divine Solutions (UK) Ltd* [2004] BCC 325).

Any creditor who wishes to enforce his or her rights during the administration must either persuade the administrator to permit enforcement (unlikely in most circumstances but, for example, repossession of hire purchase machinery may be permitted where the administrator has no use for it) or obtain leave of the court. In deciding whether to allow a creditor to enforce rights against the company in administration, the Court of Appeal in *Re Atlantic Computer Systems plc* [1992] Ch 505 laid down a number of guidelines, namely:

- If the enforcement of rights is unlikely to impede the purpose of the administration, the court would normally grant leave. In other cases, the court must undertake a balancing exercise.

- The interests of the applicant creditor must be balanced with the interests of other creditors. Due weight must be given to the applicant creditor's proprietary rights. If the owners of property have their property used to finance the administration but are not being paid, the court will usually give leave.

- If significant loss would be occasioned by the applicant creditor if leave was refused, this would tend to sway the balance in favour of granting leave.

In making any decision, the court will consider the company's financial state, its ability to make payments to creditors, the administrator's proposals, the likely effect of giving leave on those proposals, the duration of the administration and the conduct of the parties.

22.4.8 Administrators' proposals

An administrator's job is to put together a proposal in an attempt to satisfy one of the three statutory purposes of the administration. The administrator has eight weeks from appointment to prepare the proposal (this period may be extended by the court). A meeting of the company's unsecured creditors is called to consider the proposal within 10 weeks of appointment (again, this time period may be extended by the court). In certain circumstances, the administrator need not call a meeting of unsecured creditors: for example, if the company's financial position is such that there will be no money available ultimately to make a distribution to the unsecured creditors. The proposal cannot affect the priority rights of secured or preferential creditors without their consent. If the administrator is proposing a rescue package for the company this may take the form of a company voluntary arrangement (discussed below).

22.4.9   Duties of administrators

An administrator is subject to various statutory duties. He or she must take control of the company's property and must manage the company in accordance with any proposal approved by the creditors. An administrator must act in the interests of the company's creditors as a whole.

A creditor or member of the company may bring an action against an administrator if it can be shown that the administrator is acting in a way which unfairly harms the interests of the creditor or member (either alone or in common with other creditors or members). This right is largely untested in the courts but appears to bear some resemblance to CA 2006, s.994 (discussed in **Chapter 19**). In the case of *Re Charnley Davies Ltd* [1990] BCC 605, the court held that administrators owed a company the same duties owed by all professionals, namely, to exhibit the standard of care one would expect from an ordinary skilled practitioner. As agent of the company an administrator owes the company fiduciary duties and must consequently act within his or her powers, not act where there is a conflict of duty and must carry out the functions of an administrator with reasonable skill and care (including using reasonable care in choosing when to sell – unlike a receiver who may sell at any time). If it can be shown that the administrator acted in breach of duty to the company by, for example, misapplying company property, an application may be brought against the administrator by, among others, a creditor of the company (see IA 1986, Sched.B1, paras.74 and 75).

In *Oldham* v. *Kyrris* [2004] BCC 111, the Court of Appeal concluded that administrators owe no general duty of care to individual creditors. They do owe a duty to act in the best interests of creditors generally and this duty is similar to the duty that directors of a solvent company owe to its shareholders. If that duty is breached, a creditor may bring a form of representative action on behalf of all creditors.

22.4.10   Powers of administrators

An administrator acts as an agent of the company. The administrator has the power to do 'anything necessary or expedient for the management of the affairs, business and property of the company' (IA 1986, Sched.B1, para.59). In addition to this very wide power, administrators have the same specific powers as administrative receivers as listed in IA 1986, Sched.1. Additional powers are littered throughout IA 1986, Sched.B1, such as the power to remove or appoint directors, call meetings of creditors or members and the power to apply to court for directions in connection with the administration. An administrator has the same powers as a liquidator to apply to the court to upset transactions at an undervalue (IA 1986, s.238), preferences (IA 1986, s.239), extortionate credit bargains (IA 1986, s.244) and floating charges (IA 1986, s.245). An administrator may dispose of assets subject to a floating charge and, with the consent of the court, dispose of assets subject to fixed charges or even hire purchase goods.

Frequently, the only realistic option for an administrator will be to attempt to sell the company's business quickly. Rescue may be out of the question. There may be a buyer present who will not wait. The nature of the business may be that its goods are perishable and continuing to trade for any length of time may be financially out of the question. If a quick sale is the best way forward, the administrator has a problem in that if the sale goes ahead, it makes the drafting of proposals and calling of meetings of creditors rather redundant. After some judicial wavering, it is now possible for an administrator in this position to exercise professional judgment and to opt for a quick sale. In order to prevent allegations of negligence or breach of statutory duty an administrator should consider taking the following steps to protect himself or herself from personal liability (taken from Neuberger J's judgment in *Re T & D Industries plc* [2000] BCC 956 and approved under the new regime in *Re Transbus International Ltd* [2004] BCC 401):

- In normal circumstances a creditors' meeting should be held as soon as possible.
- Administrators may have to make urgent and important decisions. This is their job. Administrators cannot come to the court for guidance every time a difficult decision needs to be made. The court cannot be used as 'sort of bomb shelter'.
- Administrators should not take unfair advantage of creditors. Some consultation with major creditors should be possible even where time is short.
- An application to the court may still be necessary, where, for example, the administrator is convinced the sale is essential but the creditors are not in agreement.
- If a court hearing is needed, it will usually need to be an *inter partes* hearing.
- If there is an issue of sufficient importance and there is time, the court may be asked to call a creditors' meeting on short notice.
- In making a decision to sell the whole of the company's undertaking, the administrator must bear in mind that such a sale effectively renders a subsequent creditors' meeting meaningless.

22.4.11 Pre-packaged administration

A pre-packaged administration ('pre-pack') extends the idea underpinning *T & D* and *Transbus* by permitting an administrator to take office and immediately sell the business to a purchaser (who is often a person connected to the company in administration). There is often a perception that if a business is to be sold on as a going concern, the sale will need to happen extremely quickly and without a company's creditors or employees becoming aware of the proposed sale before-hand. The goodwill of the business may suffer irreparable damage if the company spends any time trading in administration while a proposal is prepared and voted upon by creditors. In a pre-pack there is unlikely ever to be a meeting of creditors held. Any proposal sent to the creditors will be sent long after the company's business has been sold on. The creditors will not get to vote on the proposal prior to the deal being executed and are essentially disenfranchised from the process. As soon as the pre-pack deal is executed the administrator will distribute the sale proceeds according to the statutory order and will usually take steps to dissolve the company or put the company into liquidation (often with the same insolvency practitioner acting as liquidator who acted as administrator).

Under the terms of Statement of Insolvency Practice 16, pre-pack administrators must inform creditors of, among other things, how the pre-pack came about, the sale price, the details of any independent valuations of the business and the identity of the purchaser. This information will inevitably be passed on after the deal has been executed. It increases transparency of the process but in a situation where the administrator has been appointed by the company's directors (usually with the consent of any secured creditors), and the sale is in favour of the company's directors, unsecured creditors often feel there is an inherent conflict of duty present.

Despite concerns as to whether pre-packs lead to a proper price being paid for the business (see, e.g. *Clydesdale Financial Services Ltd* v. *Smailes* [2009] BCC 810), the courts have on a number of occasions given their blessing to pre-packs, recognising that they are often the best option available to realise full value for the business and to save jobs (see, e.g. *DKLL Solicitors* v. *HMRC* [2008] 1 BCLC 112, *Re Kayley Vending Ltd* [2009] BCC 578 and *Re Hellas Telecommunication (Luxembourg) II SCA (No.2)* [2011] EWHC 3176 (Ch)).

22.4.12 Contractual liability of administrators

Similar rules apply to administration contracts as apply to contracts when the company is in administrative receivership, with one major difference, namely that an administrator is not made personally liable on any contractual liability of the company (see IA 1986, Sched.B1, para.99). Under Sched.B1, para.69, the administrator acts as agent of the company. This agency cannot be terminated by the company. The appointment does not, in itself, terminate any contracts with third parties, although as with receivership, some contracts will specify that a company entering administration will bring the contract to an end. An administrator may decide to continue existing contracts. If creditors are not paid under such contracts, they are prevented by the moratorium from enforcing their rights against the company without leave of the court. Having stated this, it is usual for an administrator to pay such creditors, at least for liabilities arising during the administration.

If new contracts are entered into by the company during the administration, the administrator incurs no personal liability. Only the company is liable. However, creditors owed money under such contracts are entitled to what is sometimes called 'super priority' in that such debts are paid ahead of the administration's expenses and even of the administrator's own remuneration. In respect of employment contracts, as with administrative receiverships, much turns upon whether the contracts have been adopted by the administrator. If an employee is kept on for more than 14 days after the commencement of the administration, the contract of employment is deemed to be adopted. The employee is then entitled to be paid 'wages or salary' for the period worked after the contract has been adopted. The administrator is not personally liable to pay this amount but the employee is entitled to 'super priority', that is the employee will be paid this amount before the administrator can claim his or her fees and expenses. Employees may also be entitled to payment for work carried out prior to the administration, in part anyway, due to their claim as preferential creditors in the administration and may also have a statutory claim for redundancy under the Employment Rights Act 1996.

22.4.13 Ending administration

Under the new regime an administrator has the power to make distributions to secured and preferential creditors. An administrator can only make distributions to unsecured creditors with leave of the court or if the administrator thinks it is likely to assist in the achievement of the purpose of the administration. Such distributions must be made in accordance with what is essentially the same statutory order of priority which applies in administrative receivership (which was mentioned above). The administrator's remuneration and expenses are charged upon and payable out of any property held under the administrator's control at the end of the administration and are paid out in priority to, first, any preferential creditors and, secondly, any floating charge holder. If the floating charge was created on or after 15 September 2003, the administrator will first need to deduct the 'prescribed part' under IA 1986, s.176A, which is set aside for unsecured creditors.

An innovation of the new regime is that following the completion of administration, the administrator may, by notice, convert the administration into a creditors' voluntary liquidation or by notice merely dissolve the company. This leads to a saving of fees and expenses. If, for example, distributions have been made by the administrator to secured and preferential creditors and no money is left, there is no point in going through the procedure to put the company into liquidation. It is more sensible for the administrator to send a notice to the registrar of companies requesting him to dissolve the company (see, e.g. *Re GHE Realisations Ltd* [2006] 1 All ER 357). If there is money left to be distributed to unsecured creditors, it is usual to convert the administration into a creditors' voluntary liquidation with the administrator usually acting as liquidator. This saves time and money and the liquidator will not have to become familiar with the company's background as he or she will have previously conducted the administration.

If the company has survived administration and has been successfully rescued, the administrator merely notifies the registrar of companies that the administration has finished and hands back control of the company to the directors (for detail of termination of administration see IA 1986, Sched.B1, paras.76–86).

22.5 COMPANY VOLUNTARY ARRANGEMENTS

When a company finds itself in financial difficulty, its directors may attempt to refinance its obligations or come to some other arrangement with the company's creditors. The arrangement may be formal or informal. The company may be forced into receivership, administration or liquidation. The company may wish to go into a formal insolvency procedure. If there is time and the company is looking to restructure itself, a scheme of arrangement under Part 26 of the Companies Act 2006 may be considered. Depending on how dire its financial problems are, the company may also consider a company voluntary arrangement (CVA) under IA 1986, Part 1.

The problem with negotiating with creditors in an informal way is that any deal agreed will not bind all the creditors. If one creditor decides to break ranks and take action against the company, the whole arrangement may come tumbling down. Getting all the company's creditors to agree to a deal will also be no mean feat. The Cork Report recognised that there was a need for the introduction of a simple procedure whereby the will of the majority of the creditors could be given effect, even where some creditors disagreed. This became, in 1986, the CVA. (A similar form of procedure was introduced for individual debtors called an individual voluntary arrangement (IVA). The case law decided in relation to CVAs is generally authoritative in the area of IVAs and vice versa.)

Back in 1986, it was part of the plan that administration and CVAs would operate together. A company would have the benefit of the moratorium on actions and, during this period of protection, the administrator could draft a proposal for a CVA. It did not quite work out that way. The old regime of administration became very expensive and time consuming. It was only really available to large companies with substantial assets. Small and medium-sized companies were priced out of administration. This problem was recognised belatedly. IA 2000 created a procedure specifically for small companies considering a CVA to obtain a 28-day moratorium on creditor action to facilitate the CVA (introduced as IA 1986, Sched.A1). Unfortunately, events rather overtook this initiative, as the 2000 Act's provisions only came into force shortly before the Enterprise Act 2002's new regime for administration. The consequence of this is that it is far easier and cheaper for a company considering a CVA to go first into administration (with the concomitant moratorium) than it would be to consider using the 2000 Act moratorium procedure. The 2000 Act procedure is dead in the water and will rarely, if ever, be used. It will not be mentioned further in this chapter.

A company in distress may put forward a proposal for a CVA itself or first go into administration and put forward the CVA from that protected environment (it is also possible but extremely rare for a liquidator of a company to propose a CVA). A CVA can take a variety of forms. It may be a composition of debts where the company promises to pay only a percentage of the debt owed. This is frequently referred to as a promise to pay, for example, 10p in the pound. The CVA may be in the form of a scheme of arrangement which in this context means that the creditors will be paid in full but they will have to wait a certain period of time. A CVA may take the form of a debt equity swap, where the creditor agrees to swap some or all of the debt owed for a shareholding in the company. The CVA may be a mixture of the above.

The exact legal nature of a CVA is not entirely clear. It is usually viewed as a form of statutory contract. It binds all the company's members and unsecured creditors and is supervised by a supervisor who usually holds CVA assets or money on trust for the creditors bound by the CVA. The courts tend to call it a contract, a statutory binding or a trust depending on the context (see, e.g. *Johnson* v. *Davies* [1998] 2 BCLC 252, *Re Arthur Rathbone Kitchens Ltd* [1998] BCC 450 and *Re Bradley-Hole* [1995] BCC 418). There would appear to be few practical consequences to this divergence in terminology.

The CVA may last for a short period of time or go on for years. It may be funded by the sale of company assets, by benevolent third-party funders, or be based on monthly payments by the company from its trading profits. An insolvency practitioner will act as supervisor of the CVA to ensure adherence to its terms.

22.5.1   Procedure to approve a CVA

The procedure may be initiated either by the company's directors or if the company is in administration (or liquidation) it may be commenced by the administrator (or liquidator). If the directors commence the procedure, they must approach an insolvency practitioner to act as 'nominee'. IA 1986 states that the directors will approach the nominee with a proposal for a CVA, but in practice the nominee will usually assist in the drafting of the proposal. The nominee will then report to the court whether the proposal has a reasonable prospect of being approved and implemented. The report to the court is a matter of record. There is no hearing. If the nominee's report is positive, the nominee will proceed to call meetings of members and creditors to consider the proposal. If the company is in administration or liquidation, the administrator or liquidator acts as nominee. No report to the court is made. The administrator or liquidator proceeds directly to calling meetings of members and creditors.

22.5.2 Approval of the CVA

The CVA becomes effective when it is approved. The proposal cannot affect the rights of secured or preferential creditors without their consent. At the members' meeting, an ordinary resolution is needed to approve the CVA. Votes at the creditors' meeting are calculated according to the value of the creditors' unsecured debt. A creditor owed a debt for an unliquidated amount, such as a contingent creditor, may vote and will have the value of £1 placed upon the debt unless the chairman (who is usually the nominee) agrees to put a higher figure on the debt. The creditors' meeting must approve the proposal by a majority of 75 per cent or more in value of those creditors present and voting. Providing the creditors approve the proposal, it binds the company even if the members have voted against it. The CVA is implemented with the nominee usually continuing to act as supervisor of the CVA. If the company is in administration, the administration will usually be terminated at this point, as the terms of the CVA will usually contain a provision continuing the block on creditors enforcing their rights. If the company is in liquidation, the winding up will usually be stayed by the court.

Once approved, the CVA takes effect as if made by the company at the creditors' meeting and binds every person who was entitled to vote at either meeting (whether or not present or represented at the meeting) or would have been entitled if he or she had received notice of the meeting, as if he or she were a party to the CVA. If approved, the CVA will therefore bind creditors with no notice of the meeting or creditors who were in fact unknown to exist at the time of the meeting. A disgruntled creditor or member has the right to apply to the court, under IA 1986, s.6, on the grounds that the CVA unfairly prejudices the interests of a creditor, member or contributory of the company or that there has been some irregularity at the meeting.

22.5.3 Unfair prejudice or material irregularity

Unfair prejudice may be towards a particular creditor or a specific class of creditors or to all the creditors generally. The unfair prejudice must be brought about by the terms of the arrangement itself, not from some external agreement. It must relate to some discriminatory treatment of a creditor or creditors. It may be possible to explain why members of the same class of creditors have been treated differently but such an explanation will need to be very convincing.

The court in *Prudential Assurance Co Ltd* v. *PRG Powerhouse Ltd* [2007] BPIR 839 explained that the position of a creditor may be compared with that of others from both a 'vertical' and a 'horizontal' angle. The vertical angle requires the court to compare the creditor's position under the CVA to the position the creditor would have been in under a winding up. On the facts in *Powerhouse*, the terms of the CVA left the guaranteed landlords in a worse position than if the company had been wound up and so was unfairly prejudicial. Horizontal comparison is with other creditors or classes of creditors under the terms of the CVA. This latter type of comparison may also include comparing the creditor's position under the CVA with the position the creditor would have been in under a scheme of arrangement under Part 26 of the Companies Act 2006.

In recent years the courts have been asked to consider whether the operation of the so-called 'football creditor rule' is unfairly prejudicial in the context of CVAs. The effect of the rule is that when a club enters a formal insolvency procedure, usually administration, the respective internal rules of the Football Association Premier League (FAPL) and the Football League (FL), require that the club exit administration via a CVA. The terms of the CVA must ensure that all the club's football creditors (including the FAPL, the FL and the club's players but not ordinary unsecured suppliers) are paid in full, otherwise the club will forfeit its membership of the FAPL or FL. A liquidation of the club will lead to forfeiture of the league place and the player registrations (which together are usually the most valuable assets of the club). The deal for the sale of the club under the terms of a CVA will usually provide for the purchaser to pay the football creditors in full without any reduction in the purchase price paid for the club itself. As the money raised by the sale would be the same, whether or not the football creditors were paid, the CVA itself cannot be said to be unfairly prejudicial to the non-football creditors. They would get no more in a liquidation and probably would get less as the club would be virtually without value if it entered liquidation and lost its league place. The football creditors' rule is therefore not unfairly prejudicial (for a full examination of the law on this point, see, e.g. *HMRC* v. *Football League Ltd and Football Association Premier League Ltd* [2012] EWHC 1372 (Ch)).

A 'material irregularity' in relation to a meeting called to consider a CVA requires an irregularity that would or could have made a material difference to the way the CVA was assessed by those voting upon it. Minor breaches of IA 1986 will not normally be viewed as material. If a significant creditor is not given notice of the meeting, even though the creditor's existence is known about, this would normally be an irregularity in relation to the meeting. If the creditor in question is owed only a small amount and therefore his or her vote would make no difference to the result, the irregularity would not be material.

22.5.4 Duties owed by nominees/supervisors

Nominees and supervisors owe various statutory duties to appraise the initial proposal, call and hold meetings and supervise the CVA in accordance with IA 1986 and the terms of the CVA. Any breach of these statutory duties gives creditors a right to apply to the court. The court has wide powers, for example, to remove and replace a supervisor, to overturn a decision of the meetings and to regulate the supervision of the CVA generally (see IA 1986, ss.6 and 7). There is a general duty to exercise independent professional judgment (see, e.g. *Re a Debtor (No.222 of 1990)* [1993] BCLC 233). Where nominees (and subsequently supervisors) had allowed a CVA proposal to be put forward which they knew was unfairly prejudicial to certain creditors, the court, as well as revoking the CVA, also took the extraordinary step of reporting the insolvency practitioners to their professional body (see *Mourant* v. *Sixty UK Ltd* [2010] BCC 882).

Although the supervisor may be characterised as holding assets on trust for the creditors, the supervisor holds no private law duties to the creditors. No action for breach of trust, duty or contract is available against a supervisor. A supervisor cannot be sued for negligence because the courts view the nominee/supervisor as being under the control of the courts, and as the courts have ample power to control their respective activities, no private law action is needed (see *King* v. *Anthony* [1998] 2 BCLC 517). This seems a little strange, especially when receivers, administrators and liquidators may be sued in private law actions.

The nominee/supervisor does need to be careful though. Frequently, the nominee/supervisor may also be advising the client company as well as acting in an official capacity. If negligent advice is given to the client in the capacity of adviser rather than as nominee/supervisor, a private law action will be available (see *Prosser* v. *Castle Sanderson Solicitors* [2003] BCC 440).

22.5.5   Variation of a CVA

Commonly it is the case that, as circumstances change, the terms of a CVA may require some amendment. The company may need more time to pay, or less money than expected may have been realised by the sale of an asset. As a CVA is usually viewed as a form of contract, its terms cannot be changed unilaterally. Any attempt to vary its terms must either be under a specific variation clause contained within the CVA or be agreed to by all the persons bound (see, e.g. *Raja* v. *Rubin* [1999] BCC 579). In practice, a variation clause is invariably contained within a CVA stating that its terms may be changed if 75 per cent or more of the unsecured creditors agree. Such a clause will generally be valid (see, e.g. *Horrocks* v. *Broome* [1999] BPIR 66).

22.5.6   Termination of a CVA

A CVA may be a success or a failure. It may run its course and the company may pay off all its debts and thereafter return to profitable trading. This is the intention of the legislation, albeit that there is not always such a happy ending. A company may run up substantial post-CVA debts with new creditors who may petition for the company's winding up. The company may not make the profits it expected. The supervisor or a creditor may petition for the company's winding up on the basis that the CVA has been breached. Frequently, a company in CVA enters liquidation. If this occurs, one important issue is what happens to assets being held by the supervisor? Are they held on trust for the CVA creditors or must they be handed over to the liquidator for the benefit of all the company's creditors? The answers to such questions may be taken from the decision of the Court of Appeal in *Re N T Gallagher & Sons Ltd* [2002] BCLC 133, namely:

- Where a CVA provides for monies or assets to be paid to CVA creditors, this will create a trust of those monies or assets for those creditors.
- The effect of the liquidation of the company on a trust created by the CVA will depend upon the terms of the CVA.
- If the CVA provides what is to happen on liquidation, or other failure of the CVA, effect must be given to it.
- If the CVA does not so provide, the trust will continue notwithstanding the liquidation or failure.
- The CVA creditors can prove in the liquidation for so much of their debt as remains after payment of what has been recovered under the trust.

Once the final distributions are made by the supervisor, the CVA comes to an end. The supervisor gives notice to the registrar of companies, the court, the creditors and the members either that it has been fully implemented or that it has terminated prematurely (whichever is the case).

22.6 LIQUIDATION

Liquidation is the process by which a company's assets are realised, the proceeds distributed to creditors as far as possible and finally the company is dissolved, that is, it ceases to exist. If a company is 'unable to pay its debts' either in the 'balance sheet' sense, where its liabilities outweigh its assets (see IA 1986, s.123(2)) or, in the 'cash flow' sense, where the company is unable to pay its debts as they fall due (see IA 1986, s.123(1)), the court may order the company to be wound up. Although a company may have been through receivership or administration, and these procedures may have been a success, with the business being sold to a buyer, the endplay may still be that the company (which is often left as an empty shell) is wound up.

The main purposes of the liquidation of an insolvent company are:

- to provide for the equitable and fair distribution of the assets of the company among its creditors;
- to put an end to the continued existence of hopelessly insolvent companies;
- to allow for the investigation of the company's affairs with particular regard being paid to the events leading to the company's failure (such investigation may lead to civil liability of the company's directors, for example, for breach of fiduciary duty or wrongful trading; or to criminal liability, for example, fraudulent trading or to quasi-criminal proceedings under the Company Directors Disqualification Act 1986).

There are two types of winding up: voluntary and compulsory. Although the vast majority of liquidations occur following a company's insolvency, voluntary and compulsory windings up are equally applicable to solvent companies. The procedure for placing a company into compulsory winding up (or winding up by the court; see generally IA 1986, ss.122–130) is essentially the same whether the company is solvent or insolvent. It will begin with a winding-up petition to the court. With voluntary windings up (which occur without any court involvement), there is a marked difference in the procedure for the winding up of a solvent company (referred to as a 'members' voluntary winding up'; see generally IA 1986, ss.90–96 and ss.107–116) and an insolvent winding up (referred to as a 'creditors' voluntary winding up'; see generally, IA 1986, ss.97–116).

The main differences between the various types of liquidation relate to the procedure up to and including the appointment of the liquidator. The duties owed by the liquidator and the process of liquidation after appointment are broadly the same for both types of liquidation. All liquidators are required to be licensed insolvency practitioners.

22.6.1 Voluntary winding up

As the name suggests, voluntary liquidation is where the company voluntarily decides to wind itself up. It is usually a quicker and cheaper process than compulsory winding up, as neither the court nor the Official Receiver are involved. The procedure begins with the company in general meeting passing a special resolution to wind up the company (IA 1986, s.84). If the company is insolvent, the liquidation will be called a 'creditors' voluntary liquidation'. In a creditors' voluntary liquidation, the policy of IA 1986 is to permit the creditors' interests to be treated as paramount. In effect, the creditors exercise a degree of control over the progress of the liquidation. As there will be no surplus money left in the company after creditors have been paid, and therefore there will be no capital to return to members, the members have no financial interest in the liquidation. The creditors have a clear interest in how the liquidation progresses. Depending on how it proceeds, they may see more or less of the money owed to them. Following the members' meeting, where the resolution to wind up is passed, a creditors' meeting will be held. Although a liquidator may have been appointed at the members' meeting (by an ordinary resolution), the creditors' meeting has the power to overrule that appointment, that is, the creditors may choose their own liquidator (voting at the creditors' meeting is based upon the amount of unsecured debt owed to each creditor). The creditors may also decide to form a liquidation committee which has various powers including sanctioning certain types of legal action being proposed by the liquidator, fixing the remuneration of the liquidator and the right to inspect financial records kept by the liquidator (see, e.g. IA 1986, s.101).

If, on the other hand, the company is solvent, the liquidation will be a 'members' voluntary liquidation'. Here the members effectively control the winding-up process. The creditors have no say in how the winding up progresses, as they will be paid in full. The interests of the members are paramount because, depending upon how efficiently the company's assets are realised, they stand to receive a larger return on their capital investment. Accordingly, there is no meeting of creditors in a members' voluntary winding up (unless the liquidator becomes aware that the company is in fact insolvent, in which case the liquidator will call a meeting of creditors and the liquidation will thereafter progress as a creditors' voluntary liquidation).

In the period of five weeks prior to the general meeting that is held to pass the resolution in a members' voluntary liquidation, the directors of the company are required to make a statutory declaration of solvency (IA 1986, s.89). This declaration must state that the directors have made full enquiry into the affairs of the company and, having done so, have formed the opinion that the company will be able to pay its debts in full within a stated period of time of not more than 12 months from the date of the resolution. The directors will have committed a criminal offence if, having made the statutory declaration of solvency, the company is unable to pay its debts within the specified period of time, unless the directors can show they had reasonable grounds for making the statement. There is a statutory presumption that the directors did not have reasonable grounds for making the statement if the company is found ultimately to be insolvent.

22.6.2 Compulsory winding up

IA 1986, s.122 lists the grounds upon which a winding-up order may be made. IA 1986, s.124 lists the persons eligible to present a petition. The most common type of petition is one brought by a creditor on the ground that the company is unable to pay its debts. Under IA 1986, s.123, a company's inability to pay its debts may be proved by a creditor if it is proved to the satisfaction of the court either that the company is unable to pay its debts as they fall due ('cash flow' insolvency) or that the value of the company's assets is less that the amount of its liabilities ('balance sheet' insolvency), taking into account its contingent and prospective liabilities.

Cash flow insolvency may be proven by:

- a creditor who is owed a debt exceeding £750, serving a statutory demand on the company requiring payment within three weeks, and the creditor does not receive payment or some other form of reasonable satisfaction within that time; or
- a creditor who is a judgment creditor of a company and has issued execution on the judgment has had the execution returned wholly or partly unsatisfied.

In respect of establishing balance sheet insolvency, until recently it was considered that the court required evidence, not merely that the company's liabilities outweighed its assets but that the company has reached the 'point of no return'. However, following the decision of the Supreme Court in *BNY Corporate Trustee Services v Eurosail* [2013] 1 WLR 1408, the 'point of no return' test is now discredited. The Supreme Court held that the ability of a company to meet its liabilities, both prospective and contingent, was to be determined on the balance of probabilities with the burden of proof on the party asserting 'balance-sheet insolvency'.

The statutory demand procedure is most commonly used method of proving to the court that a company is unable to pay its debts. If the demand is correctly served and the company has no genuine grounds to dispute the debt (the leading case on which is *Mann* v. *Goldstein* [1968] 1 WLR 1091), a petition will generally be successful and the court will usually make the winding-up order. Once a winding-up order is made, the Official Receiver (an employee of the Department for Business, Innovation and Skills) will take control of the company's assets. The Official Receiver will investigate the reasons for the company's liquidation. If there are sufficient assets, the Official Receiver will call meetings of members and creditors to appoint a private sector liquidator (if the members and creditors cannot agree who should be appointed, the creditors' candidate is appointed). If the company is effectively an empty shell with few, if any, assets, there will be no meetings and the Official Receiver will continue to act as liquidator.

22.6.3   General effect of a winding up

Initially, the corporate personality of the company remains unaffected by its being placed in liquidation. The affairs of the company are wound up by the liquidator who takes over the powers of management of the company. The liquidator acts as agent of the company. One consequence of entering liquidation is that the company's business may no longer be carried on except for the limited purpose of the winding up (see, e.g. IA 1986, s.87 and Sched.4, and *Re Great Eastern Electric Co Ltd* [1941] 1 Ch 241). To safeguard the company's goodwill, it may prove necessary to continue the business for a short period, in the hope that the business may be sold as a going concern. Once in liquidation, all business letters, invoices and orders for goods issued by the company must contain a statement that the company is being wound up.

Winding up severely affects the company's powers to deal with its assets. Under IA 1986, s.127, any disposition of property by a company in compulsory winding up (a more limited provision, IA 1986, s.88, applies to voluntary windings up) made after the commencement of the winding up will be void (unless the court orders otherwise). A compulsory winding up is deemed to commence on the date the petition was presented to the court. Section 127 effectively avoids any transfer of money or property made by the company after the presentation of the petition. The purpose of the section is to prevent the improper disposal of companies' assets by the directors once a petition has been served. Section 127 has been the subject of a significant amount of case law, especially in the area of payments out of a company's bank account (see, e.g. *Re Gray's Inn Construction Co Ltd* [1980] 1 WLR 711 and *Hollicourt (Contracts) Ltd* v. *Bank of Ireland* [2000] 2 WLR 290). It is normal and prudent practice for banks to freeze existing company bank accounts when they become aware of a winding-up petition against the company in question. The bank may require any subsequent dealings to be made through newly set up accounts which have been validated by the court. Generally speaking, the courts will retrospectively validate a transfer of property made by a company (which at the time of the transfer, is subject to a winding-up petition which is ultimately success-ful) if the transfer is made honestly in the ordinary course of business and for the benefit of the company (see, e.g. *Denney* v. *John Hudson & Co Ltd* [1992] BCLC 901).

Although winding up does not, in itself, terminate contracts with outsiders, it will usually result in the contract being frustrated or terminated by the company's inability to continue its terms. The contract may specifically deal with what is to happen upon the company's winding up. Any party who suffers loss due to the termination of the contract will be able prove in the liquidation, usually as an unsecured creditor (see, e.g. *Ogdens Ltd* v. *Nelson* [1905] AC 109).

Winding up will usually terminate all contracts of employment. In a compulsory winding up, the publication of the winding-up order operates as a notice to dismiss all employees (see, e.g. *Re General Rolling Stock Co* (1866) 1 Eq 346). The position is not so clear cut in voluntary liquidations but it seems likely that a creditors' voluntary winding up has the same effect (see, e.g. *Midland Counties Bank* v. *Attwood* [1905] 1 Ch 357 and *Fowler* v. *Commercial Timber Co Ltd* [1930] 2 KB 1).

When a winding-up order is made, all proceedings and actions against the company are automatically stayed (IA 1986, s.130). In a voluntary winding up, the liquidator may apply to the court to exercise its power to stay actions and proceed-ings (IA 1986, s.112). The purpose of these provisions is to ensure a fair distribution of the company's assets among its creditors and to prevent some creditors jumping the queue.

22.6.4 Duties of liquidators

As with the agencies of receivers and administrators, the agency of the liquidator is not a normal type of agency. The liquidator controls the principal's assets and cannot usually be dismissed by the principal. The liquidator's fiduciary duties to the company (principal) are limited by overriding statutory duties to get in the com-pany's assets, realise them and to pay the proceeds out to the company's creditors. The liquidator is not usually liable on any contracts entered into as agent of the company (see, e.g. *Stead Hazel & Co* v. *Cooper* [1933] 1 KB 840).

As a fiduciary officer, the liquidator must act honestly and exercise his or her powers *bona fide* for the purpose for which they are conferred (see, e.g. *Ayerst* v. *C & K (Construction) Ltd* [1976] AC 167). The liquidator's personal interest must not conflict with his or her duty to the company (see, e.g. *Silkstone Coal Co* v. *Edey* [1900] 1 Ch 167). A liquidator must act in a totally impartial way as between the persons interested in the company's property and those interested in the company's liabilities (see, e.g. *Re Lubin, Rosen & Associates Ltd* [1975] 1 WLR 122).

A liquidator owes a duty of skill and care and must display a level of competence reasonably expected of a well-paid professional (see, e.g. *Re Windsor Steam Coal Co* [1929] Ch 151). An action in negligence may lead to the liquidator being liable in damages and he or she may lose all or part of his or her claim to be remunerated (see, e.g. *Re Silver Valley Mines* (1882) 21 Ch D 381).

A number of more specific duties are owed under IA 1986. Notice of a liquidator's appointment must be filed with the registrar of companies. A liquidator must settle a list of contributories. This refers to a list of company members who are liable to contribute in the winding up, for example, if they have only partly paid-up shares. In a compulsory liquidation, the Official Receiver must provide creditors and contributories with a statement of affairs of the company and a report on the statement. Importantly, a liquidator must take custody or control of all company property (IA 1986, s.144) and ensure that it is protected or preserved. If assets are missing, an investigation will need to be carried out. To realise certain assets or to maximise the assets available to the company's creditors, the liquidator may have to commence legal proceedings. An investigation of how and why the company failed must be carried out to assist the liquidator in locating assets of the company and identifying any action available to the liquidator. The investigation may also lead to a report being prepared which may be used in subsequent disqualification proceedings against unfit directors.

Crucially, the liquidator is under a duty to realise the assets. The liquidator has a power to sell or otherwise dispose of all or any part of the company's property (IA 1986, Sched.4, para. 6). There is also a general obligation to pay all liabilities (as far as is possible). Frequently, assets subject to fixed charges will have been enforced prior to the liquidator taking office. Any distribution to creditors will be subject to the same statutory priority order mentioned above in the context of receivership and administration. The one significant difference is that the liquidator must also, if funds allow, pay unsecured creditors (who come at the bottom of the list after fixed charge holders, preferential creditors and floating charge holders). If the company in liquidation is subject to a floating charge created on or after 15 September 2003, the liquidator will need to deduct the prescribed part under s.176A in favour of the unsecured creditors prior to making any distribution to the floating charge holder (discussed in **Chapter 11**).

22.6.5 Powers of liquidators

The powers enjoyed by liquidators in compulsory and creditors' voluntary liquidations are essentially the same, although different provisions apply to each form of winding up. Most powers can be found in IA 1986, Sched.4. Some of these powers can only be exercised with the approval of the court or the liquidation committee. Liquidators are given powers to effect compromises, to defend or commence proceedings, to sell company assets, to appoint agents (but not to delegate the exercise of any discretion), to call meetings of members or creditors, to apply to the court for directions and to do all such things as are necessary for winding up the affairs of the company and distributing its property.

The liquidator may take action against directors for breach of duty under IA 1986, s.212 (discussed in **Chapter 5**). Importantly, the following proceedings under IA 1986, cannot, *inter alia,* be commenced by the liquidator without the sanction of the court or liquidation committee:

- Section 213 action for fraudulent trading (discussed in **Chapter 5**).
- Section 214 action wrongful trading (discussed in **Chapter 5**).
- Section 238 action to attack a transaction at an undervalue.
- Section 239 action to avoid a preference.

(Reference could also usefully be made to liquidators' powers under IA 1986, s.178 (to disclaim onerous property), ss.216–217 (directors' personal liability under the 'phoenix syndrome' (discussed in **Chapter 5**), s.244 (to attack extortionate credit bargains), s.245 (avoidance of floating charges) and s.423 (to avoid transactions designed to defraud creditors).)

22.6.6 Transactions at an undervalue

Under IA 1986, s.238, a court may make any order adjusting a transaction at an undervalue. A liquidator or an administrator has the power to apply to the court for such an order. The office holder must establish that the transaction in question was entered into during the two years preceding the onset of insolvency (which in a compulsory winding up is the date of the petition, in a voluntary winding up is the date of the special resolution and in an administration is the date of appointment of the administrator). At the time the transaction was entered into, the company must have been unable to pay its debts (within the meaning of IA 1986, s.123, considered above) or became unable to pay its debts as a result of entering into the transaction. If the transaction is in favour of a person connected to the company, there is a rebuttable presumption that the company was unable to pay its debts at the time. The meaning of 'connected person' is defined in IA 1986, s.249 and includes, for example, directors and their spouses.

A transaction is at an undervalue where the company makes a gift or enters into a transaction where the value of the consideration provided by the company, in money or money's worth, is significantly less than the value of the consideration received by the company. In *Re MC Bacon* [1990] BCLC 324, it is explained that for a claim to be successful, the liquidator must establish in monetary terms what the value of the consideration was, passing to and from the company. If it can be shown, for example, that the company has paid £20,000 for an asset, worth at the time only £10,000, this would appear to satisfy the test that the company has received significantly less consideration than it provided.

Transactions may take many forms, and the more complex the details the more difficult it may be to establish the value of the consideration in monetary terms. If the value of a transaction is speculative, then the party who relies upon the consideration must establish the value (see, e.g. the decision of the House of Lords in *Phillips* v. *Brewin Dolphin Bell Lawrie Ltd* [2001] 1 WLR 143). In assessing whether the consideration received is significantly less than that provided, the court must form a view as to what the value of the consideration would have been in the open market. This gives the 'correct valuation' (see, e.g. *National Westminster Bank plc* v. *Jones* [2001] 1 BCLC 98 – a case decided under IA 1986, s.423, but the reasoning of which applies equally to IA 1986, s.238). Following the valuation of the consideration, the court will assess in percentage or proportionate terms, how much less is the value of the consideration transferred than that received. As yet, the courts have not given any clear indication of how much the discrepancy has to be to constitute 'significantly less'.

The substantive law under IA 1986, s.238 has proven difficult. The liquidator may have difficulty in establishing the open market value of the assets involved. It may be difficult to prove that the company was insolvent at the time of the transaction. The presumption of insolvency against a connected person is useful in this context but does inhibit actions against company outsiders. It is a defence to a s.238 action to show that the company entered into the transaction in good faith, for the purpose of carrying on its business, and that when entering into the transaction there were reasonable grounds to believe that the transaction would benefit the company. If the company is experiencing extreme cash flow problems, it is perhaps arguable that a sale of assets even if at a very low price, would indeed, benefit the company.

If the court decides that a transaction falls within IA 1986, s.238, it may make such order as it deems fit to restore the position to what it would have been if the transaction had not been entered. Although the court has a wide discretion, it will usually order that the transaction be, in effect, rescinded. Any order made by the court must not prejudice any interest in property acquired by a third party from a person who is not the company, providing the third party acquires the interest in good faith and for value.

22.6.7 Preferences

To ensure that creditors are all treated equally in the distribution of a company's assets, IA 1986, s.239 allows an administrator or a liquidator to apply to the court to avoid a preference. A preference is some action by the company which, in the event of the company entering insolvent liquidation or administration, has the effect of putting a creditor of the company into a better position than he or she would otherwise be in. As with IA 1986, s.238, where the court establishes a preference it may make any order to restore the position to what it would have been if no preference had been given. Any security which constitutes a preference under s.239 will usually be avoided by the court.

Liquidation and administration are designed to be collective procedures, whereby duties are owed to all creditors to ensure an equal distribution of the company's assets. It would offend this basic *pari passu* principle if, for example, one creditor was given the benefit of security just prior to the company entering insolvent liquidation. The office holder must prove that the transaction in question was entered into by the company within the period of six months prior to the onset of insolvency (which has the same meaning as that under IA 1986, s.238) or, if the transaction is in favour of a person connected to the company, the period is extended to two years prior to the onset of insolvency. The other party to the transaction (the person being preferred) must be one of the company's creditors or a surety or guarantor of the company's debts.

It must be shown that the company was 'influenced by a desire' to prefer the other party. It must also be established that the company was unable to pay its debts (within the meaning given under IA 1986, s.123), at the time of, or as a result of, the transaction. The office holder does not have the benefit of a presumption of insolvency if the preference is in favour of a person connected to the company. Instead, there is a presumption, if the transaction is in favour of a connected person, that the company was influenced by the requisite desire to prefer. It must be noted that it is not always straightforward to establish that a company was insolvent at the time of the preference because companies that are struggling do not always keep complete and accurate financial records of their dealings.

In order to establish whether a creditor has been preferred, the court will need to compare the position the creditor would have been in, if the alleged preference had not taken place, with the creditor's ultimate position. If the preference has the effect of disturbing the statutory order of priorities as regards payments in an insolvency, then *prima facie*, the creditor will have been preferred. One of the main problems faced by office holders under IA 1986, s.239 is proving that the company was influenced by a desire to prefer the creditor. The leading case on this issue is *Re MC Bacon* [1990] BCLC 324. It is clear from this case that the word 'desire' is to be construed subjectively, so that it must be shown that the company positively wished to prefer the creditor in question. Establishing what the mind of an artificial creation such as a company is thinking is notoriously difficult (see, e.g. *Re Transworld Trading Ltd* [1999] BPIR 628). Although the requisite desire may be inferred from the facts of the case, the desire must have influenced the decision to prefer. There must be a connection between the desire and entering into the transaction. The desire need not be the only or main motivation for the decision but it must have been influential. The desire may have been only one of several factors. If a company is put under pressure by a lender to provide, for example, some security for existing indebtedness, the decision to provide the security will not usually satisfy the requirement of desire. If the desire is to keep the company's business going, and a necessary by-product of that desire is to put the lender in a preferred position, that is not a preference because such a decision is not influenced by a desire to prefer the lender, rather, it is influenced by a desire to keep the company going. Such commercial pressure will therefore prevent any claim by an office holder that the company's actions constitute a preference (by analogy, see the bankruptcy case of *Rooney* v. *Das* [1999] BPIR 404).

Therefore, proving that a transaction falls within IA 1986, s.239 is a difficult proposition. Proving the company was insolvent at the time of the transaction and establishing what a company is thinking is far from straightforward. Further, in the absence of express admissions by the company's directors, proving the requisite subjective motive of the company will be particularly difficult. Indeed, unless the preference is in favour of a person connected to the company (for examples of which, see *Re DKG Contractors Ltd* [1990] BCC 903 and *Wills* v. *Corfe Joinery Ltd*

[1997] BCC 511), there is little chance of proving a preference. If the preferred creditor can point to some commercial pressure placed upon the company forcing it to enter the transaction in question, the s.239 action will usually fail (for rare exceptions, see, e.g. *Re Living Images Ltd* [1996] BCC 112 and *Re Agriplant Services Ltd* [1997] BCC 842).

22.6.8 Dissolution

A company continues in liquidation until it is dissolved. Dissolution is the final act in the life of the company and will constitute the final act to complete the liquidation. In a compulsory liquidation, dissolution occurs automatically at the end of a three-month period following the registration by the registrar of companies of a receipt to the effect that a private liquidator has held a final meeting of creditors or, in the case of the Official Receiver, that the winding up is complete. In a creditors' voluntary liquidation, dissolution takes place automatically three months after the registrar of companies registers receipt of the liquidator's final account and return stating that a final meeting has been held.

22.7 INTERACTION BETWEEN THE DIFFERENT INSOLVENCY PROCEDURES

22.7.1 Administrative receivership and administration

These two procedures are mutually exclusive. A company can be in either administrative receivership or administration, it cannot enter both at the same time, and it would be almost impossible to conceive of a scenario whereby a company may enter these two procedures sequentially.

22.7.2 Administrative receivership to liquidation

It is very common for a company to enter administrative receivership and at the same time, or shortly thereafter, to enter liquidation. It is also possible, but less common, for a company to enter into liquidation and for an administrative receiver to be appointed during the liquidation.

22.7.3 Administration to liquidation

A company cannot be in administration and liquidation at the same time. When the administration ends, the company may have been successfully rehabilitated. If the company cannot continue to trade, but it has sufficient assets to finance payments to unsecured creditors, the administration may be converted into a creditors' voluntary liquidation. If there is no money left to pay out to unsecured creditors, the administration may proceed straight to dissolution.

22.7.4   Administration to CVA

It would be most strange for a company to go from administrative receivership into a CVA. It is possible but also rare for a company to go from liquidation into a CVA. IA 1986 is designed to encourage a distressed company to enter administration and to take advantage of the moratorium on actions to allow it to enter into a CVA, usually with the former administrator acting as supervisor of the CVA.

Index